RETHINKING THE REASONABLE PERSON

Rethinking the Reasonable Person

*An Egalitarian Reconstruction of the
Objective Standard*

MAYO MORAN

OXFORD
UNIVERSITY PRESS

OXFORD

UNIVERSITY PRESS

Great Clarendon Street, Oxford OX2 6DP

Oxford University Press is a department of the University of Oxford.
It furthers the University's objective of excellence in research, scholarship,
and education by publishing worldwide in

Oxford New York

Auckland Bangkok Buenos Aires Cape Town Chennai
Dar es Salaam Delhi Hong Kong Istanbul Karachi Kolkata
Kuala Lumpur Madrid Melbourne Mexico City Mumbai Nairobi
São Paulo Shanghai Taipei Tokyo Toronto

Oxford is a registered trade mark of Oxford University Press
in the UK and in certain other countries

Published in the United States
by Oxford University Press Inc., New York

© M. Moran, 2003

The moral rights of the author have been asserted
Database right Oxford University Press (maker)

Crown copyright material is reproduced under Class Licence
Number C01P0000148 with the permission of HMSO and
the Queen's Printer for Scotland

First published 2003

British Library Cataloguing in Publication Data

Data available

Library of Congress Cataloging in Publication Data

Data available

ISBN 0-19-924782-X

1 3 5 7 9 10 8 6 4 2

Typeset by Newgen Imaging Systems (P) Ltd., Chennai, India
Printed in Great Britain on
acid-free paper by
T.J. International, Padstow, Cornwall.

For Bridget

Acknowledgements

It is a pleasure to acknowledge the considerable support, input, and assistance I received while writing this book.

Work on this book was generously supported by the Social Sciences and Humanities Research Council of Canada, the Laidlaw Foundation, the Canadian Law Scholarship Foundation, the Connaught Fund of the University of Toronto, and the Cecil A. Wright Foundation for Legal Scholarship of the University of Toronto Faculty of Law.

The book has also benefited from the comments of participants in the Oxford-Toronto jurisprudence colloquium at Oxford University, at the University of Michigan Legal Theory Workshop, at the University of Western Ontario Jurisprudence Conference at Tort Law Symposium in Montreal, and at the Canadian Judicial Institute, where I presented parts of the book. I owe a special debt of thanks to Dean Ron Daniels and to my colleagues at the University of Toronto Faculty of Law who always managed that elusive but ideal combination of support and constructive criticism. I have also been extremely fortunate to teach much of the material of this book at the University of Toronto and have benefited from the input of thoughtful students and the unfailing intellectual acuity and enthusiasm of my co-teacher, Bruce Chapman. I also received excellent research support from the librarians at the Bora Laskin Law Library at the University of Toronto and from my research assistants Alissa Hamilton, Sarah Loosemore, and Alia Hussey. I am especially indebted to Pauline Rosenbaum who not only did extensive research on the book but also coordinated the other research and finalized the manuscript while she was clerking. When I served as Associate Dean of the Faculty of Law, my assistant, Georgina Phillips, created as much space, support, and tranquillity for this book as possible.

Ernest Weinrib supervised the doctoral dissertation out of which this book grew. His wisdom, encouragement, and guidance were, and have remained, vital to this project. Bruce Chapman, Jenny Nedelsky, and Arthur Ripstein also supervised the dissertation and each of them contributed enormously well after the completion of the original project. I also benefited from the input of Jules Coleman who served as my external examiner. This book would not be here without the incredible efforts and generosity of Joe Carens, David Dyzenhaus, and Marty Friedland who provided invaluable advice and guidance at important moments.

The comments of the reviewers of this manuscript were also invaluable for their insight and guidance. Many other people also read and commented on parts of this manuscript in its various versions including Alan Brudner, Bruce Chapman, Denis Klinchuk, Karen Knop, Denise Reaume, Arthur Ripstein, and Marianna Valverde. Karen Knop's support and encouragement, both intellectual and beyond, was vital to this project. I would also be remiss if I did not thank Stephen Perry, who first inspired my interest in tort law and in the puzzle of the reasonable person.

Very early in this project, my little boy Aidan was born, and he is an important part of the inspiration for this book. The dedication and attentiveness of our caregiver, Tessie Pahimna, enabled me to have the intellectual space to complete this work. My father Patrick, my sister Roseanne, my brothers Patrick and Michael, my wonderful Aunt Eileen, and my partner Doug Cunningham all encouraged me with their unfailing enthusiasm, support, and willingness to believe in me. My dear mother, Bridget, who died during this project, would perhaps have been proudest of all. Before her time and often in a world too small for her, she was a scholar, a writer, and a visionary with a passion for justice. Though no gift could be adequate to her gifts to me, this is for her.

M.M

Contents

Table of Cases

Table of Legislation

Introduction
'Personal' Problems:
Rethinking the Reasonable Person

I. THE PROBLEM WITH THE REASONABLE PERSON

AP Herbert's 1935 classic *Uncommon Law* opens with the judgement in *Fardell v Potts*, a fictional case where the court is faced with the puzzle of applying the reasonable man standard to a woman.[1] After noting that among the many authorities there is 'no single mention of a reasonable woman', Herbert's judge continues that this must be more than a coincidence and concludes that 'legally at least there is no reasonable woman'. Thus, he holds that the learned trial judge should have instructed the jury that while there was evidence that the defendant had not come up to the standard of a reasonable man, the conduct was only what was to be expected of a woman, as such!

For well over a century the reasonable person—or perhaps, more accurately, the reasonable man—has been a central figure in the landscape of the law. The reasonable person has, for instance, embodied the fault component of the law of negligence and played an important role in criminal law, particularly in the defences. He has also come to personify the appropriate level of care in various aspects of contract law (in mitigation of damages, for example), in administrative law (as in the regulation of sexual harassment), and elsewhere. In this respect, the reasonable person is ubiquitous. He has, however, recently come under increasing suspicion. But as Herbert's parody illustrates, criticism and suspicion of the reasonable person are by no means entirely new.

In fact, the 'new' criticisms of the reasonable person—however different their inspiration—share something with Herbert's perceptive mockery of the difficulties inherent in fashioning a legal standard by reference to some idealized person. *Fardell v Potts* in this sense presages the insight later voiced by feminists, critical race theorists, and others, that there is something troubling about using an idealized person as a legal standard. Indeed, an implicit recognition of the tension between the descriptive components of the infamous reasonable man and his normative task is the source of much of the humour in Herbert's account. And the renowned comment that no reasonable woman is to be found in all of the law finds an unlikely echo in much later feminist and other 'critical

---

[1] AP Herbert, *Uncommon Law* (London: Metheun, 1935) 4.

egalitarian' anxiety about the normative significance of the 'default characteristics' of the reasonable person and the difficulty posed when those characteristics do not represent the person actually judged. Indeed, implicit both in Herbert and in later feminist commentators is the recognition that only so far as the reasonable person resembles the person actually judged does the standard render unproblematic its complex mixture of descriptive and normative characteristics.

Yet for all of this concern, virtually no systematic work has been done on the reasonable person. Feminists and other critics do pick up on the rhetorical significance of Herbert's point and note that the test has historically been framed in terms of what 'men' do. Unfortunately, though, these suspicions tend to move between—and sometimes even combine—the extremely general and the *ad hoc*. The consequence is that the critique rarely progresses beyond these important though relatively limited insights. Nonetheless, critical egalitarians do gesture towards a set of broader concerns about the reasonable person. In a legal world dominated by the reasonable man, how is the behaviour of women to be judged? Similarly, how ought one to judge the behaviour of other individuals, including many men, who do not possess the default characteristics of the reasonable man?

The way that the reasonable person seamlessly intertwines the normative and descriptive may be one source of his appeal, but this very feature makes disentanglement difficult when the actual person no longer so closely resembles his 'legal' counterpart. Gender is perhaps the most straightforward illustration of this difficulty, and early courts and commentators—by no means feminist—thus call attention to the difficulty of figuring out how the standard of the reasonable man applies to a woman. But conventional legal debates have also addressed other variations on this problem. Thus, at least at one end of the spectrum, an age differential between the actual person being judged and the 'reasonable' person makes overtly problematic the relation between the two. More controversial is the question of what to do with a divergence between the 'mental' qualities of the actual person and the reasonable man. The reasonable man can, it seems, suffer from various forms of physical ailments—like a heart condition, for instance— but can the reasonable person suffer from a mental disability or insanity? The wider—and perhaps more fundamental, though we will require a theory of what that means—the disparity between the actual and the legal person, the more puzzling these questions become. What, for instance, can the reasonable person be assumed to know? A bored student of tort law can easily amuse herself by the attempts to catalogue the store of knowledge possessed by the reasonable person.[2] But the difficulty of describing even an uncontroversial core of human knowledge is inevitably as daunting as it is amusing. Thus, it is perhaps not surprising that in the face of far more complex and contentious judgements about the significance of various levels of intelligence, character, or emotional make-up, the very murkiness of the reasonable person may sometimes seem like a refuge.

[2] Note on 'Negligence' (1938) 23 Minn L Rev 628.

In fact, the dominant response to a divergence between the legal and the actual person preserves this murkiness but circumvents the difficulty it poses by simply making the legal person look more and more like the actual person. In the case of children, for instance, this is what the law chooses to do. Unsurprisingly, critical egalitarians themselves have inclined towards a similar solution in the face of a troubling relationship between the reasonable and the actual person. Thus, one finds attempts to remedy the defects of the reasonable person by creating a 'legal' person with the gender, age, race, class status, occupation, religion, linguistic capacities, etc. of the actual person—in essence, bringing the reasonable person into closer alignment with the actual person. And while it may be tempting to criticize feminists and others for the seemingly endless specification of the qualities of the reasonable person, it is worth noting the continuity with the traditional approach as exemplified in the treatment of children, for instance. In fact (though this typically goes unnoticed in the case of children) the danger threatened in both moves is the same: without a clear sense of which qualities of the reasonable person matter normatively and which do not, the standard threatens to disappear into a description of the actual person. So understood, the reasonable person threatens to elide the important difference between particularizing a general standard and subjectivizing it.

The riddle of the reasonable person is thus ultimately the question of why he matters at all. What is it exactly we are trying to capture through reference to him? And how effective is he as a means of achieving that end? While his centrality as a legal device certainly underscores the importance of his task, it does not answer the question of just what it is that he accomplishes. Nor does it tell us whether, in a more complex and more inclusive world, he remains the best means of accomplishing that end. It is to those questions that this work addresses itself.

II. THE SCOPE OF THIS ANALYSIS

It is therefore perhaps unsurprising that a central focus of this work is the operation of the reasonable person standard in the law of negligence. After all, the law of negligence is the central and most important instance of the reasonable person standard. The reasonable person is critical to negligence liability for he determines fault and thus sets an important threshold for liability. Oddly enough, though, the reasonable person is actually less examined and theorized in the law of negligence than in his other contexts, such as in criminal and even administrative law. And this suggests the utility of bringing together various instances and controversies surrounding the reasonable person. For while we ought not diminish the different roles the reasonable person may occupy in his various settings, something may be gleaned from bringing together these roles and their accompanying controversies to examine both the commonalities and the differences. Indeed, such an examination suggests that there are valuable lessons to be taken from this particular—and particularly important—instance of the reasonable person to the issue of the reasonable person more generally, and perhaps even to broader ideas of reasonableness. So although this inquiry focuses on the use of the reasonable person for assessing responsibility in civil and in criminal law, it also contains some lessons for thinking more systematically about his other appearances.

In fact, the extent to which this analysis brings together civil and criminal negligence may seem at odds with the traditionally sharp conceptual divide between criminal and civil standards of liability. But tradition notwithstanding, there are important lessons to be learned in bringing together these two central instances of the reasonable person. Most obviously perhaps, the reasonable person standard serves a similar culpability-related function in civil and criminal negligence, in the standard of care in negligence and in the criminal defences in particular. And since the reasonable person embodies (quite literally) the fault of inadvertent wrongdoing, bringing these two central cases together helps to shed light on this important but somewhat obscure form of fault.

A related though more significant reason to bring together the central civil and criminal instances of the reasonable person is the fact that most of the detailed theorizing about the nature of culpability for negligence or inadvertence is found in discussions of criminal negligence. Similar difficulties relating to the standard are posed in the civil and criminal context. However, the centrality of fault in the criminal context forces consideration of the normative core of the standard in a way that the civil law manages to avoid. But though questions about the composition of the standard may be posed more sharply in the criminal setting, they are equally central in the civil context. The consequence is that conceptual work on criminal negligence is illuminating for the civil law of negligence, even though it may not play out in exactly the same way.

There are also other more complex benefits of juxtaposing civil and criminal negligence. Negligence is the thinnest form of criminal culpability and is in that respect most closely related to its civilian counterpart. Thus, to connect the reasonable person in his civil and in his criminal contexts is to link civil and criminal law at their point of closest relation. This, however, ought not to be taken to mean that such relation generally exists between the two bodies of law. After all, it is the very conceptual and normative proximity between civil and criminal law here that makes the reasonable person so controversial as a basis of criminal culpability and generates the important scholarly discussions concerning the exact nature of culpability in negligence. Even beyond this, though, the debate about the controversial status of negligence in criminal law uncovers deeper continuities between the civil and the criminal standards.

Indeed, part of the argument of this work is that it is difficult to understand the shortcomings of either instance of the standard without looking at them together, for their fates are, in an important sense, intertwined. This should hardly be surprising. Civil and criminal law theorists frequently point to the other sphere of liability when faced with questions about the limitations of their own inquiries. But this, I shall argue, is too easy. While there are telling links between the two applications of the standard, it is misleading to read these links too literally. A closer examination of the relationship between the two applications of the standard suggests that their fates are more related to complementary mistakes than to complementary missions (though those may indeed exist). In this sense then, even apart from the conceptual links and the well-developed nature of the criminal law analyses, the civil and the criminal instances of the reasonable person can quite literally not be understood without reference to each other and in this sense must be brought together.

III. OVERVIEW OF THE ARGUMENT

The first (and in some ways most daunting) task in addressing the question of the reasonable person is to clarify the nature and variety of intertwined puzzles involving the standard. In order to begin assessing the allegedly problematic nature of the reasonable person, this analysis takes as its point of departure the core reasonable person cases in the law of negligence. And the central question of these cases reminds us of the perceptiveness of Herbert's parody of the problematic relation between the reasonable person and the person being judged. An idealized person is undoubtedly a convenient device, often serving as a kind of shorthand for intuitive judgements about the appropriateness of a whole range of human behaviour. When judgement becomes more complex, though, as in the case of a disjuncture of age or intelligence, the utility of such a tool is less obvious (even if it may for that very reason be more appealing). Think, for instance, of the apparently simple question of age. The age of the reasonable person would have barely been conceived of until the age of the actual litigant renders its problematic. Only in that moment would the presumed age of the reasonable person—presumptively an adult somewhere between the extremes of youth and advanced years—even have been apparent. But once divergences between these 'default characteristics' of the imagined and the actual person open up, the intuitive judgements that form the basis of the reasonable person standard are put to a difficult test: which characteristics of the reasonable person really matter and which ones should be treated simply as default characteristics that can be displaced when that characteristic is not possessed by the person whose behaviour is being judged? An examination of the case law on how the reasonable person standard treats just such divergences provides a fitting starting point for the examination of this problem.

Perhaps the most vexing such problem for the reasonable person standard concerns whether the court ought to hold the person whose behaviour is being judged to the same level of intelligence as the reasonable person. The court in the landmark case of *Vaughan v Menlove* seemed to respond with an emphatic 'yes' to this question. And subsequent commentators have confirmed that liability in negligence is not negated simply because the risk springs from diminished intelligence for which the defendant cannot be blamed. If an intellectual shortcoming prevents him from acting as a reasonable person would have, then it is simply his bad luck. This position might lead us to assume that the reasonable person is simply an unvarying standard to which all are uniformly held regardless of their personal characteristics. Yet courts reject this approach in the other 'test case' of divergence: children. There, by contrast, they insist that fault in negligence actually demands that the characteristics of the legal person closely mirror those of the actual person whose behaviour is being judged. And despite the striking difference between the hostility to the 'stupid' and the generosity to the child, courts and commentators alike are widely agreed on the correctness of both approaches, thus confirming the centrality of both cases to the reasonable person's conception of fault. Examining the problematic relationship between these two core cases thus sheds light on the operation of the reasonable person.

It is commonplace for tort theorists to tackle the problem of the treatment of the mentally disabled. And virtually all of them defend the *Vaughan v Menlove* approach. Yet whatever their various insights, these justifications are not noteworthy for their success. In fact, I argue that no one who has attempted to justify the treatment of the mentally disabled under the reasonable person standard actually manages to do so. Nonetheless, the attempts are revealing. They illuminate how the reasonable person standard shapes the boundary between the core concerns of negligence: liberty and security. From Holmes and others it is clear that avoidability is somehow central to negligence. Indeed, Honoré's notion of general capacity as a precondition to liability in negligence is a more precise articulation of this concept and thus provides at least part of the justification for objective liability. The most powerful defences of the reasonable person also indicate that equality is somehow deeply implicated in the standard.

Despite these powerful links to equality, though, the defences of the treatment of the mentally disabled also give some reason to credit egalitarian worries about the reasonable person. Perhaps because of the curious embodiedness of the reasonable person, even the most sophisticated tort theorists pay little heed to the question of which latent qualities of the reasonable person can be displaced and individualized, and which cannot. This may initially not seem troublesome—concepts like Holmes's notion of avoidability or Honoré's general capacity test may do all the work needed with the mentally disabled, even if they do not recognize this. But we should hesitate before travelling too far down this path. There is a lingering worry, after all, about just what it is that accounts for the 'systematically unsystematic' treatment of the mentally disabled. And indeed, close examination of the other 'test case' for the reasonable person standard—that of the child—heightens the egalitarian concern about the reasonable person.

While the case of the mentally disabled illuminates one aspect of the reasonable person's claim to distinctiveness, the treatment of child defendants points up something very different. Liberty, fault, and equality play an important role in both of these situations, but they play out in contrasting ways. In the case of the mentally disabled, the law of negligence refuses to privilege the *liberty* interests of the defendant: it justifies this by pointing to the way that the fault requirement in negligence instantiates the equality between the plaintiff and the defendant. This claim to distinctiveness points to the difference between fault in negligence and criminal law fault: the law of negligence, commentators and courts point out, does not require moral blameworthiness. However, in the case of the child defendant—almost inevitably, the playing boy—the law refuses to privilege the *security* interests of the plaintiff: it justifies this by pointing to the imperative of applying the fault requirement in negligence equally across cases as between *defendants*. In this case, the claim to distinctiveness contrasts negligence as a fault-based regime with the older regime of strict liability: the distinctive feature of the law of negligence here is said to be its attachment to the fault principle. So in contrast with the mentally disabled, in the case of the child defendant we instead find the widest possible reading of avoidability. Indeed, courts insist that the latitude granted to the playing boy defendant is as critical, as implicated in the reasonable person's notion of culpability, as the latitude withheld from the mentally disabled. But the playing boy cases also hold broader lessons for understanding the reasonable person.

In fact, in these cases courts do provide a language for thinking about two very different components of the reasonable person standard, which they describe in terms of foresight and prudence. This distinction between what are essentially the biographical or descriptive components of the reasonable person (i.e. physical ability, age, and cognitive capacities such as foresight) and the normative elements (such as prudence or attentiveness to others) holds the promise of remedying some of the weaknesses inherent in less normatively differentiated concepts like avoidability and capacity. Yet while courts and commentators advert to this distinction, they unfortunately make little use of it. So, in the case of the mentally disabled, they arguably fail to distinguish those shortcomings that have normative significance from those that do not. And in the case of the child defendant, rather than articulating a fully normative idea of care, courts instead invest the idea of carefulness with some conception of normalcy or ordinary prudence. But this temptation—perhaps induced by the personification of the standard—threatens to fatally undermine any egalitarian promise the standard may hold. The troubling consequence, amply illustrated in the cases involving the child defendant, is that individual behaviour may end up being judged against a standard of 'normal' treatment, rather than reasonable treatment. There may be many cases where this will not matter because normal behaviour will be reasonable. But in certain kinds of cases—often just the ones critical egalitarians are worried about—this will not be so. If boys are characteristically careless, for instance, then a normatively undifferentiated standard that draws on some conception of ordinary behaviour yields a standard that fails to be critical enough. This is because the standard will be calibrated even for normative shortcomings to the extent that those shortcomings are normal or widely shared.

In this way at least, the reasonable person standard seems to operate in a troubling way even in its defining moments. Perhaps the most dominant contemporary worry about the reasonable person concerns gender. Feminist commentators, for instance, routinely treat the reasonable person standard as inherently suspicious, in part because of its genealogical link to the reasonable man. But since virtually all of the child defendant cases involve boys, few lessons about the broader treatment of gender issues can be drawn from these cases alone. Thus, it is necessary to identify a group of cases that involve female as well as male litigants and that allow for at least somewhat systematic comparison. Only then can we begin to investigate whether, for instance, courts are prepared to extend the kind of latitude to the playing girl that they make available to the playing boy. At least a partial answer to this question can be found in the examination of cases on the doctrine of allurement. The primary significance of this doctrine is to determine whether child plaintiffs can recover despite the dangerous activities they may themselves have engaged in; it thus centrally concerns the 'reasonableness' of certain kinds of childish behaviour and provides a counterpoint to the cases of the child defendants. And since there are allurement cases involving both boys and girls (though again, far fewer involving girls), this body of law provides an opportunity to systematically compare how determinations of reasonableness apply to boys and to girls.

The title of the chapter on allurement—Fun with Dick and Jane—not incidentally echoes the infamous school book. Like that childhood reader, the allurement cases exhibit familiar patterns in the treatment of boys and girls. Here too, courts routinely exonerate playing boys for their dangerous behaviour. Their language is telling—they speak of boys yielding to the overwhelming temptation to play with dangerous things, things which appear 'calculated to attract or allure' them or which are 'flaunted' in front of them, making it almost inevitable that they will 'succumb'. Warnings to such boys appear futile: one court even suggests that 'fruit may actually be more tempting when it is forbidden'. In this sense, the treatment of playing boys under the doctrine of allurement confirms what we saw in the child defendant cases: boys who exhibit prudential failings, to the extent that their failings are 'normal' or natural, have the benefit of a very expansive understanding of 'innocence'.

The contrast with playing girls could hardly be more dramatic. In response to an argument that a 13-year-old girl killed by a backing train engine should be judged by a lower standard, a court responds by noting that 'if we judged ordinary care for a woman by what was commonly looked for from one of her sex, we would hold her to a higher standard of prudence and vigilance than a man'.[3] And indeed in cases involving girls injured while at play, courts show little or no sympathy for the playing girl, routinely holding her to a higher standard than her male counterpart. They describe what seem like relatively subtle dangers as 'obvious' and plain. So even in the absence of a warning, a playing

---

[3] *Michigan v Hassenyer Central Railroad* 48 Mich 205, 208 (SC 1882) per Cooley J.

girl is less likely to recover any damages than is a playing boy. Similarly, with girls courts rarely if ever mention the concepts of temptation, attraction, and allurement that work so much in favour of playing boys. Instead, courts apply to girls rigid and even anachronistic versions of the very doctrines that they routinely reject as outmoded in cases involving playing boys. So unlike boys, girls are almost never allowed failures of prudence, even when those failures are self-directed. And the rare occasions where the language of naturalness is invoked with playing girls actually confirm these suspicions: courts forgive the girl who responds with panic or alarm to a dangerous situation (even when this does not seem a very adequate description on the facts). Thus, boys are granted much more latitude because they can invoke a broader conception of 'normal' prudential failures—failures which turn out to be exculpatory because of the tendency to read reasonableness as normalcy. And because reasonableness draws on underlying conceptions of normalcy, girlish failures of prudence are judged relatively harshly, since no similarly expansive understanding of 'normal' prudential failings comes to their aid.

Indeed, the picture that emerges is relatively clear: the reasonable person in practice turns out to be deeply indebted to troubling conceptions of what is normal or ordinary. The shortcomings, both cognitive and normative, of the mentally disabled are not widely shared and so are not seen as normal, nor therefore reasonable. It is however normal, and hence reasonable, for boys to be inattentive not only to their own safety but also to that of others. By contrast, it is not normal and therefore not reasonable for girls to be imprudent, even when it is only their own security at stake. Because of the way that the reasonable person embodies intuitive and undifferentiated judgements about appropriateness, it should hardly be surprising that it often draws deeply on ideas about what is normal or natural. But this means that the application of the standard actually works to reinforce exactly the stereotypes that equality seekers are worried about—reasonableness gets read as normal or natural with all of the difficulties that this implies.

In fact, the language used to account for this often troubling treatment serves to confirm the worry about equality. Thus, for instance, commentators justifying the special standard of care for children routinely refer to how normal and ordinary childhood is, and the gendered nature of these notions comes to the fore when we compare the treatment of boys and girls. In contrast, mental disability is depicted as an idiosyncrasy or peculiarity, an abnormality, confirming the worry that the mentally disabled continue to find themselves excluded from the ranks of full membership. Indeed, the defences of the seemingly anomalous treatment of the mentally disabled are replete with references to the stupid, to congenital fools and morons. And this rhetoric illustrates the indebtedness of the reasonable person to a certain kind of 'common sense' reasoning. So it seems that the personification of the standard, its infusion with an unreflective conception of ordinariness, and the distinctive impatience of common sense reasoning together characterize the troubling yet tenacious intuitive judgements that are the hallmark of the reasonable person.

This does suggest that there is indeed a problem with the reasonable person standard. As we have seen, the standard operates very differently for different groups of litigants: the mentally disabled are held to a fixed or invariant standard even for non-normative shortcomings such as lack of intelligence, both boys and girls have the benefit of a standard closely tailored to their non-normative shortcomings, and for the playing boy alone is reserved the privilege of a standard tailored to his normative as well as non-normative failings. The rhetoric and its reliance on unreflective ideas of what is normal only serve to exacerbate concerns about how the reasonable person operates. But how ought we to conceptualize this problem? Although feminist and critical writing on citizenship may seem the most obvious place to look for insight, even those debates take as relatively uncontroversial the aspect of citizenship implicated here—civil equality or equality under law. Instead, the most fundamental idea of our legal system—the rule of law—provides a powerful articulation of what seems to be going wrong with the reasonable person. John Rawls's discussion of the rule of law draws out the egalitarian demands of the idea of civil equality and calls attention to the complex and subtle ways that it can be undermined. The Rawlsian formulation, which notes how 'the subtle distortions of bias and prejudice' can effectively 'discriminate against certain groups in the judicial process'[4] seems to capture a vital dimension of the problem with the reasonable person standard. Rawls clarifies that under a system of the rule of law, judicial decision-making must at a minimum exhibit a certain kind of equality across cases. And his formulation of the rule of law serves to illuminate the critical link between constitutional (and other) norms of equality and the operation of a system of private law.

But if, as Rawls suggests, the rule of law is undermined by bias or prejudice in the application of the law, then it seems very unlikely that that bias or prejudice is confined to gender. Indeed, work which explores the complexity of discrimination is useful for fleshing out the full implications of Rawls's intuition about how the rule of law can go wrong. And this more developed picture of discrimination points towards re-examination of the category of 'boy': who exactly is the privileged boy? Most certainly, his privilege—and the courts' willingness to excuse his indiscretions—is not due only to his gender but also to his race and to his class. Discrimination analysis suggests that if gender is implicated in determinations of reasonableness, in all likelihood so is race. However, the difficulty of determining the race of the litigants means that it is extremely difficult to systematically assess its impact. But at least some of the class implications are a bit easier to identify. In fact, a group of cases involving the contributory negligence of working children from the early decades of the twentieth century enables comparison of the treatment of the working boy with that of the playing boy. And this reveals that working children are almost never given the latitude granted to the playing boy. The rhetoric here is also illuminating. In

---

[4] J Rawls, *A Theory of Justice* (Cambridge, Mass: Harvard University Press, 1971) 235.

the work setting, childhood appears virtually irrelevant, and working children who are injured are chided for not being more careful. Indeed, on more than one occasion, courts actually suggest that the fact that an injured child is working in and of itself means that he should not get the benefit of the relaxed standard of care normally extended to children. These cases thus reinforce our concerns about the troubling relationship between the reasonable person and common sense ideas of what is normal or ordinary. In stark contrast with its egalitarian ambitions, the standard actually seems to undermine one of the most basic tenets of equality—civil equality or equality under law. The question thus posed is whether the reasonable person standard is so hopelessly and fundamentally flawed that it must be jettisoned.

On this question, the feminist debate, which forcefully articulates both the virtues and the vices of the reasonable person standard, proves illuminating. At first blush, this may appear unlikely since feminists often seem conflicted, if not downright incoherent, on the question of the reasonable person. So, in the case of provocation and self-defence, many feminists criticize the reasonable person test, arguing that it is inherently biased on the grounds of gender, race, and class. A move to subjectivity, they suggest, is the only solution. Yet in sexual assault, feminists advocate an objective standard and decry any subjectivization of the *mens rea* requirement on the ground that it exacerbates women's inequality and misses an important dimension of blameworthiness. However, it is possible to make sense of this feminist ambivalence without completely giving up on the egalitarian promise of an objective standard. Indeed, recognition of the way that an invariant normative standard like reasonableness instantiates the fundamental legal requirement of equal respect, actually connects the feminist and critical egalitarians to their more traditional counterparts who defend the standard on equality grounds. But though we may affirm the conceptual centrality of an objective reasonableness standard to an egalitarian legal order, this by no means implies that feminist worries about the way such a standard works in practice can be ignored. In this important sense, critical egalitarians sharpen our sense of what is at stake: without the reasonable person's insistence on an invariant or objective normative standard, there is no check on the corrosive influence that discriminatory stereotypes (among other things) have on the imperative of equal respect. Yet if an objective standard holds such important promise for equality seekers that it cannot be jettisoned, the feminist debate also confirms the worry noted earlier that that promise will remain illusory unless something is done to correct the standard's conventional operation. In this way, the feminist debates both elucidate the normative significance of the reasonable person and highlight the difficulty of realizing that significance, at least in the absence of a major reworking of the standard.

Work on reasonableness standards in criminal law provides a useful point of departure for thinking about how the standard could be reformulated so as to live up to its egalitarian promise. The attentiveness to fault in the criminal setting and the controversial nature of inadvertence as a basis for criminal liability means that criminal law theory is pressed to provide a more precise account of the objective standard. In part because of the controversial status of inadvertence as a form of *mens rea*, its defenders devote considerable energy to explicating the conditions under which inattentiveness to others is blameworthy. And the conditions criminal theorists identify as central echo the very features adverted to, though not fully attended to, in the private law setting. So here too we see an emphasis on avoidability, awareness of the difference between the normative and non-normative elements of the standard, and the importance of an invariant normative standard to equality interests. Thus, in the criminal law setting, Hart echoes Holmes and Honoré in his insistence that the accused must have both the capacity required to comply with the law and a fair opportunity to exercise that capacity. However, Hart—like Holmes and Honoré in the private law context—arguably asks avoidability to do too much work and thus fails to fully elucidate the normative core of the reasonable person standard. Accounts of the culpability of inadvertence that look to customary practices may also seem promising for they are clearly influential but their egalitarian implications are deeply troubling. In fact, the very weaknesses of both the avoidability-based and the customary accounts point to the importance of articulating a more fully normative account of culpable inadvertence.

Fortunately, there are important resources in the theory of criminal negligence that aid in the development of this kind of an account. Most useful on this score is the work of theorists such as Duff, and those inspired by him, who have been developing an account of when heedlessness of others can be culpable. This 'indifference' account fixes its sights directly on the normative failing exhibited in culpable inadvertence: indifference to the interests of others. The standard's promise of egalitarianism takes hold here, and we can now understand it as the insistence that all, whatever their varying characters and normative make-ups, must appropriately attend to the interests of others. In this way, the strength of the standard's egalitarian claim is premissed on its entrenchment of an invariant standard of attentiveness to others. Thus, I cannot insist that my selfish character should diminish the care I owe others. In this sense then, the 'fixity' of an invariant *normative* standard like the objective standard is essential to ensuring interpersonal equality.

Because an indifference account treats as culpable only those actions that betray indifference to the interests of others, it demands an understanding of the 'proper relation' between the normative and what I have referred to as the descriptive parts of the standard. So the indifference account enables us to understand both the concern with the different components of the standard and the insight of avoidability-based theories. Indifference accounts ultimately demand attentiveness to the reason why a particular risk was imposed. And assessing whether indifference explains the inattentiveness to risk requires that we pay attention to the context and to the non-normative qualities of the litigant, such as whether he has the cognitive capacity to reach the standard. Otherwise, as Hart, Honoré, and Holmes at times all admit, we risk condemning those whose shortcomings betray no indifference to others. Focusing on indifference also helps to account for the limitations on the inquiry into avoidability that are difficult to explain on other grounds. Because the account focuses on when heedlessness betrays indifference, it does not ask whether the agent could have avoided his indifference. After all, at least in the absence of insanity, it is just as blameworthy to fail to possess the capacity to be attentive to others as it is to fail to exercise it. In this way, an indifference account ensures the objectivity of the normative component of the standard. At the same time, however, the focus on the normative demands of the objective standard makes it possible to particularize the standard without subjectivizing it. This is because it calibrates the standard only for those features of the agent that are not related to his indifference. An objective standard so understood should capture only, but *all*, culpable inadvertence.

By providing the groundwork for a more defensible understanding of the fault that the objective standard aims to capture, an indifference-based understanding can serve as a basis for critically assessing the rough intuitive judgements that often characterize determinations of culpability under the reasonable person standard. We can now begin to see which qualities of the reasonable person are contingent and cannot be insisted upon (her 'default characteristics', properly understood), but we can also identify those latent 'moral' qualities of the reasonable person which we must hold fast. Ironically, this account suggests that in many difficult cases, the conventional reasonable person analysis leads us astray. The mentally disabled are held to an invariant standard, despite the fact that cognitive shortcomings alone betray no indifference to the interests of others. We might say that a normatively indifferent 'default' characteristic of the reasonable person—her level of intelligence—is erroneously treated as though it had the kind of significance that enables us to properly demand it of all and condemn those who lack it. The case of the privileged playing boy (and frequently also the man in sexual assault) seems to exhibit just the opposite kind of problem. Here, the *moral* character of the reasonable person is too often varied to reflect that of the litigant, allowing variation just where there should be none simply because the particular form of indifference is common or pervasive. So ironically, the standard often seems to hold firm those qualities that it should particularize or vary with the person judged (non-normative qualities, intelligence, foresight, etc.) and subjectivize what it should hold firm (normative or moral qualities—respect for others). But if in this way, the reasonable person standard seems paradoxical as a fault standard in that it 'catches' some behaviour that is not culpable and misses some that is culpable, this paradox is not simply a series of *ad hoc* mistakes.

As their rhetoric suggests, courts tend to infuse the reasonable person with the qualities, normative and non-normative, of the ordinary person. The unsurprising result is that the standard too often operates as an (unjustifiable) standard of ordinariness rather than as a (justifiable) standard of reasonableness. In this way, the reasonable person may act as an invitation to draw on underlying stereotypes that are often played out through unreflective ideas of what is normal or ordinary.

Too often the inquiry thus ends up turning on the ability of a particular litigant to draw on a capacious concept of normal imprudence or carelessness. The dangerous playing boy and the oblivious sexual aggressor both have access to relatively broad understandings of normal imprudence or carelessness, with the result that exoneration is much easier, even when the shortcoming in question is normative in the sense that it betrays indifference to others. In contrast, the developmentally disabled person, the woman who kills her abuser out of anger, and the girl at play have even at best very limited access to such a notion and thus find it much more difficult to be exonerated. The result is a deeply conventional account of what is reasonable—it is what people ordinarily or customarily do. But so understood, a reasonable person standard will rarely assist an equality seeker. To the extent that people commonly treat others in ways that are discriminatory or disrespectful, reading reasonableness as ordinariness will do nothing but replicate—with the force of law—existing inequalities.

The question then is whether it is possible to realize the egalitarian promise of the objective standard by somehow disentangling the reasonable person from the ordinary person. This is particularly pressing because the mistakes that result from the entanglement of the ordinary or normal and the reasonable are typically not *ad hoc* but are instead systematic in nature. This is because discrimination is actually constituted by 'widely shared' or normal mistakes about the equal worth of others. But it can be very difficult to recognize the moral quality of the mistake when it is a mistake that is commonly made. Indeed, typically neither a judge nor a 'wrong-doer' will be aware of the fault or indifference, precisely because it is so common. The temptation then will be to hold, as is commonly argued in the sexual assault context, that while the perpetrator did something wrong, he cannot be held accountable for that wrong because he did not subjectively know the act was wrong. This will not be a problem in ordinary mistake of law cases because where the mistake is idiosyncratic it will seem unproblematic to insist that the law, not the individual judged, is the arbiter of values. Unfortunately, where a similar kind of mistake of law is normal or widespread, our confidence begins to fail. But the troubling consequence of this is that common or ordinary mistakes threaten to escape the mistake of law effect, which is the means by which the law insists on the primacy of its own values. And this is despite the fact that the mistake of law rule has particular salience in the context of discrimination because of its insistence that assessments of the value of others be set by the law, rather than by the varying characters and predilections of individuals. So the systematic nature of discriminatory mistakes may effectively create an exception to the mistake of law rule. But given the rule of law implications, it is essential to ensure that 'objective' reasonableness standards do not end up counting widely shared mistakes as 'reasonable'.

This means that for the objective standard to provide the kind of normative fixity that is so essential to equality, it must be capable of consistently capturing the fault of indifference even in situations involving discriminatory background beliefs. For as we have seen, although an objective standard premised on indifference theoretically holds promise for equality seekers, it will not make good on this unless we ensure that it does not merely reflect conventional understandings. On this point, law reform efforts in the area of sexual assault help to illustrate how we might go about disentangling the reasonable and the normal in a context where customary beliefs threaten to undermine the egalitarian normative content of reasonableness. Thus, as a general matter it will often be possible to considerably improve the negligence inquiry simply by articulating and focusing on the centrality of the normative failing of indifference. Because this better captures what would count as a proper relation between the normative and the non-normative components of the inquiry, it should assist for instance in dealing with cases involving mental disability and the like. However, where the normative content of reasonableness is more controversial, where there is deeper tension between the legal and the customary norm, the literature on sexual harassment and sexual assault both suggest that more normative specificity will be required. Thus, for instance, in the context of sexual interactions it is probably critical to insist on the centrality of the right to sexual autonomy. Furthermore, where judges may be tempted to draw on troubling background understandings in interpreting what kinds of actions are and are not reasonable, the 'call to context' will not provide a solution. Instead, as sexual assault reform efforts illustrate, it may be necessary to use specific provisions to counteract the most prevalent discriminatory understandings and to draw attention to and try to rule out customary errors.

This analysis, though it focuses specifically on the objective standard, may also have some small contribution to make to legal theory. Legal theory, in both its traditional and its critical postures, has been preoccupied with the problem of judicial discretion, at least since the Hart–Fuller debate. But the worry has focused on the difficulties that the existence of discretion poses for the institutional competence of the judiciary. Partly because of this institutional focus, legal theory has made relatively few connections with critical egalitarian work on the problem of discretion. But critical egalitarian theory may actually have something important to contribute to the somewhat formulaic debate about discretion that proceeds elsewhere in the world of legal theory. The focus of critical egalitarians is not so exclusively on *who* exercises discretion, but increasingly on *how* it is exercised. In part this is because similar problems of exclusion apply to legislatures as well as courts. So one pressing question from this perspective, and a question that is virtually ignored in the traditional debate between legal theory and critical legal studies, is a more complex one about how discretion should properly be exercised. In particular, how, given its open-textured nature, can we ensure that discretion does not simply create room for bias and discrimination? This is a problem for an open-textured standard like the reasonable person, but the problem is of course far more wide-ranging. There are undoubtedly important institutional components to such a problem. However, while the solutions will necessarily be tailored to the kind of institution in question, they are not the kind of primarily institutional responses found in the standard legal theory debate. Instead it seems at least as crucial to address how the exercise of judgement or discretion can be both constrained to rule out common (and often discriminatory) mistakes, and positively shaped by deeper values. This necessarily implicates a more integrated way of thinking about the relationship between public and private law and perhaps other normative regimes as well. It may ultimately raise questions about the proper stance towards the past as well.

IV. CONCLUSION

Taking seriously the egalitarian concerns in a core problem of fault and responsibility in this sense proves illuminating. It reveals the serious equality and rule of law problems associated with the tendency to conflate the reasonable person with her ordinary counterpart. Thus conceived, the reasonable person can never achieve the ideal of reasonableness to which it aspires; in that important sense it is therefore rightly criticized on equality grounds. But since abandoning the ideal of reasonableness to a realm of purely subjective standards is even more corrosive of equality, a more constructive response is necessary. The analysis though ultimately raises more profound worries about the standard. It seems at least conceivable that adopting some ideal person as a standard of behaviour creates an almost irresistible opening to endow that imaginary person with all sorts of qualities that are not in fact prudential. Indeed, it is perhaps not accidental that the common law's famous lyricism about the reasonable man rarely if ever speaks to the normative qualities that this analysis identifies as the heart of the standard. Instead, the common law has been transfixed with where the reasonable man lives, his mode of transportation, what kinds of clothes he wears, and what activities he engages in. But this personification, while undoubtedly entertaining, also carries with it certain dangers.

The most important such danger is the extent to which personification encourages the conflation of 'descriptive' attributes of the person with the normative standard of behaviour. Indeed, personification may tempt the judicial imagination precisely because of how it integrates different aspects of the standard. This may seem to improve our access to reasonableness by making it familiar and knowable. However, as we have seen, it also makes it extraordinarily complex to figure out which latent qualities of the reasonable person matter and which do not. So while personification holds out the promise of relatively uncomplicated—and intuitively plausible—judgements about the reasonableness, these judgements begin to seem flawed when it is necessary to have a sharper sense of just what it is about the reasonable person that matters. Even more troublingly, perhaps, the confusion that personification actually invites about what such embodied reasonableness can mean, undoubtedly makes it all too easy to read the reasonable man as the infinitely more knowable 'ordinary' man. Thus, perhaps unsurprisingly, the reasonable person often turns out to bear a rather suspicious similarity to the judge. The solution that many of the critics have suggested has been to substitute the biographical qualities of the litigant for those of the judge. But this may be misguided. In the end, although critics have often suggested jettisoning the 'reason' part of the standard, it seems more likely that we can actually fortify the reason by instead abolishing the person created so long ago in *Vaughan v Menlove*.

1

Living on the Fault Line: The Reasonable Person and the Developmentally Disabled

Just who is the reasonable person? Revered and vilified, he is perhaps the common law's most enduring and expounded upon fiction. And notwithstanding contemporary suspicion, the reasonable person remains a central figure in the literary imagination of the common law, reassuring us with his very ordinariness. The biography of the reasonable person is thus understandably renowned: he is the man who mows the lawns in his shirtsleeves in the evening and takes the magazines at home; he rides the Clapham omnibus; he is, in short, that 'excellent but odious' character that A. P. Herbert deplores.[1] Some have extolled his virtues, describing him as having 'the agility of an acrobat and the foresight of a Hebrew prophet',[2] others have focused on his limitations among which number the fact that 'he has not the courage of Achilles, the wisdom of Ulysses or the strength of Hercules'.[3]

As the common law's tool for identifying behaviour that attracts neither censure nor legal liability, the reasonable person plays a central role in the law of negligence. The actions of the litigant (plaintiff or defendant) are compared to what the reasonable person would have done in like circumstances. Only those who emulate the reasonable person will be considered 'faultless' and hence relieved of the consequences of their actions. In this sense then the behaviour of the reasonable person defines the content of the renowned objective standard of the law of negligence: a standard that, though it does not demand perfection, does insist upon a certain level of prudence or attentiveness to the interests of others. Thus, most prominent among the reasonable person's many roles is his embodiment of the fault element or standard of care in negligence: the objective standard. And it is because of his personification of this normative demand that the reasonable person has been described as 'the anthropomorphic conception of justice'.[4]

Yet though his role is in this way a normative one, the reasonable person's judgement and attentiveness are not prominent among the qualities about which judges and commentators have waxed lyrical. Indeed, these are not the qualities that dominate the many 'biographies' of the reasonable person. In fact,

---

[1] AP Herbert, *Uncommon Law* (London: Metheun, 1935) 4.
[2] RE Megarry, *Miscellany-at-Law: A Diversion for Lawyers and Others* (London: Stevens & Sons Ltd, 1955) 260 (quoting Lord Bramwell).   [3] ibid (quoting Sir Percy Winfield).
[4] *Davis Contractors Ltd v Fareham UDC* [1956] AC 686, 728.

we often glean our understanding of these most vital aspects of the reasonable person indirectly, through encounters with *who he is not*. And his erratic approach to those who—like the developmentally disabled and children—fail to resemble himself is such that it may actually tempt us to question whether he is best understood as a model of excellence. Indeed, while the stature of the reasonable man may have convinced us of his importance, at bottom he remains something of a mystery. This is at least in part because of his complicated relationship to blameworthiness. In fact, the treatment of the various forms of incapacities or shortcomings—age, physical or mental ability, informational deficits—that do not trouble the reasonable person seem more noteworthy for variability than for coherence. Yet this obscure corner of the law of negligence holds broader lessons for our understanding of the crucial relationship between fault and blameworthiness.

Unease with the way the reasonable person conceives of the relationship between fault and blame has traditionally taken the defendant's claim in *Vaughan v Menlove*[5] as its point of departure. There Menlove, the defendant, was found liable after his hayrick caught on fire and destroyed several cottages belonging to his neighbour. On appeal, Menlove challenged the charge to the jury arguing that if he had acted to the best of his judgement, then he ought not to be responsible for the misfortune of not possessing the highest order of intelligence. The facts of the case may make it easy to dismiss our misgivings.[6] But nonetheless there remains a lingering sense that there is after all something in the argument made by the wily Menlove even if it was not persuasive in his own case. And we would do well not to ignore these misgivings, for the defendant's claim in *Vaughan* prompts re-evaluation of what the orthodoxy that negligence is fault-based[7] really means. Indeed *Vaughan v Menlove* has long served as the focal point for discussions of the reasonable person precisely because it sharply poses the question of how someone of limited intelligence can be held liable for that misfortune in a system that allocates liability based on fault.

---

[5] (1837) 3 Bing NC 468, 132 ER 490 (CP).

[6] The court upholds the trial judge's charge to the jury that the defendant was 'bound to proceed with such reasonable caution as a prudent man would have exercised under such circumstances' and thus rejects the defendant's claim that he ought not to be blamed for deficits of intelligence. The case, however, is more complicated than it appears at first glance. In part this is because the real difficulty in the case was a credibility problem, not a moral dilemma. Repeatedly the defendant was advised to dismantle the perilous rick because of the danger of fire. However, perhaps in part because his own stock was insured, he responded that 'he would chance it'. So the defendant's insistence that he should not be blamed 'for not possessing the highest order of intelligence' seems like straightforward bad faith. Unsurprisingly, two of the three judgments refer to these credibility problems and suggest that the charge to the jury was, if anything, too favourable to the defendant who was probably guilty of gross negligence: ibid 476–477, Park and Vaughan JJ. Significantly, all three judgments refer to, and two rely on, the non-fault-based duty, apparently sounding in nuisance, that 'everyone takes upon himself the duty of so dealing with his own property as not to injure the property of others': ibid 477, Vaughan J.

[7] JB Ames, 'Law and Morals' (1908) 22 Harv L Rev 97. Ames describes the transition from strict to fault-based liability. Similarly, in *The Common Law* Oliver Wendell Holmes provides an energetic defence of tort law as a species of liability founded on fault or blameworthiness: (ed. MD Howe) (Cambridge, Mass: Harvard University Press, 1963) 64–103.

In fact, beginning an analysis of the reasonable person with this problem of the 'developmentally or cognitively disabled'[8] uncovers deep tensions and ambiguities in the law of negligence. An overview of the actual configurations of the standard illustrates that in fact the law does forgive certain failures to attain the standard of the reasonable person. But it is not similarly generous to those who lack intelligence. Tort theorists almost uniformly defend this apparent anomaly. And their accounts are worth examining closely, although ultimately they are all unsuccessful. For as they defend holding the unintelligent to the same level of intelligence as that of the reasonable person, they illuminate the constitutive tension between liberty and security in a case where the law of negligence is pressed to a choice between them. And from their accounts it is possible to take both something to work from and something to worry about. The defences of imposing the objective standard on the developmentally disabled do suggest some possibilities for reconstructing a more adequate account of the basis of liability in negligence. At the same time, however, they point to where we ought to be wary of the reasonable person.

I. Tracing the 'fault line'

As noted above, the law of negligence determines whether or not the individual in question is at 'fault' by measuring his or her behaviour against what the 'reasonable man of ordinary prudence would do in the circumstance'. A glance through leading texts suggests that commentators agree on the wisdom of holding individual actors, more or less regardless of their competence,[9] responsible for the harm they cause by virtue of their failure to behave as a 'reasonable man' would have.[10] So in theory at least, the objective standard 'eliminates the personal equation and is independent of the idiosyncrasies of the particular person whose

---

[8] The term 'developmentally disabled' denotes individuals who suffer from cognitive or intellectual limitations, disorders, or disabilities. This term is in this sense a more respectful reference to what used to be called 'mental retardation'. For an overview of the various issues related to terminology and legal issues, see GB Robertson, *Mental Disability and the Law in Canada* (2nd edn, Scarborough: Carswell Thomson Professional Publishing, 1994) 2 and ch 10 (Tort Liability). See also J Parry, *Mental Disability Law: A Primer* (5th edn, Washington: American Bar Foundation, 1995) 1–2 discussing terminology. This term is thus narrower than either the colloquial term 'stupid' or ignorant often used in the literature, which may encompass not only cognitive or intellectual impairments but also 'moral' ignorance. Similarly, it is narrower than the common term 'mentally disabled', which refers both to cognitive or intellectual limitations as well as various forms of mental illness. As discussed below, mental illness is best viewed as posing a set of issues distinct from those involved in claims like the defendant's in *Vaughan*, and perhaps for that reason is treated as a separate legal problem as well. Thus, the term 'developmentally disabled' does not encompass emotional or social disorders, though such disorders may, of course, appear either in conjunction with a developmental disability or on their own in persons of otherwise 'normal' intellectual abilities.

[9] Competence is distinct from capacity. While capacity is in general a precondition for legal liability, competence is not: T Honoré, 'Responsibility and Luck: The Moral Basis of Strict Liability' in *Responsibility and Fault* (Oxford: Hart Publishing, 1999) 17.

[10] M Brazier and J Murphy (eds), *Street on Torts* (10th edn, London: Butterworths, 1999) 239; JF Clerk, *Clerk and Lindsell on Torts* (ed AM Dugale) (18th edn, London: Sweet and Maxwell,

conduct is in question'.[11] However, the actual workings of the objective standard are more complex than this suggests. A uniform norm of reasonableness is not applied to every individual regardless of his or her abilities. Instead, in practice the reasonable person standard often—though as we shall see, not invariably—borrows heavily from the qualities of the actual litigant. The result, far from a single straightforward norm of behaviour, is rather a densely textured set of considerations that together constitute the complex fault line of negligence.

The first category of problems for the reasonable person arises because liability in negligence requires a minimum capacity for rational agency. Thus, individuals who lack that capacity pose a set of threshold problems for the reasonable person. The easiest and least controversial of these problems is the case of very young children. Because they cannot meet the threshold 'agency' requirement, children of 'tender years' (approximately 5 years and below) are typically totally immune from liability in negligence.[12] But beyond this category, courts and commentators are divided over what is sufficient to negate the presumption of agency and thus preclude liability in negligence. Nonetheless, certain patterns that turn out to be recurrent features of the reasonable person are apparent even in the considerations of what kinds of incapacities will negate the presumption of agency.

Thus, we see, for instance, that outside of the case of very young children, courts and commentators are more disposed (perhaps somewhat surprisingly) to allow physical than mental incapacities to negate the presumption of agency and thus liability. Similarly, temporary incapacities are more likely to receive leniency than permanent ones. Thus, for instance, the 'normal' defendant who suffers sudden collapse or other involuntary conduct, including the sudden onset of incapacitating physical and even mental conditions, will be excused from liability in negligence.[13] And although in the case of driving, *Roberts v Ramsbottom*

2000) 389–397; JG Fleming, *The Law of Torts* (9th edn, Agincourt: The Law Book Company, 1998) 117; GHL Fridman, *The Law of Torts in Canada* Vol I (Toronto: Carswell, 1989) 287, 297; Holmes (n 7 above) 87; WP Keeton (gen ed), *Prosser and Keeton on the Law of Torts* (5th edn, St Paul, Minn: West Publishing Co, 1984) 173–175; AM Linden, *Canadian Tort Law* (6th edn, Toronto: Butterworths, 1997) 126; WVH Rogers, *Winfield and Jolowicz on Tort* (15th edn, London: Sweet and Maxwell, 1998) 171.

[11] *Glasgow Corp v Muir* [1943] AC 448, 457 (Lord MacMillan) in Fleming (n 10 above) 119. However, Edward Green has suggested that in fact the objective standard has a limited impact on the actual outcome of particular cases: 'The Reasonable Man—Legal Fiction or Psychosocial Reality?' (1968) 2 Law & Soc Rev 241, 256. See also Leon Green, 'The Negligence Issue' (1927–28) 37 Yale LJ 1029, also discussed below, n 110. Note, however, both writers are discussing American tort law where the role of juries is far more extensive.

[12] Linden (n 10 above) 136; Prosser (n 10 above) 180; RFV Heuston and RA Buckley, *Salmond and Heuston on the Law of Torts* (21st edn, London: Sweet and Maxwell, 1996) 411–412; Winfield (n 10 above) 832; Fridman (n 10 above) 298.

[13] Fleming (n 10 above) 126–127. See nn 68–69 below. See also Fridman (ibid) 298–299, noting in reference to incapacitating illnesses of which the defendant has no warning, '[t]he fact that the defendant behaved as he did by reason of an attack which made him incapable of observing the appropriate standard of care will mean that he was not negligent'. In support of this position he cites cases involving epilepsy [*Gootson v R* [1948] 4 DLR 33 (SCC)], sudden illness [*Slattery v Haley* [1923] 3 DLR 156, 52 OLR 95 (Ont CA)], dizzy spells [*Dessaint v Carrière* [1958] OWN 481 (Ont CA)],

held that nothing less than a complete loss of consciousness would negate liability, that view has been revisited by the Court of Appeal in *Mansfield v Weetabix* on the ground that it comes perilously close to strict liability.[14] The corollary though is that courts and commentators are unlikely to negate the presumption of agency where the litigant's incapacity is mental not physical, and chronic rather than sudden and temporary. Thus, although one might automatically presume the opposite, in fact the negligence liability of the 'insane' remains controversial.[15] Some courts and commentators have suggested that since negligence presupposes a capacity for rational choice, there should be no liability in negligence for defendants whose insanity is so extreme as to preclude them from appreciating that they had a duty to take care.[16] However, this position may not be the

blackouts [*Hagg v Bohnet* (1962) 33 DLR (2d) 378 (BC CA)]. Fridman does not mention *Roberts v Ramsbottom* [1980] 1 All ER 7 (QBD). Winfield notes that the negligence standard is said to eliminate the individual characteristics of the defendant, 'but this does not mean, for example, that a driver who suffers a sudden, unexpected and disabling illness is liable for the damage he does: even the reasonable man can have a heart attack': (n 10 above) 840 [footnotes omitted]. Salmond (n 12 above) 416 states that '[m]ischief done by an epileptic in one of his paroxysms, or by a fever patient in his delirium, or by a somnambulist in his sleep is presumably not actionable' [citing *Morriss v Marsden* [1952] 1 All ER 925, 927]. Prosser notes that '[s]imilar to the cases involving sudden illness or unconsciousness, there is some sentiment for treating a sudden delirium or loss of mental faculties as a "circumstance" depriving the actor of control over his conduct, thus shielding him from liability, provided that the lapse was unforeseeable': (n 10 above) 178 [footnotes omitted, citing *Breunig v American Family Insurance Co* (1970) 173 NW 2d 619 (US Wis), *Buckley v Smith Transport* [1946] 4 DLR 721 (Ont CA), and comparing *Restatement (Second) of Torts*, ss 283C Comment B (1965) and *Kuhn v Zabotsky* 224 NE 2d 137 (SC Ohio 1967)]. Linden (n 10 above) 143 [citing test in *Buckley*].

[14] In *Roberts* (ibid), the defendant who had had a stroke was held liable for an accident he caused despite the fact that the court accepted that the stroke rendered him 'unable to appreciate that he should have stopped'. Neill J held that '[o]ne cannot accept as exculpation anything less than total loss of consciousness'. As discussed in the text however in *Mansfield v Weetabix* [1998] 1 WLR 1263 (CA), the Court of Appeal refused to find liability on the part of a man who partially lost consciousness as a result of a hypoglycaemic state caused by a serious malignancy he did not know he had. The Court found that that state must be taken into consideration in assessing the defendant's negligence.

[15] Fleming (n 10 above) 126. The kind of confusion to which Fleming refers is apparent throughout the discussions of the application of the objective standard to the developmentally disabled defendant. For instance, Clerk (n 10 above) 136, first states that the liability in negligence of a person of unsound mind is basically on the same footing as that of a young child. For both, 'it is a question of fact whether he was sufficiently self-possessed to be capable [of] taking care.' However, this is immediately followed by, '[t]his should not, however, be taken too far in view of the objective standard normally applicable in cases of negligence': ibid. It is noteworthy that the cases used to support the latter proposition deal solely with automobile drivers and thus perhaps are rationalized on different grounds: see n 19 below.

[16] Fleming (n 10 above) 126–127 refers to but does not support this position and cites as relevant *Buckley* (n 13 above). Picher's 1975 comparative analysis of the tort liability of the insane notes that in Canada, an insane person will be held liable for unintentional torts such as negligence only if he appreciates the duty upon him to act in a particular way and is able to discharge that duty: P Picher, 'The Tortious Liability of the Insane in Canada . . . with a Comparative Look at the United States and Civil Law Jurisdictions and a Suggestion for an Alternative' (1975) 13 Osgoode Hall LJ 193, 214–216, relying on *Slattery* and *Buckley* (n 13 above). On similar grounds, the English authorities appear reluctant to subject the insane to liability in tort, particularly given the Court of Appeal decision in *Mansfield* (n 14 above). So while unsoundness of mind does not render the insane immune from tort liability, it may affect liability where it defeats the requirement that the defendant possess

predominant view. In the United States, rather than relaxing the standard for mental incapacities, the law has held 'the developmentally deranged or insane defendant accountable for his negligence as if the person were a normal, prudent person'.[17] Increasingly this seems to be the view that is winning the support of Canadian courts and commentators.[18]

In fact, similar complications are evident even where the litigants have satisfied the minimum 'agency' threshold for liability. Indeed, it is possible to identify certain continuities between when courts refuse to recognize mental incapacity and when, more generally, they refuse to take the qualities of the litigant into consideration under the reasonable person standard. Thus, for certain groups of individuals the standard is subjectivized in order to avoid the perceived unfairness of imposing an unattainable standard. Thus, the law has been most hesitant to impute liability to children. The result is that even children beyond tender years are not held to the standard of the reasonable person. Instead, they need exercise only that degree of care to be expected 'from a child of like age, intelligence and experience'.[19] This holds true for child defendants

the requisite state of mind for the tort in question: Winfield (n 10 above) 839–840; Clerk (n 10 above) 4–68. English commentators also note that the shift from the relatively 'strict' interpretation of the negligence standard in *Roberts* (n 13 above) to the more capacity-oriented standard in *Mansfield* (n 14 above) may well have implications for those of unsound mind though these are as yet unclear: Winfield (ibid); Clerk (ibid). Fridman states that the key question regarding the liability of the insane concerns 'whether the mental state of the defendant rendered him incapable of appreciating that he had a duty to take care, or, if he was aware that he was under such a duty, made him incapable of discharging it': (n 10 above) 299. See also E Weinrib, *The Idea of Private Law* (Cambridge, Mass: Harvard University Press, 1995) 183 n 22 rationalizing *Slattery, Buckley*, and *Bruenig* (n 13 above) on similar grounds.

[17] Prosser (n 10 above) 177. Prosser and Fleming (ibid) both distinguish cases involving 'developmentally deranged' defendants from cases involving 'a sudden delirium or loss of mental faculties'. They suggest that in these latter cases there is reason to treat the disability 'as a "circumstance" depriving the actor of control over his conduct, thus shielding him from liability, provided that the lapse was unforeseeable': Prosser (ibid) 178. They provide no reason for the difference in treatment, but simply point to the similarity between sudden disability cases and the sudden illness or unconsciousness cases.

[18] Linden (n 10 above) 143–144 states that the best solution may be to treat the 'insane in the same way as everyone else'. He cites fairness to the victims as the main rationale for this. However, in his ensuing discussion (at 144), he cites only cases involving automobiles, so it is unclear how far beyond this he wishes his 'solution' to extend. Some courts at least are adopting a similar position. For instance, in *Wenden v Trikha* a driver who had injured a woman while he was suffering from an insane delusion was found liable: (1991) 8 CCLT (2d) 138 (Alta CA). In that case, Murray J explicitly rejects the application of the M'Naughten rules to civil actions and on this ground rejects the holdings in *Buckley* (n 13 above) and in *Canada (Attorney-General) v Connolly* (1990) 41 BCLR (2d) 162, 64 DLR (4th) 84 (BCSC). Murray J states that a person whose mental state is such that he does not appreciate that he owes a duty of care to others while operating a motor vehicle should be subject to the objective standard of a reasonable driver: *Wenden* (above) 174–175. In support of this position he cites Robertson (n 8 above) 243 and Linden (n 10 above) 40–42, 142–145, as well as the majority position in the United States as set out in 'Torts—Insanity as Defense' 49 ALR (3d) 193. Murray J also distinguishes the case of the mentally ill defendant from the exception available for 'the person who suddenly and without warning suffers an affliction which results in physical incapacity': *Wenden* (above) 176 citing and discussing on this point cases including *Slattery* (n 13 above); *Gootson* (n 13 above); *Boomer v Penn* (1965) 52 DLR (2d) 673 (Ont HC); *Roberts* (n 13 above); and *Waugh v Allan* [1964] 2 Lloyd's Rep 1.

[19] *McEllistrum v Etches* [1956] SCR 787; *Heisler v Moke* [1972] 25 DLR (3d) 670 (HC); *Restatement* (n 13 above) ss 283A. See also Linden (ibid) 138; Fridman (n 10 above) 299; Prosser

as well as child plaintiffs.[20] This relaxation of the standard is subject, however, to an 'adult activities' exception that holds children who are engaged in 'adult' activities, such as driving, to the ordinary standard of care.[21]

The qualities of the reasonable person are also typically tailored to mirror the physical attributes of the litigant, again repeating the leniency we saw towards physical incapacities. Physically, the reasonable person is said to resemble the actor. The result is that the person who is blind, deaf, lame, or otherwise physically disabled is entitled to 'live in the world and have others make allowances for his disability'.[22] This is because under a fault standard 'the person cannot be required to do the impossible by conforming to physical standards which he cannot meet'.[23] Consequently, the physically disabled person is simply required to act reasonably in the light of his or her knowledge of the disability, which is treated as merely one of the circumstances under which the person acts.[24]

(ibid) 179 (child must exercise the degree of care that it would be 'reasonable to expect of a "child of like age, intelligence and experience" ' [footnotes omitted]).

Slight variations on this test are found in the leading case of *McHale v Watson* (1966) 115 CLR 199 (Aust HC) (child to be compared to normal children of similar age and experience). See Winfield (n 10 above) 832 (child's behaviour must fall below the standard of an ordinarily reasonable and prudent child of his age); Salmond (n 12 above) 411 (child must exercise the amount of care reasonably to be expected from a child of that age); Clerk (n 10 above) 396 (standard of care to be expected of a boy of that age and maturity); Fleming (n 10 above) 126 (child is expected to conform to the standard appropriate for normal children of similar age, intelligence, and experience).

[20] *McHale v Watson* (ibid); *Mullin v Richards* [1998] 1 All ER 920 (CA); *Vaillancourt v Jacques* [1975] 1 SCR 724; *Christie v Slevinsky* (1981) 12 MVR 67 (Alta QB). American courts have also explicitly rejected a double standard for children plaintiffs and child defendants with the result that defendants also receive the benefit of a relaxed standard of care so long as they are not engaged in 'adult' activities: *Purtle v Shelton* 474 SW 2d 123 (SC Ark 1971); *Hamel v Crosietier* 256 A2d 143 (SCNH 1969); *Daniels v Evans* 224 A 2d 63 (SCNH 1966); *Charbonneau v MacRury* 153 A 457 (SCNH 1931). See also Salmond (n 12 above) 411–412; Street (n 10 above) 237; Fleming (ibid) 126; Winfield (ibid) 172, 827–832; Prosser (ibid) 181.

[21] *Ryan v Hickson* (1974) 7 OR (2d) 352 (Ont HC); *Dellwo v Pearson* 107 NW 2d 859, 863 (SC Minn 1961); *Daniels v Evans* (ibid). As these cases suggest, the rationale for this 'exception' may have less to do with 'adult activities' than with the heightened liability imposed on drivers. This seems consistent with the stricter form of liability imposed on drivers generally: *Roberts* (n 13 above); *Wenden* (n 18 above). Commentators have also noted that courts tend to be particularly stringent when the harm results from the use of a vehicle: Salmond (n 12 above) 224, 234–235; Fleming (n 10 above) 125–127; Linden (n 10 above) 142–144; Clerk (n 10 above) 413. Thus, a driver—particularly a defendant driver—who requests a somewhat subjectivized standard of care may have less success than other litigants. This reluctance to be lenient to defendant drivers may be due at least in part to the presence of mandatory insurance: Fleming (ibid) 127; Winfield (ibid) 172; Linden (ibid) 140; Clerk (ibid) 512. However, there has been some debate over the position of learner drivers: Winfield (ibid) 172, referring to *Nettleship v Watson* [1971] 2 QB 691 and the Australian High Court's criticism of it in *Cook v Cook* (1986) 68 ALR 353. A similar explanation also seems to be at work in cases involving drivers who are physically or developmentally infirm or elderly: Fleming (ibid) 126; Linden (ibid) 144; Prosser (ibid) 176; Street (ibid) 238–239. However, despite cases like *Roberts* (n 13 above), even here the situation is unclear, for courts often refuse to impose liability on the driver who is subject to a sudden incapacitating attack: *Buckley* (n 13 above); *Connolly* (n 18 above); Fleming (ibid) 125.

[22] Prosser (n 10 above) 176. See also Clerk (ibid) 395–396; Fleming (ibid) 125; Linden (ibid) 134; Street (ibid) 203. However, a closer examination of the cases cited in support of this fairly broad proposition leaves it unclear just how far the exception would apply to defendants, rather than plaintiffs.

[23] Prosser (ibid).

[24] ibid; Clerk (n 10 above) 395–396; Fleming (n 10 above) 125; Linden (n 10 above) 134; Street (n 10 above) 238–239.

However, courts have not been similarly willing to consider developmental limitations as 'circumstances' that must be incorporated into the reasonable person in order to appropriately tailor the standard to the defendant. Indeed, the generosity extended to children both below and above the minimum agency threshold contrasts with the distinct lack of similar generosity for any mental incompetence. Thus, the treatment of such incompetence under the reasonable person more generally mirrors the reluctance to relieve the insane of liability in negligence even where it seems impossible to impute the minimum capacity requirement.[25] So in the case of the 'capable' individual with some kind of mental incompetence that falls short of complete insanity, the reasonable person standard is typically applied without employing the person/circumstance distinction that is relied on in the case of physical disabilities and without any kind of latitude of the kind made for children.

According to John Fleming, the weight of authority rejects making any allowance for the 'defendant's mental abnormality' on the ground that it would be unfairly prejudicial to accident victims.[26] In direct contrast to the predominant approach to insanity, commentators sometimes sound as though it is actually the minor nature of the mental disability that precludes legal consideration. Thus, Alan Linden argues that while individuals with mental disabilities need not comply with the reasonable person standard on the basis that it is unfair to hold someone liable for accidents he is incapable of avoiding, the law makes no allowance for 'those who are merely deficient mentally'.[27] And Prosser confirms that, with regard to any 'mental deficiency of a minor nature' the objective standard applies.[28] Interestingly though, both Linden and Prosser actually support holding both the completely insane and the 'merely' deficient or incompetent to the reasonable person standard.[29] Thus, in the law of negligence an individual who has some kind of mental incompetency will be liable even where the disability makes compliance with the standard impossible. Unlike children and the physically disabled who will not be liable for harm that was not in their power to avoid, for those with mental incompetencies, avoidability does not

---

[25] See above nn 15–18.

[26] Fleming (n 10 above) 126–127, citing *Adamson v Motor Vehicle Insurance Trust* (1957) 58 WALR 56; *Wenden* (n 18 above); *Restatement* (n 13 above) ss 283B. Despite his acknowledgement that this position is inconsistent with how 'normal' defendants are treated when they lose consciousness, Fleming celebrates it as a welcome recognition that moral considerations are out of place in accident law, particularly where there is insurance: ibid.

[27] Linden (n 10 above) 142. Linden goes on to advocate that the insane be treated the same way as everyone else. He reasons, '[a]lthough this might be somewhat hard on them, it is harder still on their victims to excuse them': ibid 144. He places particular emphasis on automobile accidents.

[28] Prosser (n 10 above) 177, citing *Vaughan* (n 5 above) 471. For similar statements, see Street (n 10 above) 239 and Clerk (n 10 above) 185.

[29] Indeed, Prosser is interesting on this point, noting that 'where an actor entirely lacks the capacity to comprehend a risk or avoid an accident, one might expect a relaxation of the standard similar to the physical disability rule. Yet, for a variety of reasons, the law has developed the other way, holding the developmentally deranged or insane defendant accountable for his negligence as if the person were a normal prudent person': (ibid) 177 [footnotes omitted].

serve as a precondition to liability.[30] This thus confirms the common reading of
Vaughan v Menlove: those with developmental disabilities can be held liable in
negligence even when their disability precludes them from foreseeing and avoiding the relevant harm.

II. Defending the 'fault line'

In this sense, the 'fault line' delineated by the reasonable person is actually quite
complex. Thus, as we have seen, in some hard cases the reasonable person is
understood and applied in a manner that ensures a tight relationship between
blameworthiness and legal fault. In the case of children and the physically disabled, for example, the reasonable person is sufficiently infused with the characteristics of the litigant that the standard captures only blameworthy
behaviour. And though these cases have attracted little attention, in fact some
of them may be more troubling than they seem. In contrast, controversy
abounds in those cases where the reasonable person standard is not so attentive
to the relationship between legal fault and blame. Indeed, the interest in cases
that involve the liability of the insane, the developmentally disabled, and those
who suffer various other kinds of incapacities seems attributable primarily to
what such cases reveal about the relationship between legal and moral fault and
the light that this may cast on the underlying theory of liability in negligence.

Given that negligence professes to be fault-based, it seems unsurprising that,
out of the broad category of incapacities, particular interest is bestowed on the
problem that the 'developmentally disabled' pose for the reasonable person—
a problem typically associated with *Vaughan v Menlove*. Because the shortcomings of the developmentally disabled are cognitive or intellectual in nature, they
tend to impair the individual's ability to perceive, and hence avoid, risk. But the
literature tends to locate this problem within a broader undifferentiated category of 'mental' shortcomings. This category thus includes both the kinds of
problems of responsibility that arise in the case of developmental disabilities per
se as well as problems relating to mental illness or claims that essentially turn
on inability to care about others. And perhaps because of this categorization,
commentators and judges tend to be rather inattentive to possible differences
between these different kinds of shortcomings. But we should be hesitant to
accept this approach, for the reluctance to take apart the components of agency
may well obscure important differences in the normative significance of different
kinds of shortcomings. For instance, we would probably want to respond very
differently to a credible claim by an individual that he did not have the intellectual capacity to perceive the relevant risk, as opposed to a similarly credible
claim that an individual did not have the moral resources to care about imposing

---

[30] Prosser (ibid). However, as discussed below, jurisprudential support for this position is not as
strong as one would expect from the confident conclusions of the commentators and even the theorists.

the harm. Even if we were to decide that liability should follow in both cases, presumably the justification for that conclusion would vary greatly as between them. This suggests that we may want to be more attentive to possible differences in different kinds of mental shortcomings as we consider the defences of the reasonable person standard.

But if *Vaughan v Menlove* is the point of departure for consideration of such shortcomings, we would do well to be alert to the ambiguity of the problem of stupidity or ignorance as it appears in *Vaughan*, for it may actually be partially responsible for some of the subsequent confusion. Although the defendant presents his problem in *Vaughan* as developmental (not possessing the highest order of intelligence), the facts suggest that he simply did not value the interests of others enough to be bothered sparing them from harm (hence he decided to 'chance' the risk). In fact, as I shall argue, liability seems justified in *Vaughan* precisely because the risk was the result of the defendant's moral obtuseness, not his cognitive or intellectual limitations. So courts and commentators may rightly be suspicious of the defendant's claim to be judged according to a standard that simply requires that he did his best. But because in this way *Vaughan* actually rests on a claim by the defendant to be judged according to his own normative standard, not according to his own cognitive abilities, it may be a poor, even misleading, vehicle for examining the claims of the developmentally disabled. We will return later to the complex problem of how the reasonable person does—and should—respond to the class of normative shortcomings that we will term 'imprudence' or indifference to the interests of others, including the difficult problem of 'moral ignorance'. Here, though, the focus will be on the more obvious challenge that a credible version of Menlove's developmental disability claim poses for the reasonable person: how should it deal with someone who lacks the cognitive and intellectual abilities that are such an important part of the 'standard equipment' of the reasonable person?

Let us for the moment assume a more credible variation on *Vaughan* in which the defendant truly was developmentally disabled in a way that meant that he did not understand that there was a risk. We should further assume that he had no warning (and perhaps no insurance!). The difficulty that this kind of example brings up, which is of course the very attribute that awakens the interest of theorists and commentators, is that the individual who has a developmental disability cannot be blamed for that shortcoming. And it is for this reason that developmental disabilities pose a profound difficulty for the fault element of negligence. The reasonable person, as we have seen, does encounter other kinds of shortcomings that do not seem to implicate the normative make-up of the agent, such as age, physical disability, and the like. But the response to these normatively indifferent shortcomings diverges sharply from the response to the problem of developmental disabilities. In this we perhaps begin to trace the complicated legacy of *Vaughan*'s unwillingness to 'parse' the different elements of agency. Thus, since *Vaughan*, courts and commentators have insisted that the reasonable person standard hold developmentally disabled individuals to a certain level of cognitive and intellectual skill regardless of their capacity to achieve it. Commentators and theorists recognize this case as one of significant difficulty for the theory of negligence and, in particular, for its fault requirement. Nonetheless, they are nearly unanimous in defending this treatment as not merely acceptable, but as constitutive of the meaning of fault in negligence.

But while the works are various, the arguments are not. Instead, a few arguments dominate attempts to justify this treatment of the developmentally disabled under the reasonable person standard. Most common but least promising of these is the 'unmanageability' argument, which suggests that evidentiary and administrative constraints justify this treatment of the developmentally disabled. More sophisticated but equally ubiquitous is the argument that the treatment of the developmentally disabled is justified on the ground that it furthers the general welfare by deterring dangerous behaviour and by compensating innocent victims. Beyond these well-worn arguments, though, there are also some more ambitious attempts to justify the treatment of the developmentally disabled under the reasonable person standard. So, for instance, one important defence is found in the argument that the standard does indeed impose a form of strict liability, but that strict liability itself can be justified. Finally, the reasonable person standard has been defended on equality grounds. As we shall see, although all of these arguments are ultimately unsuccessful, they are nonetheless important for the light they cast both on the underpinnings of the law of negligence and on how we might go consistently wrong in translating those underpinnings into practice.

A. The unmanageability argument

The reasonable person's refusal to take the developmental limitations of the actual agent into consideration is frequently defended on the ground that it would be unmanageable to have a more nuanced standard of care. According to this justification, any attempt to take account of lack of intellectual competence would hopelessly burden the courts. There are typically two closely linked arguments at work here. The evidentiary argument suggests that such claims of lack of competence are inherently difficult to prove. And the administrative argument develops this point, noting that this evidentiary difficulty is such that it would be impossibly burdensome for courts to permit claims of lack of intellectual competence. So, according to the unmanageability rationale, we are justified in holding the developmentally disabled to the standard of the reasonable person because only thus can we ensure the continued functioning of the judicial process that is so central to the law of negligence.

In a classic formulation of this argument, Oliver Wendell Holmes states that because legal standards are of general application, they do not take account of the 'infinite varieties of temperament, intellect, and education which make the internal character of a given act so different in different men'.[31] According to Holmes, the evidentiary difficulties inherent in making finely tuned assessments

---

[31] Holmes (n 7 above) 86. Similarly, Fleming states, '[b]ecause of administrative limitations, the law can only work within the sphere of external manifestations of conduct': (n 10 above) 119.

of fault on the basis of an individual's powers and limitations serve as one of the primary reasons why the law does not attempt to assess the internal character of the act in question.[32] This concern, along with the related fear that claims of mental disability would be abused, remains one of the major justifications for imposing the objective standard on the developmentally disabled.[33] The unmanageability argument also plays an important role in justifying the exceptions to the objective standard that courts will countenance. Once again, the influential Holmesian formulation is the best illustration of a far more widely cited justification. Thus, Holmes's insistence that the objective standard will only be displaced where there is 'a clear and manifest incapacity' or 'a distinct defect of such a nature that all can recognize...as making certain precautions impossible'[34] is echoed by many other commentators who also justify exceptions for 'obvious' incapacities such as blindness, physical disabilities, and youth, while simultaneously refusing to extend similar treatment to mental disabilities.[35]

However, although it is widely cited, on closer inspection this unmanageability argument is unpersuasive as a justification for the treatment of the developmentally disabled under the reasonable person standard. To begin with, Holmes's argument that laws of general application cannot take account of individual variations seems unsustainable. The *mens rea* requirement of criminal law may be the most glaring counter-example, but even Holmes's own discussion illustrates that the law of negligence is attentive to certain individual 'variations', such as physical disabilities and youth. Nonetheless, the response may be that the developmentally 'abnormal' actor creates all sorts of evidentiary and therefore administrative difficulties that are not presented by the 'normal' actor, difficulties that would virtually debilitate courts.

However, it is far from obvious that developmentally disabled litigants present evidentiary and administrative difficulties significantly different from those

[32] Holmes apparently distinguishes between 'internal' and 'external' aspects of an act. He insists that '[h]owever much [the law] may take moral considerations into account, it does so only for the purpose of drawing a line between such bodily motions and rests as it permits, and such as it does not': (ibid) 86. But his phrasing of this apparently limited view of the role of moral considerations belies the centrality of what he himself describes. It is difficult to imagine a more important role than that of distinguishing between what is permitted and what is not. Holmes's discussion of the exceptions to the rule also suggests that moral considerations are used to draw the line to which he refers. Thus, in most instances he suggests that the ability to avoid the harm in question should be a precondition to liability in negligence (in the case of children or the insane) or contributory negligence (the blind). As discussed below in n 61, Honoré and others also rely on an internal–external distinction.

[33] Linden (n 10 above) 142–143; Prosser (n 10 above) 177; GJ Alexander and TS Szasz, 'Mental Illness as an Excuse for Civil Wrongs' (1967) 43 Notre Dame L Rev 24, 36–38. In this sense, it seems symbolic that the leading case on the negligence liability of the developmentally disabled should be *Vaughan v Menlove* (n 5 above), since there the claim of 'stupidity' seems a very strategic choice by an actor who intelligently planned for his own protection and was obtuse only when it came to the interests of his neighbours.   [34] (n 7 above) 87.

[35] R Parsons, 'Negligence, Contributory Negligence and the Man Who does not Ride the Bus to Clapham' (1957) 1 Melb U L Rev 163, 180; Fleming (n 10 above) 125; Charles V Barrett III, 'Negligence and the Elderly: A Proposal for a Relaxed Standard of Care' (1984) 17 John Marsh L Rev 873; WF Schwartz, 'Objective and Subjective Standards of Negligence: Defining the Reasonable Person to Induce Optimal Care and Optimal Populations of Injurers and Victims' (1989) 78 Georgetown LJ 241, 269–275.

with which courts already contend. Medical malpractice and environmental torts present issues of daunting complexity, yet courts deal with the attendant difficulties, presumably because they are essential to a fair resolution of the issues. The continual references to possible abuses point to an underlying belief that allowing consideration of mental disabilities may open the door to serious credibility concerns. But even if this were true (and there is no indication that it is[36]), there seems no persuasive reason why credibility cannot be treated as it typically is—a case by case assessment by the trier of fact. And research developments that have greatly increased our understanding both of mental illness and of mental disabilities should further undermine the worry that such incapacities would be subject to uncontrollable abuse.[37] If they fail to do so, perhaps it is worth asking whether the pervasive credibility concerns are not instead serving as a way of expressing some other—perhaps less speakable—anxiety.

Consideration of the cases where the reasonable person standard *is* tailored to the litigant only aggravates this difficulty of justifying the treatment of the developmentally disabled on the basis of the unmanageability rationale. The underlying assumption of the unmanageability argument seems to be that, unlike mental disabilities, childhood is an obvious comprehensible condition, which therefore does not present courts with evidentiary or administrative difficulties. But the superficial appeal of this argument disappears on closer inspection. Even granting the assumption that courts have a firm understanding of what a reasonable 7-year-old, for example, would do, they will most certainly have to receive evidence about the particular child's maturity, experience, and intelligence[38] and then factor those in to come up with an appropriately tailored version of the reasonable person standard. Indeed, in the case of children courts seem to deal with very serious complications without bringing the machinery of justice to a halt. In fact, perhaps the most serious challenge to the unmanageability rationale is found in the fact that courts actually do take developmental disabilities into consideration in the case of children.[39] But if determining the appropriate standard for children is actually far more complicated than the 'common sense' rhetoric implies, and if courts actually do take developmental disabilities into consideration in the case of children, then it seems very difficult

---

[36] Several commentators have challenged the assumption that a defence of mental disability would be seriously abused. For instance, James Ellis notes in response to the concern about feigned mental disability that recent strides in understanding mental illness have considerably undermined this rationale, although imprecise diagnoses will still be a problem: 'Tort Responsibility of Developmentally Disabled Persons' [1981] Am B Found Res J 1079, 1086–1087. See also F Bohlen, 'Liability in Tort of Infants and Insane Persons' (1924–25) 23 Mich L Rev 9.

[37] See eg Ellis (ibid). On this and the many legal issues, see, for instance, Parry (n 8 above) and Robertson (n 8 above).

[38] In most jurisdictions, courts considering the negligence of children must factor in not only age but also the child's experience, maturity, and even intelligence: Linden (n 10 above) 138, citing *McEllistrum v Etches* (n 19 above); Fleming (n 10 above) 126; *Restatement* (n 13 above) s 283A; Prosser (n 10 above) 179–180; Street (n 10 above) 238.

[39] When courts are faced with the problem of a developmentally handicapped child, they do not seem to have any difficulty factoring that handicap into the appropriate standard of care by which to judge the child's actions: *Laviolette v Canadian National Railway* (1986) 36 CCLT 203 (NBQB)

to justify the treatment of adults with developmental disabilities on the basis of the exceptional evidentiary or administrative difficulties.[40]

Further, if the unmanageability argument is correct, it also seems to make it extremely difficult to account for the other exceptions to the objective standard besides the exception for children. Parallel to the assumption that, unlike developmental disabilities, childhood is a comprehensible obvious incapacity is the assumption that physical disabilities are obvious in a way that mental ones are not. However, it is not at all clear that the distinction between mental and physical disabilities is even sufficiently stable to support this kind of generalization. How would one deal, for example, with an individual who suffered brain lesions as a result of an attack and was subsequently developmentally disabled? In such a case a brain lesion seems to be both a physical characteristic of the individual and the cause of a developmental disability. Indeed, the cases themselves illustrate this difficulty all too well. For instance, *Buckley v Smith Transport*, which involved delusions arising from the sudden onset of syphilis of the brain, is discussed by commentators both as a case involving insanity[41] and as a case involving physical conditions.[42] But if the line between physical and mental disabilities is not itself clear this undermines treating the two categories very differently on the ground that one is so much more obvious and comprehensible than the other is.

Thus, despite widespread reliance on the unmanageability argument, it does not ultimately seem equal to the task of justifying the treatment of the developmentally disabled under the reasonable person standard. Its general premiss that the law takes account only of external factors seems both untenable and inaccurate. And the unmanageability argument does not seem able to distinguish on its own terms between the kinds of factors—internal or external—that are taken into consideration in developing the relevant standard and those that are not. Thus, it is necessary to look elsewhere to find a more promising justification for the treatment of the developmentally disabled.

B. The deterrence rationale

Another widespread argument relies on deterrence considerations to justify the imposition of an 'unreflective' reasonable person standard on the developmentally disabled. According to the classic version of this argument, a standard that does

(developmentally handicapped 12-year-old boy held not contributorily negligent); *Garrison v St Louis, IM & S Ry Co* 123 SW 657 (Ark SC 1909) (16-year-old boy 'of inferior intelligence' held not contributorily negligent); *Zajczkowski v State* 71 NYS 2d 261 (Claims 1947) (6-year-old girl with a mental age of 2½ years found not contributorily negligent).

[40] Francis Bohlen notes that courts already consider insanity in addressing the scope of liability and that courts have been willing to deal with the complexities of capacity when it comes to children: (n 36 above) 34 n 38. Similarly, James Ellis argues that Holmes's point about the unmanageability of the subjective standard would be more persuasive if the law did not already take account of certain kinds of 'subjective' qualities of children and the physically disabled: (n 36 above) 1088. In addition, as Charles Barrett points out, accepting the unmanageability rationale at face value would suggest that the elderly should also receive the benefit of a relaxed standard of care, but this is not the case: (n 35 above) 883.

[41] *Buckley* (n 13 above) discussed in Fleming (n 10 above) 126; Linden (n 10 above) 143; *Wenden* (n 18 above).   [42] Linden (ibid) 134 n 147.

not in matters of intelligence reflect the capacities of the individual, furthers the general welfare because it deters individuals who cannot meet the standard of care from engaging in potentially injurious conduct.[43] Because it reduces the amount of substandard conduct and also presumably the injuries arising therefrom, such a standard enhances general security. Another version of the deterrence argument holds that imposing the objective standard on the developmentally disabled is justified because it will deter their guardians from allowing them to engage in potentially injurious activities. However, there are serious difficulties with both versions of the deterrence rationale.

The classic version of the deterrence argument suffers from a fatal defect. The treatment of mental disabilities is controversial precisely because of the disconnect that occurs between legal fault and moral blame when actors whose disabilities preclude them from appreciating the risks inherent in their choices are nonetheless subject to liability in negligence. But this very fact almost completely undermines the deterrence rationale. Pound claims that those who have limited capacity to perceive risk should be held to a standard that they cannot meet because they will then be deterred from pursuing risky conduct. But if those with limited mental abilities cannot appreciate when their conduct imposes risks on others, then they will not be able to make rational choices about what activities they should avoid.[44] And in the absence of this threshold ability to perceive risk, it is difficult to see how the preconditions for effective deterrence could ever prevail. A deterrence theorist may respond that imposing a higher standard would nonetheless protect general security, since it would deter those with diminished mental capacities from engaging in *any* activity. However, assuming that the same difficulties with the preconditions for deterrence would not exist, this also seems untenable. Even without addressing the draconian and possibly unconstitutional nature of this argument, it is hard to see how it could prevail in the absence of mass institutionalization.[45] But this

---

[43] R Pound, *An Introduction to the Philosophy of Law* (New Haven: Yale University Press, 1954) 89–91. Although Schwartz's argument focuses on the high process costs in dealing with the developmentally disabled, he also discusses—but ultimately does not rely on—the question of incentives and deterrence: (n 35 above).

[44] Jules Coleman also notes that individuals with mental defects are unlikely to possess the cognitive skills required for effective deterrence. Ironically, however, imposing an objective standard on the physically disabled could be justified on deterrence grounds: Jules L Coleman, 'Mental Abnormality, Personal Responsibility, and Tort Liability' in BA Brody and H Tristram Engelhardt, Jr (eds), *Mental Illness: Law and Public Policy* (Boston: D Reidel Publishing Co, 1980) 107. For a similar argument with regard to the elderly, see Barrett (n 35 above) 888. Caroline Forell notes how the deterrence rationale is used in favour of, rather than to the detriment of, children despite similar conceptual problems: C Forell, 'Reassessing the Negligence Standard of Care for Minors' (Summer 1985) 15 New Mexico L Rev 485, 498. According to this rationale, children require a more subjectivized standard because a higher (objective) standard would deter them from engaging in the activities that are essential to their learning processes. However, Forell states that there is no evidence to suggest that minors would be deterred from learning because of a higher standard of care. So, in the case of children, despite the fact that they apparently would not be deterred by a higher standard they are nonetheless given the benefit of a lower standard, partially on deterrence grounds.

[45] In fact, Alexander and Szasz argue that the effect of relaxing the standard in the case of the developmentally disabled would in effect be large-scale incarceration of the developmentally

would obviate the need to achieve deterrence through the manipulation of the negligence standard.

There are also serious difficulties with the argument that a rigid reasonable person standard furthers general welfare because it deters those who have control over the lives of the developmentally disabled. The most common version of this argument is that such a standard will encourage the guardians of those with diminished mental abilities to restrain the risky activities of their charges.[46] However, here too the argument faces serious difficulties. Not only does it assume that guardians have a far greater degree of control over developmentally disabled individuals than they legally possess,[47] but it also seems to be at odds with basic common law principles. Since guardians are not vicariously liable for the acts of their charges, it is not at all clear how imposing liability on the developmentally disabled furthers the goal of controlling the *guardians'* behaviour. Even in situations involving maximum control (as in, for instance, some form of institutionalization), the duty of the guardian remains a duty of reasonable care or supervision.[48] But a duty of supervision is not contingent on a finding of legal carelessness on the part of the developmentally disabled person him- or herself. Even apart from these difficulties, it is far from clear that it would be desirable for guardians to exercise the kind of control that this version of the deterrence rationale contemplates. And if the desired focus of deterrence is actually the guardian, then it seems that the more appropriate way of achieving this would be by making the guardians themselves liable.[49] Thus, it seems clear that if the true goal is deterring the guardians of those with developmental disabilities from allowing them to engage in risky conduct, then imposing an objective standard on the developmentally disabled is an unlikely and ineffective means of achieving it.

Further, even if the deterrence justification were as effective in its application to the developmentally disabled as its defenders suggest, there appears to be no reason to confine it to that case. Indeed, if the goal of negligence is to protect general security, and if an unreflective reasonable person standard accomplishes

disabled. They state that 'a person enjoying the liberties of a sane citizen, but licensed at law to commit tortious acts with impunity, is unthinkable': (n 33 above) 38. They see this as the main deterrent to extending criminal responsibility to civil law. Ellis notes in such an approach the vestiges of the view that the developmentally disabled should not live freely in society: (n 36 above) 1085.

[46] James Ellis characterizes this argument as among the most frequently cited rationales for the imposition of the objective standard on the developmentally disabled: (ibid) 1084. So, for example, Linden states, 'If liability is imposed, "the relatives of the lunatic may be under inducement to restrain him" ': (n 10 above) 143 [quotation marks without an accompanying citation].

[47] See Robertson (n 8 above) 171 (legislation in various jurisdictions provides that 'a guardian must exercise authority in the least restrictive manner possible, and in such a way as to encourage the dependent adult to become capable of self-care' [citations omitted]). See also Ellis (n 36 above).

[48] See Robertson (n 8 above) 173–174; Fleming (n 10 above) 171–172; *Watts v Watts* [1989] BCJ No 2032 (SC).

[49] Bohlen (n 36 above). Coleman, for instance, also argues that if the goal is to deter the developmentally 'defective', then it would be better achieved by holding their employers liable because this would give employers an incentive to restrict the faulty conduct of people who have mental handicaps by changing their work or by refusing to hire them: Coleman (n 44 above) 117–118.

that by deterring individuals from engaging in risky conduct, then it is hard to see why this rationale would countenance any 'tailoring' of the reasonable person standard. But this would mean that the deterrence rationale would equally support a rigidly objective reasonable person standard for children and those suffering from sudden physical incapacities, among others.[50] In fact, to the extent that such persons have a superior ability to perceive and even predict risk compared to that of the developmentally disabled, the deterrence argument actually seems more persuasive in their cases. Yet defenders of the current treatment of the developmentally disabled on deterrence grounds do not adopt this position, instead typically supporting the existing common law. The puzzling fact that the deterrence rationale seems to countenance imposing the rigid standard on only one group of 'incapable' individuals, and on the group for whom the deterrence is least persuasive, only serves to confirm the inability of that rationale to justify the treatment of the developmentally disabled.

C. The compensation rationale

One of the most prominent and persuasive justifications for imposing the objective standard on the developmentally disabled looks to the perceived fairness of compensating the person injured by substandard behaviour. Again, in his classic *The Common Law*, Holmes provides an early formulation of this justification when he argues that the objective standard should be applied even in the absence of moral fault because the 'slips' of the awkward individual cause the same injury to his neighbours as 'if they sprang from guilty neglect'.[51] Thus, the objective standard is justified because it accords fair treatment to those injured by imprudent conduct. For this reason it furthers general welfare.[52]

Many writers justify the objective standard on compensation grounds. However, Jules Coleman forwards the most sustained and sophisticated version of this rationale and does so in the context of providing a theoretical justification for the application of the objective standard to the 'mentally abnormal', including those whom we have termed developmentally disabled. Coleman describes the objective test as 'a tool for identifying faulty *action*, the harmful consequences of which warrant compensation'.[53] He argues that the objective standard can be squared with our conceptions of justice only if tort law is understood primarily as a compensation scheme and fault is seen as an appraisal of acts, not actors.

Coleman's first argument in favour of imposing the objective standard on the developmentally abnormal (as he puts it) is essentially a restatement of the

---

[50] Schwartz (n 35 above) responds to this difficulty by combining considerations of deterrence and incentive with considerations about information costs. These costs, he says, help to explain the subjective standard for the physically disabled but the objective standard for the developmentally disabled. However, as noted above, this analysis seems incapable of explaining major features of the objective standard and seems to rest on unsubstantiated assumptions.

[51] Holmes (n 7 above) 86.   [52] See also Pound (n 43 above) 89–91; Fleming (n 10 above) 119.

[53] Coleman (n 44 above) 125 [emphasis in original].

traditional argument that allowing consideration of the defendant's mental abnormality would be unfairly prejudicial to accident victims.[54] Thus, he states, 'If a loss must fall on either of two *morally* blameless parties, in order to protect the innocence of the completely faultless individual, liability ought to be imposed on the party who has failed to comply with the standard of reasonable care'.[55] Coleman supports this first argument, which he admits is a somewhat weak thesis, by arguing that its deeper justification is that it comports with tort law's fundamental ambition of identifying and compensating 'a certain class of victims for whom compensation *is a matter of justice*'.[56] Thus, tort law seeks to identify and eliminate 'unjustifiable losses', that is those injuries caused by the faulty conduct of another.[57] So this second argument establishes that 'the fault of the injurer is not *just* a morally relevant distinction between victims and injurers, but where it contributes causally to the victim's injury, it suffices to ground the victim's claim to compensation as a matter of justice'.[58] In this way, the second argument complements the first.

Throughout this analysis, Coleman reiterates the crucial characterization of the injurer as 'faulty' and the victim as 'innocent'.[59] And partly because of this, his two arguments initially seem uncontroversial. However, without more, neither argument can justify the treatment of the developmentally disabled under the reasonable person standard. This is because the persuasiveness of both rationales turns on the prior issue of whether it is appropriate to term the developmentally abnormal injurer 'faulty'. After all, as Coleman himself notes in the first quotation above, both the injurer and the injured are 'morally blameless'. Nonetheless, he concludes in the second quotation that the 'fault' of the injurer is a 'morally relevant distinction' that is capable of providing the reason of justice needed to ground the victim's claim to compensation. But then Coleman needs some reason to treat an admittedly morally blameless act as morally relevant—and to distinguish such a blameless act from other morally similar acts. Thus, in order for this argument to succeed, he must establish that the developmentally disabled individual who cannot meet the standard of care is, though not blameworthy, at fault in some 'morally relevant' sense of that term.

Coleman's discussion of the fault of the developmentally abnormal injurer begins with a distinction between fault that involves culpability or blameworthiness, and fault that does not.[60] Thus, he argues that those with mental abnormalities 'are expected to satisfy the objective standard, and their failure

---

[54] See eg Holmes (n 7 above) 68; Fleming (n 10 above) 119, 126; Prosser (n 10 above) 177–178.
[55] Coleman (n 44 above) 121 [emphasis in original].   [56] ibid 122 [emphasis in original].
[57] ibid 123.   [58] ibid 124 [emphasis in original].
[59] So, for instance, '[i]f the choice is between a faultless victim—that is, one whose conduct fails to contribute causally to the harm or one whose conduct, though it contributes to the occurrence, in every way complies with community ideals—and a faulty injurer, one whose conduct not only contributes to the occurrence but falls below our ideals as well, the loss ought to be imposed on the party at fault': ibid 120–121. See generally discussion at 120–125.
[60] Coleman also distinguishes both sorts of judgements from judgements about moral fault on the ground that with moral fault, the standard the act fails to satisfy must be a moral one: ibid 119. Similarly in 'Tort Law and the Demands of Corrective Justice' (1992) 67 Ind LJ 349, 370, Coleman

to do so constitutes a fault in their *action* but not necessarily in them'.[61] But what exactly is the content of this non-culpable fault? Coleman responds, 'That the injurer is at fault implies no more than that his conduct is in an appropriate sense undesirable'.[62] But presumably any conduct that injures someone is in some sense 'undesirable'. However, clearly Coleman cannot intend this broad meaning, since it would obliterate the objective standard in favour of a system of strict liability. Yet if only some conduct that injures others is 'undesirable' in Coleman's sense, what exactly delineates tolerable injury-inflicting conduct from conduct that is undesirable 'in an appropriate sense'? Given Coleman's definition of what counts as fault in negligence, culpability cannot be the distinguishing factor. Instead, he seems to give the following answer: 'Conduct that falls below our standards of proper care and foresight, whether or not non-compliance marks a personal weakness in the actor, is in a suitably narrow sense undesirable or at fault.'[63]

But there is a difficulty with this argument. Coleman defends the treatment of developmentally abnormal individuals on the ground that there is an appropriate sense in which they can be considered at fault. However, it turns out that their fault consists of breaching the objective standard, which is, after all, the 'standard of proper care and foresight'. But simply pointing to the fact that the conduct of the developmentally disabled breached the objective standard can at best *explain* liability under the standard but cannot *justify* it. In order to actually justify this treatment of the developmentally disabled, Coleman needs to give us a reason for the treatment that comports with the fundamental principles of negligence—that, in his own words, explains the 'moral relevance' of this understanding of fault. Coleman does seem confident that '[h]owever we unpack the standard of the reasonable man, we will provide a reason why failure to live up to the standard is undesirable'.[64] But unfortunately he does no more than point to two theories that he suggests could explain why non-conforming behaviour is undesirable—first, the economic theory that treats sub-standard conduct as inefficient, and second, the reciprocity in risk-taking theory. But without a further elaboration of why we should label conduct that fails to conform to the objective standard faulty in

argues that the objective standard is concerned with 'the shortcoming in the doing, not in the doer'. See also *Risks and Wrongs* (Cambridge, New York: Cambridge University Press, 1992).

[61] Coleman (n 44 above) 120 [emphasis in original]. Note the similarity here to Holmes's insistence that the law does not look to that internal character of an act that makes 'a given act so different in different men': (n 7 above) 86. Similarly, Holmes later argues that 'the standards of the law are external standards, and, however much it may take moral considerations into account, it does so only for the purpose of drawing a line between such bodily motions and rests as it permits, and such as it does not. What the law really forbids, and the only thing it forbids, is the act on the wrong side of the line, be that act blameworthy or otherwise': ibid 88.

[62] Coleman (ibid) 124. There is a striking similarity between Coleman's argument here and an argument by Honoré in 'Responsibility and Luck' (n 9 above). Both Coleman and Honoré use examples from games to try to draw attention to a cleavage between notions of moral fault and the assignment of responsibility for the consequences of action. However, it is worth questioning whether examples of inadvertent goal scoring do anything to illuminate the connection (or lack thereof) between moral fault and legal responsibility.   [63] Coleman (ibid) 123.

[64] ibid.

some 'morally relevant' sense, Coleman's defence of the objective standard amounts to little more than a complicated restatement of the rule that he is purporting to justify.

There is also a broader difficulty with Coleman's argument. He claims that his defence of the reasonable person standard ultimately makes sense because it rests on a general understanding of tort law as a system of compensatory justice that looks primarily to acts rather than to actors. But this theory does not seem to be able to explain major features of even the objective standard itself. If the compensatory aims of tort law require a definition of fault that looks solely to acts that injure others as a result of conduct that falls below our standards of proper care, then the standard should apply to any actor that injures another as a result of a failure to meet the standard of proper care. But this is not the case. In the case of children in particular, the actual workings of tort law diverge from what Coleman's account suggests. The focus of the negligence inquiry in these cases is not simply on the nature of the act but is rather on the ability of the particular actor to avoid the harm in question. But this suggests that the law of negligence is, of necessity, as concerned with the actor as with the act. Similarly, these cases do not focus on compensating an objectively defined class of unjustifiable losses. Were that the case, it would surely be necessary to compensate those who are injured by the risky conduct of children. Yet negligence law does not do this, instead typically defining the 'unjustifiable losses' that Coleman discusses with reference to the ability of the actor to avoid the harm in question.

If this is correct, it suggests fault in negligence cases does typically focus on a certain kind of culpability or blameworthiness. In fact, Holmes seems to capture a crucial element in this notion of culpability when he notes that reference to a moral standard of liability is not designed to improve men's hearts, but rather 'to give a man a fair chance to avoid doing the harm before he is held responsible for it'.[65] In this way, avoidability enables us 'to reconcile the policy of letting accidents lie where they fall, and the reasonable freedom of others with the protection of the individual from injury'.[66] Thus, Holmes later concludes that the law requires that 'the defendant must have had at least a fair chance of avoiding the infliction of harm before he becomes answerable for such a consequence of his conduct'.[67] Because, by definition, most defendants will be 'normal', they will be able to foresee and avoid the same injuries that the reasonable person could avoid. Thus, the simple application of the reasonable person standard will generally satisfy the avoidability requirement, thereby ensuring that there will be no liability unless the actor is at fault in some 'morally relevant' sense.

However, in cases like those involving children and the developmentally disabled, applying the reasonable person standard will not automatically satisfy the avoidability requirement. In negligence, the ordinary response to a divergence between the dictates of the avoidability requirement and those of a strict application of the

---

[65] Holmes (n 7 above) 115.   [66] ibid.   [67] ibid 129.

reasonable person test is to prefer the avoidability requirement. So in the case of children the primary inquiry is directed to whether the particular child had a fair chance of avoiding the injury (to either self or others). And this concern with whether the particular actor in the particular circumstances had a fair chance of avoiding the harm is not confined to children. Thus, for instance, in cases of emergency[68] or where ignorance is unavoidable because of the background of the agent,[69] the reasonable person is typically reshaped to take those 'circumstances' into account.

But this focus of the common law on the avoidability of harm seems to undermine Coleman's claim that as a system of compensation negligence is concerned only with the quality of the act and not with the actor. Coleman's alternative characterization instead seems more apt: negligence aims to compensate individuals for 'unjustifiable losses'. But the difficulty here is that without a morally significant notion of fault, it turns out to be extremely difficult to account for what counts as an unjustifiable loss under negligence. And any morally significant conception of fault surely yields Coleman's own characterization: that someone whose mental abnormality prevents them from recognizing and hence avoiding the harm in question cannot be morally blameworthy. Coleman attempts to address this difficulty by loosening up the language of

---

[68] For instance, courts have held that an actor may not have to meet the ordinary standard of care in an emergency situation that is 'sudden and unexpected, and such as to deprive the actor of reasonable opportunity for deliberation and considered decision': Prosser (n 10 above) 197. So, for example, in *Cordas v Peerless Transportation Co* 27 NYS 2d 198 (NY City Ct 1941) the court found no negligence when a cabdriver in Manhattan leaped from his moving vehicle when he was confronted by an armed bandit making his getaway, despite the fact that the car struck and injured a pedestrian and her two children. In these cases, actors may be exonerated from liability even though they may have made a choice that 'no reasonable person could possibly have made after due deliberation': Prosser (ibid) 196. The rule is typically stated as requiring adherence to an objective standard of conduct, with the sudden emergency being a factor in determining reasonableness: *Restatement* (n 13 above) s 296. Thus, even where an act is 'objectively' culpable in that it falls below the standard of due care, if the person in question was put into a situation where they could fairly not be expected to avoid the harm, they will not be liable in negligence.

[69] So where ignorance that would otherwise amount to a breach of the standard of care is unavoidable, it has often been held not to constitute negligence: *Prasad v Frandsen* (1985) 60 BCLR 343 (SC) (non-negligent for a person from England not to wear a seatbelt); *Geier v Kujawa* [1970] 1 Ll Rep 364 (QB) (failure to wear a seatbelt not contributory negligence on part of a German girl who had not seen one before); *Lorenzo v Wirth* 49 NE 1010 (1897) (Spanish woman stepped into a coal hole found not contributory negligent on other grounds but court indicates it would have taken her reason for ignorance into account); WA Seavey, 'Negligence—Subjective or Objective?' (1927) 41 Harv L Rev 1 states 'a hermit, hearing without explanation, a radio for the first time; or a savage, suddenly dropped from his native swamps into the streets of New York, cannot be judged except with reference to what he knows' (at 19); F James, Jr, 'The Qualities of the Reasonable Man in Negligence Cases' (1951) 16 Missouri L Rev 1 argues that where an individual is a stranger or has an unusually limited background there may be 'genuine and reasonable ignorance [which] will be considered in all but a very few situations' (at 12); L Klar, *Tort Law* (2nd edn, Scarborough: Carswell, 1996) 255. But see Prosser (ibid) 184, who suggests that the individual must conform to the community and citing cases for both views. See also H Shulman, 'The Standard of Care Required of Children' (1927) 37 Yale LJ 618, 621 n 16. Similarly, while intoxication may amount to negligence in certain situations, commentators have suggested that allowances should be made for involuntary intoxication: James (above) 20; Prosser (ibid) 178. So most commentators suggest that where ignorance that would otherwise be negligent is unavoidable, it will not be negligent.

fault, but ultimately cannot generate the kind of morally relevant account that he himself admits that he needs. And since his definition of fault therefore ends up restating the standard, Coleman's account also falls short of the task of justifying the treatment of the developmentally disabled under the reasonable person standard.

D. Luck and responsibility

Coleman's defence of the treatment of the developmentally disabled runs up against a fundamental difficulty—how can this treatment be reconciled with the commonplace understanding that liability in negligence is fault-based? This difficulty also plagues Holmes's classic defence of the reasonable person standard. In response to the strict liability argument, Holmes argues that '[t]he general principle of our law is that loss from accident must lie where it falls', and relative to a given human being, 'anything is an accident which he could not fairly have been expected to contemplate as possible, and therefore to avoid'.[70] But this seems directly at odds with his insistence elsewhere that the standard should ignore 'peculiarities' such as being stupid, hasty, or awkward apparently regardless of whether they make it impossible to avoid the harm in question. And even Coleman's ambitious effort to resolve this tension by developing an objective notion of fault is ultimately unsuccessful.

This makes it difficult to resist the conclusion that there is something incoherent about an apparently fault-based standard that in fact imposes a form of liability without fault on the developmentally disabled. Indeed, the reasonable person standard has been condemned on such grounds, including by Richard Epstein who takes the tension between the moral requisites of fault and the reasonable person standard to indicate a deeper incoherence running through the law of negligence.[71] Epstein's controversial solution argues that the fault standard should be abandoned in favour of a general strict liability standard.[72]

However, Tony Honoré has raised an interesting alternative possibility. Unlike other defenders of the objective standard, he admits that the reasonable person standard does in fact impose a form of strict liability on those who suffer from unavoidable shortcomings. But Honoré argues that this does not mean that either the objective standard or the general fault regime need be abandoned. On the contrary, he insists that under certain circumstances strict liability can coherently coexist with a general fault standard. Honoré begins by pointing out that while the objective standard typically assigns responsibility on the basis of blame, it also penalizes the bad luck of those who suffer from unavoidable shortcomings, including limited intelligence. This raises the question of when it is justifiable to

---

[70] Holmes (n 7 above) 76.

[71] R Epstein, 'A Theory of Strict Liability' (1973) 2 J Leg Studies 151.

[72] For a persuasive view that Epstein's argument for strict liability in fact builds an implicit fault standard into its account of causation, a fault standard that is necessary to avoid the pervasive indeterminacy problems that a general theory of strict liability would otherwise generate, see SR Perry, 'The Impossibility of General Strict Liability' (1988) 1 Can J Law & Jur 147.

hold individuals responsible for things beyond their control—in essence for the consequences of bad luck. Holmes also points to this issue, but as Honoré notes, in fact Holmes gives no morally convincing reason for his insistence that if we lack the 'gifts' of the average man, it is simply 'our misfortune'.[73]

Honoré begins his own attempt to offer a more adequate defence of the reasonable person standard by arguing that the standard cannot be defended in the absence of a justification for strict liability, which accounts for why 'people should sometimes bear the risk of bad luck'.[74] Honoré then goes on to argue that bearing the risk of bad luck is inherent in the most basic form of responsibility in any society— 'outcome responsibility'. Under outcome responsibility, we are forced to make implicit bets on our choices and their outcomes, and just as we receive credit for good outcomes we must also bear the responsibility for harmful outcomes that may be due solely to bad luck rather than to any fault on our part. Outcome responsibility, according to Honoré, can also be defended on the deeper ground that it is inescapably tied to our personal identity. And because we are likely to gain more from outcome responsibility than we lose by it, the system is not unfair. However, this means that outcome responsibility can fairly be applied only to individuals who possess a minimum capacity for choosing and acting, measured by whether they generally succeed in performing given actions when they try. Since civil liability is justified because it reinforces outcome responsibility with formal sanctions, Honoré concludes that it is legitimate for the legal system 'to impose strict liability for risky activities alongside fault liability for conduct which discloses an uncooperative disposition'.[75]

Much of Honoré's argument in 'Responsibility and Luck' is taken up with the justification for outcome responsibility. However, while interesting and complex, this discussion is not as crucial as Honoré suggests to the justification of the objective standard. The heart of Honoré's argument concerning outcome responsibility is the conclusion that the outcomes of one's action, regardless of fault, are themselves of some moral significance.[76] One might expect, particularly given the subtitle 'The Moral Basis of Strict Liability', that Honoré would proceed from this to defend a general regime of strict liability of the kind that Epstein envisages. Instead, Honoré insists that responsibility for a harmful outcome should not automatically give rise to a legal duty to compensate. As he somewhat obliquely puts it, '[a]n extra element is needed to ground the legal sanction. Sometimes the extra element is fault.'[77] However, in the case of strict liability the extra element is instead the fact that 'the conduct of the harm doer carries with it a special risk of harm of the sort that has in fact come about.'[78] Honoré argues that the justification for strict liability, which is a 'species of enhanced responsibility for outcomes', therefore depends in part 'on the fairness

---

[73] Honoré (n 9 above) 24, commenting on Holmes (n 7 above) 87.

[74] Honoré (n 9 above) 24.   [75] ibid 40.

[76] For an analysis of both the tensions and the possibilities of Honoré's notion of outcome responsibility, see SR Perry, 'The Moral Foundations of Tort Law' (1992) 77 Iowa L Rev 449, 488–ff.

[77] Honoré (n 9 above) 27.   [78] ibid 27.

of outcome responsibility'.[79] But while this seems correct, it does not address the central difficulty that Honoré has identified with the objective standard.

This is because Honoré's justification of outcome responsibility primarily goes to the moral significance of causation.[80] Let us assume that Honoré's argument establishes that producing a harmful outcome gives some reason to hold the defendant responsible. But Honoré also acknowledges that while this may be necessary for legal liability, it is not sufficient for it. If there were not an additional element needed to ground legal liability, then the position of the shortcomer would not provoke any particular unease because, like everyone else, he would simply be liable for the harm caused by his actions.[81] However, the problem that Honoré sets for himself is to reconcile the objective standard's treatment of the person with unavoidable shortcomings with the ordinary fault basis of liability in negligence. On his own terms Honoré must justify the fact that the standard imposes on this shortcomer '*enhanced* responsibility for outcomes', while the 'normal' individual will be liable only if he or she is at fault.[82] On outcome responsibility grounds alone, there is no basis for distinguishing between an individual with a mental disability and a 'normal' person, both of whom count as proximate causes of harm to another. Presumably both injurers have the same moral connection with the injured that arises out of the mere fact of causing harm to another. But then it is hard to see how Honoré's defence of outcome responsibility can justify using the fault requirement to limit outcome responsibility for the 'normal' person while not similarly limiting (indeed, enhancing in outcome responsibility terms) the liability of the developmentally disabled.

This suggests that we must look to other aspects of Honoré's analysis to see how he defends the displacement of the fault requirement in the case of the developmentally disabled. Honoré suggests that strict liability is appropriate when the conduct involves some sort of enhanced risk. However, his examples, which are straightforward instances of textbook strict liability, such as storing

---

[79] ibid.

[80] This does not necessarily mean that causation and outcome responsibility are simply to be equated: Perry, 'Moral Foundations' (n 76 above) 494. However, Honoré's argument can be taken in part as a response to the query raised by Judith Jarvis Thomson in 'Remarks on Causation and Liability' 13 Phil & Publ Aff 101, reprinted in JJ Thomson, *Rights, Restitution, and Risk: Essays in Moral Theory* (Cambridge, Mass: Harvard University Press, 1986) 192. In a variation on *Summers v Tice* 199 P 2d 1 (Cal SC 1948), Thomson asks why, if two defendants acted equally negligently, only the one who actually caused the harm should be liable. Why should the law exonerate one of two equally faulty parties merely because, through luck, his carelessness did not result in injury? Honoré's defence of outcome responsibility argues that causation is not in fact morally neutral, although it may be a matter of luck. Instead, the fact that the injurer produced a harmful outcome itself creates a morally significant link between injurer and injured regardless of fault.

[81] This is not to suggest that there would not be other problems with such a general regime of strict liability: Perry, 'Strict Liability' (n 72 above). The point is simply that it would not count as problematic under such a regime to impose liability on an individual who, through no fault of his own, caused an injury to another.

[82] Honoré (n 9 above) 27 [emphasis added]. The fault requirement that Honoré envisages here seems satisfied where the injurer imposed a risk on the injured that the injurer could fairly be expected to have avoided. However, the shortcomer will be liable even for harm that he or she could not have avoided, and this is the enhanced responsibility that Honoré must justify.

explosives, running nuclear power stations, and selling dangerous products,[83] seem unhelpful in justifying the application of the objective standard to the developmentally disabled. Honoré's position here is further obscured because he does not explain the crucial step in his argument, namely, how the conduct of the developmentally disabled poses an enhanced risk of the kind that displaces the fault requirement and thus brings strict liability into play. What Honoré does do is note that while 'ordinary' strict liability often merely makes it easy to prove negligence on the part of someone who is in fact at fault, sometimes it also punishes bad luck, including both ordinary (presumably unforeseeable) accidents and being saddled with shortcomings. He then goes on to argue that, since the objective standard in negligence has a 'like dual effect', the principle involved in imposing ordinary strict liability and in applying the objective standard of negligence is the same.

However, Honoré's assumption that justifying ordinary strict liability also makes out the case for the objective standard seems to elide crucial differences between the two situations. The analogy between imposing liability for the harm caused by running a nuclear power plant and imposing liability for harm arising out of unavoidable shortcomings, such as developmental disabilities, is surely not so obvious as to require no explanation. Ordinary strict liability is imposed on lawful activities that are abnormally dangerous.[84] Unsurprisingly, therefore, most of the cases of ordinary strict liability that Honoré discusses involve an assumption of responsibility, typically within a heavily regulated context.[85] Even a nuanced approach to luck itself suggests that responsibility for bad luck in such situations calls for a very different form of justification than where, for example, a developmentally disabled individual runs across a street and thereby causes an accident in which a third party's vehicle is damaged.[86]

[83] Honoré (ibid) 23, 28.

[84] Fleming (n 10 above) 367–374. The risk must be extraordinary in either the seriousness or the frequency of the harm threatened: ibid. Fleming suggests that under the common law, the activity must also be abnormal, as with the rule in *Rylands v Fletcher* (1866) LR 1 Ex 265 (Ex Ch) (Blackburn J). Similarly, in the United States, strict liability applies to abnormally dangerous activities (defined as those activities in which the risks cannot be eliminated by the exercise of reasonable care, such as aviation and products liability). Fleming points to two similar categories of strict liability: cases involving products that are of an unusually dangerous nature (such as flammable materials and chemicals), and cases involving risks of very serious and extensive casualties (such as stadiums and bridges): ibid.

[85] See William H Rodgers, Jr, who argues that such cases involving rational decision-makers are typically treated as instances of strict liability 'regardless of the nominal differences accorded to recognized categories of strict liability, intentional tort, and negligence': 'Negligence Reconsidered: The Role of Rationality in Tort Theory' (1980) 54 S Cal L Rev 1, 12. Thus, he treats *Vaughan v Menlove* (n 5 above) as falling within this class of cases, along with *Rylands v Fletcher* (n 84 above), vicarious liability in the employment setting, *Vincent v Lake Erie Steamship Co* 124 NW 221 (Minn SC 1910), and various other bodies of case law: Rodgers (above) 12–16. According to Rodgers, rational injurers 'weigh their own convenience against risks of injuries to others': ibid 12. He thus notes that in such cases strict liability is justified because there is typically 'foreknowledge, time for study, and a deliberate choice of procedure': ibid 15.

[86] Rodgers treats this type of case as involving a non-rational actor and therefore advocates that rather than 'imposing liability for the excessively rash response, the better starting point is to identify the injurer's capabilities and to condemn a departure from those capabilities': ibid 22. Rodgers also

Presumably, Honoré would respond by saying that with the actions of the developmentally disabled, as with other instances of strict liability, there is a special risk that there will be a harmful outcome. However, this superficially appealing argument deserves closer scrutiny. While ordinary strict liability proceeds on the basis that particular *activities* are especially dangerous, this defence of the objective standard proceeds on the assumption that particular *individuals* are especially dangerous regardless of the activities in which they engage. Honoré glosses over this difference when he says that in order to justify strict liability it is necessary to show 'why people should sometimes bear the risk of bad luck'.[87] But the challenge of justifying the form of strict liability imposed by the objective standard, as opposed to 'ordinary' strict liability, is really to explain why *some people* should always bear the risk of bad luck.

Honoré's special risk argument seems to assume that the developmentally disabled pose a heightened risk to society. Is this assumption sound? Honoré offers neither evidence nor argument to support it, perhaps believing its veracity is self-evident. But in what sense can it be said that, for example, a person with a mental disability imposes more risks on others than so-called normal individuals? The actual imposition of heightened risks on others does not follow automatically from a diminished ability to perceive risks. A developmentally disabled individual may have a diminished ability to perceive risk but may also be very timorous so that in fact he imposes very few risks on others. Perhaps his ill-conceived attempt to cross the street is in fact one of the very few times that he has engaged in risky conduct. Conversely, an individual with average or even superior ability to perceive risks may also be very careless of—or indeed enjoy—imposing them.[88] So it seems difficult to justify enhancing the outcome responsibility of the developmentally disabled on the ground that they are especially dangerous. And in order to justify the operation of the common law in the way that Honoré contemplates, he would need to go further than this and show not only that developmentally disabled individuals impose special risks but also that *only* such shortcomers and not 'ordinary individuals' impose special risks. Unfortunately, Honoré offers neither evidence nor argument to support either proposition. And without some persuasive reason to accept this point, the special risk justification cannot account for enhancing the outcome responsibility of *all and only* the developmentally disabled. Thus, even if strict liability can justifiably be imposed when an activity imposes heightened risks of harm to others, in the absence of evidence that all and only individuals with developmental disabilities fall within the group of heightened risk imposers, this argument cannot justify the imposition of the objective standard on such individuals.

notes that in situations including those where ordinarily rational actors are incapable of rationally responding to an emergency situation, negligence law supports the view that 'non-rational actions in tort conflict should be adjudged by a subjective "best efforts" standard of behaviour': ibid 19.

[87] Honoré (n 9 above) 14.

[88] The adolescent male seems to afford a very obvious example of this category of individuals. In this regard, see also the child defendant cases discussed ch 2. below

Another possible response proves similarly unfruitful. It may initially seem tempting to infer from the fact that a shortcomer has had an accident that there is something especially risky—in general as opposed to in this particular case— about his or her activities. However, not only is this kind of *ex post* risk assessment out of keeping with negligence methodology,[89] but again there seems no reason to confine the inference to the case of the shortcomer. If the heightened risk imposer designation is inferred from the fact of an accident in the case of a developmentally disabled individual, it would logically seem that it could be inferred in any case where there has been an accident. But this would transform negligence into a general regime of strict liability and Honoré's aim is to defend the objective standard.

There is however one more possibility open to Honoré. Perhaps the inference of heightened risk arises not from the fact of an accident itself but rather from an accident that resulted from a failure to act as a reasonable person would have in similar circumstances. So anyone who breaches the standard of care will be liable regardless of fault, although of course 'normal' individuals who find their capacities and abilities mirrored in the qualities of the reasonable person will be 'lucky' in that only when they are at fault will they breach the objective standard and thus be liable. Indeed, this may be what Honoré is referring to when he says that the objective standard has a dual effect similar to strict liability, in that while it sometimes simply makes it easy to prove negligence on the part of a person who is in fact at fault, it may also penalize the bad luck of someone who suffers from shortcomings. So the standard is like strict liability in that it is concerned with the imposition of a heightened level of risk on others regardless of the culpability of any individual's mental state. The standard only looks fault-based because for the vast majority of individuals legal liability will in practice coincide with a blameworthy mental state. But it is the fact of causing harm as a result of conduct that falls below a certain level specified for community safety, rather than the fact of being subjectively careless, which is the central concern of the law of negligence.

Initially, this seems a promising way of explaining both the operation of the objective standard generally and the treatment of the shortcomer in particular. In fact, it seems similar in certain significant ways to Coleman's suggestion that the standard relates to fault in the doing rather than in the doer, although Honoré frankly admits that the standard is not fault-based, rather than attempting to develop a notion of objective fault. However, if Honoré's defence of the objective standard is best understood in terms of this notion of risky conduct, then his statement that the objective standard imposes a form of strict liability on those who suffer unavoidable shortcomings is a bit confusing.

---

[89] By this I mean that inferring risk from the fact of causation would alter the fundamental method of tort law. As Ernest Weinrib explains it, the assessment of wrongdoing focuses on the period before the accident in order to determine whether the injurer knew or should have known that his or her activity imposed a risk on other individuals: 'Causation and Wrongdoing' (1987) 63 Chi-Kent L Rev 407. As noted in the text, inferring risk from injury would in effect eviscerate the inquiry into wrongfulness and transform negligence into a regime of strict liability.

The statement seems to grant too much, in the sense that while the form of liability suggested by Honoré's argument relies heavily on the fact of risky conduct and consequently has a very attenuated notion of fault, it is nonetheless significantly different from ordinary strict liability. Perhaps most importantly, this variation on strict liability does not look to the fact of harm per se but rather to harm caused by particularly risky conduct. So, it does not face the pervasive indeterminacy problems of ordinary strict liability. However, Honoré's suggestion that the objective standard imposes a form of strict liability on the shortcomer, although it seems too broad in some ways, also seems too limited in others. If Honoré's best defence of the reasonable person standard is that like strict liability it is non-fault-based because it is really concerned only with compensation for unreasonably risky conduct that harms others, then surely the standard also imposes this kind of 'strict liability' on individuals who are not shortcomers. And if the argument is that the standard is not concerned with fault—although its operation may in fact track fault to some degree—then it surely follows from this that the basis of liability must be the same for both shortcomers and 'normal' individuals, even though the actual coincidence of fault and liability will vary.

Even granting these qualifications, however, this interpretation of Honoré's defence of the objective standard still faces a very serious hurdle. Unsurprisingly, given the similar thrust of the argument, it is a difficulty shared by Coleman's attempt to reconstruct fault. The argument that the standard in fact looks to conduct that poses an unreasonable risk of harm to others regardless of the culpability of the actor seems a more plausible description of what is at stake in the law of negligence than Coleman's attempts to defend the objective standard as going to a fault in the doing rather than in the doer. The concept of harm arising from unreasonably risky conduct[90] also helps to explain why only certain kinds of harmful consequences are of concern to the law of negligence and why negligence does not therefore collapse into a general scheme of strict liability, a fact that Coleman's causation-based notion has difficulty addressing.[91] Despite these advantages, Honoré's variation on strict liability ultimately faces the same hurdle that Coleman's does: it does not accurately describe the contours of the common law. The problem for Honoré is that the common law does not in fact ignore culpability and look simply to the fact of objectively risky conduct. Instead, as the case of children in particular illustrates,[92] the common law is centrally concerned with the very form of culpability that Honoré's reconstruction of the objective standard should rule out as irrelevant.

---

[90] This notion does not necessarily call for one standard for all of the interests protected by the law of tort, but is instead capable of being sensitive to the nature of the interest protected by the right. For a discussion of the interest-sensitive nature of negligence, see SR Perry, 'Protected Interests and Undertakings in the Law of Negligence' (1992) 42 U Toronto LJ 247.

[91] SR Perry, 'Comment on Coleman: Corrective Justice' (1992) 67 Indiana LJ 381, 398–400.

[92] As discussed at nn 68–69 above, the subjectivization of the objective standard to account for various kinds of inabilities to avoid the harm in question is not confined to the case of children.

Let us consider the responses that seem open to Honoré to counter this difficulty. Honoré's use of the term 'capacity' to refer to children could imply that, unlike the shortcomer who merely lacks competence, the child lacks the minimal rational agency required for liability in negligence. However, the notion of capacity (as Honoré himself defines it) seems to explain only the most unproblematic case—that of infants of tender years. It is competence rather than capacity that is at issue in the childhood cases that Honoré discusses, none of which involves an infant of tender years.[93] But if the incapacity of childhood serves only to explain the complete negligence immunity of children of tender years but not the subjectivized standard that applies to children above that age, then Honoré still needs to come up with an explanation for the objective standard's attentiveness to childhood incompetence in order to save this defence of the standard.

A solution may be found in Honoré's reconstruction of the sense in which the 'capacity to act otherwise' is relevant to liability in negligence. Honoré suggests that the required capacity should be construed as 'a *general* ability to perform the sort of action that would in the instant case have led to a different outcome'.[94] An individual possesses the requisite general capacity if 'it is usually the case that when he tries he succeeds'.[95] So perhaps Honoré could be read as saying that the objective standard imposes a form of strict liability on all who breach it provided that they have the general ability to succeed at the sort of thing that would, on that occasion, have avoided the breach. This seems to account for the treatment of children.[96] The puzzle concerns its implications for the 'shortcomer' including, prominently, the developmentally disabled.

[93] In fact, Honoré himself distinguishes between capacity and competence and says, 'In most systems a child is regarded as wholly or partly incapable, in some the insane, in some the elderly': (n 9 above) 17–18 [footnotes omitted]. He states that shortcomings are the defects and deficiencies from which the shortcomer's lack of competence stems. Competence, as Honoré describes it, seems to be a matter of degree. However if he hopes to retain some meaningful distinction between capacity and competence (and to reflect the position of the common law), then one would think that capacity cannot also be a matter of degree but must instead refer to the minimal requirement of rational agency that is a precondition to liability in negligence. But then lack of capacity only helps to explain the treatment of those who are completely exempt from liability in negligence because they lack the minimal necessary rational agency, like children of tender years, sometimes the totally insane, and those who suffer from some form of automatism. However, it would not then be possible to say, as Honoré seems to, that older children and the elderly are partly incapable. Partial incapacity seems to go to questions of competence—a 'deficiency in intelligence, learning or experience' or a 'defect of physique' that prevent someone from being able to reach the objective standard: ibid 17–18. It is true that the law adjusts the objective standard to meet the limitations of those whom Honoré calls 'partly incapable', but it is not the distinction between capacity and competence that is doing the work here despite Honoré's attempt to draw a distinction.   [94] ibid 37 [emphasis in original].

[95] ibid 38.

[96] I am purposely ignoring a possible difficulty that arises out of Honoré's discussion of the novice surgeon: ibid 36. On a straightforward application of Honoré's test, a novice surgeon would seem to lack the requisite general capacity because he would not succeed most of the time. However, Honoré says that the novice surgeon's inexperience need not be treated as a circumstance that limits liability. Instead, Honoré suggests that he can fairly be held liable for mistakes arising from his inevitable inexperience because 'taking his professional life as a whole, he is likely to be an overall winner': ibid 36 n 41. However, this reasoning also seems to suggest that 'normal' children should be held to an objective standard, since presumably, considered over a whole life, they too would profit by their

According to Honoré's own definition, a shortcomer is someone who lacks the qualities 'physical, intellectual, or emotional, needed to attain the standard set for the task in question'.[97] But then by definition shortcomers will lack the general capacity that Honoré identifies as a precondition to the application of the objective standard. If they do not have the qualities needed to attain the standard, they will not generally succeed no matter how hard they try. So the general capacity test seems to exonerate rather than inculpate the individual who, for example, suffers from 'stupidity'. So long as he is generally unsuccessful despite his best efforts, the test precludes, rather than justifies, holding him to the standard of the reasonable person. The shortcomer would, by definition, be someone whose limited capacities make him a consistent loser such that it is not fair to hold him responsible.[98] So while Honoré's general capacity test seems capable of explaining the treatment of children in the law of negligence, it does not—contrary to his own conclusion—justify imposing an rigid objective standard on the shortcomer. And it is not possible to argue that this general capacity is irrelevant to strict liability, for Honoré insists that it is a prerequisite for both strict and fault-based liability.

It does not seem to aid Honoré's argument here to have recourse to the distinction he initially draws between general capacity and the more specific capacity needed for fault-based liability. He says of the additional capacity needed for fault-based liability that it requires 'the ability to succeed most of the time *in doing the sort of thing that would on this occasion* have averted the harm'.[99] However, not only would reliance on this distinction undermine the argument that the objective standard in fact imposes a general form of strict liability, but the examples that Honoré uses to flesh out his notion of general capacity leave little room for the specific capacity that he identifies as distinguishing fault-based liability.[100] So, for example, Honoré says that 'general capacities can be measured by how people generally perform when they try to execute a given type of action, like shutting the door or crossing the street'.[101] But given that

experience and ultimately enjoy an overall benefit. In contrast, if the mistakes arising from a shortcomer's chronic incompetence will not disappear with experience, then the general capacity test, applied over the course of a life, would suggest that they should not be held to the objective standard.

[97] ibid 16.

[98] Nor is it clear that Honoré's overall benefit point would justify holding the shortcomer to the objective standard even if the shortcomer in question had sufficient capacity to succeed slightly more often than he failed. Even assuming that Honoré can establish in some workable way that such a shortcomer receives an overall benefit from the system of responsibility, this does not provide a complete answer to the question of the fairness of the system. Can the system really be justified as fair if, although everyone to whom it applies benefits overall, some groups benefit much more than others for whom the benefit is marginal? Even Honoré's general principles suggest that an individual who by virtue of his shortcoming always acts at his peril will gain far less from the system than his 'average' counterpart. But if the distribution of benefits arising from the system of responsibility is significantly unequal, it may not exhaust the fairness inquiry simply to point out that everyone benefits overall from the system of outcome responsibility.   [99] ibid 15 [emphasis added].

[100] Unfortunately, Honoré offers neither further elaboration nor any examples to elucidate his reference to the specific capacity required for fault-based liability. The rest of his discussion of this point focuses exclusively on the general capacity required for both strict and fault-based liability.

[101] ibid 38.

Honoré apparently judges general capacity on the basis of the task at issue,[102] it is difficult to see how exactly the specific capacity necessary for fault could differ significantly from general capacity.

This difficulty is reinforced by the role general capacity plays in Honoré's analysis. The general capacity requirement provides the crucial assurance that the system of outcome responsibility is fair because it limits the application of the system to those who stand to win most of the time. Individuals who have met the general capacity requirement will receive an overall benefit because it will be 'true by definition that, when they try, they usually perform up to their ability'.[103] But since there seems to be no meaningful way to make the overall benefit requirement work in the aggregate, the only way that Honoré can in fact ensure fairness is by limiting liability to those acts where the individual in question has the general ability to perform successfully. However, this reinforces the specificity suggested by Honoré's examples of general capacity and renders virtually meaningless his allusion to a more specific capacity required for fault-based liability. As a result, it seems unlikely that Honoré can invoke the idea of specific capacity to argue that the objective standard should apply in the way he suggests to shortcomers of various kinds.

There are also other related difficulties with Honoré's general capacity test. While it may seem appropriate that under such a test the developmentally disabled would not be held liable for that shortcoming, its operation is more troubling when applied to other types of shortcomings. For instance, despite Honoré's confident assertions to the contrary,[104] the 'can general' test seems to exculpate the consistently and uncontrollably bad-tempered individual because it would not be the case that he usually succeeds when he tries to control his temper. Honoré may have room to introduce a more constructive notion of what it means to 'try', but it then seems likely that he would have to begin to recognize distinctions between different types of shortcomings.[105] This points to an underlying difficulty with the 'can general' test: it assimilates the various different kinds of 'mental' shortcomings discussed earlier. In the case of children, Honoré implicitly recognizes a potential difficulty with the different elements that together form the standard of what can be 'expected' of a particular child. Thus, he insists that the child's usual behaviour bears upon but does not answer this question.[106] However, when Honoré goes on to discuss his general capacity test he seems to ignore this potential divergence. And his examples of the test

---

[102] What Honoré does not require, however, is the ability to succeed on the particular occasion in question. The 'general' in Honoré's general capacity seems to go not to the specificity of the task, but rather to the fact that an individual's 'general ability need not have been exercisable in all the concrete conditions, external and internal, of the case': ibid 37. So, to use Honoré's own example, we should look to an individual's general capacity as a driver rather than his or her ability to remain alert every moment at the wheel.   [103] ibid 38.

[104] ibid 35.

[105] In his analysis, Honoré does not distinguish between various types of shortcomings. Instead, he treats as normatively equivalent defects of physique, character, intelligence, learning, or experience as well as accident-proneness, bad coordination, and slow reactions: ibid 16–17.

[106] ibid 33–34.

are unhelpful because instead of showing how it would resolve the liability of shortcomers, Honoré applies it to golfers attempting six-foot putts and to drivers who are generally capable but who suffer momentary lapses of concentration. These easy cases, however, shed little light on the treatment of those whom it is the point of his analysis to address. Indeed, his examples assume that all shortcomings should be treated in the same way. But a closer examination suggests that this may not be desirable. We may well think that we should not hold the person with a cognitive impairment liable for failing to perceive a risk that a person with standard cognitive skills would view as obvious. But do we really want to similarly exonerate the consistently bad-tempered person for failing to control his outbursts? It does not seem intuitively obvious that we do, but Honoré's analysis of general capacity ignores these complications entirely.

So, while Honoré's discussion of the objective standard illuminates some important dimensions of the standard, it too is ultimately unsuccessful. Treating the objective standard as imposing a form of strict liability on all who breach the standard of care initially seems like a helpful way of accounting for the treatment of the shortcomer that seems anomalous by the fault standard. However, this approach to the reasonable person standard faces its own difficulties, including its inability to account for significant elements of the common law that Honoré appears to find unproblematic. And exploring whether Honoré's justification has the resources to remedy this reveals further difficulties with his analysis. These difficulties ultimately call into question whether, according to Honoré's own principles, shortcomers such as the developmentally disabled would be held to the kind of rigid objective standard that Honoré takes himself to be defending. And perhaps more troubling, the failure of the general capacity test to distinguish between different types of shortcomings raises the troubling possibility that it is just as likely to forgive an agent's characteristic moral failings as it is to forgive her cognitive limitations.

E. The equality rationale

As Honoré's strict liability argument illustrates, part of the intuitive appeal of the reasonable person standard lies in its uniformity. The standard appears fair because at least notionally it requires all individuals to observe the same level of care in their dealings with others. In fact, this equality justification is apparent as early as Tindal CJ's insistence in *Vaughan v Menlove* that allowing Menlove's claim would result in a rule of liability that would be unacceptable in part because it 'would be as variable as the length of the foot of each individual'.[107] Such a rule would not only be unfair but also unworkable, too uncertain to act upon, and so vague 'as to afford no rule at all'.[108] And ever since *Vaughan* much

[107] (n 5 above) 465.
[108] ibid 474–475. A similar concern is also apparent in Holmes's argument that legal standards are external and cannot attend to 'individual peculiarities': (n 7 above) 86.

of the support for the reasonable person standard has ultimately rested upon the perceived fairness of a uniform rule.[109]

But how plausible is it to defend a standard as vague as the reasonable person standard on the ground that it specifies a single evident standard that applies uniformly to all? If the point of the standard is to specify a uniform rule of conduct that individuals can easily comprehend and follow, the reasonable person of negligence law seems an extraordinarily unlikely vehicle. Indeed, commentators have argued that the reasonable person is actually the response to the very *impossibility* of dealing 'by way of [a] precise anticipatory rule with each of the infinite number of cases which can be classified as "negligence" cases'.[110] The result is that while the reasonable person standard may sound like—and indeed often be characterized as—a uniform standard, it is in fact highly variable (perhaps even as variable, Leon Green suggests, as the foot of each individual).[111] And given the variability of the standard, it seems unlikely that it can be formulated in a sufficiently precise way to serve as the kind of forward-looking, action-guiding norms that Tindal CJ extols.[112] These are not necessarily flaws in the reasonable person standard, but they do make it unlikely that it could be adequately defended on the ground that, unlike its alternative, it specifies a single knowable standard to both guide and judge human conduct. However, this does not fatally undermine the equality defence of the objective standard. For while Tindal CJ's notion of identity of treatment may ultimately rest on a shallow and perhaps even an indefensible view of equality, there are deeper accounts available. And Ernest Weinrib elaborates such an account in his important defence of the objective standard.[113]

Weinrib insists that the equality of treatment entailed by the reasonable person standard is in fact the basis of the standard's legitimacy. According to Weinrib, tort law exhibits its own special morality that derives from the moral relationship of doer to sufferer. But in order to count as a moral relationship, the parties must stand on a footing of equality 'as between doer and sufferer'.[114]

---

[109] Prosser (n 10 above) 174; Fleming (n 10 above) 117. An implicit appeal to the fairness of an identical standard also undergirds many of the justifications for the objective standard discussed here, including the appeal to fairness to the victim, Coleman's attempt to reconstruct fault, and Honoré's strict liability argument discussed above.   [110] Leon Green (n 11 above) 1029.

[111] ibid 1037–1039. In fact, in his classic work on tort law, *Judge and Jury* (Kansas City: Vernon Law Book Co, 1930), Green puts the point more bluntly and rejects the notion that the qualities and characteristics of the persons in litigation are irrelevant to the jury's deliberations: 180–181. Indeed, as discussed below, Green argues that many individual characteristics including sex, race, and income level are influential.

[112] But this weakness is not necessarily fatal. Perry suggests that 'it is a mistake to think that [the moral evaluation of action] must always be carried out on the basis of norms that are generally capable of antecedently guiding action': 'Moral Foundations' (n 76 above) 511–512.

[113] As discussed below, an account that defends *Vaughan* along lines similar to Weinrib's (though it differs in the larger point) has been elaborated by Arthur Ripstein in *Equality, Responsibility and the Law* (Cambridge: Cambridge University Press, 1999), especially at 84–87 (*Vaughan* as a particularly dramatic example of the more general principle of treating the parties as equals).

[114] E Weinrib, 'The Special Morality of Tort Law' (1989) 34 McGill LJ 403, 409.

However, this equality is threatened by the person who claims that 'he ought not to be held liable for the injuries caused by his stupidity'.[115] Weinrib argues that allowing the defendant to be the judge of reasonableness would undermine the equality of the parties because then the defendant's capacities would unilaterally set the terms of the relationship between individuals who should be equals. So the significance of the objective standard is found in the fact that it reflects the formal equality of the rights holders by setting terms on which they can interact as equals.[116] Seen in this way, the objective standard is egalitarian in that it prevents the doer's personal qualities from unilaterally determining the terms of the relationship.[117] The egalitarianism of the objective standard also contrasts with the inequality of strict liability in which one person's property sets the bounds within which others must act.[118] According to this understanding, negligence is the failure to conform one's behaviour to the equal status of others, and the objective standard is the unique embodiment of this equal status.

Weinrib's defence of the objective standard cannot be adequately understood, however, unless it is placed in the context of his discussion of Kantian right. For Weinrib, this idea of right specifies the form of equality that is implicit in corrective justice. It is, according to Weinrib, corrective justice that lends private law relationships their distinctive structure. However, there is a troubling omission in Aristotle's articulation of corrective justice. While it presupposes the equality of two parties to a transaction, it fails to specify the respect in which the parties are equal.[119] Weinrib rejects Aquinas's assertion that the law simply treats the parties as equals 'however much they may be unequal'[120] and instead insists that the parties 'cannot rightly be treated as equals unless they are equal in some relevant sense'.[121] And according to Weinrib, only the Kantian idea of right can respond to this omission in the Aristotelian account of corrective justice.[122]

Weinrib locates the distinctiveness of corrective justice in three essential ideas: the abstraction from particulars such as social status and moral character; the equality of the parties; and the correlativity of doing and suffering.[123]

---

[115] Weinrib, 'Causation and Wrongdoing' (n 89 above) 427. Weinrib notes that this example is based on the defendant's claim in *Vaughan* (n 5 above).

[116] Weinrib, 'Causation and Wrongdoing' (n 89 above) 428.

[117] Weinrib, 'Morality of Tort Law' (n 114 above) 410; 'Causation and Wrongdoing' (n 89 above) 428; *The Idea of Private Law* (n 16 above) 178.

[118] Weinrib, 'Causation and Wrongdoing' (n 89 above) 428; *The Idea of Private Law* (n 16 above) 177–179.   [119] *The Idea of Private Law* (ibid) 57.

[120] ibid 80, quoting Aquinas, *Commentary on the Nicomachean Ethics* Vol I (trans CI Litzinger) (Chicago: H Regnery Co, 1964) 411.

[121] ibid. Partly for this reason, Weinrib rejects the notion that the equality requirement would be satisfied by any liability rule so long as it was uniformly applied: 'Morality of Tort Law' (n 114 above) 409.

[122] *The Idea of Private Law* (n 16 above) 80–83. Weinrib argues that something like the Kantian concept of right is implicit in Aristotle's notion of corrective justice, which is concerned with equality, abstraction from particularity, and the correlativity of doing and suffering. Thus, Weinrib does not conceive himself to be imposing the Kantian notion of agency on the Aristotelian structure of corrective justice. Rather, he is drawing out the 'conception of agency presupposed in corrective justice': ibid 83.   [123] ibid 80–82.

Thus, the necessary conception must link equality both with abstraction and with the correlativity of doing and suffering. Weinrib argues that only the Kantian account of right accomplishes this. Aristotle's concern to abstract from particulars finds its expression in Kant's negative freedom, the capacity 'to rise above the givenness of inclination and circumstance'.[124] Aristotle's equality requirement corresponds to the Kantian insistence on the normative irrelevance of the 'particular features—desires, endowments, circumstances, and so on—that might distinguish one agent from another' and thus form the basis of 'judging them unequal'.[125] And Aristotle's correlativity accords with Kant's treatment of doing and suffering as a single normative sequence that disregards the particularities of the doer and the sufferer.[126] Once the inchoately Kantian nature of corrective justice is thus uncovered, the relevant form of equality emerges. The equality of corrective justice derives its normative force from Kantian right. Kantian right is the juridical manifestation of self-determining agency. And the fundamental feature of self-determining agency is the capacity of an agent to 'abstract from—and thus not to be determined by—the particular circumstances of his or her situation'.[127] Thus, it is with reference to this capacity to abstract from particularity, to rise above inclination and circumstance, that all self-determining agents are equal.

Clearly this is a sophisticated and complex defence of the objective standard. However, without addressing the complex issues of equality it implicates, it is possible to query its significance for the reasonable person standard. This is because it is difficult to understand how the objective standard, which requires only that an individual behave as a reasonable person would in the circumstances, comports with a Kantian view of agency. Even in its core case, the standard does not demand that individuals rise above every inclination and circumstance.[128] Indeed, through the use of the qualifier 'in the circumstances' the objective standard explicitly recognizes certain circumstances that the agent need not transcend. And the emergency cases also illustrate that the standard does in fact make allowances for certain inclinations, including common human failings.[129] Similarly, agents are not in fact expected to rise above all 'endowments' in the way that Weinrib's rendering of Kantian right would seem to demand. The limited physical abilities of the physically disabled and the limited mental abilities of children are not treated as the kind of particularities that must be overcome. Thus, something beyond Kantian right seems to be required in order to justify the application of the objective standard to the developmentally disabled. In particular, if not all endowments are irrelevant, if not all circumstances need be transcended, why it is justifiable to require the developmentally

---

[124] *The Idea of Private Law* (ibid) 82.   [125] ibid.   [126] ibid.   [127] ibid 81.

[128] Perry notes a similar difficulty with the argument that abstract right requires the adoption of the objective standard. Why, he asks, would it not attribute omniscience to the actor rather than simply the knowledge possessed by the reasonable person: 'Moral Foundations' (n 76 above) 486.

[129] As the *Restatement* puts it, 'The fact that this judgment is personified in a "man" calls attention to the necessity of taking into account the fallibility of human beings': (n 13 above) s 283, Comment A.

disabled person either to 'rise above' his or her limited intelligence or to be liable in negligence?

Answering this question seems vital to Weinrib's equality-based defence of the objective standard. At least a partial response can be found in his discussion of the exceptions to the objective standard. There Weinrib argues that the exceptions accord with Kantian right because they 'allow subjective factors to exonerate when their presence precludes seeing the plaintiff's injury as a consequence of the defendant's self-determining agency'.[130] Naturally enough, it is on this ground that he accounts for cases involving blackouts and insane delusions. In the case of children, Weinrib argues that the law 'must accommodate the development of self-determining agency'.[131] With regard to the physically disabled, he states that the common law treatment simply recognizes physical characteristics as 'part of the context within which, under conditions of human existence, agency occurs'.[132] But then why are developmental disabilities not similarly understood?

Weinrib's answer to this question is somewhat oblique. He states that the defendant's physical embodiment is 'distinguishable from the intellectual processes through which agency operates as a causality of concepts'.[133] Unlike a physical disability, lack of intelligence is 'part of the act itself'.[134] However, it is difficult to see why this kind of dichotomy should be given such normative significance. But what it does reveal is the same kind of reluctance that we noted earlier to parse the elements of agency. And without this, it is very difficult to account for the possibility that different components of action and choice, or different kinds of shortcomings, may vary in their normative significance. Indeed, Kant here seems to provide one way to think about the significance of such matters in his emphasis on the normative significance of 'self-determining' agency. And according to Weinrib's own analysis, it is the capacity to act as a self-determining agent that gives action normative significance and thus permits judgement of it. But if a developmental disability is not only not the result of the exercise of self-determining agency, but actually limits the ability to exercise such agency, it is hard to see why this kind of account would treat it in the way Weinrib suggests. Why is it not instead treated as part of the context within which the exercise of agency—albeit constrained—occurs? Indeed, this is precisely what happens in the case of the cognitive and intellectual shortcomings of children. Weinrib's account of why there should be this difference seems to rest on the notion that the treatment of children is justified because the law is simply reflecting the natural process of the development of agency. But what precisely is the basis of the normative distinction here? The fact that it is 'natural'? The fact that it is a process? Even without problematizing what these terms might mean, it seems unlikely that either of these factors alone or in combination is sufficient to

---

[130] *The Idea of Private Law* (n 16 above) 183 n 22.

[131] ibid 183 n 22(4). He also notes with approval comments to the effect that childhood is not an idiosyncrasy.   [132] ibid 183 n 22(3).

[133] ibid.   [134] ibid.

justify the difference between the legal treatment of children and that of the developmentally disabled. Perhaps Weinrib could explain how this discrepancy accords with Kantian right, but to date he has not done so. And in the absence of such an account his equality-based justification of the objective standard falls short of its goal.

III. CONCLUSION

Vaughan v Menlove, despite its antiquity, nonetheless remains the most fitting place to begin an examination of the reasonable person. Indeed, *Vaughan*'s strengths and weaknesses continue to exert formidable influence on the nature and meaning of fault in negligence. There one can see, for instance, the reluctance to take apart the components of agency that has been one of the hallmarks of the reasonable person ever since. In fact, Menlove himself arguably trades on this very feature when he argues that the appropriate solution to the problem of failing to 'possess the highest order of intelligence' would be to judge him by a standard that simply demands that he do his best. *Vaughan*'s important affirmation that it is not a defence to a claim of negligence to act to the best of one's judgement thus ends up inextricably linking the very different problems of moral ignorance and intellectual or cognitive deficiency. And in part for this reason, it has seemed to courts and commentators ever since *Vaughan* that holding on to the normative heart of negligence requires us to demand that even those with developmental disabilities must exercise the same level of intellectual prowess as the reasonable person. It may seem that the reasonable person has the resources to respond to some of the complexity that has resulted from this link. But this would require us to delve more deeply into the exercise of agency, and in the context of the civil law of negligence, courts and commentators have been reluctant to do so for fear that negligence would be infected with the subjectivism of the criminal law.

And even apart from Menlove's own claim, this undifferentiated approach to agency is confirmed by the very articulation of the standard. Thus the court in *Vaughan* sets out two alternatives: saying that the liability for negligence should be co-extensive with the judgement of each individual (Menlove's claim), or adhering to the rule that 'requires in all cases a regard to caution such as a man of ordinary prudence would observe'.[135] Capturing a standard of reasonable judgement in terms of what some idealized person (the man of ordinary prudence) would do by now no doubt seems entirely unremarkable. But at least since *Vaughan*, courts and commentators have puzzled to articulate just what kind of relation ought to exist between the idealized person and the person actually judged. The way that the reasonable person seamlessly links the normative qualities of the idealized person with his biographical or empirical qualities may

---

[135] (n 5 above) 475.

often seem to pre-empt the need to examine agency more closely. But if this 'intuitiveness' frequently seems like a strength of the reasonable person, it comes to look more like a shortcoming in the face of a claim that the standard needs to be reshaped in order to establish a proper relation between it and the person actually judged.

In such cases the reasonable person seems to give decision-makers little but their intuitions to turn to, and these may lead them seriously astray. Ironically, here too *Vaughan* still speaks to contemporary observers. The Court there famously states that allowing liability to be co-extensive with the judgement of each individual would result in a standard 'as variable as the length of the foot of each individual'.[136] But students of the law will recognize in the Court's pronouncement an echo of the traditional criticism of the discretionary justice characteristic of Equity—that such a system made liability as variable as the Chancellor's foot. The concern is thus rather that such a variable standard permits the decision-maker too much discretion and gives too little in the way of guidance. And indeed, the treatment of the developmentally disabled under the reasonable person standard cannot help but awaken the concern that decision-makers, left unaided by the reasonable person just where they most need assistance, too easily incorporate their own preferences, biases, and stereotypes into the vacuum left by the standard. Despite the efforts of prominent theorists and commentators, it seems extremely difficult to find a persuasive reason for the radically different way the reasonable person approaches children and the developmentally disabled. Indeed, in a different but arguably relevant context, Mr Justice La Forest specifically noted the danger of decision-makers undervaluing the interests of the developmentally handicapped: history tells us, he reminds us (and himself) that we have consistently perceived them as 'somewhat less than human'.[137] And given that even today those with developmental disabilities struggle to enjoy the full rights of citizenship, it is difficult to dismiss the worry that something troubling may be behind the fact that the law of negligence is selectively inattentive to their concerns.

Despite the weaknesses of the defences of imposing the reasonable person standard on the developmentally disabled, commentators attempting to justify what they take to be the implications of *Vaughan* do illuminate a critically important dimension of the law of negligence (even if it does not entail the consequences that they suppose follow from it). *Vaughan* insisted that a fault standard is not to be equated with a simple demand that each individual exercise her best judgement. Such an approach, as *Vaughan* notes and subsequent commentators affirm, would actually obliterate the core of the fault standard and eviscerate the equality that animates the law of negligence. The challenge then—taken up, though not in fully satisfactory ways, by subsequent commentators—has been to articulate a defensible conception of responsibility for heedlessness, a conception that preserves the

---

[136] ibid.

[137] *Re Eve* (1986) 31 DLR (4th) 1, 29 (SCC) (Application for the involuntary non-therapeutic sterilization of a developmentally disabled young woman).

insistence that the standard of judgement must be found in the law, not in the individual agent. Our examination of the defences of *Vaughan* may help to rule out certain possibilities, but the task of outlining a more positive conception proves somewhat elusive. Nonetheless, the defences of the treatment of the developmentally disabled do provide us with some elements that seem important to any such conception.

The account of Weinrib is perhaps in this respect the deepest, providing insight into the core ambition of the reasonable person standard. Throughout discussions of the reasonable person standard, one can trace the sense that equality is somehow central to the justification of the objective standard. Weinrib thus gives the moral defence of the holding in *Vaughan*, noting the link between the refusal to allow the subjective powers of judgement of the defendant to define the standard of care and the fundamental legal commitment to equal moral worth. And the force of his account in this respect suggests that an idea of equality, and the concomitant refusal to allow individuals' varying assessments of the worth of others to calibrate the standard of care, must be a central element in a more adequate account of fault and responsibility.

There are also other indications of elements that may be important to such an account. Holmes's powerful articulation of the centrality of avoidability seems to capture something essential to the conception of fault in negligence, even if Holmes himself did not follow through on its full implications in his discussions of the developmentally disabled. For the 'normal' person whose qualities are mirrored in the reasonable person, the mere application of the objective standard will generally preclude liability in the absence of a fair chance to avoid the harm. It is therefore telling that where the reasonable person test fails to ensure this because of some important difference between the reasonable person and the actual agent, the typical response of the law of negligence is to prefer a more nuanced reading of avoidability to a strict application of the objective standard. Thus, it takes into consideration the shortcomings of children, the physically disabled, and those facing emergency situations to ensure that they will not be liable unless they had a fair chance of avoiding the harm in question. Indeed, it is this general preference for avoidability that makes it so troubling that the law refuses to extend the same treatment to the developmentally disabled.

Honoré's discussion of the general capacity test as a precondition to liability in negligence also parallels in significant ways the Holmesian insistence on avoidability. For that reason, Honoré's general capacity test, though it does not serve the purpose to which he puts it, may be a useful place to begin developing a more egalitarian interpretation of avoidability. However, here too there are perils as well as promise. At times Honoré suggests that the notion of 'normal' behaviour will not be determinative of general capacity and thus of liability. However, his analysis—based as it is on an assessment of whether someone can usually succeed when they attempt something—actually seems to accord troubling significance to normal or ordinary behaviour. In this sense, the general capacity test does indeed seem to provide a compelling reason why the developmentally disabled cannot be judged according to an unreflective reasonable person standard, but it does so at a high price. For the general capacity test also seems to require that we accede to the defendant's claim in *Vaughan* that all we can demand of him is his best. More nuance, it seems, may be needed if we are to make use of something like general capacity without this danger, but this kind of nuance is just what the reasonable person is designed to forestall. Admittedly, this danger may seem to pale in comparison with the difficulty of the developmentally disabled, but our next case study, the child defendant, suggests that this may not be so.

2

'Boys Will Be Boys': The Child Defendant and the Objective Standard

The problem of how to judge individuals with cognitive or intellectual shortcomings illustrates one aspect of the 'trouble' with the reasonable person and thus raises a series of questions implicated in objective standards more generally. Scholarly interest in this problem turns in part on the belief that the treatment of such shortcomings distinguishes the objective standard's conception of fault from the subjectivist understanding of the criminal law. So, part of the justification for the treatment of cognitive disabilities calls attention to the divergence between the notion of fault under negligence law's objective standard and more thoroughgoing conceptions of blameworthiness such as those found in the criminal law. Thus, what might initially appear as the reasonable person standard's 'failure' to capture only blameworthy behaviour is actually posited as its distinctive strength. As we have seen, in part this is because this 'failure' to attend to blame is seen as crucial to maintaining the core of the objective standard. In this way, the reasonable person's rigidity in the face of the intellectual shortcomings of the defendant is taken to exemplify its distinctively egalitarian conception of fault. By focusing on the perspective of the injured plaintiff and the need to repair or compensate for injury, the argument goes, the reasonable person of the law of negligence complements criminal law's focus on the importance of the defendant's liberty interests.

But interestingly, the treatment of the child defendant forms the mirror image of this. In stark contrast to the treatment of mentally disabled defendants, courts and commentators addressing the application of the objective standard to the child defendant insist that the basis of liability in negligence actually requires taking account of the limitations of childhood. Here, there is also an emphasis on the distinctive basis of liability in negligence, but the point of contrast is different: negligence in the child defendant cases tends to be distinguished, not from criminal law, but rather from strict liability. Analysing the treatment of intellectual disabilities provided an opportunity to examine the justifications for and some constitutive elements of the objective standard's distinctive notion of fault, but it also alerted us to potential dangers in the way in which that notion of fault is articulated. By illuminating the opposite facet of the standard's claim to distinctiveness, the child defendant cases enable us to examine another critical aspect of the reasonable person and its justifications. Here too we see dangers as well as promise, for this examination reveals just how indebted the norm of reasonableness is to some conception of what is normal or ordinary.

I. JUDGING THE PLAYING BOY: *McHale v Watson*

Reported cases involving child defendants are rare indeed. It is not difficult to speculate why this might be the case. Rarely will children have sufficient resources to warrant a plaintiff's pursuit of a costly negligence action. And since parents are not vicariously liable for the torts of their children, only the resources of the child defendant himself will typically be subject to any judgment.[1] Nonetheless, the reported cases involving the claims of the child defendant are illuminating. A survey of the negligence cases involving child defendants reveals a remarkable pattern. Almost all of the child defendants are boys. Thus, for example, in the section of *The Canadian Abridgement* that summarizes the cases on child tortfeasors, nine of the ten negligence cases involve boys.[2] Similar patterns prevail in other jurisdictions where the vast majority of child defendants are also boys.[3] But what exactly can we learn from the treatment of the child defendant? In order to answer this, let us examine the leading common law case on this question: *McHale v Watson*.[4]

---

[1] This is assuming, of course, that no insurance is involved. It may be that where such insurance is implicated—as in many of the adult activities cases discussed at nn 96–108 below—litigation is more common.

[2] *Canadian Abridgement*, Family Law, XII, 'Status and Capacities of Children', s 2 (Torts) ss a (Child as Tortfeasor) (Toronto: Carswell, 1995, 2001). I did not include in my calculations from this section those children so young that they were below the age of tender years. Because of their extreme youth, such actors are incapable of rational agency and thus seem to raise different considerations. The one case in the *Abridgement* section on the Child as Tortfeasor that fell into this category involved a 3-year-old boy who dragged a baby along the ground and severely injured her: *Tillander v Gosselin* [1967] 1 OR 203; affd (1967), 61 DLR 2d 192n (Ont CA).

[3] The few child defendant cases that I found from other jurisdictions also confirmed this pattern. Thus, all of the child defendant cases discussed by Fleming involve boys (JG Fleming, *The Law of Torts* (9th edn, Agincourt: The Law Book Company, 1998) 126–127), as do all of the cases discussed in Gary L Bahr's 'Tort Law and the Games Kids Play' (1978) 23 S Dak L Rev 275. However, it is not entirely clear what lessons can be drawn from the absence of cases involving girls as defendants. The most obvious one would be that girls simply do not take the kinds of risks with the security of others that boys do. However, it may be more complex than that given that our 'results' are reported cases. For instance, it could be the case that when girls are potential defendants, parents or guardians do not even consider litigating but instead simply pay the claims or settle because they do not view the girls as having plausible defences. In this way, stereotypes can feed back into the litigation process and can affect even the numbers of reported and unreported cases, as well as settlement patterns. Nonetheless, accident rates more generally do reflect gender differences. Thus, the Statistics Canada breakdown of leading causes of death among Canadians reveals that males consistently suffer more deaths by accident. For example, in the year 1994 the number of deaths by accident under age 1 were relatively similar for both genders (male 22; female 19) but after this the numbers begin to diverge. Between the ages of 1 and 4, 104 boys died but only 75 girls; ages 5 to 9, 80 boys died and only 44 girls; ages 10 to 14, 85 boys and only 52 girls. After age 15, the differences become even more marked, with male deaths typically over 400 and female deaths just over 100. No doubt this is in part due to motor vehicle deaths: JR Colombo, *The Canadian Global Almanac, 1998* (Toronto: Macmillan Canada, 1997) 71.

[4] *McHale v Watson* (1964) 111 CLR 384, Windeyer J [hereinafter *McHale*, Trial]; (1966) 115 CLR 199 (Aust HC), McTiernan ACJ, Kitto, Menzies, Owen JJ [hereinafter *McHale*, Appeal].

A. The facts and holdings of *McHale*

The leading common law case on the standard of care to be applied in negligence cases against child defendants is the decision of the High Court of Australia in *McHale v Watson*. In fact, the English Court of Appeal recently adopted the reasoning of *McHale* in *Mullin v Richards*.[5] *McHale* is important in part because it contains by far the most detailed justification for modifying the objective standard to take account of the limitations of youth, as well as the most detailed discussion of what the application of such a standard entails. In fact, other cases that extend the protections of the relaxed standard to the child defendant do so in terms strikingly similar to those employed in *McHale*, although typically without such detailed reasoning. And the implications of the reasoning in *McHale* also help to explain why certain categories of child defendants do not benefit from a relaxed standard.

McHale thus provides a useful place to begin to unravel the mystery of why courts faced with the task of applying the objective standard treat children so differently from the developmentally disabled. How, first of all, does the court justify extending a subjectivized standard of care to the child defendant? And once the court decides on the reasonable child standard, how does it give content to that standard? What, in short, convinces the court that a 12-year-old boy should not be responsible for throwing a metal rod at a 9-year-old girl and destroying the sight in her eye? In order to answer these questions let us examine *McHale* more closely.

The relevant events took place on a day in January of 1957. Several children, including 12-year-old Barry Watson and 9-year-old Susan McHale, were playing in Portland, Australia. After a game of tag, the children were standing near portable wooden guards designed to protect young ornamental trees. In his pocket Barry Watson had a six-inch long piece of metal welding rod that he had earlier sharpened to a point in order to spear starfish on the beach. He took this rod out of his pocket and threw it. It struck Susan McHale and pierced her right eye with the result that her sight in that eye was virtually destroyed. Susan McHale brought an action against both Barry Watson and his parents. In the aspect of the action with which we are concerned, she alleged that when Barry Watson injured her with the dart he was guilty either of assault and battery and trespass to the person or of negligence. Her negligence claim required the court to determine first the appropriate standard of care for a child defendant, and then to consider how to give effect to that standard in the particular circumstances of the case.

At trial, Windeyer J found in favour of the defendant Barry Watson. He insisted that it was not necessary 'to disregard altogether the fact that the defendant Barry Watson was at the time only twelve years old'.[6] Windeyer J then held that, in the light of the defendant's age, the 'injury to the plaintiff was not the

---

[5] [1998] 1 All ER 920 (CA).   [6] Trial (n 4 above) 397.

result of a lack of foresight and appreciation of the risk that might reasonably have been expected, or of a want of reasonable care in aiming the dart'.[7] Thus, he dismissed the case against Barry Watson. He also dismissed the case against Barry's parents.

Susan McHale appealed Windeyer J's finding that Barry Watson was not liable in negligence for the injury to her eye. She argued that Windeyer J erred when he held that Barry Watson was not to be judged by the standard of the reasonable man but was instead entitled to have his age taken into consideration in determining his liability. In the alternative, she asked the High Court to find that regardless of whether the standard was that of the reasonable 12-year-old or the reasonable man, on the facts Barry Watson should have been found negligent.

A majority of three members of the High Court of Australia dismissed Susan's appeal. McTiernan ACJ, Kitto J, and Owen J agreed with the trial judgment of Windeyer J both on the appropriate standard of care and on the conclusion that Barry was not liable under that standard. In dissent, Menzies J held that child defendants, unlike child plaintiffs, were required to take the same care as the 'ordinary reasonable man' in their dealings with others.[8] Further, Menzies J argued that even if Barry were given the benefit of a reasonable boy test, his actions were still so unreasonable as to be negligent.

B. The standard of care for a child defendant

The most far-reaching question addressed by the courts in *McHale v Watson* concerned the appropriate standard of care for child defendants. Since there was no directly applicable authority for taking the defendant's age into consideration in determining the appropriate standard of care, the court was in somewhat uncharted terrain. The commentary supporting special treatment for children did not deal with the negligence of a child above tender years but instead concerned either contributory negligence or children of tender years. Similarly, the Canadian case of *Walmsley v Humenick*[9] was apparently on point but in fact dealt with a child under 5 and so actually turned on the lack of capacity of a child of tender years. And, as Kitto J himself noted, American and Canadian judicial opinions on the negligence of children are 'varied both in result and in reasoning'.[10] How then did the courts determine that child defendants are entitled to have their age taken into consideration in fashioning the appropriate standard of care?

At trial Windeyer J seems to find the issue of the appropriate standard of care unproblematic. After quoting the classic formulations of the objective standard from *Vaughan v Menlove*[11] and *Glasgow Corporation v Muir*,[12] Windeyer J states that he must determine what the defendant ought to have foreseen in the circumstances of the particular case. Since the question of what circumstances

---

[7] ibid.   [8] Appeal (n 4 above) 226.   [9] [1954] 2 DLR 232 (BCSC).
[10] Appeal (n 4 above) 214.   [11] (1837) 3 Bing NC 468, 132 ER 490 (CP).
[12] [1943] AC 448.

to consider is, in his opinion, a 'question of fact', he reasons that it must be determined not 'by regarding the facts of other cases, but by regarding all the circumstances of this case'.[13] Based on this, Windeyer J holds that he is not 'required to disregard altogether the fact that the defendant Barry Watson was at the time only twelve years old'.[14] This, he insists, is not contrary to Lord Macmillan's injunction from *Glasgow Corporation* that the standard must be 'independent of the idiosyncrasies of the particular person'[15] because '[c]hildhood is not an idiosyncrasy'.[16] Similarly, in the High Court two of the three judgments that uphold Windeyer J's decision on the relevant standard of care do so largely without any reasoning of their own.

Substantive arguments about the appropriate standard of care for the child defendant can be found only in the majority judgment of Kitto J.[17] He relies on two principal arguments in favour of extending a relaxed standard of care to the child defendant. His first argument is that a relaxed standard for children is necessitated by the form of fault upon which the system of negligence is based. Determining the appropriate standard of care for the child defendant, Kitto J points out, inevitably implicates 'the true theory of liability in negligence'.[18] He notes that while historically liability for causing harm to another was absolute, in time liability became limited 'to acts involving a shortcoming on the part of the defendant'.[19] Under such a system, 'inherently proper' acts cannot give rise to liability.[20] But propriety should not be equated with lack of moral blameworthiness. Instead, propriety asks whether the individual exercised the degree of 'care reasonably to be expected in the circumstances from the normal person'.[21] This notion of propriety does not preclude a child from raising a defence of limited capacity, so long as the relevant limitations upon the capacity for foresight or prudence are 'characteristic of humanity at his stage of development and in that sense normal'.[22] In relation to those qualities that bear on foresight and prudence, normality for children—in contrast with adults—is 'a concept of rising levels until "years of discretion" are attained'.[23] Thus, before adulthood, 'normal' capacity

---

[13] Trial (n 4 above) 397.   [14] ibid.   [15] (n 12 above) 457, quoted at ibid.

[16] Trial (n 4 above) 397.

[17] The dissenting judgment of Menzies J also contains a substantive discussion of this issue, although his argument is not in support of the trial judgment of Windeyer J. The arguments made in the dissent will be discussed when relevant to the majority analysis.

[18] Appeal (n 4 above) 212.

[19] ibid 213, citing WS Holdsworth, *A History of English Law* Vol III (gen edn, London: Metheun, Sweet and Maxwell, 1966) 379.   [20] ibid.

[21] ibid. Kitto J also states that consequently it is no more open to a child than to an adult to escape liability by arguing that he is 'abnormally slow-witted, quick-tempered, absent-minded or inexperienced', for instance. However, Menzies J argues that any holding that a child's conduct is to be judged by a child's standards would logically also require that 'there should also be special standards of care applicable to other classes of persons having less capacity than the ordinary reasonably prudent man—e.g. the mentally defective or the senile': ibid 219. As noted above, in the case of children, courts have shown themselves more willing to consider 'subjective' factors such as mental capacity, at least in contributory negligence cases: see ch 1 above, nn 38–39 and accompanying text.

[22] ibid. In fact, Kitto J states that a person who relies on such a defence is actually appealing to 'a standard of ordinariness, to an objective and not a subjective standard': ibid.   [23] ibid.

for foresight and prudence means 'the capacity which is normal for a child of the relevant age'.[24] To hold otherwise, Kitto J states, would be 'contrary to the fundamental principle that a person is liable for harm that he causes by falling short of an objective criterion of "propriety" in his conduct—propriety, that is to say, as determined by a comparison with the standard of care reasonably to be expected in the circumstances from the normal person'.[25] Thus, according to Kitto J, the shift from strict liability to the fault system actually requires that a child be judged by a standard that makes reference to the capacity for foresight and prudence, not of an adult, but of a normal child of his age.[26]

In addition to insisting that a calibrated standard for the child defendant is required by the underlying concept of fault in negligence, Kitto J also argues that considerable support—albeit indirect—for such a standard can be found in the cases on contributory negligence of children. These cases hold that normal childhood deficiencies of foresight and prudence are relevant in determining what care it is reasonable to expect a child to take for himself. And, while contributory negligence is not a breach of a legal duty but only a failure to take reasonable care for one's own safety, Kitto J nonetheless argues that there is no basis for distinguishing between the two in terms of the relevant standard of care.[27] His principal argument in favour of this conclusion points to the fact that formally the relevant standard is objective both for negligence and for contributory negligence. The consequence, according to Kitto J, is that a child defendant's behaviour ought to be measured against 'the standard to be expected of a child, meaning any ordinary child, of comparable age'.[28]

---

[24] ibid 214.   [25] ibid.

[26] Other child defendant cases also state that the 'special' treatment accorded the child defendant under the objective standard is in fact required by the very basis of liability in negligence. So, for example, in *Vaillancourt v Jacques*, Rivard J relies on the fact that there cannot be responsibility without fault in challenging the trial judge's finding of negligence: [1972] CA 197, 199 (Que), aff'd [1975] 1 SCR 724, Pigeon J dissenting. And he notes the 'subjectvisme relatif de la faute', particularly with respect to the power to foresee and avoid the dangerous act: ibid 200, citing R Savatier, *Traite de la responsabilité civile en droit français civil, administratif, professionel* (2nd edn, Paris: Librairie générale de droit et de jurisprudence, 1951) nos 167, 208, 209.

[27] Appeal (note 4 above) 214. In dissent, Menzies J argues that there is 'no justification for deciding whether a defendant has been negligent by the test which the law adopts for ascertaining whether a plaintiff has been guilty of contributory negligence in the sense that he has failed to take reasonable care for his own safety': ibid 224. He points out the difference between negligence, which is the duty of care that the law imposes upon one man in his relationship with others, and contributory negligence, in which no such duty is implicated. These issues are discussed by Kenneth W Simons, 'Contributory Negligence: Conceptual and Normative Issues' in David G Owen (ed), *Philosophical Foundations of Tort Law* (Oxford: Clarendon Press, 1995) 461–485. Simons suggests that the absence of a formal distinction between a plaintiff's and a defendant's negligence may obscure actual differences in treatment, and in particular the more lenient attitude to victims than to injurers: ibid 469–470. He also notes that courts occasionally suggest—as does Menzies J in *McHale*—that creating an unreasonable risk to others is more faulty than exposing oneself to such a risk: ibid. Simons explores these and other difficult questions and notes that under any view 'the issues resist easy analysis': ibid 485.   [28] Appeal (n 4 above) 215.

C. Sense and sensibility: Applying the standard of care

In addition to providing a detailed justification for the nature of the standard of care applicable to child defendants, *McHale v Watson* also affords an opportunity to closely examine how courts give content to the standard of care. How does the court determine whether or not Barry Watson behaved reasonably in the circumstances? In this, the heart of the negligence inquiry, the court must specify what the legal requirement of reasonableness entails in the concrete circumstances of the case. And despite the centrality of this process of judgment, it is remarkably mysterious. Examining *McHale v Watson* more closely, however, does shed some light on what considerations courts weigh when they determine whether or not someone acted as a reasonable person would have in their circumstances.

In this sense, *McHale* repays analysis in part because it contains more than the usual cursory assessment of whether the behaviour in question was reasonable. And because the court explicitly struggles with just how far and where the standard of care ought to be tailored to reflect the capacities of the defendant, the reasoning in *McHale* is actually more attentive to the very different components that together make up the reasonable person standard. Thus, for instance, Kitto J characterizes the standard as requiring that degree of care 'reasonably to be expected in the like circumstances from the normal person exercising reasonable *foresight* and *consideration for the safety of others*'.[29] And this reference to foresight and prudence is but one of a series of references to these different components of the objective standard.[30] By describing the standard in this way, *McHale* makes room for the possibility of distinguishing between foresight, which implicates the defendant's cognitive and perceptive abilities, and prudence, which turns on the defendant's normative abilities or attentiveness to others. And by in this way noting the complexity of the standard, *McHale* can be seen as providing at least the beginnings of a more nuanced vocabulary for understanding the objective standard. Unfortunately, despite the fact that the *McHale* courts point to the availability of such a vocabulary, they do not actually make use of it in their analysis.[31] Nonetheless even noting the distinct elements of the standard of care and then paying little attention to the difference between them is telling.

[29] Appeal (note 4 above) 213 (emphasis added).

[30] Similarly, Windeyer J states 'the injury to the plaintiff was not the result of a lack of foresight and appreciation of risk that might reasonably have been expected': Trial (n 4 above) 397. Owen J refers to 'the capacity of the particular child to appreciate the risk and form a reasonable judgment': Appeal (n 4 above) 231, quoting WL Prosser, *Handbook of the Law of Torts* (2nd edn, St Paul: West Pub Co, 1955) 127–128.

[31] So, for instance, in the judgment at trial, Windeyer J concludes 'on the facts of this case' that 'the injury to the plaintiff was not the result of a lack of foresight and appreciation of risk that might reasonably have been expected, or of a want of reasonable care in aiming the dart': Trial (n 4 above) 397. Similarly, Kitto J routinely links the two concepts as though they were actually one. In his judgment, this occurs at least nine times, both in his discussion of the relevant standard of care and in his application of that standard to the facts: Appeal (n 4 above) 212–215.

However, it is not possible to completely avoid the question of what significance should attach to the nature of the shortcoming. The *McHale* court does note that the reasonable person inquiry potentially implicates both shortcomings that ordinarily have some normative significance (like the failure to attend to the interests of others) and those that do not (like the intellectual limitations of children). But although it identifies these separate elements, the court then goes on to treat them as indistinguishable from each other. The implication is thus that there is no basis for according different types of shortcomings different treatment. The court prefers, as we shall see, to read the reasonable person stand-ard as demanding propriety or ordinariness, rather than some more thorough-going moral conception. This undifferentiated approach to fault plays out in the fact that the majority decisions hold that both the degree of foresight and the degree of prudence that children are required to exercise should be modified. As Kitto J puts it, an individual can defend against liability in negligence by point-ing to a limitation 'in the capacity for foresight or prudence' so long as that defi-ciency is normal or ordinary.[32] So those justices who find that Barry Watson was not negligent first hold that he did not have the foresight to recognize the risk. However, perhaps partly as a response to the dissent's challenge, the majority justices also indicate that even if Barry's action did result in part from a lack of prudence, that lack of prudence would also be excused because it is an ordinary incident of youth.

1. *Foresight of harm*

In support of the conclusion that Barry Watson lacked the requisite foresight for liability in negligence, both Windeyer J at trial and the majority decisions in the High Court rely on descriptions of the risk that imply that Barry's careless act resulted from the limited foresight of childhood. So, for instance, Windeyer J stresses the technical and complex knowledge required to recognize risk when he describes it in the following terms: 'It may be that an adult, knowing of the resistant qualities of hardwood and of the uncertainty that a spike, not properly balanced as a dart, will stick into wood when thrown, would foresee that it might fail to do so and perhaps go off at a tangent.'[33] And this very character-ization implies that a child of 12 would be unlikely to recognize the risk and thus helps to ground the conclusion that Barry was not negligent. This conclusion is also furthered by Windeyer J's insistence that the defendant lacked not merely foresight of the risk but also the more complex '*appreciation* of the risk'.[34] In affirming Windeyer J's judgment, Kitto J also emphasizes the sophisticated

---

[32] ibid 213. See also similar statements at 214–215.   [33] Trial (n 4 above) 397.

[34] ibid. Other cases on child defendants also distinguish between bare foresight of harm and true 'appreciation' of the risk. In *Christie v Slevinsky* (1981) 12 MVR 67 (Alta QB), the plaintiff sustained injuries after he was struck by a dune buggy driven at a high rate of speed by 11-year-old Paul Slevinsky. McFayden J notes that Paul continued to drive the vehicle 'without reducing speed, although his vision was substantially obstructed by dust and by the natural lighting conditions':

cognitive apparatus required to identify the risk.[35] Like Windeyer J, Kitto J makes this important point largely through specific and technical descriptions of the risk:

> To expect a boy of that age to consider before throwing the spike whether the timber was hard or soft, to weigh the chances of being able to make the spike stick in the post, and to foresee that it might glance off and hit the girl, would be, I think, to expect a degree of sense and circumspection which nature ordinarily withholds till life has become less rosy.[36]

Thus he implies the unlikelihood of a boy foreseeing such a danger.

But the persuasiveness of the conclusion that Barry Watson lacked the foresight to avoid inflicting the harm on Susan McHale depends heavily on the characterization of the facts. The description of the same facts in Menzies J's dissent makes this clear. Not only does Menzies J stress the contentious nature of the evidence concerning Barry's intent,[37] he also diverges from the other judges in his description of the risk involved in the boy's action. In fact, Menzies J implicitly disputes their characterization of the risk, suggesting that it was of a much more obvious nature when he states that what Barry did 'was to throw with force a piece of metal like a blunt, headless nail in the general direction of the appellant'.[38]

---

ibid 71. However, rather than therefore concluding that the boy should have foreseen the harm in question, McFayden J indicates that what one must look to is not simply foresight but rather something more complex—appreciation of the risk. Thus, he concludes that 'an 11 year old, of like experience and intelligence would not be likely to *appreciate* the danger inherent in driving' in such conditions: ibid 72 [emphasis added].

[35] Similar reliance on the characterization of the risk as unforeseeable in order to exonerate the playing boy is apparent in *Vaillancourt v Jacques* (n 26 above). The trial judge held that the defendant was responsible for putting out his playmate's eye during the course of a game of 'cowboys' among the three boys, aged 12 to 14. The judge noted that the dangers inherent in the boy's use of the broken pistol with the 'sharp, sharp point' were so manifestly obvious that to continue to use the toy amounted to culpable imprudence. However, Rivard J, whose Court of Appeal decision was affirmed by the majority at the Supreme Court, overturned this conclusion. Rivard J insisted that the law does not treat as foreseeable all possible dangers ('tout ce qui est *possible*') but instead only those dangers that are quite probable ('*assez probable*'): [1972] CA 200, quoting *Ouellet v Cloutier* [1947] SCR 521, 526 [emphasis in original]. The implication is that the danger inherent in the use of the broken pistol, far from being obvious as the trial judge (and Pigeon J in dissent at the Supreme Court) suggest, is in fact obscure and difficult to foresee and thus the playing boy is not culpable.

[36] Appeal (n 4 above) 215–216.

[37] So, for instance, Menzies J uncovers the factual dispute underlying the case on appeal. At trial there was a serious dispute about whether Barry threw the dart at the wooden post or whether he actually threw the dart at Susan, intending either to hit or simply to scare her so that he could catch her. Menzies J highlights the contentious nature of the facts when he notes that the 'weight of the oral evidence was that the missile did not hit the post. His Honour's finding was that it probably hit the post and bounced off': ibid 217–218. Later Menzies J states that 'in the face of the evidence I would not infer, as did his Honour, that the missile hit the post and was deflected'. And Menzies J intimates the relationship between the evidence and the question of Barry's intent when he states that 'no boy of twelve could reasonably think that he could hurl a nail into a post': ibid 226. However, as one commentator puts it, 'The combination of ample judicial discretion and appellate respect for the trial judge's findings of fact means that the vision of reality which takes hold at the first level is difficult to influence and to change': M Eberts, 'New Facts for Old: Observations on the Judicial Process' in R F Devlin (ed), *Canadian Perspectives on Legal Theory* (Toronto: Emond Montgomery Publications Limited, 1991) 467, 494.   [38] Appeal (n 4 above) 217.

Describing the facts in this way suggests that, far from being complicated or technical, the risk inherent in Barry's action should have been clearly apparent to any 12-year-old attentive to the safety of others. So Menzies J concludes that, even if the appropriate standard is that of a reasonable child, Barry Watson should still be judged negligent because 'a reasonable boy would not throw a three-inch piece of metal, head high, in the direction of another person'.[39]

In this sense, there is considerable normative significance in the manner in which the risk is described. The legal conclusion that Barry could not reasonably have been expected to have had the foresight to avoid the harm is made plausible only because of the characterization of the facts—here, the risk involved in his behaviour. Morris persuasively argued decades ago that the foreseeability of any particular risk is intimately linked to the level of specificity with which that risk is described.[40] But what guides the choice of how to characterize the risk? Such choices are crucial and yet, as *McHale* suggests, both the process by which they are arrived at and the justification for the chosen characterization ultimately seem mysterious. However, examining *McHale*'s treatment of the prudential element of the objective standard may shed some light on the court's choice of characterization.

2. *Prudence*

There is more to *McHale* than the suggestion that the risk was sufficiently complicated for Barry, as a 12-year-old, to lack reasonably the foresight to recognize the danger posed by his actions. The judgments in Barry's favour also implicitly recognize that justifying the dart-throwing may require something beyond this. Indeed, much of the language actually cuts against the suggestion that Barry's shortcoming was straightforwardly cognitive, thus implying that inattentiveness to the security of others or lack of prudence also played a role in Susan's injury. And as noted above, the majority decisions suggest that this lack of prudence, like the lack of foresight, is attributable to childhood and thus non-culpable.

This is particularly evident in the High Court judgment of Kitto J. So, for instance, Kitto J routinely suggests that the boy's age limits not only his ability to foresee harm ('not yet of an age to have an adult's realization of the danger of edged tools'), but also his capacity for prudence ('or an adult's wariness in the handling of them').[41] Similarly, even in the passage cited above where Kitto J characterizes the risk as sufficiently complicated to excuse a 12-year-old's lack of foresight, the conclusion actually turns as much on prudence as on foresight. For instance, he states that to expect Barry to foresee the danger to Susan would

---

[39] ibid 226.   [40] C Morris, 'Custom and Negligence' (1942) 42 Col L Rev 1147.

[41] Appeal (n 4 above) 215. Similar comments are made throughout Kitto J's discussion of the relevant standard of care for a child: 213–215. Thus, for instance, he expresses his disagreement with those who think that 'the deficiencies of foresight *and prudence* that are normal during childhood are irrelevant in determining what care is it reasonable for a child to take': ibid 214 [emphasis added].

be to demand of him the 'sense and circumspection' of an adult.[42] But since 'circumspection' is the quality of prudence—that is essentially a normative quality rather than a cognitive one—the implication is that Susan's injury was at least partially due to Barry's lack of attentiveness to others. A similar ambivalence about whether limited foresight is alone sufficient to account for Barry's actions is also apparent in Windeyer J's analysis. Thus, after the technical description of the risk discussed above, Windeyer J allows that a person who could foresee such a risk might be held negligent 'if he were *not more circumspect* than was this infant defendant'.[43] Again this implies that the injury suffered by Susan McHale was in fact the result of a complicated mix of deficiencies in both foresight and prudence.

The suggestion therefore seems to be that even if Susan's injury was due to Barry's lack of prudence, the standard of care should also be adjusted to take account of such a shortcoming. However, this conclusion raises a serious concern with *McHale* and perhaps with the standard of care more generally.[44] The argument in favour of a standard of care that reflects the cognitive and perceptive powers of the child—encapsulated in the phrase 'foresight'—seems straightforward enough. In fact, both Holmes's notion of avoidability and Honoré's general capacity test provide persuasive accounts of why children who lack the cognitive abilities relevant to the recognition of risk should not be liable under the objective standard. So, for instance, under Honoré's formulation, such children would not be liable because it would not be the case that, when they tried, they would usually succeed in recognizing the relevant risk.[45] However, it seems crucial to this conclusion that we cannot normally blame people for deficiencies of intelligence, perhaps particularly when they arise out of something like childhood. But why should we also be willing to weaken the degree of attentiveness to others, as the standard requires? After all, we normally feel justified in blaming those whose actions reveal that they do not care about others. In fact, some version of this is what we ordinarily call 'fault'. Taken literally, however, it seems that Honoré's general capacity test would actually exonerate those (including children but not limited to them) if, when they try, they do not usually succeed in acting prudently. Those who are routinely heedless seem on this understanding to be

---

[42] Appeal (n 4 above) 215–216.

[43] Trial (n 4 above) 397 [emphasis added]. Similarly, Windeyer J later insists that the plaintiff's injury was not the result of 'a lack of foresight and *appreciation of the risk* that might reasonably have been expected': ibid [emphasis added].

[44] As discussed below, other cases involving child defendants also seem prepared to exonerate playing boys for their lack of prudence on much the same terms as *McHale*: see n 69 below, discussing *Vaillancourt* (n 26 above); *Christie* (n 34 above); *Briese v Maechtle* 130 NW 893 (Wis 1911); and *Hoyt v Rosenberg* 173 ALR 883 (Cal App 1947).

[45] Ironically, it is this very utility of the test in explaining when the shortcomings of children should be exonerated that precludes Honoré from successfully arguing that exoneration on the same basis should not be extended to those with cognitive or intellectual shortcomings: see discussion in ch 1 above. This is because the test specifies that the '*general* ability to perform the sort of action which would in the instant case have led to a different outcome' is a precondition for liability under the negligence standard: T Honoré, 'Responsibility and Luck: The Moral Basis of Strict Liability' in *Responsibility and Fault* (Oxford: Hart Publishing, 1999) 17, 37 [emphasis in original].

able to claim a relaxed standard. And the fact that we also noted similar difficulties with Holmes's idea of avoidability and that these same difficulties show up in *McHale* suggest that they are not simply *ad hoc*. But this approach is puzzling. As Kitto J himself points out, the fault-based understanding of negligence limits liability to acts involving a *shortcoming* on the part of the defendant. And since carelessness of others seems to be just the kind of shortcoming that ordinarily grounds (rather than precludes) legal liability, the conclusion that such shortcomings may not be culpable is surprising.[46]

Although both Windeyer J at trial and the majority of the High Court on appeal indicate that the objective standard should be relaxed to take account of childish lack of prudence as well as lack of foresight, they do not explicitly justify this rather striking conclusion. Nonetheless, their judgments do suggest why they believe that Barry should be exonerated even if his actions betray a lack of prudence. Indeed, the language of 'boyish impulse' and the frequent descriptions of the behaviour as 'normal' actually form the justification—however implicit—of this conclusion. Barry's lack of prudence is seen as non-culpable because it is the result of 'boyish impulse'. And the courts view boyish impulse as non-culpable because they see it as normal.

3. *Boyish impulse*

The language of 'boyish impulse' appears in both the trial level and the High Court decisions in *McHale* and plays a significant role in justifying the exoneration of Barry's lack of prudence. This language cuts against the attribution of responsibility because of its implication both of the innocence of youth (boyishness) and of the absence of choice (impulse). The extent to which these two dimensions of boyish impulse play a role in relieving Barry Watson of responsibility is apparent throughout the majority decisions in *McHale*. Those judges that rule in Barry's favour convey his innocence by employing the concept of boyish impulse. And in addition to making specific use of this notion, they also stress its separate components. Thus, they imply Barry's innocence both by emphasizing his youth and by characterizing his actions as involuntary reactions to forces beyond his control.

To begin with, the language of boyish impulse is used to convey the essential innocence of Barry's action. Despite the facts that gave rise to the case, boyhood and boyish play are presented as purely harmless and innocent fun. Indeed, the very facts of the case are structured to protect this image of boyhood. Thus, in his trial decision, Windeyer J rejects evidence, given by both Susan and her cousin, that Barry actually threw the spear directly at Susan, either to scare or to actually injure her. In his response to the girl's evidence, Windeyer J finds it

---

[46] Indeed, if the deterrence argument has any purchase, it surely supports the liability of children who have the foresight but not the prudence to avoid the harm. As noted above, the deterrence argument is not persuasive with cognitive shortcomings that impair foresight (including many mental disabilities). However, unlike limitations in foresight, deficiencies of prudence do not undermine the preconditions for deterrence: see discussion in ch 1 above, nn 43–50.

'most unlikely' that a boy like Barry Watson would 'do anything so likely to hurt'.[47] Instead, he accepts Barry's evidence that he threw the 'missile at the post expecting it to stick in it'.[48] The reason Windeyer J gives for preferring this innocent account of Barry's motivation is that it 'does not put any strain on one's memory of boyhood to see this as a boyish impulse'.[49] So it is his image of the state of boyhood that enables Windeyer J to reach the conclusion that Barry's actions were innocent. Similarly, when querying whether Barry acted reasonably in the circumstances of this case, Kitto J responds by echoing the same language of boyish impulse that Windeyer J invoked at trial. Thus, he proclaims Barry's innocence by stating that this was simply 'the unpremeditated, impulsive act of a boy'.[50] So, Kitto J holds that the action against Barry must be dismissed.

Beyond this use of the concept of boyish impulse per se, *McHale* also implies Barry's innocence by emphasizing his youth. This is accomplished not only by the description of his impulse as 'boyish' and hence apparently innocent, but also by the characterization of Barry's age. For example, in describing the facts of the case, McTiernan ACJ states that Barry 'played as a child' and insists that it was 'right for the learned trial judge to refer to him in common with Susan and other playmates as young children' even though Barry was 12 and Susan and the other children were only 9.[51] McTiernan ACJ also refers to Barry as a 'young boy',[52] and describes the issue as involving the standard of care applicable to 'young children'.[53] He also uses the most age-minimizing legal term for someone below the age of majority when he states that the 'age and experience of an *infant*' should be considered in determinations of reasonableness.[54] Although this use is technically acceptable, it is interesting that the court preferred the term whose ordinary use is confined to a 'child during the earliest period of life'[55] to another legal term like minor that also tracks ordinary use.

In addition to drawing attention to Barry's youth, both Windeyer J and Kitto J at the High Court also insist on his innocence by specifically stressing the non-culpability that 'impulse' implies: Barry's actions are not the result of his considered choice but are instead activated by external forces.[56] Barry's actions are characterized as beyond his control, the result of an 'impelling force'.[57] So Barry appears essentially innocent because he is depicted not as an actor but rather as the instrument of nature. Elsewhere in the decisions, Barry's innocence is

---

[47] Trial (n 4 above) 396.   [48] ibid.   [49] ibid.   [50] Appeal (n 4 above) 215.
[51] ibid 210.   [52] ibid 210–211.   [53] ibid 204–205.
[54] ibid 205 [emphasis added]. Other child defendant cases also rely on the term 'infant' rather than other more age-appropriate terms. For instance, in *Vaillancourt v Jacques* (n 26 above) 200, Rivard J insists that an analysis of the foresight and avoidability of this accident must be considered in the light of the age of the boys whom he refers to as 'enfants' despite the fact that they are between 12 and 14 years old.
[55] *The Compact Oxford English Dictionary* (2nd edn, Oxford: Clarendon Press, 1994) 844.
[56] Trial (n 4 above) 396; Appeal (n 4 above) 215.
[57] *The Compact Oxford English Dictionary* (n 55 above) 826 under the definition of 'impulse': 'the application of sudden force causing motion'.

conveyed by language that similarly implies that his actions are largely beyond his own control. For instance, McTiernan ACJ characterizes the wooden corner post as 'an allurement or temptation to him to play with the object as a dart'.[58] This description however depicts Barry as responsive rather than active. The true genesis of Barry's action is not his free choice but the seductive suggestions of the objects that surround him—it is the wooden post that 'allures' and 'tempts' the playing Barry into seeing the dartlike possibilities of the object he is holding.

A similar view of responsibility is apparent in Kitto J's analysis of why Barry's actions were not culpable. Kitto J justifies his finding of Barry's innocence in part by noting that 'the ordinary boy of twelve suffers from a feeling that a piece of wood and a sharp instrument have a special affinity'.[59] That the boy again has the mere appearance of being an actor is signified by the choice of the verb to 'suffer', with its complication of subject and object. In 'suffering', the apparent actor—the individual in the subject position—is in fact the object of the action of another. He is thus subjected to something evil or painful, something that is 'inflicted or imposed' upon him.[60] And in addition to locating the real genesis of the boy's action outside his control,[61] the term 'suffer' also symbolically re-creates the sufferer—the one who deserves our sympathy—as Barry the injurer rather than Susan the injured. So the judicially recognized pain here is suffered by Barry, who is impelled to act by his too-keen sense of the intrinsic— and perhaps also gendered—affinity between a sharp instrument and a receptive object like a piece of wood.

However, the intimation of innocent irresponsibility contained in the concept of 'boyish impulse' only takes the court a certain distance toward justifying Barry's exoneration. It is true that the language of impulse tends to remove the actor from the position of agent and hence from exposure to liability. Nonetheless, given that we often condemn rather than condone impulsive behaviour, it is unclear why these impulses are treated as exculpatory. So even if Barry threw the dart because he succumbed to a 'boyish impulse', the question remains—why should a boy's impulsive heedlessness preclude rather than ensure liability?

---

[58] Appeal (n 4 above) 210.   [59] ibid 215.

[60] *The Compact Oxford English Dictionary* (n 55 above) 1953.

[61] A similar pattern of calling attention to the difference between the apparent actor—the child defendant—and the 'real' actor is also found in other child defendant cases. For instance, in the Court of Appeal decision in *Vaillancourt*, Rivard J gives subtle support to his characterization of the injury as nothing more than an unfortunate accident by removing the child defendant from the subject position and placing the plaintiff in that position instead. Thus, he describes how the plaintiff, in turning his head, 'hit himself on the plastic pistol which Christian held in his right hand and hit his right eye on the point of that pistol': (n 26 above) 198 [author's translation]. Similarly, in *Christie v Slevinsky*, when McFayden J concludes that 'an 11-year-old, of like experience and intelligence would not be likely to appreciate the danger' in operating a vehicle in the circumstances, he cites as one such 'circumstance' the fact that the boy's 'attention was not fully directed to the task'. But treating lack of attention as a circumstance—along with poor visibility conditions—implies that Paul's inattention to the task of driving is simply another factor beyond his control that must be taken into consideration when assessing his liability: (n 34 above) 72.

4. *The innocent ordinary boy*

The decisions in *McHale* do not directly address this question. Nonetheless, their reasons do help to illuminate why the court may view such behaviour as non-culpable. As noted above, in justifying the special standard of care applicable to child defendants, Kitto J discusses the changing basis of liability in negligence. Thus, he notes that liability came to be limited to acts involving a 'shortcoming', with the result that there would be no liability for acts that were 'inherently proper'.[62] But as we have discussed, for Kitto J propriety is not a matter of 'a morally blameless state of mind' but is instead a standard of 'ordinariness'.[63] Certain things follow from this characterization of the objective standard as a standard of 'ordinariness'. To begin with, this concept of propriety results in a rather different sphere of liability than that suggested by a standard of moral blameworthiness. In fact, the sphere of behaviour that propriety condemns as giving rise to liability in negligence is in one sense larger, and in another sense more limited, than the sphere delineated by a more thoroughgoing conception of blameworthiness.

One important difference between the standard of propriety or ordinariness outlined in *McHale* and one of blameworthiness is that an ordinariness standard will countenance liability for certain acts even though they may not be morally blameworthy. Thus, there will be liability for acts arising out of limitations on the capacity for foresight or prudence, but which are 'abnormal'. The consequence of this, as Kitto J states, is that it will be no answer to an action in negligence for a defendant to say that he is 'abnormal in some respect which reduces his capacity for foresight or prudence'.[64] Under this conception of the objective standard it is therefore irrelevant that an individual is 'abnormally slow-witted, quick-tempered, absent-minded or inexperienced'.[65] In this sense, the concept of what is normal or ordinary seems to expand the range of actions that will give rise to liability in negligence beyond those that would be condemned by a more robust standard of moral blameworthiness. Indeed, this aspect of the reasoning in the *McHale* majorities may provide an account of fault in negligence that explains the insistence, discussed above in Chapter 1, that those with intellectual limitations ought to be held to the same standard as the reasonable person. For so long as their limitations are abnormal, a standard of propriety as understood in *McHale* will condemn them as unreasonable.

However, if the standard of propriety in this way reads liability more broadly than would a standard of blameworthiness, in another sense it reads liability more narrowly. And this is the effect of 'propriety' that is most germane to *McHale v Watson*. Under a standard of propriety, responsibility turns on whether a shortcoming is proper—that is, ordinary or normal. This opens up not only the possibility of liability for abnormal limitations that are not morally blameworthy, but also of exoneration for ordinary or normal behaviour which *is* morally blameworthy. Thus, as Kitto J states repeatedly in *McHale*, so long

---

[62] Appeal (n 4 above) 213.   [63] ibid.   [64] ibid.   [65] ibid.

as the failure is normal or ordinary there will be no liability even where there is a lack of prudence. But it is important to remember that lack of prudence or attentiveness to others is a normative shortcoming to which we normally attach blame.[66] And it seems to be precisely this 'contracting' effect of the standard of propriety that underpins the majority decisions in *McHale*. Thus, Kitto J insists that it is open to a defendant to defend against an action in negligence by pointing to 'a limitation upon the capacity for foresight *or prudence*, not as being personal to himself, but as being characteristic of humanity at his stage of development and in that sense normal'.[67] Similarly, McTiernan ACJ considers it relevant to the question of Barry's liability that he is not 'other than a normal twelve year old boy' and, being a normal 12-year-old, lacks the 'maturity of mind' to avoid the injury to Susan.[68] So it seems that the standard of propriety necessitates the conclusion that even if Barry Watson's actions were in part attributable to lack of prudence—and were in that sense morally blameworthy—he would nonetheless be exonerated if he could establish that his carelessness was normal or ordinary.

However, so characterized this is a startling conclusion. In part this is because the divergence between the objective standard and a more thoroughgoing moral standard is typically thought to operate only in the first sense—allowing the imposition of liability even in the absence of moral fault, as in the case of those with intellectual shortcomings. However, the fact that the objective standard draws so heavily on ordinariness means that in the case of at least some child defendants it may actually have the opposite effect. The fault sanctioned by the law of negligence is carelessness of others. Yet *McHale v Watson* suggests that the objective standard will not sanction such carelessness if it is sufficiently common to be seen as ordinary or normal.[69] But why should this be so? *McHale*

---

[66] ibid 213–216.   [67] ibid 213 [emphasis added].   [68] ibid 210.

[69] Other cases that exonerate playing boys also exhibit a similar reliance on the notion of normal or ordinary behaviour. For instance, in the Court of Appeal decision in *Vaillancourt*, Rivard J addresses the issue of whether the child defendant behaved imprudently with the observation that the boy took part in the game 'in a normal and proper manner' and notes that there is no indication that the defendant Christian 'behaved any differently from his companions': (n 26 above) 200. So the fact that Christian behaved 'normally' seems to settle the issue of the propriety of his actions from the point of view of negligence. And the majority of the Supreme Court dismisses the appeal by quoting these comments on the normal and ordinary character of the boy's acts and proclaiming its 'respectful agreement with that finding': [1975] 1 SCR 724, 726, Abbott J. Pigeon J in dissent challenges this characterization of Christian's action as 'normal and proper' by pointing out that the boy was 'imprudent enough to use a toy that had become manifestly dangerous': ibid 727. Similarly, in *Christie v Slevinsky*, in considering whether the boy was negligent because his excitement and inattention distracted him from safety concerns, McFayden J treats it as relevant that the child defendant is a 'typical 11 year old': (n 34 above) 72.

An even more striking reliance on ordinariness as a basis for forgiving boyish imprudence is apparent in *Briese v Maechtle* (n 44 above). In that case, a boy was kneeling down to shoot a marble when another boy, engaged in a game of tag, came running around the corner of the school house and ran into him. As a result of the collision, the boy's eye was injured and his sight completely destroyed. In the Supreme Court of Wisconsin, Winslow CJ rejected the allegation of negligence in the following terms: 'The rule is that a child is only required to exercise that degree of care which the great mass of children of the same age ordinarily exercise under the same circumstances, taking into account the experience, capacity, and understanding of the child': ibid, quoting *Cooley on Torts* (3rd edn) 823.

implies rather than states the response to this question. Underlying both the language of 'boyish impulse' and the related concept of normal or ordinary behaviour is the implication that Barry's act was not culpable because his behaviour was natural. The suggestion seems to be as follows: Barry Watson is not culpable because his imprudent act was the result of boyish impulse; imprudent boyish impulses, in turn, are forgivable if they are normal or ordinary; and such normal or ordinary impulses are non-culpable because they are natural—their true author is nature, not the boy.

Indeed, the significance of the 'natural' is apparent throughout the decisions in *McHale v Watson*. For instance, in the trial decision of Windeyer J, the view that childhood is natural and its limitations non-culpable seems to account for the insistence that '[c]hildhood is not an idiosyncrasy'.[70] Thus, there will apparently be no liability for limitations that we all inevitably suffer due to the course of nature. A similar understanding is implicit in Kitto J's statement that the boy can rely on a limitation so long as it is 'characteristic of humanity at his stage of development'.[71] In this sense, exoneration seems to turn on the limitation being an inevitable incident of human nature. Kitto J also specifically attributes to nature the reason for Barry's imprudence. Thus, he states that to expect Barry to have acted more carefully would be 'to expect a degree of sense and circumspection which *nature* ordinarily withholds till life has become less rosy'.[72] So responsibility for the injury seems to lie not with Barry's lack of attentiveness to others, but rather with nature, which has 'withheld' from Barry the means necessary to exercise care.[73]

He also implicitly invokes notions of normalcy and ordinariness by repeatedly referring to the venerable game of tag: ibid 893–894.

The view that normal behaviour cannot be the basis of a claim in negligence is also apparent in *Hoyt v Rosenberg* (n 44 above). There, an 11-year-old girl lost her eye when she was hit in the face by a can kicked by a 12-year-old boy during a game of 'kick the can'. The evidence suggested that had he looked, he would have seen the girl standing in a gateway ahead of him. At trial the jury returned a verdict for the plaintiff, but this was reversed on appeal. Barnard PJ noted that the defendant would only be liable if he 'did something while playing this game that the ordinary boy of like age and experience would not have done': ibid 887. It is, he argues, 'unreasonable to expect a boy of that age to stop in a moment in such a game, at the risk of losing his advantage, in order to look for something that was apparently outside his field of action': ibid 888. So any lack of prudence on the part of the boy defendant was sufficiently ordinary or normal to exonerate him from liability in negligence.

[70] Trial (n 4 above) 397. Of course, Windeyer J is also pointing out that in taking the age of the child into consideration, he is not running afoul of Holmes's admonition that the objective standard takes no account of the 'idiosyncrasies' of the individual.

[71] Appeal (n 4 above) 213.   [72] ibid 216 [emphasis added].

[73] A similar attribution to nature of the real responsibility for the imprudent actions of the playing boy is apparent in *Hoyt v Rosenberg*. There Barnard PJ uses some version of the modifier 'natural' in conjunction with Jack's actions at least seven times: (n 44 above) 886 (twice), 887 (twice), 888 (3 times). He seems particularly at pains to stress the 'naturalness' of Jack's focus on winning and his consequent inattentiveness to the possibility that kicking the can without looking when other children were around could hurt someone. So, for instance, he states that '[w]hile he did not look to see where Marlene was during the time he was running, it was *natural* that he would not do so and that he would bend all his efforts to winning the race to the can. While he knew that Marlene, if she entered the alley, would come through the gateway it would hardly be *natural* to expect him to delay his kicking of the can until she appeared': ibid 887 [emphasis added]. So Jack cannot be held liable because he was simply acting in accordance with the dictates of nature, which exert particular control over

Another indication that Barry is exonerated because his limited prudence is seen as 'natural' is the reiteration of the idea that it would be ridiculous—even 'unnatural'—to impose a higher standard on the boy because it would amount to demanding something of him that nature does not allow. The language throughout the decisions suggests that the limitations due to the boy's age are simply a 'fact' of nature that a judge is not at liberty to ignore. So, for instance, Windeyer J argues that the boy's age must be relevant to the standard of care by insisting that a judge can surely not be required to disregard the 'facts' of the case—in particular that the boy was only 12.[74] This insistence on the factual nature of the issue implies that any other conclusion would have the ridiculous effect of deciding *this case* on the basis of the facts of *other cases*. Similarly, Owen J insists that refusing to take into account the limitations arising out of the defendant's age would be 'contrary to common sense' and would create the impression that 'the law was an ass'.[75] And in his conclusion Kitto J notes that we must all bear risks that ordinary care on the part of others cannot eliminate. He continues: 'One such risk is that boys of twelve may behave as boys of twelve; and that, sometimes, is a risk indeed'.[76] In this way Kitto J conveys the naturalness and hence absolute inevitability of the behaviour of boys. He also implies the ridiculousness of any other view, which would thus necessarily demand that boys not be what nature has emphatically declared they are— boys. The subtle play of gender also underscores the unnaturalness of any alternative to Kitto J's approach.

Yet however eloquent the defence of Barry's carelessness, *McHale* seems to leave the most critical questions unanswered. It never becomes clear why, even accepting that Barry's behaviour is both normal and natural, he should on that account be exonerated. The emphasis on normal and natural limitations could function as something like a presumption that the act in question was not within the control of the individual and thus as an expression of something like Honoré's notion of general capacity or Holmes's notion of avoidability. However, at bottom these arguments, and the idea that responsibility turns on control, assume a tighter relation between legal and moral responsibility than Kitto J seems willing to allow. And a control-based view also seems to undermine Kitto J's insistence that abnormal deficiencies like lack of intelligence should nonetheless ground responsibility, presumably regardless of the absence of control. As we have seen, Kitto J specifically insists that the notion of propriety that informs the objective standard is not a 'matter of a morally blameless state of mind'.[77] Ultimately it seems that both Kitto J and the other judges who rule in Barry's favour assume that the fact of normal or natural behaviour itself has some normative status, even apart from whether it functions as an indicator

boys. The 'naturalness' of Jack's actions is also stressed at the end of the opinion when Barnard PJ insists, quoting *Briese* (n 44 above) 894, that Jack only did what 'healthy' boys have been doing since 'time immemorial': ibid 889. Responsibility therefore really lies with 'nature', not with the individual boy.

[74] Trial (n 4 above) 397. [75] ibid 229. [76] Appeal (n 4 above) 216. [77] ibid 213.

of the ability to do otherwise. However, the exact nature of that normative content remains unclear.

In this sense, perhaps the most troubling of the problems that *McHale* leaves open is a serious question about what we can hold people responsible for. The majority judgments do suggest that Honoré's general capacity test has some significant explanatory power. But they also point to a troubling way to read this relatively 'undifferentiated' approach to responsibility. The majority decisions exonerate Barry's limited prudence as well as his limited foresight because they see them as normal and natural. *McHale* in this way provides an illustration of a worry noted earlier. If, for example, boys routinely are heedless of the security of others, do we really want to relieve them of liability simply because of the commonness of their failing? The opinions in *McHale* raise a profound question about what level of care towards others we can legitimately require. The implication of *McHale* is both that we *can* demand what is normal (even from those who lack normal cognitive or intellectual capacities) and that we can *only* demand what is normal (even when it comes to attentiveness to others). Thus, the objective standard seems intimately bound up with the idea of the normal, expressed as a standard of propriety. But why the 'normal' should be so determinative of the obligations we owe each other remains mysterious. *McHale* itself provides an illustration of the dangers of exonerating common normative mistakes but leaves unanswered the question of why the prevalence of such mistakes should excuse them. The court gestures toward nature, but ultimately gives us no more than that.

5. Determining the 'normal'

Whatever the justification for the role of a conception of normal behaviour under the objective standard, *McHale* illustrates that such a conception is undeniably significant. But if 'normal' behaviour does play a central role in determinations of the propriety of conduct, then how judges decide what behaviour is and is not normal becomes crucial. *McHale* gives us some insight into this process. After all, the majority judges do not seem to have difficulty concluding that Barry Watson's behaviour was sufficiently normal or ordinary to count as proper for the purposes of the objective standard. Yet ascertaining whether Barry's injury to Susan resulted from a limitation sufficiently widely shared to count as 'characteristic of humanity at his stage of development'[78] would seem, at least superficially, a rather daunting task.

It is central to the inquiry in *McHale* that the judges consider the characteristics of 12-year-old 'humanity' as sufficiently within their general knowledge to be the subject of judicial notice. In fact, Kitto J specifically adverts to this when he describes as 'a matter for judicial notice'[79] the 'fact' that the ordinary boy of 12

---

[78] Appeal (n 4 above).

[79] ibid 215. As Morgan describes it, this dimension of judicial notice is based on the assumption that the judge's 'fund of general information must be at least as great as that of all reasonably well-informed persons in the community'. Thus, we take judicial notice of 'what everyone knows and uses

suffers from a sense of the affinity between a piece of wood and a sharp instrument. And other evidence that Barry's actions are normal and natural is also clearly based on judicial notice. There is no indication that Barry put forward or that the court received evidence concerning the normal 12-year-old's capacity for either foresight or prudence, even though the legal conclusion regarding Barry's negligence turned on his carelessness being 'normal' and not an 'idiosyncrasy'. The judges must therefore have concluded that Barry's carelessness was normal through recourse to that 'fund of general information' that they share with other well-informed members of the community. Indeed, the court underscores the appropriateness of judicial notice when it refers to the boy's limited capacities for prudence and foresight as 'normal', as 'natural', and as a 'fact'.

The appeal to common sense that underlies judicial notice seems to play an important role in the court's conclusions. But this very fact also gives rise to worries about the implications of the relationship between judicial notice and the idea of the 'normal' that animates the objective standard. If a 'fact' is seen as so obvious that it is an apt matter for judicial notice, it may for that very reason also be especially impervious to challenge. Indeed, as one commentator notes, on matters where 'common sense' lends them confidence, judges often refuse to admit expert testimony, preferring instead their 'own totally untested view of contemporary society'.[80] And because judicial ideas about what is normal are so crucial to the outcome of the negligence action, the problem is an especially pointed illustration of a larger set of evidentiary issues about how such assumptions can be subjected to an appropriate degree and kind of scrutiny.

McHale also illuminates the extent to which the judge's own memories of childhood form the major wellspring of judicial notice. The general arguments in the case and the justifications for the subjectivized standard of care refer to childhood.[81] However, when assessing Barry's actions, the majority judges

---

in the ordinary process of reasoning about everyday affairs': EM Morgan, 'Judicial Notice' (1944) 57 Harv L Rev 269, 272.

[80] Eberts in the context of discussing the case of *Rose v The Queen* (1972) 19 CRNS 66 (Que KB), which considered whether it was discriminatory not to require jury service of women. Eberts also notes that judicial reluctance to admit complicating facts can sometimes be 'explained by the decider's unwillingness to take the time necessary to hear such evidence'. There may also be a connection to the 'authoritative' world-view of common sense: 'there may well be no time, literally or figuratively, for an alternative view of reality, because the decider is very skeptical about there being any need to hear it: reality is already very nicely and very authoritatively described and understood. The problem is exacerbated by the fact that carefully unpicking and reworking the stuff of knowledge can indeed take a long time': (n 37 above) 475.

[81] Thus, Windeyer J's statement that '[c]hildhood is not an idiosyncrasy': Trial (n 4 above) 397, and Kitto J's reference to what is 'characteristic of humanity at his stage of development': Appeal (n 4 above) 213. Similarly, Kitto J later states that it would be 'a misuse of language, to speak of normality in relation to persons of all ages together. In those things normality is, for children, something different from what normality is for adults': ibid 213. And he summarizes by stating that the standard must be based on the capacity for foresight and prudence 'which is normal for a child of the relevant age': ibid 214.

invoke their own memories and speak specifically of boyhood, not childhood. So, for instance, Windeyer J recognizes that Barry's action is subject to those irresistible impulses that characterize 'boyhood' through recourse to his own 'memory of boyhood'.[82] Similarly, on appeal, McTiernan ACJ finds Barry's response to the dart symbolic, not of childhood, but instead of 'boyhood'.[83] Barry should succeed, he concludes, because 'an ordinary *boy* of twelve'[84] would not have appreciated the risk to Susan McHale. And although Kitto J speaks of children rather than boys during his discussion of the legal standards, when he poses the 'question of fact' he asks whether the respondent, 'did anything which a reasonable *boy* of his age would not have done in the circumstances—a *boy*, that is to say, who possessed and exercised such degree of foresight and prudence as is ordinarily to be expected of a *boy* of twelve, holding in his hand a sharpened spike and seeing the post of a tree guard before him?'[85] When exonerating Barry, Kitto J attributes his action to the impulsiveness of a 'boy' rather than a child. Similarly, what he takes judicial notice of is the particularly keen sense of things suffered by a 'boy'.[86] And his conclusion insists we must all bear the risk that 'boys will be boys'. So, although the justifications for the standard of care discuss taking account of the behaviour of children, the majority judges at both levels in *McHale* in fact rely very specifically on the behaviour of *boys* in evaluating whether Barry's actions were normal and therefore non-negligent.[87] And through judicial notice, their understanding of boyhood—gleaned in part from memories of their own boyhood—becomes a central part of the negligence inquiry.

---

[82] Trial (n 4 above) 396.   [83] Appeal (note 4 above) 210.   [84] ibid 211 [emphasis added].
[85] ibid 215 [emphasis added].   [86] ibid.

[87] ibid 216. The judge's own memory of boyhood plays a similarly central role in other boy defendant cases. In *Briese* Winslow J opens his analysis by '[c]alling back to the mind for a moment the old schoolyard at recess': (n 44 above) 894. And this setting enables him to ask whether any man who 'recalls the scene' can truthfully blame the young defendant: ibid. Here too the behaviour of *boys* is used to determine ordinariness. The schoolyard is repeatedly described as involving 'the sudden dash of *boys* here and there' and '*boys* darting here and there': ibid 894 [emphasis added]. Similarly, Winslow J asks 'any *man*' whether he can deny that the boy here was simply doing what 'healthy *boys* of his age' have always done: ibid [emphasis added].

Judicial memories of boyhood also play a pivotal role in *Hoyt v Rosenberg*. There Barnard PJ endorses *Briese* and then condemns the 'fallacious' notion that the boy should have kicked the can in a less dangerous direction. Anyone who believes otherwise 'not only does not know boys of that age, but either never played similar games, including "shinny" or played them too long ago': (n 44 above) 889. And this appeal to memory gives similar confidence to his conclusion that '[t]here is no room here for a reasonable difference of opinion as to what the normal and ordinary boy of that age would have done': ibid. (One cannot help but think of Eberts's worry about the inviolability of common sense here: (n 37 above) 475.) When Barnard PJ poses the legal question, he refers to 'the standard of care that is reasonably to be expected of *boys* of similar age and development'. He states that the plaintiff's contention is that 'this appellant did something while playing this game that the ordinary *boy* of like age and experience would not have done': ibid 886–887 [emphasis added]. The idea, Barnard PJ concludes, 'that this appellant should, or that the ordinary *boy* would, have seen Marlene and turned around and kicked this can in the other direction is fallacious': ibid 889 [emphasis added]. It may be worth asking whether these same statements would seem as persuasive had they referred to children rather than boys.

6. *The re-creation of boyhood*

> In the sun born over and over,
> I ran my heedless ways,
> My wishes raced through the house-high hay
> And nothing I cared, at my sky blue trades, that time allows
> In all his tuneful turning so few and such morning songs
> Before the children green and golden
> Follow him out of grace.[88]

Perhaps because the judges' own memories infuse judicial notice, boyhood is cast in a nostalgic—even romantic—light. Since the attempt to understand Barry's actions engages the judges in the imaginative re-creation of their own boyhood, it seems unsurprising that they identify with Barry's perspective. It is as if the facts of the case recall for them an image, illuminated by memory, of themselves as small boys playing as Barry does here. The version of boyhood that thus emerges from the collective judicial memory in *McHale* depicts an innocent boy engaged in a complicated struggle with nature. The boy attempts to assert his mastery over nature, yet is also curiously caught in the sway of its impulses. And because of this, the courts indicate, he deserves our empathy and understanding. Further, as we shall see, the judicial re-creation of boyhood ultimately depicts a world where heedlessness of others is constitutive of that golden state.

Given the nostalgic vision of boyhood that emerges from judicial memory in *McHale*, it hardly seems remarkable that the judges identify so closely with Barry, the boy who plays as they once did. In fact the judges invoke their own memories in large part to emphasize the innocent nature of Barry's actions.[89] And even their understanding of the 'facts' illustrates the strength of their identification with Barry's perspective. Thus, the majority judges at both levels prefer the version of the facts most favourable to Barry, even where the account seems rather unlikely. For instance, Barry stated that although he aimed at the post, he missed and hit Susan. But the difficulty with this account was that he was standing within four or five feet of Susan and so close to the tree guard post that he could almost touch it.[90] In fact, Windeyer J actually admits the difficulty

---

[88] From 'Fern Hill' by Dylan Thomas, *FT Palgrave's Golden Treasury* (Centennial Edn, New York: Mentor Books, 1961) 525, lines 39–45.

[89] Similarly, in *Briese*, the language celebrates boyhood play in the strongest terms: 'The venerable and exhilarating game of tag in its various forms must have been one of the primal games of the race, and it still occupies an honored place among the sports of childhood': (n 44 above) 894. Similarly, Winslow J's descriptions of his own memory of the 'old school yard at recess' dwell fondly on the happy details—the sights and sounds—of play. He describes play in the most approbatory terms despite the events that inspired this case; it is 'to be encouraged on account of its wholesome activity and stirring of the blood'; 'perfectly lawful and even laudable', it is repeatedly—even insistently— described as innocent, harmless, and lawful: ibid. And this elegiac language from *Briese* is specifically relied on by Barnard PJ in *Hoyt v Rosenberg*, to support his conclusion that this boy cannot be culpable, since he did nothing 'more or less than healthy boys of his age have done from time immemorial': (n 44 above) 889. It would be unhealthy, it seems, to require a boy to be more careful of others.

[90] Trial (n 4 above) 395.

that the evidence presents for Barry but resolves it by finding it most likely that the dart hit Susan after it glanced off the post. In the High Court, however, Menzies J points out in dissent that this account—which tracks Barry's evidence—is both physically somewhat unlikely and is contradicted by the weight of the oral evidence.[91] And at other points in the evidence, the majority judges show a similar preference for the testimony of Barry, dismissing evidence about the dart given by the girl by noting that 'young children often remember things are larger and seemingly more significant than they really were'.[92]

Nostalgia also helps to account for the focus of judicial concern in *McHale*. Throughout the majority judgments but particularly in the decision of Kitto J, the real empathy is reserved for Barry, the boy who 'suffers' the impulses of nature. In contrast, concern for—or for that matter even interest in—Susan McHale is minimal. The terse expressions of empathy for her are typically reserved for the last few lines in the judgment and seem more *pro forma* than truly felt. So, for instance, Kitto J concludes his decision with a paragraph that opens '[s]ympathy with the injured girl is inevitable'.[93] And immediately pre-ceding this blunt pronouncement is the empathetic evocation of the feelings of the boy. The contrast in the language is revealing—it suggests that since anyone can feel sympathy for the injured girl, the judge's task is to evoke the more com-plex, esoteric, and ultimately more relevant sympathy due the 12-year-old boy. Thus, despite the explicit expression of sympathy for the injured girl, the real beneficiary of judicial concern seems to be the playing boy. A similar implica-tion is apparent in Kitto J's remark that 'one might *almost* wish' for a modern rule of absolute liability.[94] The term 'almost' here does not seem incidental, for Kitto J then closes his decision by stating that boys will be boys, a 'truism' that in Kitto J's phrasing celebrates the lost freedom of boyhood and does not seem moved by the injury that 'freedom' may do to others.

As this suggests, the place occupied by freedom in this nostalgic reconstruc-tion of boyhood is also critical to *McHale*. The empathy that the judges have for Barry seems to spring at least in part from their view about just why boyhood must be protected. And this understanding ultimately helps to explain why the imprudence of boyhood has to be forgiven. Indeed, the majority judges suggest that one could not impose liability on boyish imprudence without risking the loss of what is most valuable in that happy state. Throughout *McHale* the boy appears as the child of nature—specially responsive to the whims and impulses

---

[91] Appeal (n 4 above) 217–218, 226.

[92] Trial (n 4 above) 392. While Windeyer J later insists that the size of the dart is actually of no importance, his attentiveness to the evidence of the girls belies this. Further, his intimation that the girls did not perceive the dart as it 'really was' again underscores the weight given to Barry's account of the events. A similar affinity for the perspective of the playing boy is apparent in *Christie v Slevinsky* (n 34 above). There, McFayden J is at pains to justify the boy's failure to see the pedes-trian, repeatedly suggesting that the boy's powers of judgement were overcome by the 'excitement' of driving the dune buggy: ibid 71.

[93] Appeal (n 4 above) 216. See also the conclusion of the judgment of Windeyer J that states 'I feel great sympathy for the plaintiff. I find for the defendants': Trial (n 4 above) 401.

[94] Appeal (n 4 above) 216 [emphasis added].

of the natural world. Beyond this implicit assertion of what the state of boyhood *is*, however, one can discern a deeper commitment, a commitment to a certain understanding of what is both constitutive of and most valuable in the state of boyhood. The characteristic freedom of boyhood is, it seems, defined by the absence of any constraints arising out of the interests of others. So one could not impose liability for boyish imprudence without destroying the most fundamental and valuable characteristic of boyhood itself.

According to the majority opinions in *McHale*, freedom and irresponsibility are constitutive features of boyhood. And this joyous 'heedlessness' springs from the fact that the boy is not concerned with the presence of others and is therefore not constrained by their needs. Thus does McTiernan ACJ see Barry's conduct with the dart as 'symbolic of the tastes and simplicity of boyhood'.[95] Nostalgia thus transforms even so obviously dangerous an instrument as the metal dart that put out Susan's eye into to a spiritual 'symbol' of boyhood. And Barry's act of throwing the dart becomes emblematic of the happy days of freedom and irresponsibility of boyhood. Indeed, viewed in this light it seems that the characteristic 'simplicity' of boyhood actually *is* the lack of prudence, the single-mindedness in the literal sense, that characterizes Barry's action. And it is this single-mindedness that makes boyhood a happy state. The delightful freedom of boyhood springs, it seems, from the liberty to ignore the interests of others.[96]

---

[95] ibid 210.

[96] Freedom also plays a similarly critical role in the notion of boyhood in *Briese* (n 44 above). It is because boyhood seems essentially bound up with heedlessness that the court refuses to impose liability on the 'time-honored and innocent games of youth in the schoolyard': ibid 893. Such liability would 'make it necessary for children to stand about the schoolyard with folded hands at recess for fear they might negligently brush against one of their fellows, and become liable for heavy damages': ibid 894. Thus, boyhood depends on the ability to act without regard for the security of others, for once the standard of prudence is imposed on boys, they are condemned to a life of dull carefulness and passivity. The 'venerable and exhilarating game of tag' cannot be made 'safe' without transforming boyhood into a nervous lethargic state. And such games implicate not only the vigour of individual boys, but also thereby the future of the entire 'race'. Tag, Winslow J insists, is one of 'the primal games of the race', to be encouraged for its wholesomeness and 'stirring of the blood'. So, 'healthy boys' will continue to play tag 'as long as the race retains its activity': ibid. And the larger dangers of restricting boyhood games are also implied here. Since boys will only be healthy and active so long as they are not hindered by the need to worry about injuries to others, imposing liability on such games will sap the vigour of the 'race' and imperil its future.

Many of these themes are echoed in *Hoyt v Rosenberg* (n 44 above). There, the court stresses the 'naturalness' of the boy's drive to win the game. One simply cannot imagine the game occurring were there a requirement for prudence, the judge suggests. In fact, if the safety of others figured in the player's calculations, the game would be ruined. While it was the spectre of a passive and inactive boyhood that Winslow CJ conjured up in *Briese*, in *Hoyt*, Barnard PJ seems concerned that requiring a boy to be careful would cut against his drive to win. Thus, he frequently points to the apparent ridiculousness of the idea that a boy would be expected to jeopardize his possible advantage in a game simply to ensure that he does not injure others: 'at the moment of accomplishing his object of kicking the can, [a boy] would not stop to look around, and much less would he take a chance on stopping his run, turning around and going back in order to kick the can the other way': ibid 887. As in *Briese*, the implication seems to be that if one requires boys to be careful of others, one must be content with a 'race' of boys neither healthy nor normal—a passive, cautious lot. Indeed, as the close association between the boyhood and heedlessness suggests, one can perhaps only impose prudence at the risk of transforming boys into 'sissies', giving them, in other words, the attributes of girls.

Kitto J also seems to view freedom as the defining feature of boyhood. It would be contrary to nature, he insists, to require Barry to consider the danger and foresee the harm inherent in his action of throwing the dart for this would be to 'expect a degree of sense and circumspection which nature ordinarily withholds till life has become less rosy'.[97] What is interesting is the equivalence this statement implies between the rosiness of boyhood and lack of circumspection. Indeed, it seems that the price one pays for circumspection or attentiveness to others is the irrevocable loss of the rosiness of boyhood—a 'rosiness' that thus seems to depend upon heedlessness of others.

D. The lessons of *McHale*

McHale v Watson illuminates how the objective standard actually works in at least one important set of cases. Through the vocabulary of foresight and prudence, the case provides us with what is at least potentially a richer and more complex set of ideas about fault and responsibility. In this perhaps lies the beginning of a more differentiated account of fault that may help to respond to some of the difficulties that we see in the treatment of intellectual shortcomings as well as in *McHale* itself. But *McHale* also directs our attention to the deep and complicated relationship between the notion of what is reasonable and conceptions of what is normal and natural, conceptions that are themselves infused with views about what is valuable. Reliance on these conceptions enables judges to accord the playing boy a significant amount of latitude in determining what will count as reasonable care. Thus, in *McHale* not only are the majority judges willing to tailor the foresight requirement to the capacities of boys, they are also willing to hold that even boyish imprudence—far from being a violation of the standard of care—may well be considered reasonable so long as it is 'normal' or 'natural' for a boy to act without regard for the security of others.

McHale also illustrates how judges, in giving content to the notion of reasonable care, may use judicial notice to draw on common sense notions of what is normal and natural. And this process allows the judge to rely on his own experiences, understandings, and, in the case of boyhood, memories in order to flesh out what is normal and therefore apparently reasonable. In the case of the child defendant—here perhaps significantly the playing boy—judges re-create a nostalgic image of boyhood that depicts the boy's action as essentially innocent. And beyond this there is a deeper current at work. Ultimately, it seems that the very essence of boyhood is carelessness of others, which means that we cannot impose liability for boyish imprudence without taking the unnatural and dangerous step of destroying boyhood itself. And this signals a potentially troubling relationship between the idea of reasonableness and that of normalcy. Indeed, as it gets played out in *McHale* and in other boy defendant cases, this complication of the reasonable and the normal ends up lending tremendous normative

[97] Appeal (n 4 above) 216.

(and legal) significance to a certain understanding of masculinity. On this view, it seems, prudence is a virtue that has no bearing on—or is potentially even destructive of—at least some pre-eminently masculine activities. The sphere of liberty accorded such imprudence is thus correspondingly large.

II. THE 'ABNORMAL' CHILD DEFENDANT: ADULT ACTIVITIES, BULLIES, AND GIRLS

As it turns out, many of these elements of *McHale* are also apparent in the child defendant cases more broadly. The concern for the playing boy in *McHale* turns on the fact that the limitations of childhood are seen as normal. The consequence is that *McHale* extends forgiveness only to 'normal' imprudence. And *McHale* identifies as paradigmatic of such normal imprudence the carelessness of the boy at play. When one looks beyond *McHale* to the child defendant cases more broadly, it is possible to identify thematic similarities with the majority analysis in *McHale*. Let us begin by briefly examining the adult activities exception.

A. The adult activities exception

One important parallel to the reasoning found in *McHale* is apparent at the doctrinal level in the adult activities exception. This exception echoes *McHale*'s enshrinement of the principle of protecting the 'normal' indiscretions of childhood because it excludes categorically from the benefit of the relaxed standard of care any child engaged in an activity that is not 'normal' to childhood. The image of the child who benefits in *McHale* is thus mirrored—literally in that the images are reversed—by the children who do not benefit because they are precluded from relying on the relaxed standard of care due to the adult activities exception. The adult activities exception accomplishes this by imposing an adult standard of care on any child who engages in an activity 'normally undertaken by an adult' even if the relevant risk arose as a result of the limitations of childhood.[98] What this suggests is that the generosity extended to the child defendant is not based solely on recognition of the 'normal' limitations of childhood, since these limitations presumably persist regardless of the activity in which the child is engaged. Thus, it is not enough to be young to claim the benefit of a specialized standard of care—it is also necessary to be engaged in 'childish' activity, at least to the minimal extent that the relevant activity is not seen as one 'normally undertaken by adults'.

The way that this requirement works out at the level of adjudication is illuminating for it reinforces *McHale*'s identification of the playing boy as the centrepiece of childhood. In order to apply the adult activities exception, courts must have some notion of what activities are normally undertaken only by adults and what activities, in contrast, are constitutive of childhood. Various

---

[98] WP Keeton (gen ed), *Prosser and Keeton on the Law of Torts* (5th edn, St Paul: West Publishing Co, 1984) 181.

rationales have been forwarded for this exception, including the argument pointing to insurance. However, the failure of such rationales to account for the scope of the exception suggests that in fact the primary reason for refusing to extend the children's standard of care does turn on the idea that the child is engaged in 'an activity which is normally one for adults only'.[99] And perhaps unsurprisingly, in the course of identifying what kinds of activities are so inherently 'adult' that even children engaged in them cannot rely on the limitations of childhood, courts construct a certain image of childhood, an image in which, like *McHale*, the unfettered freedom to play is the central and defining feature.

The centrality to childhood (or perhaps boyhood) of the unfettered freedom to play is also confirmed negatively through the adult activities exception: to the extent that an activity looks 'serious' as do, for instance, transportation or especially work, it is seen as 'adult'. In contrast, the more that an activity looks like 'play', the more it is seen as inherently childish, with the consequence that the child engaged in it is granted special protection from legal liability. So, for example, one of the major categories of the adult activities exception involves driving motorized vehicles. But the distinctions even within this category are telling. Thus, courts are most willing to apply the adult activities exception where the use of the vehicle involves what they see as typically adult pursuits like transportation or work.[100] However, to the extent that the use of the

---

[99] *Prosser* (ibid). The *Restatement (Second) of Torts* (1965) expands somewhat on the scope of the exception by stating that the activity must be one that 'is normally undertaken only by adults, and for which adult qualifications are required': s 283A, Comment. It is also frequently suggested that the adult activities exception may be explained on the basis that the activities in question are typically covered by insurance: L Klar, *Tort Law* (2nd edn, Scarborough: Carswell, 1996) 257; Prosser (ibid) 181; AM Linden, *Canadian Tort Law* (6th edn, Toronto: Butterworths, 1997) 130. However, while the insurance and licensing rationales do help to explain some of the adult activities exceptions—driving automobiles in particular—the exception also covers a wide range of activities that do not necessarily have either licensing or insurance requirements such as snowmobiling [*Ryan v Hickson* (1974) 7 OR (2d) 352 196 (Ont HC); *Mont v Black* (1988) 6 MVR (2d) 231, 83 NSR (2d) 407 (QB); *Robinson v Lindsay* 598 P 2d 392 (Wash 1979)], motorboats [*Dellwo v Pearson* 107 NW 2d 859 (SC Minn 1961)], and go-carts [*Ewing v Biddle* 216 NE 2d 863 (Ind App 1966)] to name but a few counter-examples. The argument is also made that the adult activities exception removes from the protections of childhood especially dangerous activities in which children may engage. However, this rationale seems undermined by the fact that many of the cases where the children's standard of care *was applied* involve activities every bit as dangerous as those activities typically included in the adult activities exception [*Chaisson v Hebert* (1986) 74 NBR (2d) 105, 187 APR 105 (QB) (no negligence for 13-year-old who had a collision while driving an all-terrain vehicle); *Christie v Slevinsky* (n 34 above) (no negligence for an 11-year-old who hit a pedestrian while driving a dune buggy); *Purtle v Shelton* 474 SW 2d 123 (SC Ark 1971) (no negligence found on basis of application of 'reasonable minor' standard to teenager using gun)]. Further, it seems arguable even when one looks at what are apparently the 'core' cases of the application of the special standard of care for children that the application of a more generous standard could not be explained on the basis that the activities posed minimal risk for others.

[100] Thus, as discussed in *Dellwo v Pearson* (ibid) 863, the adult activities exception should apply to minors driving automobiles. Courts have followed this advice finding that the exception applies not only to minors who drive cars [*Gunnells v Dethrage* 366 So 2d 1104 (Ala 1979); *Constantino v Wolverine Insurance* 284 NW 2d 463 (Mich 1979); *Reiszel v Fontana* 312 NYS 2d 988 (1970); *Tucker v Tucker* [1956] SASR 297] but also those who drive more work-oriented vehicles like trucks [*Betzold v Erickson* 182 NE 2d 342 (Ill App 1962)] and tractors [*Goodfellow v Coggburn* 560 P 2d 873 (Idaho 1977); *Jackson v McCuiston* 448 SW 2d 33 (Ark 1969)].

motorized vehicle looks like 'play' courts seem more ambivalent about applying the adult activities exception. Thus, cases that involve vehicles that may be used either for play or for transportation are divided on the application of the adult activities exception. They seem to turn to some degree on how 'play-like' the activity appears and on the age of the defendant.[101] Once the activity in question looks more clearly like play and therefore apparently paradigmatically 'childish', courts are unlikely to apply the adult activities exception. Thus, allowances are made for the limitations of childhood where the child in question is riding a bicycle,[102] skiing,[103] and perhaps even using a gun.[104]

In this sense, the adult activities exception parallels *McHale* in its implicit invocation of a model of childhood that depends upon an idealized image of the ordinary boy. It seems to be this image that prevents courts from seeing work as any part of the life of a child even if it is the case that many children do spend childhood engaged in labour.[105] And this idealized image of the ordinary boy also seems at work in another dimension of the adult activities cases, for according to these cases not all 'play' or recreation counts as a 'childish' activity. Thus, courts also seem to exclude the 'Richie Rich' character from the ranks of ordinary childhood, holding for instance that the 11-year-old golfer in *Neumann v Shlansky* should be held to the same standard of care as an adult because golf is a sport 'ordinarily played by adults'.[106]

---

[101] For example, the adult activities exception was applied and liability found in *Ryan v Hickson* (n 99 above) (14-year-old driver of a snowmobile); *Mont v Black* (note 99 above) (minor snowmobile driver on highway); *Daniels v Evans* 224 A 2d 63 (NH 1966) (19-year-old motorcyclist); *Cleworth v Zachariuk* (1985) 32 MVR 23 (BCSC), affd 11 BCLR (2d) 125 (CA) (16-year-old snowmobile driver). However, courts did not apply the adult activities exception to minor plaintiffs in *Christie v Slevinsky* (n 34 above) (no negligence found where 11-year-old boy struck plaintiff while riding dune buggy); *Chaisson v Hebert* (n 99 above) (no negligence found where 13-year-old operating an all-terrain vehicle collided with a similar vehicle). Concerning the actual effect of the adult activities exception, however, at least one commentator has queried its significance for the outcome of particular cases, noting that in many cases even the more generous children's standard of care would have resulted in liability: Klar (n 99 above) 256–258 discussing *Ryan v Hickson* (ibid), *Mont v Black* (ibid), and *Robertson v Butler* (1985) 32 CCLT 208 (NSTD) among others.

[102] *Caradori v Fitch* 263 NW 2d 649 (Neb 1978); *Davis v Bushnell* 465 P 2d 652 (Idaho 1970).

[103] *Goss v Allen* 360 A 2d 388 (NJ 1976).

[104] *Thomas v Inman* 578 P 2d 399 (Or 1978); *Prater v Burns* 525 SW 2d 846 (Tenn App 1975); *Purtle v Shelton* (n 99 above). However, Canadian jurisprudence on negligence by minors with regard to the use of guns suggests that the boy's 'right to hunt' may be peculiar to the United States. Thus, for instance, Canadian courts appear to be far more willing to impose liability for injuries that arise out of inexperience or carelessness with guns even when the minor is relatively young. For instance, in *Hatfield v Pearson* [1956] 1 DLR (2d) 745 (BCSC), a 13½-year-old boy who seriously injured a playmate while carrying his father's loaded automatic rifle without the safety catch was found negligent. The court reasoned that he had failed to take such precautions as 'a reasonably careful person of his age in such a situation would have taken': ibid 749.

[105] As discussed in ch 5 below, the effect of the adult activities doctrine seems to be to prevent working children from claiming the benefit of the children's standard of care on terms similar to their playing counterparts. This is evident not only in the way that the exception itself is constructed but particularly in the inclusion of the use of work vehicles such as tractors and trucks as part of the adult activities doctrine. As discussed below, courts seem similarly unlikely to apply the children's standard of care to child plaintiffs who are injured when they are at work.

[106] 312 NYS 2d 951 (SCAD 1970).

B. The bully

As noted above, almost all of the child defendants are boys. However, as the adult activities exception illustrates, not all boys who injure others will benefit from being judged according to the standard of care applicable to children. And in line with the somewhat romantic notion of 'normal' play apparent in *McHale*, courts in child defendant cases also place other limits on what they will include within the protected scope of normal boyish play. The limits reinforce the essential innocence of the normal boy—however dangerous his actions—by excluding from the protections of childhood a narrow class of boyish behaviour that verges on the intentional infliction of harm.

Thus, for instance, in *Michaud v Dupuis*[107] Richard J found negligent an 11-year-old boy who threw a rock at a 4-year-old girl and destroyed the sight in one of her eyes. There is no sympathy here, either in the Court's description of the boy as having 'a propensity for throwing rocks', or in its finding that he acted 'in a reckless manner with complete disregard for the safety of other people'.[108] The Court refuses to treat the boy's action as normal childhood carelessness in large part precisely because his behaviour went beyond 'ordinary' careless disregard for the safety of others. Instead, the boy's actions here are distinguished in part because it is so difficult to construe the events as an instance of mutual play (in part because the victim was so much younger than the defendant). But it is also the fact that the actions are not simply careless but rather verge on the intentional infliction of harm. Thus, Richard J distinguishes the injury here from the 'purely accidental' injury in *Vaillancourt v Jacques*.[109] Similarly, in *Pollock v Lipkowitz*[110] the court feels little affinity for a 13-year-old boy who threw nitric acid at an 11-year-old girl, describing his act as a 'senseless act of folly' and finding him liable.[111]

Drawing attention to the behaviour of these boys as *not* normal, precisely because the infliction of harm looks almost intentional, has the effect of stressing the innocence of the normal playing boy, however careless his actions might appear. By defining as the 'other' the abnormal boy who wilfully injures, the character of the normal boy as essentially innocent is thus reinforced. And by insisting that a 'normal' boy would not intentionally injure another, especially a girl, especially a young girl, and especially outside the context of mutual play, these cases also confirm *McHale*'s idealized image of boyhood.[112] Courts

---

[107] (1977) 20 NBR (2d) 305 (SC).   [108] ibid 308.

[109] ibid 308–309 discussing *Vaillancourt* (n 26 above).

[110] (1970) 17 DLR (3d) 766 (Man QB).   [111] ibid 768.

[112] Indeed, case law suggests that the more the injury looks like the result of even 'overly enthusiastic' play, the more courts seem willing to see the risks as mutual and thus to exonerate the careless boy. For example, in *Barrett v Carter* 283 SE 2d 609 (Ga 1981), the court refused to impose liability on a 12-year-old boy who hit a girl in the eye during an 'ice-throwing spree': ibid 609. Although the court cited a Georgia law that it found provided immunity from tort liability to 'infants under 13', it also noted that 'to rule otherwise would permit lawsuits between children who fail to exercise due care while at play': ibid 610. Interestingly, however, the girl was not part of the ice-throwing spree, but was struck as she came out of a restaurant.

thereby place outside the protected sphere of normal boyhood those boys who seem to intend harm to others, even if such behaviour could be considered quite statistically 'normal' for boys. In so doing they reinforce the place of innocence in *McHale*'s vision of normal boyhood. And by almost paradoxically limiting the *negligence* liability of the normal playing boy to situations that verge on *intentional* harm, courts create an extensive sphere of 'innocence' to foster the development of the playing boy.

The broader case law involving the child defendant also reinforces *McHale*'s image of normal boyhood as constituted by the innocent pursuit of play unfettered by the presence or needs of others. These cases do so negatively by identifying what activities do not count as part of boyhood—wilful injuring of another—thus reinforcing the crucial role innocence or ordinary heedlessness plays in the image of boyhood. Within these limits the play of the boy is depicted as normal, natural, and thus innocent. And as an inherently valuable activity—not just individually but socially—it must be protected from the destructive scrutiny of the law.

C. The girl defendant

If it is possible to begin to develop from this one 'hard case' a picture of what reasonable behaviour might demand, and of what the reasonable person standard might thus enshrine, that picture is as yet partial. It is partial, as we have seen, because of its focus on the child at play. But it is also partial in the fact that virtually all of the reported cases involving the child defendant involve boys. What lessons can be drawn from this? And is there anything that can be gleaned from the very few child defendant cases involving girls? The lessons, as we shall see, are bound to be rather limited but they may nonetheless help to think about the implications of the picture of childhood developed in *McHale* and its companion cases for that almost absent class of defendants—girls.

The section in the *Canadian Abridgement* discussed at the outset of this chapter contains only one case that involves a girl defendant and that case turns out to be very different than the other child defendant cases. In *Saper v City of Calgary*,[113] an unidentified 5-year-old girl crossed a street at a cross walk without looking to see if there was oncoming traffic. A city bus was forced to stop quickly and an elderly woman who had just boarded and was still standing fell down and was injured. She sued the bus company. The 5-year-old girl 'Mary Doe' was added as a defendant. Moshansky J found that the driver was negligent in starting the bus before the elderly woman was seated, in failing to see the little girl in time, and in not taking adequate care in an area frequented by children. Moshansky J dismissed the action against 'Mary Doe', who was represented by counsel for the Administrator of the Motor Vehicle Accident Claims Fund of the Province of Alberta, on the ground that as a child of tender years she was incapable of negligence. But *Saper* differs in such significant ways from

---

[113] (1979) 21 AR 577 (QB).

the other child defendant cases that it proves difficult to compare. To begin with, Mary Doe is extremely young, right on the boundary of 'tender years' where no responsibility can be imputed. But even beyond this, unlike the cases examined above in which boys took serious risks with the security or property of others, 'Mary Doe's' primary carelessness seems to be toward herself. Indeed, it is perhaps because the facts read so much more like contributory negligence that Moshansky J states that he would have assessed at 50 per cent the child's degree of culpability if he had found evidence that she 'was of sufficient age and intelligence to be capable of *contributory negligence*'.[114] Moshansky J's telling mischaracterization underscores that, although the little girl was not injured here, her mistake seems to turn less on foreseeable risks to others and more on inattentiveness to her own safety.

A more recent and more interesting instance of a case involving a girl defendant is found in *Mullin v Richards*,[115] a case that more closely parallels those involving boys. The litigation arose as a result of an injury that occurred when two schoolgirls, Teresa Mullin and Heidi Richards, were engaged in a play sword fight with plastic rulers. One of the rulers snapped and a fragment of the broken plastic entered Teresa's eye, causing her to lose all sight in that eye. She brought proceedings against Heidi and the education authority. At trial, the judge dismissed the claim against the education authority. He found that both Heidi and Teresa had been negligent and accordingly allowed Teresa's claim to succeed again Heidi subject to a 50 per cent reduction for Teresa's contributory negligence. Heidi appealed this holding, arguing among other things that the judge had failed to take account of the fact that she was not an adult.

The Court of Appeal unanimously allowed Heidi's appeal. While they found that the judge had taken proper account of her age for the purposes of the standard of care inquiry, they also held that there was insufficient evidence to support his finding that the accident was foreseeable. The practice of such sword fights was widespread and there was no evidence that it was banned or even frowned upon. Further, the Court noted there was no evidence to suggest that either of the girls had used excessive or inappropriate violence. The trial judge 'readily and almost without question accepted that on his findings of fact there was negligence on the part of the young ladies' even though, as the Court of Appeal found, there was no evidentiary support for such a conclusion.[116] Instead, as Hutchison LJ puts it, 'This was in truth nothing more than a school girls' game such as on the evidence was commonplace in this school and there was, I would hold, no justification for attributing to the participants the foresight of any significant risk of the likelihood of injury.'[117] In his brief concurrence Butler-Sloss LJ quotes the passage from Kitto J's judgment in *McHale* that describes the standard of the reasonable person as a standard of propriety. After endorsing this as entirely appropriate, he quotes the closing 'Boys will be boys' passage and strikingly continues: '—and I would say that girls of 15 playing

---

[114] (1979) 21 AR 577 (QB) 583 [emphasis added].   [115] n 5 above.   [116] ibid 927.
[117] ibid.

together may play as somewhat irresponsible girls of 15. I too would allow this appeal.'[118]

In many respects then, *Mullin* bears important similarities to some other child defendant cases discussed above. However, it is difficult to develop a deeper sense of its significance without placing it in the context of other cases involving the playing girl. As we shall see shortly, it suggests some interesting lessons when juxtaposed to other cases involving the playing girl, albeit the girl plaintiff, which we shall discuss next.

The continuities with *McHale* are interesting. First, in giving content to the standard of care, the court seems to treat the standard of prudence in particular as though it is gender-specific—thus, Hutchinson LJ repeatedly describes the standard as requiring him to ask what a reasonable 15-year-old schoolgirl would have foreseen, 'whether an ordinarily prudent and reasonable 15-year-old schoolgirl'[119] would have realized the danger etc. Similarly, it seems telling in this respect that, in addition to citing *McHale*, he cites *Gough v Thorne*[120] despite the fact that this case concerns contributory negligence. But presumably the reason he does so is that the case involves the question of how a reasonable person standard might apply to a girl rather than a boy. Thus, he quotes: 'The question of whether the plaintiff can be said to have been guilty of contributory negligence depends on whether any ordinary child of thirteen and a half can be expected to have done any more than this child did. I say "any ordinary child". I do not mean a paragon of prudence; nor do I mean a scatter-brained child; but the ordinary girl of thirteen and a half.'[121]

If in this way, *Mullin* may seem a counterpoint to a number of cases we will examine involving the playing girl, in other ways it exactly tracks some of the worries about *McHale*. As we saw, the court in *Mullin* does explicitly rely on the reasoning in *McHale*. And the *Mullin* court seems to take from *McHale* the very point we noted above—that is, that the objective standard is essentially a standard of ordinariness and normalcy. There are at least two ways to read the holding in *Mullin*. One is, as the Court of Appeal critically comments regarding the trial decision, that in the absence of foreseeability of such harm no attribution of negligence can be made. But the Court goes further than this. Both substantive opinions at the Court of Appeal place tremendous significance on the commonness, the normalcy of the game that the girls were playing. Indeed, it is possible to read the judgment of Hutchinson LJ in particular as endorsing the very conception of the standard that we noted may be troubling. This is because he seems to rely heavily on the commonness of the practice of play sword fights to support his conclusion that there was no culpable behaviour here.

In this sense then, the meanings of *Mullin* seem to be quite complex. At first blush, and especially with the playing boy defendant cases in mind, *Mullin* reads as a revelation—posed against the nostalgia about the playing boy,

---

[118] ibid 928 quoting *McHale* Appeal (n 4 above) 213.   [119] ibid 924.
[120] [1966] 3 All ER 398 (CA).
[121] n 5 above, 925 quoting *Gough v Thorne* (n 120 above) 400.

Butler-Sloss LJ's insistence that girls will also be irresponsible girls seems almost revolutionary. And indeed as we shall see when we turn to the allurement cases, there is much to this reaction. Without a significant (and ongoing) change in our underlying conceptions of boyhood and girlhood, this conclusion would be impossible. Yet the conclusion, though it seems to extend the possibilities of irresponsibility to at least some girls, also gives reason to pause. The court seems, in its emphasis on girlhood as the touchstone for the standard of care, to suggest that inherently gendered notions of ordinary behaviour will determine what can count as reasonable. Here we see the rather remarkable fact that some courts may be coming to see that this may also work in favour of girls. But the underlying worry about the implications of gender remains. And beyond this, we also see the deeper idea that the fault standard is essentially conventional here. Reasonableness *is* ordinariness on this view and so the standard will excuse common mistakes and condemn abnormal ones. But even if the result in *Mullin* is in its own way egalitarian, it nonetheless poses the same worry about the ordinariness standard that we noted in *McHale*. Girls may indeed benefit here (although with a girl on both sides of the sword, so to speak, it is not entirely easy to sort out the play of gender), but this does not inevitably lead us to conclude that this is the appropriately egalitarian solution. For as we shall see, the terms on which such benefit is extended ought to continue to provoke egalitarian concern.

III. Conclusion

The cases on child defendants help to uncover another important dimension of how the objective standard actually operates. Several elements of this operation are illuminated by these cases. In contrast to their treatment of the developmentally disabled, the courts are capable of being extraordinarily generous to the child defendant. And as we have seen, courts seem particularly inclined to excuse what they see as the normal heedlessness of the playing boy. Indeed, the exculpatory conditions available to the playing boy include not only the lack of foresight expressly ruled out in the case of the developmentally disabled, but also failures of prudence so long as they are normal or ordinary among boys. In their opinions judges reveal that, in evaluating the harm-imposing actions of the playing boy, they often rely heavily on their own memories of boyhood, which are deeply romantic and nostalgic. And in this universe, 'childhood' is replaced by boyhood so that it is the norms of boyhood that apply—thus, the courts ask what would the normal or ordinary boy have done in this situation. In answering the crucial question of what the normal boy of a given age would have done in the situation, several threads of reasoning come to the fore. The boy is seen as the instrument of nature, subject to its whims and impulses and therefore not responsible for his actions. And the essence of boyhood seems ultimately to reside in freedom from concern about others.

But what do these cases say about the treatment of the child litigant more generally and how do they illuminate the workings of the objective standard? They do illustrate that the reasonable child standard seems to be powerfully intertwined with conceptions of what is normal—so much so that courts seem to be prepared to exonerate even blameworthy or imprudent behaviour where it is sufficiently normal. But—and this surely is significant in its own right—virtually all of the child defendants are boys. So one cannot help but wonder how girls fare under the objective standard. To evaluate this it is necessary to look to contributory negligence cases. What are the continuities with the child defendant cases, and what are the differences? As we shall see, when we put together the implications of *McHale*, its companion child defendant cases, the treatment of the developmentally disabled and that of the child plaintiff, we arrive at a crucial though typically obscured dimension of the objective standard.

3

Fun with Dick and Jane

To return, however, as every judge must ultimately return, to the case which is before us—it has been urged for the appellant, and my own researches incline me to agree, that in all that mass of authorities which bears upon this branch of the law *there is no single mention of a reasonable woman*. It was ably insisted before us that such an omission, extending over a century and more of judicial pronouncements, must be something more than a coincidence; that among the innumerable tributes to the reasonable man there might be expected at least some passing reference to a reasonable person of the opposite sex; that no such reference is found; that legally at least there *is* no reasonable woman, and that therefore in this case the learned judge should have directed the jury that, while there was evidence on which they might find that the defendant had not come up to the standard required of a reasonable man, the conduct was only what was to be expected of a woman, as such.

Fardell v Potts[1]

As Herbert's fictional dilemma indicates, the law of negligence is notably silent on the standard of conduct to which a woman should be held. Indeed, so far in our inquiry, the female population has been almost absent. Yet feminists and others, including perhaps Herbert himself, suspect there is something troubling about applying the 'reasonable person' to women. Thus far we have examined two groups of litigants to illuminate what counts as reasonable behaviour. The treatment of those with intellectual disabilities reveals the complex interrelationship between the reasonable and the normal, and suggests that even failures of foresight will not be forgiven if they are not normal. At the other extreme, it seems, is the child defendant. In contrast with the developmentally disabled, the child defendant is typically forgiven not only for failures of foresight but also for failures of prudence so long as those failures are normal. Here too, the conception of what is normal seems to play a crucial role in determining what is reasonable. Because there is a conception of a normal failure to exercise prudence (at least for boys), the normal often comes to the fore to forgive not merely the cognitive shortcomings but even the moral mistakes of the child defendant.

Nonetheless, so far we have learned little about how the objective standard deals with the puzzle of women because that troublesome class of litigants, the child defendant, turns out to be composed almost exclusively of playing boys above the age of tender years. In order to untangle how the objective standard works, we need to look at a broader category of cases. If courts

[1] AP Herbert, *Uncommon Law* (London: Metheun, 1935) 5 [emphasis added].

are prepared to forgive a 'normal' lack of prudence on the part of the playing boy who injures others, are courts similarly generous with girls? The recent decision in *Mullin*[2] suggests that courts may also have a conception of normal girlish play that may sometimes work to the benefit of the playing girl, but beyond this it tells us little. Is the decision characteristic or unusual? It is difficult to answer this question, and to think more systematically about the treatment of gender, without a broader context. In order to develop a more nuanced understanding of how the reasonable person standard deals with the puzzle of gender, we need to find a parallel group of cases to those involving the child defendant. As it turns out, an analogous group of cases that involves judging the reasonableness of the behaviour of both boys and girls at play is found in the contributory negligence cases that deal with the doctrine of allurement.

The leading case on allurement is *Lynch v Nurdin*.[3] In that case, the Court of Queen's Bench upheld a jury award to a boy of 7 who was injured while playing with an unattended horse and cart that the defendant's servant had left in the street. The court refused to find that the boy's wilful misconduct prevented him from recovering, instead stating that since the defendant's servant's 'most blameable carelessness has tempted the child', the defendant therefore 'ought not to reproach the child with yielding to that temptation'.[4] After all, the court reasoned, the boy had 'merely indulged the natural instinct of a child, in amusing himself with the empty cart and deserted horse'.[5] Since *Lynch v Nurdin*, the doctrine of allurement has been widely used to defeat the argument that the playing child is precluded from recovering damages because of his or her own carelessness. Allurement therefore occupies a central place in assessing the reasonableness of the behaviour of the playing child.[6]

---

[2] *Mullin v Richards* [1998] 1 All ER 920 (CA).
[3] (1841) 10 LJQB 73, [1835–42] All ER 167, 1 QB 29.   [4] ibid 76.   [5] ibid.
[6] For instance, in *Gough v National Coal Board* [1953] 2 All ER 1283, 1295 (CA), Hodson LJ describes *Lynch* as the decision 'from which all the cases on allurement to children descend'. As *Lynch* illustrates, a finding of allurement resolves the question of contributory negligence in favour of the playing child. Thus, allurement cases are properly characterized as contributory negligence cases even though they do not invariably present themselves as such. Historically, allurement (or attractive nuisance as it is commonly known in the United States) was important in part because of the now-defunct rule that an occupier need only refrain from intentionally harming a trespasser. There was no duty to take reasonable care nor to protect from concealed danger: *Robert Addie & Sons (Collieries) Ltd v Dumbreck* [1929] AC 358, 365 (HL). However, an exception existed where dangers arising from allurements caused injuries to children—even trespassing children: J Fleming, *The Law of Torts* (9th edn, Agincourt: The Law Book Company, 1998) 509, citing *Latham v Johnson* [1913] 1 KB 398, 416, Hamilton LJ. In *Cooke v Midland Great Western Railway of Ireland* [1909] AC 229 (HL), Lord Atkinson ruled that an owner would be liable for injuries caused by unguarded dangerous items that were 'calculated to attract or allure' children: ibid 237. Allurement enabled circumvention of the harsh *Addie* rule.

The allurement cases are also doctrinally complex because sometimes the legal issue is described in terms of duty of care rather than standard of care or contributory negligence. Richard Kidner comments on the tendency to confuse these kinds of questions by approaching them as problems of duty of care rather than standard of care: 'The Variable Standard of Care, Contributory Negligence

However, the concept of allurement is sufficiently ambiguous to lead judges to stress the importance of the facts of each case and to resile from the difficult task of articulating any general rules.[7] In part this is because although allurement is presented as a unitary concept based on the notion of 'alluring traps',[8] this description actually confounds two distinct rationales for exoneration—entrapment and temptation. Recognizing this does help resolve some of the difficulties in the allurement case law, but it also reveals deeper worries about that body of law and the light it casts on the standard of care more generally. This is because while both bases of exoneration for allurement are theoretically open to any playing child, in fact the particularly powerful temptation rationale seems to be much more accessible to boys. Indeed, the implications of the language of seduction that we saw in *McHale v Watson*[9] begin to appear anything but accidental. As in the child defendant cases, the view that it is normal for the boy to yield to temptation once again comes to the fore to excuse the prudential mistakes of boys. It is reasonable, it seems, and thus non-culpable, for boys to be seduced into danger. But there does not appear to be a similar apparatus to forgive the girl who is careless of her own safety. Thus, the nominally identical standard for boys and girls often seems to result in very different treatment of boy and girl plaintiffs. And, echoing *McHale*, this treatment ultimately seems to turn on the complicated relationship between the reasonable and the normal. Thus, because reasonable is read as normal and because courts intimate that normal masculine behaviour involves significantly more imprudence, boys are more likely to be exonerated despite the risks they take. While *Mullin* may point to an emerging sense of normal girlish imprudence, the allurement cases reveal just how exceptional that holding is. Beyond this, *Mullin's* reliance on the normal and on gender-specific notions of reasonableness actually seem characteristic of the treatment of the playing child more generally, and only serve to heighten egalitarian concern about the reasonable person.

and *Volenti*' (1991) 11 Legal Stud 1. He notes the difficulties that arise where either the plaintiff or the defendant is incapable of achieving the usual standard of care and concludes that the central question in such cases really concerns whether the standard of care should be varied: ibid 2. However the issue is framed though, to the extent that judges find the behaviour of the allured child 'reasonable', recovery is allowed. Conversely, if the child's behaviour is not seen as reasonable, recovery will be denied. Thus, the essential issue is the 'reasonableness' of the behaviour and the extent to which courts will make allowances for 'shortcomings' in this assessment. And though there are, as discussed in ch 2 above, serious doctrinal questions about whether the same standard applies to plaintiffs and defendants, they are not central to this analysis because it compares the treatment of boy plaintiffs and girl plaintiffs.

  [7] A detailed discussion to this effect is found in *Jolley v Sutton London Borough Council* [2000] 3 All ER 409, 416–417 (per Lord Steyn) and 419 (per Lord Hoffman). Similarly, in *Gough* (n 6 above), Birkett LJ stresses that everything turns on the particular facts of each case: ibid 1291. Singleton J similarly quotes from *Latham* to the effect that '[c]hildren's cases are always troublesome': ibid 1287.

  [8] Fleming (n 6 above) 509; *Pinkas and Pinkas v Canadian Pacific Ry Co* [1928] 1 WWR 321 (Man KB).   [9] (1964) 111 CLR 384.

I. Entrapment and Temptations:
Making Sense of Allurement

Two other terms must be alluded to—a 'trap' and 'attraction' or 'allurement.' A trap is a figure of speech, not a formula. It involves the idea of con-
cealment and surprise[,] of an appearance of safety under circumstances
cloaking a reality of danger. Owners and occupiers alike expose licensees and
visitors to traps on their premises at their peril, but a trap is a relative term.
In the case of an infant, there are moral as well as physical traps. There may
accordingly be a duty towards infants not merely not to dig pitfalls for them,
but not to lead them into temptation.

Hamilton LJ, *Latham v Johnson*[10]

Although courts and commentators addressing the allurement of the playing
child speak as though they were working with a unitary concept, they often
identify very different and even inconsistent requirements of the allurement
doctrine. For instance, while courts commonly refuse recovery by pointing to a
warning or awareness of danger, just as frequently they treat such warnings or
awareness as irrelevant to the child's culpability. Similarly, at times any dangerous activity on the part of the child seems to be sufficient to preclude recovery;
in other cases, children recover despite the most blatantly dangerous acts,
including the child's own creation of danger. While some courts have suggested
that a defendant will be liable for an allurement only to children of tender
years, other courts have not hesitated to find allurement even with plaintiffs
as old as 15. As noted above, courts themselves have pointed with some frustration to the difficulty of articulating the general principles implicit in the
allurement case law. But these problems are not attributable to any failure of
judicial imagination. In fact, the source of many of these apparent contradic-
tions of allurement jurisprudence can be traced to the ambiguity of the concept
itself. Two very different rationales are actually at work under the rubric of
allurement. Although the different rationales are not explicitly acknowledged,
they are actually conceptually distinct bases for exonerating the playing child.
As Hamilton LJ's description from *Latham* obliquely suggests, one rationale
relies on the notion of 'pitfalls' or entrapment. The other very different rationale for allurement focuses instead on the notion of a 'moral trap' or temptation.

With this distinction in mind, it is possible to identify a group of cases in
which playing children are exonerated because of some kind of 'pitfall' or hidden danger—presumably the 'physical traps' to which Hamilton LJ refers. In
these cases an allurement is described as something 'dangerous, although not
apparently so—something insidious'.[11] Accordingly, the entrapment cases typically insist that allurement claims will not succeed unless the relevant danger

---

[10] (n 6 above) 415.
[11] *Perry v Thomas Wrigley Ltd* [1955] 3 All ER 243, [1955] 1 WLR 1164, Oliver J.

was hidden from the child. The underlying idea turns on the notion of mistake or even deception, and in the archetypal case the child's youth means that he or she lacks the information necessary to identify the source of danger—it is in this sense that the trap in question is 'physical'.[12] Thus, the 'hidden' nature of the danger arises primarily from the cognitive limitations of childhood. Exoneration under entrapment therefore turns on recognition of the non-culpable limitations on foresight that attend childhood. Courts treat warnings to the child—at least to a child above very tender years—as germane to entrapment because warnings counteract the argument that the child had insufficient foresight to recognize the danger. The centrality of limited foresight is also apparent in the fact that evidence that the child was particularly intelligent or had prior experience with the source of the danger tends to defeat the entrapment argument. It is telling that children significantly above the age of tender years rarely succeed on entrapment grounds.[13] In this sense, within the allurement case law it is possible to identify a significant and conceptually unified body of cases that revolve around the notion of entrapment.

However, the allurement case law also contains another rationale, conceptually distinct from these entrapment cases. These cases involve 'temptations'—the 'moral traps' that Hamilton LJ describes. Central to the temptation cases is the notion that the child was enticed or lured into a dangerous situation.[14] Because the premiss of the temptation rationale is that there are conditions under which it is non-culpable for children to 'yield' to the temptation to play with things they recognize as dangerous, awareness of the danger itself does not undermine a temptation claim. In fact, while *unawareness* of danger is crucial to entrapment, both *awareness* of danger and some degree of attraction to it are central to the

---

[12] An illustration can be found in *Glasgow Corp v Taylor* [1922] 1 AC 44, where the House of Lords held in favour of a 7-year-old boy who died as a result of eating poisonous berries growing in a fenced area beside a playground in public gardens. The House of Lords emphasized the misleading and deceptive nature of the berries and found that they constituted a trap. They also noted that there was no warning that the berries were deadly even though the defendants were aware of it.

[13] The exception is where the allurement argument turns on deception rather than on the child's limited foresight. This is the case, for instance, where children are injured when they climb trees that conceal high voltage wires. In such cases, the entrapment arises not so much from the child's limited foresight as from the deceptive nature of the situation itself. Unsurprisingly, in such cases courts do exonerate older children on entrapment grounds: *Buckland v Guildford Gas Light and Coke Co* [1948] 2 All ER 1086 (KB) (13-year-old girl who was electrocuted when she climbed a tree which concealed high voltage wires was held not contributorily negligent. The situation was described as one involving a 'hidden peril', a 'lurking, unseen danger': ibid 1095); *Amos v New Brunswick Electric Power Commission* (1976) 70 DLR (3d) 741 (SCC) (9-year-old boy who was injured when he climbed a tree that concealed high voltage wires was allowed to recover damages). Presumably, however, this ground of exoneration is not limited to children, although childhood does make it easier to establish the reasonableness of the absence of awareness of danger.

[14] An illustration can be found in the leading case of *Lynch v Nurdin* (n 3 above). There, the court found that since the servant of the defendant had tempted the injured child with the empty cart and deserted horse, he could not relieve himself of liability by simply pointing to the fact that the child had yielded to that temptation. Although the boy who yielded to the temptation acted 'without prudence or thought', he nonetheless showed those qualities 'in as great a degree as he could be expected to possess them': ibid 76.

idea of temptation.[15] In the temptation cases, neither the obviousness of danger nor explicit warnings about it nor even the child's own participation in the creation of the danger are, in and of themselves, sufficient to preclude the child from recovering. Similarly, because exoneration here rests not on the cognitive limitations of childhood but rather on its 'mischievous' propensities, the temptation argument marks out those cases where the child's failure of prudence is nonculpable. Thus, superior intelligence will not necessarily preclude success under the temptation rationale. Indeed, the child with superior intelligence may even be granted more leeway under this rationale. Perhaps unsurprisingly, then, the temptation rationale operates primarily to exonerate children who are above the age of tender years.

Recognizing the difference between entrapment and temptation does help to explain elements of the allurement case law. However, it also raises broader questions. Principal among these is the question of when courts will confine a playing child to the relatively narrow entrapment rationale and when courts will be willing to rely on the more generous temptation rationale. This inquiry has considerable practical significance because the chance of recovery is far greater under the temptation rationale than if one is confined to the more limited rationale of entrapment.

The threshold consideration for the application of either branch of the doctrine of allurement is the age of the child. When children are above a certain age, typically around 14, courts will rarely find any version of the doctrine of allurement persuasive.[16] There is also a limit below which the courts will be

---

[15] This element of temptation is apparent in the definition of the verb 'to tempt': 'To try to attract, to entice (a person) to do evil; to present attractions to the passions or frailties of; to allure or incite to evil with the prospect of some pleasure or advantage': *Compact Oxford English Dictionary* (2nd edn, Oxford: Clarendon Press, 1994) 2024. In this sense, the concept of temptation turns on both recognition of and yet attraction to the evil and enticing source of temptation. Shakespeare played on the fact that 'tempter' is a synonym for 'the devil' (ibid) when he wrote in 'Troilus and Cressida' 'And sometimes we are devils to ourselves / When we will tempt the frailty of our powers, / Presuming on their changeful potency' (Act IV, scene iv, 95).

Temptation concerns the struggle between the reason (the knowledge of what is right) and the passions (the strong—almost irresistible—desire to do something other than what reason dictates). It is unsurprising that man often pleads to be spared from temptation: 'Watch and pray, that ye enter not into temptation: the spirit is indeed willing but the flesh is weak' (Matthew 26: 40–41). And for this reason perhaps, triumph over temptation is equated with strength and even greatness. As Dryden expressed it, 'Dare to be great, without a guilty crown; View it, and lay the bright temptation down'. Similarly, Browning wrote 'Why comes temptation, but for man to meet / And master and make crouch beneath his foot, / And so be pedestaled in triumph' (*The Ring and the Book* [1868–69] bk X, The Pope l.1185.

Thus while conquering temptation is laudable, it is understandable if the 'ordinary' man, the man on the Clapham omnibus or the 'man who mows the lawn in his shirtsleeves' is unequal to such feats.

[16] So, for instance, where boys of 15 or 16 are injured when playing with hydro wires, courts generally refuse to apply the doctrine to them: see *Barnes v Newfoundland Light & Power Co* (1982) 36 Nfld & PEIR 422 (Nfld TD) (doctrine of allurement not applying to intelligent 16-year-old boy who was injured when he grabbed a live wire hanging from a hydro pole); *Partridge v Etobicoke (Township)* [1956] OR 121 (CA) (doctrine of allurement not applying to intelligent 15-year-old boy who was injured when he jumped into the air to grab a wire attached to a electric power pole). However, courts occasionally apply the doctrine of allurement to exonerate boys as old as

reluctant to find allurement. When children are younger than 3 or 4,[17] courts may exonerate them on the ground that they are incapable of contributory negligence, but they will not ordinarily apply the doctrine of allurement, since it presupposes some minimal capacity for rational choice.[18] Thus, it seems that playing children between 3 or 4 and 14 or 15 may be able to rely on the doctrine of allurement. However, within this broad category it is possible to identify two distinct groups of children.

The first group is composed primarily of children who are within or just on the border of what is traditionally referred to as tender years. These children— typically between about 4 and 6—do have some minimal capacity for rational agency. But because they have very limited abilities to foresee harm, they often fail even to recognize situations that are dangerous. Since their primary short-coming thus relates to foresight rather than prudence, courts that exonerate such children under the doctrine of allurement do so primarily by relying on the concept of entrapment. Indeed, case law reveals that the entrapment branch of the

15: *Makins v Piggott & Inglis* (1898) 29 SCR 188 (15-year-old boy who was injured while playing with a detonating cap that had been left in a public cemetery could recover damages). It is worth noting that cases involving children this old often seem to turn on other more general rationales that would equally apply to adults, such as strict liability or unforeseeability of harm. Generally, however, courts and commentators suggest that the upper limit for the application of this doctrine is probably about 14. See e.g. *Hurd v City of Hamilton* (1910) 1 OWN 881 (HC): 'In this case [child of 7 falling to death while walking along wall] there was that which had the child been 14 years of age or over, and of the ordinary capacity and intelligence of children of that age, would have precluded recovery for his death': ibid 882.

[17] See *Clyne v Podolsky* [1942] 1 DLR 577, [1942] 1 WWR 100 (Alta TD) (doctrine of allure-ment inapplicable to 3½-year-old boy who removed inflammable cleaning fluid from owner's pre-mises); *Pedlar v Toronto* (1913) 29 OLR 527, 15 DLR 684 (HC) (doctrine of allurement did not apply to 2½-year-old boy who drowned after he fell from a platform leading from the shore to a tower about one hundred feet from the shore); *Penner v Bethel Hospital Society* (1981) 8 Man R (2d) 310 (QB) (hospital not liable for injury sustained by a young child when coat rack on which the child was swinging fell over); *Bonne v Towes* (1968) 64 WWR 1 (Man QB) (doctrine of allurement did not apply to 4-year-old boy injured by sparks from apparently dead fire); *Gwynne v Dominion Stores Ltd* (1963) 43 DLR (2d) 290, 45 WWR 232 (Man QB) (automatic door in which 20-month-old boy caught his hand not a trap); *Marshall v Sudbury (Hydro-Electric Commission)* [1959] OWN 63 (HC) (doctrine of allurement did not apply to 3-year-old boy who fell into excavation on building site near his home); *Richardson v Canadian National Railway* (1927) 60 OLR 296, [1927] 2 DLR 801 (CA) (doctrine of allurement did not apply to 4-year-old boy who was injured while playing on a pile of crushed stone near defendant's railway tracks).

[18] The doctrine of allurement seems to require that the child be old enough to be left unsupervised. This means that the child must have a sufficient degree of agency that, though its actions may not be fully rational, they are at least sufficiently comprehensible to be foreseeable. Where the child is not old enough to be left unsupervised, courts tend to attribute primary responsibility for their safety to their parents. So, for instance, in *Pianosi v CNR* [1944] 1 DLR 161 (Ont CA), the court held that a licence of a general character does not extend to children too young to take care of themselves. Similarly, in *Sproat v Magistrates of Prestwick* [1955] Sess Cas 271 (Scot), the court rejected the neg-ligence action by the father of two children aged 2 and 4 against the owner of a water-filled pit in which the children had drowned. See also *Hache v Savoie* (1980) 31 NBR (2d) 631 (QB) (parent of injured 2-year-old 50% contributorily negligent for injuries sustained by child when tampering with an exercise bicycle); *Beckerson and Beckerson v Dougherty* [1953] 2 DLR 498 (Ont HC) (the absence of supervision of a very young child injured on a busy street constitutes negligence on the part of the parent).

doctrine of allurement has been applied to enable many boys[19] and some girls[20] aged 6 and under to recover damages for the injuries they sustained while at play. These cases tend to involve children who are attracted to something unusual and interesting—something that contains an unrecognized source of danger.

Within the case law on the doctrine of allurement, it is also possible to identify another group of children. These older children, typically above the age of tender years but below the maximum threshold for the application of the doctrine of allurement—so between approximately 6 or 7 and 14—ordinarily suffer from defects not of foresight but of prudence. Because they are generally capable of recognizing the relevant danger, the allurement inquiry is directed to whether, even if the child was aware of the danger, it would be reasonable to expect him to avoid it. This means that older children who are injured will typically not find success under the doctrine of allurement unless they can invoke the temptation rationale. But the cases reveal that whatever else is needed for a successful invocation of the temptation rationale, such an invocation seems quite unlikely unless the playing child is a boy. As in the child defendant cases, courts are prepared to excuse as normal a whole range of boyish imprudence. However, as we will see, the powerful temptation branch of the doctrine of allurement seems to play virtually no role in cases involving girls. But if the standard for determining whether or not a child is culpably careless is nominally identical for boys and girls—as all the discussions of children suggest it is—why should this be so? An examination of the temptation cases helps to cast light on the extent to which conceptions of reasonable behaviour are gendered.

A. Temptation and gender

To begin with, it is worth noting that there are far fewer allurement cases involving playing girls than involving playing boys.[21] Although this might suggest that

---

[19] See e.g. *Brignull v Grimsby (Village)* (1925) 56 OLR 525, [1925] 2 DLR 1096 (CA) (5½-year-old boy injured while playing on a disabled road-grader left on highway); *Clement v Northern Navigation Co* (1918) 43 OLR 127, 43 DLR 433 (CA) (6-year-old boy crushed when climbing on a crate left on a public wharf); *Whaling v Ravenhurst* (1977) 16 OR (2d) 61 (CA) (4-year-old boy injured by rotary lawn mower); *Seamone v Fancy* (1923) 56 NSR 487, [1924] 1 DLR 650 (CA) (5-year-old boy kicked by unattended horse); *Howard v R* [1924] Ex CR 143 (boy who fell through a hole in the defendant's bridge and drowned in river would have been allowed to recover because the hole was a trap, but the action was dismissed on other grounds).

[20] See *Daneau v Trynor Construction Co* (1971) 24 DLR (3d) 434 (NSTD) (6-year-old girl not responsible for injuries she sustained when she and her younger brother climbed down into trench on city street and played in a pile of sand that collapsed on her); *Leadbetter v R* [1970] Ex CR 260, 12 DLR (3d) (3-year-old girl not a trespasser because improperly levelled group mail box that fell on her while her older sister and friend were climbing on it was an allurement, particularly given its location on a public street, near a trailer court and a school).

[21] This is true for children both below and above the age of tender years. Thus, for instance, the Canadian Abridgement section on the doctrine of allurement has 64 cases involving children: *Canadian Abridgement* (Toronto: Carswell, 1995, 2001), Family Law, Status and Capacities of Children, s 2 Torts, ss b Child's Action Against Tortfeasor (XII.2.b). (One case applied the allurement rule for children to horses: *Futton v Randall* [1918] 3 WWR 331 (Alta Dist Ct)). Of these, only 14 cases involved girls. The remaining 50 cases involved boys. Eight of the 14 cases involving girls

girls are more careful than boys, playing girls seem to be denied recovery more often than their male counterparts. Once they are above the age of tender years, it seems extremely difficult for playing girls, in contrast with playing boys, to find exoneration under the doctrine of allurement. And the very exceptional cases where older playing girls are exonerated actually reinforce the general inaccessibility of the temptation rationale to the playing girl.

Playing boys above the age of tender years are allowed to recover damages in a striking number and variety of situations. Thus, courts frequently rely on the doctrine of allurement to award damages to boys who are injured or even killed while engaged in a variety of clearly dangerous activities. For instance, the doctrine is frequently applied to exonerate boys who are injured when they gain access to, play with, touch or even swing on electrical equipment such as light poles or wires, substations, and transformers.[22] Similarly, allurement is often used to excuse boys who injure themselves while playing with matches or with explosive materials, and this includes boys who intentionally ignite the explosive materials themselves.[23] Boys are also frequently exonerated when they are injured while playing around trains, including around moving trains.[24] Damages have also been awarded to boys who were injured as a result of climbing on fences and walls,[25] or playing with various types of equipment, animals, vehicles,[26] as well as

had girl plaintiffs aged 6 or younger. Of the 50 cases involving boys, 21 involved boys age 6 and under, while 29 involved boys over age 6 but under age 15. In addition, as discussed in ch 2 above, general accident statistics confirm that boys are involved in far more accidents than girls.

[22] *Mayer v Prince Albert* [1926] 4 DLR 1072 (Sask CA) (9-year-old boy electrocuted when he climbed an electric light pole); *Amos v New Brunswick Electric Power Commission* (n 13 above); *Van Oudenhove v D'Aoust* (1969) 8 DLR (3d) 145 (Alta CA) (8-year-old boy electrocuted when he crawled under a neighbour's cottage and came into contact with an unconnected electrical ground wire); *Nixon v Manitoba (Power Commission)* (1959) 21 DLR (2d) 68 (Man QB) (boy playing on CP Railway property seriously injured when loose guy-wire on which he was swinging became energized); *Jones v Calgary (City)* (1969) 67 WWR 589 (Alta SC) (9-year-old boy inserted his arm through the door of an electrical transformer located in an alley way near a shopping centre); *Lengyel v Manitoba Power Commission* (1957) 12 DLR (2d) 126 (Man CA) (7-year-old boy climbed over a snow fence and onto a portable substation).

[23] See *Fergus v Toronto* [1932] OR 257, [1932] 2 DLR 807 (HC) (10-year-old boy allowed to recover from City for severe injuries sustained when he and his 14-year-old brother were playing and placed a lit firecracker in a disused gasoline drum left in a ditch on the roadway); *Dainio v Russell Timber Co Ltd* (1924) 27 OWN 235 (HC); *Yachuk v Oliver Blais Co Ltd* [1949] 3 DLR 1 (JCPC) (9-year-old boy suffered serious burns igniting bulrushes with gasoline that he purchased from a gas station attendant saying it was for his mother's stalled car).

[24] *Paskivski v Canadian Pacific Ltd* [1976] 1 SCR 687, 57 DLR (3d) 280 (railway owed a common law duty of care to a 7-year-old boy of low intelligence who was injured when he reached out and touched a moving train); *Geall v Dominion Creosoting Co* [1918] 55 SCR 587 (respondent's employees negligent when they failed to prop freight cars on blocks and apply air brakes, such that when schoolboys took off handbrake the train cars rolled downhill and collided with passenger coach).

[25] See *Arnold v Gillies* (1978) 8 Alta LR (2d) 21, 93 DLR (3d) 48 (Dist Ct) (two brothers, one aged 8, exonerated for injuries received when a concrete wall on which one child was walking collapsed); *Hurd v City of Hamilton* (n 16 above) (boulevard and stone retaining wall were allurements to a 7-year-old boy who fell to his death while walking along the wall).

[26] *Burbridge v Starr Manufacturing Co* (1921) 54 NSR 121, 56 DLR 658 (CA) (water wheel with an unguarded shaft held to be an allurement to boy of between 6 and 8 who was killed after he went into the wheel house); *Lynch* (n 3 above); *Gough* (n 6 above).

in other situations.[27] This is not to say, of course, that every boy above the age of tender years who claims damages on the basis of the doctrine of allurement will win. The case law on allurement suggests that roughly half of the boy plaintiffs above the age of tender years, but still within the age limits for the doctrine of allurement, were able to claim damages in negligence because of their successful invocation of the doctrine of allurement.[28] Thus, allurement seems to be a powerful option available to boys above the age of tender years who are injured while at play.

However, the same cannot be said for playing girls of a similar age. In fact, of all of the cases listed in *The Canadian Abridgement* on the doctrine of allurement, only one girl between the ages of 7 and 14 is exonerated. Of the sixty-four cases listed under the doctrine of allurement, only fourteen involve girls as plaintiffs—in itself an interesting fact. And all but one of the girls over 7[29] failed in their attempts to obtain exoneration under the doctrine of allurement. It must be frankly admitted that drawing conclusions from such figures is hazardous. This is in part a problem inherent in comparing the outcome of any two legal cases, since it is virtually impossible to find two identical cases. The possibility always exists that there is some internal reason why the cases in question were treated differently. Attempting to compare the treatment of boy and girl plaintiffs under the doctrine of allurement faces another serious hurdle: there are so many fewer cases involving girls that the numbers cannot be given too much weight. This does not mean however that it is futile to attempt to understand the patterns that might exist in the cases that we have before us. But it does make it necessary to look to other features, including the nature of the justifications and the rhetoric of judicial decisions, in order to try to understand what courts are doing with the notion of reasonable behaviour. Further, some humility is always useful in trying to characterize a wide-ranging set of issues in a fair way. Nonetheless, these limitations ought not to prevent us from attempting to understand how judges work within this particular body of law.

As we have seen, boys are often exonerated in situations that they knew to be dangerous on the basis that they reasonably yielded to temptation. In contrast, however, the claims of playing girls are routinely rejected even when the girl's behaviour does not seem nearly as dangerous as that of her male counterpart. In fact, the cases suggest that unless the playing girl can bring herself within the notion of entrapment she is unlikely to recover damages under the doctrine of allurement. The possibility of exonerating the playing girl on the

[27] *Laverdure v Victoria (City)* (1952) 7 WWR 333 (BCSC) (open ditch in a field held to be an allurement to 10-year-old boy).

[28] Thus, of the 29 cases in the Abridgement section on the doctrine of allurement involving boys over age 6, 16 cases allowed the boy to recover under the doctrine of allurement and 13 refused to award damages to the boy: n 21 above.

[29] That is, in 5 cases involving six girls age 7 or over: *MacKeigan v Peake* (1971) 20 DLR (3d) 81 (BCCA); *Nelson v The Pas (Town)* (1969) 67 WWR 580 (Man QB) (two girls aged 9 and 10); *Koehler and Koehler v Pentecostal Assemblies of Canada* (1956) 7 DLR (2d) 616 (BCSC); *O'Connell v Town of Chatham* (1949) 24 MPR 36 (NBCA); *Humeny v Chaikowski* [1931] 3 WWR 398 (Man KB).

ground that she was—like her male counterpart—tempted into a situation of danger rarely seems to occur to courts even as an option. For girls, it seems, it is much more difficult to access any notion of normal, non-culpable temptation. This apparent difference in treatment is corroborated by the justifications and the rhetoric that courts rely on in cases involving boys compared to those involving girls. With playing boys, there are constant echoes of *McHale*, most obvious perhaps in the nostalgic romantic language and in the generosity towards the boy in interpreting both the facts and the law. This leniency towards the indiscretions of 'childhood' is extremely difficult to find in the case of playing girls. Instead, when assessing the carelessness of the playing girl, judges tend to rely on very rigid interpretations of both the facts and the law, often seeming to overlook the youth of the girl in question. Far from being nostalgic and generous, the language and reasoning that predominates in the cases of playing girls is perfunctory, even dismissive, despite the fact that the girls here are plaintiffs, not defendants.

B. See Dick run, run Dick run!, or the temptation of playing boys

The case law that deals with playing boys above the age of tender years is replete with indications that courts are willing to permit recovery on the basis that they were tempted into danger. This is by no means confined to situations in which the playing boy is the unsuspecting victim of hidden danger. Instead, as we have seen, courts routinely relieve the playing boy of responsibility for injuries that occur as result of his own dangerous activities. The parallels with *McHale v Watson* are strong here. Thus, courts accept that under some circumstances it may be so normal or natural for a boy to 'succumb' to temptation that he cannot be held responsible. Underlying these cases is a conception of the playing boy as a curious and mischievous little fellow whose instincts impel him to pursue danger, often to his detriment. As in *McHale*, courts here invoke the language of seduction to relieve the playing boy of responsibility for his failure to exercise prudence. This language implies that to require the boy to resist the dangerous temptress would be contrary to nature, and manifestly the reasonableness standard does not require perfection but only normal or ordinary prudence. As we saw in *McHale*, in the cases involving the playing boy, prudence does not figure prominently as a 'normal' masculine virtue.

1. *A paradigm case*: Gough v National Coal Board[30]

The widely cited English Court of Appeal decision in *Gough v National Coal Board* serves as a useful example of how the courts rely on the temptation rationale to exonerate the playing boy for his imprudence. In *Gough*, a $6\frac{1}{2}$-year-old boy was seriously injured when he jumped off a tram on which he had caught a ride. The tram belonged to the defendant National Coal Board and was

---

[30] n 6 above.

used to transport waste from the colliery to a pit. The track on which the trams ran was unfenced. There was only one warning sign at the foot of the slope. No one accompanied the trams and no one was on duty on the track when it was in use. The track ran near houses and the public routinely crossed it. The evidence revealed that children frequently played on the tracks and even rode on the trams, but that they there were chased away or told not to when they were discovered.[31] Further, the children of the town were routinely warned off the trams both by their parents and by the townspeople more generally. In fact, one witness agreed that for many years it had been 'an almost constant battle' to keep the children off the tramlines.[32] Both the plaintiff and his father testified that 'the boy had been warned by his father not to ride on the trams, and also had been told many times of the danger of so doing'.[33] Indeed, the boy himself testified that he knew it was wrong to ride on the trams because his father had told him not to do it.[34] At trial, Finnemore J gave judgment in favour of the young plaintiff on the basis that slow-moving trams were singularly tempting to small boys, that the defendants had not done everything they could to prevent such boys from jumping on the trams, and that the plaintiff did not appreciate the real danger of what he was doing.[35] He awarded the boy £4,000 in damages. On appeal, the Court of Appeal unanimously upheld the judgment of Finnemore J.

The most troublesome of the issues in *Gough* concerns the boy's awareness of the danger. Despite this, both courts permit the boy to recover on the ground that some situations present boys with such irresistible temptations that they should not be responsible for succumbing to them. Indeed, the idea of temptation is deeply embedded into the description of the facts of the case. Thus, for example, after explaining the location of the tramway, Finnemore J at trial states that 'boys used to yield to the temptation of getting a ride on this tramway'.[36] Similarly, he says that he could think of 'few things more likely to tempt small boys than a slow-moving set of trams on which a boy can get for a little distance a pleasant and unusual ride. From time immemorial boys have always been anxious to get rides, and it has always been a very real allurement to them'.[37] Finnemore J describes the status of the boy after he had jumped on the tramway in the following terms: 'if the child, as I find he was in this case, was a licensee over the whole of that land through which the tram track ran, he did not cease to be a licensee when he succumbed to the very temptation against which he ought to have been protected'.[38] Finnemore J later finds that the fact that the boy was warned does not harm—and indeed may actually assist—his chances of recovery.[39] He concludes that regardless of the many warnings

---

[31] Testimony of the retired colliery worker Peter Jones (ibid 1285), and the witness Mr EJ Rees and the colliery manager Mr Ronald Williams (1290).   [32] ibid 1286 (testimony of Mr Rees).
[33] ibid 1290.   [34] ibid.
[35] ibid 1289–1290 (per Singleton LJ summarizing the judgment of Finnemore J at trial).
[36] ibid 1287 (quoted in the judgment of Singleton LJ).
[37] ibid 1289, 1292 (quoted with approval by Singleton LJ and Birkett LJ).
[38] ibid 1292–1293 (quoted with approval by Birkett LJ).
[39] ibid 1293 (quoted with approval by Birkett LJ).

given to the boy, 'he was extremely likely to succumb to the temptation' of the slow-moving tramway.[40] Thus, the concept of temptation seems inextricably interwoven into the decisions in *Gough*. As we shall see, in its depiction of temptation as a dangerous seductress and the succumbing boy as her hapless prey, *Gough* is typical of the decisions that exonerate the tempted boy. There are also powerful continuities here with *McHale*, particularly in the dominance of a romantic language of boyhood that comes to the fore to exonerate boyish imprudence.

2. *The dangerous temptress and the playing boy*

The view of the boy as the plaything of dangerously seductive impulses that was so central to *McHale* also figures prominently in allurement cases on the temptation of the playing boy. The judgments in *Gough* impute invidious intention to the source of the temptation. They also rely on language more typical of sexual situations than of childhood play. So the tramline is 'dangerous but very tempting and attractive',[41] a deadly and seductive force that is actually 'flaunted' in front of the tormented boy who eventually and perhaps inevitably 'succumbs'.[42] In fact, Finnemore J even suggests that '[f]orbidden fruit is not less tempting than when permissible: in fact it is often more tempting'.[43] Indeed, characterization of the source of temptation as a cunning and dangerous seductress is also apparent in other cases that exonerate the playing boy.

For instance, in *Cooke v Midland Great Western Railway of Ireland*, Lord Atkinson describes unguarded vehicles or machines as '*calculated to attract or allure*' boys or children to intermeddle with them.[44] The attribution of invidious intention and the (apparently inextricable) language of seduction are also apparent in *Lengyel v Manitoba Power Commission*. There, the court describes the portable substation as 'a device *calculated to attract* small boys, to *arouse* their curiosity'.[45] It is 'fascinating and fatal'.[46] As in *Gough*, the very fact of the inaccessibility of the dangerous object seems to translate into that object's increased desirability. Thus, in *Lengyel* the fence surrounding the substation, which is 'leaning *invitingly* inward',[47] serves not as a warning but rather as a further enticement. Similarly, in *Holdman v Hamlyn* the English Court of

---

[40] Gough (n 6 above) 1293.

[41] ibid (per Birkett LJ quoting with approval the judgment of Finnemore J).

[42] ibid 1293 (per Singleton LJ quoting with approval the judgment of Finnemore J).   [43] ibid.

[44] (n 6 above) 237 [emphasis added]. See also Lord Collins's use of the notion of an 'irresistible attraction' to ground the defendant's potential liability to the injured child.

[45] *Lengyel* (n 22 above) 132 [emphasis added]. Similarly, in *Van Oudenhove*, the court found that a crawl space under a cabin was 'an almost ideal hiding place for children playing hide-and-seek and in that sense the crawl space might be said to constitute an allurement or enticement to children': (n 22 above) 156. Later, Allen JA also notes that the doctrine of allurement must be interpreted in the light of the fact that 'the law recognizes that children may be less careful than adults and they may be tempted to play with things or climb onto things capable of causing them harm, but which would present neither an attraction nor deception to adults who would probably avoid them as being both dirty and dangerous': ibid 158.   [46] *Lengyel* (ibid) 133.

[47] ibid (per Tritschler JA quoting Freedman J at trial) [emphasis added].

Appeal upholds a judgment in favour of a 10-year-old boy who was seriously injured after he failed to follow the defendant's instructions to get down off of a stack of grain. According to the Court of Appeal, the boy's disobedience did not preclude him from recovering because, as Scott LJ puts it, 'there was a terrible allurement there to tempt the boy'.[48] Once again, the boy's awareness that he ought not to do something actually seems to increase that activity's allurement. Thus, Scott LJ states that 'the presence of possible danger—not too obvious to frighten—is of itself an exciting attraction'.[49] It all adds up, in the Court of Appeal's assessment, to a 'perfectly irresistible temptation' to the boy.[50]

As in *McHale*, this depiction of the source of danger as a powerful seductress is closely related to the portrayal of the boy as a non-agent—an object upon which this seductress inevitably works her power. Thus, in *Gough* the judgments continually reiterate the description of the boy as yielding or succumbing to the temptation to ride the trams.[51] Similarly, Singleton LJ's reference to the 'wantonness of infancy',[52] with its implication of actions that are 'random, heedless, reckless or purposeless',[53] underscores the view that the boy's behaviour is essentially impulsive rather than purposive. Other cases that exonerate the tempted boy also suggest that an external force impels the boy to act dangerously. In fact, in *Lynch v Nurdin* itself, Lord Denman CJ responds to the argument that the boy was responsible for his own injury by stating that since the defendant's carelessness tempted the child, 'he ought not to reproach the child with yielding to that temptation'.[54] This kind of 'duress' analysis is often relied upon to exonerate playing boys in similar situations. For instance, in *Yachuk v Oliver Blais Co Ltd*,[55] the House of Lords refused to impute contributory negligence to two boys aged 9 and 7, one of whom was severely burned when they dipped a bulrush into a pail of gasoline. Although the boys had lied to obtain the gasoline, Lord du Parcq applied the principle from *Lynch* and held that since the gas station attendant culpably tempted the boys, he could not now reproach the boys for yielding to that temptation. Indeed, the House of Lords found that the gas station attendant was the 'real and only cause of the mischief'.[56] Similarly, in *Dainio v Russell Timber Co Ltd*, Wright J held that the plaintiff's act of setting fire to the fuse 'could not be said to be his voluntary act so as to incapacitate him from recovering'.[57] In *Arnold v Gillies*, the court found that it was the boy's 'inquisitive and frequently mischievous disposition' that '*prompted him*' to climb the fence.[58] Thus, the concept of temptation, with its implication that the culpable exercise of agency lies elsewhere, comes in to exonerate the imprudence of the playing boy.

---

[48] *Holdman v Hamlyn* [1943] KB 664 (CA).   [49] ibid.   [50] ibid.

[51] *Gough* (n 6 above) 197.

[52] ibid 1287–1288, quoting *Latham* (n 6 above) 413 (per Hamilton LJ).

[53] *The Concise English Dictionary* (London: Cassell/Omega Books, 1982) 1261 [entry under 'wanton'].   [54] (n 3 above) 76.

[55] n 23 above.

[56] ibid 6, quoting Lord Denman CJ in *Lynch* (n 3 above) 38–39.   [57] (n 23 above) 235.

[58] (n 25 above) 56 [emphasis added].

The decisions in *Gough* are also characteristic of the case law on the playing boy in their suggestion that the overwhelming nature of the temptation in question destroys the boy's mental independence, reducing him to an automaton. By stressing the boy's appreciation of danger rather than his bare knowledge or awareness, the courts in *Gough* are able to conclude that the boy was effectively 'trapped', although it was the temptation rather than lack of knowledge that ensnared him. For instance, Singleton LJ states that '[t]he slowly moving trucks were an attraction to boys. Boys knew they ought not to get on them, but can it be said that this boy appreciated the risk he was running?'[59] Similarly, in *Culkin v McFie* the court awarded damages to the 7-year-old boy who was injured while trying to catch sugar that was falling from sacks on a passing lorry. The description is illuminating: 'This is not a mere lorry, but a species of juggernaut dropping sugar into the roadway as it goes and blinding children of such tender years as the plaintiff's to the danger of too close an approach to it'.[60] In these circumstances, the court found that the danger 'to this plaintiff was in effect a concealed one'.[61] A similar point is eloquently made by Justice Holmes in *United States Zinc & Chemical Company v Britt*: '[W]hile it is very plain that temptation is not invitation, it may be held that knowingly to establish and expose, unfenced, to children of an age when they follow a bait as mechanically as a fish, something that is certain to attract them, has the legal effect of an invitation to them although not to an adult'.[62] The very temptation has the effect of so overcoming the plaintiff's understanding that he cannot appreciate the risks inherent in what he admittedly knew was wrong. In this sense, as in *Gough*, the risks are hidden or concealed to him. This emphasis on appreciation rather than bare knowledge of the risk is also more generally characteristic of the case law on tempted boys.[63]

---

[59] *Gough* (n 6 above) 1288.   [60] [1939] 3 All ER 613, 620 (KB).   [61] ibid.
[62] 258 US 268, 275 (1921).
[63] Thus, for instance, in *Mayer*, Martin JA upheld the jury's conclusion that a warning to the 9-year-old boy who was later electrocuted while climbing an electric light pole 'was not sufficient to warrant a finding that the child appreciated the nature of the risk he was incurring by climbing the pole': (n 22 above) 1078. Similarly, in *Dainio v Russell Timber Co Ltd*, the court found that the 12-year-old boy who was injured when he set fire to the fuse 'did not appreciate the danger': (n 23 above) 235. In *Jones v Calgary (City)*, in the course of exonerating the 9-year-old boy who was injured when he put his hand into an electric transformer box, Kirby J cites with approval the statement that occupiers must take reasonable care to protect children who are 'too young to appreciate the danger of some attractive object': (n 22 above) 600, citing *Winfield's Law of Torts* (9th edn) 587. The court in *Lengyel* (n 22 above) also relies on this passage from Winfield as well as on Birkett LJ's discussion of lack of appreciation and traps from *Gough* (n 6 above). In *Lengyel* the court exonerated the 7-year-old plaintiff who, along with his two 10-year-old brothers, climbed over a fence and onto a portable electric transformer. The boys admittedly knew they should not have done so but the court nonetheless concluded that the boys' knowledge of wrongdoing was not an obstacle to their success: ibid 133–134, citing Birkett LJ in *Gough* (ibid) 1292. Similarly in *Paskivski*, Dickson J (as he then was) upheld the trial judgment in favour of the 7-year-old plaintiff who was injured when he reached out and touched a passing train, in part on the basis that the evidence tended to establish that even where they were warned such children 'were incapable of understanding and comprehending the hazards to which they were exposed by the slowly moving train': (n 24 above) 708. See also *Walker v Sheffield Bronze* (1977) 77 DLR (3d) 377, 384–385.

3. *The plaything of nature*

Nonetheless, one might ask why the boy who succumbs to these impulses (how-ever seductive they might be) should be exonerated. Once again the parallels with *McHale* are strong. When courts exonerate boys on the ground that they could not help but yield to the dangerous temptation, they justify doing so on the basis that it is natural or normal for a boy to respond to seductive impulses. The boy is not responsible for yielding to the temptation because his action is dictated by his 'nature'. Thus, the court in *Gough* insists that boys have been behaving this way since 'time immemorial'.[64] The virtual inevitability of the boy's behaviour suggests that it is simply a law of nature. Indeed, in *Lynch v Nurdin* itself the court insists that the boy should not be reproached for yield-ing to temptation since he 'merely indulged the natural instincts of a child in amusing himself with the empty cart and deserted horse'.[65] The notion that the boy's actions were 'natural' and thus presumably beyond his control thus justi-fies the refusal to impute culpability. This is despite the fact that the court itself describes the boy as having 'indulged' his instincts and having acted 'without prudence or thought'.[66] This suggests that at bottom the temptation defence turns on the view that in a particular situation the child is merely the instrument of 'natural instincts'—instincts so powerful that we cannot reasonably expect the child under their sway to exercise prudence or thought, so irresistible that it is 'natural' for the child to indulge them.[67]

It seems that the underpinning of this willingness to exonerate boys on the basis of temptation is found in the view that boys are by nature curious and mischievous. In a passage strikingly similar to *McHale*'s discussion of judicial notice, Lord Atkinson opens his oft-quoted decision in *Cooke* by referring to the very qualities of childhood that are germane to the temptation argument: 'every person must be taken to know that young children and boys are of a very inquisitive and frequently mischievous disposition, and are likely to med-dle with whatever happens to come within their reach'.[68] Similarly, in *Holdman v Hamlyn*, in the course of finding for the 10-year-old plaintiff, the English Court of Appeal frequently refers to the boy's 'natural childish propensity to stray beyond the stack-top'.[69] In *Culkin v McFie* the court notes that the 7-year-old plaintiff 'merely indulged in the natural instincts of a child in chasing this tantalising offer of a free sweetmeat'.[70] Dickson J, speaking for the major-ity of the Supreme Court of Canada in *Paskivski*, finds that a slowly passing train is an allurement to a 7-year-old boy because it 'would test the patience of children and afford them ample opportunity to indulge their natural propensity

---

[64] (n 6 above) 1289, 1292.   [65] (n 3 above) 76.   [66] ibid.

[67] As one court has put it, there will be no exoneration 'unless the temptation which it presents is such that no normal child could be expected to restrain himself from intermeddling even if he knows that to intermeddle is wrong': *O'Leary v John A Wood Ltd* [1964] IR 269, 277 (SC Ireland).

[68] *Cooke* (n 6 above) 237.

[69] (n 48 above) 140, Scott LJ. See also ibid 139, Scott LJ; 141–142, DuParcq LJ.

[70] (n 60 above) 621, citing *Lynch* (n 3 above) 38.

for play or mischief'.[71] These are but a few of the many references to the mischievous nature of children so often called forth to exonerate the playing boy.[72]

One of the subtler ways in which the case law depicts the tempted boy as the plaything of nature is through its reliance on causation and reasonable foreseeability. By invoking such concepts rather than the kind of duty analysis that ordinarily applies with the acts of intervening agents,[73] courts reinforce the notion that the boy's dangerous behaviour is akin to a causal regularity of the natural world. As the court in *Gough* puts it, children like Gerwyn Gough 'often are only links in a chain of causation extending from such initial negligence to the subsequent injury'.[74] Similarly, because courts see the dangerous behaviour of the playing boy as so natural that it can be predicted as easily as other natural events, reasonable foreseeability plays an important role in how courts approach these cases. Thus, for instance, in *Jolley v Sutton London Borough Council*, the House of Lords rejected the argument that *novus actus* defeated the claim of the 14-year-old boy whose back was crushed when a boat, abandoned on the defendant's property, collapsed on him.[75] The boy and his friend had jacked up the boat to repair it. The House of Lords rejected the Court of Appeal's finding that, *inter alia*, the boys' actions 'broke the chain of causation' and restored the trial judge's finding that the accident was foreseeable.

---

[71] (n 24 above) 709.

[72] In *Arnold v Gillies* the court found that a fence in a state of disrepair was an allurement because the defendant should have known of 'the inquisitive and mischievous disposition of children and their likelihood to meddle with anything within their reach': (n 25 above) 54. And in *Mayer v Prince Albert*, Lamont JA argues that the steps and the fire alarm box on the electric light pole were allurements to the 9-year-old, since the boy 'did only what a boy would naturally do': (n 22 above) 1075. In the same case, Martin JA states that the 'unfortunate boy did only what boys would naturally do in climbing the electric light pole': ibid 1079. The notion that it is natural or instinctual for boys to engage in imprudent activities is also found in *Dainio v Russell Timber Co Ltd* (n 23 above). There the court granted damages to a boy who was injured when he set fire to a fuse with a cap attached, which he had found in a field. In his one-page decision, Wright J emphasizes that the boy's actions were due to 'boyish curiosity' and to 'natural curiosity on the part of a boy who did not appreciate the danger': ibid 235. Similarly, in *Hurd v City of Hamilton*, Britton J finds that the boulevard and retaining wall were tempting to the 7-year-old boy who fell to his death. In arriving at this conclusion, the court states that a child would 'quite naturally and without motive or reason other than childish playfulness, go to the wall and look over, and might, as in this case the child did, walk backwards, not appreciating the danger': (n 16 above) 882. In *Bouvier v Fee* the Supreme Court of Canada relieved the 7-year-old boy of any responsibility for injuries he sustained when he put his hand in a cement mixer. The Court noted that the 'allurement of a piece of machinery in motion for a small child is notorious': [1932] SCR 118, [1932] 2 DLR 424, 427.

[73] This contrasts with the ordinary treatment of intervening acts as going to either contributory negligence (for acts of the plaintiff) or *novus actus* (for other intervening acts): Fleming (n 6 above) 246, 302 ff. Ordinarily, deliberate intervening acts absolve the defendant of part or all his responsibility: ibid 246–250. But as Clerk points out, '[i]ntervening conduct by a third party not responsible, or not fully responsible, for his actions will be much less likely to constitute a *novus actus*. An act of a child is much less likely than an act of an adult to break the chain of causation, albeit the child may have acted deliberately and voluntarily.' JF Clerk, *Clerk and Lindsell on Torts* (gen ed AM Dugdale) (18th edn, London: Sweet and Maxwell, 2000) 78.

[74] (n 6 above) 1288, quoting from the judgment of Hamilton LJ in *Latham* (n 6 above) 413.

[75] (n 7 above) 415–416.

Similarly, in *Lynch v Nurdin*, Lord Denman CJ held that since the boy's action was easily foreseeable, he was entitled to recover.[76] In *Yachuk v Oliver Blais Co Ltd*, the House of Lords finds that the boy cannot be precluded from recovering simply because 'he was tempted to do that which a child of his years might be reasonably expected to do'.[77] In *Davis v St Mary's Demolition & Excavation Co Ltd*, the English Court of Queen's Bench relied on foreseeability to establish liability on the part of a demolition company for injuries the 12-year-old plaintiff sustained when a wall he and other boys were pulling apart collapsed on him. In arriving at this conclusion, Ormerod J states that if boys of 12 go to a building site like the one here, 'it does seem one of the most likely things that in the course of an afternoon's play there will be interference in some way or another with some part of the building, which must offer a constant allurement and temptation to any child who is within sight of it'.[78] These are but a few illustrations of a very common strand of reasoning in the case law on tempted boys.[79]

The understanding of the tempted boy as ultimately the plaything of nature rather than as an agent seems to account for a somewhat surprising feature of the cases that exonerate playing boys on the basis of temptation. As *Gough* itself illustrates, courts in these cases routinely refuse to hold that warnings about the relevant danger necessarily work to prevent playing boys from recovering in negligence.[80] In fact, this aspect of the temptation cases is nicely summarized

---

[76] Closely related is the idea that '[a] prudent man will guard against the possible negligence of others, when experience shows such negligence to be common': Clerk (n 73 above) 110, citing Lord du Parcq in *Grant v Sun Shipping Co* [1948] AC 549, 567 (HL). And in the case of children, the law commonly holds that adults must be prepared for children to be less careful than adults would be in similar situations: Clerk (ibid) 574: an occupier must be prepared for children to be less careful than adults, citing Occupier's Liability Act 1957, s 2(3)(a). As noted, the finding that the actions of the tempted boy are 'common' and therefore reasonably foreseeable also relies to a significant extent on the willingness to take judicial notice of the curious and mischievous nature of boys. Because an understanding of the likely actions of the playing boy is seen as part of the common sense apparatus of the ordinary person, they are both the subject of judicial notice and seen as sufficiently common and reasonably foreseeable to ground an enhanced duty of care.

[77] (n 23 above) 8.   [78] [1954] 1 All ER 578, 580 (QB).

[79] See also *Fergus v Toronto* (n 23 above) 808; *Jones v Calgary* (n 22 above) 603; *Culkin v McFie* (n 60 above) 621; *Laverdure v Victoria (City)* (n 27 above) 335; *Dainio v Russell Timber Co Ltd* (n 23 above) 235; *Paskivski v CP Ltd* (n 24 above) 709; *LeBel v Edmunston* [1954] 1 DLR 377, 385 (NBSC); *Holdman v Hamlyn* (n 48 above) 141; *Cooke v MGW Ry of Ireland* (n 6 above) 238–239; *Pannett v McGuinness & Co* [1972] 3 All ER 137 (CA) 142, 144; *Van Oudenhove* (n 22 above) 156; *Bouvier* (n 72 above) 426–427; *Walker* (n 63 above) 63; *Seamone v Fancy* (n 19 above) 652; *Lengyel* (n 22 above) 132.

[80] Thus, for example, in *Jolley* the 14-year-old boy was awarded damages despite the fact that the boat that crushed him had a sign on it warning 'Danger do not touch this vehicle unless you are the owner': (n 7 above) 411. In *Mayer*, the court awarded damages to the 9-year-old boy even though his father had specifically warned him not to climb light poles: (n 22 above) 1077. Similarly, in *Yachuk*, the fact that the injured boy had been warned to keep away from his father's gasoline torch did not preclude him from recovering for the injuries he suffered when playing with gasoline: (n 23 above) 7–8. In *Walker*, the court similarly refused to find culpability on the part of the 9½-year-old boy who placed a lighted match in a barrel, even though he admittedly knew that playing with matches was wrong: (n 63 above) 384. In *Lengyel* the court held that it was no defence that the 7-year-old plaintiff and his older brothers knew they should not have been climbing on the portable substation, since they were 'entitled to more than a warning that they should not be upon this inviting

in *Mueller*. There, Macdonald JA insists that it is 'idle' to warn 'a boy whose curiosity is excited'. He continues: 'The fact that he was a bright boy, in my opinion, increased his danger. Such a boy is naturally keen to investigate the unusual, and is therefore more liable to put himself in the way of injury from things which excite his youthful curiosity than is the dull and less enterprising boy'.[81] Thus, the qualities that make the boy more imprudent, more prone to pursue—and even to be enticed by—danger, are paradoxically the very qualities that are most valued in the boy and thus most in need of judicial protection.[82] As in *McHale*, it seems that it is the best in a boy's nature that makes him vulnerable to imprudence.

Powerful means are available to exonerate playing boys for their dangerous activities. As *Gough* illustrates and other cases on the tempted boy confirm, this is not by any means confined to situations in which the playing boy is the unsuspecting victim of hidden danger. In the cases that find for the playing boy, courts rely on the language of seduction to relieve the playing boy of responsibility for his pursuit of what is often patently dangerous. Thus, the boy is described as yielding or succumbing to an overwhelming temptation, enticement, or allurement. The source of danger is often portrayed as a dangerous and even malevolent seductress, inviting the boy, enticing him, tempting him, and using her attractions to blind him to the danger. And since he is a boy—curious, mischievous, and perhaps a bit contrary—he is often drawn in at least in part by that which is forbidden. Courts insist that he cannot be held responsible for it is only natural that a boy will succumb to the temptation. To hold such a boy responsible would not only require him to do the impossible and triumph over nature, it would also punish him for possessing in abundance the best elements of boyhood—curiosity, intelligence, and daring.

C. See Jane watch!, or the allurement of the playing girl

> [N]o case, so far as we know, has ever laid it down as a rule of law that less care is required of a woman than of a man. Sex is certainly no excuse for negligence, and if we judge ordinary care by the standard of what is commonly looked for and expected, we should probably agree that a woman would be likely to be more prudent, careful and particular in many positions and in the

and attractive apparatus': (n 22 above) 133. Similarly, if a warning is not sufficient to deter the 'intermeddling' of a curious boy, then at least where playing boys are concerned a warning may not discharge one's duty of care: *Jones v Calgary* (n 22 above) 604. Indeed, these are but a few examples of the fact that the court is willing to apply the concept of temptation even where the boy engaged in dangerous play was warned about or knew about the danger: *Paskivski v CP Ltd* (n 24 above) 697–698; *Pannett v McGuinness* (n 79 above); *Holdman v Hamlyn* (n 48 above); *Laverdure v Victoria (City)* (n 27 above); *Culkin v McFie* (n 60 above); *Baker v Flint & PMR Co U* 35 NW 836 (Mich 1888); *Arnold v Gillies* (n 25 above); *Bouvier* (n 72 above); *Burbridge v Starr Manufacturing* (n 26 above).

[81] *Mueller v BC Electric Railway* [1911] 1 WWR 56, 58 (BCCA) (11½-year-old boy who was killed while playing with dangerous wires about which he had just been warned was permitted recovery).

[82] Here note the similarity with the child defendant cases where the imprudent behaviour of boys is so often linked to the very qualities—specifically male, I think—that are most prized in boys.

performance of many duties than a man would. She would, for example, be more vigilant and indefatigable in her care of a helpless child; she would be more cautious to avoid unknown dangers; she would be more particular to keep within the limits of absolute safety when the dangers which threatened were such as only great strength and courage could venture to encounter.[83]

If the cases on the temptation of the playing boy illustrate judicial generosity to the indiscretions of childhood, closer inspection reveals that this conception of childhood may actually be quite exclusive. The language of childhood with its invocation of seduction and attendant view of the child as the plaything of nature, so dominant in the case of playing boys, is all but absent in the case of girls. Indeed, the gendered implications of seduction seem borne out by the case law: the notion that children are so prone to being seduced by danger that they must be forgiven for their heedlessness seems both predicated on and confined to boyhood. In this sense, Lord Atkinson's discussion of childhood culpability in *Cooke* seems strangely—though no doubt unintentionally—apt. There, he repeatedly refers to the 'inquisitive and frequently mischievous disposition(s)' of 'young children and boys', features which make them vulnerable to attraction or allurement. But Lord Atkinson's description of who inhabits the 'playground' of childhood contains a significance absence—what of the girl who is not a young child? This might simply be a rhetorical oddity were it not for the fact that it so accurately describes the reach of the doctrine of allurement. For as we shall see, the words Cooley J uttered so long ago in *Hassenyer* seem prophetic: because judges ask 'what is commonly looked for from one of her sex', they do seem to hold the playing girl to a higher standard of prudence than that required of the playing boy. Thus, while the temptation argument offers a useful option for the playing boy who engages in dangerous activities, it is extremely difficult to find a case in which it is similarly deployed to the advantage of a playing girl.

1. *A paradigm case:* O'Connell v Town of Chatham[84]

Once again, it is helpful to begin by focusing on a paradigm case—a case in which a playing girl may have had a plausible allurement claim. *O'Connell v Town of Chatham* serves as a useful example. For years, children in the Town of Chatham had been coasting on Queen Street. Citizens concerned with the safety of the children eventually approached the Mayor who advised them that Council would 'try to accommodate the children in this winter pastime'.[85] Eventually, the town approved the erection of barricades across the street. These barricades were not permanent but were removed and then placed back in position when conditions were good for coasting on Queen Street. They were designed to check the flow of traffic on the street and thereby lessen the danger to the children coasting down the street. On a December night, after the illuminated

---

[83] *Michigan Central Railroad v Hassenyer* 48 Mich 205, 209–210 (SC 1882) (per Cooley J, footnotes omitted) (13-year-old girl killed by a backing engine).   [84] n 29 above.
[85] ibid 30.

barricades were set up for the evening, an 8-year-old girl named Dolores O'Connell went coasting on Queen Street with her friend. Unfortunately, she was struck and seriously injured by a car that slid across the partially barricaded icy intersection. She brought an action in negligence against the town of Chatham claiming, *inter alia*, that by erecting the barricades the town set up an allurement for children who were thereby led to believe that coasting on the street was safe. In the circumstances, she alleged that the town had failed to discharge the duty it owed her.

At trial, Michaud CJKBD held in favour of Dolores O'Connell on the ground that the town had failed to take reasonable care to ensure that the coasting street was safe for invitees like her.[86] Having allured her to believe that the street was safe for coasting, the town came under an obligation to make the street safe. On appeal, however, the majority of the New Brunswick Court of Appeal allowed Chatham's appeal and dismissed Dolores O'Connell's claim. Justices Harrison and Hughes held that the barricades could not constitute an invitation and therefore the children who were coasting on Queen Street were not doing so as invitees. Instead, at best Dolores O'Connell was a licensee and thus was entitled to be protected only from hidden dangers.[87] They also found that Chatham did nothing to create an allurement to the plaintiff. This was because the barricades and lights were simply a warning and that warning was 'plain to anybody to see [sic]'.[88] Thus, there was 'no hidden danger and therefore no trap'.[89] They therefore dismissed Dolores O'Connell's claim against the town. Richards CJ in dissent would have affirmed the trial judge's holding. He points out that the street presented an allurement and trap, noting that the barricades were 'erected for the purpose of protecting coasting and were intended to be, and were in fact, so regarded'.[90]

Even this cursory description suggests the contrast between the treatment of the playing boy in *Gough* and that of the playing girl in *O'Connell*. Unlike courts in *Gough* and other cases involving the playing boy, here the courts do not even seem aware of the possibility that the girl could rely on temptation. Instead, they treat the doctrine of allurement as if it were exhausted by the notion of entrapment. Thus, after stating that as a licensee the girl was entitled to be protected only from hidden dangers, the majority decisions then go on repeatedly to characterize the danger involved in sliding down Queen Street as obvious and familiar, not hidden, as plain or apparent,[91] with the result that Dolores O'Connell is not entitled to recover. The implication seems to be that unless the town had actually set a trap for the girl, they would not have been liable for her injuries. The result, in contrast with *Gough* and many other cases

---

[86] ibid 52. Interestingly, however, Michaud CJKBD assessed the girl's damages at only $1,500. This was despite the fact that she suffered several injuries including a broken vocal cord, she was hospitalized for over a month, lost a year of school, and still had only partially recovered her voice three years after the injury. She had claimed $31,000 in damages for these injuries.

[87] ibid 63, Harrison J, quoting *Clerk and Lindsell on Torts* (gen ed H Potter), (9th edn, London: Sweet and Maxwell, 1937) 658; ibid 67, Hughes J, quoting Lord Sumner in *Mersey Docks and Harbour Board v Proctor* [1923] AC 253, 274 (HL).   [88] ibid 68.

[89] ibid 69, Hughes J.   [90] ibid 59–60.   [91] ibid 63–64, Harrison J; 68–70, Hughes J.

involving the playing boy, is that any indication that the girl knew of the danger seems to operate to preclude her recovery. *O'Connell* thus suggests that the playing girl may have considerable difficulty gaining judicial forgiveness where any girlish imprudence may be involved. Unlike her male counterpart, it seems the reasonable girl would never be tempted.

Whatever the court's straightforward rhetoric implies, the analysis seems more complex when compared with the decision in *Gough* and other playing boy cases. As with any two cases, *Gough* and *O'Connell* are not perfectly identical. Nonetheless, the similarities between the two cases are significant enough to justify comparison. In *Gough* and in *O'Connell* the defendants owned as well as occupied the relevant property. Both defendants were aware of and implicated in the dangerous play of the children on their property. Although the question of immunities or legal protections arising from the status of public authorities is not discussed in either case, both cases involve defendants who are public authorities and thus enjoy similar legal protections as a result thereof. Accordingly there does not seem to be much reason to distinguish the cases on that ground. Further, the cases were decided within a few years of each other and the courts rely on many of the same precedents.[92] *O'Connell* may however seem more complex than *Gough* in one respect: it may look like liability for non-feasance, since another agent—the driver—caused the actual injury to Dolores. However, as pointed out by the trial and Court of Appeal dissent decisions in Dolores's favour, the town in *O'Connell* took positive action that created the dangerous situation. So both cases do involve misfeasance claims. And unlike in *Gough*, which involved activities on private property, the property in Chatham was public so there could be no question of trespass. To some degree, the characterization of both children as licensees actually obscures the fact that it was only the allurement that transformed Gerwyn Gough from a trespasser to a licensee, whereas Dolores O'Connell was entitled to be on public property and so could not have been classified as a trespasser. Further, whereas the NCB had a warning sign and its employees routinely chased children away, Chatham actually put up protective barricades and lanterns when conditions were good for sliding. In fact these measures were designed to 'accommodate' children and may have enticed children who would not otherwise have thought of sliding on a city street. Thus, while the two cases are not perfectly identical, there is more than sufficient similarity between them to justify comparison.

---

[92] These include *Latham* (n 6 above), *Winfield on the Law of Tort* (4th and 5th edns), and *Liddle v Yorkshire (North Riding) County Council* [1934] 2 KB 101. However, even when the courts quote from similar sources, they emphasize very different elements. So, for instance, in *Gough*, Singleton LJ quotes *Winfield on the Law of Tort* to the effect that '[a]n occupier must take reasonable care to see that children . . . are protected against injury from that danger either by warning which is intelligible to them or by some other means': (n 6 above) 1289, quoting *Winfield* (5th edn) 587. A very different tone is apparent in the quote from *Winfield* in the judgment of Hughes J in *O'Connell*: 'The only respect in which a child differs from an adult is that what is reasonably safe for an adult may not be reasonably safe for a child, and what is a warning to an adult may be none to a child': (n 29 above) 68, quoting *Winfield* (4th edn) 576.

Yet despite these similarities, the approach to the dangerous play of the injured children is different in the two cases. To begin with, the court seems much more willing to impute awareness of danger to the playing child in *O'Connell* than it did in *Gough*. In *O'Connell* Dolores testified that she was not afraid of sliding on the hill because the cars slowed down when they came to the barricades.[93] However, because she agreed with counsel's statement that if a car failed to stop it would be dangerous for a coasting child, Hughes J concludes that 'she was familiar with the danger, there was no hidden danger and therefore no trap'.[94] Yet in *Gough* there was a warning sign, the boy himself had also been warned many times of the danger involved in riding on the trams, and had been told not to do so. He admitted to being aware both of the danger and of his disobedience.[95] But even in these circumstances, the English Court of Appeal found that the moving trams were a 'concealed danger to the boy, and, therefore, properly described as a trap'.[96] In *Gough*, the court finds that the boy was effectively trapped despite his awareness of the danger. This finding is supported by the court invoking the notion of a 'moral trap' from *Latham* and thus the prohibition on leading children 'into temptation'.[97] But *O'Connell* actually seems easier to reconcile with the notion of being tempted into danger. Indeed, at trial Michaud CJKBD found that the town should have 'anticipated that children would be tempted or attracted or allured by the placing of the barricades and the lanterns', which led them 'to believe that they were protected while coasting on Queen Street, while in fact they were not'.[98] Yet the Court of Appeal majority in *O'Connell* does not even consider the moral trap or temptation option and straightforwardly finds that if the girl admitted under questioning that the situation could be dangerous, then the danger was sufficiently obvious that she cannot claim entrapment.

This failure to consider the moral trap argument is closely related to other, more subtle, differences between the two cases. Rather than calling attention to and articulating the special characteristics that attend childhood, *O'Connell* seems either to ignore the qualities of childhood or to treat them as irrelevant to the resolution of the issues. In *Gough* the judgments repeatedly insist that even the boy's subjective awareness of the danger will not preclude him from recovering so long as his youth prevented him from properly appreciating that danger. But in *O'Connell*, there is no hint of this very child-centred approach to imputing foresight of danger. So although Dolores did not even have subjective awareness of the danger much less true 'appreciation', the court refuses to award her damages because it finds that the danger was objectively foreseeable. Harrison J states, 'The licensee is not entitled to be protected from the existing risks of premises unless there is [*sic*] hidden dangers. Here there was no hidden danger. The danger was of a kind that *could be apprehended by children* as well as by

---

[93] These include *Latham* (n 6 above), *Winfield on the Law of Tort* 68–69, evidence of Dolores O'Connell as quoted by Hughes J.   [94] ibid 69.

[95] See discussion above, and text accompanying nn 28–38.   [96] (n 6 above) 1292.

[97] ibid 1288, Singleton LJ, quoting Hamilton LJ in *Latham* (n 6 above) 415.

[98] (n 29 above) 52, Michaud CJKBD.

adults. I refer now to children eight years of age such as the plaintiff.'[99] Similarly, after finding that the lights and barricades served as a warning of the danger of sliding on the street, Hughes J insists that the danger is 'plain to anybody' and thus '[c]hildren are in the same position as adults in that respect.'[100] The two cases also adopt strikingly different approaches to consequentialist considerations. *Gough* appears very child-centred in its worry that adopting a narrow definition of allurement would destroy 'the whole doctrine of allurement to children'.[101] In *O'Connell*, however, consequentialist concerns play a very different role. There, Harrison J quotes Farwell J's warning in *Latham* that 'we must be careful not to allow our sympathy with the infant plaintiff to affect our judgment', for too broad an interpretation of the duties that landowners owe to children would have 'disastrous' results.[102]

Ultimately, it may be possible to gain some insight into the judicial treatment of the playing girl by paying attention to the most intangible and yet perhaps the most eloquent absence of all. As noted above, the cases involving playing boys, both as defendants and as plaintiffs, are marked by their invocation of a common vision of childhood, a vision in which the playing boy is by nature peculiarly subject to being seduced by that which is dangerous and forbidden. But both the vision and the language that play such a strong role in exonerating boys are entirely absent from the decisions in *O'Connell*. There are no references to the seductive pull of danger, to the impulsiveness of childhood, or to what is natural or normal for the playing child. The judges who consider the injuries of Dolores O'Connell do not speak of the childish thrill of tobogganing on new-fallen snow. Indeed, the one timid suggestion that Dolores O'Connell may have been allured is instructive: she was allured, the trial judge suggests, not by the thrill of danger nor even by the sheer delight of the activity, but rather by the semblance of safety.[103] So as Cooley J indicated so long ago in *Hassenyer*, courts do seem to believe that the reasonable girl will be 'more cautious to avoid unknown dangers' and 'more particular to keep within the limits of absolute safety'.[104] *O'Connell* suggests that courts are also prepared to give legal expression to this image of the reasonable girl.

2. *Playing with fire: Temptation and the playing girl*

O'Connell may look anomalous set against the backdrop of the cases involving the playing boy, but further examination of the few cases that involve injuries to playing girls above the age of tender years suggests that *O'Connell* is actually quite characteristic of these cases. The implication of *O'Connell*, confirmed in the subsequent case law, is that playing girls will find it very difficult to

---

[99] ibid 64 [emphasis added].   [100] ibid 68.   [101] (n 6 above) 1295, Hodson LJ.

[102] (n 29 above) 64, quoting *Latham* (n 6 above) 408. Interestingly, the judgment in *Gough* requires exactly what the court in *Latham* finds unacceptably burdensome, namely that landowners may be forced 'to employ a groundkeeper to look after the safety of their licensees': *Latham* ibid. The injured plaintiff in *Latham* was a very young girl.   [103] (n 29 above) 47, 52, Michaud CJKBD.

[104] *Hassenyer* (n 83 above) 209.

recover unless they can bring themselves within the restrictive confines of the entrapment branch of allurement. As in *O'Connell*, courts in these cases routinely point to the obviousness of the danger as a reason to reject recovery. And like in *O'Connell*, courts in cases involving the playing girl rely on particularly narrow and rigid interpretations of both the facts and the law. Similarly, courts routinely ignore or minimize the youth of the playing girl, often apparently failing to attach any significance to the fact that she is a child. Perhaps unsurprisingly, then, the robust and romantic language of childhood that characterizes the cases on the temptation of the playing boy is nowhere to be found in the cases on the playing girl. Instead, there is at best impatience with the playing girl who may at times be daring, curious, and dangerously blind to her own safety, just like her male counterpart.

O'Connell's approach to the temptation branch of the doctrine of allurement is more broadly characteristic of the case law on the playing girl in a number of ways. To begin with, as in *O'Connell*, courts routinely deny girls damages in situations that involve even the mildest hint of temptation. So, in contrast with playing boys, it is extremely difficult to find any cases in which a playing girl was allowed to recover damages even though she was warned, had notice, or (much more weakly) as in *O'Connell*, might have noticed the danger had she turned her mind to it. As one of the very few cases on point, *Humeny v Chaikowski* illustrates this apparent unwillingness to invoke the temptation branch of the doctrine of allurement for a playing girl who was warned of the relevant danger. In that case, the Manitoba Court of King's Bench dismissed the claim of a girl who was injured when she got her fingers caught in a bread-mixing machine in the defendant's bake shop. There was evidence that children were in the habit of playing in the vicinity, and Kilgour J accepted that they ran back and forth between the public bake shop and the stairway behind the shop that lead to the plaintiff's sister's apartment.[105] In fact, the children testified that they were invited into the room by the man in charge of the machine. As in *O'Connell* it is the obviousness of the danger, here conclusively established by the fact of a prior warning, that precludes the playing girl from recovering damages. Despite the fact that the children seem to have been attracted by the mixing machine, the word 'allurement' does not even appear in the decision. Instead, the court insists, there is 'no reason for supposing that the children of the neighbourhood would regard this room as a playground'.[106]

In another parallel with *O'Connell*, courts deciding allurement cases involving playing girls typically find that objective foresight of danger is sufficient to disentitle the girl to damages. In contrast with the treatment they often afford to playing boys, courts appear unwilling to permit playing girls to recover damages even when there is much weaker evidence that they were—or more constructively, could have been—aware of the relevant danger. An illustration can be found in *Nelson*. In that case, two girls aged 9 and 10 drowned in a large excavation hole

---

[105] *Humeny* (n 29 above) 399.   [106] ibid 400.

dug by the town of The Pas on land at the edge of the town's limits that was being developed as a park. Workmen 'had consistently chased children away from the park area when they were observed'[107] and the town had been prosecuted, convicted, and fined under a provision of the Criminal Code for failing to protect the excavation by fencing, warnings, or supervision.[108] Counsel for the plaintiff argued that by digging the ditch and permitting it to fill with water, the town created a dangerous allurement. Since the town failed in its duty to protect this allurement with fencings, warnings, or supervision, counsel argued that the town was responsible for the damages that ensued. However, Hunt J summarily dismissed these arguments. He reasoned that the two girls were trespassers and therefore 'the only duty owed to them was not to set a trap. An excavation filled with water is not a trap. That it is dangerous is obvious even to children younger than these two unfortunate girls.'[109] Hunt J found the town's conviction under the Criminal Code irrelevant because '[i]t is obvious that the children did not fall into the excavation by accident and also that they were fully aware of its existence'.[110] Yet he notes that the pits were 'used to dump trees, stumps, rocks, and other material grubbed from the area when it was cleared'.[111] Water accumulated in the excavation in which the girls were drowned because, unlike the other two holes in the area, it had not been completely filled in. But this suggests that the danger may not have been so obvious. There were no warning signs about the dangerous nature of the bottom, no depth indications, and no evidence about the nature of the shoreline. In such circumstances, even in the absence of the 'moral trap' argument, it is not at all clear that the danger was in fact as obvious as Hunt J's conclusory remarks suggest. Further, there was no evidence that these girls were ever warned or chased away from the area. And unlike in *Gough* and other cases involving the playing boy, here Hunt J makes no attempt to ascertain whether these girls actually knew of, much less 'properly appreciated', the danger.[112] Instead, he simply repeats that the dangers of the excavation are 'obvious'.[112] There is no consideration of the temptation argument that is so effective for playing boys. Once again it is the obviousness of the risk, objectively determined, that seems to preclude girls from succeeding in their allurement claim.

It is worth comparing *Nelson* not only to *Gough* but also to the factually similar case of *Laverdure v Victoria (City)*. There, the Supreme Court of British Columbia awarded damages to a 10-year-old boy who fell into an open ditch that the city had dug on a field adjoining the boy's home. This was despite the fact that the boy had been specifically warned by his father to keep away from the ditch. In *Laverdure*, the court does not even mention the obviousness of the

---

[107] (n 29 above) 581.   [108] ibid 583, referring to Criminal Code RSC 1953–54, c 51 s 228(2).
[109] ibid 581.
[110] ibid 583. See here the use of *East Crest Oil*: 'The owner must protect the trespasser on the land from a trap, but he is not called on to protect against a subsequent danger from trespassing on the guard itself raised against that trap. The duty is not to prevent a person from falling into an opening but from falling in "accidentally", that is, accidental as to the existence of the thing holding the threat': *Nelson* (n 29 above) 583, quoting *R v East Crest Oil Co* [1945] SCR 191, 197, Rand J.
[111] ibid 580.   [112] ibid 583.

danger to the boy. Indeed, the notion of what is obvious plays an entirely different role. Thus, Macfarlane J states: 'I think it should have been obvious to the city employees that to leave this hole uncovered, unfenced and unguarded in a place in such close proximity to where children were accustomed to play was a failure to use ordinary care in the circumstances.'[113]

In addition to rejecting the claims of playing girls where the danger is seen by the court as obvious or apparent, courts also routinely reject such claims where the girl's play involves any element of danger. In none of these situations does it seem to occur to judges—nor perhaps to counsel—to rely on the temptation or 'moral trap' aspect of the doctrine of allurement to analyse the apparently dangerous activities of the playing girl. So, for instance, in *Koehler and Koehler v Pentecostal Assemblies of Canada*,[114] the court rejected the claim of a 7-year-old girl who was burned by a pile of hot ashes deposited on the edge of the defendant's property near a set of swings on which children frequently played.[115] The court notes the evidence of a little boy who testified that he told the girl 'not to go up there; that there was smoke up there'.[116] The little girl 'said "okay" but continued on'.[117] While the court rejects the little girl's claim on the ground that she was a trespasser, it nonetheless seems significant that the court found it necessary to draw attention to the apparently irrelevant fact that she may have had some inkling of danger. Yet in a similar—but superficially at least less compelling—situation, a court was willing to allow a much older boy to recover. *Commissioner for Railways (NSW) v Cardy*[118] is an Australian case which was decided only a few years after *Koehler* and which relied on many of the same background rules of English law and cited many of the same sources.[119] Yet in *Cardy* the court allowed a 14-year-old boy to recover for burns he sustained while running over part of the defendant's land that had been used for depositing ashes. In allowing the boy's action against the landowner, the court did not focus on the boy's knowledge but rather stressed that the landowner knew that children and adults frequently walked over the dangerous terrain.[120]

MacKeigan v Peake[121] also suggests that it will be difficult for the playing girl to recover damages when her play involves any element of danger. There, the British Columbia Court of Appeal refused to find any allurement in the case of a 7-year-old girl who was impaled when an abandoned porch blew over on her. As in *O'Connell*, the British Columbia Court of Appeal seems remarkably unsympathetic towards the little girl, who was injured while tobogganing in an

---

[113] (n 27 above) 235.   [114] n 29 above.

[115] In the course of rejecting the girl's claim, the court remarked on the fact that the girl was playing 'cops and robbers' and chasing a little boy. Interestingly, the court also saw fit to point out that all of the other children playing 'were boys except the infant plaintiff': ibid 619. As discussed below, in drawing attention to the fact that all of the children were boys except the plaintiff and that the plaintiff was the one chasing the boys, there may be some implication of gender-inappropriate play: ibid 617.   [116] ibid.

[117] ibid.   [118] [1961] ALR 16, 34 ALJR 134 (Aust HC).

[119] Including *Latham v Johnson* (n 6 above), *Glasgow Corp v Taylor* (n 12 above), and *Addie v Dumbreck* (n 6 above).   [120] (n 118 above) 19.

[121] n 29 above.

abandoned trailer stall only a hundred yards from her home and a 'short distance' from the trailer park's playground for children. Here too the court disposes of the claim by characterizing the girl as a trespasser. McFarlane JA then summarily dismisses the allurement argument by simply stating: 'I cannot regard the temporarily abandoned porch situated as it was as an allurement of such a nature as to constitute an implied invitation or licence.'[122] This is despite the fact that there was evidence that the children played in the porch and described it as 'their fort'. Once again, this analysis seems particularly noteworthy when juxtaposed with case law involving playing boys. While the factual situation in *Davis v St Mary's Demolition* is reminiscent of *MacKeigan*, the result is not. In *Davis*, the 12-year-old plaintiff was injured when he and some friends entered the site of a partially demolished house. The boys began pulling loose bricks away from the wall with the result that a wall of the house collapsed, killing one boy and injuring the plaintiff. Although Ormerod J held that the boys were trespassers, he went on to hold that the defendant nonetheless owed them a duty of care because the partially demolished site offered 'a constant allurement and temptation to any child who is within sight of it'.[123] While in both circumstances children had been observed playing in the partially abandoned structures, only the court in *Davis* was willing to interpret this as evidence of allurement. In fact, although the children in *Davis* had been warned away, there was no evidence that the children in *MacKeigan* had been. Even though *MacKeigan* was decided in 1971, fifteen years after *Davis*, it relies on a much more anachronistic interpretation of *Addie*'s 'no duty to a trespasser' rule—the very rule whose demise Lord Denning authoritatively chronicled only one year later in 1972.[124]

If courts are quick to treat dangers as 'obvious' and thus to impute knowledge to the playing girl, they are correspondingly reluctant to find that the landowner in cases involving playing girls had knowledge either of presence of children or of danger. In cases involving playing boys, courts often justify a finding of allurement by referring to evidence that children frequented the area in which the allurement was located. So, for instance, in *Arnold v Gillies* the court found as evidence of allurement the fact that children frequented the street where the fence that the boys were injured on was located.[125] In *Lengyel* the court rejected the defendant's argument that the portable substation was not an allurement because it was placed in an area not frequented by children and where there was no reason to expect children. In response, the court stated that the fact that witnesses 'had not seen children in the area is not evidence that the area was not one frequented by children'.[126] In fact, the court went on to find it foreseeable that 'children would be attracted to the strange apparatus' despite

---

[122] ibid 84.   [123] *Davis* (n 78 above) 580.

[124] As discussed below, in *Pannett v McGuinness* (n 79 above) 139, Lord Denning held as follows: '*Addie v Dumbreck* was wrongly decided. It proceeded on principles which were considered right at the time, but which must now be discarded'.

[125] (n 25 above) 54. See also *Jones v Calgary*, where the court indicated that '[t]he allurement which the transformer had for the infant plaintiff is indicated by his evidence that he and his friends had often played around it, climbed on top of it, and played with the padlocks and imagined it as a space ship': (n 22 above) 603.   [126] (n 22 above) 132.

the lack of any evidence that children had been seen in the area.[127] In recent jurisprudence, the House of Lords explicitly considers the question of the appropriate description of the risk in cases of allurement and adopts the wider more inclusive description.[128] Thus, in the case of boys, courts seem willing to find allurement and foreseeability even when there is no evidence that children had been seen in the area of the alleged allurement.

However, courts seem less willing to draw such inferences in the case of playing girls. For instance, in *MacKeigan*, although there was evidence that a number of children lived in the trailer park and that the defendants 'knew in a general way of their existence', the court found that they had no specific knowledge of children going onto the abandoned porch[129] and thus were not aware that the porch could constitute an allurement. Similarly, McFarlane JA rejects allurement because, although the plaintiff was playing on the lot on which the abandoned porch was situated and was within a few feet of the porch itself, evidence that children played in the porch and used it as 'their fort' could not be used to infer that the plaintiff was allured to the abandoned structure. This was because while those children were 'attracted to and had entered the porch on its open north side', the plaintiff was injured while playing 'in the area south of the porch and between it and the fence when the porch fell'.[130] In *Nelson*, Hunt J relies on a similarly narrow understanding of what counts as evidence of allurement. Thus, he states that although children were chased away from the park area, '[t]here is no evidence that anyone had ever seen children swimming in the excavation.'[131] Similarly, in *Koehler* the court justifies the finding that the girl was a trespasser by insisting that the defendants did not know that children routinely played in the area. This was despite the fact that the hot ashes were routinely deposited in a gully on the edge of the defendant's property less than twenty feet from a back-yard set of swings on which children often played, that the defendant's property was not fenced or marked in any way, that the children routinely played on the defendant's lots and that it was 'in the natural course of their play' to do so,[132] and that the men dumping the ashes saw the children playing. In *Humeny*, Kilgour J also adopts this approach when he concludes that the injured girl was a trespasser regardless of how much 'running to and fro there may have been by these children between the front bake shop and the back hall and stairway, or even possibly the room where the doughnuts were made'.[133]

In the cases with playing boys, courts also rely on evidence that boys had been chased away from the putatively alluring object to infer that the situation involved allurement.[134] Interestingly, however, the very evidence which in the

[127] (n 22 above).

[128] *Jolley* (n 7 above) 418–419 (per Lord Hoffman). On the complexity of the various holdings in this case, see the discussion in ch 5 below.   [129] (n 29 above) 85.

[130] ibid 84. This is the very kind of argument the House of Lords rejected as inappropriate to such cases in *Jolley* (n 7 above).   [131] *Nelson* (n 29 above) 581.

[132] *Koehler* (n 29 above) 619.   [133] *Humeny* (n 29 above) 399.

[134] See e.g. *Gough* (n 6 above) 1290–1293; *Davis* (n 78 above) 580; *Van Oudenhove* (n 22 above) 156. To this effect but on another legal issue, see *Shiffman v Order of St John* [1936] 1 KBD 557.

case of boys is relied upon to infer allurement seems more likely to be used to support the conclusion that the playing girl is a trespasser. For instance, in *Nelson*, Hunt J refers to the fact that 'workmen had consistently chased children away from the park area when they were observed'.[135] However, far from establishing that the girls were 'lured' to the excavation ditch, this evidence actually forms the basis of the conclusion that the children 'were certainly not invitees', and indeed, were trespassers.[136] In *Humeny*, Kilgour J relies on evidence that the girls had previously been chased out of the room to conclude 'that being so, the plaintiff was a mere trespasser'. Thus, in contrast with cases like *Gough, Mayer, Bouvier*, and many other cases where being warned away from the alluring object simply serves as evidence of allurement to the playing boy, warnings to girls conclusively establish that they are trespassers.

3. *'What to justice shall appertain'*

As discussed above, the court in *O'Connell* adopts a particularly rigid approach to the available legal rules, an approach that has the effect of excluding the application of the moral trap or temptation branch of the doctrine of allurement. Once again, this is not unique to *O'Connell*. As *Nelson, MacKeigan, Koehler*, and other cases involving the playing girl illustrate, courts adjudicating the claims of playing girls often invoke very strict interpretations of the 'no duty to a trespasser' rule from *Addie*. This is despite the fact that in many contemporaneous cases involving playing boys courts refuse to hold that merely classifying the child as a trespasser disposes of the matter.[137] In 1972, just three years after Hunt J so unproblematically rejected the claims of the drowned girls in *Nelson* by asserting the 'no duty to a trespasser' rule and only one year after *MacKeigan*, Lord Denning noted the slow demise of that harsh rule and described 'the ways and means by which we used to get around *Addie v Dumbreck*':

One of the most useful fictions was that by which we used to turn child trespassers into licensees. Another device of proved worth was the distinction we used to draw between the static condition of the premises and current activities on the land. Lastly, if we could not make a man liable as an occupier, we used to do so by making him a contractor. In each of those cases we held that in the special circumstances of the case there was a duty to take reasonable care. No one has suggested that the actual decisions were wrong. On the contrary, they did 'what to justice shall appertain'.[138]

---

[135] *Nelson* (n 29 above) 581.   [136] ibid 582.

[137] See, to cite but a few such examples, *Bird v Holbrook* (1828) 4 Bing 628; *Lynch* (n 3 above); *Mayer v Prince Albert* (n 22 above) 1079 ('In cases of nuisance, however, where children of tender years are involved, the authorities show that trespass does not apply.'). As discussed above, this principle was applied to permit recovery on behalf of a 9-year-old boy who was electrocuted when he climbed an electric light pole: *Lengyel* (n 22 above) 131. See also *Jones v Calgary* (n 22 above) 59; *Walker v Sheffield Bronze* (n 63 above) 382–384; *Pannett v McGuinness* (n 79 above) 139–141; *Davis v St Mary's Demolition* (n 78 above).   [138] *Pannett* (ibid) 140.

Lord Denning, with characteristic flair, may have been putting the point somewhat dramatically. Nonetheless, the case law on the temptation of the playing boy illustrates that the plaintiff was often permitted to recover on the basis of exactly the 'fictions' that Lord Denning identifies.[139] However, with playing girls courts did not exert the same ingenuity to 'get around' the rule in *Addie*. Instead, whenever there was even a possibility of a moral trap argument, courts seem to dispose of the claims of the playing girl by invoking the full rigor of the rule in *Addie*. Thus, we are left with a sense of unease about what may be at work in the courts' sense of 'what to justice may appertain'.

Tracing the difference in the construction of the legal rules in cases involving boys and those involving girls seems to provide further reason for this unease. *Humeny v Chaikowski* and *Bouvier v Fee*, a case decided by the Supreme Court of Canada in the same year as *Humeny*, serve as useful points of comparison. Both cases involved playing children injured by moving equipment from which they had previously been chased away. In both cases, the equipment was located in an area in which children habitually played. In *Bouvier* the cement mixer was located partially on a private lot and partially on a laneway. In *Humeny* the bread machine was located in premises that were partly private and partly public. In both cases there was evidence that the defendants knew that children habitually played in the vicinity, and were entitled to do so. In finding in favour of the playing boy in *Bouvier*, Anglin CJC states,

The allurement of a piece of machinery in motion for a small child is notorious, and anybody, operating such machinery upon, or so accessible from, a highway or public place as to make it dangerous to children lawfully about the neighbourhood, assumes the burden of so guarding the same as to make it practically inaccessible to them.[140]

Despite the fact that the playing boy in *Bouvier* had already been chased away from the mixer at least once, the court does not even mention trespassing. Instead, it stresses that the defendant knew children played in the vicinity and suggests that the fact that the boy had already been chased away simply served to establish the 'notorious' allurement of such moving machinery to a young child.[141] This contrasts with the treatment of the playing girl in *Humeny*. If the court in *Humeny* had applied the *Bouvier* principle, it seems clear that it would

---

[139] So, for instance, boys are often not classified as trespassers even when it seems at least equally persuasive to treat them as such: *Gough* (n 6 above); *Lynch* (n 3 above); *Laverdure v Victoria (City)* (n 27 above); *Jones v Calgary* (n 22 above); *Bouvier* (n 72 above). Similarly, courts adjudicating the claims of playing boys often find that the defendant was 'in the special sense, the occupier of the land' on which the injury occurred: *Davis* (n 78 above) 580; *Lengyel* (n 22 above) 131; *Jones* (n 22 above) 603; *Laverdure* (n 27 above). In the cases involving playing boys, courts also soften the implications of the rule in *Addie* by emphasizing either more recent case law questioning the rule or the many exceptions to it that were developed to take account of special circumstances involving the trespassing child. See, for instance, *Jones* (n 22 above) 596; *Lengyel* (ibid) 131; *Laverdure* (n 27 above) 333–334. The effect of invoking these 'fictions' was that the relevant child's claim was governed by the much more generous general principles of negligence rather than by the restrictive terms of the rule in *Addie*.

[140] *Bouvier* (n 72 above) 427.   [141] ibid 425–427.

have found the defendant liable. Instead, however, the court in *Humeny* finds that the girl was a 'mere trespasser'. Kilgour J thus concludes:

even if the omission to provide a guard for the revolving gears of the bread-mixing machine, on which the plaintiff with perhaps childish incautiousness let her fingers be caught, might in some circumstances be held to be negligence as against an invitee or even licensee, there was no duty to take such a precaution against a trespasser.[142]

And unlike *Bouvier* where the centrepiece of the decision is the 'notorious' allurement that a piece of moving machinery holds for a small child, in *Humeny* the word 'allurement' does not even appear.

The treatment of the playing girl contains many other illustrations of the harsh application of the rule in *Addie*. Unlike many cases involving playing boys, courts in cases involving playing girls are quick to conclude that the landowner owes only the most minimal duties. So although the court in *Van Oudenhove* states that 'the distinction between invitees and licensees is rarely of importance in cases involving children',[143] in fact the distinction and its implications seem to be rigorously applied in cases involving playing girls. For instance, this very distinction seems to play a crucial role in *Nelson* despite the fact that it was decided in the same year as *Van Oudenhove*. As noted above, in *Nelson* Hunt J refuses to find that the two girls who drowned in the pit were invitees. He holds that even if they were not trespassers, they were nothing but 'mere licensees' so that 'the only duty owed to them was not to set a trap'.[144] Another example of the harsh application of legal rules that seems to characterize the treatment of playing girls can be found in *MacKeigan v Peake*.[145] In that case, decided in 1971, the British Columbia Court of Appeal adopts a particularly narrow understanding of how the rule 'no duty to a trespasser' applied to the case of children. In fact, McFarlane JA cites an exception that treats 'trespassing' children with more generosity,[146] but he does not even seem to recognize its applicability to the playing girl. Instead, he concludes that the girl plaintiff 'must be regarded in law as having been at that time and place a trespasser'[147] with the consequence that she is owed only the most minimal duty. This is despite the fact that in 1952 in *Laverdure* another British Columbia court outright rejects the proposal that the playing boy who fell into a water-filled pit on neighbouring property is a

---

[142] *Humeny* (n 29 above) 399.   [143] *Van Oudenhove* (n 22 above) 158.
[144] *Nelson* (n 29 above) 581.   [145] n 29 above.
[146] Many cases involving playing boys either explicitly or implicitly invoke the exception for children to the rule that there is no duty to a trespasser: *Lynch* (n 3 above); *Harrold v Watney* [1898] 2 QB 320, 324–325 (CA) ; *Van Oudenhove* (n 22 above) 157. In *Lengyel*, the Manitoba Court of Appeal upheld an award to a 7-year-old boy who was severely burned when he climbed over a snow fence and onto a portable substation that was located near a public highway. Tritschler JA insists that the principle 'no duty to a trespasser' ought not to be extended 'with relentless disregard of consequences to a "dryly logical extreme"': (n 22 above) 131, quoting Cardozo J in *Hynes v New York Cent R Co* (1921) 131 NE 898, 900. He goes on to hold that the defendant cannot 'escape liability upon the ground that it did not intentionally injure the infant plaintiff': ibid.   [147] n 29 above.

trespasser and similarly refuses to invoke the rule in *Addie* as an obstacle to his success.[148]

Cases on the temptation of playing girls reveal other patterns that parallel those found in *O'Connell* and contrast with the cases involving playing boys. In addition to their rigid interpretation of the *Addie* rule, courts also seem to take an uncharitable approach to the 'facts' of cases involving the playing girl. Indeed, courts often seem suspicious of the idea that the playing girl may have been tempted into danger. Thus, for instance, in *Humeny v Chaikowski* although the children claimed they were invited into the room by the man in charge of the mixing machine and gave evidence to the effect that they were in the habit of 'running to and fro' from the bake shop to the back hall,[149] the court concluded that they were trespassers. The language is instructive. There is no hint of indulgence towards the curiosity or 'mischievousness' of children in Kilgour J's statement that they were '*furtively* drawn into the room by curiosity'.[150] In contrast with the open, energetic quality of boyish curiosity so often described in cases involving playing boys, the girl's curiosity here is 'furtive'— underhanded, sly, and even dishonest, as indicated by its synonym 'thievish'.[151] In fact, the implication of sly criminality conveyed by the use of 'furtively' is confirmed later in the same paragraph where the court states that the evidence of the children raises 'an unpleasant suspicion of collaboration'.[152] The view that there is something untrustworthy about the playing girl is also apparent in *Koehler* where the court points out very minor differences in the accounts of the accident,

not because the difference in these facts is significant but because I think it must be realized that these children's minds are open to suggestion and their evidence where it is not precise is to be considered in that light. I do not accuse them at all of being dishonest, rather the contrary[,] but imprecise and compliant to suggestion in the emphasis to be placed on certain factors.[153]

The girl, it seems, is not to be believed.

This harshness of the application of the *Addie* rule also points to a deeper contrast between the treatment of the playing girl and that of the playing boy. As noted in the discussions of *McHale* and the other cases involving the playing boy, courts tend to invoke a particular view of boyhood and of the mischievous indiscretions that are part of that golden state. In contrast, the playing

---

[148] (n 27 above) 334.   [149] *Humeny* (n 29 above) 399 [emphasis added].   [150] ibid 398.
[151] *The Compact Oxford English Dictionary* (n 15 above) 646. The term 'furtive' also implies foreknowledge of guilt, in contrast with impulsive boys who are innocently carried away by curiosity and enthusiasm.   [152] (n 29 above) 399.
[153] *Koehler* (n 29 above) 618. Note how this echoes the statements in *McHale* about the evidence of the girls: see discussion in ch 2 above. In another echo of *McHale*, courts also seem more likely to reject the evidence of witnesses favourable to the girls. Thus, for instance, in *MacKeigan* the court states that 'no witness save one felt that the porches standing where and when they were constituted a source of possible danger to anyone. The evidence of that one witness was rejected, and in my opinion quite properly, by the trial Judge [*sic*]': (n 29 above) 86.

girl cases are marked by the virtual absence of the rhetoric of childhood. As the treatment of *Addie* suggests, often courts do not seem to even notice that the girl is a child. Perhaps related to this failure to see the playing girl as a child is the most intangible of the elements missing from cases involving the playing girl: unlike the sympathy that one finds for the playing boy and the nostalgia for the lost state of boyhood, the rhetoric in the cases involving the playing girl is dismissive. Indeed, the perfunctory judicial tone suggests that there is something implausible about the playing girl's claim—as if the reason that it must fail is so evident that it barely deserves articulation.[154] Unlike the language in the playing boy cases, language which powerfully evokes the world of childhood from the child's point of view and re-creates the child's experience of the events, the language in the cases involving the playing girl is straightforward and matter-of-fact. The impatience of the judges in cases involving playing girls is reflected not simply in the cursory dismissive rhetoric, but also in the lack of imaginative effort—effort that they seem so willing to make in the case of playing boys. The cases involving the playing girl virtually never re-create the world of the playing child—a world filled with wonder, curiosity, and also danger.

4. *The ordinary girl: 'Neither a paragon of prudence nor a scatter-brained child'*

The failure even to notice that the girl is a child is subtly corroborated by the absence of the rhetoric of childhood from the cases involving the playing girl. In the contributory negligence cases, the realm of mischievous play and daring is the realm of boys. For boys, as we have seen, it is normal and indeed natural to be seduced by danger. On this basis, courts find it possible to forgive the prudential mistakes of boys. But courts do not seem prepared to extend similar generosity to girls, perhaps because there is no sense that curiosity and mischief are normal or natural for a girl. Indeed, the infrequent references to girlish curiosity depict it as unnatural and perhaps underhanded. It is possible to trace the tentative outline of a vision of girlhood in the few cases that find for the playing girl, but this vision is entirely unlike that of boyhood. Because curiosity, mischief, and daring are natural for the boy, he is forgiven for his attraction to and pursuit of danger. But what emerges as natural and normal for the girl is very different. Indeed, the cases on the playing girl seem to confirm what the court in *Hassenyer* suggested so long ago: the normal girl 'would be more cautious to avoid unknown dangers; she would be more particular to keep within the limits of absolute safety when the dangers threatened were such as only great strength and courage could venture to encounter'.[155] Where the girl is not particularly timid or cautious, courts refuse to excuse her indiscretions. But the corollary of this, as we shall see, is that courts do in fact forgive the playing girl

---

[154] Ironically, in cases involving the temptation of the playing boy, it is just the opposite claim that receives such dismissive treatment—that is, courts seem to find ridiculous the notion that the boy should have resisted the dangerous temptation.　　[155] *Hassenyer* (n 83 above) 209–210.

when her actions exhibit the timidity and caution that is 'commonly looked for and expected' in one of her sex.[156] It is commonly looked for, it is normal, and it is therefore reasonable, for the girl to be 'scatterbrained' or to panic in the face of danger.

In this light it is revealing to consider one of the extremely rare cases in which a girl above the age of tender years was exonerated under the doctrine of allurement. In *Coley v CPR*,[157] the doctrine of allurement was applied to a 9-year-old girl who was seriously injured while she was playing on a turntable located on the property of the defendant railway. The court found that the turntable was an allurement to children as evidenced by the fact that children were frequently in the immediate vicinity of the turntable.[158] However, the case is more complicated than it first appears. A 15-year-old boy, Gilbert Sykes, had ridden on the turntable earlier on the day of the accident. Gilbert then decided to take his own younger brother, and his friend Florence Coley and her younger sibling to the turntable. He 'placed' Florence and her sibling on the turntable and then he and his brother proceeded to turn it. The court describes the accident in the following terms: 'Florence E Coley, having become somewhat alarmed, requested the boy Sykes to stop the turntable, but, before he had succeeded in doing so, the said child Florence E Coley, attempted to step off the turntable'.[159] The result of this was that the girl's foot was caught and so badly crushed that it had to be amputated.

Florence Coley was awarded damages, but given what we have seen of the judicial attitude towards the playing girl, it seems significant that she did not herself embark on the risky initiative. Rather Gilbert Sykes not only took her to the turntable but also placed her upon it and turned it. Indeed, Florence's passivity is reflected in the fact that in Hutchinson J's description of the accident, she does not even appear in the subject position until, in a state of alarm, she attempts to get off the moving turntable. In fact, Hutchinson J's description of the doctrine of allurement and his subsequent references to the case law are all sufficiently vague that it is impossible to tell whether the references to allurement apply to Florence or to Gilbert.[160] So, while the girl here is exonerated, it is clear that her injury did not spring from her attraction to risk and danger. *Coley* thus suggests that while courts may not be prepared to forgive girls for being attracted to risk or danger—in essence for yielding to temptation—they will forgive the girl who, through no fault of her own, responds with alarm or panic to a dangerous situation.[161]

---

[156] *Hassenyer* (n 83 above) 209.

[157] (1906) 29 Que SC 282, affirmed by the Quebec Court of Appeal (1907) 16 Que KB 404.

[158] ibid 285, Hutchinson J.   [159] ibid.

[160] So, for example, Hutchinson J states that 'the turntable was evidently an allurement to children': ibid. Following this, he simply paraphrases or quotes a number of authorities on the contributory negligence of children or the doctrine of allurement and then applies them to the facts in one oblique sentence: ibid 285–287.

[161] Note, however, the similarity to the adult emergency doctrine. This may suggest that this case and others like it have little or nothing to do with the girl being a child.

The implications of *Coley* are confirmed in the few other cases that forgive or even partially forgive the indiscretions of the playing girl. For instance, in *Holmes and Burke v Goldenberg*,[162] a majority of the Manitoba Court of Appeal attributed 15 per cent responsibility to an 8-year-old girl who was struck by a car while playing hockey. What is most interesting about that case, however, is the basis on which the dissent at the Court of Appeal would have been prepared to exonerate the girl. Coyne JA rejected attributing any responsibility to the girl by arguing that she had expected the car to stop and she had panicked in the face of an emergency. Thus, he concludes, 'she was not negligent in the emergency in running to the north instead of the south.'[163] This willingness to exonerate the girl who panics in the face of an emergency is also apparent elsewhere in the case law on the contributory negligence of playing girls. In fact, as noted earlier, a similar impetus is apparent in the trial judgment in *O'Connell* where the judge finds it plausible that Dolores had in fact been allured by the semblance of safety rather than the thrill of danger.

Similarly, in *Gough v Thorne*[164] the English Court of Appeal allowed the appeal of a 13-year-old girl who had been found one-third contributorily negligent for the injuries she suffered when she was hit by a car while crossing the road. The terms on which the Court of Appeal was prepared to exonerate the girl are illuminating. As Lord Denning MR puts it, 'I have no doubt that there was no blameworthiness to be attributed to the plaintiff at all. Here she was with her elder brother crossing a road. They had been beckoned on by the lorry driver. What more could you expect the child to do than to cross in pursuance of the beckoning?'[165] Similarly, in one of the very rare appeals to what is natural or normal to exonerate a girl, Salmon LJ states, 'I think that any ordinary child of thirteen and a half, seeing a lorry stop and let her cross and the lorry driver, a grown-up person in whom she no doubt has some confidence, beckoning her to cross the road would naturally go straight on, no one in my view could blame her for doing so.'[166] Salmon LJ even goes on to articulate the range of possibilities encapsulated in the reference to his ordinary child: 'I do not mean a paragon of prudence; nor do I mean a scatter-brained child; but the ordinary girl of thirteen and a half.'[167] Indeed, it does not seem surprising that Salmon LJ refers specifically to the 'ordinary *girl* of thirteen'.[168] The court finds it easy to conclude that it is natural and therefore normal and reasonable that the girl, beckoned by older and wiser males, naturally follows their lead. In fact Salmon LJ's description of the range of possibilities open to the playing girl does seem borne out by the case law: the ordinary (and thus reasonable) girl is somewhere between a paragon of prudence and a scatterbrained child. In this sense, the possibilities present to the judicial imagination are dramatically different for

---

[162] (1952) 7 WWR (NS) 109 (Man CA).

[163] ibid 117, Coyne JA (dissenting). Note that unlike in the boy defendant cases discussed above, it does not seem to occur to the court here that a playing girl's judgment could be clouded by her interest in the game or desire to win. [164] [1966] 3 All ER 398 (CA).

[165] ibid 399. [166] ibid 400. [167] ibid. [168] ibid [emphasis added].

boys and for girls. For boys the extreme of irrationality is the boy who is dangerous, rash, attracted to risk. The extreme of irrationality for girls is a scatterbrained child, a skittish creature who panics in the face of danger. Interestingly, even when this does not seem on the facts to be a convincing description of a particular girl, courts find it a plausible understanding of their behaviour.[169] Attraction to risk or danger simply forms no part of the motivations of the ordinary girl.

This understanding of the playing girl's characteristic timidity does not spring from fond memories and is not, at bottom, a romantic vision. Indeed, in the perfunctory nature of these courts' analyses, it is possible to discern a sense that dangerous play—while perhaps normal, natural and even desirable for a boy— is undesirable and even somewhat unnatural for a girl. From this one can begin to trace the tentative outline of a vision of girlhood. It is a pale thin vision, to be sure, but it is nonetheless as central to the assessment of the claims of the playing girl as is the more romantic and robust vision of boyhood to the claims of the playing boy. This understanding of the girl's natural timidity means that the playing girl will find it very difficult to be exonerated on the basis of temptation. Thus, as we have seen, she is all but confined to entrapment branch of the doctrine of allurement. In this sense, then, the quote from *Hassenyer* may not be as anachronistic as it seems: as it suggests, the girl may in fact be required to be 'more cautious to avoid unknown dangers' and 'more particular to keep within the limits of absolute safety'.[170] In effect then, she may have to meet a higher standard of care in attending to her own safety than that demanded of the playing boy.

II. Conclusion

The allurement case law provides additional insight into the actual workings of the concept of reasonable behaviour. The cases involving those with intellectual disabilities and the child defendant pointed to a deep and complicated entanglement between the reasonable and the normal, and this is corroborated by the allurement cases. In order to assess what a reasonable agent (person or child) might do in any particular situation, judges typically invoke some notion of normal or natural behaviour. But although such concepts may seem useful, they also have a troubling dimension. Because ideas of normal or ordinary behaviour tend to be gendered, for instance, filling out the reasonable child standard by looking to ordinary or normal behaviour results in a gendered legal standard. In this way, as we see in the child plaintiff cases, assumptions about what kind of behaviour is natural for girls as opposed to for boys effectively results in different standards for contributory negligence. The normal boy, it seems,

---

[169] This is the case, for instance, in *Holmes* (n 162 above), as well as in the trial judgment in *O'Connell* (n 29 above).   [170] *Hassenyer* (n 83 above) 209–210.

seeks risks and is therefore not chastised for so doing; in contrast, the normal girl seeks safety and avoids risks and is held to that standard. The consequence is that the range of situations in which the playing girl will be able to recover damages from a tortfeasor will be far more limited than the situations in which the boy will be permitted to recover.

Comparing the treatment of playing girls and playing boys corroborates our suspicions about the entanglement of the reasonable and the normal. So, as the treatment of those with intellectual impairments suggests, some litigants are seen as so outside of the purview of the normal or natural that their mistakes can never fall within any conception of 'reasonableness', even when the mistakes are cognitive and do not normally attract blame. Regardless of that, they act at their peril. At the other end of the spectrum, as the child defendant illustrates, some defendants can call on such extensive understandings of what kinds of mistakes are normal for them that they will be forgiven, not merely for cognitive shortcomings, but even for moral or prudential failings. Thus, careless boys can frequently invoke the belief that they are easily seduced by that which is dangerous or forbidden. And the view that boys are peculiarly susceptible to being overwhelmed by their passions operates to normalize a whole range of typically boyish mistakes. In contrast, as we have seen, the judicial understanding of the nature of girlhood does not allow girls access to such a basis of exoneration, resulting in exactly the kind of elevated standard described so long ago by Judge Cooley in *Hassenyer*.[171]

In this sense, oddly enough, it seems that the reasonableness standard actually does operate as the reference to 'ordinary prudence' suggests.[172] In many cases the standard of attentiveness does seem to turn on some conception of what degree of care is normal or ordinary in the circumstances. Both the child defendant cases and the allurement cases strongly suggest that one of the factors taken into consideration is the gender of the agent in question. As we noted, even in *Mullin*, the gender of the idealized agent seems to be one of its most prominent attributes. Thus, the boys in *McHale, Gough*, and the other playing boy cases are compared to the ordinary boy; similarly, the girls in the allurement cases, in *Gough v Thorne*, and even in apparently more progressive *Mullin* are faced with the comparison with what ordinary *girls* would do. This approach to the standard of care, which understands carelessness in terms of a gender-specific ordinariness standard, heightens the concern noted earlier. If, for example, boys are routinely less attentive to the interests of others than are girls, then the effect of this reading of reasonableness is that they are held to a lower standard. This parallels the worry that both Holmes's idea of avoidability and Honoré's of general capacity, though they articulate something that seems important to fault in negligence, also seem to risk too much emphasis on ordinary behaviours and capacities in determining what we can reasonably demand of people. What is commonly done is thus accorded pride of place in

---

[171] ibid.   [172] Fleming (n 6 above) 118.

assessing what ought to be done. The patterns we see in the case law on the playing child suggests how problematic it may be to rely on the concept of what is normal or natural to determine what level of prudence it is reasonable to expect. This in turn raises a deeper worry about the entanglement of the reasonable and the normal that seems to characterize our efforts to give content to the reasonable person.

4

Just the Facts: Common Sense Ideas of the Normal and the Reasonable Person

The cases involving children thus reveal the extent to which the reasonable person standard, at least in that context, turns on conceptions of what is normal or ordinary and what is natural. Perhaps this should not be surprising: the idea of the normal is deeply intertwined with the idea of the reasonable more generally. Indeed, the standard's reliance on a conception of what is normal often seems uncontroversial. But the cases involving children also suggest a more problematic dimension to the idea of normal behaviour. In those cases, invoking some apparently uncomplicated notion of what is normal or natural often seems to exhaust the inquiry into what is reasonable. Returning to the justifications of the treatment of cognitive or intellectual disabilities with this intertwining of the reasonable and the normal in mind only reinforces the central role normalcy seems to play in the reasonable person inquiry. As we shall see however, the history of assumptions about who is 'normal' is itself cause for concern. Indeed, even a brief review of this history suggests why it may be so problematic to give content to notions of reasonableness through recourse to the concept of what is normal or ordinary. This difficulty is both reinforced and complicated by the fact that as a rhetorical matter, the invocation of the normal often derives its justificatory force from the powerful though frequently hidden tenets of common sense. In this way, the idea of the normal and the rhetoric of common sense work together to give content to and justify the operation of the reasonable person standard. But they do so, as we shall ultimately see, in a troubling way. In fact, by tracing out the details of this complicated relationship between the reasonable, the normal, and common sense, we can begin to uncover how the reasonable person and perhaps the operation of the objective standard more generally may raise serious equality concerns.

I. REASONABLE MEN OF ORDINARY PRUDENCE

In some sense, it should hardly be surprising that there are deep connections between the conception of what is reasonable and underlying assumptions about normal behaviour. Indeed, it often seems difficult to extricate the reasonable person from his ordinary counterpart. Thus, for instance, the reasonable and the ordinary or normal are closely intertwined in the formulation of the standard of care, in the way custom gives content to the standard, and in the elaboration of what the reasonable person knows and believes. The very ordinariness of his conduct is often taken to be the hallmark of the reasonable person. So, in descriptions of the reasonable person, references to what is normal and ordinary abound. In fact, determinations of normalcy are often treated as definitive of negligence. As Fleming notes, the reasonable person of '*ordinary* prudence' is the central figure in formulating the standard of care required by the law of negligence.[1] Commentators frequently refer to the fact that the reasonable person is not free from all shortcomings and thus those individuals who have 'normal' shortcomings will not be negligent.[2] And personifications of the reasonable man are remarkable for their insistent ordinariness: the reasonable man is the man on the Clapham omnibus or the Bondi tram,[3] he is 'the man who takes the magazines at home, and in the evening pushes the lawn mower in his shirt sleeves'.[4] The reasonable person, it seems, the perfectly ordinary middle-class citizen going about his own business:

In foresight, caution, courage, judgment, self-control, altruism, and the like he represents, and does not excel, the general average of the community. He is capable of making mistakes and errors of judgment, of being selfish, of being afraid—but only to the extent that any such shortcoming embodies the normal standard of community behaviour.[5]

As F. W. Edgerton eloquently puts the link, 'to say that an act is negligent is to say that it would not have been done by the possessor of a normal mind functioning normally.'[6] Similarly, he later notes that behind the 'Pickwickian' formulations of the standard there is 'the general idea of a mentally normal person'.[7] And Weinrib

---

[1] JG Fleming, *The Law of Torts* (9th edn, Agincourt: LBC Information Services, 1998) 118 [emphasis added]. The original formulation along these lines is normally attributed to Baron Alderson in *Blyth v Birmingham Waterworks Co* (1856) 11 Ex 781, 784. Other similar formulations are legion: F Pollock, *The Law of Torts* (13th edn, London: Stevens and Sons Ltd, 1929) 453–458; L Green, 'The Negligence Issue' (1927–28) 37 Yale LJ 1029, 1034–1039; WL Prosser, *Handbook of the Law of Torts* (4th edn, St Paul: West Publishing Co, 1971) 150.

[2] Indeed, the *Restatement (Second) of Torts* puts the point in a probably unintentionally illuminating way when it notes that the fact that the negligence judgment 'is personified in a "man" calls attention to the necessity of taking into account the fallibility of human beings': American Law Institute (St Paul: American Law Institute Publishers, 1965) s 283, Comment b (1965) (quotations in original). Similarly, Prosser notes that the reasonable person has 'only those human shortcomings and weaknesses which the community will tolerate on the occasion': (ibid) 150. Fleming also notes that even the reasonable man is not 'a model of perfection', although he may be rather closer to such a model than any of us are: ibid.   [3] Fleming, ibid.

[4] *Hall v Brooklands Club* [1933] 1 KB 205, 224.

[5] FV Harper, F James, Jr, and OS Gray, *The Law of Torts* Vol III (2nd edn, Boston: Little, Brown and Company, 1986) 389. See also F James Jr, 'The Qualities of the Reasonable Man in Negligence Cases' (1951) 16 Missouri L Rev 1, 4–5.

[6] FW Edgerton, 'Negligence, Inadvertence and Indifference: The Relation of Mental States to Negligence' (1926) 39 Harv L Rev 849, 858.

[7] ibid 862. See also GHL Fridman, who describes the reasonable person as someone who is 'supposed to act in accordance with what is normal and usual': *Introduction to the Law of Torts* (Toronto: Butterworths, 1978) 142; Prosser (n 1 above) 152.

also describes the objective standard as a standard of 'ordinariness'.[8] In this sense, then, the very formulation of the objective standard reveals the close— often definitional—link between conceptions of what is normal or ordinary and what is reasonable.

The relationship between the reasonable and the normal or ordinary is also apparent in the elaboration of the knowledge and beliefs of the reasonable person. Generally, the reasonable person is held to be aware of matters of common knowledge.[9] In elaborating on this somewhat cryptic phrase, Fleming James, Jr notes that people will be held to know 'certain fundamental facts and laws of nature which belong to universal human experience' such as the laws of gravity and leverage and the properties of common substances.[10] In addition, people will be treated as if they have knowledge of many other things that are normal or ordinary features of their lives. The various attempts to delineate the kinds of things that reasonable people are required to know also seem somewhat 'Pickwickian': thus an adult may be held to know of 'the proneness of mules to kick', the 'viciousness of bulls' (especially during breeding season), and 'the propensity of mad dogs to bite',[11] 'the dangers inherent in common modes of travel', and 'the dangers incident to common sports'.[12] Indeed, some commentators have undertaken the probably impossible task of exhaustively identifying the facts that 'reasonable' individuals are required to know.[13] The crucial point here is simply that the touchstone for identifying these qualities of the reasonable person is some notion of the normal or ordinary human being.[14]

However, the role accorded to custom in determinations of negligence is perhaps the most straightforward example of the relationship of normal or ordinary behaviour to determinations of reasonableness. Here, ordinary behaviour is actually given explicit doctrinal significance. Fleming nicely elucidates the conceptual connection to negligence itself: 'Since the standard of care is determined by reference to community valuations, considerable evidentiary weight attaches to whether or not the defendant's conduct conformed to standard practices accepted as normal and general by other members of the community in

---

[8] E Weinrib, *The Idea of Private Law* (Cambridge, Mass: Harvard University Press, 1995) 183 quoting Justice Kitto in *McHale v Watson* (1966) 115 CLR 199, 213 (Aust HC).

[9] Fleming (n 1 above) 119–120. The individual who has greater knowledge or skill will, however, be held to a higher subjectivized standard: ibid. [10] James (n 5 above) 9.

[11] ibid 10 [citations omitted]. [12] ibid 11 [citations omitted].

[13] See, for instance, Note on 'Negligence' (1938) 23 Minn L Rev 628; *Restatement* (n 2 above) s 290.

[14] Interestingly, although there are few cases that turn on it, commentators seem to agree that where an individual can conclusively establish genuine and reasonable ignorance, he will not be held to the standard of ordinariness: James (n 5 above) 12; WA Seavey, 'Negligence—Subjective or Objective' (1927) 41 Harv L Rev 1, 19; *Lorenzo v Wirth* 49 NE 1010 (1897) (Spanish woman stepped into a coal hole in Boston); *Geier v Kujawa* [1970] 1 Ll Rep 364 (QB) (German girl excused for not using seat belt because she had never seen one before). It is perhaps worth noting however, that the few cases that do consider this do so in the context of contributory negligence. Nonetheless, these cases do seem to suggest that avoidability, at least in the context of non-normative attributes, takes into consideration the qualities of the individual litigant.

similar circumstances.'[15] Thus, defendants often marshall evidence that they acted in a way that people in their position normally act as an indication that they were not negligent.[16] And indeed, although the nuances of the role of general practice vary somewhat from jurisdiction to jurisdiction, the general rule is that a defendant charged with negligence can clear himself if he shows that he has acted in accordance with general and approved practice.[17] The corollary of this, of course, is that failure to adopt a general practice is often the strongest evidence of negligence.[18] Nonetheless, while custom or ordinary practice plays a significant role in the determinations of negligence, it is not conclusive, and judges retain the power to find even an established practice negligent. As Learned Hand J stated in what is widely viewed as the *locus classicus* regarding the role of custom:

Indeed in most cases reasonable prudence is in fact common prudence; but strictly it is never its measure; a whole calling may have unduly lagged in the adoption of new and available devices. It never may set its own tests, however persuasive be its usages. Courts must in the end say what is required; there are precautions so imperative that even their universal disregard will not excuse their omission.[19]

So while custom or ordinary practice will be important as an evidentiary matter, it cannot be determinative of the legal question regarding the existence of negligence. It is equally clear, however, that while courts retain this power to 'overrule' custom, they may be hesitant to employ this power, particularly in specialized areas that involve issues of professional negligence.[20]

Thus, it seems that reference to some conception of what is normal or ordinary often plays a crucial role in determinations of what is reasonable and therefore non-negligent. And in many of these cases, using a conception of what is normal to give content to reasonableness may seem unproblematic. Indeed, as Learned Hand J suggested in *The TJ Hooper* it may typically be appropriate to treat common prudence as reasonable prudence.[21] However, the case law involving children also suggests ways in which reference to a conception of what is normal or natural seems more troublesome. Taking this worry about the entanglement of the reasonable and the normal back to the situation of

---

[15] Fleming (n 1 above) 133, citing *Paris v Stepney Borough Council* [1951] AC 367, 382 (HL); *Kauffman v TTC* [1960] SCR 251; *Vancouver Hospital v MacDaniel* [1934] 4 DLR 593 (PC). See also C Morris, 'Custom and Negligence' (1942) 42 Col L Rev 1147; AM Linden, *Canadian Tort Law* (7th edn, Markham: Butterworths Canada Ltd, 2001) 187.

[16] FA Trindade and P Cane, *The Law of Torts in Australia* (3rd edn, Oxford: Oxford University Press, 1999) 453.

[17] RFV Heuston and RA Buckley, *Salmond & Heuston on the Law of Torts* (21st edn, London: Sweet and Maxwell, 1996) 236 (citations omitted); Fleming (n 1 above) 133.

[18] Fleming, ibid.   [19] *The TJ Hooper* 60 F 2d 737, 740 (2nd Cir 1932).

[20] Fleming (n 1 above) 133–134; Heuston (n 17 above) 236; M Brazier and J Murphy (eds), *Street on Torts* (10th edn, London: Butterworths, 1999) 245; Trindade and Cane (n 16 above) 453. For a recent Canadian decision on the subject of when custom may itself be negligent, see *Ter Neuzen v Korn* (1995) 127 DLR (4th) 577 (SCC).   [21] n 19 above.

people with intellectual disabilities serves only to confirm it. As we shall see, the idea of the normal is also deeply implicated in discussions of intellectual impairments and developmental disabilities more generally. Examination of its role in those discussions reveals another troubling dimension of reliance on the normal and suggests a more systematic difficulty with the application and justification of the reasonable person standard.

II. OF MICE AND MEN: DEVELOPMENTAL DISABILITY AND THE NORMAL

As we saw in Chapter 1, the imposition of the objective standard on those with cognitive or intellectual shortcomings proves extraordinarily difficult to justify. Despite this difficulty, the persistence of the rule itself seems relatively uncontroversial. However, it is illuminating to examine the arguments typically taken to be persuasive. For while the justifications may be unsuccessful in defending the current configurations of the objective standard and the liability of the developmentally disabled in particular, they do reveal certain assumptions that may help to account for the readiness to impose the standard on such individuals and for the lack of critical scrutiny directed towards this problem. And if the general discussions of the reasonable person reveal the least problematic aspect of reliance on the normal, looking back to the case of the developmentally disabled illuminates a much more troubling dimension of that reliance. In fact, discussions of developmental disabilities confirm the egalitarian concern about invoking the normal and make visible the initial outlines of a disturbing pattern of treatment.

A. Normal shortcoming or idiosyncrasy?

Throughout the justifications of the objective standard, there is an implicit distinction between those whose shortcomings are 'normal' and those who suffer from shortcomings that are seen as 'abnormal' or peculiar. As we have seen in the case of the developmentally disabled and children, characterization as normal or abnormal plays a particularly important role in explaining what kinds of shortcomings will and will not count as circumstances that affect the standard of care. And in those discussions, the justification for calibrating the standard (or not) often refers explicitly to the ordinariness of the shortcoming in question. Thus, the standard will normally be calibrated for shortcomings that are seen as normal or ordinary. But the corollary of this is that courts refuse to adjust the standard for the peculiar, perhaps because they are located outside the 'normal' community.

We have already seen this concept of normal shortcomings at work in the cases involving children. And like judges and theorists, commentators also rely on the idea that childhood is a normal state to justify relaxing the standard of care for children. This reinforces the fact that the emphasis that we have seen on normalcy is anything but accidental. So Linden, for instance, defends the relaxed standard of care that applies to children on the ground that it is hardly open to the court to ignore 'the facts of life'.[22] After all, he argues, 'a minor's *normal condition* is one of recognized incompetency and, therefore, indulgence must be shown.'[23] Similarly, Seavey advocates a relaxed standard of care for children on the ground that childhood is a period 'through which all *normal* persons pass'.[24] Prosser also defends the relaxed standard of care for children 'because "their *normal condition* is one of incapacity".'[25] And Weinrib quotes with approval the passage from *McHale v Watson*, which states that a child can rely on the defence of childhood 'not as being personal to himself, but as being characteristic of humanity at his stage of development and in that sense normal'.[26] Thus, children are notionally placed on the side of the 'normal' population whose shortcomings will be taken into consideration when formulating the standard of care.

Nor is childhood the only shortcoming that is identified as normal and thus capable of being incorporated into the reasonable person standard. Indeed, to the extent that other shortcomings are seen as weaknesses that could afflict a normal person, they are also capable of affecting the standard of care. So, for instance, F. James and J. J. Dickinson suggest that there should be some leniency towards young drivers because their actions are due to 'natural exuberance and the wish to test one's ability'.[27] Thus, while inexperience may be related to accidents, it is like youth in that it is 'common to many and is temporary'.[28] A similar reliance on notions of normal and natural incapacities is also apparent in Seavey's distinction between the inexcusable 'clumsiness beyond the normal' and the excusable clumsiness that arises out of 'the shaking hand of age or the faltering steps of infancy'.[29] And Weinrib's references to the process of the development of self-determining agency also implicitly draw on a sense that immaturity, as part of a natural and normal process, cannot be treated as blameworthy.[30]

However, this generosity towards normal shortcomings also has a dark side. If those who have the benefit of a standard that more closely resembles them are defined in terms of how normal they are, the abnormality of those who do

---

[22] Linden (n 15 above) 140, citing H Shulman, 'The Standard of Care Required of Children' (1927) 37 Yale LJ 618.

[23] ibid 140 [emphasis added], citing *Charbonneau v MacRury* 153 A 457, 462 (SCNH 1931). *Charbonneau* was overruled in *Daniels v Evans* 224 A 2d 63 (SCNH 1966). Although the court in *Daniels* approved of *Charbonneau*'s reasoning on the standard of care to which a child should be held, it found that this did not apply when the activity was one that was normally undertaken by adults. Driving an automobile or similar vehicle fell within this exception.

[24] Seavey (n 14 above) 12 n 12 [emphasis added].

[25] Prosser (n 1 above) 155, citing *Charbonneau* (n 23 above) 463 [emphasis added].

[26] Weinrib (n 8 above) 183 n 22(4).

[27] F James and JJ Dickinson, 'Accident Proneness and Accident Law' (1950) 63 Harv L Rev 769, 775. As noted above, however, this lenient approach to young drivers does not represent the current legal position: ch 2 above, n 101.   [28] James and Dickinson (ibid).

[29] Seavey (n 14 above) 16.   [30] Weinrib (n 8 above) 183 n 22(4).

not receive such generosity is frequently adverted to as part of the reason why they cannot be given similar treatment. Indeed, these individuals are constantly placed outside the community of the 'normal', and are consistently described as peculiar or idiosyncratic. Holmes's famous passages reconciling the fault principle with the treatment of those with inexcusable shortcomings serve as a case in point—the characterization of the shortcoming as abnormal or peculiar substitutes for some more thoroughgoing justification. Thus, Holmes argues, 'when men live in society, a certain average of conduct, a sacrifice of *individual peculiarities* going beyond a certain point, is necessary to the general welfare.'[31] But the power of this argument depends on the rhetorical force of Holmes's insistent characterization of these qualities as idiosyncratic, peculiar, or strange. By notionally juxtaposing these odd and somehow private qualities with the comprehensible public nature of 'normal' shortcomings, Holmes lends force to the argument for placing responsibility on the errant individual rather than relaxing the standard of care, even though he forwards little in the way of substantive justification.

Characterizing certain shortcomings as abnormal or peculiar in order to justify a refusal to take them into consideration is actually quite pervasive. So, for instance, Prosser concludes the discussion of physical deficiencies by noting that the standard 'is sufficiently flexible to take the actor's physical defects into account'.[32] But immediately following this sentence, Prosser begins the section on 'Mental Capacity' by stating 'As to the *mental attributes* of the actor, the standard remains of necessity an external one.'[33] And one of the most common ways of explaining the operation of the objective standard is to suggest that it simply eliminates the personal equation by ignoring the 'idiosyncrasies' of the defendant.[34] Indeed Fleming welcomes (on grounds of fairness to the victim) the refusal to make any allowance for a defendant's '*mental abnormality*'[35] despite the tension that he himself recognizes between this and the practice of excusing loss of consciousness by 'normal' defendants.[36] Fleming even describes as 'peculiar'[37] those risks created by the physically handicapped that cannot be tolerated by the general public. Similarly, G. J. Alexander and T. S. Szasz justify the application of the objective standard to the mentally ill in part by

---

[31] OW Holmes, *The Common Law* (ed MD Howe) (Cambridge, Mass: Harvard University Press, 1963) 108 [emphasis added].   [32] Prosser (n 1 above) 152.

[33] ibid [emphasis added]. Unsurprisingly, Prosser then quotes Holmes.

[34] Fleming (n 1 above) 119; Fridman (n 7 above) 142; LD Rainaldi (ed), *Remedies in Tort* Vol II (Toronto: Carswell, 1987) 16.I-52.3; Pollock (n 1 above) 457; Prosser (n 1 above) 153; SI Splane, 'Tort Liability of the Mentally Ill in Negligence Actions' (1983) 93 Yale LJ 153, 153 n 1. Weinrib relies on a similar characterization when he defends the subjectivized standard for children partly on the ground that '[c]hildhood is not an idiosyncrasy': (n 8 above) 183 n 22, quoting the trial judgment of Windeyer J in *McHale v Watson* (n 8 above) 204. The language of idiosyncrasy is also found in Lord MacMillan's statement in *Glasgow Corp v Muir* [1943] AC 448, 457.

[35] Fleming (ibid) 126, citing *Adamson v Motor Vehicle Insurance Trust* (1957) 58 WALR 56 [emphasis added].   [36] ibid.

[37] ibid 125.

characterizing mental illness as a deviation 'from normal moral and social standards'.[38]

The crucial role of the normal is also apparent in the arguments in favour of extending the relaxation of the standard to other shortcomings. For instance, Charles Barrett argues that the elderly should receive the same generosity as children because for both groups the diminished capacities are a result of 'conditions expected of *normal* human beings during their lives'.[39] Barrett distinguishes the elderly from the 'insane or retarded' on the ground that the latter conditions are 'derangements'.[40] Indeed, Barrett's repeated insistence that the elderly are a large portion of our population and that ageing is a normal aspect of human life rests on the idea that since ageing is not a 'peculiarity' it should count as a circumstance that calibrates the standard of care. In this sense, the underpinnings of Barrett's argument also imply the non-culpability of normal behaviour. Lewis Klar similarly underscores the normal and natural quality of certain unavoidable infirmities when he argues for more generous treatment of the elderly on the ground that 'the infirmities of old age are just as debilitating to defendants accused of negligence as are the weaknesses of youth'.[41]

B. Peculiarity and its Problems

The justification for relaxing the objective standard for those shortcomings that are 'normal' is never fully articulated. However, discussions of this problem are replete with suggestions that the individual with normal shortcomings is somehow more credible than individuals with abnormal or peculiar shortcomings. The contrast between the 'obvious' credible claims of those who are normal and the suspect claims of those who are peculiar can be seen at work in Holmes's influential discussion of the evidentiary argument. According to Holmes, the law will require a man to possess ordinary capacity 'unless a clear and manifest incapacity be shown',[42] or as he earlier puts it, unless 'a man has a distinct defect of such a nature that all can recognize it as making certain precautions impossible'.[43] As examples of the 'distinct defects' that will exonerate, Holmes points to physical disabilities including blindness and youth.[44] This seems to leave open the possibility that a cognitive impairment, for instance, could be so manifest that all could recognize it as making certain precautions impossible and that adjustments to the reasonable person standard may thus be required. Despite this, Holmes unequivocally states that the law will not take account of defects in intelligence.[45] So he must believe that 'stupidity', for instance, can never be a sufficiently 'distinct' defect to affect the standard.

---

[38] GJ Alexander and TS Szasz, 'Mental Illness as an Excuse for Civil Wrongs' (1967) 43 Notre Dame L Rev 24, 26 [footnote omitted].

[39] CV Barrett III, 'Negligence and the Elderly: A Proposal for a Relaxed Standard of Care' (1984) 17 John Marsh L Rev 873, 879–880 n 39 [emphasis added].   [40] ibid.

[41] L Klar, *Tort Law* (2nd edn, Scarborough: Carswell, 1996) 258.   [42] Holmes (n 31 above) 88.

[43] ibid 87.   [44] ibid.   [45] ibid 86.

Instead, low intelligence is simply treated as a misfortune of the individual.[46] Holmes's conclusion thus implies the mutual exclusivity of 'distinct defects' and 'individual peculiarities' of intelligence. He never explains why he construes the two categories in this way. But his assumption seems to be that while 'normal' incapacities are sufficiently clear to be the touchstone of liability, peculiar shortcomings are inherently suspect and thus can never be sufficiently obvious to play this role.

Holmes is not alone in implicitly distinguishing between the credible obvious claims of those with normal shortcomings and the unfathomable claims of those whose shortcomings are 'peculiar'. So, for instance, R. Parsons argues that while courts will take account of 'patent physical disabilities', they will 'boggle at a general investigation of the will-power and intelligence of the actor' except where there is a 'ready reckoner'.[47] Thus, while 'youth, senility and insanity are obvious circumstances which may affect the qualities of the actor',[48] beyond this the actor's mental and emotional qualities can 'be assessed only by the psychologists and the Almighty'[49] (apparently equally inaccessible!). A contrast between comprehensible normal shortcomings and incomprehensible abnormal ones is also apparent in the *Restatement*. According to that text, familiarity with the shortcomings arising out of childhood and physical disabilities means that for children, 'there is a wide basis of community experience upon which it is possible, as a practical matter, to determine what is to be expected of them.'[50] Similarly, physical illnesses can be proved with 'comparative ease and certainty'.[51] Thus, according to the *Restatement*, 'the explanation for the distinction between such physical illness and the mental illness dealt with in s 283B probably lies in the greater public familiarity with the former, and the comparative ease and certainty with which it can be proved.'[52]

Arguments about expert evidence also reveal assumptions about the relationship between normalcy and credibility. Advocates of a relaxed standard of care for cognitive or intellectual shortcomings, or for mentally disability more generally, frequently point to the availability of expert evidence as a response to the pervasive evidentiary uncertainty objections.[53] However, what

---

[46] ibid.

[47] R Parsons, 'Negligence, Contributory Negligence, and the Man Who does not Ride the Bus to Clapham' (1957) 1 Melb U L Rev 163, 179.   [48] ibid 181.

[49] ibid 179.   [50] *Restatement* (n 2 above) s 283A, Comment b.

[51] ibid s 283C, Comment b.   [52] ibid.

[53] So, for example, Ellis responds to the apparent evidentiary difficulties with the mentally disabled by noting the increased possibility of using expert evidence, as well as by pointing out that courts have no trouble with the asserted difficulties when the litigant is a child: JW Ellis, 'Tort Responsibility of Mentally Disabled Persons' [1981] Am B Found Res J 1079, 1085, 1103. Barrett makes a similar point with regard to the availability of expert evidence for the elderly: Barrett (n 39 above) 884. Intriguingly, Barrett also argues in favour of a relaxed standard of care for the elderly partly on the ground that the elderly are a large segment of our population: ibid 882. Although one might initially think that this observation would argue against extending a relaxed standard of care to the elderly, presumably he introduces it in part to assure the credibility of their claims. Like childhood, he suggests, being elderly is a normal condition shared by many and so it is easily

is most interesting about this argument is its unstated premises. Even critical commentators do not recommend expert evidence concerning what it is reasonable to expect, for example, from an average 9-year-old child with a given level of intelligence, experience, and perhaps even maturity. Instead, as the passage from the *Restatement* suggests, this is treated as the kind of information that the trier of fact has at hand, part of the common store of knowledge to which we all have ready access. It is the very 'ordinariness' of the shortcoming that locates such 'knowledge' within the realm of judicial notice[54] and simultaneously renders it so invisible as to be below the level of criticism, justification, and even discussion. 'Normal' shortcomings are thus seen as so obvious and apparent that no one could mistake either their credibility or their significance. Conversely, the 'peculiar' shortcomings of the mentally disabled seem so impenetrable that they cast a cloud of suspicion over those that raise them. Thus, we see, for example, that references to the danger of feigning mental disabilities are common and are commonly relied on as reasons to reject any claims of mental disability.[55] Yet discussions of claims of shortcomings by children or the physically disabled are virtually never accompanied by concerns about the possibility of feigned claims.

The language of 'normal' and 'natural' shortcomings also seems to import unstated assumptions about culpability. And while no one actually asserts that those with intellectual impairments, for instance, are actually responsible for those impairments, much of the rhetoric that justifies their treatment subtly implies this. Once again, the influential Holmesian argument provides an illustration. Holmes justifies the operation of the objective standard partly on the basis that the general welfare simply requires that individuals sacrifice their peculiarities.[56] Describing the demands of the objective standard in terms of a sacrifice (the surrender of a possession[57]) implies both that it is within the power of the individual to give up the shortcomings, and that the individual somehow prefers to hold on to the shortcoming rather than give it up. Yet the problem for those with developmental disabilities arises precisely because they cannot alter their behaviour to conform with the standard: indeed this conflict with the fundamental idea that 'ought implies can' is the whole reason that commentators

understood and not prey to credibility concerns. See also DE Seidelson, 'Reasonable Expectations and Subjective Standards in Negligence Law: The Minor, the Mentally Impaired, and the Mentally Incompetent' (1981) 50 Geo Wash L Rev 17, 39.

[54] That is, 'what everyone knows and uses in the ordinary process of reasoning about everyday affairs': EM Morgan, 'Judicial Notice' (1944) 57 Harv L Rev 269, 272. In fact, on occasion the reliance on judicial notice is explicit. Thus, as discussed, in *McHale v Watson* (n 8 above), Kitto J finds that it is 'a matter for judicial notice that the ordinary boy of twelve suffers from a feeling that a piece of wood and a sharp instrument have a special affinity': ibid 215.

[55] See eg *Restatement* (n 2 above) s 283B, Comment b2; Prosser (n 1 above) 153; but see Seidelson (n 53 above) 38–39, discussing *Breunig v American Family Insurance Co* 45 Wis 2d 536, 173 NW 2d 619 (Wis 1970), and arguing that fabrication is unlikely given the stigma attached to mental illness.   [56] Holmes (n 31 above) 86.

[57] *The Compact Oxford English Dictionary* (2nd edn, Oxford: Clarendon Press, 1994) 340.

and theorists puzzle over and attempt to justify their treatment. It thus seems inapt to treat their lack of intelligence as a 'peculiarity' to which they are oddly attached, a 'minute difference of character' that they are reluctant to 'sacrifice'. And Holmes's is not simply an isolated phrase, a chance remark with problematic implications. Instead, it is emblematic of a much broader, though similarly submerged, line of justification that incorporates deep-seated assumptions about the relationship between normalcy, peculiarity, and responsibility.

A similar intimation of responsibility also shows up in language that imputes intention to the 'abnormal,' implying that in some sense they choose their condition. Holmes's statements about the 'sacrifice' of individual peculiarities can be read in this way, but he is not alone in choosing language that attributes a certain kind of wilfulness to those with abnormal shortcomings. For instance, Weinrib describes this kind of defendant as 'claiming an entitlement to realize his projects in the world while retaining the exclusively internal standpoint applicable to projects as mere possibilities.'[58] Indeed, he suggests that under a subjectivized standard 'the defendant subordinates the plaintiff to the operation of the defendant's moral abilities'.[59] Weinrib also describes the subjective standard as an insistence by the defendant that he be the sole judge of reasonableness: 'Here you wish to make your subjective powers of risk assessment the standard to which you must conform when exposing others to injury.'[60] This suggests some form of self-preference—a clear justification for attributing responsibility. As discussed below, given that the point of departure for Weinrib and many others is *Vaughan v Menlove*, this characterization is hardly surprising for it is an apt description of the defendant in that case.[61] The difficulty is justifying the extension of this approach to those whose shortcomings are cognitive or intellectual, rather than moral. A similar but stronger attribution of intent is also found in the analysis of Alexander and Szasz. They argue that a mentally disabled defendant should not be exonerated simply because he has 'less capacity to resist inflicting harm than a more inhibited person'.[62] In addition to imputing wilfulness to the mentally disabled by suggesting that their fundamental problem is failure to exercise moral restraint, this language also implies culpability and thus justifies liability.[63]

---

[58] Weinrib (n 8 above) 180.   [59] ibid 183.

[60] E Weinrib, 'Causation and Wrongdoing' (1987) 63 Chi-Kent L Rev 407, 427. Similarly, he later says 'You allow me property but you demarcate the border between your holdings and mine': ibid.

[61] See the discussion of *Vaughan v Menlove* (1837) 3 Bing NC 468, 132 ER 490 (CP) in ch 8 below. As Rodgers also notes, *Vaughan* is perhaps best understood in terms of an exercise of rational choice: WH Rodgers, Jr, 'Negligence Reconsidered: The Role of Rationality in Tort Theory' (1980) 54 S Cal L Rev 1, 15. But as discussed in ch 1 above, the difficulty is generalizing these concerns to all cases of unintelligent individuals.   [62] Alexander and Szasz (n 38 above) 33.

[63] In fact, Alexander and Szasz go on to make explicit the imputation of guilt at least to the insane when they argue that the insanity defence should be rejected as an excuse for civil wrongs 'because of our belief that acts ascribed to insanity are not blameless in the way in which indifferent accidents are': ibid 35, citing TS Szasz, *The Myth of Mental Illness: Foundations of a Theory of Personal Conduct* (New York: Harper & Row, 1961) 142–143.

In addition, assumptions about culpability are frequently apparent in the use of rhetoric that distinguishes between the blameworthiness of the developmentally disabled injurer and that of the injured party. As noted earlier, commentators repeatedly describe the injured party as innocent—as if the other party is somehow not. The effect of this is to cast an aura of moral blameworthiness around the developmentally disabled actor, making legal responsibility seem more justifiable. For instance, despite the circularity of J. Coleman's defence of the objective standard,[64] his discussion seems plausible in large part because of his repeated characterization of the intellectually disabled injurer as faulty. In contrast, Coleman repeatedly refers to the plaintiff as innocent or faultless.[65] Other commentators similarly imply the culpability of those with intellectual disabilities by the insistent characterization of the victim as innocent or deserving.[66] These commentators express the view that the developmentally disabled are in some nebulous way culpable when they stress the blameless quality of 'normal' disabilities. So, for example, D. E. Seidelson makes allowances for faultless physical disabilities but not for mental disabilities.[67] Similarly Barrett argues for generosity towards the elderly on the ground that their infirmities are natural, clearly blameless, and thus distinguishable from 'derangements'.[68] Thus, while it seems clear that few if any commentators would actually argue that those with developmental disabilities are responsible for their shortcomings, these discussions do reveal deeper assumptions about culpability and normalcy that seem to underlie much of the debate.

Another indication that a certain kind of culpability is imputed to those with abnormal shortcomings is found in the ease with which the ordinary principles of fault-based liability are displaced in their cases.[69] So, for instance, Holmes confirms the centrality of a certain understanding of fault when he makes 'the power of avoiding the evil complained of a condition of liability'.[70] Thus, for Holmes it is crucial that 'the defendant must have had at least a fair chance of avoiding the infliction of harm before he becomes answerable for such a consequence of his

---

[64] As discussed in ch 1 above, Coleman's definition of fault turns out simply to mean breach of the very standard that his argument purports to justify: J Coleman, 'Mental Abnormality, Personal Responsibility, and Tort Liability' in BA Brody and HT Engelhardt, Jr (eds), *Mental Illness: Law and Public Policy* (Boston: D Reidel, 1980). [65] ibid 120–126.

[66] *Restatement* (n 2 above) s 283B, Comment b3 (reference to '*innocent* victims'); Alexander and Szasz (n 38 above) 35 ('*deserving* victims'); James (n 5 above) 1–2 ('*innocent* victims').

[67] Seidelson (n 53 above). [68] Barrett (n 39 above) 879–80.

[69] Pound's argument that the law of negligence is really concerned, not with the 'culpable exercise of the will' but rather with the 'danger to the general security' seems on point here. Pound notes: 'Whenever a case of negligence calls for sharp application of the objective standard, fault is as much a dogmatic fiction as is representation in the liability of the master for the torts of his servant. In each case the exigencies of the will theory lead us to cover up a liability irrespective of fault, imposed to maintain the general security, by a conclusive imputation of fault to one who may be morally blameless': R Pound, *An Introduction to the Philosophy of Law* (New Haven: Yale University Press, 1954) 91. But *contra* Pound, the argument here is that fault is much more a fiction with some litigants than with others and that there is indeed something selective about when the law of negligence attends to moral blameworthiness and when it does not. [70] Holmes (n 31 above) 77.

conduct'.[71] But this powerful reasoning is curiously absent from his untroubled conclusion that for those who lack normal powers, the law simply considers 'what would be blameworthy in the average man, the man of ordinary intelligence and prudence, and determines liability by that. If we fall below the level in those gifts, it is our misfortune.'[72] And other commentators are quick to follow Holmes's lead. For instance, after affirming the principle of avoidability, Linden states that no allowance will be made 'for those who are merely deficient intellectually and therefore cannot live up to the objective standard'.[73] Similarly, although Seavey acknowledges the difficulties with an objective standard for intelligence,[74] he has no hesitation in concluding that the person with limited intelligence should simply bear the consequences of that shortcoming.[75] Perhaps unsurprisingly, then, it is typically in the context of discussion of the liability of those with intellectual limitations that commentators point to and often praise the disjunction between moral and legal fault.[76] But though it may indeed reveal the underlying identity of the standard, this insistence may also lead us to worry more generally about the basis of the distinctiveness of the objective standard.

Thus, the identification of certain kinds of shortcomings as normal or natural and others as peculiar plays an important—although unacknowledged—role in justifying the operation of the objective standard. This is despite the fact that there is an obvious sense in which having a cognitive or intellectual disability is as much a result of the processes of nature as is youth. While the underlying idea may be that childhood is normal because every human being passes through it, in fact childhood as we think of it is not something so unproblematically normal and natural.[77] But even if we were inclined to allow that childhood is normal or natural in some way that developmental disabilities are not, there is still a pressing question about why such a characterization should be relevant to the standard of care. Perhaps the normative power of the idea of the

---

[71] ibid 129.   [72] ibid 87.   [73] Linden (n 15 above) 146.   [74] Seavey (n 14 above) 12.
[75] ibid.

[76] Fleming (n 1 above) 114; Linden (n 15 above) 134; Klar (n 41 above) 254; Holmes (n 31 above) 86 (law does not attempt to see men as God sees them, necessity of attending to the external quality of the act only); Prosser (n 1 above) 153, citing Holmes; *Remedies in Tort* (n 34 above) 16.I-49 (first point under section entitled 'Moral Qualities and Knowledge' insists that defendant's blameworthiness is irrelevant).

[77] P Ariès, *Centuries of Childhood: A Social History of Family Life* (trans R Baldick) (New York: Vintage Books, 1962). So Ariès notes that '[i]n medieval society the idea of childhood did not exist': 128. Thus, they had no concept of 'the particular nature of childhood, that particular nature which distinguishes the child from the adult, even the young adult': ibid. And it is precisely this awareness of the particular nature of childhood that is the basis of the subjectivized standard of care for children. Yet, as Ariès's study illustrates, for most of our history, there was no awareness of the supposedly natural and normal distinctiveness of childhood. Of course, the mere fact that something has not been attended to in the past is not in itself conclusive proof that it cannot be labelled natural or normal. But Ariès's analysis should alert us to the difficulties with uncritical application of labels like 'natural' and 'normal' to biological differences. As his work indicates, many of the differences that we think of as natural and normal may in fact be more contentious than these labels suggest.

normal is nowhere so evident as in the fact that this question is not even addressed in the literature. G. E. Moore's perceptive discussion of how terms like natural and normal tend to be infused with ethical meaning seems on point here: 'But is it so obvious that the normal must be good? ... It is, I think, obviously in the first place, that not all that is good is normal; that, on the contrary, the abnormal is often better than the normal: peculiar excellence, as well as peculiar viciousness, must obviously be not normal but abnormal.'[78] As Moore notes, this use of terms like normal and natural to convey attributions of value is in fact deeply problematic, though this may be obscured by the appealing rhetoric. Thus, as Moore insists: 'We must not, therefore, be frightened by the assertion that a thing is natural into the admission that it is good; good does not, by definition, mean anything that is natural; and it is therefore always an open question whether anything that is natural is good.'[79] In much the same way, labelling shortcomings as either normal and natural or as peculiar *implies* moral judgements but does not *justify* them. And as we shall see, infusing the norm of reasonableness by recourse to some conception of what is normal or ordinary also has deeper problems.

III. NORMAL MEN, NATURAL WOMEN, AND THE FOOL'S MISFORTUNE

> objective, a.& n. (Philos.) belonging not to the consciousness or the perceiving or thinking subject but to what is presented to this or the nonego, external to the mind, real; (of person, writing, picture, &c.) dealing with outward things & not with thoughts or feelings.[80]

As our earlier discussion of *McHale* and other cases suggests, the most common understanding of the source of the reasonable person's objectivity seems to be found in the fact that it appeals not to personal or individual qualities, but rather to an interpersonal standard of ordinariness. The determinations of what is normal or ordinary that infuse the standard are 'objective' in the sense that they are external to the actor. But a closer examination of the idea of the normal undermines at least one aspect of the standard's claim to objectivity: it does not seem possible to argue that the treatment of various groups under the

---

[78] GE Moore, *Principia Ethica* (ed T Baldwin) (Revised edn, Cambridge: Cambridge University Press, 1903) 94–95. In Moore's discussion of Naturalistic Ethics he discusses the 'vague notion' underlying Stoic Ethics that 'Nature may be said to fix and decide what shall be good': ibid 94. Indeed, Moore goes on to connect the ethical assumptions commonly made about the natural with assumptions about the normal. He points out that, for instance, health may be thought to be good because it is natural. But since disease is certainly also a natural product, what can natural mean here but 'the *normal* state of an organism': ibid [emphasis in original]. The implication, he continues, is that 'the normal must be good': 94–95. But he argues that language that uses words like 'natural' and 'normal' to connote value judgments is 'fallacious, and dangerously fallacious': ibid 95.

[79] ibid 94.

[80] *Webster's Dictionary of the English Language* (Toronto: Wordsworth Editions, 1989) 781, entry under 'objective'.

standard is justified because it simply reflects reality, an uncontroversial reflection of the world. Even a cursory examination of the idea of normalcy suggests that it is unlikely that it can do this work. But the second and deeper problem is that the idea of the normal, invoked to justify and give content to the operation of the objective standard, is not just value-laden in some undifferentiated and untroubling way. Instead, behind the veneer of common sense one can trace the complicated hierarchy of a deeply inegalitarian world-view. And history suggests that notions of what is normal, natural, or ordinary have long been, and continue to be, one of the primary vehicles for inequality.

As we have seen, terms like 'normal' and 'natural' tend to surreptitiously import attributions of value.[81] In fact, even in what would seem to be the least problematic realm of science, concepts of what is normal are far from uncontroversial. In his classic work on the history of science, Georges Canguilhem analyses how concepts of the normal and the pathological are not determined by science or statistics, but instead depend fundamentally on contestable attributions of value.[82] Thus, he notes the difficulties inherent in using the 'average state of the characteristic studied' as a substitute for objectivity in biometrical profiles of the normal or average man, pointing out that determinations of what counts as the 'average state' are inevitably arbitrary.[83] So given the inadequacy of the biometrical data and the more fundamental uncertainty about what principles are to be used in distinguishing between normal and abnormal, Canguilhem describes 'the scientific definition of normality' as 'beyond reach'.[84] Similarly, he points out the discretion inevitably involved even in determining which physiological behaviours are normal and notes that selection of the norm 'whose antiquity makes it seem natural' is often the response to this difficulty.[85] Thus, like Moore he concludes that our determinations of what is normal or average, 'our image of the world[,] is always a display of values as well'.[86] Ultimately, conceptions of normality and abnormality depend on each other. In this way, 'the normal man knows that he is so only in a world where every man is not normal'[87] Thus, the idea of the normal is problematic even in its scientific application.

Prominent postmodern and feminist critics of science have also pointed to the way that apparently neutral 'scientific' categorization imports both hierarchy and disadvantage. Perhaps the most celebrated such discussion is found in Michel Foucault's work on the 'normalizing' gaze of modern scientific reason. Foucault notes that such reason 'differentiates individuals from one another' in the following way:

It measures in quantitative terms and hierarchizes in terms of value the abilities, the level, the 'nature' of individuals. It introduces, through this 'value-giving' measure, the

---

[81] Thus, as discussed earlier, Moore stresses the difficulties with arguing that a thing is good because it is natural or bad because it is unnatural: (n 78 above) 97.

[82] *The Normal and the Pathological* (trans Carolyn R Fawcett with Robert S Cohen) (New York: Zone Books, 1991). [83] ibid 155.

[84] ibid, quoting H Laugier, 'L'Homme normal', *Encyclopédie française* 4 (1937) 4.56–4.

[85] ibid 175. [86] ibid 179. [87] ibid 286.

constraint of a conformity that must be achieved. Lastly, it traces the limit that will define difference in relation to all other differences, the external frontier of the abnormal.[88]

Similarly, feminist critics of epistemology and science point out how much scientific thought actually distorts our understanding both of the natural world and of social relations by rendering it in a partial and often troubling way.[89] But if giving 'objective' non-value laden content to the concept of what is normal is so difficult, even in the seemingly less complex case of human physiology, how can an unreflective version of this concept be used to attribute responsibility under the objective standard?

The problem is not simply that the concept of what is normal and therefore reasonable is not objective because it is inevitably value-laden. Indeed, were this the case, it would simply be a particular instance of the now-general recognition of the difficulty inherent in drawing any uncontroversial fact/value distinction. But this difficulty might not be so troubling in and of itself were its impact randomly distributed, so to speak. The problem, however, is deeper and more complex. This is because what we have seen so far suggests that the impact of the values imported through the idea of the normal is anything but random. Indeed, Foucault (among others) draws attention to the way that concepts like the normal are not value-laden in some relatively uncontroversial way:

Like surveillance and with it, normalization becomes one of the great instruments of power at the end of the classical age. For the marks that once indicated status, privilege and affiliation were increasingly replaced—or at least supplemented—by a whole range of degrees of normality indicating membership of a homogeneous social body but also playing a part in classification, hierarchization and the distribution of rank.[90]

Thus, the problem associated with the invocation of the normal goes beyond Moore's point that notions of what is normal are inevitably value-laden. What is more worrisome is the unstated conceptions of value that so often accompany ideas of the normal. The concern in philosophy and the history of science, as we have seen, is that ideas of the normal or natural typically both imply and create a troubling hierarchy in which the normal are privileged and the abnormal are not. And this concern is by no means confined to those disciplines.

---

[88] M Foucault, *Discipline and Punish: The Birth of the Prison* (trans Alan Sheridan) (New York: Vintage Books, 1979) 183.

[89] Prominent examples include S Harding, *The Science Question in Feminism* (Ithaca, NY: Cornell University Press, 1986); G Lloyd, *The Man of Reason: 'Male' and 'Female' in Western Philosophy* (London: Methuen, 1984); E Keller, *Reflections on Gender and Science* (New Haven: Yale University Press, 1984).

[90] Foucault (n 88 above) 184. See also M Foucault, *Power/Knowledge: Selected Interviews & Other Writings 1972–1977* (trans Colin Gordon, Leo Marshall, John Mepham, and Kate Soper) (New York: Pantheon, 1980) 107–8, 131. Thus, despite the similarities noted in the text, this is the major point of divergence between Moore and later philosophers like Foucault. Indeed, Moore's claim about the invocation of terms like 'normal' and 'natural' is primarily that they are simply sloppy arguments in the search for the good: n 78 above. He does not argue that there is anything more deeply troubling about how such arguments operate—whose interests they privilege and whose they ignore.

In fact, legal history also suggests that wariness about reliance on ideas about the normal or natural is not misplaced. Indeed, such concepts have been the mainstay of justifications for the unequal treatment of both the developmentally disabled and women, among others. Invidious ideas of what is normal and natural have often been invoked to justify exclusion from the privileges of full membership, and often from the formal rights of citizenship itself.

A. The unfortunate fool

A powerful illustration of the dangers of invoking unreflective or common sense ideas about what is natural or normal can be found in the history of the treatment (in law and otherwise) of the developmentally or cognitively disabled (often called 'retarded'). In fact, their treatment also provides insight into the deep link to membership and citizenship. Throughout this history we also see how legal force is given to inegalitarian social hierarchies through ideas of what is normal and natural. In the Supreme Court of the United States, Justice Marshall summarized it in this way:

[The] mentally retarded have been subject to a lengthy and tragic history of segregation and discrimination that can only be called grotesque.... By the latter part of the [nineteenth] century and during the first decades of the new one, however, social views of the retarded underwent a radical transformation. Fuelled by the rising tide of Social Darwinism, the 'science' of eugenics, and the extreme xenophobia of those years, leading medical authorities and others began to portray the 'feebleminded' as a 'menace to society and civilization... responsible in a large degree for many, if not all, of our social problems'. A regime of state-mandated segregation and degradation soon emerged that in its virulence and bigotry rivalled, and indeed paralleled, the worst excesses of Jim Crow.[91]

Justice Marshall went on to note how such individuals have also suffered recent and in some cases continuing exclusion from the fundamental rights of citizenship, including voting and education. He concluded by pointing out that the

---

[91] *City of Cleburne v Cleburne Living Center* 473 US 432, 461–462 (1985) (dissenting in part) [internal citations omitted]. *Cleburne* concerned an equal protection challenge to a zoning ordinance that prevented construction of a group home for people with developmental disabilities in a residential neighbourhood. Justice White, writing for the majority, rejected the argument that mental retardation was a quasi-suspect classification. Thus, the classification did not engage heightened scrutiny under the equal protection clause. Nonetheless, the majority found that the zoning ordinance was unconstitutional because it could not even survive low-level (rational basis) review. Justice Marshall, along with Justices Brennan and Blackmun, concurred in the result. However, they found that in the light of the history of discrimination that the 'retarded' had suffered, the equal protection clause required heightened scrutiny for such a classification. For a more recent case involving deinstitutionalization, see *Olmstead v LC* 119 S Ct 2176 (US Ga 1999) (meaning of 'undue institutionalization' under Americans with Disabilities Act of 1990, s 202, 42 USCA 12132). For a more general overview of this extensive topic, see Mary C Cerreto, '*Olmstead*: The *Brown v Board of Education* for Disability Rights: Promises, Limits and Issues' (2001) 2 Loyola J Publ Int L 47. In Canada, s 15 of the Charter enumerates 'mental disability' along with race, gender, religion, and other traditional categories as prohibited grounds of discrimination.

'lengthy and continuing isolation of the retarded [*sic*] has perpetuated the ignorance, irrational fears, and stereotyping that have long plagued them'.[92] Similarly, in *Re Eve*[93] Justice La Forest, speaking for the Supreme Court of Canada, rejected an application for the involuntary non-therapeutic sterilization of a young woman with a cognitive disability. In the course of his judgment, Justice La Forest pointed out that this kind of decision must be approached with 'the utmost caution', in part because it involved 'values in an area where our social history clouds our vision and encourages many to perceive the mentally handicapped as somewhat less than human'.[94] Courts themselves are beginning to recognize their own complicity in treating those with cognitive or intellectual limitations as abnormal, indeed in some sense sub-human, thus fuelling their discriminatory treatment and exclusion from society.[95]

Even such a brief examination of this history serves to increase the uncomfortable sense that there is something troubling about how the reasonable person standard both treats those with developmental disabilities and justifies that treatment. The ideology of exclusion referred to by both Justice Marshall and Justice La Forest seems perpetuated by the reasonable person's untroubled assertion that, unlike other members of society, the developmentally disabled simply have to participate in social life at their peril. And the fact that their liberty is not accorded the same protection as that of 'normal' members of society dovetails with the historical treatment of the developmentally disabled, and in particular with their incarceration and exclusion from the ordinary rights of citizenship.[96] The 'welfare' arguments made in the context of those with developmental limitations are also ominously echoed in history. Thus, invoking our concern with the welfare of children and noting their importance to society as a justification for relaxing the standard to which they are held[97] also intimates those whose welfare we have never cared about.

The unusual ease with which the liberty interests of those with developmental disabilities are subordinated to social welfare concerns also has historical

---

[92] *Cleburne* (n 91 above) 464.   [93] (1986) 31 DLR (4th) 1 (SCC).   [94] ibid 29.

[95] See, for instance, *Muir v Alberta* (1996) 132 DLR (4th) 695, Veit J, and in particular Appendix A, the Report of the Expert Witness Gerald Robertson, on the Sexual Sterilization Act, SA 1928, c 37 (the 'Act'): 744–762. Robertson notes that detailed studies of the administration of the Act show that 'it had a disproportionate impact on females, the unemployed, people of minority ethnic backgrounds, and those in lower socio-economic groups': 745, citing Tim Christian, *The Mentally Ill and Human Rights in Alberta: A Study of the Alberta Sexual Sterilization Act* (Edmonton: Faculty of Law, University of Alberta 1974) and Law Reform Commission of Canada, *Sterilization: Implications for Mentally Retarded and Mentally Ill Persons*, Working Paper No 24 (Ottawa: Minister of Supply and Services Canada, 1979).

[96] As discussed below, those who were considered 'feeble-minded' form one of the recurring categories of exclusion: n 151 below.

[97] So, for instance, the *Restatement (Second) of Torts* indicates that the special standard for children arises in part 'out of the public interest in their welfare and protection': (n 2 above) s 283A, Comment b. Wilderman also attributes tort law's generous treatment of children to the 'social urge to protect children': LH Wilderman, 'Presumptions Existing in Favour of the Infant in Re: The Question of an Infant's Ability to be Guilty of Contributory Negligence' (1935) 10 Indiana LJ 427, 427.

resonance. In *Buck v Bell*, Justice Holmes justified the compulsory sterilization of 'mental defectives' on the following grounds:

We have seen more than once that the public welfare may call upon the best citizens for their lives. It would be strange if it could not call upon those who already sap the strength of the State for these lesser sacrifices, often not felt to be such by those concerned, in order to prevent our being swamped with incompetence.[98]

Even a strong aversion to *ad hominem* arguments is not enough to dispel the uneasy sense of some connection between Justice Holmes's position in *Buck v Bell* and his untroubled conclusion in *The Common Law* that those who are 'merely stupid' must simply make certain sacrifices in the interests of the general welfare. Indeed, the point is in an important sense not *ad hominem*: the hostility to those with developmental disabilities, though betrayed here by Justice Holmes, is most certainly not confined to him.[99] Because of the prevalence of incarceration, the developmentally disabled were historically quite literally outsiders. But even when they were not, the terms in which their interests are discussed reveals that they inhabit a world far beyond the community of care and concern that encompasses the playing child. And this is undoubtedly important to the ease with which the developmentally disabled are subjected to unfavourable treatment under the objective standard. Indeed, the uncritical way in which the reasonableness standard is infused with notions of what is normal makes it all too easy for these kinds of discriminatory stereotypes to seep into the standard of care and thus to affect how those with developmental limitations fare under that standard.

Thus, even beyond the pejorative labels routinely used to designate those with developmental limitations, the justifications for their treatment under the objective standard reveals a deep sense in which they are excluded. Courts and commentators say that there are limits on what can be attributed to the reasonable man. So, although he may be susceptible to heart attacks, emergencies and other exigencies, the reasonable man can nonetheless not be a moron or an idiot—and this is true by definition. On the standard reading, the reasonable man is defined by his ordinariness or commonness. The person with a developmental disability is defined by his idiosyncrasies, his peculiarities. There is no conception of ordinariness that can apply to him. Instead, he is a moron or an idiot. But the words 'idiot', 'idiosyncrasy', and 'peculiarity' all derive from the Greek 'idios' meaning 'own' or 'private'—thus the labels themselves mark the developmentally disabled person's interests as essentially private rather than

---

[98] 274 US 200, 207 (1926).
[99] In fact, Justice Holmes was not writing an opinion for himself alone in *Buck v Bell* but rather for Court. Only Justice Butler dissents and he does so without a written opinion. For a history of such views and their prevalence among the medical community, political leaders (including feminists like Nellie McClung and Emily Murphy), the media, and the public, see Robertson (n 95 above) and the sources discussed therein. See also the sources cited in the dissenting opinion of Justice Marshall in *Cleburne* (n 91 above). See also *SL (by her litigation friend, the Official Solicitor) v SL (her mother)* [2000] EWCA Civ 162.

common or shared.[100] So he can never be a citizen in the true sense of the word, for a citizen is defined by his public role, while the idiot is by definition private. In this way then, the treatment of people with developmental disabilities under the objective standard actually seems to echo their historic exclusion from the formal rights of citizenship. The essence of the reasonable man is possession of those ordinary shared qualities that are accessible to common sense. Left alone in the prison of his peculiarity, the idiot cannot inhabit this shared world of ordinariness. This is reflected in the treatment he receives under the objective standard—treatment that seems intimately connected to a broader history of isolation and exclusion from even the most basic rights of membership, including his liberty.

B. The natural woman

In this sense, the way that ideas about what is normal or natural play out to the disadvantage of the developmentally disabled re-enacts a now largely discredited history of formal exclusion. But commentators on membership and exclusion note that this is but one of the recurring categories of exclusion justified by recourse to what is normal and natural. Thus, Ursula Vogel notes that within the context of the modern state in the last two centuries, there are certain recurring categories of exclusion: incapacity to exercise rights and perform obligations (children, insane persons, criminals); ascribed social status (slaves, serfs); racial and ethnic identity (Jews, blacks); religion (Dissenters, Catholics, Huguenots, etc.); status of aliens (foreigners, immigrants, refugees, guest workers); lack of property.[101] Similarly, Iris Marion Young points out that liberalism traditionally asserted the right of all rational autonomous agents to equal citizenship.[102] But the consequence of assumptions about 'nature', rationality, and dependence meant that 'poor people, women, the mad and the feebleminded, and children were explicitly excluded from citizenship and many of these were housed in institutions modeled on the modern prison: poorhouses, insane asylums, schools'.[103] This suggests that we should not be surprised if the reliance on the idea of the normal that we saw at work more broadly under the objective standard also raises other serious egalitarian concerns.

One particular such concern is found in the gender implications of incorporating this kind of idea of the normal into the workings of the objective

---

[100] The term 'idiot' comes from the Greek 'idiotes' meaning 'private person, layman, ignorant person' from whence came its more modern meaning 'person so deficient in mind as to be permanently incapable of rational conduct; utter fool': *Webster's Dictionary of the English Language* (n 80 above) 563. Similarly, 'peculiar' has the implication of privacy rather than commonness or publicity, 'belonging exclusively to the individual': ibid 843.

[101] 'Is Citizenship Gender-Specific?' in U Vogel and M Moran (eds), *The Frontiers of Citizenship* (London: MacMillan, 1991) 62.

[102] *Justice and the Politics of Difference* (Princeton: Princeton University Press, 1990) 54.

[103] ibid 54, referring to C Pateman, *The Sexual Contract* (Stanford, Calif.: Stanford University Press, 1988) ch 3.

standard. As we saw in the cases involving the playing girl, appealing to a conception of what is normal or natural allows the reasonable person standard to effectively extend more generous treatment to the boy—more liberty with himself and with others—than to the girl. This should hardly be surprising. If anything, the history of the treatment of women betrays an even more sustained illustration of the dangers of appeals to ordinariness, to the natural, and normal.[104] So speaking of women's access to the basic rights of membership and the formal rights of citizenship, Vogel notes: 'Within the parameters of the common law, for example, married women were—until the end of the nineteenth century—placed in the same category of legal incompetence as children, minors and idiots. Because they were presumed to lack the capacities of agency, the language of the law might...refer to them as "aliens in the state".'[105] And once again we see the centrality of ideas of natural and normal feminine qualities as justifications for limiting female participation in the public world. Psychology, philosophy, and law alike are replete with such appeals. As Dr Benjamin Spock put it,

Women are usually more patient in working at unexciting, repetitive tasks...Women on the average have more passivity in the inborn core of their personality.[106]

I believe women are designed in their deepest instincts to get more pleasure out of life—not only sexually but socially, occupationally, maternally—when they are not aggressive. To put it another way I think that when women are encouraged to be competitive too many of them become disagreeable.[107]

In fact, the overriding conception of what is natural for women—a conception that shows up in remarkably similar terms in twentieth-century cases—is perhaps most eloquently stated by Jean-Jacques Rousseau: 'A perfect man and a perfect women should no more be alike in mind than in face. The man should be strong and active; the woman should be weak and passive; the one must have both the power and the will; it is enough that the other should offer little resistance.'[108] Girls, Rousseau later insists, should become accustomed to restraint

---

[104] But this may only be because the history of women's exclusion is far more chronicled than that of the mentally disabled. Perhaps this is in part because, as Young notes, often the exclusion of the mentally disabled was accomplished not through the direct denial of the franchise and civil rights, but rather through more extensive exclusion, principally institutionalization: (n 102 above) 54. In addition, because they have traditionally been characterized as non-agents, the exclusion of the mentally disabled from the rights of citizenship may not be viewed as similarly problematic: Note, 'Mental Disability and the Right to Vote' 88 Yale LJ 1644 (1979). So although women have begun to write the history of their silence, for the mentally disabled, one might say, the silence remains quite literally deafening.　　　　　　　　　　　　　　　　　　　　[105] Vogel (n 101 above) 62–63.
[106] B Spock, *Decent and Indecent: Our Personal and Political Behaviour* (New York: McCall Publishing, 1969) 32.　　　　　　　　　　　　　　　　　　　　[107] ibid 47.
[108] J-J Rousseau, *Émile, or on Education (1762)* (trans Barbara Foxley) (London: JM Dent & Sons Ltd, 1955) 322. Note the similarity of Rousseau's suggestion that being brought under authority is not in fact a hardship for women to the reasoning of Justice Holmes in *Buck v Bell*. There, after arguing that the incompetents should make sacrifices for the greater good, Holmes notes that these sacrifices are 'often not felt to be such by those concerned': (n 98 above) 207. Yet this remark was made in a case where Carrie Buck challenged her involuntary sterilization all the way to the Supreme Court of the United States.

early for it will characterize their lives. They must 'be trained to bear the yoke from the first, so that they may not feel it, to master their own caprices and to submit themselves to the will of others'.[109] Thus, whether they are made or trained to be such, girls must be passive and gentle in contrast to their masculine counterparts.

This kind of appeal to a passive feminine nature has also played an important role in justifying the refusal to admit women to 'masculine' professions and to the public world more generally. As Carl Jung commented:

[N]o one can evade the fact, that in taking up a masculine calling, studying, and working in a man's way, woman is doing something not wholly in agreement with, if not directly injurious to, her feminine nature…[110]

[Female] psychology is founded on the principle of eros, the binder and deliverer; while age-old wisdom has ascribed logos to man as his ruling principle.[111]

Indeed, this conception of what is natural or normal for women has often played an overtly important role in legal determinations. To cite but one of myriad examples, in *Bradwell v State*,[112] the Supreme Court of the United States sustained legislation that denied women the right to practice law. An appeal to nature is crucial to the oft-cited concurrence of Justice Joseph P Bradley in that decision:

[The] civil law, as well as nature herself, has always recognized a wide difference in the respective spheres and destinies of man and woman. Man is, or should be, woman's protector and defender. The natural and proper timidity and delicacy which belongs to the female sex evidently unfits it for many of the occupations of civil life. The constitution of the family organization, which is founded in the divine ordinance, as well as in the nature of things, indicates the domestic sphere as that which properly belongs to the domain and functions of womanhood. The harmony, not to say identity, of interests and views which belong, or should belong, to the family institution is repugnant to the idea of a woman adopting a distinct and independent career from that of her husband.[113]

Such appeals to nature have not only been used to exclude women from important professional aspects of the public world; they have also played a central role in denying women other civil and political rights including the right to be educated, and the right to vote and participate in public life.[114] Thus, for instance,

---

[109] ibid 332.

[110] *Contributions to Analytical Psychology* (trans HG and Cary F Baynes) (London: K Paul, Trench, Trubner & Co Ltd, 1928) 169.   [111] ibid 176.

[112] 16 Wall (83 US) 130 (1873).

[113] ibid 141. For an analysis of the impact of the law and such discriminatory conceptions on the professional lives of women more generally, see Constance Backhouse, *Petticoats and Prejudice: Women and Law in Nineteenth Century Canada* (Toronto: The Osgoode Society, 1991), especially ch 9 'Protective Labour Legislation' and ch 10 'Lawyering: Clara Brett Martin, Canada's First Woman Lawyer'.

[114] Judith Shklar points out that, whatever the appeal of the participatory Aristotelian conception of citizenship, this is not the sort of citizenship that the disenfranchised have demanded. Instead, she describes the right to vote and the opportunity to earn as the 'two great emblems of public standing',

two years after *Bradwell* the Supreme Court of the United States denied women the right to vote on the ground that it was not a right and that they already possessed all necessary civil rights.[115] Nature, it was argued, had made women so weak that they required protection and thus could not be granted suffrage.[116]

When viewed against this backdrop, we can begin to see the larger significance of the cases we examined involving children. As with the developmentally disabled, there is a disturbing reflection of history in the way that courts use conceptions of what is normal and natural to give content to the meaning of reasonable behaviour. In this sense the pattern of treatment that dominates cases involving boys and girls seems corroborated by the concepts and language invoked in those cases. In fact, the virtual exclusion of girls from access to the argument that they acted out of natural imprudence echoes the pervasive belief, articulated by Rousseau centuries ago, that female nature is—or ought to be—inherently timid and passive.[117] So, in the cases involving the playing girl we see courts invoking an all-too-familiar understanding of girlhood as characterized by appropriately cautious and passive behaviour. Indeed, if we look past the quaint language of the quote from the court in *Hassenyer*,[118] it is hard to miss how much the court there actually seems to capture about the expectations of female behaviour and the extent to which those expectations are still expressed in the objective standard. So women, unaccustomed to the ways of the world and more inclined to panic in the face of danger, may be given greater latitude

the central attributes of citizenship, around which the struggle for inclusion has centred: 'American Citizenship: The Question for Inclusion' in *The Tanner Lectures on Human Values XI: 1990* (Utah: University of Utah Press, 1989) 388.

[115] *Minor v Happersett* 88 US (21 Wall) 162 (1875). For an overview of the struggle to get the franchise, see Shklar (n 114 above); A Prenctice et al, *Canadian Women: A History* (2nd edn, Toronto: Harcourt Brace & Company, Canada, 1996) 234 ff; S Brooks, *Canadian Democracy: An Introduction* (3rd edn, Don Mills, Ontario: Oxford University Press Canada, 2000) 349 ff; C Rover, *Women's Suffrage and Party Politics in Britain 1866–1914* (London: Routledge & Kegan Paul, 1967); V Randall, *Women and Politics* (2nd edn, London: MacMillan, 1987).

[116] Shklar (n 114 above) 403. See also Vogel (n 101 above) 62–64; Backhouse (n 113 above) 293; Iris Marion Young, 'Polity and Group Difference: A Critique of the Ideal of Universal Citizenship' in Cass R Sunstein (ed), *Feminism and Political Theory* (Chicago: University of Chicago Press, 1990) 117, 120–122.

[117] It is important to note here, however, that these images of delicacy so often called forth to justify female exclusion from the public world clearly invoked only a certain group of women, privileged on grounds of class and race at least. Elizabeth Spelman offers a more contemporary example of the same phenomenon in her comment that when Betty Friedan suggested that women's problems would be largely solved if they got 'out of the house' she could not have been thinking of the millions of women that have always worked outside the house, often as domestic labour for the very women about whom Friedan was writing: *Inessential Woman: Problems of Exclusion in Feminist Thought* (Boston: Beacon Press, 1988) 8, discussing Betty Friedan, *The Feminine Mystique* (New York: Norton, 1963). Thus, the ideal of femininity that we see in both the commentary and the cases is an ideal premissed not only on gender identity but also on class and racial privilege at a minimum. For a fascinating history of how some of these issues play out in the complexities of the women's movement and female waged workers in the nineteenth century, see Backhouse (n 113 above) ch 9 'Protective Labour Legislation'.

[118] *Michigan Central Railroad v Hassenyer*, 48 Mich 205 (SC 1882).

when they react with fear to a risk not of their own making. However, as we have seen in the cases involving the playing girl, asking what 'is commonly looked for from one of her sex' will at least as often lead to a higher standard of care—requiring more vigilance in the care of others and more caution with regard to her own safety.[119] Conceptions of what is normal and natural mean that the girl must inhabit the public world with more caution: her liberty is consequently more constrained.

C. The playground of childhood

The light of history is also revealing in other ways. The absence of any romantic language and understanding of girlhood may seem surprising, but looking to the larger context is again helpful. As Philippe Ariès points out in his path-breaking social history of childhood, the idea of childhood, although phrased in general terms, was actually distinguished by its treatment of boys. Thus, the developing concept of childhood as a distinct period with its own special characteristics which must be encouraged and protected was in fact a concept of boyhood.[120] Ariès comments, 'The idea of childhood profited the boys first of all, while the girls persisted much longer in the traditional way of life which confused them with the adults.'[121] And indeed, this accords with what we see under the objective standard. The latitude under the objective standard that is notionally given to all children in fact seems to benefit boys disproportionately. So courts are prepared to forgive all sorts of boyish imprudence based on that commonsense appeal to the inevitability of nature—'boys will be boys.' Unlike the developmentally disabled or the playing girl, the boy inhabits the public world with impunity, sure that it will look with leniency on his childish excesses. Thus, as in the literature on the history of childhood, the legal understanding of childhood depicts a specially protected sphere of liberty and learning, but it is also a sphere which permits only the most privileged children to enter. In some way then, this history is repeated in the workings of the objective standard, where other children—not privileged, not boys—have struggled to access the liberty so often extended to certain boys.

---

[119] ibid 208. See discussion in ch 3 above.

[120] In *Centuries of Childhood*, Ariès chronicles the significance of education in the evolution of the modern conception of childhood: (n 77 above) 137–336. In the course of that discussion he indicates that the terms 'schoolboy', 'scholar', and 'student' were used interchangeably: 329. He also notes that schooling was 'the monopoly of one sex. Women were excluded': 331. Indeed, elsewhere Ariès states that although he discusses childhood in general terms, in fact it had very distinct gender and class lines. For instance, he points out that the change in clothing, like many of the innovations in the treatment of children, affected boys more than girls. For a very considerable period of time, girls were not differentiated from adults, as certain boys were.

Ariès also points out the relationship between the development of childhood and the rise of the modern bourgeois or middle class. After noting that the 'old ways of life have survived almost until the present day in the lower classes', he points out the impact of the demand for child labour during the nineteenth century. He continues, 'Child labour retained this characteristic of medieval society: the precocity of entry into adult life. The whole complexion of life was changed by the differences in the educational treatment of the middle-class and lower-class child': 336.   [121] ibid 61.

With his characteristic eloquence, William Wordsworth described the child as the father of the man. Rousseau was perhaps less poetic but no less apt when he noted, 'Silly children grow into ordinary men. I know no generalisation more certain than this.'[122] And since the relaxed standard for children is justified in part on the ground that we care about their welfare and want them to learn,[123] we should perhaps ask what exactly the standard tells children about how they should behave. The standard depicts a world sharply riven by gender boundaries and other divisions.[124] And it is not simply that the gender line in the playground, so to speak, exists: it exists, at least in part, because it is enforced, including by judges. But this illustrates how complicated the assertion of 'naturalness' is. The cases imply that since recklessness is part of a boy's nature because boys simply *will* behave recklessly, the standard by which such behaviour is judged must be calibrated accordingly. But looking at how judges tend to react to reckless girls casts a different light on the notion that the standard is simply reflecting 'natural' differences, for these cases suggest that at least some girls also have reckless impulses. Thus, it seems that something beyond the apparently descriptive appeal to what is natural is at work here. Rather than simple generalizations of how girls *do* behave, what we see are far more normative assertions of how girls *should* behave. And this is by no means

---

[122] Rousseau (n 108 above) 70.

[123] There are, it is worth noting, serious difficulties with these rationales beyond those discussed in the text. If (as seems likely) children behave in much the same way regardless of tort liability, then this undermines the forward-looking argument that the relaxed standard allows children room to develop. Similarly, because many cases arising out of so-called 'carefree' activities involve situations where one child injures another child, the 'protection of children' justification for relaxing the standard seems unpersuasive (for examples, see *McHale v Watson* (n 8 above); *Purtle v Shelton* 474 SW 2d 123 (sc Ark 1971) (hunting); *Hamel v Crosietier* 256 A 2d 143 (SCNH 1969) ('playing')). Interestingly, however, the romantic construction of 'carefree' child's play is so powerful that the dangerous—indeed often brutal—form that child's play may take is routinely obscured: GL Bahr, 'Tort Law and the Games Kids Play' (1978) 23 S Dak L Rev 275. Thus, Bahr advocates handling children's games on an 'exuberance model' that excuses much carelessness on the ground that then 'the kids of the world would be free to be free': 300. The freedom here is clearly the freedom of the child defendant. Indeed, it is interesting to note that this model is beginning to be challenged by parents and school authorities that are insisting, for example, that bullying be taken seriously. See, for instance, *R v DW and KPD* [2002] BCJ No 627 (female school bully convicted of death threats and bodily harm); *Jubran v North Vancouver School District No 44* [2002] BCHRTD No 10 (school board responsible for harassment of student on basis of perceived sexual orientation); *Davis v Monroe County Board of Education* 526 US 629 (1999) (school board liable because it was deliberately indifferent to student harassed by another student); *Bradford-Smart v West Sussex County Council* [2002] EWCA Civ 7 (CA) (school board that 'did what a reasonable school might be expected to do' not liable for harassment of student).

[124] This is not to say that this world is simply a fiction of the fertile judicial imagination: B Thorne, *Gender Play: Girls and Boys in School* (New Brunswick, NJ: Rutgers University Press, 1993). *Gender Play* is based on extensive observations of the children (primarily fourth and fifth grade students) at play in working-class communities. As an ethnographer, Thorne begins with the well-known phenomenon of gender segregation on the playground. She examines how 'the play of gender' organizes children and their activities. But in explicating this, she discusses the complexity of the meaning of gender, influenced by age, ethnicity, race, sexuality, social class, and the context of play. Thorne details how the complex configurations of 'separate cultures' of boys and girls are created and sustained through the activities of play.

confined to the opinions of judges. Recall Rousseau's insistence that in order to prepare them for adulthood, girls must be trained early 'to bear the yoke', to master their inclinations and submit to the will of others.[125] And as he notes, teaching the playing girl to control her reckless impulses will prepare her for womanhood. So girls must be passive or docile, perhaps because of a vague sense articulated by Dr Spock that when females are encouraged to be competitive, they become 'disagreeable'.[126] Thus, Rousseau's view that the hardship of being 'brought under authority' is inseparable from being female seems oddly echoed by judges who almost inevitably chastise the reckless girl.

But if the message to girls is that their aggressiveness and attraction to danger, their desire to do unseemly masculine things, must be brought under control, the message to boys is precisely the opposite. The message to boys is that their recklessness, their daring, their attraction to danger and even to the forbidden are all qualities that are prized in boys and thus are to be encouraged even when they result in harm to others. Boys, as we have seen, are often lauded for such displays of masculinity despite the harm they may occasion. Indeed, the role of play in preparing children for their adult roles is apparent not only in children's toys and games and literature,[127] but also in the justifications given for children's play. One of the major justifications that developed for the games of schoolboys was that 'they prepared a man for war'.[128] And in the cases involving boys, one sometimes senses that the encouragement of a certain 'warlike' nature continues to exert an influence on the understanding of boys' play. Indeed, it seems plausible that the traits that the objective standard values and protects in boys continue to mirror what the adult world counts as masculine success.

---

[125] Rousseau (n 108 above) 332.   [126] Spock (n 106 above) 47.

[127] See, for instance, Thorne (n 124 above) 2, 44–45; Ariès (n 77 above) 89–90.

[128] Ariès (ibid) 89. Interestingly, the image of the soldier runs like an almost invisible thread through the image of boyhood, the ideal of citizenship, and the problem of equality. As Ariès notes, and as we have seen in the cases involving boys, the development of masculine aggressiveness premissed on the image of the soldier has exerted a powerful influence on boys' play: ibid 89. And the 'warlike' activities identified by Ariès continue to be an important component of boy's play. Thus, the games of boys are often overtly hierarchical and competitive, and typically revolve around strength and force: see Thorne (n 124 above) 91–93. Further, boys also tend to turn other play activities into contests, invasions, and the like: ibid. The image of the ideal citizen too has often taken the form of the 'citizen-as-soldier': Shklar (n 114 above) 390. This model of patriotic virtue, 'possessed of all the military qualities of readiness to fight' is most commonly identified with Machiavelli but, as Shklar notes, it has long been important in modern Western democracies: ibid. Indeed, the implication of this ideal—that the soldier must also be a citizen—has played an important role in the struggle for full citizenship and civil equality. Thus, the fact of military service has often been used to bolster claims to full rights of citizenship. Shklar notes, 'In every war young Americans came to harbour some of these sentiments and asked whether men good enough to serve their country in war were not fit to be full citizens': ibid. The 'right' to engage in military service has therefore sometimes assumed a somewhat paradoxical significance. Thus, feminist organizations (NOW in the United States, ANMLAE in Nicaragua, and others) have fought for women's equal inclusion with men in the military, 'arguing that once women share with men the ultimate citizen's duty—to die for one's country, they would be able to gain also equal citizenship rights to that of men [*sic*]': N Yuval-Davis, 'The Citizenship Debate: Women, Ethnic Processes and the State' (1991) 39 Feminist Review 58, 64. In *Rostker v Goldberg*, the majority of the United States Supreme Court found that the male-only draft survived the equal protection challenge: 453 US 57 (1981).

It is therefore perhaps unsurprising that judges worry that imposing liability on the reckless behaviour of playing boys will penalize both that which is best in boys and the best of boys.[129] Risk-taking, it seems, is a valuable masculine trait but not similarly desirable in women. This is despite the fact that we reward many forms of risk-taking not only with high praise but also with considerable material benefits.

Thus, we see how ideas of what is natural and normal, so central to the objective standard's reasonable person, actually raise profound concerns about the justifiability and significance of such treatment. In fact, the very ideas of what is ordinary, normal, or natural that play such a central role under the objective standard have a long history of being invoked to justify the discriminatory treatment of the developmentally disabled and of women, among others. And examining the operation of such ideas more closely only confirms our initial concern: the very same kinds of invidious stereotypes about the developmentally disabled and women also infiltrate determinations of what is reasonable through untroubled appeals to some conception of what is normal, ordinary, or natural. In this way then, the reasonable person seems so intertwined with troubling conceptions of what is normal that it raises serious, and much more general, equality concerns.

IV. The rhetoric of common sense

The influence of the normal cannot be fully understood without reference to another important feature of the reasonable person. Reading through the academic and judicial discussions of the objective standard, one cannot help but be struck by their distinctive rhetoric. Indeed, perhaps what is most striking is the tone of much of the 'reasoning' about the objective standard. This distinctive tone is attributable in large part to reliance on what cultural anthropologist Clifford Geertz describes as the language of 'common sense'—a language that characterizes many of the invocations of the normal in discussions of the reasonable person. And for all the claims that common sense makes to a kind of egalitarian ordinariness, it invokes a world-view that echoes and perhaps even protects the deeply inegalitarian understanding of membership that filters into the reasonable person through the idea of the 'normal'. Moreover, being common sense, it does so in a way that makes such invocations especially impervious to challenge.

Geertz alerts us to the fact that, despite its own claims to the contrary, common sense is itself a cultural system, a loosely connected body of belief and judgement characterized above all by a special frame of mind, a distinctive tone, 'just what anybody properly put together cannot help but think.'[130] This

---

[129] As discussed in ch 2 above.

[130] C Geertz, *Local Knowledge: Further Essays in Interpretive Anthropology* (New York: Basic Books, Inc, 1983) 10–11.

attitude of common sense derives from its insistence that 'its tenets are immediate deliverances of experience, not deliberated reflections upon it'.[131] So the very language of common sense implies the self-evidence of its claims: its authority is based on its unspoken assertion that it is a 'mere matter-of-fact apprehension of reality'.[132] As Geertz notes, its characteristic 'maddening air of simple wisdom'[133] is attributable to certain qualities typical of the common sense frame of mind. The 'naturalness' that Geertz describes as the most fundamental quality of common sense has an 'air of "of-courseness"', which is cast over certain selected things, things that are depicted as intrinsic aspects of reality. The second quality of common sense wisdom that seems particularly apposite here is what Geertz terms 'thinness'. This implies that the 'world is what the wide-awake, uncomplicated person takes it to be. Sobriety, not subtlety, realism, not imagination, are the keys to wisdom; the really important facts of life lie scattered openly along its surface, not cunningly secreted in its depths.'[134] According to common sense wisdom, truth is obvious and plain. And the 'accessibleness' of common sense implies that the precepts of common sense wisdom are open and will be readily apparent to all whose faculties are reasonably intact.[135] But Geertz acknowledges that while common sense is frankly anti-expert, it is not necessarily egalitarian. Instead, common sense seems to grant authoritative interpretive power over 'reality' to the common *man*. So, although Geertz does not highlight this feature of common sense, he does note that 'children, frequently enough women, and, depending upon the society, various sorts of underclasses are regarded as less wise, in an "they are emotional creatures" sort of way, than others'.[136]

Although common sense reasoning makes itself felt primarily at the rhetorical level, the literature on the objective standard does contain some explicit references to common sense. The virtues of common sense seem to come to the fore to displace the ordinary principles of logic and analysis. They are often used to justify the treatment of the developmentally disabled despite the apparent conflict with fundamental principles of the law of negligence. Thus, for example, *The American Law of Torts* quotes *McGuire v Almy* to the effect that the rules governing insanity and various degrees of mental incapacity 'rest more upon grounds of public policy and upon what might be called a popular view of the requirements of essential justice than upon any attempt to apply logically the underlying principles of civil liability to the special instance of the mentally deranged'.[137] F. W. Pollock expresses a similar preference for the precepts of

---

[131] ibid 75.   [132] ibid 75–76.   [133] ibid 85.

[134] ibid 89. Note here the congruity of 'common sense' and the assumptions underlying the doctrine of judicial notice discussed in ch 2 above.   [135] ibid 91.

[136] ibid. There is an important ambiguity in Geertz's conclusion that 'being common, common sense is open to all, the general property of at least, as we would put it, all solid citizens': ibid. In fact, this suggests that like the notions of the normal and natural, which common sense so often invokes, the methodology of common sense *itself* replicates inequalities of membership and citizenship by granting the power to declare the normal to those 'solid citizens' that are paradigmatically normal.

[137] *McGuire v Almy* 297 Mass 323, 8 NE 2d 760 (1937), discussed in SM Speiser, CF Krause, and AW Gans, *The American Law of Torts* Vol I (Rochester, NY: The Lawyer's Co-operative Publishing Co, 1983) 823 (ss 5:17 n 79).

common sense, however flawed, as well as the characteristic anti-intellectualism of common sense when he argues that 'it is by no means suggested that theories of psychology, normal or abnormal, should be made propositions of law. The errors of common sense are more tolerable, on the whole, than those of speculation; at all events they are more easily corrected'.[138] This anti-expert stance is also explicitly associated with common sense by Alexander and Szasz, who object to the depiction of insanity as an illness partially because it would displace 'the public judgment of social conduct based on common sense' with a 'private judgment of it based on quasi-medical criteria'.[139] Thus, we see the attachment to common sense even when—or perhaps more cynically, *especially* when—it seems to contradict 'undesirable' applications of legal principles or the expert evidence of other disciplines.[140] The literature is characterized by common sense's characteristic refusal either to inquire into the facts more fully or to make the principles of liability logical and systematic, perhaps because its 'appealing' results could not withstand this kind of scrutiny.

More typically, however, the appeal to common sense takes place at the level of rhetoric and is implicit rather than explicit. Its distinctive tone thus supplements the idea that fine reasoning and expert knowledge are often not only unnecessary, but are actually sometimes positively detrimental. So the conditions that give rise to normal and natural shortcomings, particularly childhood, are characteristically depicted as uncomplicated 'facts of life'.[141] Thus, Henry Shulman opens his classic article by noting that the objective standard must be moderated for children because for the law 'to do otherwise, would be to shut its eyes, ostrich-like, to the facts of life'.[142] This attitude, according to Shulman, is not the result of complicated logic but simply a form of 'realism'.[143] *The American Law of Torts* justifies the relaxation of the objective standard in the case of physical disabilities by pointing out that 'law must meet the realities of life'.[144] The reality is simply that 'a child's normal behaviour differs from an adult's'.[145] Prosser also suggests that law is only recognizing reality when he comments that for children 'it has been necessary, as a practical matter' to depart from the objective standard, because they 'cannot in fact' meet the standard.[146] In an implicit recognition of the significance of 'facts', Barrett argues for generosity towards the elderly partly on the ground that, like the young, they are a

---

[138] FW Pollock, *Pollock's Law of Torts* (ed PA Landon) (15th edn, London: Stevens and Sons, 1951) 48.   [139] Alexander and Szasz (n 38 above) 27.

[140] These arguments seem to echo another element of common sense noticed by Geertz. As Geertz states, 'Common-sense wisdom is shamelessly and unapologetically *ad hoc.*' And it is this very 'immethodicalness' of common sense that recommends it as 'capable of grasping the vast multifariousness of life in the world': Geertz (n 130 above) 90–91.

[141] Indeed, Holmes's characterization of childhood and of physical disabilities such as blindness as 'distinct defects' that 'all can recognize' and as 'clear and manifest' incapacities can be understood as implying what kinds of incapacities are recognizable as common sense facts: (n 31 above) 87–88.

[142] Shulman (n 22 above) 618.

[143] Linden among others cites this passage with approval: (n 15 above) 140.

[144] Speiser, Krause, and Gans (n 137 above) 818.   [145] Rainaldi (n 34 above) 16.I-56.

[146] Prosser (n 1 above) 154–155.

demographic fact.[147] But this common sense emphasis on the 'fact' of incapacities like childhood and physical disabilities implies its opposite: the rhetoric of common sense that invokes the 'facts of life' as a justification for relaxing the standard in some limited category of cases subtly suggests the incredibility of the other categories of claims—indeed, it implies their 'fictional' status. In this way, the language of common sense rhetorically reinforces the same idea of the normal so implicated in determinations of reasonableness.

The notion that the workings of the objective standard are dictated by reality, straight and simple, is also apparent in the frequent admonition that law will not require the ridiculous. This echo of Shulman's insistence that law will not be blind to the facts of life[148] reinforces the status of certain limited incapacities as 'facts'. So, for example, commentators frequently make the point that 'a person with a hearing disability is not required to hear, a physically disabled person need not be nimble, nor is a person who is blind obliged to see'.[149] Persons with physical disabilities, it is often said, will not be asked to behave as though they had no disability.[150] Thus, Prosser states that the person 'cannot be required to do the impossible by conforming to physical standards which he cannot [meet]'.[151] The danger of ignoring these facts of life is nicely summarized in *Daly v Liverpool Corporation*: 'I cannot believe that the law is quite so absurd as to say that, if a pedestrian happens to be old and slow and a little stupid, and does not possess the skill of the hypothetical reasonable pedestrian, he or she can only walk about his or her native country at his or her own risk. One must take people as one finds them.'[152] Tony Honoré also intimates that the law will not require the ridiculous when he argues that someone who is too short to see over a wall 'is not to be treated as if he could see over the wall unaided'.[153] Similarly, Klar states that 'negligence law does not expect young children to possess the common sense, intelligence, and knowledge of the reasonable adult'.[154] This understanding is also reinforced in other more subtle ways. Thus, commentators often use terms which imply that certain kinds of incapacities are simply straightforward facts that no sensible person could possibly question.[155] Incapacities such as childhood are

---

[147] Barrett (n 39 above) 880–882.   [148] Shulman (n 22 above) 618.

[149] Linden (n 15 above) 138 [footnotes omitted]; Fleming (n 1 above) 125; Holmes (n 31 above) 87; James (n 5 above) 18.   [150] Rainaldi (n 34 above) 16.I-53.

[151] Prosser (n 1 above) 152. See also Seavey (n 14 above) 13.

[152] [1939] 2 All ER 142, 143 (KB). This quote is cited in Parsons (n 47 above) 178 n 55, in his discussion of the limits of the reliance rule in judging situations of contributory negligence.

[153] T Honoré, 'Responsibility and Luck: The Moral Basis of Strict Liability' in *Responsibility and Fault* (Oxford: Hart Publishing, 1999) 14, 35.

[154] Klar (n 41 above) 255. See also EB Kinkead, *Commentaries on the Law of Torts* (San Francisco: Bancroft-Whitney Co, 1903) 43.

[155] Thus, Linden states that '*[a]fter all*, a minor's normal condition is one of recognized incompetency and, therefore, indulgence must be shown': (n 15 above) 140 [emphasis added], citing *Charbonneau v MacRury* (n 23 above) 462. He later states, '*Clearly*, youth needs a buffer against tort liability for its indiscretions': ibid [emphasis added]. Similarly, Seavey states that 'of course' children should be treated differently than adults in the law of negligence: Seavey (n 14 above) 12 n 12. Prosser defends a relaxed standard of care for children partly by noting that children '*obviously* cannot be held to the same standard as adults': Prosser (n 1 above) 155 [emphasis added].

often described as *obviously* requiring some calibration of the standard of care.[156] In this sense, the relaxation of the objective standard for certain 'normal' shortcomings is presented as an uncontentious corollary of the nature of things.

But the language of common sense plays a complementary role here as well. If the relaxation of the objective standard for 'normal' shortcomings is defended in its uncompromising tones, common sense's impatience with the ridiculous is also used to justify refusing to relax the standard when the shortcomings are not seen as normal. While the language in cases involving childhood and physical disabilities suggests that law will not be so foolish as to ignore the facts, the rhetoric in the case of 'abnormal' shortcomings relies on a very different invocation of the obvious. So in discussions of the developmentally disabled, commentators invoke the common sense idea of the obvious to imply the silliness of suggesting that a developmental disability could affect the standard in negligence. Prosser's insistence that a person's mental disability '*obviously* cannot be allowed to protect him from liability'[157] is but one illustration. In support of this position, Prosser cites 'the *very obvious* difficulties of proof as to what went on in [the person's] head'.[158] Similarly, when speaking of such disabilities, Klar states that 'it is *obvious* that legal fault and moral fault cannot be expected to be synonymous concepts'.[159] Honoré also relies on similar rhetoric when he states that 'the most *obvious* factors that are not circumstances are things which are inside the agent or part of his make up, like being stupid or in a bad temper'.[160]

The distinctive tones of common sense rhetoric can also be detected in the dismissive language that characterizes discussions of abnormal shortcomings.[161] So although these problems are sometimes discussed at length, the impatience of the prose reinforces the 'obviousness' of the conclusion by implying that it is hardly worth spelling out. So, for example, Linden begins his discussion of the objective standard by simply stating that 'stupid individuals must answer for their foolish

---

[156] Holmes's description of certain defects as distinct and manifest is but one example. Parsons also argues that the limits on practicable judicial inquiry mean that courts will refuse to consider factors other than perhaps insanity, unless there is a 'ready reckoner' or an 'obvious circumstance' like age to simplify their task: Parsons (n 47 above) 179. Seavey too describes physical defects as 'obvious': (n 14 above) 23–24. See also Prosser (n 1 above). [157] ibid [emphasis added].

[158] ibid [emphasis added]. [159] Klar (n 41 above) 254 [emphasis added].

[160] Honoré (n 153 above) 35. However, as discussed in ch 1 above, Honoré's analysis does not in fact support this point. Honoré further appeals to common sense when he says that the person concerned must either overcome these difficulties or face the ensuing consequences. But this argument does not have the same force for both of his illustrations. At least where an individual's lack of control is not of clinical dimensions, the law can legitimately require someone to overcome a bad temper. But the 'shape up or ship out' argument does not seem to have the same force with individuals who lack intelligence. Can we actually demand that someone 'overcome' their lack of intelligence? And if we cannot, does it make sense to hold them liable for the consequences of the lack of intelligence as if the problem emanated from a want of willpower? Given this difficulty, it does not seem surprising that in the discussion following this statement Honoré focuses, not on the 'stupid' individual, but rather on the person who has a 'filthy temper' or is irritable: ibid 36. This despite the fact that Honoré's major objective is to defend the imposition of the objective standard on the 'stupid' person, for only with the disjunction between legal and moral fault does the strict liability concern arise.

[161] This is the equivalent, one suspects, of Dr Johnson's injunction, 'And that's an end on the matter': Geertz (n 130 above) 80.

ways to their victims, even though they may be forgiven by their Maker'.[162] Similarly, after Seavey discusses the possibility of treating the elderly in the same way as children on the ground that both represent stages in the life of 'normal' persons, he goes on to remark that it is not 'unfair that the consequences of his folly should be visited upon the fool'.[163] Or, as E. B. Kinkead matter-of-factly puts it, 'the lunatic must bear the loss occasioned by his torts, as he bears his other misfortunes.'[164] But the impatience with claims of the developmentally disabled is perhaps most evident in Prosser's statement that someone obviously cannot be exonerated from liability merely because 'the individual is a congenital fool, cursed with inbuilt bad judgment, or that in the particular instance he "did not stop to think," or that he is merely a stupid ox, or of an excitable temperament which causes him to lose his head and get "rattled" '.[165] And the impatient tone of the reasoning suggests the underlying impatience with the claims themselves. Sometimes it seems that the commentators view the claims of the developmentally disabled as so overtly unfounded that they are barely worth addressing.

This impatient tone also implies that the society's demands on the developmentally disabled are anything but unreasonable. So, for instance, Holmes invokes a kind of common sense utilitarianism when he insists that the general welfare simply requires 'individuals to sacrifice their peculiarities going beyond a certain point'.[166] The literature more generally seems to minimize what is at issue by implying that all the law requires is minimally decent behaviour.[167] Often this takes the form of an apparently simple insistence that 'everyone is required by tort law to possess a certain modicum of intelligence'.[168] Or, as James puts it, in the absence of physical impairment, insanity or youth, an individual 'will be held to see the obvious and hear the clearly audible'.[169] The reasonableness of this demand is often bolstered by drawing attention to the fact that the developmentally disabled are simply being treated like everyone else. So, as Salmond and Heuston

---

[162] Linden (n 15 above) 134.   [163] Seavey (n 14 above) 12.

[164] Kinkead (n 154 above) 63. See also *Restatement* (n 2 above) s 283B, Comment c (no allowance is made for mental deficiency; 'the actor is held to the standard of conduct of a reasonable man who is not mentally deficient, even though it is in fact beyond his capacity to conform to it'); Pollock (n 138 above) 338 (law 'peremptorily assumes that he has as much capacity to judge and foresee consequences as a man of ordinary prudence would have in the same situation', citing Holmes J in *Commonwealth v Pierce* 130 Mass 165 (1884)).   [165] Prosser (n 1 above) 135 [internal citations omitted].

[166] Holmes (n 31 above) 86.

[167] Holmes refers to 'individual peculiarities going beyond a certain point' and later to 'minute differences of character': ibid 86–87. Similarly, Linden states that the law will refuse to make any allowance 'for those who are *merely deficient* intellectually and therefore cannot live up to the objective standard': (n 15 above) 146 [emphasis added]. Rhetoric along these lines is also found in Rainaldi (n 34 above) 16.1–54 ('*Mere intellectual deficiency* does not always excuse the defendant's behaviour,' citing *Vaughan v Menlove* (n 61 above) [emphasis added]. The minimization of the interests of the intellectually disabled is also accomplished partly through the choice of examples. For instance, though they both refer explicitly to individuals who lack intelligence, Honoré's examples focus on the bad tempered individual and Holmes's on the individual who is born 'hasty and awkward': Honoré (n 153 above) 36; Holmes (n 31 above).

[168] Linden (n 15 above) 134; Prosser (n 1 above) 158–161; Fleming (n 1 above) 125; Street (n 20 above) 239; Klar (n 41 above) 251 (although Klar notes that the actual support that the case law offers for this position is in fact very weak); Rainaldi (n 34 above) 16.I-52.4; Pollock (n 138 above) 339; Edgerton (n 6 above) 868; *Restatement* (n 2 above) s 283, Comment b.   [169] James (n 5 above) 6–7.

argue, 'the foolish and the forgetful are judged by the same external standard as other defendants.'[170] And the related impatience with the notion of 'special' treatment for the developmentally disabled is palpable in Prosser's insistence that 'if [the person] is to live in the community, he must learn to conform to its standards or pay for what he breaks'.[171] Prosser also relies on the suggestion that the demands of the law are hardly unreasonable when he says that it is 'no bad policy to hold a fool according to his folly' because the harm to others is as great or greater than if the person exhibited a 'modicum of brains'.[172] Perhaps the most striking example is found in Parsons's comment that even Seavey 'stops short of suggesting that we should judge the moron by asking how the Clapham gentleman would behave if he were a moron'.[173] Such is the distinctive—almost intolerant—impatience of common sense with any demand to articulate or justify its precepts.

V. CONCLUSION

In this way, what Geertz terms 'common sense reasoning' plays an important role in discussions of the objective standard. Such reasoning comes most to the fore in articulating the importance of assumptions about what is normal under the objective standard. In fact, the rhetoric of common sense surrounding the reasonable person seems to confirm the systematic nature of features that we first noticed in the case law involving the developmentally disabled and children. Those cases are noteworthy in part because they point to an entanglement between the normal and the reasonable. Indeed, closer analysis illuminates the role of assumptions about what is normal and natural in determinations of reasonableness more generally. But as we have seen, reliance on these assumptions is actually quite difficult to justify. An even more worrisome side of the interrelationship between the reasonable and the normal becomes apparent when we reconsider the treatment of those who are seen as having 'abnormal' shortcomings, like those with intellectual or cognitive impairments. Here and in the case of gender, for example, reliance on assumptions about what is normal raises deeper concerns because of the way that it draws inegalitarian social understandings into the reasonable person inquiry. But as we have heard, the voice of the ordinary man (and sometimes perhaps the judge)—whose world-view is reflected in the idea of the normal—is impatient here, insisting the rules are simply obvious and that any other approach would make law ridiculous by contradicting the 'facts of life'. Even though we have become aware of his shortcomings, this common sense stance that the ordinary man adopts seems singularly well adapted to securing his tenure. We would do well not to overlook his tenacity as we turn to consider the broader implications of the entanglement between the reasonable and the normal.

---

[170] Salmond (n 17 above) 224. See also Kinkead (n 154 above) 67.

[171] Prosser (n 1 above) 153. See also *Restatement* (n 2 above) s 283B, Comment b3. Fridman also argues that the individual 'must meet the demands of society, not merely fulfill his own personal capacities' (n 7 above) 144.   [172] ibid.

[173] Parsons (n 47 above) 179.

5

Ordinary Prudence, Equality, and the Rule of Law

> One kind of unjust action is the failure of judges and others in authority to apply the appropriate rule or to interpret it correctly. It is more illuminating in this connection to think not of gross violations exemplified by bribery and corruption, or the abuse of the legal system to punish political enemies, but rather of the subtle distortions of prejudice and bias as these effectively discriminate against certain groups in the judicial process.[1]

As we have seen, the objective standard seems deeply indebted to certain common sense ideas about what is normal or ordinary. In fact, identifying this helps to clarify at least some of the unease with the standard. Our case studies suggest that partly because of its dependence on these ideas of the normal, the objective standard operates very differently for different groups of litigants. And while the fact of different treatment may not be inherently problematic, closer examination suggests these differences are troubling, in part because the form they take seems anything but accidental. It is significant that both the developmentally disabled and women have suffered sufficiently discriminatory histories that they are now often the focus of equality concern both in the law and in the theoretical writing. Indeed, as we have seen, even a brief review of these histories reveals important continuities between discriminatory social understandings of what is normal or ordinary and the treatment of these litigants under the objective standard.

Reading the problems with the objective standard in the light of these histories suggests that the operation of the standard actually raises a much more general difficulty with the kind of basic civil equality notionally protected by the rule of law. To the extent that the notion of what is reasonable draws on views about normal behaviour, troubling or discriminatory social understandings of particular groups thereby seep into determinations of reasonableness under the objective standard. Because these problems are accordingly not *ad hoc* but instead incorporate and thus give legal voice to existing systematic inequalities, they raise significant questions about the legitimacy of the objective standard. Indeed, when we relate this worry about the equality problems posed by the entanglement of the reasonable and the normal to the apparently advantaged boy litigant, we see that the worry may be well founded. Re-examining those cases reveals the extent to which the privileged playing boy of the case law implicates stereotypes not simply about mental ability and gender, but also

---

[1] J Rawls, *A Theory of Justice* (Cambridge, Mass: Harvard University Press, 1971) 235.

about class and perhaps other qualities. In this sense then, the operation of the objective standard seems to illustrate John Rawls's worry about how the 'subtle distortions of bias and prejudice' may discriminate against certain groups in the judicial process in a way that undermines the rule of law.

I. DIFFERENCE OR DISCRIMINATION: ASSESSING EQUALITY UNDER LAW

The negligence regime stakes its character on a distinctive understanding of the fault of culpable inadvertence or carelessness. In part because the private law of negligence seems so anxious to distance itself from the subjectivist understanding of fault in criminal law, courts and commentators routinely insist on the difference between the propriety-based conception of fault in negligence and the more thoroughgoing conception of fault as blameworthiness in criminal law. Thus, as we frequently hear, negligence is not to be equated with blameworthiness but instead turns on the propriety of the conduct in question. Yet despite this insistence, the requirement of avoidability or what Honoré calls 'general capacity'[2] often has the effect of diminishing the very distance between legal and moral fault that the law of negligence paradoxically works so hard to insist upon.

At the most fundamental level, this is evident in the fact that the standard of propriety itself is not conceived of as invariant but instead generally turns on a relatively litigant-specific understanding of ordinariness. Indeed, as the cases involving the child defendant illustrate particularly well, it is partly this that accounts for the gendered quality of the standard in those cases. Even beyond this however, the rigidity of the standard is tempered by the general willingness of the courts to calibrate the standard further in order to ensure that the litigant had the capacity to avoid the relevant harm. So, as we have seen, the standard of care—objective though it may be—often varies its demands to take into account extraordinary factors that may impede the litigant's ability to attain the standard.[3] Even at the conceptual level, avoidability plays a crucial role in important defences of the standard such as those of Holmes and Honoré.[4] We have already noted some of the difficulties that might accompany too much reliance on an undifferentiated notion of avoidability, and we will be taking these

---

[2] T Honoré, 'Responsibility and Luck: The Moral Basis of Strict Liability' in *Responsibility and Fault* (Oxford: Hart Publishing, 1999).

[3] Thus, for instance, the willingness to consider limited cognitive capacities of children even where they exceed the ordinary: *Laviolette v Canadian National Railway* (1986) 36 CCLT 203 (NBQB); *Garrison v St Louis, IM & S Ry Co* 123 SW 657 (Ark SC 1909); *Zajczkowski v State* 71 NYS 2d 261 (Claims 1947). Similarly, in cases involving children, courts typically consider the particular experience and intelligence of the child in fashioning the standard: see ch 1 above, n 38 and ch 2 above. Even beyond this, cases like emergency situations and cases involving litigants whose limited knowledge is extraordinary but non-culpable also illustrate the willingness of the standard to reshape itself to ensure that the litigant had a fair opportunity to avoid the harm in question: see ch 1 above, n 69.

[4] Honoré (n 2 above); OW Holmes, *The Common Law* (ed MD Howe) (Cambridge, Mass: Harvard University Press, 1963) 67.

up in more detail soon. Nonetheless, at this point it is worth paying somewhat closer attention to the way that the general attentiveness to avoidability actually serves to align the standard quite closely to blameworthiness and thus oddly cuts against the explicit insistence of the law of negligence that it is not concerned with moral fault. This is particularly revealing because of the light it sheds on the treatment of the developmentally disabled. Although the idea that fault in negligence is not about blame may indeed seem to account for the treatment of the developmentally disabled, the power of this account looks rather different if we pay attention to where avoidability is (and is not) invoked to mitigate the rigours of that 'distinctive' conception of fault. In this sense, tracing how avoidability operates for different categories of litigants reveals the complicated relationship between the meaning of fault in negligence and more thoroughgoing conceptions of blameworthiness, and so provides a way of assessing the equality effects of the standard.

Viewed in this light, the treatment of the child defendant—typically the playing boy—serves as the most extreme example of how reliance on avoidability undermines the standard's purported inattentiveness to blameworthiness. In the cases involving the playing boy, courts typically refuse to find negligence unless the boy defendant had both the foresight and the prudence to avoid the risk.[5] The playing boy benefits from the widest possible reading of avoidability, for he must have sufficient cognitive *and normative* capacities to have exercised the requisite degree of care before he is found to be at fault. Indeed, the willingness of the courts to extend such an expansive understanding of avoidability to the playing boy is such that notwithstanding the claim that fault in negligence is not concerned with blame, the playing boy will not be deemed faulty unless he exhibits a robust form of blameworthiness more typically associated with criminal responsibility. So in his case, avoidability realigns legal fault and blameworthiness in a way that mirrors (and sometimes even seems to exceed) the criminal law's characteristic concern with moral culpability.[6]

In the case of the playing girl we see another variation on avoidability. Here too courts often have recourse to the principle of avoidability. As we have seen, the playing girl is typically not held liable if her risky behaviour is attributable to a failure of foresight. In the allurement cases, the playing girl is ordinarily exonerated where her limited understanding or cognitive capacities resulted in entrapment. In this sense, the standard for the playing girl is to some degree premissed on avoidability, for courts will rarely find a breach of the standard where her only shortcoming is a non-culpable failure to foresee and hence avoid the risk. This means that for the playing girl, liability will generally only follow

---

[5] Thus, in *McHale v Watson* and other cases involving the child defendant, the centrality of the avoidability principle was used to justify calibrating the standard of care, with the consequence that the victim was unable to recover for her injuries: 115 CLR 199 (1966) (Aust HC).

[6] I put the relation to criminal fault in this way because as discussed below, the complication of reasonableness and ordinariness that is characteristic of the reasonable person standard sometimes seems to deem innocent the very kind of moral mistakes that would engage the prohibition on mistake of law defence in criminal law.

where she possesses the cognitive capacity to avoid the harm. Because the responsibility of the playing girl is thus to some degree contingent on the ability to avoid the relevant harm, in her case too we see a closer alignment of legal and moral fault than that which the reasonable person apparently demands. However, because she does not enjoy as expansive a reading of avoidability as the playing boy, her legal responsibility is not conditioned, as his is, on a particularly robust conception of moral blameworthiness.

With this in mind, let us consider how the standard of care deals with the developmentally disabled adult. As we have seen, despite the purported commitment of negligence law to a conception of fault independent of moral blame, avoidability in fact typically serves as a vitally important precondition to liability. Further, its insistence that the litigant possess some ability to avoid the relevant harm effectively ensures a closer relation between legal fault and moral fault than the law of negligence will admit it seeks. But while the insistence on the irrelevance of blame may generally be tempered through recourse to avoidability, this is nowhere evident in the treatment of people with developmental disabilities. Indeed, virtually alone among litigants, the developmentally disabled person is exposed to liability even where her limited cognitive abilities mean that she lacks the ordinary person's capacity to perceive or understand the relevant risk. She has virtually no ability to invoke avoidability to limit her negligence liability. Thus, for her the inability to foresee and hence avoid the harm in question is not sufficient to negate liability, even though such cognitive shortcomings are admittedly not blameworthy and so do not reflect negatively on the litigant. While with other litigants avoidability generally steps in to realign legal and moral fault, in the case of the developmentally disabled litigant we instead see adherence to the very kind of disjuncture between legal and moral fault that the standard is unwilling to countenance elsewhere.

In this sense, the treatment of litigants with developmental disabilities does indeed look exceptional, for here alone the law of negligence seems unwilling to invoke avoidability to mitigate the rigours of its purported commitment to the disjuncture between legal and moral fault. While avoidability generally works to bring legal fault into a closer relation to moral fault, it does not do so in the case of the developmentally disabled, who are thus uniquely liable without attentiveness to the kind of blameworthiness that the law of negligence normally demands. But even where avoidability has some sway, the very different way in which it is extended to different categories of litigants—and the resulting variations in the relationship between legal and moral fault—raises concern about what exactly counts as fault in negligence.

However, even acknowledging the differential access to avoidability and the resulting variability of the relation between legal and moral fault, one might still ask why it is even relevant to compare different cases in this way. After all, it seems plausible that private law adjudication is primarily a matter of doing justice between the parties to the discrete dispute. And in any event, each case has distinctive facts that defeat perfect comparison. Further complicating this is the fact that cases are decided by different judges, in different places and times. Judges in arriving at these decisions rely on a wide array of precedents in their decisions. There is after all no requirement of perfect consistency across cases, although of course judges do endeavour to treat like cases alike. Although mistakes are certainly not desirable, clearly a judge *can* make a mistake in a particular case, or indeed in many cases, without thereby undermining the rule of law. To this extent, it seems right to insist that there is no robust general requirement of equality that cuts across individual cases. Yet however persuasive these arguments are, they must be weighed against the fact that a conception of equality is central to the rule of law and hence to our understanding of justice.

Equality is often thought of as conceptually entailed by the very idea of a general rule. Rawls describes the link in the following terms:

> If we think of justice as always expressing a kind of equality, then formal justice requires that in their administration laws and institutions should apply equally (that is, in the same way) to those belonging to the classes defined by them. As Sidgwick emphasized, this sort of equality is implied in the very notion of a law or institution, once it is thought of as a scheme of general rules.[7]

Similarly, Ronald Dworkin insists that whatever the varying obligations of equality that may attach to individuals, government has 'an abstract responsibility to treat each citizen's fate as equally important'.[8] There are, of course, different conceptions of equality that may infuse this abstract obligation, but a commitment to equality is understood as central to a system of law. Indeed, the centrality of equal enjoyment of legal or civil rights is such that citizenship theory typically treats civil equality or equality under law as a definitional element of full citizenship.[9] And our legal system at least partially reveals its commitment to these broader ideals in its doctrine—however flawed—of precedent. Indeed

---

[7] Rawls (n 1 above) 58, quoting H Sidgwick, *The Methods of Ethics* (7th edn, London: MacMillan, 1907) 267.

[8] Ronald L Dworkin, *Law's Empire* (Cambridge, Mass: Belknap Press of Harvard University Press, 1986) 296. Dworkin elaborates on the legal and political (including distributional) ramifications of this commitment to equality in a series of articles including 'In Defense of Equality' (1983) 1 Social Philosophy and Policy 24; 'What is Equality? Part I: Equality of Welfare' (1981) 10 Phil & Public Affairs 185; and 'What is Equality? Part II: Equality of Resources' (1981) 10 Phil & Public Affairs 283.

[9] TH Marshall, *Citizenship and Social Class* (London, Concord, Mass: Pluto Press, 1992) describes the right to justice, which is a part of the civil element of citizenship as 'the right to defend and assert all one's rights on terms of equality with others and by due process of law': 8. Citizenship itself is defined in terms of the equality of full members: 18. Similarly, K Karst, *Belonging to America: Equal Citizenship and the Constitution* (New Haven: Yale University Press, 1989) states that 'the very idea of citizenship implies some measure of equality [under the law]': 34. A similar understanding of the centrality of equality to citizenship is generally characteristic of the literature. See, for instance, K Fierlbeck, 'Redefining Responsibility: The Politics of Citizenship in the United Kingdom' (1991) 24 Can J Political Science 575, 590 ('The principle underlying citizenship in the modern context has increasingly been one of equality in principle, if not in fact—'); U Vogel, 'Is Citizenship Gender-Specific?' in U Vogel and M Moran (eds), *The Frontiers of Citizenship* (Houndmils: Macmillan, 1991) 62 ('The concept of membership...is inseparably linked to the presumption of equality. The rights and obligations that define citizen status are the same for all members, just as they mark the boundaries against non-members.'); J Shklar, *American Citizenship: The Quest for Inclusion* (Cambridge,

this broader significance of the requirement of equality across cases is apparent in the fact that Rawls terms the requirement of treating like cases alike as going to 'justice as regularity', which he describes it as the 'least controversial element in the common sense idea of justice'.[10] The very centrality of some idea of equality across cases (not only to civil equality but also to full membership and to the rule of law itself) suggests that we must attend to the possibility that there will come a point at which inequalities in the application of the law do raise a rule of law concern. The question to which we now turn is how to determine when this point has been reached.

There is no doubt that equality plays a complex and multifaceted role— perhaps because of its importance—in our legal system. This centrality of equal- ity to the rule of law and to fundamental rights is apparent in the fact that equality guarantees are core elements in international and supra-national rights- protecting regimes.[11] Unsurprisingly, equality guarantees are also one of the most foundational elements of democratic constitutional orders and figure importantly in democratic constitutions.[12] Beyond governing the behaviour of public actors, the principle of equality also places some restrictions on pri- vate relations and thus is typically a cornerstone of domestic human rights

Mass: Harvard University Press, 1991) 387; W Kymlicka, *Multicultural Citizenship: A Liberal Theory of Minority Rights* (Oxford: Clarendon Press, 1995) 174 ('For [some liberals], citizenship is by defi- nition a matter of treating people as individuals with equal rights under the law. This is what distin- guishes democratic citizenship from feudal and other pre-modern views that determined people's political status by their religious, ethnic, or class membership.'); IM Young, 'Polity and Group Difference: A Critique of the Ideal of Universal Citizenship' (1989) 99 Ethics 250 (full citizenship status is understood to be 'equal political status and civil rights').

[10] (n 1 above) 504–505. Aquinas, *Commentary on the Nicomachean Ethics* Vol I (trans CI Litzinger) (Chicago: H Regnery Co, 1964). Although this procedural understanding of equality has been criticized (not only by philosophers but also by courts including the Supreme Court of Canada: *Law Society of British Columbia v Andrews* [1989] 1 SCR 143), it certainly does provide at least a partial understanding of what equality requires.

[11] European Convention for the Protection of Human Rights and Fundamental Freedoms (Rome, 4 November 1950; TS 71 (1953); Cmd 8969, art 14); African [Banjul] Charter on Human and Peoples' Rights (27 June 1981; OAU Doc CAB/LEG/67/3 rev 5; 21 ILM 58 (1982); entered into force 21 October 1986, preamble and art 3, 13); American Convention on Human Rights (OAS Treaty Series No 36; 1144 UNTS 123; entered into force 18 July 1978; preamble, art 8(2), 17(4), 23(1)(c), 24); Declaration on the Elimination of All Forms of Intolerance and of Discrimination Based on Religion or Belief (GA Res 36/55; 36 UN GAOR Supp (No 51) 171; UN Doc A/36/51 (1981)); Declaration on the Rights of Persons Belonging to National or Ethnic, Religious or Linguistic Minorities (GA Res 47/135, annex 47 UN GAOR Supp (No 49) 210; UN Doc A/47/49 (1993)); Universal Declaration of Human Rights (GA Res 217(A); UN Doc 810 (1948) preamble and art 1, 7, 10, 16, 21, 23, 26); International Covenant on Civil and Political Rights (19 December 1966; 999 UNTS 171, preamble, art 3, 14(3), 25, 26); International Covenant on Economic, Social and Cultural Rights (16 December 1966; 993 UNTS 3, preamble, art 3, 7, 13, 31); United Nations Convention on the Elimination of All Forms of Discrimination against Women (GA Res 34/180 (18 December 1979)); International Convention on the Elimination of All Forms of Racial Discrimination (660 UNTS 195; entered into force 4 January 1969, preamble, art 1, 2, 5).

[12] Canadian Charter of Rights and Freedoms, being Part I of the Constitution Act, 1982, Schedule B, Canada Act 1982, 1982, c 11 (UK), ss 15 and 28; US Const amend XIV [Privileges and Immunities, Due Process, Equal Protection (1868)]; Bill of Rights of Constitution of the Republic of South Africa Act 108 of 1996, s 9; United Kingdom, Human Rights Act 1998, c 42 (incorporates sections of the ECHR into British law).

regimes.[13] Further, even in the absence of constitutional guarantees of equality, the common law itself also enshrines a conception of equality or non-discrimination.[14] Given the fact that the principle of equality seems to be foundational to the very idea of a rule of law and of human rights, and given the complex series of roles equality plays in various dimensions of democratic legal orders, it is unsurprising that there is voluminous literature on the principle of equality and considerable debate about the exact scope and significance of the principle.[15]

However, it is not necessary to canvass all of the intricacies of equality law and literature in order to develop an equality analysis suitable to the problem at hand. This is because it is possible to identify certain fundamental aspects of the idea of equality before the law in the Anglo-American legal systems with which we are primarily concerned. This fact is what underlies Rawls's confidence that the percept that like cases must be treated alike is one of the least controversial aspects of the rule of law. Indeed, a brief examination seems to bear out Rawls's view. Thus, we see this idea playing a central role in shaping and constraining the behaviour

[13] See, for instance, in Australia, Racial Discrimination Act 1975, Sex Discrimination Act 1984, Disability Discrimination Act 1992, Human Rights and Equal Opportunity Act 1986; in Canada various provincial codes, including Ontario Human Rights Code, RSO 1990 c H-19 and the federal Canadian Human Rights Act, RS 1985 c H-6; in the United States, Civil Rights Act, 42 USC Chapter 21 (1964) (Title VII); Equal Pay Act, 29 USC s 206 (1963); Americans with Disabilities Act, 42 USC Chapter 126 (1990); in the United Kingdom, the Disability Discrimination Act 1995, c 50; Sex Discrimination Act 1975, c 65; Race Relations Act 1976, c 74 (as amended); in New Zealand, Human Rights Amendment Act 2001; and in South Africa, Human Rights Commission Act, No 54 (1994).

[14] *Mabo v Queensland (No 2)* (1992) CLR 1, 35.

[15] For instance, in Canada, see M Liu, 'A Prophet with Honour: An Examination of the Gender Equality Jurisprudence of Madam Justice Claire L'Heureux-Dubé of the Supreme Court of Canada' (2000) 25 Queen's LJ 417; J Cameron, 'Dialogue and Hierarchy in Charter Interpretation: A Comment on *R v Mills*' (2001) 38 Alberta L Rev 1051; MA Irvine, 'A New Trend in Equality Jurisprudence?' (1999) 5 Appeal 54; P Hughes, 'Recognizing Substantive Equality as a Foundational Constitutional Principle' (1999) 22 Dalhousie LJ 5; C Sheppard, 'Of Forest Fires and Systemic Discrimination: A Review of *British Columbia (Public Service Employee Relations Commission) v BCGSEU*' (2001) 46 McGill LJ 533; G Brodsky, 'Recent Graduate Student Dissertation and Thesis Abstracts: Transformation of Canadian Equality Rights Law' (2000) 38 Osgoode Hall LJ 669. In the United States, the literature is voluminous. For an important recent overview, see Iris Marion Young, *Justice and the Politics of Difference* (Princeton: Princeton University Press, 1990); Karst (n 9 above); KM Sullivan, 'Constitutionalizing Women's Equality' (2002) 90 CALR 735; KL Karst, 'Why Equality Matters' (1983) 17 Ga L Rev 245; Peter Westen, 'The Empty Idea of Equality' (1982) 95 Harv L Rev 537; Ronald Dworkin, *Sovereign Virtue: The Theory and Practice of Equality* (Cambridge, Mass: Harvard University Press, 2000); Angela P Harris, 'Equality Trouble: Sameness and Difference in Twentieth-Century Race Law' (2002) 88 CALR 1923; Claire L'Heureux-Dubé, Justice of the Supreme Court of Canada, 'A Conversation about Equality' (2000) 29 Denver J Intl Law and Policy 65; Kent Greenawalt, 'Prescriptive Equality: Two Steps Forward' (1997) 110 Harv L Rev 1265; Gay Moon (ed), *Race Discrimination: Developing and Using a New Legal Framework: New Routes to Equality?* (Cambridge, Mass: Harvard University Press, 2000). For Europe, see Mark Bell, 'Mainstreaming Equality Norms into European Union Asylum Law' (2001) 26 E L Rev 20; Pedro Cabral, 'A Step Closer to Substantive Equality' (1998) 23 E L Rev 481. For Australia, see Kristie Dunn, ' "Yakking Giants": Equality Discourse in the High Court' (2000) 24 Melb U L Rev 427. For the UK, see Bob Hepple, Mary Coussey, and Tufyal Choudhury, *Equality: A New Framework: Report of the Independent Review of the Enforcement of UK Anti-Discrimination Legislation* (Oxford, Portland: Hart Publishing, 2000). For South Africa, see Arthur Chaskalson, 'Equality & Dignity in South Africa' (2002) 5 Greenbag 2d 189.

of public actors through the doctrine of precedent in the common law, as a basic analytical tool in defining the meaning of constitutional equality guarantees, and in the most foundational elements of the rule of law as described by Rawls and others. However, perhaps the most developed legal analyses of this relatively minimal idea of equal treatment are found in the constitutional realm. For this reason, even though constitutional guarantees of equality will not necessarily straightforwardly apply to private disputes decided under the common law,[16] the most basic attributes of those guarantees, often described in terms of fundamental or core values, assist us in thinking through how to assess whether the operation of the common law comports with justice as regularity or equality under the law.

As a point of departure in this equality analysis, it may seem particularly relevant that the objective standard clearly does treat different groups of litigants very differently. This is despite the fact that many justifications of the objective standard locate the virtue of the standard in its insistence on uniformity or identity of treatment.[17] However, we should not make too much of this, because the fact that the standard treats different groups of litigants differently is not inherently problematic. This is because no plausible account of equality posits that its demands are satisfied by mere identity of treatment. Instead, the principle of equality at a minimum necessarily encompasses an account of justifiable differences, commonly formulated as requiring that likes be treated

---

[16] For general discussions of the issue, see M Moran, 'Authority, Influence and Persuasion: *Baker* and the Puzzle of Method' forthcoming in D Dyzenhaus (ed), *The Unity of Public Law* (Oxford: Hart Publishing, 2003); Lorraine E Weinrib and Ernest J Weinrib, 'Constitutional Values and Private Law in Canada' in Daniel Friedmann and Daphne Barak-Erez (eds), *Human Rights in Private Law* (Oxford: Hart Publishing, 2001) 43; A Barak, *Constitutional Human Rights and Private Law* (1996) 3 Rev Const Stud 218. In Canada, see *RWDSU v Dolphin Delivery Ltd* [1986] 2 SCR 573, 33 DLR (4th) 174 (SCC) 603 ('the judiciary ought to apply and develop the principles of the common law in a manner consistent with the fundamental values enshrined in the Constitution'); *CBC v Dagenais* [1994] 3 SCR 835; *Hill v Church of Scientology* [1995] 2 SCR 1130 (SCC) (Charter values influence the development of the common law); *R v Salituro* [1991] 3 SCR 654. In South Africa, see *DuPlessis v De Klerk* (1996) CCT 8/95 and South African Constitution, Article 8(1): the Bill of Rights applies to all law and binds the legislature, the executive, the judiciary, and all organs of state. In the United States, see *New York Times Co v Sullivan* 376 US 254 (1964) and *Shelley v Kraemer* 344 US 1 (1948). On the changing situation in the UK, see Murray Hunt, *Using Human Rights Law in English Courts* (Oxford: Hart Publishing, 1997); KD Ewing, 'A Theory of Democratic Adjudication: Towards a Representative, Accountable and Independent Judiciary' (2000) 38 Alb L Rev 708; Sir Richard Buxton, 'The Human Rights Act and Private Law' (2000) 116 Law Q Rev 48; D Oliver, 'The Human Rights Act and the Public Law/Private Law Divide' (2000) EHRLR 343; M Hunt, 'The "Horizontal Effect" of the Human Rights Act: Moving Beyond the Public/Private Distinction' in J Jowell and J Cooper (eds), *Understanding Human Rights Principles* (Oxford, Portland: Hart, 2001). In Israel, *Hevra Kadisha, Jerusalem Burial Company v Kestenbaum* [1992] 46 (2) PD 464, 530. In the European Union, F Raday, 'Privatising Human Rights and the Abuse of Power' (2000) 13 Can JL & Juris 103. In Europe, Guido Alpa, 'The European Civil Code: "E Pluribus Unum"' (1999) 14 Tul Eur & Civ L F 1.

[17] RFV Heuston and RA Buckley, *Salmond and Heuston on the Law of Torts* (21st edn, London: Sweet and Maxwell, 1996) ('the foolish and the forgetful are judged by the same external standard as other defendants': 224); EB Kinkead, *Commentaries on the Law of Torts* (San Francisco: Bancroft-Whitney Co, 1903) 67; Honoré (n 2 above). More conceptual accounts that also rest on equality include those of E Weinrib, *The Idea of Private Law* (Cambridge, Mass: Harvard University Press, 1995) and Arthur Ripstein, *Equality, Responsibility and the Law* (Cambridge: Cambridge University Press, 1999), discussed in ch 1 above.

alike and unalikes unalike.[18] Thus, even the most minimal principle of equality will not count simple differences in treatment as violations.[19] Instead, it will ask whether there is some account of relevant similarities and differences that justifies the treatment accorded different groups. Differences in treatment will, of course, not be justified simply by finding any difference between groups: instead, the difference must provide an acceptable basis on which to draw the relevant distinction.

In order to investigate whether such a basis exists, we must assess whether individuals are similarly situated with respect to the purpose of the law.[20] To determine what kinds of similarities and differences are normatively relevant to treatment under the rule, it is necessary to develop an account of the purpose of the rule. However, this is not simply a matter of taking the stated or commonly accepted purpose of the rule at face value and then asking whether the treatment under that rule accurately reflects that purpose. The result that one would get with such an approach will often be either empty or tautological. Instead, one must ask what the rule seeks to achieve, in the light of its actual operation. This involves a process of formulating the purpose of the rule and examining that against its application, perhaps reformulating the purpose and then taking that reformulated purpose back to the cases involving the rule, and so on. Analysis may reveal that the logic of the rule itself requires some reformulation of its actual operation. Ultimately, the aim is to provide the most coherent possible explanation of the ambition of the rule.[21] Then, one must take that ambition back to see the extent to which the rule achieves or falls short of its own best

[18] Rawls (n 1 above) 237 ('The rule of law also implies the precept that similar cases be treated similarly.')

[19] Most accounts of equality also hold that the principle imposes substantive as well as procedural demands. Otherwise, a law that was evenly applied yet discriminatory in its purpose, as for instance in the case of an evenly administered system of slavery or segregation, could be consistent with equality: Rawls (ibid) 59, quoting Sidgwick (n 7 above) 496. And since this principle of equality rests on equal moral personality, it cannot be purely procedural but must also put some restrictions on what grounds could be offered to justify inequalities: ibid 507. Similarly, the constitutional jurisprudence of egalitarian democracies also treats something like a principle of equal human dignity, equal moral worth, or equal moral personality as the foundation of equality guarantees: Karst (n 9 above) 3–5; *R v Keegstra* [1990] 3 SCR 697, 764; Young (n 15 above) 37.

[20] The *locus classicus* regarding the application of the similarly situated component of the equality principle is J Tussman and J tenBroek, 'The Equal Protection of the Laws' (1949) 37 Calif L Rev 341, discussing the meaning of the equal protection branch of the Fourteenth Amendment to the Constitution of the United States. The Canadian Supreme Court has been at the vanguard of criticizing the sufficiency of the similarly situated test as an understanding of the equality guarantee of the Canadian Charter: *Andrews* (n 10 above). But even the Supreme Court of Canada continues to affirm the centrality of some sort of comparative analysis to determinations of equality: *Andrews* (ibid) and *R v Turpin* [1989] 1 SCR 1296. As McIntyre J stated in *Andrews*, equality 'is a comparative concept, the condition of which may only be attained or discerned by comparison with the condition of others in the social and political setting in which the question arises': 164. See more recently *Law v Canada (Minister of Employment and Immigration)* (1999) 170 DLR 4th 1.

[21] Of necessity I am simplifying an extremely complex process here. The distinctions drawn by the rule itself may undermine the availability of certain formulations of purpose because, at a certain point, the fit between the stated purpose of the rule and its operation is so tenuous that it calls into question whether one can actually say that the purpose is the purpose of *that* rule. This is one way

formulated ambition. This inquiry thus forms the 'means-ends' analysis of the operation of the rule, which is typically a crucial part of any equality analysis. With this aspect of an equality analysis in mind, let us reconsider the workings of the objective standard.

II. EQUALITY, FAULT, AND RESPONSIBILITY: LIABILITY UNDER THE OBJECTIVE STANDARD

> Nevertheless, the precept that like decisions be given in like cases significantly limits the discretion of judges and others in authority. The precept forces them to justify the distinction that they make between persons by reference to the relevant legal rules and principles. In any particular case, if the rules are at all complicated and call for interpretation, it may be easy to justify an arbitrary decision. But as the number of cases increases, plausible justifications for biased judgments become more difficult to construct. The requirement of consistency holds of course for the interpretation of all rules and for justifications at all levels. Eventually reasoned arguments for discriminatory judgments become harder to formulate and the attempt to do so less persuasive.[22]

Let us consider what such an equality analysis might yield in the cases of the reasonable person standard that we examined in previous chapters. Do the patterns in the use of avoidability that we noted earlier have any significance for the equality demands of the rule of law? Rawls's description of how one might assess whether there is a concern with the precept that like cases be treated alike provides us with a useful guide to thinking through this analysis. First, we must determine what it is that the reasonable person is trying to accomplish. What set of interests is protected by the standard? To employ the Rawlsian terms, what legal rules and principles are invoked for the treatment of different categories of litigants, and do those rules and principles actually serve to justify the treatment? An inquiry of this kind takes up the Rawlsian insight that the requirement of equality across cases limits judicial discretion by forcing decision-makers to justify distinctions in treatment with reference to the relevant legal rules and principles. Only with such purposes or principles in mind can we evaluate the justifiability of the distinctions in treatment we have noted.

At the most basic level, the reasonable person in the law of negligence provides a standard of conduct, of due care, against which the behaviour of

---

to understand the problem with the equality analysis in the United States Supreme Court decision in *Hirabayashi v US* 320 US 81 (1943). Although the Court upheld the constitutionality of a curfew order imposed on all persons of Japanese ancestry living on the West Coast, the classification seems both underinclusive and overinclusive when measured against the purported purpose of responding to the dangers of sabotage discussed in Tussman and tenBroek (n 20 above) 352–353.

[22] Rawls (n 1 above) 237.

individual litigants may be assessed.[23] In this sense, as Weinrib puts it, the standard 'demarcates the boundary between the defendant's freedom to act and the plaintiff's interest in security by treating certain risks as unreasonable'.[24] The reasonable person in negligence prescribes the appropriate boundary between liberty and security: determinations of reasonableness under the standard of care specify the terms on which individuals can exercise their liberty in interactions with others, as well as delineating the correlative amount of security people can reasonably expect. And as we have seen, the standard defines the boundary between the appropriate liberty of the defendant and the security of the plaintiff by recourse to its propriety-based understanding of the fault of culpable inadvertence. However, as we have also discussed, the notional strictness of this conception of fault is often modified by emphasizing the centrality of avoidability. Where the reasonable person standard attends to avoidability, the effect is to inject into fault in negligence the insistence that the relevant actions exhibit some minimal form of personal fault before they can give rise to liability.

While the workings of the reasonable person standard and the invocation of avoidability may sometimes seem quite puzzling, closer analysis of the basis of liability suggests that the role of avoidability is anything but accidental (although it may of course be imperfectly realized). Indeed, as Honoré, Holmes, and others indicate, in addition to capturing much of the actual operation of the law of negligence, attentiveness to avoidability has the advantage of providing a morally attractive basis for allocating liability. This is because conditioning liability on blameworthiness is generally understood as more liberty-enhancing than is strict liability.[25] It is for this reason that some conception of avoidability is seen as integrally linked to the liberty interests protected by the rule of law. Thus, this principle occupies a central place in Rawls's articulation of the rights of persons protected by the rule of law:

Let us begin with the precept that ought implies can. This precept identifies several obvious features of legal systems. First of all, the actions which the rules of law require and forbid should be of a kind which men can reasonably be expected to do and to avoid. A system of rules addressed to rational persons to organize their conduct concerns itself with what they can and cannot do. It must not impose a duty to do what cannot be done.... It would be an intolerable burden on liberty if the liability to penalties was not normally limited to actions within our power to do or not to do.[26]

This in turn suggests that an important principle may underlie the primacy that the reasonable person ordinarily gives to the avoidability inquiry. Avoidability

---

[23] JG Fleming, *The Law of Torts* (9th edn, Agincourt: LBC Information Services, 1998) 118. The original formulation along these lines is normally attributed to Baron Alderson in *Blyth v Birmingham Waterworks Co* (1856) 11 Ex 781, 784. Other similar formulations are legion: FW Pollock, *The Law of Torts* (13th edn, London: Stevens and Sons Ltd, 1929) 453–458; L Green, 'The Negligence Issue' (1927–28) 37 Yale LJ 1029, 1034–1039; WL Prosser, *Handbook of the Law of Torts* (4th edn, St Paul, Minn: West Publishing Co, 1971) 149–150.

[24] EJ Weinrib, *Tort Law: Cases and Materials* (Toronto: Emond Montgomery, 1997) 47.
[25] Holmes (n 4 above).   [26] (n 1 above) 236–237.

seems crucial to ensuring that the conception of fault in negligence, though stricter than its criminal law counterpart, is nonetheless respectful of fundamental liberty interests. Thus, even as negligence liability tends to the security interests of the plaintiff, it employs avoidability to ensure that it is also appropriately attentive to the liberty interests of the defendant and so comports with basic rule of law values. Avoidability also helps to account for why, in contrast with strict liability, which entails that 'people go about at their peril', the negligence regime is typically credited with being more liberty-protecting.[27] Given this important connection between avoidability, blameworthiness, and liberty interests, it is unsurprising that Rawls, Holmes, Honoré, and others argue that liability in negligence is defensible only where the litigant possesses some capacity to avoid the harm in question. As we have seen, the negligence regime does generally demonstrate its commitment to this by limiting liability to those situations where inadvertence is accompanied by that minimum level of blameworthiness inherent in the ability to foresee and avoid the relevant harm. Indeed, it is because avoidability in this way protects a key value to the individual—liberty of action—that the failure to employ it in an egalitarian manner may raise rule of law worries.

Clearly, the precept that like cases be treated alike does not in and of itself specify which form of avoidability the law of negligence ought to adopt. What it does do, however, is insist that whatever idea is adopted be applied in an egalitarian way. Accordingly, in order to ensure that all who are subject to its terms benefit from the same attentiveness to their liberty interests, this would therefore seem to require (for instance) that the fundamental principle of avoidability be similarly extended to all who are judged by reference to the reasonable person. Presumably this requires either that the same form of avoidability be extended to all litigants, or that some principled basis be found for the differential application of this fundamental principle. Such justification is particularly important given the connection between avoidability, blameworthiness, and the liberty interests protected by the rule of law.

Because the qualities of the reasonable person by definition mirror the qualities of the ordinary citizen or litigant, the simple application of the reasonable person standard itself will typically ensure that, for the 'ordinary' population, liability will only follow where there is some minimal degree of avoidability.[28] This means that for such litigants the conception of fault in negligence will be sufficiently based on blameworthiness that it will respond to the concern of Rawls, Holmes, Honoré, and others regarding the liberty interests of the defendant.

---

[27] See, for instance, Holmes (n 4 above); R Epstein, 'A Theory of Strict Liability' (1973) 2 J Leg Studies 151. Other 'liberty-preferring' features of the law of negligence include the fact that the plaintiff bears the burden of proof and thus the risk of uncertainty. There are of course significant areas within negligence where the fault principle does not hold sway, as Epstein notes and celebrates. But these are clearly exceptions to the general rule and perhaps for that reason are controversial.

[28] As noted in ch 1 above, Honoré notices this feature of the objective standard, although as discussed there, his conclusions on the larger issue differ from those here: (n 2 above) 32.

But where the litigant differs in some significant way from the ordinary person, equal attentiveness to avoidability will require deviation from the rigid reasonable person standard. In the case of children, the absence of the foresight necessary to avoid the harm is sufficiently relevant to the underlying principle of responsibility that in order to ensure equality in the application of that principle, there must be a difference in treatment.[29] Indeed, as we see in those cases, the reasonable person standard is replaced with a standard premised on the capacities of the child.

But this calibration of the standard to ensure that it is appropriately attentive to avoidability, and hence premised on some degree of personal fault, rules out justifying the treatment of the developmentally disabled by appealing to the apparent justice of an inflexible rule of identity of treatment. Indeed, as we have noted, the law itself implicitly recognizes the inequality and injustice that would be occasioned by such a rigid rule and generally calibrates it accordingly. In fact, virtually the only place where the rigid reasonable person rule is adhered to in the face of significant tension with the underlying principle of avoidability is in the case of people with developmental disabilities. Thus, the equality analysis demands that we locate some basic principle of negligence to justify this refusal to allow the avoidability inquiry to condition the negligence liability of the developmentally disabled. For, as Rawls suggests, it is this kind of consistency in the application of principles and in the justification for that application that is so crucial to safeguarding against bias and arbitrariness in the application of the law.

Analysing the justifications given for the treatment of the developmentally disabled under the objective standard actually heightens rather than diminishes the concern about equality. Some attempts to justify identity of treatment, such as Coleman's, do posit a normatively relevant similarity between the developmentally disabled and the ordinary injurer—that is, fault.[30] However, as discussed in Chapter 1, these justifications ultimately fail because they cannot come up with a plausible sense in which the developmentally disabled injurer is at fault.[31] Related problems plague other attempts to justify the difference in treatment of litigants who seem similarly situated with respect to the principle of avoidability. If, as courts insist, the very meaning of fault in negligence

---

[29] In *Andrews* (n 10 above) 164, McIntyre J speaking for the majority on s 15 noted that the principle of equality was as capable of demanding differences in treatment as identity of treatment.

[30] Jules L Coleman, 'Mental Abnormality, Personal Responsibility, and Tort Liability' in BA Brody and H Tristram Engelhardt, Jr (eds), *Mental Illness: Law and Public Policy* (Boston: D Reidel Publishing Co, 1980) 107.

[31] Indeed, this feature of the objective standard has been noted by other commentators. Both Epstein and Honoré acknowledge that the objective standard is not wholly fault-based in that it does impose a form of strict liability on the 'shortcomer', including prominently, the mentally disabled: Honoré (n 2 above) 27; Epstein (n 27 above) 153. Both Epstein and Honoré suggest, in different ways, that this is to some degree justified because the fault principle is not as salient to liability in negligence as other commentators suggest. But, as noted in ch 1 above, the weakness of this argument is apparent in the case law, and in particular in the fact that we are not prepared to dispense with the fault principle for litigants whose welfare and liberty we value, such as children.

requires that the standard for the child defendant be reshaped to take into consideration the child's inability to foresee and therefore avoid the harm, why would the same principle not apply to the developmentally disabled individual who has a similar inability to perceive risk?

In the face of the failure of more theoretical defences of this treatment, we are left with the repeated insistence that childhood and the incapacities that attend it are normal and natural and, not inconsequentially, that developmental disability and its attendant incapacities are somehow not. Similar problems beset the treatment of children. The reasonable child test presents itself as a 'facially' neutral rule. But in fact the rule is applied very differently to boys and girls. Here the requirements of equality also demand a principled justification for that treatment. Once again, however, instead of such justifications, we get something all too familiar: appeals to a conception of what is normal and natural in the unchallengeable precepts of common sense.

We have seen that the justificatory force of appeals to the natural and normal is extremely limited. As Rawls reminds us, it is only the ability to justify variations in treatment on the basis of the relevant rules and principles that provides the crucial safeguard against the kind of arbitrary and biased judgments that undermine justice as regularity. It seems difficult to argue that there is an underlying principle of the law of negligence that counts normal or natural behaviour as non-culpable and abnormal behaviour as culpable. Indeed, the fact that the law of negligence refuses to treat customary or common practices as negating fault amounts to an explicit rejection of this very equation.[32] There is however an even deeper problem. As Rawls suggests, much of the discipline of adjudication, and its safeguard against the influence of bias and prejudice, comes from the demand for a particular kind of justification—that is, that distinctions be justified with reference *to the relevant legal rules and principles*. But not only are unreflective ideas about what is normal and natural not 'legal rules or principles', they are actually often the very mechanisms by which bias and prejudice work. So, far from being a bulwark against discriminatory judgments, justifications forwarded in these terms bring to mind the observation that 'eventually reasoned arguments for discriminatory judgments become harder to formulate and the attempt to do so less persuasive'.[33] The need to forward a justification in face of the fact that 'reason' seems to have run out in these cases may help to account for the distinctively impatient tones we noted earlier in the discussion of common sense.

It may be argued, however, that courts and commentators who invoke ideas of what is natural or normal for gender differences may implicitly be invoking

---

[32] See ch 4 above, nn 18–20. However, as discussed below in the chapters on criminal law, there may be a subtler version of this position that lurks behind many of these issues.

[33] Rawls (n 1 above) 237. Perhaps also germane to our discussion here, Rawls notes that 'the sufficient condition for equal justice, the capacity for moral personality, is not at all stringent': 506. Thus, there will not be a race or recognized group of people who lack this capacity. Further, where 'scattered individuals' lack the capacity for justice it is because of 'unjust and impoverished social circumstances, or fortuitous contingencies', and thus is not a reason for depriving those with lesser capacities of the full protection of justice: ibid.

the kind of gender-based conceptions of moral reasoning associated with the work of Carol Gilligan.[34] In her ground-breaking work, Gilligan claims that in the process of moral reasoning girls use a voice of relation, of care and connection, which differs from boys' emphasis on abstract rules and what Gilligan terms an ethic of justice. Thus, her work suggests significant gender differences in moral reasoning. An analysis of the negligence cases involving playing children does reveal very different behaviour patterns for boys, and so may seem fertile ground for a 'Gilliganesque' analysis. For the narrower purposes of this discussion, however, it seems relevant that girls do cross the 'gender divide' and engage in risk-taking behaviour.[35] And where they do so, they are routinely sanctioned in a way that boys tend not to be. Unless we are at a minimum persuaded both that there are systematic gender differences in moral reasoning[36] and that such differences should be accorded not only normative but legal force, a 'Gilliganesque' account seems unlikely to justify the differences we see in the legal treatment of boys and girls. So, beyond appeals to the natural and the normal, it is extremely difficult to identify any justification for such gendered treatment of children.

Examining the workings of the objective standard in the light of even the most minimal rule of law equality demands uncovers serious difficulties. As we have seen, the reasonable person typically tempers its apparent strictness by ensuring that the litigant in question had at least a minimal capacity to foresee and hence avoid the relevant harm. For this reason, even though more than avoidability

[34] C Gilligan, *In a Different Voice: Psychological Theory and Women's Development* (Cambridge, Mass: Harvard University Press, 1982).

[35] Interestingly, however, at least as revealed by the case law, the major boundary-crossing in which girls engage takes the form of imprudence about their own security, not about the security interests of others. As noted above, one should not be too quick to draw conclusions from this fact. Nonetheless, even given the ambiguousness of the evidence, it may be worth considering whether there is some significance to the fact that the riskiness of girls' behaviour seems primarily directed towards themselves, not others. Since the imprudence of girls seems to be with regard to their own security, the cases could be read to suggest that girls actually give more weight to the interests of others than boys do. Of course, even if true, the question is why. Perhaps girls do have a 'different' moral sense, at least to the extent that they weigh the interests of others more heavily than do their male counterparts. But the cases involving the playing child also reveal that what children are taught about appropriate behaviour is deeply gendered.

[36] It is worth noting that in general, despite the many merits of her articulation of a broader conception of the domain of moral reasoning, Gilligan's observations about how these different voices are used by men and by women have not been supported by subsequent research. Instead, research has suggested that both men and women use both justice and care-based reasoning: C Tavris, *Mismeasure of Woman* (New York: Simon & Schuster, 1992) 85, citing LD Cohn, 'Sex Differences in the Course of Personality Development: A Meta-Analysis' (1991) Psychological Bulletin 109; A Colby and W Damon, 'Listening to a Different Voice: A Review of Gilligan's *In a Different Voice*' in MR Walsh (ed), *The Psychology of Women: Ongoing Debates* (New Haven: Yale University Press, 1987) 321; WJ Friedman, AB Robinson, and BL Friedman, 'Sex Differences in Moral Judgments' (1987) Psychology of Women Quarterly 11; PD Lifton, 'Individual Differences in Moral Development: The Relation of Sex, Gender and Personality to Morality' in AJ Stewart and MB Lykes (eds), *Gender and Personality* (Durham, NC: Duke University Press, 1985); MT Mednick, 'On the Politics of Psychological Constructs: Stop the Bandwagon, I Want to Get Off' (1989) 44 American Psychologist 1118; SJ Thoma, 'Estimating Gender Differences in the Comprehension and Preference of Moral Issues' (1986) 6 Developmental Rev 165.

alone will be necessary to articulate an appropriately egalitarian conception of inadvertent wrongdoing, avoidability does animate much of the jurisprudence and the commentary. Some attentiveness to avoidability seems crucial to developing a morally attractive account of responsibility for heedlessness. But measured against this important principle, certain aspects of the objective standard seem unjustifiable. The treatment of people with developmental disabilities particularly stands out for its distinctive refusal to employ avoidability to realign responsibility and blame as it does with other litigants. Similarly, the very different uses of avoidability in the cases of boys and those involving girls seems hard to justify under any egalitarian conception of responsibility. In these cases, as we have noted, the increasingly difficult task of justification gives way to an unproblematized appeal to common sense understandings of what is normal or ordinary. Indeed, common sense seems to be invoked in these cases to refute the need for the kind of justification that the rule of law demands. But, as Rawls predicted, the more these cases are brought together, the more unpersuasive the reasoning looks. If these cases do accordingly look like 'mistakes', the question now is how we should assess their significance.

III. Equality and the Pitfalls of Tradition

> Age, sex, color, temperament, indifference, courage, intelligence, power of observation, judgment, quickness of reaction, self control, imagination, memory, deliberation, prejudices, experience, health, education, ignorance, attractiveness, weakness, strength, poverty, and any of the other possible assortments of qualities and characteristics of the persons involved may each be a factor in the jury's judgment on the negligence issue.[37]

In a day when such admissions were perhaps less troubling, Leon Green acknowledged that the qualities and characteristics of the litigants in a negligence action were of undoubted importance. Despite this, these factors seldom actually come to the surface. In fact, Green suggested that they are so common that 'they are virtually ignored', lying as they do 'beneath the formal statements of pleading, and ...above the rules of evidence'.[38] Green concludes that since the law cannot deal with these factors in detail, it ignores them.[39] However, to the extent that the factors outlined by Green actually compromise equality under law, the law cannot afford to be inattentive in this way and also remain consistent with its own values. But if not every illegitimate consideration, every mistake or unfairness in the legal process undermines the rule of law, then we must find some way to identify the kinds of mistakes that do have this deeper systemic significance.

One important clue to identifying the kinds of mistakes that have significance for the rule of law is found in Rawls's reference to the corrosive effect of 'bias', 'prejudice', and 'discrimination' on justice as regularity. What these terms suggest

---

[37] Green (n 23 above) 1044.   [38] ibid 1045.   [39] ibid 1046.

is that particular kinds of mistakes are especially likely to undermine the rule of law. So, consistent with equality analysis more generally, the rule of law significance of such mistakes seems to be partially a function of their frequency (their systematic quality) and partially a function of the nature of the mistake. Thus, *ad hoc* judicial mistakes, in contrast with systematic ones, typically hold limited significance for the rule of law. So, to use one of Green's examples, if a decision-maker dislikes me because of my temperament, 'mistakes' that she makes in applying the law, though they may be unfair and reviewable on various bases, will probably not undermine justice as regularity. In part this is because this kind of mistake is unlikely to be made systematically. Equally important, however, a mistake like excessive focus on the temperament of the litigant does not engage traditional equality concerns because it is not directed against a group that has long been the subject of legal discrimination, and exclusion. The references to bias, discrimination, and prejudice, and to the significance of 'groups' in Rawls's discussion, point to this quality of the relevant mistake and thus draw broader equality analyses into the assessment of justice as regularity.

To see how this might operate, we can contrast the person with the unpleasant temperament with another individual, the treatment of whom more deeply implicates long-standing discrimination and exclusion. Take for instance a decision-maker who is hostile to and hence harsher with litigants who are women or who are aboriginal or black, for instance. Legal systems like all of those discussed here are characterized in part by an unfortunate history of racial and gender discrimination, among others.[40] So, one implication of this is that the kinds of mistakes that draw on these entrenched views about the lesser humanity of some individuals are far more likely to be systematic than other kinds of views. Such discriminatory views are systematic not only because they occur more frequently but also because their content is systematic. As the language of bias, prejudice, and discrimination suggests, these mistakes find their genesis in certain kinds of damaging and widespread beliefs and attitudes. Because these kinds of mistakes seldom appear on the face of the decision (and are therefore unlikely to emerge unless one reads many cases in an effort to discern whether there is a pattern), they are extremely difficult to track. However, a few relevant examples of how this kind of dynamic might undermine justice as regularity can be found in the literature.

For instance, a considerable body of recent work suggests that tort damages to female plaintiffs are routinely and significantly lower than awards to male plaintiffs.[41] Commentators have argued that these patterns are attributable to

---

[40] For an overview of this, see Young (n 15 above).

[41] For a sample of this literature, see Martha Challamas, 'The Architecture of Bias: Deep Structures in Tort Law' (1998) 146 U Penn L Rev 463; Martha Challamas, 'Questioning the Use of Race-Specific and Gender-Specific Economic Data in Tort Litigation: A Constitutional Argument' (1994) 63 Fordham L Rev 73; Judith Resnik, 'Asking about Gender in the Courts' (1996) 21 Signs 952; Jamie Cassels, '(In)equality and the Law of Tort: Gender, Race and the Assessment of Damages' (1995) 17 Advocates' Quarterly 158; KA Clarke and AI Ogus, 'What is a Life Worth' (1978) Brit J L & Soc 1; R Graycar, 'Women's Work: Who Cares?' (1992) 14 Sydney L Rev 86. As Challamas

the effect of systematic beliefs about the lesser value of women's lives and women's work.[42] Indeed, the link to a history of discrimination is apparent in the fact that the patterns that emerge from the exercise of judicial discretion under facially neutral rules often bear a suspicious similarity to overtly discriminatory rules that used to characterize the legal treatment of women, especially married women.[43] Thus, the literature on the gendered nature of damage awards serves as an illustration of how systematic and prejudicial beliefs about the inferior value of women's lives can effectively discriminate against injured women in the judicial process and thereby raise a worry about justice as regularity. As this suggests, the kind of beliefs that are likely to have this rule of law effect have a systematic quality both in their frequency and in their content that replicates broader inegalitarian beliefs.

Another example of how the systematic effects of bias might undermine justice as regularity can be found in the Baldus study that formed the evidentiary backdrop to the United States Supreme Court decision in *McClesky v Kemp*.[44] Professor Baldus examined over two thousand murder cases that occurred in Georgia in the 1970s. After taking non-racial variables into account, he concluded that defendants charged with killing white people were much more likely to receive the death penalty, and that black defendants who killed white victims had the greatest likelihood of receiving the death penalty. McClesky, a black man who was sentenced to death for killing a white, used the Baldus study to argue that Georgia's capital sentencing scheme was administered in a racially discriminatory manner and thus violated the equal protection clause of the Fourteenth Amendment. The Supreme Court rejected this argument on the ground that the study was insufficient to establish racially discriminatory intent in any particular sentencing case. Mr Justice Powell also noted that the implications of McClesky's argument could throw 'into serious question the principles that underlie our entire criminal justice system'.[45] However, the four dissenting justices noted that the study established that the jury likely would have spared McClesky's life if his victim had been black and pointed out that for many years the State of Georgia 'operated openly and formally precisely the type of dual system the evidence shows is still effectively in place'.[46] But the merits of the constitutional argument aside, the Baldus study provides another example of how widespread beliefs about the different values of white and black lives might infect the administration of justice and undermine the rule of law.

notes, a number of jurisdictions have also undertaken studies on the effect of gender and racial bias in the courts: 'Architecture of Bias' 464–466 nn 8–13 discussing studies by the Ninth Circuit Gender Bias Task Force, the Washington State Task Force on Gender and Justice in the Courts, and the Illinois State Task Force on Gender Bias in the Courts among others. See also Law Society of British Columbia, *Gender Equality in the Justice System* (1992).

[42] See, for instance, Challamas, 'Architecture of Bias' (n 41 above) 467, 474 ff.

[43] Reva B Siegel, 'Home as Work: The First Women's Rights Claims Concerning Wives' Household Labor, 1850–1880' (1994) 103 Yale LJ 1073; Richard H Chused, 'Married Women's Property Law: 1800–1850' (1983) 71 Geo LJ 1359; C Backhouse, 'Married Women's Property Law in Nineteenth-Century Canada' (1988) 6 Law & History Rev 210.

[44] 481 US 279 (1987).   [45] ibid 315.   [46] ibid 329.

Indeed, as with gendered damage awards in tort law, the nature of the mistake is revealing: the dissenting justices in *McClesky* found the discrimination claim credible in part because the numbers in the study were 'consonant with our understanding of history and human experience'.[47]

These examples illustrate how prejudicial beliefs about the lesser value of some human lives can be sufficiently systematic that their influence on the application of the law will enable us to conclude, as Rawls suggests, that some groups are effectively discriminated against in the judicial process. These errors have rule of law significance when it becomes apparent that the application of the law is contingent upon attributes of individuals that are actually irrelevant to the legal rules and principles. To go back to Rawls's reference to Sidgwick, such an implication undermines the very idea of law as a system of general rules applied impartially. In this important respect, at least some kinds of systematic mistakes compromise the rule of law in a way that *ad hoc* mistakes, however unfortunate, do not. The 'mistakes' we have noted in the treatment of developmental disability and of gender under the objective standard do seem systematic in just this way. Like the beliefs about the lesser values of women's lives in the damages context and of the superior value of white lives in the Baldus study, these beliefs also reflect deeply entrenched social and civil inequalities as well as historical limits on formal rights of citizenship. Thus, we find considerable congruity between the groups that fare poorly under the standard and a broader history of exclusion and discrimination. In this respect then, the patterns of treatment under the objective standard that we have identified do seem to possess the very kind of deeper significance that jeopardizes the characteristic impartiality of the rule of law.

But if women and the developmentally disabled are in this way linked to similar histories of discrimination and exclusion, they are not alone in this. Indeed, both the example of race from the Baldus study and the nature of equality problems more generally suggest that our examples are merely illustrative of a broader problem. So although the developmentally disabled and women are among the categories of individuals routinely denied the full rights of membership, they are certainly not alone in that fact. If these are essentially problems of discrimination, then it seems likely that other groups subjected by prejudice to similar historical, social, and legal disadvantage will also suffer under the objective standard because of the way that determinations of reasonableness end up incorporating stereotypes about what is normal or ordinary. This means that in order to think more systematically about the equality effects of the standard of care, we will need a fuller account of what other kinds of mistakes we might expect to find exerting their influence on the standard.

As we have seen, attending to the nature of these kinds of systematic mistakes already draws the broader history of equality and discrimination into the analysis of justice as regularity. It is neither possible nor necessary however to provide

[47] 481 US 279 (1987) 328.

a full account of that history here. But what the rule of law analysis does require is a more general examination of that history to see where else we might expect the kinds of systematic mistakes that undermine justice as regularity. We can begin by recalling the fact that histories of the idea of citizenship identify common categories of exclusion from full membership, including full legal rights. So, as Vogel points out, the history of the modern democratic state is characterized by certain recurring bases of exclusion such as legal incapacity (children, women, the feeble-minded or insane), social status (slaves and serfs), racial, religious or ethnic identity (Jews, Catholics, Blacks), and status as aliens, among others.[48] Unsurprisingly, given their explicitly remedial aspirations, the equality provisions of constitutions and other similar documents and the relevant jurisprudence also tend to identify similar bases of egalitarian concern. Thus, post–World War II rights protecting regimes share a number of important features, among which is the general nature of their equality guarantees.[49] The relatively recent enumeration of the bases of discrimination contained in s 15 of the Canadian Charter serves as an example of such equality provisions. Section 15 prohibits discrimination, not only based on mental disability and sex, but also based on race, national or ethnic origin, colour, religion, age and disability.[50] This enumeration, though not in itself exhaustive,[51] reproduces at least in its general outlines the predominant bases of discrimination found in many other post-war human rights protecting instruments.[52] Theoretical work on the nature of equality and discrimination also commonly invokes bases of discrimination similar to those found in s 15.[53] Thus, for example, Iris Marion Young takes as the focus of her equality analysis the conditions of groups including 'among

[48] Vogel (n 9 above) 62. See ch 4 above, nn 101–103.

[49] LE Weinrib, 'Canada's Constitutional Revolution: From Legislative to Constitutional State' (1999) 33 Israel L Rev 13.

[50] The general equality guarantee, s 15(1) of the Charter (n 12 above) reads as follows: 'Every individual is equal before and under the law and has the right to the equal protection and equal benefit of the law without discrimination and, in particular, without discrimination based on race, national or ethnic origin, colour, religion, sex, age or mental or physical disability.' Other relevant examples of constitutional equality guarantees are discussed n 12 above.

[51] Thus, courts have held that the equality guarantee under s 15 of the Charter covers not only the enumerated grounds of discrimination but also 'analogous grounds': *Andrews* (n 10 above) (citizenship); *Egan v Canada* [1995] 2 SCR 513 (sexual orientation); *Miron v Trudel* [1995] 2 SCR 418 (marital status). Indeed, a principled approach to equality will always leave open the possibility that any enumeration will fail to capture all of the possible categories of discrimination. Thus, in the United States, one finds extensive—and in many ways similar—debate about the scope of the much more general wording of the Fourteenth Amendment, and in particular about the extent to which its protection extends to bases of discrimination not contemplated by the framers: these include gender (see *Bradwell v State* 16 Wall (83 US) 130 (1873) and *Minor v Happersett* 88 US (21 Wall) 162 (1875)); mental disability (see *City of Cleburne v Cleburne Living Center* 473 US 432 (1985)); alienage (*Sugarman v Dougall* 413 US 634 (1973)); and sexual orientation (*Bowers v Hardwick* 478 US 186 (1986)).

[52] Canadian Charter (n 12 above). See also n 11 above for international instruments. The fact of some general congruence, however, should not lead us to ignore the possibilities that some groups may be subjected to more virulent discrimination in certain jurisdictions than in others and that the actual form that the discrimination takes may vary.

[53] In *Justice and the Politics of Difference*, Iris Marion Young discusses the concept of oppression and its relationship to injustice: n 15 above. Young aims to systematize and provide a normative

others women, Blacks, Chicanos, Puerto Ricans and other Spanish-speaking Americans, American Indians, Jews, lesbians, gay men, Arabs, Asians, old people, working class people, and the physically and mentally disabled'.[54] Here too we see that discriminatory stereotypes about various groups have typically taken the form of arguing that certain kinds of negative characteristics are part of the 'nature' of what it means to be Black, Jewish, Oriental, Hispanic, Irish, etc. Thus, Young notes how women were sexualized, and other groups (Blacks, Jews, homosexuals, and the poor) were classified as degenerate and often criminal.[55] Given the general similarity among these various enumerations of the groups traditionally subjected to discrimination it seems possible to view the traditional bases of discrimination as 'warning signs', telling us where to be particularly careful by pointing to the places where history and tradition show we have consistently gone awry. Heeding these warning signs suggests that we need to be concerned about the operation of the objective standard not just with the developmentally disabled and women, but also with a number of other groups that have traditionally been disadvantaged.[56] With this in mind, let us re-examine the cases involving children.

A. Re-examining the privileged child

When we first looked at the category of children, they appeared relatively advantaged in comparison with the developmentally disabled. However, when we began to examine the nature of that advantage more closely, a more complicated picture emerged. Children were indeed advantaged as a group relative to the developmentally disabled,[57] but the bulk of the advantage actually went

account of the meaning of oppression. She suggests that oppression in fact comprises several concepts and conditions, which she analyses in terms of five categories: exploitation, marginalization, powerlessness, cultural imperialism, and violence. Oppression, she states, is a condition of groups: ibid. For reasons that I take to be related primarily to certain aspects of American constitutional equality doctrine, Young distinguishes between oppression and discrimination. On the varying bases of discrimination and the relations between them, see also E Spelman, *Inessential Woman: Problems of Exclusion in Feminist Thought* (Boston: Beacon Press, 1988).

[54] Young (n 15 above) 40.

[55] ibid 129. Young also notes how these assumptions were used interchangeably, with degenerate males (including black males and Jewish males) depicted as effeminate: ibid.

[56] The concept of a disadvantaged group is complex. Young points out that there are almost infinitely varying forms and combinations of oppression. For instance, a working-class man may be exploited economically and powerless, but may not be subject to cultural imperialism or violence. Gay men, on the other hand, may experience cultural imperialism and violence but not exploitation and powerlessness: ibid 64. Many, but not all Blacks and Latinos in the United States, suffer all five forms of oppression.

[57] It may well be that girls are rarely advantaged relative to ordinary adults under the objective standard. Interestingly, Ariès repeatedly notes how for a very long period after the invention of 'childhood', girls were in all important respects treated as adults, not children. Thus, they wore adult clothing, did not play games or participate in education, and entered the adult world of marriage and childbearing at a very early age: 'Moreover, by the age of ten, girls were already little women: a precocity due in part to an upbringing which taught girls to behave very early in life like grown-ups': P Ariès, *Centuries of Childhood: A Social History of Family Life* (trans R Baldick) (New York: Vintage Books, 1962) 332.

to a privileged group of children—boys. But our discussion above suggests that it may be important to look again at that privileged category of boys to see whether the notion of what behaviour is normal or natural and therefore reasonable may be premissed on troubling stereotypes—not only about gender and mental ability, but also about other factors including race and class.

1. *Race and the reasonable child*

As both our earlier discussion of the Baldus study and the various enumerations of the bases of discrimination suggest, the race of the litigant may be the most obvious other candidate for concern under the reasonable person standard. Indeed, constitutional guarantees of equality and the relevant jurisprudence tend to give a prominent place to the danger of racial discrimination.[58] In fact, in American equality jurisprudence, the highest degree of constitutional scrutiny ('strict scrutiny') is reserved for racial classifications.[59] Further, at the international level a separate convention, the International Convention on the Elimination of all Forms of Racial Discrimination,[60] is designed to respond to the danger of racial discrimination. Similarly, as noted above, concerns about racial discrimination and stereotypes play a prominent role in most theories of equality and thus are widely discussed in the literature. Recently, scholars have turned their attention to the operation of the judicial process and particularly to the danger that discretion will be exercised in a racially biased manner.[61] *McClesky v Kemp* is illustrative in the sense that much of this literature focuses on the operation of the criminal justice system and the possible constitutional significance of racial bias.[62] Scholars are also beginning to turn their attention

[58] Canadian Charter, s 15 (n 12 above); Fourteenth Amendment (n 12 above); ECHR, Article 14 (n 11 above).

[59] *Korematsu v United States* 323 US 214 (1944). Ironically, although *Korematsu* established that racial classifications triggered the most rigid scrutiny, the majority in that case sustained a conviction for violating a military order issued during World War II that excluded all persons of Japanese ancestry from designated West Coast areas.   [60] n 11 above.

[61] The literature is too extensive to summarize but some prominent examples include Derrick Bell, *Faces at the Bottom of the Well: The Permanence of Racism* (New York: Basic Books, 1992); Charles Lawrence, 'The Id, the Ego, and Equal Protection: Reckoning with Unconscious Racism' (1987) 39 Stanford L Rev 317; Richard Delgado, 'Shadowboxing: An Essay on Power' (1992) 77 Cornell L Rev 813; Alex Aleinikoff, 'The Constitution in Context: The Continuing Significance of Racism' (1992) 63 Colo L Rev 325; P Williams, *The Alchemy of Race and Rights* (Cambridge, Mass: Harvard University Press, 1991).

[62] Once again the literature is voluminous but some important works include: Sheri Lynn Johnson, 'Race and the Decision to Detain a Suspect' (1983) 93 Yale LJ 214 and 'Black Innocence and White Jury' (1985) 83 Mich L Rev 1611; 'Developments in the Law—Race and the Criminal Process' (1988) 101 Harv L Rev 1473; Jody D Armour, 'Race Ipsa Loquitur: Of Reasonable Racists, Intelligent Bayesians, and Involuntary Negrophobes' (1994) 46 Stan L Rev 781; Richard Delgado, 'Rodrigo's Eighth Chronicle: Black Crime, White Fears—On the Social Construction of a Threat' (1994) 80 Va L Rev 503; A Alfieri, 'Defending Racial Violence' (1995) 95 Columbia L Rev 1301; Nancy J King, 'Postconviction Review of Jury Discretion: Measuring the Effects of Juror Race on Jury Decisions' (1993) 92 Mich L Rev 63; ML Nightingale, 'Judicial Attitudes and Differential Treatment: Native Women in Sexual Assault Cases' (1991) 23 CJWL 71; C Backhouse, *Petticoats and Prejudice* (Toronto: The Osgoode Society, 1991); Audrey Kobayashi, 'Do Minority Women Judges Make a Difference?' (1998) CJWL 10; Regina Graycar, 'The Gender of Judgments: Some

to the operation of private law, including the law of tort.[63] Even in the criminal context, however, there are serious debates about how to assess the extent and operation of racial bias and how to respond to it.[64] But in the criminal context it is often possible to track the race of the litigant.

The same cannot be said of the system of private law. Thus, while ordinarily (though not invariably) it is possible from the description of the case itself to identify the gender of the litigant, the race of the litigant, particularly in more recent cases, is extremely unlikely to be mentioned on the face of the decision.[65] Unfortunately, this means that in the absence of an extremely ambitious study with extensive access to court records and the like, it is almost impossible to track the kinds of patterns that we were able to identify in the treatment of people with developmental disabilities and of boys and girls. A few more ambitious studies have been done of the civil litigation system in the United States, such as in New York State and in Oregon. However, as commentators acknowledge, the significance of many of these studies is extremely limited because they tend to focus on reported *perceptions* of racial bias, rather than undertaking a systematic study of the verdicts and other outcomes.[66] The consequence is that in the civil law context at least, commentators are largely confined to using individual cases or constructed narratives to suggest points of broader significance.[67]

Reflections on "Bias"' (1998) 32 UBC L Rev 1; Sherene Razack, *Looking White People in the Eye: Gender, Race, and Culture in Courtrooms and Classrooms* (Toronto: University of Toronto Press, 1998); Tony Storey, 'Right to a Fair Trial by an Impartial Tribunal: Trial by Jury—Ethnic Minority Defendant—Suspected Racial Bias among Jurors' (2000) 5 J Civ Lib 244.

[63] Challamas, 'Race-Specific and Gender-Specific Economic Data' and 'The Architecture of Bias' (n 41 above); Frank M McClellan, 'The Dark Side of Tort Reform: Searching for Racial Justice' (1996) 48 Rutgers L Rev 761; Cassels (n 41 above); andre douglas pond cummings [*sic*], '"Lions and Tigers and Bears, Oh My" or "Redskins and Braves and Indians, Oh Why": Ruminations on *McBride v Utah State Tax Commission*, Political Correctness and the Reasonable Person' (1999) 36 California Western L Rev 11; Amy H Kastely, 'Out of the Whiteness: On Raced Codes and White Race Consciousness in Some Tort, Criminal and Contract Law' (1994) 63 U Cinn L Rev 269.

[64] See ch 8 below, n 34.

[65] Indeed, this is apparent in the fact that the studies of gender and racial bias in the assessment of damages have much more difficulty drawing conclusions about race precisely because of the inadequacy of the data and the fact that the cases rarely 'announce' their racial implications in the way that they announce gender: Cassels (n 41 above) 190–196; McClellan (n 63 above); Challamas 'Race-Specific and Gender-Specific Economic Data' (n 41 above) 87–89.

[66] The exceptions are Audrey Chin and Mark Peterson, The Institute for Civil Justice, *Deep Pockets, Empty Pockets: Who Wins in Cook County Jury Trials* (1985) (published for the Rand Corporation Institute for Civil Justice, R-3249-ICJ), which found that African Americans received only 74% as much money in damages as white plaintiffs for the same injuries. Similar findings were made by the Washington State Minority and Justice Task Force, Final Report (1990), which noted substantial disparities between settlement amounts in asbestos cases involving minority and non-minority plaintiffs. However, the studies conducted in New York State and Oregon focused on the *perception* of racial bias, which both studies found to exist: The Oregon Supreme Court Task Force on Racial/Ethnic Issues in the Judicial System, 'Report of the Oregon Supreme Court Task Force on Racial/Ethnic Issues in the Judicial System' (1994) 73 Or L Rev 823; *Report of the New York State Judicial Commission on Minorities* (1991). Unfortunately these studies did not attempt to assess the validity of these perceptions, and so while they are useful for some purposes these studies do not speak directly to the existence of the kind of racial skewing that would raise a rule of law concern.

[67] For instance, Kastely in 'Out of the Whiteness' interprets how a number of discrete cases are 'racially coded' and suggests that this means that 'legal language is permeated with white racial

Indeed, this approach is often brought forth to criticize the reasonable person as inherently problematic on race-based grounds. Though it is rarely spelled out in much detail, the underlying argument seems to run as follows: the reasonable person is essentially the ordinary or average person and, given the prevalence of racism, it is plausible that the reasonable person holds objectionable beliefs about race.[68] The difficulty, however, which candid commentators note, is that it is extremely difficult to identify systematic patterns because of the general silence of the reported private law cases on the race issue.

This difficulty should not lead us to conclude that we need not be concerned about the reasonable person on race grounds. After all, as discussed above, the treatment of the developmentally disabled and of women under the reasonable person standard is by no means accidental. Indeed, it exhibits significant continuities with a long history of exclusion from basic legal and political rights—a history that undeniably also implicates race at least as prominently as gender and disability. And for this reason, as discussed above, race figures prominently among the various guarantees of equality. Further, it is worth noting briefly that the nature of the underlying stereotypes about race are such that it is not difficult to see how they influence the standard in much the same way that we saw with gender and disability. Much of the work on stereotypes and how they might feed into the judicial process has explored the impact of stereotypes of Blacks in the American criminal justice system. In this context, the literature points to a fairly pervasive set of social beliefs that tend to view Blacks as inherently violent and criminal.[69] Concerns about how these stereotypes might feed into conceptions of reasonableness are particularly played out in the analysis of self-defence, especially in the wake of the Bernard Goetz trial. Indeed, many

consciousness': (n 63 above) 314. But she also notes the gulf between the individual cases she discusses and the broader conclusion she suggests is vast—she suggests that although race is often central, including to determinations of reasonableness, race is also 'ineffable in public discourse' including in law: ibid 313. Similarly, McClellan is candid about the inadequacy of the empirical data and so discusses narratives concerning specific cases he was involved in in order to explore the ways that race can play out in the litigation process: n 63 above.

[68] See, for instance, Kastely (ibid) and McClellan (ibid).

[69] Again, the literature is extensive but some particularly relevant examples include: Delgado (n 61 above); Alfieri (n 62 above); R Majors and J Mancini Billson, *Cool Pose: The Dilemmas of Black Manhood in America* (New York: Lexington Books, 1992); Cynthia KY Lee, 'Race and Self-Defence: Toward a Normative Conception of Reasonableness' (1996) 81 Minn L Rev 367; Armour (n 62 above); Erick L Hill and Jeffrey E Pfeifer, 'Nullification Instructions and Juror Guilt Ratings: An Examination of Modern Racism' (1992) 16 Contemp Soc Psychol 6; Studs Terkel (ed), *Race: How Blacks and Whites Think and Feel about the American Obsession* (New York: New Press, 1992); Joe R Feagin, Hernan Vera, and Pina Batur, *White Racism: The Basics* (2nd edn, New York: Routledge, 2001); Linda Hamilton Kreiger, 'The Content of Our Categories: A Cognitive Bias Approach to Discrimination and Equality Employment Opportunity' (1995) 47 Stan L Rev 1161; Marc Mauer, *The Sentencing Project, Young Black Men and the Criminal Justice System: A Growing National Problem* (Washington, DC: Sentencing Project 1990); Marc Mauer and Tracy Huling, *The Sentencing Project, Young Black Americans and the Criminal Justice System: Five Years Later* (Washington, DC: Sentencing Project 1995); David A Sklansky, 'Cocaine, Race and Equal Protection' (1995) 47 Stan L Rev 1283; Randall Kennedy, 'The State, Criminal Law, and Racial Discrimination: A Comment' (1994) 107 Harv L Rev 1255; Paul Butler, 'Racially Based Jury Nullification: Black Power in the Criminal Justice System' (1995) 105 Yale LJ 677.

commentators have discussed whether the reasonable man in a self-defence situation would hold a similar belief about the dangerousness and criminality of Black men in particular.[70] We will return to consider some of these questions in our later discussion of the reasonable person in criminal law.

For the moment however we should simply pause to note that, although the invisibility of race in civil cases may make it extremely difficult to track how such beliefs might play out in the fault standard, it does seem plausible to assume that they figure in a significant way. Let us briefly consider what we have already seen in the cases involving children in the light of the nature of stereotypes about Blacks and the findings in the Baldus study. It seems plausible that decision-makers faced with a Black boy defendant in a situation like that of *McHale* may be significantly less likely to see the boy's aggressiveness in such idealized terms. So instead of viewing the boy's play as innocent and harmless, much like what the judge himself remembers about boyhood, a judge (especially perhaps a white judge) faced with a Black boy who injured another child (especially, perhaps a non-Black child) may be more likely to see the boy as dangerous and threatening. Thus, it is not difficult to imagine that in such a case the judge may be less likely to wax lyrical about the innocent charms of boyhood and more likely to lecture the boy about carelessness. Indeed, it is certainly possible that these kinds of racial dynamics were at work in cases involving children we looked at previously. The difficulty, though, is that given the silence on race, we are generally left with the unsatisfying need to speculate. As many other commentators have noted, this points to the importance of conducting some empirical studies. In the mean time, however, the conclusions about the impact of race and other potentially significant factors are bound to be tentative.

2. *Hard times for the working boy*

Even if tracing the impact of race on assessments of reasonableness proves very difficult, it is nonetheless possible to get a bit more insight into how other kinds of stereotypes and biases might play out in the treatment of the boy. Given that gender stereotypes so pervasively influence the interpretation of what kind of behaviour is normal and hence reasonable for a boy, it seems likely, as Green pointed out, that a whole array of factors are implicated in this way. Indeed, the complexity of the stereotypes at play in discrimination and the way they feed into the idea of the normal makes it extremely unlikely that the assumptions imported into the objective standard about the boy's nature are confined to assumptions about gender and mental ability. In fact, as discussed above, history and theory suggest that we should be at least as concerned about the effect of assumptions about race. Another ground of discrimination identified by much citizenship and equality literature concerns class status, especially poverty.[71]

---

[70] See eg Armour (n 62 above).

[71] Although it does not affect the rule of law analysis, it is worth noting that the significance of class is complex relative to race, at least in terms of constitutional guarantees of equality. While many

In contrast with race, exploring some of the possible class implications of the reasonable person seems more tractable. We therefore turn to consider cases involving children injured while at work to see what else they might reveal about the standard of care.

A suitable place to begin is with the adult activities exception to the relaxed standard of care for children. Fleming describes the exception as follows: 'a minor who engages in dangerous adult activities, such as driving a car or handling industrial equipment, must conform to the standard of a reasonably prudent adult.'[72] Similarly, Prosser states that according to the adult activities rule, whenever a child engages in an activity that is normally one for adults, then 'the child must be held to the adult standard, without any allowance for his age.'[73] This may sound uncontroversial, and unrelated to the problem we are addressing, but it is worth noting how uneasily it sits with the logic underlying the relatively generous treatment of children that we saw in cases involving the playing boy, such as *McHale*. This may prompt us to ask what exactly counts as an adult activity.

There is controversy about both the basis and scope of the adult activities exception. Indeed, some commentators have suggested that most of the cases can be explained without recourse to the exception on the ground that the children would have been liable even under a subjectivized standard.[74] Further,

theories do identify poverty as a source of discrimination (eg Young (n 15 above); Spelman (n 53 above)), it is not commonly included in constitutional guarantees. Indeed, to begin with, Canadian courts were hesitant to interpret the Canadian Charter's guarantee of liberty in s 7 to include economic liberty: *Reference re ss 193 and 195.1(1)(c) of the Criminal Code* [1990] 1 SCR 1123. However, Canadian courts seem increasingly willing to consider at least certain basic economic rights as implicit in ss 7 and 15 of the Charter. In *Falkiner v Ontario* [2002] OJ No 1771 (Laskin JA), the Ontario Court of Appeal found that receipt of social assistance was an 'analogous ground' of discrimination under the Charter. There is also a scholarly debate about whether the Charter might protect some very basic economic rights, either under s 7 or under s 15: DM Beatty, 'Canadian Constitutional Law in a Nutshell' (1998) 36 Alberta L Rev 605; M Jackman, 'The Protection of Welfare Rights under the Charter' (1988) 20 Ottawa L Rev 257 and 'Poor Rights: Using the Charter to Support Social Welfare Claims' (1993) 19 Queen's LJ 65; R Howse, 'Another Rights Revolution? The Charter and the Reform of Social Regulation in Canada' in P Grady, R Howse, and J Maxwell (eds), *Redefining Social Security* (Kingston: School of Policy Studies, Queen's University, 1995). In the United States, classifications based on wealth have been considered more often but their constitutional significance is no clearer. In the leading case, the Court narrowly sustained Texas's manner of financing public education, which disproportionately benefited wealthy children: *San Antonio School District v Rodriguez* 411 US 1 (1973). Speaking for the majority, Mr Justice Powell found that the poor had 'none of the traditional indicia of suspectness: the class is not saddled with such disabilities, or subjected to such a history of purposeful unequal treatment, or relegated to such a position of political powerlessness as to command extraordinary protection from the majoritarian political processes': 28. Compare *Plyler v Doe* 457 US 202 (1982) (legislation denying free public education to undocumented children struck down on the basis of a fundamental right not to be absolutely denied education); but see *Martinez v Bynum* 461 US 321 (1983) (sustaining residence requirement for tuition-free education to minors); *Kadrmas v Dickinson Public Schools* 487 US 450 (1988) (permitting a user fee for transporting students to and from public schools).

[72] Fleming (n 23 above) 126.

[73] WP Keeton (gen ed), *Prosser and Keeton on the Law of Torts* (5th edn, St Paul, Minn: West Publishing Co, 1984) 181.

[74] DE Seidelson, 'Reasonable Expectations and Subjective Standards in Negligence Law: The Minor, the Mentally Impaired, and the Mentally Incompetent' (1981) 50 Geo Wash L Rev 17.

it seems possible that many of the cases can be explained on the basis that the nature of the activity subjects all of the participants to a stricter form of liability, with the consequence that the child is simply being treated as any other participant in that activity. Since many of the core adult activities cases involve the operation of a licensed motor vehicle, this seems plausible.[75] But even given this, some important puzzles remain. The most troubling ones centre on the treatment of the child who works. As we saw in the cases involving children, the archetypal childish activity is play.[76] But if this is correct, then it seems to suggest that the most 'adult' activity that a child can undertake is work. Indeed, the case law sometimes reveals an assumption that if a child is working, he is somehow not a child and thus not judged according to a child's standard. For instance, in discussing the adult activities doctrine, Fleming mentions the operation of industrial equipment, and Prosser's notes refer to the operation of farm equipment such as tractors. The court in *Jackson v McCuiston* stated of the boy tractor operator that 'unquestionably he was performing a job normally expected to be done by adults'[77] and accordingly was held to an adult standard. Though this may seem unremarkable, we should pause to consider how this approach squares with the justifications for the treatment of children: if the attribution of liability in negligence is fault-based, and if in cases like *McHale v Watson* the relaxation of the standard is justified on the basis that it is necessary to bring the avoidability-based conception of fault into line with the limited capacities of childhood, it seems odd that the child at work would not benefit from this rule.

Examining the cases involving the standard applied to children at work in the light of the cases involving the playing boy is revealing. As we shall see, in many work situations the child is forgiven neither for failures of prudence nor for failures of foresight. The courts actually seem remarkably untroubled about the implications of the limited capacities of working children, often reacting with impatience rather than sympathy to their claim to be judged by a relaxed standard. At law, it seems, the working child is almost indistinguishable from the adult. Thus, courts are quick to find either that such children are contributorily negligent or that no duty is owed to them, thereby barring them from recovering damages.[78]

---

[75] See discussion in ch 1 above. See also WH Rodgers, Jr, 'Negligence Reconsidered: The Role of Rationality in Tort Theory' (1980) 54 S Cal L Rev 1.

[76] However, the list of activities that does and does not fall within the exception is interesting, for it reveals much not only about conceptions of what kinds of play are childish (bicycling and skiing are, for instance, while golf is not: Prosser (n 23 above) 181), but also about what kinds of activities need to be encouraged in children. Thus, significantly, in the United States the use of guns is not an adult activity so children benefit from a relaxed standard: *Purtle v Shelton* 474 SW 2d 123 (SC Ark 1971); *Thomas v Inman* 578 P 2d 399 (Or 1978). See also WR Habeeb, 'Annotation: Weapons: Application of Adult Standard of Care to Infants Handling Firearms' (1973) 47 ALR 3d 620. However, the use of a tractor by a child is an adult activity: *Jackson v McCuiston* 448 SW 2d 33 (Ark 1969); *Goodfellow v Coggburn* 560 P 2d 873 (Idaho 1977).   [77] (n 76 above) 35.

[78] Many of these cases are situated in the early period of this century when the status of both working children and industrial workers was in transition. Thus, the contributory negligence cases involving child workers are situated at the intersection of two difficult issues in the history of

An illustration can be found in *Dominion Glass*[79] where a majority of the Supreme Court of Canada refused to find a company liable for the death of a 14-year-old boy. The company was employing the boy in contravention of the child labour provisions of the Industrial Establishments Act. Further, the foreman had imposed extra work on the boy, who was working the night shift. Because of the extreme heat in the factory, the boy had climbed over a barricaded door that had been left open for ventilation. He fell to his death when he stepped onto a smoke flue that gave way. Chief Justice Anglin, writing for the majority, found that while the employer did have an obligation to keep a watchful eye on mischievous boys, a 'factory is not a kindergarten'.[80] In contrast with the cases involving the boy at play, he described the boy's attempt to get fresh air as entirely unforeseeable. In dissent, Justice Brodeur pointed out that the foreman had threatened the boy and was making him work considerably harder than usual because of the absence of another worker. He also pointed out that since the only purpose of the door was ventilation, it should have had a grill over it. Nonetheless, the majority refused to award any damages for the boy's death.

A similar approach to the boy at work is found in *Ouellet v Cloutier*.[81] There, a boy of about 10 was helping out on a threshing crew. At the end of the day, while trying to stop a piece of machinery, his arm was caught and badly broken. The Supreme Court of Canada unanimously found against the boy. Justice Rand's description of Marcel is typical of the various judgments in the case:

Boys at farms, as part of their practical education as well as a satisfaction of their natural propensity to imitate their elders, assist at small jobs . . . He had the ordinary boy's discipline and dependability in these practical situations. But here was an impulsive act of wantonness indulged in a few moments before the last motion of the machinery would have ended. Normally, in such circumstances, particularly the presence of men, a boy of that age

---

negligence law. As both *Dominion Glass Company v Despins* (1922) 63 SCR 544 and *Berdos v Tremont & Suffolk Mills* 95 NE 876 (1911 Mass) illustrate, legislatures in this period were increasingly introducing laws prohibiting the use of child labour. Thus, for instance, the US Congress finally responded to a decade of lobbying by enacting the Keating–Owen Child Labor Act of 1916. The legislation was challenged by the father of two children, one under 14 and the other 16 employed in a cotton mill in North Carolina: *Hammer v Dagenhart* 247 US 251 (1918). A narrow majority of the Court found the Act an unconstitutional invasion by Congress into the powers of the States.

The negligence litigation in this period also reveals the struggle over the status of working-class children. While legislatures attempted to limit the use of child labour, employers continued to find it lucrative to employ children. Consequently, many accidents involving child workers came before the courts. As indicated in the text, judicial attitudes towards the working child tended to reflect the view that they were somehow not children in the full sense of the term. Ariès notes that for a considerable period of time working-class children 'kept up the old way of life which made no distinction between children and adults, in dress or in work or in play': (n 57 above) 61. And since education was not generally extended to the children of the 'lower classes', 'child labour retained this characteristic of medieval society: the precocity of entry into adult life': 336. In this sense, as Ariès points out, being treated as a child was a benefit of the privileged. The difficult exit of working-class children from that world and into the privileged ranks of childhood (a struggle by no means complete) is partly chronicled in this litigation.   [79] ibid.

[80] ibid 548. Since the master did not have to guard against dangers that could not be anticipated and that did not rise out of employment, there was no liability.   [81] [1947] SCR 521.

would not touch a revolving shaft, but certainly he would be expected to drop the belt instantly upon a sharp command to do so; and the injury suffered by him is due to that momentary wilfulness in disobedience.[82]

Like Justice Rand, the other members of the Supreme Court emphasize the fact that Marcel was a 'farm boy.'[83] The Court's approach here to what is normal and natural is diametrically opposed to that found in the cases involving the boy at play, even though Marcel is the same age as many of those children. Here we find the natural propensity is not to mischief or disobedience but rather to imitation of one's elders, to work, and indeed, to discipline and obedience. In direct contrast to the playing boy who is simply expected to ignore warnings and instructions, here courts insist that obedience to authority is characteristic of the working child. Although Marcel was actually trying (in a misguided fashion) to stop the machinery, not to play with it, his act is repeatedly described as an indulgence, an impulsive act of wantonness. As we have seen, courts are willing to find as foreseeable the danger that playing children of around Marcel's age will set torches, firecrackers, and drums on fire and play with sources of electricity even when explicitly warned not to.[84] But here where it is a working child, the court finds the boy's act entirely unforeseeable.

Indeed, during this period working children were routinely refused damages if allowing recovery would have required a relaxed standard of care for the child. This is despite the fact that these are cases in which the working child is a *plaintiff*, and so any shortcomings on the part of the child go solely to contributory negligence. In fact, even in the most egregious cases, there are controversies between higher and lower courts, reflecting the reluctance to extend the ordinary negligence treatment of children to the working child. An example is found in *Berdos v Tremont & Suffolk Mills*.[85] The plaintiff was a boy under 14 who had

---

[82] [1947] SCR 528.

[83] Interestingly, however, as Justice Rand notes, Marcel did not in fact live on a farm, although he did live in a farming district.

[84] See, for instance, *Mayer v Prince Albert* [1926] 4 DLR 1072 (Sask CA) (court awarded damages to a 9-year-old boy even though his father had specifically warned him not to climb light poles); *Yachuk v Oliver Blais Co Ltd* [1949] 3 DLR 1 (JCPC) (fact that injured boy had been warned to keep away from his father's gasoline torch did not preclude him from recovering for the injuries he suffered when playing with gasoline); *Walker v Sheffield Bronze* (1977) 77 DLR (3d) 377 (court refused to find culpability on the part of the $9\frac{1}{2}$-year old-boy who placed a lighted match in a barrel, even though he admitted knowing that playing with matches was wrong); *Fergus v Toronto* [1932] 2 DLR 807 (HC) (10-year-old boy allowed to recover from City for severe injuries sustained when he and his 14-year-old brother were playing and placed a lit firecracker in a disused gasoline drum left in a ditch on the roadway); *Dainio v Russell Timber Co Ltd* (1924) 27 OWN 235 (HC) (12-year-old boy injured when he set fire to a fuse he found in defendant's field). These are but a few examples of the fact that the court is willing to exonerate the playing boy even where he is engaged in dangerous play and was warned about or knew about the danger: *Paskivski v Canadian Pacific Ltd* [1976] 1 SCR 687, 57 DLR (3d) 280; *Pannett v McGuinness & Co* [1972] 3 All ER 137 (CA); *Holdman v Hamlyn* [1943] KB 664 (CA); *Laverdure v Victoria (City)* (1952) 7 WWR 333 (BCSC); *Culkin v McFie* [1939] 3 All ER 613 (KB); *Baker v Flint & PMR Co U* 35 NW 836 (Mich 1888); *Arnold v Gillies* (1978) 8 Alta LR (2d) 21, 93 DLR (3d) 48 (Dist Ct); *Bouvier v Fee* [1932] SCR 118, [1932] 2 DLR 424; *Burbridge v Starr Manufacturing Co* (1921) 54 NSR 121, 56 DLR 658 (CA).   [85] n 78 above.

been in the country for less than seven weeks. He had never worked in a factory and could not read or speak English. He had not been given instructions or a warning. While working, his hand was severely cut by some gears. Like the boy in *Dominion Glass* he was employed in contravention of a statute that prohibited child labour. At trial, the judge directed a verdict for the defendant on the ground that the child was contributorily negligent. On appeal to the Supreme Judicial Court of Massachusetts, Rugg J overturned this directed verdict and ruled that the plaintiff was entitled to go to a jury on the question of his contributory negligence. In addition to discussing the significance of the statutory violation, Rugg J also pointed out that as a child the plaintiff may have been 'so restless, heedless and active as to be naturally incapable of appreciating the dangers of the position in which he was placed by the defendant.'[86] But as he also points out, it is still open to the defendant to argue that the boy failed to exercise the degree of care that a normal child of his age, intelligence, and experience ought to have exercised.

A similar pattern is apparent in *Moore v The JD Moore Co.*[87] There, a boy of 15 who was employed to clean up around the machines in the defendant's factory had his arm taken off by the blades of one of the machines. The boy had been attempting to brush some dust off the machine, but the blades were unguarded and revolved so quickly that it appeared that they were not in motion when the machine was in fact operating. At trial, the jury found for the boy on the ground that the machine was not properly guarded and was not being attended by its operator. They also found that, given his age, the boy had used reasonable care. However, the trial judge then directed a verdict for the defendant on the ground that there was no evidence of negligence and that the plaintiff was responsible for his own injury. Street J betrayed a distinct impatience with the idea that the boy should recover. He wrote: '[the plaintiff] had no business to touch the machine; he put his hand on it designedly and not by accident. He was between fourteen and fifteen years of age, and it was not pretended that he was lacking in intelligence.'[88] Street J noted that an adult would be liable for doing the same thing.[89] He then insists that a 'line must be drawn somewhere' and states that since the Factories Act permits boys over 14 to be employed and since that is the age at which the Criminal Code presumes the full capacity to commit crimes and give consent, a boy over 14 is certainly beyond that line.[90] However, the Ontario Court of Appeal reversed the trial judge and restored the jury's finding in favour of the plaintiff. Armour CJO found that the defendants were indeed negligent and in contravention of their duty under the Factories

---

[86] ibid 880.   [87] (1902) 4 OLR 167 (CA).   [88] ibid 169.

[89] It is worth noting on the facts that this is by no means clear. In fact, it is implicit in the reasoning of the Court of Appeal that an adult may well not have been liable. In the Court of Appeal judgment, Armour CJO noted: 'A person may be exercising reasonable care, and in a moment of thoughtlessness, forgetfulness or inattention, may meet with an injury caused by the deliberate negligence of another, and it cannot be said that such momentary thoughtlessness, forgetfulness, or inattention will, as a matter of law, deprive him of his remedy for his injury': ibid 174.

[90] He also suggests that children under 14 may similarly be held to the standard of a reasonable adult: ibid 170–171.

Act to guard all dangerous machinery securely. He also stated that there would not have been a reason to withdraw the question of the plaintiff's own negligence from the jury, even if he were an adult—and given that he was only 15, there was still less reason to do so.

Reading these judgments, one almost has the sense that courts are inclined to judge the working child more harshly than they would even judge an adult. The archetypally boyish traits of imprudence and mischievousness that helped to exonerate the playing boy actually seem to have the opposite effect where the boy is working. Perhaps because they believe boys to be characteristically imprudent, courts are inclined to blame the working child for the accident even when, as in *Moore* or *Dominion Glass*, it is unclear that an *adult* would have been held liable.[91] So while it sometimes seems that the language of boyhood is all but absent, just as frequently courts invoke the language of childhood playfulness to defeat the working boy's claims. In fact, boyish behaviour seems so inevitably linked to recklessness that working boys in cases like *Dominion Glass*, *Berdos*, and *Ouellet* are termed 'mischievous' and the like, even though it seems extremely inapt to describe their actions in those terms. So the cases involving the working boy seem to rest on the idea that while the working boy has the same boyish impulses as the boy at play, he is simply not permitted to indulge them—as Justice Anglin stated, a 'factory is not a kindergarten'.[92]

Superficially, this may not seem untenable. After all, the consequences of imprudence to the working child are often devastating. However, when set against the playing boy cases, this rationale raises serious questions. The argument in favour of more generous treatment of children in *McHale* and other cases derives much of its force from the argument that it is simply taking account of the very nature of childhood—that boys will simply be boys. The cases involving the playing girl called this apparent truism into question. The cases involving the child at work also raise suspicions about the operation of the idea that boys will simply be boys. If the boy at work can properly be required to control his innate tendency to mischievousness and imprudence, why is the boy at play not also required to do so? This query seems yet more pointed when one

[91] There is, of course, a larger question in the background here about the treatment of the negligence claims of workers in this period more generally. So the working boy may simply be treated with the same unfairness that characterized the treatment of the working adult during this period, when the law of negligence to some degree functioned to subsidize industrial development and thus drastically undercompensated injured workers: C Woodard, 'Reality and Social Reform: The Transition from Laissez-Faire to the Welfare State' (1962) 72 Yale LJ 286; PWJ Bartrip and SB Burman, *The Wounded Soldiers of Industry: Industrial Compensation Policy, 1833–1897* (Oxford, New York: Oxford University Press, 1983); E Tucker, 'The Law of Employers' Liability in Ontario 1861–1900: The Search for a Theory' (1984) 22 Osgoode Hall LJ 213. Even so, the treatment of the working child provides an important contrast to the treatment of the playing boy, in part because of the light it sheds on the meaning of the 'natural' and normal qualities of the child.

[92] *Dominion Glass* (n 78 above) 548. It is worth noting that many of these cases were decided at the same time as cases involving playing boys: thus, *Dominion Glass* was decided in 1922, the same year as *Dainio* (n 84 above). Similarly, *Ouellet* (n 81 above) was decided in 1947 and the final decision in *Yachuk* (n 84 above) came in 1949.

recalls that in the child defendant cases the playing boy was not required to restrain his natural imprudence even when it adversely affected the bodily integrity of others. The working child is denied this latitude, even though his alleged heedlessness implicates no one's security but his own.

Thus, both judicial sympathy and the privileges of childhood look yet more confined from this standpoint. If the nature-based argument was hard-pressed to justify the treatment of playing children, this difficulty is exacerbated by paying attention to the treatment of the working child. Since the special treatment of children is clearly not extended to all children who possess the distinctive and limited capacities of childhood, what determines who receives this benefit and who does not? It begins to look more like the benefits of liberty and security go to a far more selective group of children: boys but not *all* boys, and not, for instance, boys who must labour through their childhood. Underlying the treatment under the objective standard we can see a complex set of ideas not simply about who *will* take risks, but also who *is entitled* to take risks. As we have seen, this implicates assumptions about what is normal and natural for particular groups or individuals, as well as about what is appropriate given their station in life.

IV. CONCLUSION

The reasonable person standard purports to derive its objectivity from an appeal to shared rather than individual qualities, and to the extent that it thus relies on customary norms it is essentially a standard of ordinariness. However, if the objective standard draws its notion of what is reasonable in large part from a conception of what is normal or ordinary, then we can expect many problems with these conceptions to 'seep' into determinations under the objective standard. In fact, while in the law of negligence reference to what is customary may seem useful in identifying behaviour long regarded as reasonable, there are also significant dangers here. This is because conceptions of what is normal or ordinary have also exhibited serious and systematic defects: they have consistently located some people beyond the innermost enclave of concern. For many groups including women, those disadvantaged on racial, religious, or ethnic grounds, the poor, and those with mental and physical disabilities, conceptions of what is normal or natural have been and continue to be used to justify discriminatory treatment. Indeed, liberal democracies implicitly recognize the threat these kinds of invidious assumptions pose to the rule of law by entrenching various kinds of equality guarantees. These guarantees can serve as important indications of the places where we have made and are most likely to continue to make these kinds of systematic mistakes that ultimately jeopardize the rule of law.

In fact, there seems to be a significantly differential treatment of various groups under the objective standard. This is particularly troubling given whose interests are implicated, and how. Indeed, the treatment of different groups under the objective standard seems to mirror problematic differences in the treatment of those groups more generally. Thus, we see in the operation of the reasonable person standard the persistent effect of the very kind of damaging social conceptions that equality guarantees aim to counteract. It is therefore unsurprising that the hierarchy under the standard bears important similarities to now outmoded formal distinctions in membership. The rules may change, it seems, but at least in its subtler forms the instinct to inequality persists. Thus, those who have always been the very definition of the full citizen—privileged males—receive the most generous treatment in the form of the greatest sphere of liberty. In contrast, the groups who have historically been excluded from citizenship rights receive some sort of diminished protection for their interests. The nature of that treatment both reflects and reinforces embedded inequalities.

Ultimately, this egalitarian challenge to the objective standard might seem somewhat surprising. The equality-based defences of the standard, although not without serious difficulties, are compelling. Paradoxically though, the standard actually turns out to raise very serious equality problems. The developmentally disabled are sufficiently puzzling that they generate their own variation on the standard, with the consequence that their differential treatment is explicit. More typically, however, the unequal treatment takes the subtler— though related—form of inegalitarian assumptions about what is normal and natural influencing determinations of reasonableness. We ordinarily assume that mistakes in judicial decision-making are *ad hoc*, and hence of individual concern but not of systemic theoretical significance. But if judges make certain kinds of mistakes that are systematic in nature, they may both draw on and exacerbate inequalities in such a manner that the very legitimacy of the legal system demands a response.

Even though some reliance on a conception of what is normal may seem useful in determinations of reasonableness, our case studies illustrate that reliance on the normal can also be deeply problematic. It is possible to say something more general about the nature of the problem, and what other forms we might expect it to take, because of the way that the reasonable person inquiry often replicates the ways in which we have traditionally gone deeply wrong—where we have mistreated certain groups because of stereotypes about their capacities or attributes. Equality norms and the relevant literature provide at least a provisional guide to those places where a given tradition is likely to make mistakes and so can assist us in determining whose interests we may be most likely to undervalue or jeopardize.[93] Our examination of some of the 'hard cases' under the objective standard has certainly not given us an exhaustive list of the equality problems raised by such a standard. But it has provided us with a sense of the

---

[93] There is not necessarily any reason to think that there will be complete congruence among categories across jurisdictions, or even across time. While it may be the case that certain kinds of characteristics (eg race, gender, religion, class) seem very commonly implicated in denials of equality, even in these cases we cannot be confident that the salience of those characteristics will always be the same. This is hardly a novel observation though. All that it means is that the egalitarian will need to be attentive to the context in which particular decisions are being made and to the social meaning of various attributes.

kinds of problems that are raised by such a standard—a way to conceptualize the nature of the problems and thus to identify other places where they might plausibly exist. It may also provide a way to address these problems so that we can find a more egalitarian—and ultimately more defensible—way of judging responsibility. Does such a goal mean that we jettison objective standards on the ground that they are inherently inegalitarian and therefore hopelessly flawed? Examining the feminist debate concerning objective standards will assist our deliberations about this question.

6

Are Objective Standards Worth Saving? Exploring the Feminist Debate

There is indeed reason for suspicion about the reasonable person. The problem is not simply that there are 'irregularities' in the standard. As we have seen, the nature of these irregularities is such that the standard actually raises profound rule of law concerns. Since such concerns cannot simply be dismissed or ignored, we must ask what can be done to resolve the problem. But there is no simple answer to this question. Indeed, as we shall see, the attempts of egalitarian critics to respond to these difficulties are bedevilled by such weaknesses of their own that the 'solutions' often seem to exacerbate rather than resolve the equality problems. But while the feminist and egalitarian debates concerning objective standards may sometimes seem incoherent or contradictory, exploring them provides a helpful point of departure for thinking through the equality effects of the reasonable person.

There is no doubt that feminists are awkwardly positioned on the question of the reasonable person. Feminist thought has traditionally expressed wariness, both about the reasonable man and more broadly about fashioning any defensible form of the objective standard. Indeed, feminists have been among the most prominent critics of the very idea of objectivity. In the context of provocation and self-defence, and more recently sexual harassment, feminists have decried reference to the reasonable person as an appropriate way of fashioning a standard of behaviour. A subjectivized standard, they often suggest, would be more inclusive and hence equality enhancing. Yet in the context of sexual assault or rape (and even some tort injuries), feminists object to any subjectivization of the standard and instead defend the use of objective standards. Is there some way to make sense of this ambivalence? And what further light can such an endeavour shed on the objective standard?

I. THE FEMINIST CRITIC AND THE REASONABLE MAN

The feminist literature is an obvious point of departure for considering the broader question of whether objective reasonableness standards are worth saving. After all, feminists have been among the most powerful critics of the reasonable man. Feminists were on the vanguard of illustrating how the idea of what is reasonable often privileges the powerful and their world-view.[1] Thus, feminists, and increasingly other critical egalitarians, have analysed the actual operation of standards of reasonableness not only in tort law, but also more prominently in the criminal context. Provocation and self-defence have been a particular focus of feminist concern. Indeed, feminist findings in this area parallel the difficulties highlighted in the previous chapters. Thus, feminists and other critical theorists have illustrated how standards of reasonableness end up benefiting the powerful and too often fail to deliver on their implicit promise of equality. The resulting wariness about standards of reasonableness forms one pole of the feminist debate on the appropriate standards of responsibility.

The suspiciously masculine nature of the reasonable person is one of the most long-standing topics of discussion in the general literature on feminism and the law. Feminist critiques of the reasonable person standard often begin by pointing to its history.[2] Until very recently the standard was avowedly male in the sense that it was premissed on the behaviour of the reasonable *man*, rather than the reasonable *person*.[3] Indeed, it is precisely this somewhat odd feature of the standard that is parodied by Herbert in the fictional *Fardell v Potts*.[4] And feminists have frequently suggested that the recent conversion of the reasonable man to the reasonable person is no more than cosmetic.[5] The critique, however, is not limited to a criticism of the language. Robyn Martin describes the essential harm as

[1] To cite but a few examples, CA MacKinnon, 'Feminism, Marxism, Method, and the State: An Agenda for Theory' (1982) 7 Signs 515; 'Feminism, Marxism, Method, and the State: Toward Feminist Jurisprudence' (1983) 8 Signs 635; 'Difference and Dominance: On Sex Discrimination' in *Feminism Unmodified: Discourses on Life and Law* (Cambridge, Mass: Harvard University Press, 1987); Carol Smart, *Feminism and the Power of Law* (London: Routledge, 1989); Dale Spender, *Women of Ideas and What Men have Done to Them: From Aphra Behn to Adrienne Rich* (London: Pandora, 1982) 138–162; Genevieve Lloyd, *The Man of Reason: 'Male' and 'Female' in Western Philosophy* (London: Methuen, 1984); Sandra Harding, 'Why Has the Sex/Gender System Become Visible Only Now?' in S Harding and MB Hintikka (eds), *Discovering Reality: Feminist Perspectives on Epistemology, Metaphysics, Methodology, and Philosophy of Science* (Dordrecht, Holland: D Reidel, 1983) 311; Lynda Lange, 'Woman Is Not a Rational Animal: On Aristotle's Biology of Reproduction' in Harding and Hintikka (ibid) 1; Jean Grimshaw, 'The "Maleness" of Philosophy' in *Philosophy and Feminist Thinking* (Minneapolis: University of Minnesota Press, 1986) 36; Susan Moller Okin, 'Justice and Gender' (1987) 16 Phil & Pub Aff 42; LM Finley, 'A Break in the Silence: Including Women's Issues in a Torts Course' (1989) 1 Yale J L & Feminism 41.

[2] See, for instance, Leslie Bender, 'A Lawyer's Primer on Feminist Theory and Tort' (1988) 38 J Legal Educ 3, 20–23; Robyn Martin, 'A Feminist View of the Reasonable Man: An Alternative Approach to Liability in Negligence for Personal Injury' (1994) 23 Anglo-Amer L Rev 334, 342–345; Spender (n 1 above) 138–162. As discussed in the next chapter, similar points are made in the context of the US law on sexual harassment.

[3] See, for instance, Bender (ibid); Martin (ibid); JG Fleming, *The Law of Torts* (9th edn, Agincourt: LBC Information Services, 1998) 118–19; WL Prosser, *Handbook of the Law of Torts* (4th edn, St Paul, Minn: West Publishing Co, 1971) 149–151; Ronald KL Collins, 'Language, History and Legal Process: A Profile of the "Reasonable Person"' (1977) 8 Rut Cam LJ 311. Interestingly, although Prosser terms the test the reasonable *person*, in the commentary he exclusively uses the male pronoun and many of the footnotes actually refer to reasonable man, not reasonable person. Old habits, it seems, die hard.

[4] AP Herbert, *Uncommon Law* (London: Metheun, 1935) 1.

[5] Finley (n 1 above) 59; Bender (n 2 above) 23–25; Naomi R Cahn, 'The Looseness of Legal Language: The Reasonable Woman Standard in Theory and Practice' (1992) 77 Cornell L Rev 1398, 1404–1405; Martin (n 2 above) 341–342.

'phallocentrism'—that is, representation of the two sexes in a single model congruent only with the masculine. One version of this critique points out that the objective standard inevitably requires judges to have recourse to their own understandings of what is reasonable. And given that the bench has been, and continues to be, overwhelming male, judicial interpretations will be limited and skewed by the similarly limited life experiences of decision-makers.[6] In this way, the particularity of masculinity comes to be represented as general, delegitimizing anything distinctively female.[7] So including more women in the judiciary would assist in making the standard more truly—though certainly not completely—objective. However, many feminist critiques also seemingly[8] identify phallocentrism with a set of complex epistemological and/or metaphysical claims about the inherently male nature of the 'reason' embodied in the standard. Sometimes this appears as the claim that reason itself is somehow inherently masculine,[9] and sometimes instead as the political claim that the concept of reason is part of the ideological apparatus of patriarchy—the means by which men maintain their power over women.[10]

These general feminist concerns about objective reasonableness standards have (unsurprisingly) particularly targeted the reasonable person of tort law. Thus, one of the first major feminist critiques of tort law opens its discussion of the law of negligence with a section entitled 'Negligence Law: The "Reasonable Person" Standard as an Example of Male Naming and the Implicit Male

---

[6] A version of this claim can be found in Martin (ibid); Bender (ibid) 22–23. See also Margo L Nightingale, 'Judicial Attitudes and Differential Treatment: Native Women in Sexual Assault Cases' (1991) 23 CJWL 71, 80.

[7] Martin (ibid) 341–342, quoting E Groscz, 'Philosophy' in S Gunew (ed), *Feminist Knowledge, Critique and Construct* (London, New York: Routledge, 1990). See also Bender (ibid) 22–23; MacKinnon 'Difference and Dominance' (n 1 above); *Toward a Feminist Theory of the State* (Cambridge, Mass: Harvard University Press, 1989) 120–124, 162–163. This point is also made in the context of sexual harassment: Kathryn Abrams, 'The Reasonable Woman: Sense and Sensibility in Sexual Harassment Law' (Winter 1995) Dissent 48, 48–50; Cahn (n 5 above) 1405–1406; Nancy S Ehrenreich, 'Pluralist Myths and Powerless Men: The Ideology of Reasonableness in Sexual Harassment Law' (1990) 99 Yale LJ 1177, 1210–1214.

[8] It can be rather difficult to discern the exact scope of the critiques of the reasonableness test in part because the critiques vary in their generality and sometimes even conflict with each other. For instance, critics often make the feminist point that discretion has typically been used to benefit the powerful, and thus generally advantage men over women: Martin (n 2 above) 347. But it is not uncommon for critics to simultaneously pick up on the critical legal studies attacks on abstract rationality and thus advocate more, not less, judicial discretion: ibid 353. There may be ways to resolve these tensions, but the critics rarely seem to recognize them.

[9] The broadest epistemological claims tend to adopt a Gilligan-based view of what kinds of reasons motivate men and what kinds motivate women: Carol Gilligan, *In a Different Voice* (Cambridge, Mass: Harvard University Press, 1982). See, for instance, Bender (n 2 above) and Martin (ibid). This is also apparent in the debate over the appropriate standard for sexual harassment: Abrams (n 7 above) 48–49. However, as discussed above in ch 5, while Gilligan's work usefully names different styles of moral reasoning, subsequent studies have not confirmed the kind of gender link that Gilligan points to. Moreover, feminists have been wary of the essentializing implications of Gilligan's analysis, although not necessarily of other aspects of her work, including the significance of identifying a different and equally valuable voice in moral reasoning.

[10] The most obvious example of this version of the critique of reasonableness is found in the work of Catharine MacKinnon: see *Feminist Theory of the State* (n 7 above) and 'Difference and Dominance' (n 1 above).

Norm'.[11] In this section, Leslie Bender suggests that the change from reasonable man to reasonable person, far from exorcising the sexism inherent in the standard, simply embedded it. She notes that when the standard was converted to 'reasonable person' it continued to denote a person who was reasonable according to the perspective of a male.[12] And the implication is that behaviour that may well be reasonable from some *other* perspective may fail to be identified as reasonable because of the narrowness of the perspective enshrined in the law. Closely related in Bender's analysis is a broader critique: the law and its distinctive rationality disadvantage women because they valorize the masculine as reasonable.[13] Indeed, this critique of the reasonable person has been so influential that one feminist critic has referred to it as the 'new received wisdom'.[14] At least in a narrow category of cases, however, feminist work on the reasonable person is beginning to refine and to some degree challenge this 'received wisdom' by looking more carefully at the actual treatment of women under the standard of care.[15] Unfortunately, in the context of negligence law, most feminist critiques of the reasonable person remain so general that they do little more than point out potentially problematic areas. Indeed, even Bender's concrete recommendations for change do not seem to diverge significantly from the existing common law.[16] But if critiques of the reasonable person in the field of tort law are too general to be useful in this analysis, the same is not true of criminal law. In that context it is possible to find much more concrete analysis—explicitly feminist and otherwise—of the egalitarian implications of the reasonable person.

Before we turn to this material though, let us consider a possible objection to bringing together the civil and criminal uses of the reasonable person. Examining the reasonable person as it is employed in both civil law and in criminal law does cut across the traditionally sharp conceptual divide between these two very

---

[11] Bender (n 2 above) 20.   [12] ibid 23.

[13] The ambiguity regarding the generality of her claims is not unique to Bender. See also Martin (n 2 above).

[14] M Schlanger, 'Injured Women before Common Law Courts, 1860–1930' (1998) 21 Harv Women's LJ 79, 81 n 15.

[15] Thus, for instance, Barbara Welke's examination of a significant number of cases involving injuries to women led her to the conclusion that 'injury was a gendered event' with the consequence that courts held men and women to different standards of care: 'Unreasonable Women: Gender and the Law of Accidental Injury, 1870–1920' (1994) 19 Law & Social Inquiry 369, 369. Welke argues that the special treatment of women was ultimately premissed on a narrow and debilitating image of 'ladylike' conduct and female nature. More recently, however, Margo Schlanger has suggested that these cases demonstrate judicial sensitivity to the objectively different circumstances of women and men: Schlanger (n 14 above).

[16] Thus, for instance, the cases concerning duty to rescue cases by and large already consider the 'connectedness' of the individuals by asking whether there exists a 'special relationship' of the kind that would give rise to a duty of care: Fleming (n 3 above) 164–165 (noting that there is strong support for a duty to rescue 'incidental to certain special relations' like employer–employee, occupier–visitor, etc.). It is not clear that even Professor Bender would suggest such a duty in the absence of some kind of special relationship, since she admits that it will be necessary to determine both where 'our duty to aid would be too attenuated to enforce' and 'where the limits on our personal energies and resources to aid should be defined': (n 2 above) 34 n 120. Thus, although she may be suggesting a slightly more expansive interpretation of where a special relationship will exist, it does not seem that she is advocating significant structural change, even in a major area of her concern.

different systems of responsibility. The point however is not to elide important differences that undoubtedly exist between the two systems, but rather to take seriously the law's own use of the reasonable person as a conceptual device. To suggest, as this use does, that there may be important similarities in the function and structure of the reasonable person inquiry that cuts across the civil/criminal divide does not imply (broadly) that the two systems are identical, nor (more narrowly) that the device functions in the same way across the two areas. But given that both legislatures and courts in an important number of common law jurisdictions use the reasonable person as a device to identify a certain kind of objective culpability (among other things), it seems relevant to consider what that device itself might entail, as well as to think about how it may necessarily function in different ways in the different contexts in which it is employed. Thus, it seems at least as important to consider the commonalities that may exist across categories as to attend to the differences. And indeed, this analysis suggests that the relevant commonalities actually do have significance for the reasonable person across categories, although the details will necessarily be very context-specific. But for the moment, apart from the importance of attending to the use of the reasonable person across categories, one of the reasons to examine the criminal context more closely is that in this context we can find some of the most developed thinking about the strengths and the weaknesses of the reasonable person and objective fault.

II. SUBJECTIVIZING THE REASONABLE PERSON: FEMINIST CRITIQUES OF SELF-DEFENCE AND PROVOCATION

Dolores Donovan and Stephanie Wildman's landmark article on self-defence and provocation provides the obvious point of departure for examining feminist criticisms of the reasonableness standard in the criminal context.[17] Their explicitly egalitarian aim is to fashion a standard that is more responsive to the realities of those not in the mainstream of middle-class American life.[18] According to Donovan and Wildman, the problem is not simply the gender of the mythical person but the standard of reasonableness itself.[19] Since the areas have developed so

---

[17] DA Donovan and SM Wildman, 'Is the Reasonable Man Obsolete? A Critical Perspective on Self-Defence and Provocation' (1981) 14 Loyola LAL Rev 435. The authors view both provocation and self-defence as factors that go to *mens rea* and on that basis reduce or eliminate responsibility for the killing of another. Provocation, they argue, is a 'mitigating factor, reducing the criminal responsibility of the defendant from murder to manslaughter': ibid 440. In contrast, self-defence is a complete defence that generally results in the acquittal of the accused on any charge of intentional homicide: ibid. As they point out, some jurisdictions have 'imperfect self-defence', which reduces a charge from murder to voluntary manslaughter: ibid, citing WR LaFave and AW Scott, *Handbook on Criminal Law* (St Paul, Minn: West Publishing Co, 1972) 583. The categorization of these defences is however far more controversial than they suggest.   [18] ibid 439.

[19] Donovan and Wildman claim that 'all citizens suffer by the use of an abstract reasonableness standard': ibid 437. Similarly, it is 'the reasonableness part of the standard that is faulty, not merely the sex or class of the mythical person': ibid.

considerably since the article was written in 1981, the hypotheticals that the authors develop to explore these issues no longer seem as persuasive as they once may have. Nonetheless, it is possible to reconstruct their core concern in order to capture the enduring egalitarian worry about the reasonable person. The essence of that worry is that, precisely to the degree that it is objective, the reasonable person test may (or more strongly will) result in a failure to consider factors relevant to those whose life experiences are not fully represented in 'mainstream' society. And to the degree that such a failure occurs, the criminal liability of members of marginalized groups will be more 'strict' in nature than that of those members of 'mainstream' society whose reality is reflected in the life experiences of the reasonable person.[20] Donovan and Wildman describe the problem in terms of the unfairness of refusing to assess the personal moral culpability of the actor. But while this is clearly part of their worry, the core of the 'injustice' that they point to implicates precisely the same equality component of the rule of law noted earlier.

It is possible to understand the Donovan–Wildman position as essentially concerned not with their claim that criminal liability necessarily entails subjective fault (though it may), but rather with the worry that the effect of the reasonable person's objectivity is that criminal liability falls unevenly on individuals. Thus, rather than consistently tracking culpability, which would be a justifiable basis for responsibility, the reasonable person assigns responsibility according to criteria that are at best morally neutral, and at worst morally troubling. This is because the reasonable person test in fact allocates responsibility based on the extent to which the social reality of an individual accused resembles the reasonable person's imputed attributes (i.e. default characteristics) or life experiences. Those in 'mainstream' society—those who are not disadvantaged or marginalized—will find that their characteristics, life experiences, and constraints are implicitly built into the reasonable person. So for them, responsibility will follow only where there is personal culpability. However, for those who do not enjoy this kind of congruity with the reasonable person, responsibility may well exist even in the absence of the kind of personal blameworthiness that is the necessary precondition of the liability of those in the mainstream of society.

Viewing this kind of inequality as the core of Donovan and Wildman's concern about the reasonable person helps to explain why they advocate eliminating the reasonable person test in favour of full consideration of 'the social reality which surrounds the defendant's act'.[21] On their view, the objective component of the standard is inextricably linked to the reasonable person and its default characteristics. Thus, the reasonableness part of the standard 'by its nature, precludes consideration of the defendant's personal culpability'.[22] Focusing on personal culpability will often yield the same results as a reasonable man test (as they call it) because 'the actual life experience of the individual accused may correspond to the jury's notion of the life experience of the reasonable man'.[23] However, this will not occur where the life experience of the accused does not conform to that

---

[20] ibid 461.   [21] ibid 467.   [22] ibid 456.   [23] ibid 461.

of the reasonable man. Therefore the reasonableness part of the standard seems so inimical to equality interests that Donovan and Wildman want to eliminate it altogether. They see this as the only way to displace the troubling default characteristics of the reasonable person in favour of a more even-handed system of responsibility. Thus, 'fairness requires that the community's value judgment of personal culpability' be based on a subjective understanding of an accused's state of mind.[24] So only by taking the social reality of an accused into account, and thereby displacing the troublesome default characteristics of the reasonable person, will it be possible to have an equally realistic assessment of the culpability of all regardless of background or social station.

Much of the more recent writing about the application of the reasonableness test to the self-defence claims of women who kill their batterers does give credence to the idea that the default characteristics of the reasonable person result in a troublingly uneven relationship to moral culpability. Until very recently, the plea of self-defence was unavailable in most common law jurisdictions to women who killed their abusive partners. Women who killed their abusive partners rarely did so in the face of an imminent threat and thus the imminence requirement in the common law formulation posed a crucial obstacle to invoking self-defence.[25] There were also other difficulties created by the application of the

---

[24] Donovan and Wildman claim that 'all citizens suffer by the use of an abstract reasonableness standard' 462.

[25] *R v Lavallée* [1990] 1 SCR 852, 883; *State v Gallegos* 719 P 2d 1268 (NM 1986) (cited in Wilson J's judgment in *Lavallée*); M Shaffer, '*R v Lavallée*: A Review Essay' (1990) 22 Ottawa L Rev 607 and 'The Battered Woman Syndrome Revisited: Some Complicating Thoughts Five Years After *R v Lavallée*' (1997) 47 UTLJ 1; A McColgan, 'In Defence of Battered Women Who Kill' (1993) 13 Oxford J Legal Stud 508; C Wells, 'Domestic Violence and Self-Defence' (1990) 140 New LJ 127 and 'Battered Woman Syndrome and Defences to Homicide: Where Now?' (1994) 14 Legal Studies 266; H Maguigan, 'Battered Women and Self Defense: Myths and Misconceptions in Current Reform Proposals' (1991) 140 U Pa L Rev 379; P Crocker, 'The Meaning of Equality for Battered Women Who Kill Men in Self-Defence' (1985) 8 Harv Women's LJ 121; E Schneider, 'Equal Rights to Trial for Women: Sex Bias in the Law of Self-Defense' (1980) 15 Harv CR–CL L Rev 623; B Baker, 'Provocation as a Defence for Abused Women Who Kill' (1998) 11 Can J L & Juris 193; E Sheehy, 'Battered Women and Mandatory Minimum Sentences' (2001) 39 Osgoode Hall LJ 529.

Elsewhere however the law has long demonstrated that it has the resources to pay attention to 'circumstances', such as relative lack of strength or power, past history of threats and the like. So the important question may be why courts have not been able to 'see' that this kind of reasoning was also relevant to women. For instance, in *R v Cadwallader* [1966] 1 CCC 380 (Sask QB), the court quashed the manslaughter conviction of a 14-year-old boy who killed his father. The boy lived alone with his father, a 'strange man' who threatened to kill his son. One afternoon, after a number of such incidents, the boy heard his father state, 'I'm going to kill that God Damned little bastard.' He then heard his father load a 30-30 rifle and come up the stairs towards his room. Thinking that his father was about to finally carry out his threats, the boy grabbed the semi-automatic rifle that he kept in his room and began to shoot at his advancing father. He fired five shots at his father. The fifth and last shot was fired into his father's neck from a distance of about three inches. The Juvenile Court judge found that the boy had used far more force than was reasonable, noting that the final shots were fired from a very close range at a time at which the father was no longer in any condition to kill the boy. In allowing the appeal, Sirois J discussed the boy's growing fear of his increasingly strange and threatening father:

> The boy was trapped and he reacted in the only way it seems to me that an ordinary person would under the circumstances. Can one adequately visualize the fear, terror and confusion which would

'reasonable man' test in battered women's self-defence cases. Phyllis Crocker describes them as follows: 'If the defendant has tried to resist in the past, the court accepts this as evidence that rebuts her status as a battered woman. On the other hand, if the defendant has never attempted to fight back, the prosecution argues that the defendant did not act as a "reasonable man." '[26] In this way, as Martha Mahoney points out, the 'male-identified' rules, including the rules of evidence, 'constrain the categories within which the legal image of battered women has evolved'.[27] The introduction of expert testimony on the 'Battered Woman Syndrome' was the feminist response to the impossibility of making apparent the reasonableness of the actions of battered women who kill in self-defence under the ordinary construction of the reasonable person standard.[28] One way to account for the importance of this testimony is to note how it enabled decision-makers to recognize the contingency of some of the requirements of self-defence—most prominently the imminence requirement—because these requirements might actually be attributable to morally irrelevant default characteristics of the reasonable person (like physical strength, for instance). This in turn made it possible to see when and how those default characteristics ought to be varied rather than held constant. But despite the successes that accompanied these developments, feminists have worried about the fact that the usual basis for admitting such evidence is that the woman's behaviour is sufficiently pathological and beyond the ordinary understanding that 'jurors could not understand the issue without it'.[29] So judges and jurors hear this expert testimony 'filtered through cultural stereotypes which are *of necessity enforced* by the claim of exceptionality, of incomprehensibility, required by the requirement that the issue be "beyond the layman's ken".'[30] Thus, even the attempts to locate the agency of battered women within the confines of the reasonable person test seem compromised by the fact that the introduction of that evidence reinforces an image of 'utterly dysfunctional women' who are characterized by 'learned helplessness'.[31]

---

grip any man, let alone a 14 year old boy in a situation such as this. It is clear that he acted in self-defence. On his uncontradicted evidence he used only sufficient force as he reasonably thought necessary under the circumstances to put his assailant out of action. You cannot put a higher test on a 14-year-old boy than that known to our law. (ibid 388)

[26] ibid 145. See also ibid 152–153 on the impact of sex-neutral standards and male definitions of objectivity.

[27] MR Mahoney, 'Legal Images of Battered Women: Redefining the Issue of Separation' (1991) 90 Mich L Rev 1 36, discussing Lenore Walker's analysis of how the rules of evidence prevent more authentic explanations of women's experience: L Walker, 'A Response to Elizabeth M Schneider's "Describing and Changing"' (1986) 9 Women's Rts L Rep 223, responding to EM Schneider, 'Describing and Changing: Women's Self-Defense Work and the Problem of Expert Testimony on Battering' (1986) 9 Women's Rts L Rep 195.   [28] See the discussion in Schneider (ibid) 198.

[29] Mahoney (n 27 above) 37, quoting *Smith v State* 277 SE 2d 678 (Georgia 1981) 683, and *State v Hodges* 716 P 2d 563 (Kan 1986) ('a battering relationship is a subject beyond the understanding of the average juror') 567. For an important discussion of this, see also *Lavallée* (n 25 above) 871–872.

[30] Mahoney (n 27 above) [emphasis in original].

[31] ibid 38–39. Thus, feminists have begun to query why women who take such action can only be understood as part of a pathological 'syndrome': *Lavallée* (n 25 above); *Hodges* (n 29 above). Indeed, even in their very brief discussion of self-defence, Donovan and Wildman (n 17 above) state that the law of self-defence came to recognize that certain circumstances were relevant to the

Given these difficulties with the objective component of the reasonable person standard, it hardly seems surprising that equality seekers like Donovan and Wildman suggest that the solution lies in subjectivizing the standard. And moving to a subjective standard does seem to respond to a range of problems that arise out of the troublesome default characteristics of the reasonable person, from how to judge the responsibility of an abused woman who acts in self-defence to how to judge a developmentally disabled litigant or a playing girl. These litigants would be held responsible or not depending on whether, in the parlance of the defendant in *Vaughan v Menlove*, they 'did their best' to avoid the harm.[32] A 'best efforts' standard thus seems to ensure that there will be no legal fault without moral fault. In this sense it looks both egalitarian and normatively attractive because unlike the reasonable person, it captures *only* moral fault. And perhaps just as significantly, given the increasingly controversial status of claims to objectivity (and the lack of sympathy for such claims within feminist circles), a 'best efforts' standard also seems to eliminate the need to come up with an external standard to which the accused can properly be held. For critics like Donovan and Wildman, the equality problem arises out of the very objectivity of the standard, which they associate with the attribution to the reasonable person of normatively irrelevant and politically problematic default characteristics. And since a subjective standard incorporates the features of the person whose behaviour is being judged, it may seem likely to eliminate some of the equality problems that plague objective determinations. So now the question is whether subjectifying the standard to take 'social reality' into account will promote the kind of equality that critics like Donovan and Wildman seek.

The answer is a resounding 'no'. Subjectivizing the standard in the way Donovan and Wildman envisage does enable the trier of fact to give greater weight to the social reality in which the accused operates. But the problem is the content of that social reality. Donovan and Wildman draw on the work of the legal realists and on contemporary critical legal theorists to emphasize that legal abstractions not only hide social inequities but also work to perpetuate them.[33] But if the social world we inhabit is characterized by vast inequalities, commonly held prejudices and unequal treatment of the marginalized, then it seems to follow that these views will be reflected in the 'subjective' understandings of litigants, who after all are constituent of that social reality. This danger is obscured by Donovan and Wildman's choice of hypotheticals that focus on marginalized individuals whose social realities are misunderstood precisely because of their marginalization.[34] But if inequality is as widespread as Donovan and Wildman

---

'reasonableness' of the action—including prior threats or lack of courage on the part of the accused. But as noted above, this suggests that the law actually had the resources necessary to fashion more egalitarian interpretations of reasonableness and yet was somehow unable to recognize its potential application to women, for instance.   [32] (1837) 3 Bing NC 468, 132 A11 ER 490 (CP).

[33] (n 17 above) 462–465.

[34] For instance, Donovan and Wildman rely on examples of a Latina woman killing her rapist some time after the event, a black man victimized by racial harassment after moving into an all-white neighbourhood and subsequently shooting a person he believes is an intruder, an Asian-American

suggest—a fact I do not doubt—then subjectivizing the standard will certainly not promote the equality they seek and will almost certainly undermine it. So while it is the case that a legal standard subjectivized in the way that Donovan and Wildman suggest will capture *only* moral fault, that undoubted virtue obscures the fact that such a standard will fail to capture *all* moral fault. But the problem for equality seekers is deeper than this, since, as I shall argue, a subjectivized standard will fail to capture the very fault that is the core concern of egalitarians. This is because a radically subjectivized standard is most likely to miss the kind of fault or mistake that is widely shared—in other words, normative mistakes that find their source in discriminatory beliefs and stereotypes.

III. THE UNREASONABLE MAN: EQUALITY AND PROVOCATION

Donovan and Wildman use provocation hypotheticals to argue for abandoning the objective standard in favour of a more subjective one. However, recent developments in the law of provocation provide a powerful counterpoint to the view that subjectivizing the standard is equality enhancing. Indeed, the increased subjectivization of the provocation defence is now widely cited as one of the aspects of criminal law that poses the most significant dangers for equality seekers. And while contemporary equality seekers therefore tend to support increasing the *objectivity*, rather than the *subjectivity* of the defence, many also argue that the defence is so inherently flawed even in its most objective form that it must be abandoned. Although some of this debate turns on issues particular to provocation, it also sheds additional light on the complex relationship between equality and the reasonable person.

As we have seen, feminists and other egalitarians have long been suspicious about the role that the reasonable man/person plays in the law of provocation.[35] But these issues received no systematic consideration until Jeremy Horder's ground-breaking work on the equality implications of the provocation defence.[36] Horder's analysis of English cases indicates that issues of sexual fidelity form close to a majority of cases involving male violence towards women.[37] In the American context, Susan Estrich argues that the 'heat of passion' defence has a similar disparate impact on women.[38] Recent studies in

who had been interned killing a co-worker after repeated racial slurs, an autoworker killing the supervisor who gives him a lay-off notice, a housewife killing her violent and abusive husband: ibid 437–438.

[35] I refer here to both the man and the person formulation of the standard because the House of Lords in its 2000 decision in *R v Smith* continues to describe the standard in terms of the reasonable man rather than the reasonable person: [2001] AC 146, [2000] 4 All ER 289 (HL).

[36] J Horder, *Provocation and Responsibility* (Oxford: Clarendon Press, 1992).   [37] ibid.

[38] 'Don't Be Surprised If OJ Gets Off Easy', *USA Today*, 23 June 1994, 1A. Similarly, Susan Moller Okin notes that 30% of all female murder victims in the United States in 1986 were killed by their husbands or boyfriends, while only 6% of male murder victims were killed by their wife or girl-friend: *Justice, Gender and the Family* (New York: Basic Books, 1989) 128–129 (citations omitted).

Canada and elsewhere report similar patterns.[39] These studies all suggest that the provocation defence primarily benefits men who attempt to use violence to secure a woman's 'unconditional, unjudgmental attentive acceptance'.[40] Indeed, Horder argues that the fact that such responses are often viewed as natural or understandable—perhaps even appropriate—is further evidence of a profound gender bias in the law of provocation.

This gender bias in the law of provocation is also apparent in the fact that women who have been subjected to long-term abuse by their partners are rarely successful in invoking the provocation defence. Typically this is because of the 'temporal test' which requires that the fatal response be the result of a 'sudden and temporary loss of control'.[41] This rigidity concerning the temporal test does indeed seem to reveal how attached the standard is to specifically masculine default characteristics such as physical strength. However, more attentiveness to this may reveal the varying significance of a delayed reaction: the expression of the same anger may necessarily differ when the affronted person is much weaker than the agent provocateur. [42] Given this, it may seem significant that the temporal test actually became a matter of law in the first case in which a woman who killed her abusive partner attempted to make use of the provocation defence.[43] Recently, however, English courts have broadened the 'on the sudden' requirement in the case of women who experienced cumulative abuse.[44] Nonetheless, the current view of many commentators—including prominent feminist organizations—is that gender bias remains so intrinsic to the defence of provocation that, far from being *extended* through a subjectivized standard, the defence should be *abolished* for specifically egalitarian reasons.[45] The federal

---

[39] 'Reforming Criminal Code Defences' (1998) Department of Justice of Canada. The study found that out of the 115 murder cases where a defence of provocation was raised, 62 involved domestic homicides and of those 55 involved men killing women. As discussed below, another 16 cases involved allegations of 'homosexual advance'. See also *New South Wales Law Reform Commission Discussion Paper: Provocation, Diminished Responsibility and Infanticide* (Sydney: New South Wales Law Reform Commission, 1993); Stanley Yeo, 'Resolving Gender Bias in Criminal Defences' (1993) 19 Mon L Rev 104; Ian Leader-Elliott, 'Sex, Race, and Provocation: In Defence of *Stingel*' (1996) Crim LJ 72, 91–93; Sue Bandalli, 'Provocation—A Cautionary Note' (1995) 22 J L & Soc 398.

[40] Horder (n 36 above), quoting L Tov-Ruach, 'Jealousy, Attention, and Loss' in A Rorty (ed), *Explaining Emotions* (Berkeley: University of California Press, 1980) 465, 483.

[41] *R v Duffy* [1949] 1 All ER 932. See also Susan Lorraine Bandalli, 'Women, Spousal Homicide and the Doctrine of Provocation in English Criminal Law' Master of Laws Thesis, Osgoode Hall Law School (1993) and 'Provocation—A Cautionary Note' (n 39 above); Baker (n 25 above); Horder (n 36 above) 189.

[42] A similar point is made by D Klimchuk 'Outrage, Self-Control, and Culpability' (1994) 44 UTLJ 441, 464, discussing Bandalli 'Women, Spousal Homicide and the Doctrine of Provocation' (n 41 above) 47–48.   [43] Horder (n 36 above) 189, discussing *Duffy* (n 41 above).

[44] See, for instance, *R v Ahluwalia* [1992] 4 All ER 889 (CA).

[45] Horder (n 36 above); Bandalli, 'Provocation—A Cautionary Note' (n 39 above); National Association of Women and the Law, *Stop Excusing Violence Against Women: NAWL's Brief on Provocation* (2000) (http://www.nawl.ca/provocation.htm), which advocates abolishing provocation and discusses the consensus in favour of this position, pointing to the position not only of numerous Canadian women's and law reform organizations, but also various reports and committees in Australia and New Zealand (22–23). For the complex law reform history and impact in the US,

Department of Justice in Canada summarizes the current egalitarian view in its Consultation Paper on provocation in the following terms: 'In view of the amount of criticism the provocation defence has received in recent years, suggesting that it reflects—even perpetuates—archaic social concepts and stereotypes of gender and different groups in society, the simplest course might to abolish the defence outright.'[46]

All of this seems to undercut any suggestion that subjectivization provides the solution to the undoubted equality problems with the objective standard for provocation. In fact, it seems arguable that the critiques that have advocated the subjectivization route with a view to enhancing the egalitarian quality of the provocation defence may have actually had precisely the opposite effect. As the work of Donovan and Wildman illustrates, these critiques challenge the very possibility of any egalitarian reasonableness standard and, consequently, advocate subjectivizing the defence by aligning the standard more closely to the person being judged. But there are egalitarian reasons to be cautious about this combination of pessimism about a normatively defensible version of reasonableness, increased subjectivization of the standard, and the resultant expansion of unstructured judicial discretion. Indeed, the provocation context suggests that the equality critique may actually have backfired in ways that are inimical to the very interests that the critics sought to further. So whatever the appropriate egalitarian response might be to worries about the potentially discriminatory effects of the reasonable person, the provocation context suggests that a simple increase in the subjectivity of the standard will not suffice.

A. Ethnicity and provocation: The Australian debate

The recent Australian debate about provocation provides an appropriate place to begin to examine this question. The relevant controversy ignited when Stanley Yeo voiced strong criticism of the 1990 Australian High Court decision in *R v Stingel*.[47] In *Stingel*, a 19-year-old man killed the new boyfriend of his former girlfriend. On appeal, the High Court found that provocation should not have been left to the jury because the accused's reaction to the provocation 'fell far below the minimum limits of the range of powers of self-control which must be attributed to any hypothetical ordinary nineteen year old'.[48] *Stingel* was decided in a context where the trend had been increasing incorporation of more and more characteristics of the accused into the ordinary person standard.[49] In *Stingel*, however, the High Court raised concerns about this trend,

see Victoria Nourse, 'Passion's Progress: Modern Law Reform and the Provocation Defence' (1997) 106 Yale LJ 1331.

[46] Department of Justice Canada, *Consultations and Outreach, Reforming Criminal Code Defences: Provocation, Self-Defence and Defence of Property*, s 2 'Options for Reform', 1 (http://canada.justice.gc.ca/en/cpns/rccd/sectitons2p1.html).   [47] (1990) 171 CLR 312.
[48] ibid 337.
[49] Jenny Morgan, 'Provocation Law and Facts: Dead Women Tell No Tales, Tales are Told about Them' (1997) 21 Melb U L Rev 237.

invoking the dissenting opinion of Madam Justice Wilson in the Supreme Court of Canada decision in *R v Hill*.[50] Thus, the High Court held that while the accused's characteristics were relevant to assessing the gravity of the provocation, no personal characteristic of the accused but age could affect the level of self-control required of the accused. The High Court also followed the lead of Wilson J in *Hill* by insisting that the principle of equality before the law actually required restricting the range of considerations that could calibrate the standard of self-control.[51]

In his 1992 article, Yeo criticizes this very restrictiveness. He argues that far from furthering equality, restricting the range of characteristics that could affect the self-control dimension of the standard actually undermines it:

> [T]o insist that all these different ethnic groups conform to the one standard of behaviour set by the group having the greatest numbers (or holding the political reins of power) would create gross inequality. Equality among the various ethnic groups is achieved only when each group realizes the others' right to be different and when the majority does not penalise the minority groups for being different.[52]

This view that equality requires taking all of the personal characteristics of the accused into consideration was explicitly adopted in McHugh J's dissent in the subsequent Australian High Court decision in *Masciantonio*.[53]

Masciantonio involved a man of Italian origin who killed his son-in-law after the son-in-law had assaulted his daughter and other members of his family. In their decision, the whole court affirms its holding in *Stingel* to the effect that the age of the accused but not the sex is relevant to the capacity for self-control.[54] On the issue of the relevance of ethnicity to the self-control element of provocation, however, McHugh J alone is willing to revisit *Stingel*. He specifically invokes Yeo's equality argument in his argument that unless the 'age, race, culture and background' of the accused is incorporated into the standard, the defence of provocation will result in 'discrimination and injustice'.[55] Indeed, he echoes Donovan and Wildman in his insistence that in a multicultural society, the ordinary person is not simply 'pure fiction'—instead, it is a particularly invidious kind of fiction that privileges the values of the dominant class.

---

[50] (1986) 25 CCC (3d) 322.   [51] See *Hill* (ibid) 343–344 and *Stingel* (n 47 above).

[52] Stanley Yeo, 'Power of Self-Control in Provocation and Automatism' (1992) 14 Sydney L Rev 3, 12. Partially in response to Ian Leader-Elliott's criticism and to the concern that his argument actually had the potential to reinforce racist stereotypes, Yeo announced in a 1996 article that he had changed his position in favour of a non-subjectivized 'ordinary person' test for self-control, noting 'the law rightly insists on a common level of self-control for everyone in the community irrespective of their sex or ethnic derivation': 'Sex, Ethnicity, Power of Self-Control and Provocation Revisited' (1996) 18 Sydney L Rev 304, 305. According to Yeo's revised hypothesis, however, characteristics of the accused including sex and ethnicity were properly relevant to consideration of the response pattern that might be expected of an ordinary person of the particular sex or ethnicity, for example.   [53] *R v Masciantonio* [1995] 69 ALJR 598.

[54] ibid 602, per Brennan, Deane, Dawson and Gaudron JJ; 606, per McHugh J.

[55] ibid 606–607, citing Yeo, 'Power of Self-Control' (n 52 above).

Thus, 'unless the ethnic or cultural background of the accused is attributed to the ordinary person, the objective test of self-control results in inequality before the law.'[56] So, like Donovan and Wildman, McHugh J concludes that without significant subjectivization, the objective test is profoundly inegalitarian.

There are other indications that egalitarian critiques have been at least part of the motivation for the increasing subjectivization of the standard in provocation. In *R v Thibert*, Cory J speaking for the majority of the Supreme Court of Canada notes that the historic narrowness of the ordinary person was such that none of the characteristics or background of the accused were seen as relevant, even to assessing the gravity of the provocation.[57] He adverts to a significant egalitarian worry about the attachment to this form of objectivity when he points out that a test constructed in this way would fail to properly register the significance of a racially specific epithet.[58] He continues by tracing the gradual broadening of the ordinary person through *Hill* and concluding: 'the wrongful act or insult must be one which could, in light of the past history of the relationship between the accused and the deceased, deprive an ordinary person, of the same age, and sex, and sharing with the accused such other factors as would give the act or insult in question a special significance, of the power of self-control.'[59] And indeed, given the history of the ordinary person it is not difficult to understand why courts might identify the narrowness of the inquiry as the standard's point of weakness. Nor does it seem surprising, given the standard's incorporation of problematic default characteristics, that courts and critics would view broadening its allowable characteristics beyond those associated with masculinity and privilege as an enhancement of the equality and inclusiveness of the criminal law.

Ironically however, although the increasing 'openness' of the standard has been at least partially inspired by egalitarian concerns, it has been greeted by equality seekers not with enthusiasm but with alarm. *Thibert* itself provides ample illustration of the concerns awakened by this reconfiguration of the ordinary person. There, after Cory J affirms that the breadth of the more generous contemporary ordinary person test makes relevant the history of the relationship between the 'provoker' and the 'provoked', he finds that in the case in question there was some evidence to satisfy the objective element of the test (and hence to put that part of the question to the jury) on the following ground: 'It might be found that...an ordinary person who was a married man, faced with the break-up of his marriage, would have been provoked by the actions of the deceased so as to cause him to lose his power of self-control.'[60] This evidence in *Thibert* itself consists in the fact that the deceased held the accused's wife 'by her shoulders in a proprietary and possessive manner' while taunting the accused and preventing him from having the private conversation he was intent upon with his wife.[61] In dissent, however, Major J (Iacobucci J

---

[56] ibid.   [57] [1996] 1 SCR 37, 45.   [58] ibid 45–46.
[59] ibid 49.   [60] ibid 52.   [61] ibid 51–52.

concurring) rejects the provocation argument on the following ground:

it would be a dangerous precedent to characterize involvement in an extramarital affair as conduct capable of grounding provocation, even when coupled with the deceased's reactions to the dangerous situation he faced. At law, no one has either an emotional or proprietary right or interest in a spouse that would justify the loss of self-control that the appellant exhibited.[62]

And indeed, egalitarian critics have worried about how *Thibert*'s increased subjectivization of the standard creates even more room for gender bias to play itself out in provocation (termed by one critic, post-*Thibert*, the 'jealous husband defence'[63]).

Critics worry about how the *Thibert* majority's subjectivizing of the objective element actually weakens it to the point where, in the words of one commentator, the objective element has effectively been repealed.[64] This is precisely because the broadening of the ordinary person test effectively amounts to the 'individualization of this defence'.[65] Thus, Klimchuk comments on *Thibert* that 'killings in such circumstances are regrettably common in our culture, and the law should be loathe to permit the mitigatory cloak of the defence of provocation to cover such actions'.[66] Voicing similar worries about equality implications, Hyland notes how *Thibert* erodes the objective standard of self-control that Wilson J set out in *Hill*. The complex relationship of the standard to equality interests is apparent in the fact that the decision seems to undermine 'the very principles of equality and individual responsibility it seeks to uphold'.[67] So, far from enhancing the inclusiveness of the standard, increased subjectivization will serve simply to confirm 'men in their view that they can control women through the use of death-dealing violence with relative impunity'.[68]

In this sense then, the unstructured expansion of the standard, and particularly of its objective component, opens up the possibility that discriminatory views (such as the belief that a man's partner is his property) will be allowed to calibrate the degree of care we expect of individuals. Paradoxically, the proposed egalitarian solution to the problem with the objective standard in this way actually seems to countenance adjusting the law's ordinary demands to take account of discriminatory views. The values the law typically insists upon—including equality—are thus susceptible to being displaced by the values of particular individuals. And allowing individual beliefs to calibrate the standard in this way also means that those people undervalued by a particular accused may consequently enjoy less legal protection than they would under a standard that refused to give legal weight to such beliefs. So because of how

---

[62] ibid 65.

[63] Wayne Gorman, 'Provocation: The Jealous Husband Defence' (1999) 42 Crim LQ 478.

[64] ibid 494.   [65] ibid.

[66] D Klimchuk, 'Circumstances and Objectivity' (1996) 45 CR (4th) 24, 29 (internal citations omitted).

[67] EM Hyland, '*R v Thibert*: Are There Any Ordinary People Left?' (1996–97) 28 Ottawa L Rev 145, 168.   [68] ibid.

subjectivization creates more space in the provocation defence for stereotypes, increasing the subjectivity of the standard actually seems to undermine, rather than enhance, gender equality.

B. Provocation and homosexual advances

Although much egalitarian concern about the subjectivization of provocation has centred on the gender implications of the defence, the worries do not end there. As noted above, the troublesome place of race and ethnicity in the construction of the reasonable or ordinary person served as an initial impetus for the subjectivization of the defence—and these issues have remained controversial.[69] But other worries about the defence have also begun to surface. The 1997 High Court of Australia decision in *Green v The Queen* is the most noteworthy in a series of decisions in which the alleged provocation for deadly violence is a sexual advance by one man on another. This controversial subset of provocation claims thus became known as the 'Homosexual Advance Defence' ('HAD'). In Australia, the New South Wales Attorney-General's Department established a Working Party to review the operation of the HAD within the country.[70] The Working Party's report points to 'a strong need to limit the role that prejudice, if any, might play' when provocation is raised in a HAD trial, and emphasizes the importance of distinguishing between a sexual advance and a sexual attack.[71] During the Working Party's deliberations, *Green v R*,[72] was working its way through the Australian courts. That decision only served to heighten concerns about the egalitarian implications of subjectivizing the defence of provocation.

Green involved a sexual advance by Donald Gillies on his close friend Malcolm Green. On the evening in question, Gillies climbed into bed with Green and touched him numerous times, including on his groin. Green resisted Gillies's advances and then began hitting him. He punched him approximately fifteen times, stabbed him ten times with scissors and banged his head into the bedroom wall. At trial, Green was convicted of murder and sentenced to fifteen years' imprisonment. On appeal, Green argued that the trial judge had erred in directing the jury not to consider as relevant evidence of Green's 'special sensitivity to sexual interference' because of his father's sexual abuse of his sisters.

---

[69] In fact, in the United States similar difficulties with a more generous understanding of the defence also seem to be playing out in the relationship between race and self-defence. In fact, in contrast to the Donovan–Wildman view that a subjectivized standard would further racial equality in the criminal justice system, commentators now worry about the possibility that racist beliefs could legitimate claims of self-defence against black victims. The controversial trial of Bernard Goetz put a particularly sharp point on this issue: Jody D Armour, 'Race Ipsa Loquitur: Of Reasonable Racists, Intelligent Bayesians, and Involuntary Negrophobes' (1994) 46 Stan L Rev 781 and *Negrophobia and Reasonable Racism: The Hidden Costs of Being Black in America* (New York: New York University Press, 1997); Cynthia Kwei Yung Lee, 'Race and Self-Defence: Toward a Normative Conception of Reasonableness' (1996) 81 Minn L Rev 367.

[70] New South Wales Attorney-General's Working Party on the Review of the Homosexual Advance Defence, *Review of the Homosexual Advance Defence* (1996).   [71] ibid paras 4.10–4.12.

[72] [1996–97] 191 CLR 334.

A majority of the Court of Criminal Appeal found that the trial judge had erred in his directions as to the meaning of 'ordinary person in the position of the appellant' because evidence relating to the sexual abuse of the appellant's sisters was relevant. However, they dismissed the appeal because in their opinion the jury could not have come to a different conclusion given the 'savagery of the beating' and the 'terrible things' that Green did to the deceased.

However, a majority of the High Court reversed this result because in their view the trial judge's misdirection was a sufficiently significant error that a substantial miscarriage of justice could not be ruled out. Gummow and Kirby JJ dissented. The central issue before the High Court concerned the extent to which the ordinary person must be placed 'in the position of the accused'; in particular, should the subjective experience or attributes of the accused affect the degree of self-control expected of him? McHugh J's majority opinion insists that 'all of the accused's attendant circumstances and sensitivities are relevant in determining the effect of the provocation', including any 'particular sensitivity' that the accused might have. [73] And because the accused's 'special sensitivity to sexual assault' was relevant, the extent of his provocation must be attributed to the ordinary person for the purpose of assessing self-control.[74] On this point, McHugh J echoes his reasoning *Stingel* but applies traditional feminist concerns about sexual assault to the homosexual advance in the case before the Court. Thus, he notes that the accused 'looked up to and trusted' the deceased, and he emphasizes the element of force in the advance in order to support his conclusion that 'any unwanted sexual advance is a basis for "justifiable indignation", especially when it is coupled with aggression'.[75] So once again, egalitarian critiques seem at work in the increasing subjectivization of the standard. However, the complexity of the interplay between equality interests and the objectivity of the standard becomes fully apparent when this majority reasoning is juxtaposed with Kirby J's powerful dissent.

The core of Kirby J's objection is found in his insistence on the centrality of an objective standard of self-control to equality interests. He argues that allowing 'subjective' considerations such as family background to affect the capacity for self-control would so thoroughly subjectivize the ordinary person standard that it may just as well not exist.[76] And Kirby J explicitly links the preservation of the objective standard of self-control to equality before the law. He makes both a general argument, relying on the principle from Wilson J in *Hill*,[77] and a more specific argument about the anti-discrimination features of an objective standard. Thus, he states: 'No lesser standard of self-control is demanded by our society in the case of the appellant than of Mr Stingel, simply because the sexual conduct of the deceased was homosexual in character. To condone a lesser standard is to accept an inequality before the law which this Court has previously, repeatedly and rightly rejected.'[78] This judgment thus provides a

---

[73] [1996–97] 191 CLR 369.   [74] ibid.   [75] ibid 370.   [76] ibid 409–412.
[77] ibid 401 n 159, referring to *Hill* (n 50 above).   [78] ibid 415.

strong counterpoint to the view that subjectivizing the standard furthers equality interests. To the contrary, Kirby J's worry is that subjectivization of the self-control requirement would allow irrational hatred, prejudice, and fear to lower the self-control members of society are expected to exercise in their interactions with those they may abhor. And this would not only exacerbate the prejudice and physical danger to which marginalized communities are already disproportionately subjected, but would also undermine equality under the law.

As was the case post-*Thibert*, egalitarian commentators also greeted the subjectivization of the ordinary person standard in *Green* with alarm, precisely on the ground that it would damage equality interests. Thus, for instance, Adrian Howe critiques the High Court's construction of the 'ordinary person as a violent homophobe, one with a right to resort to homicidal rage, depending on their circumstances and family history'.[79] The danger, it seems, is that subjectivization of the standard will permit discriminatory attitudes on the part of the accused to affect the degree of self-control he is required to exercise in provocative situations. Thus, precisely because of their 'ordinariness', which is after all the very quality that distinguishes prejudice from more discrete and individualized forms of hostility, discriminatory beliefs such as racism, sexism, and homophobia seem likely to seep into a subjectivized standard.

Ironically, here it appears that it is the weakness of 'ordinariness' as a way of capturing the objective component of the standard that turns out to be so inimical to equality interests. Far from viewing the normative component as problematic, egalitarian commentators here struggle with how to infuse 'ordinariness' with normative leverage.[80] Perhaps the most explicit statement of this is found in the Final Report of the New South Wales Working Party on the Homosexual Advance Defence. The Report specifically notes the possibility that the 'ordinary person' could be unreasonable and states:

This 'objective' component of the defence is problematic. It has the potential to operate in a way that gives weight to perceived homophobia in cases in which HAD is raised. It can be seen that the law as it stands requires a juror to make a judgment about the response that could be evinced from an ordinary person. It should be understood that, if a juror were to find that ordinary persons are homophobic, then that juror, no matter how fair-minded and free of homophobia he or she may be, would be obliged to take

---

[79] A Howe, '*Green v The Queen*—The Provocation Defence: Finally Provoking Its Own Demise?' (1998) 22 Melbourne U L Rev 466, 489. See also G Coss, 'Editorial: Revisiting Lethal Violence by Men' (1998) 22 Criminal LJ 5; the response by Green's defence counsel T Molomby, 'Revisiting Lethal Violence by Men: A Reply' (1998) 22 Criminal LJ 116; and Coss's response: 'A Reply to Tom Molomby' (1998) 22 Criminal LJ 119. This kind of egalitarian response can also be seen in other jurisdictions: N Kathleen (Sam) Banks, 'The "Homosexual Panic" Defence in Canadian Criminal Law' (1997) 1 CR (5th) 371. The commentary on the general issue in the United States is extensive and includes GD Comstock, 'Developments—Sexual Orientation and the Law' (1989) 102 Harv L Rev 1541; GD Comstock, 'Dismantling the Homosexual Panic Defence' (1992) 2 Law and Sexuality 81; R Mison, 'Homophobia in Manslaughter: The Homosexual Advance as Insufficient Provocation' (1992) 80 Cal L Rev 133; Joshua Dressler, 'When "Heterosexual" Men Kill "Homosexual" Men: Reflections on Provocation Law, Sexual Advances, and the "Reasonable Man" Standard' (1995) 85 J Crim L & Criminology 726.   [80] Morgan (n 49 above) 261, 274.

that perceived homophobia into account in determining whether or not the defence of provocation had succeeded or failed. That can hardly be a satisfactory position.[81]

Similarly, in his dissent in *Green*, Kirby J links his egalitarian concern to further subjectivization of the standard of self-control. However, the difficulty of holding on to some kind of egalitarian objective standard is exacerbated because the standard is one of 'ordinariness'. Thus, Kirby J must insist—whether it is true or not—that 'the "ordinary person" in Australian society today is not so homophobic as to respond to a non-violent sexual advance by a homosexual person as to form an intent to kill or to inflict grievous bodily harm'.[82] But the fact that Kirby J feels the need to put the phrase ordinary person in scare quotes points to its inaptness as a way of capturing the fixed normative demands of the standard that he wants to insist upon.

C. Provocation and self-control: Smith

This concern about the diminishing normative content of the standard in provocation is further exacerbated by the House of Lords' decision in *Smith*.[83] *Smith* is arguably the logical, troubling culmination of the early equality critiques of the reasonable person standard for provocation. The allegedly provocative incident in that case involved an argument between two inebriated alcoholic friends about the disputed theft of some carpentry tools. During the argument Smith stabbed the victim several times with a kitchen knife, killing him. He was charged with murder and raised the defence of provocation. He argued that the jury should be allowed to consider his severe depressive illness that reduced his powers of self-control. The trial judge rejected this and instead directed the jury that the reasonable man means a reasonable person of either sex, not exceptionally excitable or pugnacious, but possessed of such powers of self-control as everyone is entitled to expect that his fellow citizens will exercise in society as it is today.

The jury found Smith guilty of murder, in the process also rejecting Smith's claim of diminished responsibility under s 2 of the Homicide Act 1957. Smith appealed to the Court of Appeal on the ground that the judge's direction on provocation was too restrictive. The Court of Appeal found that the trial judge had misdirected the jury, and therefore they substituted a conviction for manslaughter. On further appeal to the House of Lords, a question of general public importance was certified: whether characteristics of the accused other than age and sex, attributable to the reasonable man, were relevant not only to the gravity of the provocation but also to the standard of self-control to be expected of the accused.[84]

---

[81] (n 70 above) paras 5.9 and 5.10.
[82] *Green* (n 72 above) 408–409. On this inaptness of ordinariness as a way of capturing the normative demands of the reasonable person, see also Timothy Macklem and John Gardner, 'Provocation and Pluralism' (2001) 64 Mod L Rev 815, 825 n 21.   [83] n 35 above.
[84] ibid 299.

The House of Lords split 3–2 on this important question, the majority upholding the decision of the Court of Appeal. The majority (Lords Slynn, Hoffman, and Clyde) decision revolved around the reading of s 3 of the *Homicide Act 1957*, the text of which is as follows:

Where on a charge of murder there is evidence on which the jury can find that the person charged was provoked (whether by things done or by things said or by both together) to lose his self-control, the question whether the provocation was enough to make a reasonable man do as he did shall be left to be determined by the jury; and in determining that question the jury shall take into account everything both done and said according to the effect which, in their opinion, it would have on a reasonable man.

In the opinion of the majority, the accused's mental illness (and in principle other factors as well) should go to the jury because it may be relevant to the degree of self-control to be demanded of the accused. Further the majority found that the effect of s 3 was that the jury alone determined whether the objective element in provocation was satisfied and so the judge could not direct the jury to ignore any factor or characteristic of the accused in deciding whether the objective element had been satisfied. Thus, in *Smith* the jury ought to have been told that it was up to them to determine whether to consider the effect of Smith's depression on his capacity for self-control when deciding if he met the standard. Lord Millett's dissent objects to the majority position in the following way:

this approach requires the accused to be judged by his own reduced powers of self-control, eliminates the objective element altogether and removes the only standard external to the accused by which the jury may judge the sufficiency of the provocation relied on. By introducing a variable standard of self-control it subverts the moral basis of the defence, and is ultimately incompatible with a requirement that the accused must not only have lost his self-control but have been provoked to lose it; for if anything will do this requirement is illusory. [85]

Thus, the dissent argues that the majority essentially eliminates any legal standard that could serve as the basis of directions to the jury—effectively eliminating the objective standard. Indeed, while Lord Hoffman's majority opinion acknowledges that the principle of objectivity must be upheld, that principle, he insists, is now entirely a matter for the jury.

In this sense then, *Smith* suggests that an accused could argue—and a jury could hold—that his homophobia, possessiveness, or racial prejudice could calibrate the self-control that he was required to exercise. It is true that Lord Hoffman suggests that the way to deal with jealous conduct like that at issue in *Stingel* is to direct the jury that characteristics such as jealousy or obsession should be ignored in relation to the objective element.[86] Yet this option seems ruled out by Lord Hoffman's own reasoning. In fact, he refers to the risk that the jury may find provocation on inappropriate grounds but characterizes it as

[85] ibid 346.   [86] ibid 309.

'the risk which Parliament took when it gave the jury an unfettered right to give effect to its own opinion on the objective element'.[87] But that risk, according to Lord Hoffman, is 'less likely to cause injustice than to confine the jury within the rules of law' concerning the notional characteristics of the reasonable man [*sic*].[88] Using the facts of a case in which the accused argued that the crying of a 17-day-old baby amounted to provocation,[89] Lord Hoffman says it is irrelevant if the judge thinks that a baby's crying cannot constitute an acceptable partial excuse for killing it. The matter must instead be remitted to the jury with the instruction that 'the question of whether such behaviour fell below the standard which should reasonably have been expected of the accused was entirely a matter for them'.[90] But this makes it hard to see the ground on which a judge could instruct a jury to treat a defendant's possessiveness or homophobia as irrelevant to the objective element in provocation. Indeed, the majority holding in *Smith* casts doubt on the meaning of Lord Hoffman's injunction that people ought not be allowed to rely upon their own violent dispositions.[91] After all, the facts of *Smith* cannot be understood as provocative without considering Smith's substantially diminished capacity for self-control—in essence, the 'violent disposition' that led him to kill his drinking companion over an old (and almost incomprehensible) dispute about stolen tools.

   Smith is also pertinent to the analysis here for another reason. Although the majority and the dissent obviously part company on many issues, they do agree on the difficulties with using the reasonable person standard to describe the objective element of provocation. Thus, Lord Hoffman closes his majority decision with a trenchant critique focusing on the difficult question of the kinds of characteristics that can be attributed to the reasonable man [*sic*]. Attempts to adapt this 'anthropomorphism', he suggests, have resulted in 'monsters like the reasonable obsessive, the reasonable depressive alcoholic, and . . . the reasonable glue sniffer'.[92] Particularly troublesome is the question of what 'mental characteristics' of the defendant should be attributed to the reasonable person: are attention-seeking and immaturity[93] eligible, for instance, or obsessiveness and eccentricity[94]? Unfortunately, the reasonable person—originally intended simply as a 'felicitous' explanation[95]—provides no guidance for determining which individual 'characteristics' will calibrate the required standard. The result, in provocation at least, is that the reasonable person has proven 'logically unworkable' when too many of the defendant's characteristics are taken into consideration and almost ineffective when strictly applied by juries.[96] Lord Hoffman thus suggests that the solution is to explain the principle of objectivity

---

   [87] *Green* (n 72 above) 310.   [88] ibid.   [89] *R v Doughty* [1986] Cr App R 319.
   [90] (n 35 above) 311.
   [91] On the many difficulties with *Smith*, see John Gardner and Timothy Macklem, 'Compassion without Respect? Nine Fallacies in *R v Smith*' [2001] Crim LR 623 and 'Provocation and Pluralism' (n 82 above).   [92] (n 35 above) 311.
   [93] ibid, citing *R v Humphreys* [1995] All ER 1008 (CA).
   [94] ibid, citing *R v Dryden* [1995] 4 All ER 987 (CA).   [95] (n 35 above) 312.   [96] ibid.

that the reasonable person was intended to capture. Since the law expects people to exercise control over their emotions, a 'tendency to violent rages or childish tantrums is a defect in character rather than an excuse'.[97] The loss of self-control must therefore be sufficiently excusable to reduce the murder charge to one of manslaughter. But since this is 'entirely a question for the jury', if there is some characteristic that the jury thinks it would be unjust to ignore, then they are at liberty to give effect to that view.[98] Similarly, Lord Clyde suggests that provocation is better understood as open to an accused who 'made reasonable efforts to control himself within the limits of what he is reasonably able to do'.[99] So if recourse must be had to the reasonable man, then he must be understood as 'referring to the standard of reasonable behaviour expected of a person in the situation of and with the characteristics of the accused'.[100] And although the dissents emphasize the importance of the objective standard to the 'moral basis of the defence', they too voice concerns about the utility of the reasonable person.

With its combination of concern about the inclusiveness of criminal standards and scepticism about the possibility of any defensible articulation of objective normative demands, the majority decision in *Smith* reads like the culmination of the Donovan–Wildman style of egalitarian critique of the reasonable person. Yet the move towards radical subjectivization of the standard that characterizes *Smith* and other cases is now seen as inimical by equality seekers precisely because it limits or even eliminates the ability of the law or the judge to constrain the discretion of the jury in assessing what can constitute provocation. There is no doubt that more general concerns about objectivity and reasonableness are particularly acute with provocation precisely because of the difficulty identifying the normative core of the defence. And the fact that the objective component of the standard is expressed by reference to the reasonable person exacerbates this difficulty in at least two ways. Thus, not only does the reasonable person fail to provide guidance concerning the characteristics of the accused that ought to be taken into consideration, it actually seems inconsistent with the defence because a reasonable person would not kill another because he provoked her anger, no matter how justified that anger might be.

The response has typically been, as in Canada and Australia, to invoke the ordinary person as a way of retaining an objective element in the standard for provocation while responding to the difficulty of applying a reasonable person test to someone who has killed another out of anger. Unfortunately, however, if the *reasonable* person seemed inapt and therefore incapable of providing guidance regarding the application of the provocation defence, the *ordinary* person arguably provides exactly the wrong kind of guidance. In fact the 'ordinary person' ends up legitimating the provocation defence in the very kinds of cases that concern egalitarian critics. Thus, cases like *Green* and *Thibert* illustrate how deriving the objective component of the standard from common social beliefs

---

[97] ibid.   [98] ibid.   [99] ibid 318.   [100] ibid 319.

and behaviour makes it all too easy to conclude that *ordinary* men might resort to deadly violence when faced with a female partner's infidelity or an unwanted homosexual advance. In this sense then, provocation seems to hold more negative than positive lessons regarding the reconstruction of the objective standard. The cases suggest that the equality of the defence will not be enhanced either by substituting ordinariness for reasonableness nor by subjectivizing the self-control component of the standard so that the hypothetical more closely resembles the actual person. In fact, such responses seem to make it more difficult to ensure that the standard is egalitarian, so much so that many equality seekers now suggest completely abolishing the defence, rather than opening it up.[101] So while Donovan and Wildman's critique of the reasonable person has undeniable force, the move towards subjectivization they advocate actually seems to increase the likelihood that the standard will be used to perpetuate existing disadvantage.

IV. Sexual assault and the reasonable person

The provocation debate illustrates that there is something about the reasonable person, something *not* reducible to 'ordinariness', that is important to an egalitarian conception of responsibility. However, because so many of the critics now advocate abolition of the defence, the reform proposals do little to elucidate wherein exactly the egalitarian promise lies. For this reason, it may be helpful before leaving the exploration of the feminist debates to look to other arenas where feminists have been more anxious to retain the objective standard. And no issue illustrates this impulse more clearly than the area of sexual assault or rape. Here, in contrast to self-defence and provocation, feminists have consistently decried the dangers of subjectivizing the standard. Indeed, this difference in approaches to objective standards is at least in part responsible for the impression that the feminist position is either incoherent or hopelessly *ad womanem*.[102] But while these possibilities cannot be completely dismissed, it is also the case that at least certain strains in the feminist debate on the appropriate standard for

---

[101] NAWL's Brief on Provocation discusses the egalitarian consensus in both activist and academic circles that the defence would be best abolished: (n 45 above) 22–24.

[102] Thus, for example, Gardner and Macklem say that many of those who campaign on behalf of battered women wish to make an argument that abandons standards altogether in order to make a space to excuse, whatever the method: 'Provocation and Pluralism' (n 82 above) 827. While this undoubtedly does characterize some such campaigners, and while as argued in the text, in many respects it is just this 'egalitarian' impulse that has backfired for equality seekers, it also seems likely that some of the justice-based concerns in play are rather difficult to articulate within the traditional argumentative structure of these defences. It seems possible for instance that extending some form of excuse in cases of long-term abuse may be accounted for, not on the traditional justification/excuse paradigm but rather on the deeper basis that where such social violence is persistently unaddressed by the state apparatus, the state may lose its prerogative over the exclusive use of force in those cases. So it may be that individuals in such situations are in the kind of 'state of nature' that justifies more radical forms of self-help than those expressed in the justification/excuse paradigm that pertains when the state is generally effective in its protection of key interests. Of course, as Gardner and Macklem observe, some such campaigners may be ruthlessly consequentialist.

sexual assault can be understood as contributing to our understanding of the normative role of reasonableness in an egalitarian conception of responsibility.

Examining feminist concerns around sexual assault reveals a deeper engagement than is commonly thought to exist with the traditional criminal law focus on blameworthiness. In fact, behind the consequentialist preoccupation with the impact on women, it is often possible to discern an animating worry about the way that some moves towards subjectivity result in a standard that misses a form of blameworthiness that is particularly important to equality seekers. In this sense, the feminist literature directs our attention to a potentially significant difference between culpable and non-culpable ignorance. On this reading, the feminist literature on sexual assault does more than simply express the undoubtedly important consequentialist worries about abandoning our demand for reasonableness. Drawing out and elaborating those elements of the feminist position on sexual assault that invoke an implicit concern with missed blameworthiness enables us to identify some important elements in any egalitarian reconstruction of the objective standard. Although it may seem unpromising, the feminist literature on the appropriate standard for sexual assault does voice concerns that are vital to a normative account of reasonableness.

The heart of the debate concerning the appropriate standard in sexual assault cases revolves around the availability of the defence of mistake of fact. Since sexual assault or rape is defined as sexual intercourse without consent, it is open to the accused under this defence to argue that even if the complainant did not in fact consent, he mistakenly believed that she did. The ongoing controversy in this area concerns whether it is enough that the defendant's mistake be honest (a subjective standard) or whether in order to exonerate, that belief must also be reasonable (an objective standard). Historically, an accused could not get the benefit of the defence unless his mistake was not merely honest but also reasonable.[103] However, courts and commentators began to question this approach and to incline instead towards the view that in the context of sexual assault, the belief need only be honest and need not be reasonable.[104] On this latter view, the reasonableness (or otherwise) of the belief goes only to credibility. This means the accused can defend himself by arguing that he honestly, though unreasonably, believed that the complainant was consenting to sexual intercourse. Yet even though equality seekers advocated something very like this move in other contexts, far from welcoming greater subjectivity, feminists and others voiced alarm that in the sexual assault context it would restrict women's security, exacerbate

---

[103] See the dissenting judgment of Lord Edmund Davies in *DPP v Morgan* [1976] AC 182 (HL), especially at 227–232 where he discusses the defence of mistake and other similar defences.

[104] *Morgan*, ibid; *Pappajohn v R* [1980] 2 SCR 120; *Sansregret v R* [1985] 1 SCR 570. As discussed below, in Canada this approach has been supplanted by new legislative provisions as interpreted by the Supreme Court of Canada in *R v Ewanchuk* [1999] 1 SCR 330. On the issue of honest but mistaken beliefs, see also D Archard, 'The *Mens Rea* of Rape: Reasonableness and Culpable Mistakes' in Keith Burgess-Jackson (ed) *A 'Most Detestable Crime': New Philosophical Essays on Rape* (New York: Oxford University Press, 1999) 213; Donald C Hubin and Karen Haely, 'Rape and the Reasonable Man' 18 Law & Phil 113 (1999).

their inequality, and validate the discriminatory beliefs of men.[105] And implicit in much of this literature is the belief that there is an important kind of blameworthiness that such a subjective standard fails to capture. A brief examination of this debate thus provides more insight into why equality seekers may be loathe to abandon such standards entirely, whatever their weaknesses.

Feminist writing on sexual assault, and in particular on the subjectivization of the defence of mistaken belief in consent, does tend to focus on the consequentialist fear that such a move will undermine the security interests of women and thus exacerbate gender inequality. The worry is that a sexual assault standard premissed exclusively on belief, a standard that has no capacity to reject a belief as unreasonable, will be unable to secure women's sexual—and other—autonomy. This is because, commentators insist, a subjectivized standard makes male beliefs about women's consent determinative of whether a woman was raped. And in the context of sexual assault there are particular reasons to be worried about privileging 'beliefs' in this way. Beliefs about women and consent are not *ad hoc*, but instead—like other discriminatory beliefs—are widespread and systematic in nature. Indeed, the sense that the pervasive nature of myths about women and consent poses special difficulties for the law of sexual assault accounts for the preoccupation with these stereotypes in the feminist literature on sexual assault. Although there is extensive literature on this, it is possible to draw out a few key points for the purposes of this discussion.

As provocation cases demonstrate, men often resort to physical—even deadly—force to maintain sexual proprietorship of women. But much male violence against women also takes the specifically sexual form of rape.[106] Addressing this is complicated because of the way normal consent rules seem to be displaced

---

[105] T Pickard, 'Culpable Mistakes and Rape: Relating Mens Rea to the Crime' (1980) 30 UTLJ 75; 'Culpable Mistakes and Rape: Harsh Words on *Pappajohn*' (1980) 30 UTLJ 415; Christine Boyle, Marie-Andrée Bertrand, Celine Lacerte-Lamontagne, and Rebecca Shamai, *A Feminist Review of Criminal Law* (Ottawa: Ministry of Supply and Services, 1985) 59–62; Patricia Hughes, 'From a Woman's Point of View' (1993) 42 UNBLJ 341; Dolly F Alexander, 'Twenty Years of *Morgan*: A Criticism of the Subjectivist View of *Mens Rea* and Rape in Great Britain' (1995) 7 Pace Intl L Rev 207, 236; Christine Boyle, 'The Judicial Construction of Sexual Assault Offences' in Julian V Roberts and Renate M Mohr (eds), *Confronting Sexual Assault: A Decade of Legal and Social Change* (Toronto: University of Toronto Press, 1994) 136, 147; Susan Estrich, 'Rape' (1986) 95 Yale LJ 1087, 1101. Estrich notes that if the focus were what the defendant knew, thought, or intended as to key elements of the offence, this perspective might be understandable; yet the issue has instead been the appropriateness of the woman's behaviour, according to male standards of appropriate female behaviour.

[106] Indeed, it is arguably this aspect of rape that has generated the discussion in the feminist literature about whether rape should be seen as primarily sexual or as primarily violent: Susan Brownmiller, *Against Our Will: Men, Women and Rape* (New York: Simon and Schuster, 1975); Diana EH Russell, *The Politics of Rape: The Victim's Perspective* (New York: Stein and Day, 1975); MacKinnon 'Feminism, Marxism, Method, and the State' (n 1 above) 85–92; *Toward a Feminist Theory of the State* (n 7 above) 172–183; Carol Pateman, *The Sexual Contract* (Stanford, Calif.: Stanford University Press, 1988) 224. The emphasis on the violent aspect of the crime is apparent in the language of sexual assault in the 1983 changes and the 1992 modifications to the sexual assault provisions of the Canadian Criminal Code: RSC 1985, c C-46, and An Act to amend the Criminal Code (sexual assault), SC 1992, c 38 (commonly referred to as Bill C-49).

by background assumptions about how women are allocated to 'spheres' of consent that reflect their status and relationship to men.[107] To the extent adult women know the accused, consent tends to be inferred regardless of the discrete situation. And though this may be most apparent in the increasingly outmoded marital rape exemption, it is not confined to that issue.[108] Indeed, as MacKinnon notes, any indication of a relationship, 'from nodding acquaintance to living together, still contraindicate[s] rape'.[109] The damaging legal effects of these widespread discriminatory beliefs about women and consent is also the subject of Madam Justice L'Heureux-Dubé's dissent in the decision of the Supreme Court of Canada in *Seaboyer*:[110]

similar stereotypes are held by a surprising number of individuals, for example: that men who assault are not like normal men, the 'mad rapist' myth; that women often provoke or precipitate sexual assault; that women are assaulted by strangers; that women often agree to have sex but later complain of rape; and the related myth that men are often convicted on the false testimony of the complainant; that women are as likely to commit sexual assault as men and that when women say no they do not necessarily mean no. This baggage belongs to us *all*.[111]

And these stereotypes are very influential, 'lowering the number of reported cases, influencing police decisions to pursue the case, thereby decreasing the

---

[107] *Feminist Theory of the State* (n 7 above) 175. See also Pateman, (n 106 above) 224–225.

[108] See, for instance, *R v R* [1991] 4 All ER 481, which rejected the marital rape exemption in England, and *People v Liberta* 474 NE 2d 567 (NY 1984), in which the New York Court of Appeals found that marital rape exemptions violated the Equal Protection Clause of the Constitution. On the ongoing debate in the US, see Jill Elaine Hasday, 'Contest and Consent: A Legal History of Marital Rape' (2000) 88 Cal L Rev 1373; Robin West, 'Equality Theory, Marital Rape, and the Promise of the Fourteenth Amendment' (1990) 42 Fla L Rev 45; Victoria Nourse, 'The Normal Successes and Failures of Feminism and the Criminal Law' (2000) 75 Chi-Kent L Rev 951.

[109] *Toward a Feminist Theory of the State* (n 7 above) 176.

[110] *R v Seaboyer* [1991] 2 SCR 577.

[111] ibid 659 [emphasis in original]. There is extensive literature on this issue. Some particularly influential examples include: Boyle, 'Judicial Construction of Sexual Assault Offences' (n 105 above); Hughes (n 105 above) 343–344; Alexander (n 105 above) 245; Estrich (n 105 above); L Chamzuk, 'Consent: A Relevant Distinction?' (1998) 4 Appeal 22; P Fournier, 'The Ghettoisation of Difference in Canada: "Rape by Culture" and the Danger of a "Cultural Defence" in Criminal Law Trials' (2002) 29 Man LJ 81; C L'Heureux-Dubé, 'Lecture: Conversations on Equality' (1999) 26 Man LJ 273; R Graycar, 'The Gender of Judgments: Some Reflections on "Bias"' (1998) 32 UBC L Rev 1; RJ Delisle, 'Adoption, Sub-silentio, of the Paciocco Solution to Rape Shield Laws' 36 CR (5th) 254; DM Paciocco, 'Techniques for Eviscerating the Concept of Relevance: A Reply and Rejoinder to "Sex with the Accused on Other Occasions: The Evisceration of Rape Shield Protection"' 33 CR (4th) 365; H Schwartz, 'Sex with the Accused on Other Occasions: The Evisceration of Rape Shield Protection' 31 CR (4th) 232; M Torrey, 'When will We be Believed? Rape Myths and the Idea of a Fair Trial in Rape Prosecution' (1991) 24 UC Davis L Rev 1013; S Ehrlich, *Representing Rape: Language and Sexual Consent* (London, New York: Routledge, 2001); KM DelTufo, 'Resisting "Utmost Resistance": Using Rape Trauma Syndrome to Combat Underlying Rape Myths Influencing Acquaintance Rape Trials' (2002) 22 BC Third World LJ 419; JH Aiken, 'Protecting Plaintiffs' Sexual Pasts: Coping with Preconceptions through Discretion' (2002) 51 Emory LJ 559; SH Pillsbury, 'Crimes against the Heart: Recognizing the Wrongs of Forced Sex' (2002) 35 Loy LA L Rev 845; SJ Schulhofer, *Unwanted Sex: The Culture of Intimidation and the Failure of Law* (Cambridge, Mass: Harvard University Press, 1998); GE Panichas, 'Rape, Autonomy, and Consent' (2001) 35 Law & Soc'y Rev 231; L Francis (ed) *Date Rape: Feminism, Philosophy, and the Law* (University Park: Pennsylvania State University Press, 1996).

rates of arrest, and finally, distorting the issues at trial and necessarily, the results'.[112] As we saw in the case of provocation, the danger is that subjectivizing a standard of behaviour in a context of pervasive inequality serves to give legal effect to discriminatory beliefs. But because these beliefs are systematic not *ad hoc*, giving effect to them in the legal system will also systematically diminish the protection accorded to women in certain kinds of situations.[113]

Despite these important consequentialist concerns, it is not difficult to construct reasons why the criminal law might legitimately focus on the perspective of the accused.[114] A standard rejoinder to the arguments above, forwarded by feminist commentators as well as others, admits the importance of these concerns but challenges the appropriateness of resort to the notably 'heavy hand' of the criminal law to educate men.[115] Indeed, the dominant response to such feminist worries about the consequences of a subjectivized standard is found in the view that an objective standard for mistake of fact would effectively jail men for their stupidity.[116] But this implies that a reasonableness standard for sexual assault is actually a novel and ill-advised form of criminal liability, designed to teach rather than to punish. To some extent this flows from the nature of much feminist commentary which, in its understandable concern with the impact on the female victim, may seem to ignore the interests of the accused in the criminal context. And this approach sometimes does gesture towards a radically different conception of criminal law and responsibility. Whatever the merits of such a view, however, that is not the strand of feminist reasoning regarding objective standards that I wish to pursue here. Instead, it seems more useful to draw out the submerged (though arguably more promising) egalitarian worry that there is a form of blameworthiness especially relevant to equality seekers that is missed by some moves towards subjectivization.

---

[112] *Seaboyer*, (n 110 above) 664. Justice L'Heureux-Dubé also traces the influence of these conceptions at common law and the attempts to counteract the discriminatory effects of such presumptions through legislation, including prominently the 'rape shield' provisions that were successfully challenged in *Seaboyer*. In that case, ss 276–277 of the Criminal Code (n 106 above) were challenged on the ground that they were inconsistent with the principles of fundamental justice enshrined in ss 7 and 11(d) of the Canadian Charter of Rights and Freedoms: Part I of the Constitution Act 1982, being Schedule B to the Canada Act 1982 (UK) 1982, c 11. A majority of seven justices found that the provisions of the Criminal Code did violate the guarantees in s 7 of the Charter and could not be saved under s 1.

[113] Alexander (n 105 above) 236, citing RA Duff, 'Recklessness and Rape' (1981) 3 Liverpool L Rev 49, 56, and J Temkin, 'Towards a Modern Law of Rape' (1982) 45 Modern L Rev 399; *Seaboyer* (n 110 above) 373–374.   [114] Indeed even as strong a critic as Estrich makes this point.

[115] This charge is frequently made against feminist reformers: see eg R Martin, 'Bill C-49: A Victory for Interest Group Politics' (1993) 42 UNBLJ 357, 366 and Alan D Gold, 'Flawed, Fallacious but Feminist: When One Out of Three is Enough' (1993) 42 UNBLJ 381. However, many feminists also reject the view that criminal punishment should be used to 'educate': L Snider, 'Feminism, Punishment and the Potential of Empowerment' (1994) 9 Can J L & Soc'y 75 and 'The Potential of the Criminal Justice System to Promote Feminist Concerns' (1990) 10 Studies in Law, Politics and Society 143; D Martin, 'Retribution Revisited: A Reconsideration of Feminist Criminal Law Reform Strategies' (1998) 36 Osgoode Hall LJ 151.

[116] Thus, in response to the argument that a reasonableness standard would 'educate men about sexual assault', criminal lawyers and commentators have retorted that we should not be using jail as an education: R Martin (ibid) 366.

This underlying concern with missed blameworthiness translates into a worry that subjectivizing the standard would be objectionable not simply because it would undermine the criminal law's ability to protect women, but because it would miss some culpability. So here we find attempts to articulate the sense in which an objective standard of reasonableness actually does penalize blameworthy behaviour. Thus, for instance, Boyle notes that one of the difficulties with a subjective standard is that individuals who could exercise care about consent, but do not, may escape punishment.[117] Importantly, describing misconceptions about women's consent as 'self-interested' points to the possibility that there is some blameworthy self-preference betrayed in at least some unreasonable mistakes about consent.[118] Similarly, Alexander says of the negligent rapist that someone

who is intent on intercourse without attending to the possibility that the woman does not consent, or who is prepared to take another's word, or his own preconceptions, as adequate grounds for his belief in her consent, displays what must be counted, on any proper moral view of the significance of her consent, as a serious disregard for her consent and her sexual interests.[119]

So an objective standard ensures equality in sexual relationships by refusing to allow disregard for the interests of others as a defence to a charge of sexual assault. In this sense it is important to just retribution.[120] Wells also responds to the challenge that objective standards are necessarily inconsistent with guilt by pointing to the blameworthiness of a morally obtuse defendant who thereby makes an unreasonable mistake about consent.[121] The underlying worry here seems to be that when certain forms of subjectivity are extended to the defendant, the beliefs of the accused may actually be able to diminish what the law demands of him in his interaction with others. And given the nature of the beliefs that many members of society hold about women and consent, this may result in the legal system 'missing' a significant amount of behaviour that actually is blameworthy.

Indeed, the importance of 'missed' blameworthiness to feminist critiques of a subjective standard for sexual assault is apparent in Susan Estrich's important article 'Rape'.[122] Estrich argues that American courts place so much emphasis on the victim's consent, understood in terms of force and resistance, that much of American rape law neglects the *mens rea* inquiry.[123] Given the difficulties

---

[117] 'Judicial Construction' (n 105 above) 148.

[118] ibid. Similarly, *A Feminist Review of Criminal Law* states that the central question in the mistake of fact controversy is 'whether it should be criminally culpable for someone to touch another sexually without securing consent, or at least without taking reasonable steps to ensure that consent is present': (n 105 above) 60. The *Review* then discusses the culpability of such behaviour, relying in its analysis on the work of Professor Hart.

[119] Alexander (n 105 above) 236, citing Duff (n 113 above) 60–61.

[120] Alexander (n 105 above) 246.

[121] C Wells, 'Swatting the Subjectivist Bug' (1982) Crim L Rev 209, 212–213.   [122] n 105 above.

[123] ibid 1097, discussing case law that holds that there is no *mens rea* for rape. As Estrich points out, the *mens rea* problem is to some degree dealt with in the definition of rape, which includes the

with the interpretation of blameworthiness in the context of rape, one might think that eliminating such an inquiry would actually count as progress. Indeed, feminists sometimes seem to suggest as much. However, Estrich points out how resistance 'functions as a substitute for *mens rea* to ensure that the man has notice of the woman's non-consent'.[124] The result is that it is 'virtually impossible for any man to be convicted where he was truly unaware or mistaken as to nonconsent'.[125] But because the resistance test also protects some men whose victims will not risk physical resistance, it will declare innocent some men who are actually blameworthy. In contrast Estrich comments that British courts, to their credit, have squarely confronted the true issue of blameworthiness, although their approach to it is too restrictive. Nonetheless, focusing on the key question of blameworthiness at least permits the relevant arguments about the guilt and state of mind of the accused to take place. Thus, it is crucial to 'expanding liability beyond the most traditional rape'.[126] Only a focus on blameworthiness makes it possible to see that men who possess the capacity to act reasonably but fail to do so may have made a blameworthy choice to violate the duty the law imposes on them to 'open their eyes and use their heads before engaging in sex'.[127] So by noting the dangers of failing to attend to blameworthiness, this argument illustrates the centrality of blameworthiness to feminist analysis. And while feminists often lament the exclusive focus on male blameworthiness as displacing attention from the impact on the victim, this argument points in another direction. It suggests that highlighting the centrality of blameworthiness and then challenging its limited definition will make it possible to move towards a more just law of sexual assault.

It is increasingly common to find feminist work that locates much of the egalitarian difficulty with sexual assault law not in the notion of blameworthiness per se but rather in the unduly restrictive approach taken to that idea in the law of sexual assault. So, for instance, Pickard argues that making an unreasonable mistake over such an important and simple question is sufficiently blameworthy to provide an affirmative reason for criminal sanction.[128] The nature of intercourse is such, she points out, that the man must necessarily have his mind focused on the legally relevant transaction. Because the act can be harmful without consent, he cannot answer the question of whether or not it is harmful in any particular instance without reference to the world outside him. That is why we are entitled to require the individual to inquire into consent before proceeding.[129] And this means that no accused should be able to defend himself against a rape charge by claiming that he didn't have a belief about consent because he simply didn't advert to it. A failure to inquire carefully into consent, on this account, constitutes the very kind of lack of minimal concern for the integrity of

---

element of being 'compelled by force or threat': ibid. See also Schulhofer (n 111 above) 176 pointing out that whatever is on the books, some degree of resistance remains necessary in practice; Michelle J Anderson, 'Reviving Resistance in Rape Law' 1998 U Ill L Rev 953; Nourse (n 108 above) 954–956.　　　　　　　　　　　　　　　　　　　　　　　　　　[124] (n 105 above) 1099.

[125] ibid 1098.　　　　[126] ibid 1095.　　　　[127] ibid 1104.
[128] 'Culpable Mistakes and Rape' (n 105 above) 90 n 45.　　　　[129] ibid 76.

others that is sufficiently blameworthy to ground the imposition of criminal liability.[130] This in turn makes it possible to delineate at least some of the circumstances in which the mistake itself is sufficiently culpable to amount to recklessness and thus ground liability.[131] The ultimate aim here is to bring the legal concept of *mens rea* 'into better alignment with the fundamental notions of blameworthiness it was designed to embody'.[132]

This egalitarian concern with blameworthiness is also apparent in the feminist attentiveness to moral culpability and the resulting concern not to punish those who truly suffer from non-culpable shortcomings. In this sense, although feminists do not themselves elaborate on the point, they implicitly draw our attention to possible differences between culpable and non-culpable ignorance and to the importance of distinguishing between them. So feminists frequently argue, even in the face of concerns about sexual assault, that an individual who does not have the general capacity to act reasonably should not be punished for his failure to live up to the objective standard. Boyle, for instance, notes that 'the benefit of the *Pappajohn* rule is that it avoids the danger of punishing someone who is incapable of taking reasonable care to ascertain consent and who thus does not deserve to be punished.'[133] Similarly, Wells stresses the utility of focusing on avoidability of harm as a response to the argument that an objective test would demolish the underpinning of personal guilt on which the criminal law is founded.[134] Estrich also voices her partial agreement with the traditional argument against negligence liability—that punishing a man for his stupidity is unjust. Although she stresses that such cases will be rare, she agrees that if the man in question lacks the capacity to act reasonably then it may well be unjust to punish him for it.[135] Similarly, because of the worry that negligence may entail liability without fault, Pickard distinguishes between recklessness and negligence and insists that only recklessness can afford a basis for liability in rape.[136] Only the centrality of blameworthiness to an egalitarian reconstruction

---

[130] ibid 77.

[131] 'Harsh Words on *Pappajohn*' (n 105 above) 418. As examples of the circumstances that will make unreasonable mistakes blameworthy, Pickard identifies the following: whether the actor's mind must be focused on the legally relevant transaction at the specific time, whether the risk of harm is both great and specific, and whether the inquiry into the relevant facts is simple. As discussed in the next chapter, these factors are important to liability because they signal the presence of the kind of 'moral' mistake that does justify the imposition of criminal liability.

[132] 'Culpable Mistakes and Rape' (n 105 above) 98.

[133] 'Judicial Construction' (n 105 above) 147–148.

[134] Wells quotes Fletcher's test of whether the actor could fairly have been expected to avoid the act of wrongdoing. Thus, the question is whether he had 'a fair opportunity to perceive the risk, to avoid the mistake, to resist the external pressure': Wells (n 121 above) 213, quoting GP Fletcher, *Rethinking Criminal Law* (Boston: Little, Brown, 1978) 510. For a similar point, see Alexander (n 105 above) 236. The role of avoidability in an account of culpable inadvertence is discussed in detail in ch 8 below.

[135] Estrich (n 105 above) 1103. Estrich points out that there is no evidence that the accused in *Morgan* fell within this category, at least so long as 'voluntary drunkenness is not equated with inherent lack of capacity': ibid.

[136] Thus, she queries Dickson J's suggestion in *Pappajohn* that any reasonableness requirement would make negligence the basis of rape. Pickard points out that this disregards the historical importance of

of responsibility can account for the energy feminists devote to delineating when inadvertent wrongdoing will ground criminal liability and when it will not. Developing a more nuanced account of ignorance that makes space for the fact of 'moral ignorance' therefore looks vital to an egalitarian understanding of blame.

It is also arguable that inattentiveness to the different forms of ignorance and their relationship to blame drives much of the justification for rejecting a reasonableness standard for mistake of fact among commentators more generally. Unfortunately, many of the criticisms of reasonableness standards in the sexual assault context do little more than invoke a general anxiety about 'objective standards' and criminal liability.[137] Thus, commentators often simply use the term 'subjectivist' to mean the only defensible basis for criminal responsibility and 'objectivist' to denote an unacceptable ground of criminal liability.[138] Sometimes, however, it is possible to see something more specific behind these generalized anxieties. Thus, for instance, Estrich quotes Glanville Williams defending *Morgan* in the following way: 'To convict the stupid man would be to convict him for what lawyers call inadvertent negligence—honest conduct which may be the best that this man can do but that does not come up to the standard of the so-called reasonable man.'[139] The concern that engages our sense that it would be morally inappropriate to punish this defendant turns on the fact that this defendant is 'stupid' in the sense that he cannot actually attain,

---

the difference between mere negligence and recklessness in the sense of gross deviation from a standard of care. Further, she points to the possibility of individualizing the standard and thus avoiding the application of an 'outer standard to the individual': 'Culpable Mistakes and Rape' (n 105 above) 419 n 19. However, she also warns against allowing our 'proper concern for the occasional defendant who is not capable of meeting ordinary standards of care to skew our entire view of culpability': ibid.

[137] Pickard discusses the reliance on generalized statements about what kind of mental state is required for criminal liability and notes that this is 'not a task of definition but one of discerning just bases for the attribution of criminal liability': ibid 97. She criticizes Dickson J's decision in *Pappajohn* for similar reasons, noting that his analysis rests on 'mere definitional preference' and that he 'does nothing to anchor his preference in theory or authority': ibid 417.

[138] Thus, for instance, Richard Tur criticizes the 'air of reality' test from *Pappajohn* on the ground that it injects a degree of objectivity: 'Rape, Reasonableness and Time' (1981) 1 Oxford J Legal Stud 432, 435. Relying on 'objective' recklessness, he suggests, extends the reach of crime to circumstances of decreasing moral culpability: 437. Writing of post-*Morgan* cases, PW Ferguson echoes this view: 'Rape and Reasonable Belief—A Limitation on *Morgan*?' (1986) 50 J Crim L 157, 160. Because there is no burden on judges to put the *Morgan* principle to the jury, 'the subjective principle in the law of rape' has been 'clearly subverted': ibid 160. See also Ferguson in 'Reasonable Belief in Rape and Assault' (1985) 49 J Crim L 156 discussing similar case law developments and the 'harshly objectivist view of mens rea': 156; John M Williams, 'Mistake of Fact: The Legacy of *Pappajohn v The Queen*' (1985) 63 Can Bar Rev 597. A similar point is made by John H Biebel, 'I Thought She Said Yes: Sexual Assault in England and America' (1995) 19 Suffolk Transnat'l L Rev 153, 176. Don Stuart describes the objective standard as an 'external' standard, which thus 'considerably extends the reach of the criminal law': 'The Pendulum Has Been Pushed Too Far' (1993) 42 UNBLJ 349, 353. While Stuart allows that objectively unreasonable sexual behaviour may be sufficiently culpable for criminal responsibility, he advocates a lesser offence of negligent sexual assault to reflect the difference in culpability: ibid 354.

[139] Estrich (n 105 above) 1103, quoting G Williams in a letter to *The [London] Times* (8 May 1975) 15 col 6.

however honest his attempts, the standard of the reasonable man. This therefore looks like another version of the *Vaughan v Menlove* problem in the more dramatic context of criminal liability. But it is important to note what is really engaging our moral intuitions here: it is not liability for avoidable carelessness but rather the possibility, perhaps imported from the operation of the negligence principle in the civil context, that there may be responsibility without blame. In fact Dickson J confirms this suspicion in *Pappajohn* when he writes, 'if the accused is to be punished because his mistake is one which an average man would not make, punishment will sometimes be inflicted when the criminal mind does not exist'.[140] Here again the concern seems to be that the negligence standard may attribute responsibility in the absence of blame. So Dickson J supports a subjective standard for mistake of fact in part on this ground and in part by describing the dangers that would attend an objective standard: 'if the woman in her own mind withholds consent, but her conduct and other circumstances lend credence to belief on the part of the accused that she was consenting, it may be that is unjust to convict'.[141] Dickson J's point in this example surely seems right. But as with Glanville Williams's argument, it does not tell against liability for avoidable carelessness. This is because it would almost certainly be an example of a *reasonable* belief in consent, not an *unreasonable* belief.[142] So the worry looks like it turns on liability *without* carelessness, not liability *for* carelessness.

This suggests that these examples actually tell against the point they are called on to support. In order to come up with situations in which objective reasonableness standards seem problematic, both Williams and Dickson J invoke cases where the defendant is not blameworthy. Dickson J's latter example should not be troubling: since the defendant acted reasonably, he would not be condemned by an objective reasonableness standard. But Williams and Dickson also point to a more worrisome possibility—that an objective standard may also condemn those who suffer from some shortcoming that affects their capacity to reach the standard. This anxiety is, in a certain sense, hardly surprising. As we have seen, at least in the civil context, the negligence standard does not hesitate to condemn the actions of the 'stupid'. And so subjectivists quite naturally worry about those situations where the negligence standard seems prepared to countenance a divergence between fault and blame. Interestingly, however, they have more difficulty coming up with morally engaging examples of unreasonable mistakes by actors who have the capacity to act reasonably. Feminist commentators argue that such actors are in fact blameworthy in the sense needed for criminal liability.[143] These accounts thus suggest that it may be

---

[140] *Pappajohn* (n 104 above) 150.   [141] ibid 155.

[142] Pickard makes a similar point with regard to this hypothetical. She states: 'he posits a reasonable mistake and argues that because a conviction in such circumstances would be unjust, an honest mistake (even though unreasonable) must exonerate': (n 105 above) 95 [internal footnote omitted].

[143] Indeed, commentators have suggested that this is also reflected in the case law. Thus, Boyle notes a 'functional willingness to punish for negligent sexual assault, disguised by the term wilful blindness': 'Judicial Construction' (n 105 above) 148, discussing *Sansregret* and other cases. In fact,

possible to find some common ground by developing a more refined account of what kind of ignorance or 'stupidity' will and will not exonerate. After all, concern about the criminal liability of the 'stupid' person who lacks the capacity of the average man implicitly invokes a certain kind of non-culpable shortcoming. The defendant whose 'stupidity' takes the form of moral ignorance or some kind of failure to care about others, by contrast, seems unlikely to engage our anxiety about criminal liability. The objective standard as commonly understood makes little room for such distinctions. So the question now is whether it is possible to make space in our understanding of the standard to develop a more nuanced understanding of culpable ignorance.

V. Conclusion

Even a cursory examination of those areas of criminal law where the reasonable person is implicated (such as self-defence, provocation, and sexual assault) suggests that it is unlikely that equality will be enhanced merely by moving from an objective to a subjective standard. In fact such attempts to correct systematic mistakes in assessments of liability as between wrongdoers actually come at a significant cost to equality as between victims. Both in the context of provocation and in the context of sexual assault, subjectivization of the standard enables perpetrators to invoke discriminatory stereotypes about gender relations and sexual autonomy. Without the normative leverage that an objective standard at least theoretically provides, judges are left with simple questions of credibility. And in this context, the prevalence of discriminatory beliefs will often lend sufficient credibility to exonerate or excuse the accused. The more widely held such beliefs, the more credible they will be.

Subjectivizing the standard, far from promoting equality, simply seems to give more unfettered play to the very beliefs that are most likely to undermine equality. It is presumably for this reason that even though feminists have rightly raised serious concerns about objective standards, there was widespread feminist condemnation of the move to subjectivize the standard for mistake of fact in sexual assault. In that context at least, most people concerned with women's sexual equality recognized that an objective standard of some sort—however flawed—was infinitely preferable to a subjective standard. And in the attempts to articulate just what the egalitarian promise of the objective standard might be, feminists began to invoke the fundamental criminal law concern with blame. This in turn raises the possibility that a more refined account of the culpability of inadvertence may create some important common ground between egalitarians and 'subjectivists' in the field of criminal responsibility. Unfortunately, however, while feminists and other critical egalitarians often

Boyle suggests that for this reason, the new sexual assault provisions do not in fact mark a 'stark break with the values implicit in pre-Bill C-49 case law': ibid 149.

invoke a worry about how subjectivized standards miss an important form of blameworthy behaviour, they typically do little to elaborate on this intuition. Let us therefore examine some of the theoretical literature on the issue of culpable inadvertence to see if it can aid in the development of a more refined account of its relation to blame.

7

Culpability and the Objective Standard: The Sexual Assault Debate

We must not make a scarecrow of the law,
Setting it up to fear the birds of prey,
And let it keep one shape, till custom make it
Their perch, and not their terror.[1]

Our analysis so far suggests why the feminist debate on objective standards may seem perplexing. On one hand, the use of objective reasonableness standards in cases like self-defence and provocation gives rise to serious equality concerns. Indeed, the standards appear to be problematic in ways that mirror what we saw in private law—the relation between blame and responsibility under the standard looks troublingly uneven. For this reason, in contexts like provocation and self-defence, some feminists have advocated abandonment of such standards in favour of more subjectivized measures. However the recent history of provocation where these arguments seem to have held some sway casts doubt on the desirability of such a response on equality grounds. And feminist critiques in the field of sexual assault put into yet sharper relief the dangers of such a solution. There feminists worry about subjectivized standards, not only because of their consequences for women but also because there is an important form of blameworthiness that such standards seem to miss. So in sexual assault, feminists seem as loathe to abandon such standards as they are to embrace them elsewhere.

Bringing together and trying to make sense of these critiques suggests that it may be possible to draw out an underlying worry about the inegalitarian effect of the reasonable person on the relationship between blame and responsibility. As we saw in the provocation context, some of this seems to occur because of how the standard incorporates certain default characteristics even though it is hard to see how those characteristics relate to culpability. In such a context, challenging the objectivity or fixity of the standard may look like the only way to displace those troubling characteristics and thereby achieve a more egalitarian

---

[1] William Shakespeare, 'Measure for Measure' in *The Complete Pelican Shakespeare* (gen ed A Harbage) (New York: Viking, 1979) Angelo: II i 1–4, 407.

relationship between blame and responsibility. But these critiques can equally be understood as aiming at a more modest task: to call our attention to how a rigid attribution of non-normative characteristics can actually distort the relationship between blame and responsibility. Rereading these concerns in terms of a distorted conception of blame also has the virtue of linking the feminist concerns in provocation with those in sexual assault—for here too it seems that the underlying concern can be understood in terms of blame, but the concern is the blame that the relevant legal standards miss. On this account, the subjective standard is particularly troubling from an egalitarian point of view. And while this does suggest a link between equality and objective reasonableness standards, the feminist debate is hardly sanguine on this point either. Indeed, the nature of the promise that objective standards hold for equality seekers must be carefully elucidated, since as we have seen, there are also grave equality problems with objective standards.

It therefore seems useful to examine the theoretical accounts of objective reasonableness standards to determine the promise and the perils of such standards. These accounts, primarily found in the field of criminal negligence, outline some of the conditions under which an objective standard can be justified. But the ideas of objectivity, subjectivity, and inadvertence are sufficiently complex that it is first helpful to address certain threshold issues. This in turn will assist in isolating the major conceptual challenge to the objective standard—in particular whether it is possible to provide a suitably egalitarian account of the culpability of inadvertence. There are essentially three major contenders here: the avoidability-based account, the customary account, and the indifference account. Working some of the key points through the sexual assault debate will enable us to explore how these various accounts of culpable inadvertence might respond to egalitarian concerns. In this way, we can begin to develop an understanding of the culpability of inadvertence that will uncover some of its conceptual foundations and in the process reveal its egalitarian possibilities.

I. Objectivity and inadvertence: some threshold issues

As is often the case with the most fundamental legal concepts, many of the key terms associated with the negligence standard suffer from serious ambiguity. This is starkly illustrated by one of the key distinctions in liability for negligence: the question of 'objective' versus 'subjective' standards. Almost as troublesome, and closely related, is the concept of inadvertence and the connection of that idea to objectivity, awareness, and blameworthiness. Our task of elaborating the fault element of negligence will not proceed far without greater clarity in these core ideas. Let us begin with the most tangled and difficult of these—the distinction between objective and subjective standards.

A. The objectivity of the standard

Terminology alone reveals how central the idea of objectivity is to the negligence standard, which is often referred to (including here) as the 'objective' standard. As we have seen, much of the debate in the criminal field (provocation, sexual assault, the defences) is posed as a question concerning whether, and to what extent, the standard in each case should be objective or subjective. But what exactly does 'objective' mean in the context of the negligence standard, and what is the significance of the fact that the objective or negligence standard is traditionally contrasted with the 'subjective standard' both in tort law and in criminal law? References to objectivity often seem like an attempt to capture the independent or external and hence 'fixed' dimension of the standard— the sense in which the standard refuses to treat the agent's own capacities as determinative. So, in the private law context, the negligence standard is described as objective because it is external in that it generally refuses to allow the particularities or idiosyncrasies of the defendant to diminish the degree of care she is required to exercise in her interactions with others. The court in *Vaughan v Menlove*[2] described its holding on this point as a rejection of a subjective or 'best efforts' standard. In the criminal law context, the provocation debate makes similar use of the term 'objective', which refers to a standard that is relatively fixed and independent of the agent. This is contrasted with a standard that varies with the perceptions, qualities, and capacities of the accused. Thus, for instance, as Madam Justice Wilson's famous statement from *Hill* describes it:

The objective standard...may be said to exist in order to ensure that...there is no fluctuating standard of self-control against which accused are measured. The governing principles are those of equality and individual responsibility, so that all persons are held to the same standard notwithstanding their distinctive personality traits and varying capacities to achieve the standard.[3]

The distinctive virtue of the objective standard, on this reading, seems to be found in the fixed normative demands it makes of the agent—in the provocation case, for instance, on the accused's powers of self-control. This insistence on the standard's independence from the actual normative capacities of the individual is identified as the source both of the standard's 'fixity' (or objectivity) and of the hope it holds for equality seekers.

Wilson J's passage is often thought important because it seems to capture what seems promising about the objective standard and to connect that promise to equality.[4] Despite this, however, the passage is somewhat puzzling. It insists that the normative content of the objective standard must, for equality

[2] *Vaughan v Menlove* (1837) 3 Bing NC 468, 132 ER 490 (CP).
[3] *R v Hill* (1986) 25 CCC (3d) 322, 345.
[4] See e.g. EM Hyland, '*R v Thibert*: Are There Any Ordinary People Left?' (1996–1997) 28 Ottawa L Rev 145; *Green v R* [1996–97] 191 CLR 334 (per Kirby J).

reasons, be fixed and hence agent-independent. This is undoubtedly an appealing position, but the way that Wilson J links this fixity to the objective standard seems a bit odd. This is because the quality of precluding individuals from invoking their own divergent values in response to a charge of legal liability is typically thought to be a core feature of *any* legal standard, be it subjective or objective.[5] So even the most radical 'subjectivist' in criminal law terms ought to concur with the 'objectivist' on this point: the legal duty must be independent of individual moral values or it is not a legal standard at all. Indeed, it is ordinarily seen as central to the rule of law and to its conception of equality that the ability to define and delineate wrongdoing resides with the law, not with the individual under legal scrutiny. And though this quality of the legal system is apparent in a variety of ways, it receives what is perhaps its most important expression in the prohibition on the mistake of law defence in criminal law.

It is true that the doctrine on mistake of law is hardly a model of clarity— conceptual or doctrinal. Underneath all of its complexity, however, it is possible to see how the central features of the mistake of law rule protect the legal system's insistence that the law, not the individual under scrutiny, sets the relevant norms and values. In its simplest form, the mistake of law rule prohibits an individual from defending herself on the basis that she was not aware that the act she engaged in was illegal. Thus, the prohibition enshrines the old common law rule that ignorance of the law is not an excuse.[6] But the rule against raising a mistake of law defence is limited to mistakes regarding crimes that are *mala in se* (as opposed to merely *mala prohibita*), that is to say cases where the criminalized act was 'wrong in and of itself'. This effectively limits the prohibition against mistake of law defences to those crimes where the legal rule entrenches fundamental moral values. Mistakes that have this dual 'legal-moral' quality are what is generally captured by the prohibited category of mistakes of law.[7] The assumption is that it is not unfair to bar such defences, because we are justified in requiring individuals to know that it is wrong to inflict serious harm on the core interests of others, such as life and well-being. Thus, someone could not defend herself on the ground that she did not know

---

[5] See, for instance, A Simester, 'Can Negligence be Culpable?' in J Horder (ed), *Oxford Essays in Jurisprudence* (4th Series, Oxford: OUP, 2000) 85, 93 (external imposition of values vital to the purposes of the law; individuals cannot be permitted to conduct themselves outside the norms of the law because they have different moral values); see J Horder, 'Gross Negligence and Criminal Culpability' (1997) 47 UTLJ 495, 503.

[6] For examples, see Canadian Criminal Code RSC 1985, c C-34 s 19; Ontario Provincial Offences Act RSO 1990, c P 33 s 81; US American Law Institute Model Penal Code 1985, s 2.04, especially 2.04(3); D Stuart, *Canadian Criminal Law, A Treatise* (4th edn, Toronto: Carswell, 2001) 323–324; G Williams, *Textbook of Criminal Law* (2nd edn, London: Stevens, 1983) 451; GP Fletcher, *Rethinking Criminal Law* (Boston: Little, Brown, 1978) 755; Livingston Hall and Selig J Seligman, 'Mistake of Law and *Mens Rea*' (1941) 8 U Chicago L Rev 641; Lucinda Vandervort, 'Mistake of Law and Sexual Assault: Consent and *Mens Rea*' (1987–88) 2 CJWL 233.

[7] For the sake of simplicity, I will also use the term 'mistake of law' to refer to these 'legal-moral' mistakes that possess the quality of falling afoul of both legal rules and fundamental moral injunctions.

that the intentional unprovoked killing of another human being was wrong. Such a claim rests on a mistake about a legal rule that derives its content from a basic moral value, the equal value of others. Indeed, allowing a defence of this kind would effectively permit individuals to displace the most foundational legal norms with their own divergent value systems. So by rejecting the possibility of individuals defending themselves by claiming ignorance of basic legal-moral norms, the mistake of law rule enshrines a certain set of minimum moral and legal values. One important function of the prohibition on a mistake of law defence is to preclude individuals from asserting divergent values to displace the core moral and legal minimum.

In this way then, the prohibition on mistake of law defences is an important expression of the legal system's refusal to countenance claims that challenge its norms and underlying values. Often, as we recognize, the claim 'I didn't know' will serve to exonerate. But the mistake of law rule requires us to be alert to the possibility that a claim of heedlessness may be based on 'moral' ignorance. In cases like these where a claim asserts ignorance about a basic legal-moral norm, it actually inculpates, not exculpates, the person who asserts it.[8] Regardless of how honest or credible the person may be, we are entitled to condemn those who do not understand basic legal-moral norms like those that prohibit serious harm to others. We can only properly blame someone for failing to *exercise*, but not generally for failing to *possess*, a cognitive capacity; however, the same limitation does not apply to a moral capacity. Unlike cognitive or physical capacities, the failure to possess a moral capacity also generally provides grounds for condemnation. Thus, at least in the absence of mental illness, we justifiably condemn someone who does not have the capacity to care enough about others to avoid harming them. By insisting on this baseline, the mistake of law rule protects the primacy of core legal and moral values, particularly when those values protect fundamental norms like the value of equality to which Wilson J adverts.

Reflecting on how the mistake of law rule protects core systemic values by limiting the available defences raises questions about the meaning of Wilson J's words. She suggests that, in contrast with the subjective standard, the objective

---

[8] An illustration of this function of the mistake of law rule can be found in the Supreme Court of Canada's decision in *R v Ewanchuk* [1999] 1 SCR 330. That case concerned the application of the new sexual assault provisions of the Canadian Criminal Code (ss 265 (1), (2), (3), 273.1, 273.2) to a man who, while conducting a job interview in his trailer, made a number of sexual advances on the 17-year-old woman he was interviewing. The complainant clearly said 'no' to each of his advances but, after stopping briefly, the accused then persisted with increasingly more serious advances. He was charged with sexual assault and acquitted at trial. The Alberta Court of Appeal upheld that acquittal and the theory of 'implied consent' on which it was based. The Supreme Court of Canada reversed, in the process discussing which kinds of mistakes establish the moral innocence of the accused. Mr Justice Major points out that although the accused must show that he believed that the complainant consented in order to 'cloak' his actions 'in moral innocence', not all beliefs that the accused might assert, however honestly held, will exonerate him. Instead, 'a belief that silence, passivity or ambiguous conduct constitutes consent is a mistake of law and provides no defence': 356. In this way, the prohibition on asserting mistake of law precludes the accused from exculpating himself by relying on beliefs or values at odds with the core egalitarian values of the legal system.

standard's normative 'fixity' is its particularly egalitarian feature. But the fixed moral and legal baseline protected by the mistake of law rule is as much a feature of subjective standards as of objective ones. This is reflected in the fact that the conventional *mens rea* analysis extends only to the question of whether the accused intentionally did the wrongful act and emphatically not to whether the individual believed the act to be wrong.[9] Apart from the claim of diminished responsibility or insanity, at least, the mistake of law rule limits available defences to those that are consistent with respect for the values enshrined in the legal norms. Thus, even for crimes whose *mens rea* requirements demand subjective foresight, the legal standard itself seems to be objective or independent of individual valuations of others in exactly the way that Wilson J insists is so important in her quote from *Hill*. Viewed in this light, it seems somewhat odd to insist that this independence of the legal standard from the moral make-up of the accused is the distinctive attribute of the objective standard, for this seems essential to any legal standard—including those that are uncontroversially subjective. But why then does the insistence on the agent-independent nature of the legal norm seem so important in the case of the reasonable person, and why does the reiteration of its connection to an egalitarian legal order seem to have such salience in that context?

B. The problem of inadvertence

Part of the mystery surrounding the reasonable person test seems bound up with the complexities associated with culpability for inadvertence. Although the test is used both to assess how the actor evaluates the acceptability of a known risk and to determine the culpability of failing to recognize a risk,[10] the questions about the nature of culpability seem most persistent with the failure to recognize a risk. At least in the absence of some kind of cognitive impairment, it seems likely that an agent who erroneously calculates the acceptability of a risk of which she is aware is making a normative or prudential mistake, rather than a simple cognitive one. Actual notice of the risk, therefore, generally seems to create a sufficient connection to an individual's own choices to link her to the events in a normatively significant way.[11] We could, for instance, ask her to account for her behaviour by giving reasons for her choices and actions in the light of the knowledge we know she possessed. And we can assess those

---

[9] An illustration is found in *R v Barrow* (1984) 14 CCC (3d) 470 (NSCA). In that prosecution for influence peddling, Senator Barrow argued that he was not aware of the illegality of the practice of demanding political contributions as a condition of government contracts precisely because the practice was so long-standing. The Court of Appeal characterized this as a mistake of law that accordingly afforded him no defence: see discussion in Vandervort (n 6 above) 240.

[10] GP Fletcher, 'The Theory of Criminal Negligence: A Comparative Analysis' (1971) U Penn L Rev 401, 425. As discussed below, Fletcher's view is that this unity 'obscures the essential difference between the two inquiries': ibid.

[11] I say generally because, as the discussion of *Elliott v C* below suggests, awareness may itself be an unreliable basis on which to attribute culpability: n 85 below.

reasons, choices, and actions against the law's understanding of what appropriate concern or care for others requires.[12]

Indeed, this may provide an account of why, like the Court in *Vaughan v Menlove*,[13] we are prepared to condemn the defendant even if his intellectual abilities are as limited as he suggests. Someone like Menlove with very limited cognitive or perceptive powers may well have failed to notice the risk of fire in the hayrick. We will return to this possibility below. But for the moment it seems crucial that Menlove was actually aware of the risk, which had been pointed out to him on several occasions. Because he possessed this awareness, we also have information regarding his response to the risk: he explicitly stated that he was prepared to 'chance it'. So what condemns him as careless is his egoistic response to the risk he knew he was posing to the property of someone else. His own property, the Court points out, was insured. Thus, Menlove's failure to eliminate the risk seems the product of clear self-preference. His inaction and the fact that he was willing to 'chance it' lead to the clear implication that he treated his own insured property as more important than the property of his neighbour. So even if he was as cognitively limited as he argued, his failure to eliminate the risk looks like the result of faulty moral reasoning, not limited intellectual abilities. In this way, actual knowledge of the risk helps to provide a sufficiently uncontroversial link to Menlove and his expressed values that we can analyse his reasons for not taking precautions. Because we can in this way assess the normative quality of his reason for inaction, we can condemn *him* for his response to the risk if it falls short of what attentiveness and equal respect for others requires. The fact that Menlove's response is predicated on self-preference enables us to conclude that it does indeed fall short of what respect for others requires.

This may help to explain at least part of the underlying reason why the controversial cases of criminal liability for carelessness concern inadvertence. Even orthodox 'subjectivists' take the view that once the accused has adverted to the relevant risk, it is not particularly problematic to impose criminal liability for actions taken in the light of that knowledge. The fact that the accused has actual knowledge of the risk seems to provide a sufficiently personal link to the accused to justify the imposition of criminal liability. Because we can evaluate her subsequent actions and deliberations in the light of her own knowledge, it therefore seems relatively uncontroversial to assess her personal culpability.[14] It is presumably for this reason that the fierce debate about criminal fault boils down to the narrow question of whether there can be responsibility for inadvertent as well as advertent recklessness (even though the actual

---

[12] For a discussion of the significance of a theory of practical reasoning for this kind of inquiry, see Horder (n 5 above) 502, 509 and Simester (n 5 above) 88–91.　　　　　[13] n 2 above.

[14] It is worth noting however that the exact justification and basis for the normative significance of awareness are not as simple and straightforward as they might seem: Horder (n 5 above).

doctrinal significance of this question may be quite limited).[15] So the absence of awareness or knowledge seems to be at the core of the worry that many orthodox subjectivists have about 'objective' fault. However, the focus on objective fault seems a misleading way to characterize the debate and its core issues. If legal fault is inherently objective in the sense of being external to the accused, then what is at stake in this debate seems to have more to do with the question of what normative significance can be given to unawareness of an objectively obvious risk.

We can explore this by considering a variation on *Vaughan v Menlove*: what if Menlove failed to eliminate the risk because he was completely unaware of it? It does seem that such a case would require quite a different analysis of culpability. At least some of this is due to the fact that it is more difficult to assess the normative significance of a mistake when it concerns a complete failure to recognize a risk. In part, this is because an agent might fail to notice a risk of harm to others for very different kinds of reasons. To see how this might be so, let us consider another variation on *Vaughan* in which there was no warning. Let us further assume that Menlove suffered from a serious cognitive impairment that made it difficult for him to understand the world around him, including basic ideas like cause and effect. In such a case, it is difficult to draw an inference of culpability from the inadvertence. Instead, it seems more likely that Menlove's mistake has no normative significance because it springs from a cognitive shortcoming, rather than a moral one. Yet we could equally imagine another 'Menlove' without any such shortcoming who failed to notice the risk posed to his neighbour's property because he simply did not pay any attention to anyone's property but his own. Here the inattentiveness does seem culpable because it springs from self-preference. But these varying interpretations suggest that assessing the culpability of 'pure' inadvertence requires a finer analysis of the underlying reasons than does the relatively simpler assessment of intentional or even advertent risk-imposition. For while some heedlessness reveals the agent's self-preference and thus condemns her as culpable, other kinds of reasons do not implicate culpability at all. The response of the law to this ambiguity of heedlessness has been, as we have seen, rather blunt. In the private law of negligence, courts and commentators have tended to suggest that the ambiguity does not matter because in private law legal fault is not synonymous with personal fault. In the criminal law setting, this same ambiguity has fuelled suspicion about whether inadvertence can ever properly be criminalized.

One of our tasks in this analysis is to ask whether it is possible to develop a more nuanced account of the fault of inadvertence, an account that might ground a more adequate response to these problems. Undoubtedly, at least some of the difficulty with this task is attributable to the complexity of the reasonable person as the key device for assessing culpable indifference. As we have

---

[15] Thus, the real area of controversy concerns liability for inadvertent recklessness: RA Duff, *Intention, Agency and Criminal Liability: Philosophy of Action and the Criminal Law* (Oxford: Basil Blackwell, 1990); RA Duff, 'Recklessness and Rape' (1981) 3 Liverpool L Rev 49; Horder (n 5 above).

noted, the reasonable person is 'mixed' in the sense that it encompasses both normative and non-normative attributes that sit in uncertain relation to each other and to the capacities of the agent. This fact, combined with the complexity of the reasons that may explain inadvertence, suggests that it will be challenging to ensure that the legal standard reliably captures only and all those failings that justify legal liability. But Wilson J's warning about the egalitarian significance of a fixed normative standard reminds us of the importance of this task, and perhaps points to the particular challenge inherent in a personified standard. Certainly if we cannot use a personified standard to isolate normative failings in a reliable way, it will be extremely difficult for the objective standard as ordinarily conceived to provide the kind of fixed norms that equality seems to require. This suggests a possible reason for concern about using the reasonable person to identify culpable inadvertence. We shall return to this important issue. But we will not have the tools to address it properly without a much clearer picture of when inadvertence is culpable. So let us for the moment set aside the issue of the objective standard's most common expression—the reasonable person—in order to examine more carefully the meaning of culpable inadvertence.

II. When is inadvertence culpable?

As discussed above, feminist critiques, particularly in the context of sexual assault, insist that there is an important dimension of blameworthiness that subjectivized standards miss. These critiques also echo Wilson J's above observation that the fault captured by objective standards may be particularly important to equality. We have already examined and dismissed one possible interpretation of this link: the idea that there is some kind of normative fixity that distinguishes an objective standard from a subjective one. As we have seen, the mistake of law rule insists that subjective as well as objective legal standards be independent of the vagaries of individual valuations on matters of fundamental value. And if both standards equally demand this kind of independence from the agent's values, this aspect of the objective standard seems unlikely to account for its distinctive appeal to equality seekers. Feminist critiques, especially in the sexual assault context, sometimes seem to point towards another possibility. They suggest that an objective standard is especially well suited to capturing a kind of culpability that is particularly important to equality seekers. Thus, feminist critiques often suggest that even a complete failure to notice a risk may sometimes be blameworthy. It is for this reason that the egalitarian account often seems to imply a distinction between culpable and non-culpable ignorance. So it may be helpful to see how we might develop the intuition that sometimes even pure inadvertence can be culpable in the way that criminal law properly requires. This may in turn make it possible to see why such culpability is seen as so promising by equality seekers, and how that promise may be peculiarly vulnerable.

As a starting point, it is useful to draw on more developed accounts of culpability that defend negligence or inadvertent recklessness as grounds of criminal liability by elucidating the sense in which they can be understood as targeting morally culpable behaviour. These accounts can be grouped into three broad categories according to how they understand the basis for the culpability of inadvertence. Perhaps the most common is the avoidability account, according to which inadvertence that could have been avoided is culpable. The customary account is also very influential, holding that conventional or customary practices serve as the only standard for determining when inadvertence is culpable. Finally, the indifference account takes the view that inadvertence is culpable when it springs from inattentiveness to others. With the question of their egalitarian implications in mind, let us examine these accounts in turn.

A. The avoidability account

Herbert Hart provided one of the first—and in many ways still the most influential—defences of the view that negligence can be understood, under certain conditions, as sufficiently culpable to ground criminal liability. The affinity of the Hartian account with the egalitarian project is nicely illustrated by his goal of refuting the claim, implicit in certain understandings of *mens rea*, that punishing negligence amounts to an unacceptable imposition of strict liability. [16] Hart insists however that a conclusion of negligence, properly understood, *does* implicate the culpability of the agent. The essential error in the strict liability critique of negligence, he suggests, is the idea that the subjective element in negligence is inadvertence or 'a blank mind'.[17] But Hart argues that while inadvertence is a state of mind, negligence is not. Instead, negligence makes 'an essential reference to an omission to do what is thus required'.[18] The connection between inadvertence and negligence is best understood in the following way: while an individual may be negligent in failing to advert to a situation, the negligence consists not in the blank state of mind per se but rather in 'the failure to take precautions against harm by examining the situation'.[19] In response to the challenge that this may still amount to the imposition of liability in the absence of blame, Hart responds with his famous articulation of the essential precondition for responsibility in negligence: 'What is crucial is that those whom we punish should have had, when they acted, the normal capacities,

---

[16] HLA Hart, 'Legal Responsibility and Excuses' in *Punishment and Responsibility: Essays in the Philosophy of Law* (Oxford: Clarendon Press, 1970) 31.

[17] In 'Negligence, *Mens Rea* and Criminal Responsibility' in *Punishment and Responsibility* (ibid) 146, Hart critiques the approach of Dr Turner who describes negligence as 'the state of mind of a man who pursues a course of conduct *without adverting at all* to the consequences': JW Turner, *The Modern Approach to Criminal Law* (London: Macmillan, 1945) 207. As Hart points out, Turner admits that while this state of mind may be sufficiently blameworthy to ground civil liability, he also insists it cannot amount to criminal liability (Hart 148 discussing Turner 209).

[18] Hart (n 17 above) 148.   [19] ibid.

physical and mental, for doing what the law requires and abstaining from what it forbids, and a fair opportunity to exercise those capacities'.[20]

Thus, on the Hartian account, the mental element that justifies liability in negligence is 'a failure to exercise the capacity to advert to, and to think about and control, conduct and its risks'.[21] And this in turn makes avoidability central to culpability, which, on Hart's understanding of negligence, consists in the avoidable imposition of a careless risk of harm on another.

For Hart, when negligence is properly made criminally punishable, the inquiry involves two questions: first, did the accused fail to take those precautions that any reasonable man with normal capacities would in the circumstances have taken; and second, could the accused, given his mental and physical capacities, have taken those precautions. While the first inquiry is the basis of the invariant standard of care and is hence 'objective' or agent-independent in the sense discussed above, the second goes to individual capacity ('individuated conditions of liability') and cannot be made entirely independent of the agent's capacities without risking the imposition of strict liability. On Hart's account the first stage of the negligence inquiry must therefore be invariant while the second stage must be individuated. Consequently, however, the exact relation between these two stages of the negligence inquiry is critical. In particular, it raises the question of whether an individual can argue that a 'moral' incapacity (such as a generalized inability to care about the interests of others) is the kind of factor that must be taken into consideration in individuating the conditions of liability. We need only reflect on our variation on *Vaughan v Menlove*, or on the provocation context, to see the significance of this: could a person's inability to care about others or to control her temper, for instance, count as the kind of factor that individuates the conditions of liability so that she is only held to the standard of care or self-control that she personally could meet, however low it might be?[22]

Unfortunately, Hart does not directly address this important question. Many of his examples do suggest that conditions of liability should only be individuated where the asserted incapacity is *not* normative or prudential in nature.

---

[20] Hart (ibid) 152. On this aspect of criminal negligence, Hart's remains the leading theoretical account (although as the case law on criminal negligence reveals, it has admittedly been more difficult in the application than in the conception: see, for instance, David M Paciocco, 'Subjective and Objective Standards of Fault for Offences and Defences' (1995) 59 Sask L Rev 271, especially discussing the relevance of various personal characteristics of the accused: 294. Hart's avoidability analysis mirrors Holmes's early and influential work in the context of the common law, which, as discussed in ch 1 above, also stresses the importance of avoidability as a precondition to justifiable liability in negligence: *The Common Law* (ed MD Howe) (Cambridge, Mass: Harvard University Press, 1963) 144, 163. Tony Honoré's adoption in 'Responsibility and Luck' of a 'can general' test as a precondition for liability in the private law of negligence is also reminiscent of Hart's position here, although Hart and Honoré reach different conclusions about the justifiability of punishing the 'shortcomer': T Honoré, *Responsibility and Fault* (Oxford: Hart Publishing, 1999) 14–40.

[21] Hart (ibid) 157.

[22] See ch 6 above, especially the discussion of *R v Smith* [2000] 4 All ER 289 (HL) and related cases that struggle with these questions.

Thus, he states that the inquiry into avoidability will operate in favour of an agent whose 'memory or other faculties were defective' or who 'could not distinguish a dangerous situation from a harmless one'.[23] Similarly, he views as relevant the normal capacities of 'memory and observation and intelligence' and the capacity for recognizing and assessing relevant risks.[24] Allowing individuation only for non-normative shortcomings would also account for the distinction Hart draws between those cases where an individual 'just didn't think' and those cases such as accident, coercion, and mistake where the normal capacities are absent. While the former situation actually seems to call for punishment, Hart points out that in the latter cases punishment will raise a worry about the absence of moral blameworthiness. Hart's rejection of the idea that an agent could exonerate herself for murder by stating 'I just decided to kill; I couldn't help deciding' also seems to be based on a refusal to individuate the standard for sub-standard prudential or moral capacities.[25]

Unfortunately however, Hart's account frequently blurs the distinction between prudential or normative shortcomings and those shortcomings (like cognitive and physical ones) that do not reflect upon the character of the agent. Perhaps this should not be surprising given that so much of his defence of negligence—and his great contribution to our understanding of it—is found in his insistence on the centrality of avoidability. Thus, for instance, he states: 'If our conditions of liability are invariant and not flexible, i.e. if they are not adjusted to the capacities of the accused, then some individuals will be held liable for negligence even though they could not have helped their failure to comply with the standard.'[26] Here, Hart seems to treat the ability to do otherwise as a general condition of liability. He even insists that the conditions of liability be individuated where 'repeated instructions and punishment have been of no avail',[27] although this seems to contemplate calibrating the standard to reflect the moral capacities or character of the accused. It is presumably this reading of Hart that accounts for Glanville Williams's worry that 'if every characteristic of the individual is taken into account, including his heredity the conclusion is that he could not help doing what he did'.[28] And Hart's response is telling. He dismisses Williams's worry by reiterating that what is critical is whether the individual had the capacity (inherited or not) to act otherwise than he did. Hart concludes that 'determinism' presents no greater difficulty for negligence than for intention-based liability. But all that this really seems to amount to is the admission that determinism may be equally troubling to liability for intentional *and* negligent wrongdoing.

Because Hart sidesteps these central questions, worries persist about his conception of culpability for inadvertence. He does not address an important

---

[23] (n 17 above) 150.
[24] ibid. Presumably this is also the reason that Hart calls attention to the fact that we do not generally treat the omissions of infants or mentally deficient persons as culpable: ibid.
[25] ibid 151.   [26] ibid 154.   [27] ibid 150.   [28] ibid 155–156.

difficulty suggested by Williams's critique—that where culpability (be it for careless or intentional wrongs) is so heavily premissed on avoidability, the fact that so much of our character and circumstance is beyond our control seems to threaten to obliterate all responsibility.[29] A more attentive response to this worry might have led Hart to delineate the scope of avoidability by articulating the difference that he often seems to assume between the invariant and the individuated inquiries. Instead, however, his zeal to defend the negligence standard against the strict liability challenge and the 'confused conception of the subjective element and its relation to responsibility'[30] seems to incline him to overextend the individuating conditions. Because he contemplates that an individual's own moral capacities could modify the degree of care we demand of her, Hart seems willing to allow a particularly troubling kind of individualization. In this sense, his defence of negligence leaves open the possibility that the normative content of the standard itself could vary with the capacities of the individual agent. This openness to individual divergent norms and values is such that it actually raises a worry about the mistake of law rule. And because it seems to allow individual capacities to displace legal norms, it also raises the kind of egalitarian anxiety we noted earlier. On this score, Hart's account—for all of its egalitarian ambition—points to one possible way that the egalitarian promise of the standard is especially open to being undermined. There may well be resources in the Hartian account to shape a response to such a worry. However, because Hart places such emphasis on avoidability, and because the contours of his account's application are so uncertain, it is difficult to get beyond avoidability to a closer examination of the exact nature of blameworthy inadvertence itself. Let us therefore look to some other accounts to see whether they can build on and refine Hart's great contribution to our understanding of culpable inadvertence.

B. The customary account

George Fletcher's work on criminal negligence provides a fitting place to continue our examination. Like Hart, Fletcher aims to defend negligence as a ground of criminal responsibility against subjectivists. In fact, though he largely tracks Hart on avoidability, Fletcher arguably makes more progress on the central challenge of articulating the meaning of culpable inadvertence. But the foundation Fletcher identifies for culpable inadvertence—the community's customary practices or expectations—turns out to be particularly problematic for equality seekers. Nonetheless, understanding Fletcher's account is vital to developing a more egalitarian conception of culpable inadvertence. This is because his account actually articulates more sharply than equality seekers themselves

---

[29] See, for instance, T Nagel 'Moral Luck' in Thomas Nagel (ed), *Mortal Questions* (Cambridge, New York: Cambridge University Press, 1979) 24; B Williams, *Moral Luck: Philosophical Papers, 1973–1980* (New York: Cambridge University Press, 1990).   [30] (n 17 above) 157.

do the very version of the objective standard that often animates egalitarian anxieties.

1. *Custom and culpable inadvertence*

As an initial matter, Fletcher concurs with Hart on the significance of avoidability: as he puts it, the threshold requirement for liability in negligence is that the 'running of the risk be voluntary'.[31] So 'the inadvertent actor is not culpable if he could not have informed himself of the risk he created'.[32] In this sense, Fletcher (like Hart) relies on an appeal to our intuition that avoidable negligence is blameworthy: 'The conclusion seems unavoidable that inadvertence to risk as well as choosing to take a risk might warrant the just censure of others. When the circumstances give the actor reason to think that his conduct risks harm to another, his failure to apprise himself of the risks latent in his conduct is culpable'.[33] But if Fletcher echoes Hart on avoidability, there is another respect in which his account does progress beyond Hart's.

Fletcher notes that the capacity to inform oneself of the risk, while necessary for establishing culpability, is not sufficient for it. He thus attempts to elaborate upon the aspect of the account that Hart tended to assume without much explanation. Thus, Fletcher points out that inadvertence will only be culpable where the actor is also under a duty either to avoid the harm or to inform himself of the risks. The idea of 'unreasonable mistakes'—based on 'our expectations of what other members of the community would do under the same circumstances'— is the common law's response to the conundrum of determining what should alert the actor to the need for inquiry and thus give rise to a duty.[34] By focusing on this issue, Fletcher goes beyond the threshold condition of avoidability and directly tackles the difficult question of duty: just what is it that we owe each other and why? But his answer to this question is troubling because of the extraordinary weight he accords to custom. Thus, he argues that for intentional crimes such as battery, theft, and the like, the duty is 'wholly independent of conventional practices'.[35] He continues:

In assessing the culpability of inadvertence, on the other hand, we rely heavily on community expectations. How can we determine whether a man ought to have been more attentive to the risks latent in his conduct except by gauging our expectations of what other men do in similar circumstances? We would be inclined to reprove a man for forgetting an appointment or failing to notice that someone needs aid only if it is customary in the group to take appointments seriously or to be attentive to the needs of others. Thus the duty to apprise oneself of a risk seems to derive from the demands of others, not from a principle of moral action.[36]

---

[31] (n 10 above) 423. On the avoidability inquiry, Fletcher does not significantly diverge from the basic account provided by Hart. Thus, for instance, although Fletcher uses the terminology of German and Soviet legal thought to draw a distinction between the 'legality of conduct and the culpability of the individual who engages in the conduct' (ibid 427), in essence the distinction exactly parallels that outlined by Hart discussed above. [32] ibid 423.
[33] ibid 426.   [34] ibid 425.   [35] ibid 419.   [36] ibid.

In fact, Fletcher points out that it is this emphasis on custom that leads German critic Professor Arthur Kaufmann to worry that punishing negligence exaggerates the impact of community values in the substantive criminal law. And though Fletcher himself expresses concern about granting expectations such prominence, his primary criticism is directed towards the idea that expectations are *uniquely* relevant to inadvertence rather than towards the idea that they *are* relevant. In fact, he returns to the idea that custom is definitive of duties in negligence when he says, 'Where the issue is the culpability of inadvertence, rather than the culpability of choice, the only standard of evaluation seems to be our expectations of what other members of the community would do under the same circumstances.'[37]

Thus, the strength of Fletcher's account is that it speaks to an important gap in the theoretical accounts of criminal negligence—the content and basis of the duty to take care. But it is troubling that Fletcher's articulation of the duty makes it so dependent on the 'conventional practices of the community'.[38] And though Fletcher does advert to this, he does not directly address the worrisome implications of a convention-based account of culpability. Let us consider what they might be. There are at least two obvious difficulties. First, even in the ordinary common law of negligence, courts and commentators have consistently rejected the idea that custom could be definitive of duties in negligence.[39] In his famous opinion in *The TJ Hooper*, Learned Hand J put the general position of the law of negligence as follows:

Indeed in most cases reasonable prudence is in fact common prudence; but strictly speaking it is never its measure; a whole calling may have unduly lagged in the adoption of new and available devices. It may never set its own tests, however pervasive its usages. Courts must in the end say what is required; there are precautions so imperative that even their universal disregard will not excuse their omission.[40]

And this important distinction between what is ordinarily done and what may be reasonably required as a matter of duty is consistently affirmed as central to negligence. Further, as Learned Hand J's formulation implies, this distinction is not trivial because of how it implicates the difference between the rule of law and the reign of custom. The role of courts, he insists, is not simply to enforce or apply custom, but to judge it.

As this rule of law connection suggests, there are also important reasons of principle to reject the view that custom defines the duty of care in the case

---

[37] (n 10 above) 425.

[38] ibid 419. There is another possible interpretation of Fletcher's view here—that is, that expectations and practices refer not to *actual* expectations of what people would do but rather to the *legitimate* expectations or *reasonable* practices. However appealing this view might be, it is difficult to ascribe it to Fletcher. In part this is because he does not actually qualify his understanding of expectations or practices in this way. More significantly, however, such an interpretation would render nonsensical the sharp distinction Fletcher draws between the moral basis of the duty in cases of advertence and the conventional basis of the duty in cases of inadvertence.

[39] See *The TJ Hooper* 60 F 2d 737 (2d Cir 1932); *Ware's Taxi Ltd v Gilliham* [1949] SCR 637.

[40] ibid 740.

of inadvertence. Fletcher himself notes that at least in some situations, rejection of the culpability of inadvertence 'would offend basic sensibilities of justice in cases of insensitive and arrogant perceptions of legal duties'.[41] Similarly, his conclusion that both choosing to take a particular risk and inadvertence as to risk might warrant the 'just censure of others' seems to point to a deeper, more principled, understanding of the culpability of inadvertence. But Fletcher's critique of the reasonable person suggests that his view of the customary underpinnings of culpable inadvertence ultimately wins out. The unity of the test, he insists, obscures the difference between evaluating risks and assessing the culpability of inadvertence. But for Fletcher this is not a simple matter of taxonomy precisely because on his account there is an important divergence between these two inquiries. Thus, his view is that where the issue concerns a consciously chosen risk, the reasonable person expresses the principle of balancing burdens and benefits to determine which risks are permitted. By contrast, in the case of the culpability of inadvertence, the reasonable man standard directs our attention to 'what average individuals would do if faced with the same circumstances'.[42] So 'the unity of the test is purchased at the expense of distorting the difference between a question about the utility of a risk and a question about one's expectation of inadvertence in a particular situation'.[43]

Yet the 'distortion' that Fletcher points to may actually reflect the deeper normative structure of the standard of care. The reasonable person itself may indeed be a device that obscures more than it reveals—an issue to which we shall return. But we should be loathe to dispense with the idea of reasonableness, since it can actually be understood as unifying, rather than distorting, the relationship between the various components of the standard of care. If there is truth in the reasonable person standard that helps to account for its persistence and appeal, much of that truth resides in the standard's invocation of the idea of reasonableness and with it the insistence on equal moral standing. As we have noted, work in philosophy and political theory has elaborated how the very idea of reasonableness that the standard enshrines is itself built upon a recognition of the equal standing of others and serves as one expression of our legal system's commitment to equal moral personality.[44] This link between reasonableness and the principle of equality is presumably why the most important defences of the standard invoke an egalitarian justification. Like Hart, sometimes Fletcher seems to reach for the kind of robust normative understanding of the culpability of inadvertence that the idea of reasonableness holds out. But Fletcher ultimately opts for the notionally simpler and perhaps more defensible idea of community standards. The difficulty, however, is that a standard of ordinariness or conventional practices, though it may coincidentally embody respect for equal moral standing, will not *necessarily* do so.

---

[41] (n 10 above) 422.   [42] ibid 426.   [43] ibid 426.

[44] See, for instance, John Rawls, *Political Liberalism* (New York: Columbia University Press, 1993) 50; Arthur Ripstein, *Equality, Responsibility and the Law* (Cambridge: Cambridge University Press, 1999) 7–8.

Ultimately then, Fletcher's insistence on the normative significance of conventional practices seems mistaken. But it is an important and telling kind of mistake. Fletcher makes explicit a feature of the standard that is typically only implicit, and it is a feature that helps to account for much of the egalitarian concern about it. As we have noted, courts and commentators seeking the basis of the standard often discuss reasonableness and ordinariness as though they were interchangeable. Similarly, many justifications for the standard invoke ideas of ordinariness and normalcy. One of Fletcher's contributions is to make explicit the particular role custom seems to play in delineating when inadvertence is culpable. In this way, his account of the foundation of culpable inadvertence actually articulates more sharply than egalitarians themselves do one possible—and especially troubling—understanding of the relationship between the objective standard and customary practices. For egalitarians much of the worry about the objective standard can be understood as a fear that the customary account may indeed be the only one available (or accessible). The consequence of this would be a standard that simply enforces ordinary behaviour and hence cannot condemn such behaviour as unreasonable. But much of this is not explicit. Instead, it must be reconstructed from a heterogeneous complex of anxieties about the standard, some of which are grounded in moral principle (also often unarticulated), and some of which are explicitly consequentialist. Fletcher's argument in favour of a customary standard for inadvertent fault thus provides a sharper focus for the egalitarian critique of the standard. In this way it also contributes to the possibility of a more nuanced reconstruction. Let us briefly examine the precise nature of the equality worry that a customary reading of inadvertence might pose.

2. *Customary inadvertence: An egalitarian critique*

A customary standard for culpable inadvertence may be troubling even in cases that do not raise any particularly sharp equality concerns. So while drivers may very often fail to notice crosswalks or stop signs, we would generally resist the idea that one driver could establish reasonableness simply by pointing to the similar behaviour of others. This suggests that the fact of converging choices alone cannot be given any particular moral weight. Of course, it may often be the case that common behaviour is prudent. Aberrance may, in this way, look like a useful proxy for culpability. But even if looking to commonness seems a relatively uncontroversial way of establishing reasonableness, there are serious difficulties with it. The simple example above illustrates that convergence is morally neutral in the sense that it may happen for good reasons (widespread respect for others) or for bad reasons (widespread self-preference). Thus, it seems essential to look beyond the fact of multiplicity of similar choices to the kinds of *reasons* that account for those choices. As the common law of negligence itself recognizes, the possibility of widespread carelessness is precisely what makes it so important to preserve a distinction between what is ordinarily done and what is reasonable.

But if giving too much weight to custom is worrisome even in 'garden variety' negligence cases, the problem is dramatically magnified by the existence of background discrimination. The view that common practices should be enforced as normative in the standard of care rests on an implicit confidence that the convergence of attitudes and actions will be 'positive'—that is, on the belief that people ordinarily do what respect for others requires, and that divergences from common practices will thus serve as a useful marker of wrongfulness. Although convergence is undoubtedly often positive, it has a more ominous significance where discrimination is in play. Discrimination by definition involves widely shared beliefs about the inferior worth of certain others. And the fact that discriminatory beliefs are in this way 'ordinary' means that they are extremely—even disproportionately—likely to be reflected in common or customary practices and beliefs. In this way, attentiveness to the existence of discrimination makes us alive to the possibility that convergence may be negative or positive.

Where convergence is negative, as it will be with background discrimination, basing culpability for inadvertence on customary or conventional practices will doom the standard of care to reflect the biases and prejudices of average members of the community—thus giving rise to the kind of dynamic that Rawls worried would undermine the egalitarian demands of 'justice as regularity'. An illustration can be found in the cases we examined earlier involving children. Much of what seems troubling in those cases arises because of how the standard, read as one of 'ordinariness', incorporates widespread stereotypes about gender-appropriate behaviour. The boy's action in *McHale v Watson* can be construed as 'reasonable' only where reasonableness is understood as ordinariness and where heedlessness of others is seen as a common or ordinary incident of boyhood. The backdrop of widely accepted beliefs about the growing boy's superior need for and entitlement to liberty shapes both the behaviour of the boy and the judge's understanding of it, and ultimately these beliefs receive normative expression through the standard of care. The difficulties in the companion cases involving playing girls and working children also seem indebted to too 'conventional' a reading of the standard in a context where ideas of appropriateness are strongly conditioned by gender and class, among other things.

However, it is the analysis of sexual assault that puts most sharply the worry about the equality effects of infusing the objective standard with customary norms. Let us consider the consequences of taking up Fletcher's suggestion that 'what is ordinarily done' provides the only available understanding of when inadvertence is culpable. A fitting place to begin this inquiry is with a hypothetical involving the defence of mistaken belief in consent in a jurisdiction that imposes a reasonableness requirement on the belief in consent.[45] A man who

---

[45] Such as the reasonable steps requirement in the Canadian Criminal Code provisions that were applied in *R v Ewanchuk* (n 8 above): see Criminal Code (n 6 above); see also Williams (n 6 above) 131, 549 for the position in England prior to *DPP v Morgan* [1976] AC 182.

forces sexual intercourse despite a woman's vigorous protests subsequently claims that he honestly and reasonably believed that she was agreeable despite her reaction. He expands upon this by stating that he knew she was divorced and therefore not a virgin, so it simply never occurred to him that it would be a 'big deal' for her to have sex with him. How should we assess his claim that it simply never occurred to him that the woman might not be consenting? Let us assume that he is credible (in order that we may focus on the culpability of his failure to advert to the possibility of non-consent). Are the customary beliefs of the community really the only standard against which to measure the reasonableness of his inadvertence? If so, then it will also follow that to the extent that his views about the sexual availability of divorced women are widely shared, his inadvertence will be reasonable and non-culpable. On the customary account, the standard for judging inadvertence necessarily gives legal standing to such views.

Clearly this is normatively unappealing. But allowing customary practices to determine when inadvertence is culpable also opens up the possibility of giving legal effect to views that are at odds with the fundamental concepts and values of our legal system. In order to see how a customary standard might enable this despite how uneasily it sits with the mistake of law rule, it is helpful to reflect for a moment on the general conception of consent in our legal system. This will also enable us to shape a response to one possible rejoinder to this mistake of law worry: it might be argued that basing culpability on custom cannot run afoul of the mistake of law rule precisely because, on an account like Fletcher's, customary norms are incorporated into the law and become part of the set of legal values that the mistake of law rule protects. But any such rejoinder must take the legal system to be simply a series of *ad hoc* norms with no necessary connection to each other or to underlying values—in essence not a system at all. This is certainly not Fletcher's own view. A closer examination of the concept of consent suggests that it is also an unlikely understanding more generally.

Consent, in its various guises, is generally understood as absolutely central to our legal system. Through consent, our law expresses its commitment to the equal and enduring autonomy of the individual. It is no accident that the egalitarian reforms of the twentieth century placed such significance upon legal rights to consent. These reforms were largely accomplished through expansion of the category of person to those whose entry had long been denied. The centrality of consent to full personhood is evident in the fact that the difficult shift from chattel (property) status to agent status so often centred on the effort to access the right to consent. This included various kinds of struggles for full legal rights to consent such as the right to contract, for instance, and the ability to refuse to be treated as property through rights to vindicate violations of autonomy.[46] These

---

[46] For an overview and critique, see Carol Pateman, *The Sexual Contract* (Stanford, Calif: Stanford University Press, 1988); Constance Backhouse, *Coloured Coded: A Legal History of Racism in Canada* (Osgoode Society, Toronto: Toronto University Press, 1999) and *Petticoats and Prejudice: Women and the Law in Nineteenth Century Canada* (Osgoode Society, Toronto: Toronto University

struggles are by no means complete, but the very fact that so much of the terrain has concerned access to full legal rights to consent reveals the centrality of these rights to the legal system's commitment to equal and autonomous personhood.

Because of this relation to core systemic values, the legal system cannot adopt just any notion of consent—nor does it do so. Instead, fundamental notions of autonomy and personhood demand that voluntariness be at the core of our conception of consent. We can see this expressed in the fact that the ordinary presumption of the law is non-consent; thus it is inherent in the very idea of consent that it be affirmatively given. Voluntariness also underpins other vital elements of the concept, such as the insistence that consent be personal and transactional. Thus, our legal system has a highly particularized—both as to event and as to person—understanding of consent. And the concept of consent is necessarily transactional rather than general. So we would not allow X to presume Y's consent to a transaction, say a share purchase, on the basis that Y had made an identical purchase the week before. Instead, we would insist that Y's right to withhold such agreement is not only inherent in the very idea of consent but is also crucial to the autonomy interests that consent enshrines and protects. Similarly, its significance to personal autonomy requires that consent be personal. Thus, we do not allow one adult to consent on behalf of another in the absence of a specific, structured agreement or some form of oversight.[47] Even then, the power to consent is so fundamental to personhood that any such transfer is regulated through legal devices such as fiduciary duties that are designed to protect the individual who is without this power.[48] Similarly, any abrogation of the power to consent, however well intentioned, inevitably raises concerns about paternalism, which is a way of expressing anxiety about the loss of full agency status.[49] So, a view that consent somehow extends across a range of discrete transactions or that people's agreement can generally be given by someone else would misapprehend consent in such a fundamental way that we would consider it at odds with both the basic legal concept and the values that underlie it. The invocation of the language of consent in such cases would thus probably not prevent us from seeing that such claims displace basic legal concepts

---

Press, 1991); Adrienne D Davis, 'The Private Law of Race and Sex: An Antebellum Perspective' (1999) 51 Stan L Rev 221.

[47] See, for instance, GB Robertson, *Mental Disability and the Law in Canada* (2nd edn, Scarborough: Carswell Thomson Professional Publishing, 1994); Michael L Perlin, *Mental Disability Law: Civil and Criminal* (Charlottesville, Calif: Mitchie Co 1994, Lexis Law Pub Supp 1994); *Re Eve* (1986) 31 DLR (4th) 1 (SCC) (discussing the importance of judicial oversight of substituted decision-making under the court's *parens patriae* jurisdiction).

[48] See, for instance, Wilson J in *Frame v Smith* [1987] 2 SCR 99; Robert A Pearce and John Stevens, *Pearce and Stevens: Trusts and Equitable Obligations* (London: Butterworths Law, 2002); Jill Martin, *Hanbury and Martin: Modern Equity* (16th edn, London: Sweet and Maxwell, 2001).

[49] See e.g. M Trebilcock, 'Coercion' in *The Limits of Freedom of Contract* (Cambridge, Mass: Harvard University Press, 1993) 78. Choice and autonomy are in this way so critical to our conception of the person that philosophers and legal and political theorists worry that to the extent we limit notions of choice and responsibility, we also threaten to obliterate the person: Honoré (n 20 above); Nagel (n 29 above).

and values with idiosyncratic ones—in effect just the kind of misunderstanding to which the mistake of law rule is addressed. Let us keep this in mind as we consider how certain claims and beliefs about consent might be at odds with the ordinary legal conception of consent and the values that underlie it. This in turn will help us explore how, despite similar tension with basic legal concepts and values, a customary standard might give effect to these very kinds of claims precisely because they are widespread.

We can see how a customary standard might in this way undercut the mistake of law rule and the values it protects by comparing two claims about consent— one idiosyncratic and one more widely held—that diverge from the ordinary understanding of consent outlined above. Let us begin with the idiosyncratic claim. Al has sex with Barb despite the fact that Barb is protesting. Barb subsequently claims that Al sexually assaulted her. Al defends himself by stating that he was sure that Barb was consenting because she had red hair. Al genuinely believes that all redheads are promiscuous and enjoy sex on any terms. So despite Barb's screams he proceeded. Will we allow Al to defend himself by saying that he was confident about Barb's consent because she has red hair? It seems extremely unlikely. Courts tend to dispose of particularly outlandish claims on credibility grounds.[50] Perhaps this is because in the absence of insanity courts tend not to believe that people actually hold aberrant moral views. But a want of credibility does not seem to get at the reason we cannot give legal effect to certain kinds of claims. After all, we would not want to recognize a claim like Al's even if it were honestly held. And Al will argue that since he actually believed Barb consented, he is not invoking norms at odds with the legal standard (such as a belief that women need not consent, for instance). Rather, Al will say that he accepts the legal requirement for consent and in that sense adheres to the law's values; he simply believed (wrongly as it turns out) that the standard was met in this case. But this claim needs to be examined more carefully.

If we think back to the core elements of the ordinary legal conception of consent, it becomes easier to articulate the essential reason Al's defence must fail regardless of how genuinely held his views may be. Though Al claims he believed Barb was consenting, his definition of consent turns out to lack the core legal qualities discussed above. Thus, while the core legal meaning demands that consent be personally granted for each discrete transaction, Al's conception of consent is entirely independent of what Barb says or does in the situation. Instead, Al bases his claim that Barb consented on the fact that she possesses certain personal qualities, in particular red hair. Although Al calls the inference that he draws from Barb's red hair 'consent', his use of the term has little in common with the legal category. The divergence between Al's concept of consent and the law's concept is revealed by asking whether Al's concept has space for the possibility of refusal, something which is ordinarily understood as

---

[50] An illustration can be found in *Morgan* itself (n 45 above).

conceptually central to consent. Is there anything that Barb could have done or said that Al would have counted as non-consent? The answer, it seems, is no—under Al's concept of consent, redheads cannot refuse sexual relations. In this way, Al's concept of consent denies consent's most vital attribute to a whole category of people regardless of how they respond in the discrete situation. It seems clear that the concept of consent that Al is using is neither personal nor transactional. More fundamentally, the irrebuttable presumption of consent that characterizes Al's concept fundamentally diverges from the egalitarian values that underpin the legal concept.[51] Thus, though Al uses the language of consent, we can see that his concept has little in common with the legal concept.

Al's defence rests on a claim to be judged by his own standard for consent, rather than by the legal one. Although a court in such cases may tend to invoke credibility to reject such claims, a better explanation can be found in the law's insistence that interaction be judged by law's standards, not by the idiosyncratic standards of different individuals. Al's claim reveals a fundamental mistake about the legal meaning of consent and the values of autonomy it protects. It is the nature of his mistake that justifies the conclusion that Al is culpable: his claim is based on a failure to recognize and accord respect to the important interests of others. This, then, is the underlying reason that Al cannot defend himself by claiming that all redheads consent freely to sex. Reliance on such a defence would effectively allow him to invoke norms and values at odds with those enshrined in the law—in other words, it would be tantamount to raising a mistake of law defence.

Al's case helps us see mistake of law reasoning at work in the background of the judicial refusal to allow defences that ultimately rest upon claims to be judged according to one's own concepts and values, rather than those of the law. But recall the idiosyncratic nature of Al's claim—it is unlikely to be widely held either in society or on the bench. As suggested at the outset, however, this important mistake of law effect seems prone to being unseated by a customary understanding of inadvertence. To see how, let us contrast Al's case with the situation where the views that diverge from fundamental legal concepts and values are much more widely held. Sexual assault again serves as a useful example, particularly because of the emphasis that feminist commentators place on the distortionary impact of discriminatory myths and stereotypes. Exploring how these stereotypes may feed into a customary standard for inadvertence will enable us to develop a sharper, more conceptual version of the feminist worry about reasonableness standards. We can do this by tracing how, even under a reasonableness standard, the existence of such stereotypes might work to displace the ordinary transactional and personal meaning of consent, notwithstanding the mistake of law effect that precluded just such a defence in Al's case.

---

[51] It is possible to expand upon the fundamental difficulty with Al's concept of consent by exploring whether this is a conception of consent that he would apply to himself and his personal interactions and transactions. The fact that the answer to this query will so clearly be in the negative uncovers the deep self-preference that lies at the heart of Al's position here. It is clearly also open to a Kantian objection, since his articulation of the concept is not generalizable.

As discussed above, feminists have illustrated how the construction of consent in sexual assault tends to focus on the relationship between the parties or on the use of force.[52] Thus, they point out that sexual assault by an acquaintance in almost any situation is extremely unlikely to be seen as rape.[53] If we view this in the light of the mistake of law concern, it seems plausible to say that the fact of a prior sexual relationship effectively displaces the ordinary personal and transactional meaning of consent. Thus, in contrast with the ordinary meaning of consent, here a prior relationship satisfies the consent requirement. And this is so even though a prior sexual relationship is a fact of personal history. As noted above, the transactional quality of the ordinary concept of consent means that consent in one situation cannot normally be inferred from the fact that one may have previously consented to similar interactions. But reminding ourselves of this suggests how much common ground there is between Al's claim and the claims that refer to the fact of a prior sexual relationship as relevant to consent. In both situations, the accused seeks to substitute his own conception of consent for the ordinary legal conception. But in contrast with Al's claim, we are much more likely to be tempted by a claim that infers consent from a prior sexual relationship despite a similar tension with the fundamental systemic values protected by the mistake of law rule.

This kind of analysis also seems applicable to situations where the 'mistake of fact' turns on the absence of forcible resistance. Feminists have long critiqued the fact that courts are hesitant to find a sexual assault where there was limited physical force exerted by the accused or where the complainant herself did not resist with physical force. In her opinion in *Ewanchuk*, Madam Justice L'Heureux-Dubé summarizes the essential point of the feminist literature on force and consent when she describes the stereotype that a woman has the responsibility 'not only to express an unequivocal "no", but also to fight her way out of a situation'.[54] And as discussed above, Susan Estrich notes that 'rape is most assuredly not the only crime in which consent is a defence; but it is the only crime that has required the victim to resist physically in order to establish non-consent'.[55] If we compare the ordinary legal conception of consent with the view that consent exists where there is no or little forcible resistance, it is possible to see the extent to which a forcible resistance defence invokes a concept of consent that diverges from the legal concept. So unlike the ordinary legal meaning of consent that reflects its attachment to autonomy in its general presumption of non-consent, a forcible resistance defence is premised on such a strong presumption of consent that it can be rebutted only by the exercise of physical force. However, as with the fact of a prior relationship, the forcible

---

[52] Vandervort (n 6 above) 259; Catharine A MacKinnon, 'Rape: On Coercion and Consent' in *Toward a Feminist Theory of the State* (Cambridge, Mass: Harvard University Press, 1989) ch 9; Susan Estrich, 'Rape' (1986) 95 Yale LJ 1087.

[53] Vandervort (n 6 above) 259; MacKinnon (n 52 above) 175–176. See also the discussion in ch 6 above.   [54] *Ewanchuk* (n 8 above) 374, citing Estrich (n 52 above) 1090.

[55] Estrich (ibid).

resistance defence seems to have much more credence despite this structural similarity to Al's claim. This credibility seems to derive from the fact that the forcible resistance claim invokes a stereotype about women and consent—essentially, that is, a belief that is widespread or customary.

At least some of the truth of Fletcher's customary reading of the culpability of inadvertence is found in the fact that these widespread mistakes about consent do get much greater traction from courts and commentators. To this extent, Fletcher presents exactly the account of culpability that egalitarians worry about yet rarely explicitly articulate. So, for instance, widespread mistakes may be even less likely to be seen as engaging a mistake of law concern. Even when they are, the ordinariness of the mistake seems to generate far more reluctance to condemn the divergent conception despite the very kind of tension with underlying values that engages the mistake of law rule. Thus, in cases involving a prior sexual relationship, courts often give surprising weight to the accused's claim of a belief in consent even where he has violently assaulted or abducted the complainant.[56] Similarly, where the accused did not use extreme force or where the complainant did not resist with significant force, courts are reluctant to dismiss the accused's belief in consent.[57] Comparing Al's case with these cases involving stereotypical assumptions about women and consent reveals an important egalitarian worry about a customary standard for inadvertence. The law's insistence on the 'fixity' of fundamental legal norms and values may be observed in cases like Al's which involve idiosyncratic normative views. However, the same cannot be said for cases where the divergent norms are more widely shared. If this is the case, then it may help to explain the emphasis that the feminist literature places upon stereotypes.

[56] See, for instance, the trial decision in *Sansregret v R* [1985] 1 SCR 570, where the trial judge acquitted the accused based on the argument that he had an honestly held belief that his former girlfriend had freely and genuinely consented to sexual intercourse. This was notwithstanding the fact that he had twice broken into her house and threatened her both verbally and with a knife prior to the intercourse, and that she had called the police and reported the rape subsequent to each occurrence. The Manitoba Court of Appeal overturned the trial judge's decision and entered a conviction for rape. The Supreme Court dismissed the accused's appeal, with Justice McIntyre stating that 'The appellant was aware of the likelihood of the complainant's reaction to his threats. To proceed with intercourse in such circumstances constitutes, in my view, self-deception to the point of wilful blindness': para 23. Another example can be found in *R v MacFie* [2001] AJ No 152 (CA). The accused violently abducted his estranged wife, drove her to a remote location, and had sexual intercourse with her. He murdered her three days later. MacFie was acquitted of sexual assault at trial on the basis that he had an honest belief in consent. The Alberta Court of Appeal unanimously overturned the acquittal. McFayden JA stated: 'Can the person who has violently abducted his victim claim any honest belief in consent while that abduction persists? It is difficult to imagine any circumstances in which an abductor or kidnapper would be permitted to rely on such a defence': para 27. But the trial judge's uncritical approval of the accused's belief in consent indicates exactly the circumstances in which such a claim will be given credence. The Court of Appeal implicitly reasserts the ordinary understanding of consent by pointing out that such an acquittal would be unthinkable if the accused had abducted a stranger.

[57] See, for instance, *Ewanchuk* (n 8 above) especially regarding the acquittal at trial, and the Court of Appeal decision upholding that acquittal.

If widely shared mistakes that contravene basic legal norms are particularly likely to escape the mistake of law effect, then this may account for the feminist observation that stereotypes result in some significant blameworthiness going unpunished. The difficulty in the feminist literature on stereotypes has been specifying just what their legal relevance is. For this reason the feminist emphasis on stereotypes has not always been easy to square with the legal analysis. However, a response to this apparent mismatch could be that such stereotypes may displace the important mistake of law effect that would otherwise prevent an accused from insisting on being judged by his own divergent norms. This suggests that at least some of the feminist literature's difficulty in accounting for the relationship it posits between stereotypes and missed culpability is attributable to more general difficulties conceptualizing culpability in cases of inadvertence. Fletcher's insistence on the customary basis of culpability in cases of inadvertence argues in favour of a particularly influential possibility. Exploring the egalitarian implications of such an approach helps us to articulate an important set of concerns about how we understand culpability.

Fletcher's account enables us to see why discriminatory beliefs may pose a particular challenge to developing an account of blameworthiness: because such beliefs are widely shared, they are especially likely to be incorporated into a legal standard understood in 'conventional' terms. But the fact that discriminatory beliefs are at odds with the core egalitarian values of the legal order means that any such incorporation threatens to displace in a selective manner the fundamental concepts and values that enshrine core rule of law values. In this way, infusing the standard with customary norms opens up the possibility of a limited exception to the mistake of law rule. Indeed, this seems to be exactly what feminists worry about when they emphasize the corrosive effects of stereotypes on equality and culpability. This is in and of itself problematic because of the mistake of law rule's egalitarian function. As Wilson J and others note, it is vital to equality that the normative content of the legal standard be independent from individual valuations.

However, the sexual assault example also points to a deeper problem with equality. This is because it suggests that exceptions to the mistake of law rule will be particularly likely to occur in the very cases in which they will be the most troubling. Where there is a background set of discriminatory norms, convergence will exist precisely because the underlying views are commonly held. So discriminatory norms will almost inevitably have the widely shared quality that Fletcher identifies as sufficient to lend them legal significance. Thus, although much of the appeal of a strong version of the mistake of law rule is found in the rule's ability to insist on the invariance of the legal system's egalitarian values, a customary standard for inadvertence effectively allows an exception to the rule that has particular impact on discriminatory mistakes. Yet these are the very cases that most seriously threaten the core egalitarian commitments of the legal system—commitments that the mistake of law rule aims to protect. This suggests that an account of culpability that can capture only idiosyncratic and not widespread wrongdoing, though perhaps also flawed in its own terms, is also unable to provide an egalitarian understanding of blame-worthiness. In fact, exploring the implications of the customary account of inadvertence provides us with a kind of warning: it illustrates the troubling influence custom often plays in delineating, explicitly or not, when heedlessness is culpable. If the customary account of blame is in this way too thin to be responsive to egalitarian aspirations, we need to look further to see whether it is possible to identify a foundation for culpable inadvertence that is conceptually independent of conventional attitudes.

III. The indifference account

Examining the egalitarian implications of a customary account of culpable inadvertence in a context of discrimination forces us to take apart the equation we often implicitly make between commonness and reasonableness. Developing an adequate understanding of the fault of inadvertence will require something more than either avoidability alone or simple convergence. We have made some progress: the avoidability account provides us with an important precondition for inadvertent fault, and the customary account makes us aware of how the incorporation of conventional beliefs or practices can selectively undermine important egalitarian values of the legal system. But the normative core of inad-vertence remains obscure. Despite making important contributions, the accounts of culpability for inadvertence that we have examined so far avoid the most difficult question—when are we entitled to say that failing to notice a risk is blameworthy? What is it exactly that distinguishes culpable from innocent obliviousness? The last accounts we shall examine, though they vary in a number of respects, share this important feature: they attempt to isolate the normative failing betrayed in culpable inadvertence. For this reason, they may be referred to as indifference accounts, since they focus on indifference to others as central to explicating culpable inadvertence. Because these accounts more directly engage the normative issues, they seem particularly useful to an egalitarian reconstruction of the standard.

A. When is inadvertence culpable?

Indifference accounts of culpable inadvertence largely take place in the context of the debate about whether inadvertence can ever serve as a justifiable ground of criminal liability.[58] There are several versions of the indifference account.[59] Rather than focus on the intricacies of the various accounts and their strengths and weaknesses, for our purposes here it seems more helpful to draw out the

---

[58] Duff, *Intention, Agency and Criminal Liability* (n 15 above); Simester (n 5 above) 85; Horder, 'Gross Negligence and Criminal Culpability' (n 5 above).

[59] For an overview of the various approaches to criminal fault, see J Horder, 'Criminal Culpability: The Possibility of a General Theory' (1992) 12 Law & Philosophy 193.

main thread that links them. Given the centrality of culpability to criminal liability, it is hardly surprising that these accounts share a focus on the normative content of inadvertence. Thus, indifference-based accounts argue that the distinguishing feature of culpable inadvertence is the fact that it manifests an attitude toward others that we can justifiably condemn. Though many discuss indifference as a form of *mens rea*, Tony Duff's work on the topic still provides the inspiration for most indifference-based accounts of the culpability of inadvertence.[60] Focusing on Duff's account thus provides a fitting point of departure for examining the indifference account of the culpability of inadvertence.

The indifference account seeks to elucidate the distinctive form of culpability that arises when an agent fails to notice a risk because she is indifferent to the interests of others. The challenge is to illustrate how under certain conditions heedlessness can betray culpability in the form of 'practical indifference'. Implicit in this approach is the idea that despite the importance of knowingly taking a risk, a focus on knowledge alone will be insufficient to provide a complete normative understanding of responsible agency. Although avoidability or capacity also serves as a vital precondition for responsibility here as well, the indifference account places its focus on the *attitude* displayed by any particular action: 'if I unjustifiably do what I know will injure another, I do not manifest the hostile intent which I know a direct attack on her would exhibit; but I manifest my utter indifference to her interests in being thus willing to injure her.'[61]

The core idea here is that what an agent notices and acts upon reflects what she cares about; consequently, 'failure to notice something can display my utter indifference to it'.[62] This, some subjectivists may complain, amounts to imposing liability in the absence of true culpability because it does not involve any 'positive state of mind' but rather the *absence* of a mental state of advertence or care.[63] But Duff and other defenders of indifference as a form of *mens rea* respond by noting that although the legal norm is invariant (which, as discussed above, it must be), the standard is nonetheless subjective or personal to the accused in the way required by criminal law.[64] This is because the indifference relates to the

---

[60] For a thoughtful overview, see Horder, 'Gross Negligence' (n 5 above) especially 500 ff.

[61] Duff, *Intention, Agency and Criminal Liability* (n 15 above) 141–142.   [62] ibid 163.

[63] ibid 155. See, for instance, A Brudner, 'Agency and Welfare in Penal Law' in S Shute, J Gardner, and J Horder (eds), *Action and Value in Criminal Law* (Oxford: Clarendon Press, 1993) 21 and the response by J Horder in 'Gross Negligence' (n 5 above).

[64] Duff, *Intention, Agency and Criminal Liability* (n 15 above) 163. Though negligence and recklessness are closely related in that both involve thoughtlessness, Duff insists that there remains a 'categorical distinction'. While recklessness 'displays a gross indifference to that particular risk or to the particular interests' that the action threatens, negligence involves a 'less specific kind of carelessness or inattention which does not relate the agent so closely, as an agent, to the risk which she creates': ibid 165. However, this seems to point to a distinction of degree. A more proximate relationship between the defendant and the risk she imposes is certainly relevant to the degree of culpability, but the underlying account of culpability seems the same. On this view, criminal law's insistence on the kind of proximity associated with recklessness is probably based on the principle of proportionality, not on a categorical difference between the nature of the fault requirement in civil and criminal law.

defendant's *own* attitude to the victim's protected interests. As Jeremy Horder puts it, the subjective element in indifference lies 'not in any necessary advertence to possible harmful consequences, but . . . in an uncaring attitude towards the victim's relevant protected interests'.[65] The subjectivity of indifference is thus found not in a simple cognitive state of mind, but rather in a complex affective state of mind.[66] That culpable state of mind is an 'uncaring attitude' toward the protected interests of the victim.[67] Similarly, in the sexual assault context, Duff describes indifference as consisting of 'a serious disregard or disrespect for sexual interests and integrity'.[68] And in their analysis of the 'wrongness' of rape, John Gardner and Stephen Shute also defend the form of objectivity inherent in indifference when they point out that 'the defendant's attitude, the way he looks upon others, is at the heart of our approach to his mistakes'.[69]

Recall Fletcher's criticism of the incoherence of the reasonable person test. In his view, this incoherence arose because of how the test sought to unify two conceptually distinct questions: the culpability of taking an unreasonable risk and that of failing to notice a risk. However, the indifference account may be seen as grounding the unity of the reasonable person test by revealing a deeper conceptual connection that justifies both the unification of these two inquiries and the reference to reasonableness. Thus, the unifying and underlying idea of practical indifference to the interests of others may articulate more precisely the normative content at the heart of the idea of reasonableness that the 'reasonable person' seeks to express. This kind of practical indifference is unreasonable, and ultimately culpable, because disregard of the core interests of others betrays a failure to attend to their equal standing. Given this egalitarian dimension, it is hardly surprising that the indifference account has primarily been developed and defended in the sexual assault context. As that context illustrates, the essential wrongfulness of the attitude of indifference implicates equality and personhood. It is for this reason feminist commentators and indifference theorists alike tend to identify the 'category error' of objectification—using a person as a thing—as the core of the attitude of indifference manifested in many unreasonable mistakes about consent in sexual assault.[70]

For a view of the relation of crime and tort along these lines, see J Gardner and S Shute, 'The Wrongness of Rape' in J Horder (ed), *Oxford Essays in Jurisprudence* (4th Series, Oxford: Oxford University Press, 2000) 193, 217.

[65] Horder, 'Gross Negligence' (n 5 above) 501.

[66] ibid 501. Horder points out that the simplicity of foresight or knowledge as an adequate basis for criminal liability is actually quite deceptive. Foresight alone, he suggests, is actually 'too thin and insubstantial a basis for a theory of *mens rea*': 510.

[67] ibid 501. Often this attitude is unpacked through a practical reasoning model: see Horder ibid; Simester (n 5 above); J Gardner, 'The Mysterious Case of the Reasonable Person' (2001) 51 UTLJ 273: 'reasonable person is one whose actions, beliefs, emotions and attitudes are justified'.

[68] *Intention, Agency and Criminal Liability* (n 15 above) 169.

[69] Gardner and Shute, 'The Wrongness of Rape' (n 64 above) 214, citing Duff, 'Recklessness and Rape' (n 15 above) and *Intention, Agency and Criminal Liability* (n 15 above).

[70] See, for instance, Duff, *Intention, Agency and Criminal Liability* (ibid) 171; Gardner and Shute 'The Wrongness of Rape' (n 64 above) 205, arguing that no wrong instantiates the 'central moral imperative of the Kantian argument so clearly and unequivocally as rape'. The wrongness of

The connection between reasonableness and indifference also helps explain the egalitarian demands the indifference account imposes on the kinds of reasons agents can invoke to justify their actions. Reasonableness on this view is a normative idea that embodies as its core commitment the equal standing of other agents. A belief will thus not be reasonable simply because it may seem plausible. Reasonableness refers not to the credibility of a belief but rather to 'its moral propriety as an *agent's* belief'.[71] If the idea of reasonableness in this sense provides a normative standard that constrains the kinds of reasons that agents can invoke as justification, then it may actually express the continuity between the various different tasks that the reasonable person test is asked to perform. By illustrating how culpable indifference to others can be manifested not only in an agent's response to a known risk but also in her failure to notice that a significant risk exists, the indifference account helps to reveal the underlying normative continuity of the reasonableness test across different kinds of inquiries.

If an indifference account holds out the possibility of a more egalitarian construction of the standard, the primacy it places on the normative quality of an agent's choices and reasons for action also poses an important challenge: how can we determine that an agent fails to notice a risk *because* she is indifferent to it? Most accounts of negligence, including Hart's, begin by positing the reasonable person with normal capacities—but this idea is complicated precisely because of its mixture of normative ('reasonable') and non-normative ('normal') attributes. Indifference accounts instead fix their sights on the normative core of the standard. Because they attempt to specify the relatively general idea of 'reasonableness' by articulating just what makes a mistake unreasonable in the appropriate sense, indifference accounts have the virtue of providing more guidance than the idea of reasonableness alone. Duff's 'appropriate general test of recklessness' provides an illustration: '... did the agent's conduct (including any conscious risk-taking, any failure to notice an obvious risk created by her action, and any unreasonable belief on which she acted) display a seriously culpable practical indifference to the interests which her action in fact threatened?'[72] However, since indifference accounts have generally been focused on defending indifference as a form of *mens rea*, many of the methodological questions are still rather unexplored. Nonetheless, it is possible to construct some aspects of the method by examining the various defences of the indifference account.

---

objectification on these terms is the use of people without at the same time respecting their essential non-use value—in other words, 'treating them as something other than people, it means treating them as things': ibid 204.

[71] Duff, *Intention, Agency and Criminal Liability* (n 15 above) 170. As suggested above in this chapter, there may of course be a connection in at least some cases in that beliefs that obviously lack moral propriety as an agent's belief may also be found incredible. But the danger that the discussion of Fletcher suggested is that a common belief lacking moral propriety is much more likely to be seen as credible or understandable. As discussed below, in these contexts in particular it is critical to insist on the difference between understandability and reasonableness.   [72] ibid 172.

Because of the centrality of risk to the indifference account, the analysis begins by assessing the significance of the risk that the agent failed to recognize. Essentially this inquiry asks whether the nature of the risk imposed by the agent was such that it generated a demand for caution requiring the agent to justify her failure to observe such caution. Relevant here are questions like how serious the risk was, how obvious it was, and the importance of the interest it threatened.[73] We can begin to get a clearer picture by working through an example of how an indifference account might analyse a mistake. Let us begin with the centrality of the risk to the intended action. There is an important distinction between risks that are only contingently related to an intended activity and those that are inherent in it. Thus, for instance, the risk that a driver poses to school children is inherent in the activity of driving in a school zone, since it is the *very thing* for which the driver ought to look out. We can gauge the centrality of the risk by assessing the kind of reaction we would have to a driver who said that this risk did not even cross her mind. We would demand that the driver justify her obliviousness. In the absence of such a justification, her blankness actually seems to condemn, not exonerate, her. This might be contrasted, for instance, with the risk of a tire flying off a moving vehicle and injuring someone. Here, unless there was some prior indication of risk, it seems unlikely there would be the same kind of demand for justification from the driver, for we cannot say that this was the *very thing* she should have been watching for. Where a risk is an inherent part of an intended action, heedlessness of it will generate a more pressing demand for caution and hence for justification of failure to observe that caution.

In the light of this, let us consider how we would assess the risk in Al's case. His intended activity is having sexual intercourse with Barb. As we have seen, he makes a mistake about her consent. So to begin the risk analysis we must ask whether consent is central to sexual activity or is a merely contingent circumstance that might legitimately not have been at the fore of Al's mind. Indeed, focusing on the centrality of risk helps to make sense of the emphasis that feminists and other critics place on the significance of consent. So, as several commentators have noted, mistakes about consent must be understood in the light of the fact that sexual intercourse is *essentially* a consensual activity between partners, an activity that must be structured by their mutual consent.[74] Thus, consent must be 'intrinsic to the man's intended action, rather than a merely contingent circumstance'.[75] It is the centrality of consent to sexual relations,

---

[73] ibid. Note the similarity between how the indifference account assesses the culpability of failing to recognize a risk and how cases like *Bolton v Stone* [1951] AC 850 (HL) approach the culpability of miscalculating the acceptability of a known risk. This fact seems to provide a more concrete illustration of the conceptual connection between the various standard of care inquiries that Fletcher questioned.

[74] Duff *Intention, Agency and Criminal Liability* (n 15 above) 169; T Pickard, 'Culpable Mistakes and Rape: Relating Mens Rea to the Crime' (1980) 30 UTLJ 75, 76.

[75] Duff *Intention, Agency and Criminal Liability* (n 15 above) 169.

along with the fact that attentiveness to consent can reasonably be expected of all adults, that presumably leads Gardner and Shute to suggest that rape may well be inexcusable.[76] This all suggests that when Al concludes Barb is consenting, he mistakes the absolutely central feature of his intended activity—the very thing to which he should have been most attentive. This thus generates a demand for justification: how can Al account for the fact that he missed something so central to his intended action as consent? This question leads us to the second stage of the inquiry. Can Al come up with a justification for his persistence, something that establishes that his heedlessness was not the result of indifference towards Barb's interests? He must show that his heedlessness was consistent with respect for the fundamental importance of consent.

Before we consider what is involved in this second 'indifference' stage of the analysis, however, let us briefly examine some other elements of the assessment of risk. As we have seen, failure to notice a risk that is central to the activity in question raises the prospect of indifference and hence calls for justification to rebut that possibility. However, even a peripheral risk, if sufficiently obvious, may generate such a demand. Think back to our example of the driver with the runaway tire. Even though the risk of a runaway tire is normally peripheral to driving a car, the situation seems very different if the driver had persisted despite the clunking and wobbling of her front wheel. Here, the obviousness of the risk in and of itself creates a significant reason for the driver to stop and prevent the risk from materializing. Thus, if she continues to drive, she will need to account for that decision. The obviousness of the risk also has implications for a case like Al's. Because he fails to notice a risk inherent to his intended action, he already bears a heavy justificatory burden. But the burden of accounting for his persistence will also increase, because the risk of non-consent was not merely the very thing he should have been looking out for, but was also extremely obvious given Barb's screams and protests.[77] A similar analysis also applies to the seriousness of the interest implicated. Risk analysis under an indifference account is 'interest sensitive' and in this way mirrors the standard of care more generally.[78] So where the risk threatens a central human interest—like physical integrity—its imposition may generate a demand for justification even though the risk may be less central to the intended activity, or less obvious. Thus, Al's burden of justification is also heavier because physical integrity and personal autonomy are seriously threatened whenever a person is 'used'—which is what occurs when a person is put to another's purposes without consent.[79] The risk analysis under

---

[76] Gardner and Shute (n 64 above) 213.

[77] In this way the indifference analysis helps to explain the significance of the myth that women like forced sex. The myth defeats the obviousness argument by providing a 'plausible' (though importantly, not reasonable) reason why even someone who accepted consent as central to sex might mistake non-consent for consent. The myth effectively transforms an 'obvious' indication of non-consent (screaming and protesting) into an indicator of consent.

[78] See Stephen R Perry, 'The Moral Foundations of Tort Law' (1992) 77 Iowa L Rev 449.

[79] See Gardner and Shute (n 64 above) 203–205, discussing M Nussbaum, 'Objectification' (1995) 24 Philosophy & Public Affairs 249.

an indifference account in this way helps explain the normative significance of certain features of 'mistake of fact' situations that feminists have long commented on.[80]

Thus, the first step of the indifference account consists in assessing the risk generated by the agent and asking what kind of demands for caution are thereby created. The more serious a risk is, the more obvious it is, and the more central the risk is to the agent's activity, the greater will be the demand to justify the failure to advert to it. Because it focuses on the normative failing exhibited in culpable inadvertence, the indifference account quite explicitly calls for *justification* rather than simple explanation. The agent must show that her inattention to the risk was *not* the result of indifference to the interests of the person she put in jeopardy. The risk may be such that it effectively imposes a justificatory burden on the agent, but the burden is a 'tactical' rather than a legal one.[81] That is, the evidence concerning the risk itself may impose strategic or tactical demands that the defendant provide a justification that excludes the inference of indifference that would otherwise be drawn from the facts. Although this task of justification does implicate 'character', it does so in quite a different way than in character-based theories of culpability.[82] Unlike at least some versions of character theory that inquire into the general or stable character and attitudes of the agent, an indifference account focuses on the character of the agent's choices and deliberations in imposing the relevant risk. The question therefore is whether the choices and actions that gave rise to her mistake betray her indifference towards others. Can she give an account of her inattentiveness that is consistent with proper respect for the interests of others?

Where the risk the agent misses is a serious one, assessing the 'practical attitude' an action displays requires asking whether anything other than indifference could account for the failure to notice the risk.[83] In the cases we examined earlier, for instance, an agent might argue that she failed to appreciate the risk because she was understandably distracted by an emergency or accident.[84]

---

[80] As discussed in the text, feminists like Pickard (n 74 above) point out that sexual interaction clearly is a situation that involves the risk of non-consent. Indeed, an actor with capacity who does not recognize this is surely making a prudential mistake about the sexual autonomy of women rather than some kind of cognitive mistake. Further, as discussed above, an actor who knows there is a risk of non-consent but somehow miscalculates that risk is almost certainly also making a miscalculation that rests on a prudential mistake about the relative importance of one's own needs and desires and the interests of others. This accounts for the 'self-interested' quality of such mistakes noted by Christine Boyle, 'The Judicial Construction of Sexual Assault Offences' in Julian V Roberts and Renate M Mohr (eds), *Confronting Sexual Assault: A Decade of Legal and Social Change* (Toronto: University of Toronto Press, 1994) and even by Richard Tur who benignly refers to these mistakes as 'wishful': 'Rape, Reasonableness and Time' (1981) 1 Oxford J Legal Studies 432.

[81] For a parallel in the civil law of negligence, see S Schiff, 'A *Res Ipsa Loquitur* Nutshell' (1976) 26 UTLJ 451, 454.

[82] Horder, 'Gross Negligence' (n 5 above) 504–506; Duff, *Intention, Agency and Criminal Liability* (n 15 above) 166; Gardner and Shute (n 64 above).

[83] Duff *Intention, Agency and Criminal Liability* (n 15 above) 166.

[84] See, for instance, the discussion in ch 1 above n 68.

Similarly, a child or a developmentally disabled agent could refute indifference by pointing out that she failed to recognize the risk because of her limited cognitive or perceptive capacities. An illustration can be found in Duff's analysis of *Elliott v C*.[85] That case concerned the responsibility of a 14-year-old girl of limited intelligence who burned down a shed by lighting a fire in it. The English Court of Appeal held that the objectivity of the *Caldwell* definition of recklessness was such that the girl must be convicted because the risk would have been obvious to a person of ordinary prudence.[86] But Duff suggests that where someone's age or intellectual capacity is such that she would not notice the risk even if she gave thought to it, then she should not be judged as reckless despite the fact that the risk would be obvious to an 'ordinary prudent individual'.[87] In such circumstances, heedlessness does not 'manifest a mindless indifference' to the risk.[88] An indifference account also seems to make sense of *Roberts v Ramsbottom* and the eventual demise of the holding in that case.[89] In fact, indifference seems at the heart of what was unsettling about the holding in that case, for Mr Ramsbottom did have an account of his risky driving that excluded indifference to others as a reason for his actions. This is because his stroke rendered him, in the words of the court, 'unable to appreciate that he should have stopped'.[90] Since his inattentiveness resulted from a sudden cognitive and physical incapacity, we cannot infer that he failed to avert the risk because of his disregard of others. Instead, like the girl in *Elliott*, his condition is such that he would not have understood the risk even if he had given thought to it. Consequently, an indifference-based account of culpability would not hold him responsible, for no moral significance can be attached to his failure to avert the risk.

Developing an indifference account makes it possible to sharpen our sense of what is normatively at stake in carelessness and to carry this through the analysis. Despite the sophistication of his account in other respects, Hart ultimately falls back on avoidability in order to explain the culpability of the person who says 'I just decided to kill; I couldn't help deciding'. But avoidability is so conceptually (and normatively) limited that it has difficulty providing a satisfactory answer to why a person who credibly makes such a claim is culpable. An indifference account, however, may have more success here. Suppose an agent claims that he cannot help his carelessness of others and thus should be exonerated because he lacks the moral capacity to avoid imposing the risk in question. Focusing on indifference enables us to distinguish between explanation and justification, and to note how this kind of explanation actually provides a reason to condemn the agent, not exonerate him. Unlike cognitive and physical capacities, whose absence is not generally a reason for condemnation, the absence

---

[85] *Elliott v C* (1983) 77 Cr App R 103.

[86] ibid; *R v Caldwell* [1982] AC 341. See also Duff, *Intention, Agency and Criminal Liability* (n 15 above) 146–147.   [87] Duff (ibid) 164.

[88] ibid.   [89] See ch 1 above n 14.   [90] [1980] 1 A11 ER 7 (QBD).

of moral capacity does provide a reason to condemn an agent.[91] Indeed, we may rightly blame the agent as much for a general failure to care about others as for a more localized failure to exercise a general capacity to care.

This increased normative precision also brings more clarity to concepts like ignorance or stupidity, which are often called into play in discussions of carelessness. As noted earlier, the ability to develop a more sophisticated account of ignorance seems particularly important to reconstructing a more egalitarian conception of responsibility. Current accounts of responsibility, however, tend to have rather blunt understandings of ignorance. Thus, proponents of more expansive conceptions of responsibility often seem prepared simply to condemn ignorance or stupidity.[92] On the other end of the spectrum, as we have seen, commentators like Glanville Williams seem to assume that pointing to stupidity inevitably establishes a reason for exoneration. However, paying attention to indifference helps account for the underlying sense in the feminist literature and elsewhere that terms like 'ignorance' and 'stupidity' are actually quite complex. So, as we see in cases such as *Elliott* and *Roberts*, ignorance can sometimes be non-culpable in the sense that it betrays no indifference to others. In cases like these, the agents can point to a reason unrelated to indifference to others to explain why they may have failed to notice otherwise obvious risks. They can justify their indifference as consistent with respect for others. On other occasions, however, it may be that the only explanations an agent could come up with to account for ignorance reveal the agent's actions as premissed on the kind of attitude towards others that we properly condemn.

An illustration of this kind of culpable ignorance can be found by thinking back to Al's case. There Al claims complete ignorance of Barb's non-consent. When Al attempts to account for how he could have made a mistake about something as central as consent in the face of such an obvious and serious risk, he will invoke his belief about redheaded women in sexual situations. We need to ask about the propriety of this as an agent's belief: is it a belief that an agent attentive to the end status of other agents could hold? The answer must surely be 'no'. Al's core belief is that redheads do not have the same right to withhold consent as other persons (including, undoubtedly, himself). But such a belief implicitly denies the equal personhood or end status of certain others. This is precisely the kind of attitude that we count as culpable indifference and properly condemn. A similar analysis will often hold where the mistake about consent involves a situation of obvious non-consent with the accused's former

---

[91] I say generally here because we assume that agents have a similar opportunity to develop moral capacities and thus can be held responsible for the failure to do so. In extreme situations, however, there may be a reason to displace this assumption. For a possible example, see Susan Wolf's discussion of JoJo the son of a ruthless dictator: 'Sanity and the Metaphysics of Responsibility' in Ferdinand Schoeman (ed), *Responsibility, Character, and the Emotions* (Cambridge: Cambridge University Press, 1987) 46–62 and 53–59. Wolf suggests that where an agent receives a perverse moral education, the analogue to insanity should incline us to refuse to hold him responsible for his immorality.   [92] Gardner and Shute (n 64 above) 213.

partner. Again, it is crucial to ask whether the accused's explanation has room for the former partner to refuse consent. A claim that withholds any meaningful possibility of non-consent from an individual or group necessarily denies them an important dimension of personhood (namely, sexual autonomy). A mistake that turns on a belief in the fundamental inequality of others is accordingly premissed on an indifference towards others. An indifference account thus enables us to distinguish mistakes that have this culpable character (like *Vaughan v Menlove* or *Morgan*) from those that do not (like *Roberts v Ramsbottom* or *Elliott v C*, for instance), and in so doing, helps to draw the line between culpable and non-culpable ignorance. We have noted how feminists and other egalitarians suggest that the problem of distinguishing between different types of ignorance is central to reworking responsibility along more egalitarian lines. Viewed in this light, the ability of an indifference account to bring normative precision to our assessments of mistakes and ignorance undoubtedly counts as one of its advantages.

B. Culpability and indifference: Some additional challenges

Unlike its competitor accounts based on choice and custom, an indifference-based account of culpable inadvertence better enables us to determine when heedlessness betrays disregard of others. Thus, as we saw in the sexual assault context, attentiveness to indifference helps to reveal when mistakes about consent are predicated on the kind of stereotypical assumptions that often characterize discrimination. In this sense, the culpability so often expressed in indifference or profound disregard of others may be uniquely well suited to capturing the blameworthy injuries so often suffered by the victims of discrimination. The capacity of indifference accounts to highlight underlying reasons enables them to identify wrongs that spring from widespread beliefs—beliefs that agents (and those judging them) may not think of as culpable precisely because they are so common. Infusing the objective standard with an indifference-based understanding of culpability may well assist in the development of a more egalitarian conception of responsibility.

Elaborating the potential of an indifference account also provides us with a deeper understanding of why feminists and other egalitarians may retain hope about the objective standard. As we have seen, developing an account of culpable ignorance or heedlessness seems especially important to capturing the kind of missed blameworthiness that particularly concerns egalitarians. Exploring the implications of basing the culpability of inadvertence on customary beliefs or practices alerted us to the danger that such a conception of fault poses to core legal values. By examining how this would play out in the context of sexual assault, we were able to see the particular dangers that any recourse to custom might pose to core egalitarian values, including to the mistake of law rule itself. The customary account also made us aware of the strength of the temptation to exempt common wrongs from the scope of culpability. By contrast, the indifference account rigorously focuses on the normative quality of the ignorance or heedlessness betrayed in a particular choice. This quality (at least theoretically) holds out the hope of a standard for culpable inadvertence that is capable of condemning not only idiosyncratic but also common mistakes about the equal worth of others. Thus, the indifference account looks in this way far more promising for equality seekers.

However, despite the apparent ability of the indifference account to capture the kinds of wrongs that so often characterize discrimination, its very articulation arguably provides as many reasons for worry as for hope. The most troubling of these relate to the way in which our ˌassessment of fault and responsibility is complicated by pervasive moral mistakes of the kind that characterize discrimination. Although the temptation to forgive common mistakes is conceptually built into the customary account, the force of the idea suggests that it may exert itself more generally. In fact, it is possible to see its continuing influence in two complications that equally trouble the indifference account. Most difficult perhaps is the way that the problems of responsibility and discrimination intersect to undermine our confidence in our ideas of fault. At a certain point, the pervasiveness of moral mistakes seems to complicate our ability to attribute blame. Indeed, something like this may actually lay at the heart of subjectivist anxieties about unwitting culpability. Another difficulty that is less profound, but perhaps no less damaging, is found in a set of concerns about how the commonness of the moral mistake may make it especially difficult to identify the wrong as wrong. Let us briefly consider these in turn.

1. *Should we excuse widespread moral ignorance?*

As discussed above, the fact that certain kinds of mistakes are widespread may make it more difficult to apply the ordinary mistake of law rule. Although the subjectivist's concern with awareness of risk arguably misstates the core difficulty with the objective standard, there may nonetheless be a deeper worry about culpability that perhaps accounts for at least some of the unease in these cases. Indeed, this may be why it seems so difficult to make the mistake of law point in the sexual assault context. One way to read the difficulty of 'seeing' the moral and legal quality of mistake turns on the pervasiveness of the relevant stereotypes and the fact that decision-makers are equally susceptible to them.[93] As we will discuss, this undoubtedly explains much of the difficulty of making evident the nature of many mistakes about consent in the sexual assault context. However, we should be hesitant to think that this fully accounts for these worries. Even if, as suggested above, it is possible to make a perfectly respectable mistake of law point in many cases, it is hard to deny that there remains something unsettling about culpability—something that may not be fully answered by the ordinary mistake of law analysis.

---

[93] See, for instance, Madam Justice L'Heureux-Dubé's discussion of the lower courts' reasoning in *Ewanchuk* (n 8 above) paras 82–84 and 88–96.

We can explore this unease by paying attention to a way in which the widespread nature of the moral mistake may to some degree undermine the justifications that ordinarily make the mistake of law rule relatively untroubling. Thus, for instance, the mistake of law rule is normally not afflicted with any difficulties arising out of fair notice because the *mala in se* limitation restricts the application of the rule to cases where the acts are wrong in and of themselves. This effectively eliminates any serious difficulties with fair notice because in normal circumstances we can legitimately expect people to know what is inherently right and wrong. We can therefore justifiably hold them to that knowledge without specific information. However, our confidence about fair notice may be somewhat undermined when the wrongdoing is widespread. This is because the obviousness of basic moral norms, which is what ordinarily satisfies us about the adequacy of notice, may be compromised when those norms are consistently violated or when there is some customary account (like rape myths) for why they do not actually count as wrongs. This is not to say that there is no basis for upholding the moral norm over the customary one. But it does require us to recognize that different considerations may be in play, and that different kinds of arguments may be required to make adhering to the ordinary mistake of law rule normatively compelling.

In situations where the relevant mistake is widespread, there is a second feature that complicates the relatively easy lines we typically draw from mistake of law to culpability. This relates to our ability to hold people responsible for their character flaws. The ordinary view is nicely encapsulated by David Archard in his article on the *mens rea* of rape. Archard describes the culpability of individuals who make unreasonable mistakes about consent in terms of character defects. He continues: 'Such a defect of character may be regarded as morally wrong, since the individual bears primary responsibility for knowingly allowing it to have developed in this way...he comes to believe as he does because of a character that forms beliefs in an unreasonable way.'[94] Archard seems sanguine about this even in the context of sexual assault. However, attentiveness to the normative implications of widespread wrongdoing also seems to complicate our ability to rely on a relatively simple theory of culpability for defective character. Archard justifies responsibility for normative failings by implicitly invoking the idea that everyone has a fair opportunity to develop a non-defective character. The view that individual responsibility can be grounded on control over character development is itself controversial.[95] But the context of widespread moral mistakes adds considerable difficulty to any such account of responsibility. If our moral sense turns in any way on the world around us, and if we live in a context where the same moral mistake is repeatedly

[94] D Archard, 'The *Mens Rea* of Rape: Reasonableness and Culpable Mistakes,' in Keith Burgess-Jackson (ed), *A 'Most Detestable Crime': New Philosophical Essays on Rape* (New York: Oxford University Press, 1999) 213, 224–225.

[95] See, for instance, RA Duff, 'Choice, Character, and Criminal Liability' (1993) 12 Law & Philosophy 345.

made and not recognized as a mistake, then it may be more complicated to hold individuals responsible for characters that are in this way defective. In fact, an individual who absorbs bad moral values that are pervasive in his world quite plausibly has a character that develops beliefs in a reasonable way. The problem is that the 'reasonable' method—learning from the world around him—results in an unreasonable character when the world he learns from is riddled with unreasonable beliefs about the inferior worth of others. Can we really hold him fully responsible for his unreasonable beliefs on the basis that he 'knowingly allowed' them to develop?

In this way we can begin to see how widespread wrongdoing sunders the ordinary link between criminal law and moral culpability in a way that poses serious theoretical challenges to our very concept of responsibility. The most we can do here, however, is to draw attention to how these challenges may alter our perception of what is at stake in current debates about culpability. Only through such a process will we be able to develop more nuanced accounts of responsibility. Indeed, these issues are finally beginning to receive serious theoretical attention as countries around the world begin to come to terms with the implications of widespread wrongdoing. Germany and South Africa may seem the most obvious examples, but the movement for reparation of historic wrongs illustrates that long-standing democratic regimes are by no means immune. Thus, as we see, the United States is facing a contentious legal and political debate about reparations for slavery, and Canada is embroiled in mass litigation over the implications of discriminatory taxes and residential schools for native children.[96] These are but a few examples of the increasing demands to account for pasts characterized by pervasive moral mistakes. To date, however, much of the discussion has focused on the admittedly difficult procedural questions often counted as problems of the emerging field of 'transitional justice'. The deeper substantive questions of responsibility have yet to be explored thoroughly. This is an important and difficult task beyond the scope of this work. Nonetheless, a few observations relevant to developing a more egalitarian conception of responsibility may be helpful here.

To begin with, as noted above, in thinking about how the presence of widespread moral mistakes might compromise our ordinary ability to attribute blame, it is helpful to focus more precisely on just what the culpability concerns are in order to assess their significance in the concrete situation. In the sexual assault context, for instance, we may want to ask about the extent to which questions of fair notice and responsibility for character defects actually undermine our ability to attribute blame. In essence, then, we may want to ask when we can excuse moral ignorance. Whatever our response to this question, it seems that we ought to ask it directly rather than indirectly through manipulating the

---

[96] See e.g. *In re African-American Slave Descendants Litigation* 2002 WL 31432900; *WRB v Plint* [2001] BCJ No 1446; *Rumley v British Columbia* [2001] SCJ No 39; *TWNA v Clarke* [2001] BCJ No 1621; *Mack v Canada (AG)* [2002] OJ 3488 (CA).

ordinary relationship between *mens rea* and culpability. Perhaps we should consider developing an excuse of understandable moral ignorance. Since this would only arise when ordinary *mens rea* requirements had already been satisfied, such an excuse would be structured as a defence in which the onus is on the accused to establish that the context was such that his moral mistake does not redound (or does not fully redound, since it would most likely be a partial excuse) to him.[97] For example, in the sexual assault context, an accused would need to establish that he had no fair warning that protest by a woman actually signified non-consent. Relevant here would be questions about social context, education, and the effect of widespread publicity initiatives like 'no means no' campaigns. Similarly, on the question of background, an accused would have to show that he lacked the opportunity to develop a non-defective moral character with regard to gender relations, and hence should not be held fully responsible for his moral ignorance. Once again, much would depend on the kind of evidence that the accused could marshal, but structuring this inquiry as a formal defence would impose some discipline on what has to date been a rather loosely articulated and loosely evaluated set of concerns about social context and moral responsibility.

Locating the mistake of fact argument within the structure of an excuse of moral ignorance would also place the question of responsibility on the character and moral background of the accused rather than on the behaviour and background of the complainant, where it has too often been placed. After all, presumably the underlying question of responsibility concerns what we can legitimately expect of the accused. For instance, it having been established that the complainant protested and the accused persisted, a defence of moral ignorance would focus on the accused's defective character, not on the complainant's defective protests. Rather than focusing on the plausibility of his interpretation of her protests, he would instead have to focus on the nature of, and explanation for, his moral ignorance. Undoubtedly rape myths would play a role in the arguments in both cases. But crucially, in the latter case it would be up to the accused to establish that he was so thoroughly convinced of the truth of these myths that we should at least partially excuse his moral ignorance. He would need to establish that it would be unjust to hold him liable for his moral ignorance because his social context prevented him from developing a proper character. Indeed, putting the argument in this way may help to explain why courts do routinely reject such arguments on credibility grounds even under a standard that requires only that the mistake of fact be honest.[98] Perhaps what the courts are responding to is the implausibility of the accused's

---

[97] This onus is consistent with the general assumption of the criminal law that individuals bear responsibility for their characters unless it is possible for them to demonstrate the contrary. Thus, defences like insanity and diminished responsibility are highly exceptional and the onus is on the accused to establish them.

[98] See e.g. *DPP v Morgan* (n 45 above); *R v Pappajohn* [1980] 2 SCR 120, 111 DLR (3d) 1.

implicit claim to excusable moral ignorance. But if so, this again suggests the desirability of approaching the inquiry directly rather than obliquely.

Obviously, much more work than is possible here would be necessary to develop an excuse of understandable moral ignorance. However, attending to the possibility of such an excuse has the advantage of bringing somewhat shadowy concerns into the light so that they can be properly scrutinized. If judges were to begin excusing individuals on the basis that their social context rendered moral ignorance partially forgivable, it would also force difficult questions about collective responsibility for moral education into the open. Even beyond this, such an excuse may have the benefit of eliminating some of our collective hypocrisy about when we will excuse moral ignorance. Tellingly, most of the work about when moral ignorance should be excused due to social or cultural factors has occurred in the debate about whether or not there should be a defence of culture. The standard position of criminal law theorists, including most subjectivists, has been that such a defence would undercut the egalitarian imperative of the criminal law.[99] But the analysis above suggests that our own criminal law debates about cases involving widespread moral mistakes have a structure that is surprisingly similar to the structure of the defence of culture. Indeed, the similarity forces us to ask why we are willing to take seriously the implications of widespread moral mistakes made by members of the dominant culture, yet we remain unwilling to consider the potentially similar implications for other cultures. If we think that we can demand that others overcome the moral 'blind spots' and 'errors' of their cultures, then it seems arguable that we should be making the same demands of members of the dominant culture. Beyond these inquiries there also lie deeper questions about what we are entitled to require of our fellow human beings, and how the social and moral context figure in those expectations. In fact, these difficult questions of fault and responsibility may actually underlie much of the unease in the sexual assault situation and in other cases where our accounts of responsibility struggle to come to terms with the implications of discrimination.

2. *The identification problems*

Egalitarians may also have trouble reposing confidence in an indifference account because where wrongdoing is widespread, it may be especially difficult to identify it as wrong. This problem, which can be thought of in terms of *identifying* the wrongdoing, arises because of how the pervasiveness of a moral mistake may complicate judgement. It thus poses the challenge of how to frame and apply normative standards in order to protect their egalitarian content when the widespread practice is in some important way inegalitarian. This is a complex inquiry, but at bottom it is a pragmatic matter. As we saw in the

---

[99] See e.g. C Wong, 'Good Intentions, Troublesome Applications: The Cultural Defence and Other Uses of Cultural Evidence in Canada' (1999) 42 Crim LQ 367; George Vuoso, 'Background, Responsibility and Excuse' (1987) 98 Yale LJ 1661.

discussion of the customary account of culpable inadvertence, our intuitions about moral mistakes seem to play out differently when the moral mistake—the divergent view—is not idiosyncratic. That discussion illustrated how the widespread nature of a moral mistake may complicate our recognition of it as such. But the worry that we must now address is that even though we have identified the indifference account as the best way of understanding when inadvertence will be culpable, the widespread nature of the wrongdoing may threaten to erode the difference between the customary account and the indifference account. This is because the temptation to substitute a customary standard for a normative one will be strong where the customary standard is widely shared; it will be tempting, in other words, to treat reasonableness as a standard of plausibility. So to the extent that the mistake, even though moral and legal in nature, is seen as understandable (which it will often be where it is commonly made) it may be thought to satisfy the reasonableness criteria. In fact, this may be one way in which the 'fixity' of a reasonableness standard is particularly susceptible to being eroded in cases where equality is seriously under threat.

This suggests that where there are serious background concerns about equality, it will be necessary to do more than simply state the standard as one of reasonableness. This is because it is precisely in such cases that the custom-based standard may be appealing to 'read in' to an unspecified reasonableness standard. Indeed, Fletcher's attraction to this idea, and egalitarian anxiety that this is all we can ever really expect, combine in a powerful warning: if the indifference account is particularly appealing in the context of discrimination, it is also particularly vulnerable to being 'read down' in that context. The danger here is that however attractive in theory, in practice the reasonableness standard will only ever amount to the custom-based one that we rejected for egalitarian and other reasons. This is a powerful worry, and it must be taken seriously. Fortunately, however, it is possible to develop an account of the standard that is responsive to this concern. As we shall see in the next chapter, traditional legal and criminal law theory may not have much to offer in the way of a response. Nonetheless, it is possible to extrapolate from feminist law reform efforts to develop some ways to think about shaping and constraining the discretion inevitably involved in such judgements to make them more true to the law's egalitarian ideals.

IV. Conclusion

The strength of an objective reasonableness standard comes from its ability to set an egalitarian measure for evaluating the normative quality of an individual's interactions with others. This approach to what individuals *should* do in their interactions with others is sharply at odds with the custom-based understanding, nicely encapsulated in Fletcher's insistence that the only appropriate measure for assessing the culpability of inadvertence is what other members of the community *would* do in the circumstances. This is also the kernel of truth in the equality defences of the objective standard. Thus understood, a properly constructed objective standard is vital to egalitarians because it sets an interpersonal standard of behaviour predicated on the recognition of the equal worth of all individuals. The consequent refusal to vary the demands of the standard to mirror individual moral capacities not only gives egalitarians reason for hope, it also accounts for the link so often made between equality and the objectivity or 'fixity' of the standard including in Madam Justice Wilson's celebrated passage from *Hill*. Holding all individuals regardless of their varying moral capacities and value systems to a standard that demands equal concern and respect looks crucial to an egalitarian legal order.

Measured against this ambition, the indifference account seems the most promising way of conceptualizing the culpability of inadvertence. In part, this is because of the ability of the indifference account to reveal how violation of a normative standard can implicate the blameworthiness of the agent, absence of intent notwithstanding. This capacity to identify moral ignorance makes indifference-based accounts of culpability particularly important where discrimination may be in play. We ordinarily say that if an individual consciously does an act, and that act is wrong, the fact that the actor does not subjectively believe the act to be wrong affords no defence. Indeed, the typical response is to condemn such an individual as either insane or profoundly immoral. But as we have seen, this does not seem similarly straightforward in a context where the moral mistake is widely shared. In situations involving the adjudication of widespread discriminatory beliefs such as those prevalent in the sexual assault context, assessing fault under reasonableness standards provides a local example of this difficulty. If this is the setting in which it is particularly important to hold firm to the normative content of the objective standard, it is also the setting in which the indifference account may be especially vulnerable to being elided with a custom-based account. It is therefore important to consider whether and how we might avoid this confusion.

8

Moving towards a Solution: An Egalitarian Objective Standard

Looking to the defences of negligence as a ground of criminal liability serves to highlight some reasons why feminists and other egalitarians might continue to hold out hope for an objective standard. The idea that fault in negligence might best be understood as targeting indifference to the interests of others seems to provide a more promising way to read the content of the objective standard. Moreover, insistence on the salience of attentiveness to others may seem to provide a basis for the kind of normative fixity that is so important to equality seekers. But even if we can take from the defences of criminal negligence the insistence that the standard only attach to the failing of indifference but that it attach rigidly to that failing, the remaining problems seem almost insurmountable.

Examining the theoretical accounts of criminal negligence also gives us a deeper understanding of some of the egalitarian concerns about the standard. We have already remarked upon how in operation and frequently even in theory, the objective standard too often derives its 'reasonableness' from an untroubled appeal to common sense understandings of what is normal or customary. The worry for equality seekers is that in the very kinds of cases that most concern them, the presence of widespread 'unreasonable'—non-egalitarian—beliefs will hold out an alternative reading of reasonableness that enables discriminatory beliefs to feed into the 'objective' standard. Indeed, we rejected the customary account of culpability because of its implication that there is no non-conventional basis available for understanding the culpability of inadvertence. The difficulty with that approach arose because of the way customary beliefs can effectively displace the mistake of law effect and along with it the assurance that legal norms are egalitarian. So to the extent that legal norms are infused with conventional understandings, the kind of underlying normative fixity that equality requires will remain elusive. But the influence of the customary account is such that we cannot be confident that simply insisting on an indifference-based understanding of culpability will ensure the normative fixity that equality requires.

Indeed, as the argument in the previous chapter suggests, where an inegalitarian understanding of what legal norms require is widely held, it may be equally tempting to interpret indifference itself in terms of what is ordinarily done. In this way, even a more theoretically defensible account of culpability like that found in the indifference account may be prone to being 'read down' where a widespread customary norm differs sharply from the legal norm. Because these kinds of well-entrenched customary norms are particularly prevalent where discrimination is in play, it looks like even an indifference-based account of culpability may actually hold limited egalitarian promise in the very cases where such promise most matters. This suggests that while there may be a theoretical basis for optimism about objective reasonableness standards, unless there is some way to correct for this characteristic weakness, it seems unlikely that this optimism will ever be realized.

Indeed, this tension between the promise of the standard and the difficulty attaining that promise underlies the deep ambivalence feminists and other egalitarians express about objective reasonableness standards. As we have noted, many egalitarians are prepared simply to give up on reasonableness standards largely because of their pessimism about the possibility of disentangling them from power-laden notions of what is customary or socially dominant.[1] Susan Estrich captures the central worry articulated by many when she points out the extremely limited potential of a standard in which the 'reasonable' attitude to which a male defendant is held 'is defined according to a "no means yes" philosophy that celebrates male aggressiveness and female passivity'.[2] As discussed below, these very concerns about how the reasonable person standard has incorporated 'ordinary' male sexual harassment have caused many feminists and even some courts to abandon that standard in favour of a standard premissed on the 'reasonable woman'.[3] Further, the cases involving children revealed that a certain heedlessness or inattentiveness of others is not only normalized but may even be valorized for some boys. So an indifference standard may be tempted to incorporate those moral failings that are widely shared or seen as normal, including the failure of men to treat women as sexually autonomous. Indeed it may also reflect a more general normalization of the failure of male self-control in the face of temptation or 'seduction'. To the extent that risk-taking is seen as constitutive of masculinity, this may pose a serious challenge to capturing the wrong of indifference.

But abandonment of the objective standard is not an appealing egalitarian response. Our task, therefore, is to determine whether the objective reasonableness test, which can be defended on egalitarian grounds in theory at least, can actually realize these ambitions. How can we have confidence that the objective standard properly targets the wrong of indifference, which we identified as the most egalitarian understanding of culpable inadvertence? Much

---

[1] See discussion in ch 6 above, nn 1–17.

[2] S Estrich, 'Rape' (1986) 95 Yale LJ 1087, 1103–1104.

[3] See nn 10–28 below. As discussed below, the controversy has been the subject of debate inside and outside feminist theory: K Abrams, 'The Reasonable Woman: Sense and Sensibility in Sexual Harassment Law' (Winter 1995) Dissent 48; NR Cahn, 'The Looseness of Legal Language: The Reasonable Woman Standard in Theory and Practice' (1992) 77 Cornell L Rev 1398; NS Ehrenreich, 'Pluralist Myths and Powerless Men: The Ideology of Reasonableness in Sexual Harassment Law' (1990) 99 Yale LJ 1177.

of the challenge here concerns how judicial discretion can be shaped and constrained in accordance with overall legal values, including values that spring from the constitutional framework and from the rule of law itself. Although neither traditional nor critical legal theory may have much to offer us here, we can draw some guidance from feminist law reform efforts in a number of areas. In particular, since the American law of sexual harassment has been the focus of a significant debate about the nature of the legal standard and the possibilities of restructuring it to ensure equality in a context of discrimination, it seems a useful place to begin our analysis.

I. THE SEXUAL HARASSMENT DEBATE: DO WE NEED THE REASONABLE WOMAN?

Feminist and egalitarian concerns have played an important role in the debate concerning when sexual harassment is actionable as discrimination under American law. Accordingly, much of the debate there focuses squarely on the question of the appropriate gender and other attributes of the standard of judgement. However, in this context the reasonable person plays a different kind of doctrinal role than those we have been discussing so far. The reasonable person was assigned this role because of the holding in *Meritor Savings Bank v Vinson*.[4] There, the United States Supreme Court found that sexual harassment was actionable under federal anti-discrimination law in those situations where it was severe enough to create a hostile work environment. In order to assess when harassment reached this actionable level, the court used the device of the reasonable person,[5] whose purpose was to gauge the severity of the harassment. *Vinson*'s finding that both 'quid pro quo' and 'hostile environment' sexual harassment violated employment discrimination law was seen as a major victory for feminist litigators. However, the holding was also greeted by a chorus of concerns about recourse to a reasonable man standard.

Critics of the reasonable person pointed to the clearly gendered origins of the standard, origins that seemed particularly problematic in view of the behaviour being assessed.[6] A variety of different (and often somewhat conflicting) arguments coalesced in these critiques of the reasonable person. A reasonable person

---

[4] 477 US 57, 67 (1986).

[5] *Rabidue v Osceola Refining Co* 805 F 2d 611 (6th Cir 1986), *cert denied* 481 US 1014 (1987).

[6] Abrams (n 3 above); Cahn (n 3 above) 1400–1405, discussing Susan Bordo, 'Feminism, Postmodernism, and Gender-Skepticism' in Linda J Nicholson (ed), *Feminism/Postmodernism* (New York: Routledge, 1990) 133 and Ronald KL Collins, 'Language, History and Legal Process: A Profile of the "Reasonable Person"' (1977) 8 Rut Cam LJ 311; Ehrenreich (n 3 above) 1210 ff; Toni Lester, 'The Reasonable Woman Test in Sexual Harassment Law—Will It Really Make a Difference?' (1993) 26 Indiana L Rev 227. For a challenge to the very idea in play here, see Janet Halley, 'Sexuality Harassment' in Wendy Brown and Janet Halley (eds), *Left Legalism/Left Critique* (Durham, NC: Duke University Press, 2002) 80. Other critics have suggested that alternative ways to formulate the actionable level of harassment may avoid some of the serious difficulties with the standard in this area: Gillian Hadfield, 'Rational Women: A Test for Sex-Based Harassment' (1996) 83 Calif L Rev 1151.

standard, it was argued, potentially obscured differences in the way that men and women might understand and respond to unwelcome advances. Recourse to the reasonable person in this context seemed to represent a problematic enshrinement of the male point of view and perhaps also male power to define gender relations. So adopting the reasonable person standard, given its history as the reasonable man, seemed to privilege one understanding of social interaction in the workplace (that of men) and simultaneously undermine the alternative understanding of such interaction (that of women): 'Judges might view [the reasonable person standard] as authorizing them to decide cases on the basis of their own intuition: the same "common sense" that had marked the administration of the "reasonable person" standard in tort law—and the same "common sense" that had normalized the practice of sexual harassment in the first place.'[7] Thus, as one commentator summarizes it, the worry with the reasonable person test in *Vinson* was that it would enable courts to judge the reactions of women by 'defining their reality through the eyes of the perpetrator'.[8] This worry was often linked to work in feminist and critical epistemology that challenged the very ability to invoke an unproblematic, unsituated perspective for understanding. This in turn fuelled a deeper critique of the possibility of reasonableness, which was more than simply a critique of the 'gender' or other characteristics of the idealized person.[9] It thus raised a question about the very possibility of legitimate judgement across 'difference'.

The 'solution' that many feminists initially posited to these worries about the reasonable person test came in the form of the reasonable woman standard. Initially, this proposal proved surprisingly influential. In *Ellison v Brady*[10] the Ninth Circuit commented on the dangers of recourse to the reasonable person test in sexual harassment: 'If we only examined whether a reasonable person would engage in allegedly harassing conduct, we would run the risk of reinforcing the prevailing level of discrimination. Harassers could continue to harass merely because a particular discriminatory practice was common, and victims of harassment would have no remedy.'[11] The *Ellison* court thus gave credence to the feminist worry about the entanglement of the reasonable and the ordinary. A sex-blind reasonable person standard, it suggested, tends to be male-biased and thus to systematically ignore the experiences of women.[12] Adopting a 'reasonable woman' standard accordingly seemed an appropriate response to this danger. Among its other virtues, the court suggested, a reasonable

---

[7] Abrams (n 3 above) 49–50.

[8] Wendy Pollack, 'Sexual Harassment: Women's Experiences vs Legal Definitions' (1990) 13 Harv L Rev 35, 62.

[9] See, for instance, Sandra Harding, *The Science Question in Feminism* (Ithaca, NY: Cornell University Press, 1986); Bordo (n 6 above) 133; Harding, 'Feminism, Science and the Anti-Enlightenment Critiques' in *Feminism/Postmodernism* (n 6 above) 83; Ehrenreich (n 3 above) 1216–1218.   [10] 924 F 2d 872 (9th Cir 1991).

[11] ibid 878. Interestingly, although commentators have suggested that the source of the difficulty the court identifies is found in the different male and female perspectives on this matter, it seems more likely to me that the core difficulty is instead found in something else that we have already noted— the danger that 'reasonable' may be read as ordinary and may thus simply lack critical power where the behaviour in question is common or ordinary.   [12] ibid 880.

woman standard would encourage an elaboration of how male and female perspectives in this area differed. But the *Ellison* court gave little sense of how this elaboration might proceed. Interestingly, although in the wake of the Anita Hill hearings several courts adopted the reasonable woman standard,[13] *Ellison*'s reasonable woman standard was not approved by the United States Supreme Court when it considered the question in *Harris v Forklift Systems*.[14] And so the debate among egalitarians about how best to construct the sexual harassment standard continues. Although the details of this debate are not our focus here, the controversy over how to fashion an appropriately egalitarian standard also holds broader lessons for the reasonable person. For while much of the sexual harassment debate rehearses the more general feminist arguments we have already considered, some of the discussion points to how the standard might be reshaped in a positive way to ensure its egalitarian content. In this sense, as we shall see, the sexual harassment debate dovetails nicely with feminist law reform efforts elsewhere. Further, some of the specific difficulties with reconstruction of the standard in the sexual harassment debate recall us to a larger set of concerns lurking in the background of the reasonable person analysis. Let us then briefly consider some of these aspects of the sexual harassment debate.

The early critical response to *Vinson*'s enshrinement of the reasonable person was a rare moment of feminist solidarity. But there was no similar consensus on the reasonable woman. With the rise of the reasonable woman standard as an alternative formulation of the test for sexual harassment, feminists began to voice their own concerns about this approach. They noted that a reasonable woman standard may reinforce stereotypes about women as more pure and moral than men.[15] Indeed, the very fact of a separate reasonable woman standard might allow judges to resort to their intuitions about women's difference.[16] Further, the reasonable woman standard also seemed to reinforce a view of women as victims.[17] Many feminists thus challenged the essentialism inherent in the reasonable woman standard. Unitary depictions of women, they suggested, replicated the false and exclusionary universalism that characterized the reasonable man.[18] In fact, the reasonable woman standard may itself simply

---

[13] See, for instance, *Robinson v Jacksonville Shipyards Inc* 760 F Supp 1486 (MD Fla 1991); *Burns v MacGregor* 989 F 2d 959, 965 (8th Cir 1993). Ehrenreich notes that the reasonable woman construct itself does not constrain judges' discretion in making the difficult choices involved in adjudicating sexual harassment claims: n 3 above, 1217. See also Abrams (n 3 above) 50 and Cahn (n 3 above) 1415–1420.

[14] *Harris v Forklift Systems* 114 S Ct 367, 371 (1991). In *Harris*, the court barely addresses the controversy and simply notes, in less than a sentence, that the court should review the plaintiff's claim by reference to the perspective of the reasonable person.

[15] Cahn (n 3 above) 1415–1416; Ehrenreich (n 3 above) 1218; Abrams (n 3 above).

[16] Note how this concern, expressed by Abrams, Cahn, and others, parallels exactly what we noticed about the judgment of the appropriateness of female behaviour in the case of the playing girl.

[17] Jolynn Childers, 'Is There a Place for a Reasonable Woman in the Law? A Discussion of Recent Developments in Hostile Environment Sexual Harassment' (1993) 42 Duke LJ 854, 896; Cahn (n 3 above) 1417.

[18] Cahn (ibid) 1416–1417; Abrams (ibid) 50–51; Ehrenreich (ibid) 1218 noting the standard's failure to attend to issues of race and class and arguing that this kind of inattentiveness means that

enshrine the perspective of relatively privileged women in a way that excluded disadvantaged women. Indeed, some feminists wondered whether it was tenable to suggest that women who were very differently situated could be understood to possess the homogeneity implied by the reasonable woman standard.[19] We see a similar range of feminist positions here as elsewhere on the reasonable person: while one set of feminists advocate a 'reasonable woman' standard, others insist that 'reasonableness' standards should be abandoned altogether, since they simply reinforce stereotypes, and a third group believes that much can be accomplished even with the reasonable person as currently understood.

One strain in the debate on the reasonable woman in sexual harassment will be very familiar from other issues involving the reasonable person. Indeed, as in early work on self-defence and provocation, some feminists in the sexual harassment debate suggest that the problem with the standard is precisely its insistence on reasonableness. An example of this view is found in the work of Nancy Ehrenreich. She expresses pessimism about the possibility of ever transforming the conception of reasonableness in a way that eliminates its harmful effects while retaining its benefits: 'the homogeneous image of society that results from the traditional equation of reasonableness with societal consensus is simply too harmful, excluding all but the dominant elite, to justify retention'.[20] For Ehrenreich, reasonableness—regardless of what body it is attached to—is so inextricably tied to what is commonly done that it can never be rehabilitated. In its place, she suggests 'pluralism', which requires an 'in-depth, empathic exploration of social problems'.[21] Like some of the egalitarian views we explored in the criminal law context, the underlying position here seems to be that there is simply no way to disentangle the reasonable from the normal. So only by dispensing with the element of reasonableness will it be possible to develop a more normatively defensible standard, one that is more attentive to equality issues and less connected to the ideas of 'ordinariness' that pose such difficulties for equality seekers.

However, many feminists are more reluctant to abandon the hard-won reasonable woman standard. The work of Naomi Cahn provides an illustration of this view. The 'reasonable woman' standard, she notes, is really an attempt to fashion a standard that is responsive to different social realities.[22] In keeping with this ambition, some of the difficulties with the reasonable woman might

'any unequal social conditions that affect an individual's situation are both perpetuated and condoned by such a standard' (referring to Donovan and Wildman 'Is the Reasonable Man Obsolete? A Critical Perspective on Self-Defense and Provocation' (1981) 14 Loyola LAL Rev 435.

[19] Abrams (n 3 above).   [20] Ehrenreich (n 3 above) 1232.

[21] Ehrenreich defines pluralism as basically meaning 'diversity', including 'a commitment to protecting minorities': ibid 1220. However, she limits the group's freedom to act self-interestedly to situations in which 'such conduct does not unduly harm other groups (and, implicitly, the societal interest in pluralism)': ibid 1221. As the goal of her pluralism is the elimination of inequality, it seems deeply incompatible with traditional pluralist views like those of Michael Walzer. There are arguably serious general difficulties with Ehrenreich's proposal, particularly in the light of her egalitarian goal, but only those most pertinent to the problem of reasonableness will be addressed here.

[22] Cahn (n 3 above) 1417–1420.

be remedied by further contextualizing or particularizing the reasonable woman standard.[23] The resulting standard will thus more and more closely approximate the individual being judged: her age, level of education and literacy, occupation, and many more qualities may be built into the standard on this account. But the list of potentially relevant qualities here seems impossibly long, and the standard threatens to disappear behind this endless specification of personal characteristics. Nonetheless, Cahn argues that there is considerable egalitarian potential in a standard that 'subjectively considers the pressure on an individual who is a member of a community with explicit standards for her behaviour'.[24] As we saw in the case of provocation and self-defence, it is the exclusionary nature of the 'ordinary' reasonable person inquiry that provides the impetus for insisting on greater similarity between the ideal and the actual person, particularly when that actual person is very unlikely to find herself well-represented in the ordinary person. But the provocation context also illustrated that it might actually be inimical to egalitarian goals to make the idealized person so closely approximate the actual person. In fact Cahn seems unwilling to employ this approach to judge male behaviour in cases such as sexual assault and admits that 'broader norms' may be necessary in some cases.[25] However, given her emphasis on subjective pressures on the individual and on community expectations, it is difficult to see how she could generate the kind of egalitarian norms she presumably wants.

But while neither abandoning reasonableness altogether nor modifying the idealized person through the addition of unspecified characteristics seems a promising egalitarian response to the undoubted difficulties with the reasonable person, the sexual harassment debate also contains more fruitful possibilities. The work of Kathryn Abrams is suggestive here. She argues that important feminist goals can actually be accomplished through a properly structured reasonable person inquiry.[26] Perceptions of sexual harassment, she argues, do not depend solely on biology, life experience, or gender, but rather on varied sources of information regarding women's inequality. Moreover, because these perceptions are 'a matter not of innate common sense but of informed sensibility, ... they can be cultivated in a range of women and men'.[27] Here the reasonable person can play an educative role if it is clear that it refers not to 'the average person, but the person enlightened concerning the barriers to women's equality in the workplace'.[28] So what would such reasonable people know about women, work, and sex that would enable them to assess claims of sexual harassment in a non-oppressive way?[29] Essentially Abrams is pointing to

---

[23] ibid 1435.   [24] ibid 1436.

[25] ibid 1436–1437. The significance of some of these factors may be different in the sexual harassment context, but Cahn does not confine her analysis to sexual harassment and indeed discusses the difficulties with such standards in the context of domestic violence and rape.

[26] Abrams (n 3 above) 51 ff.   [27] ibid 52.   [28] ibid.

[29] As Abrams intimates, there is a prior issue about how judges can be disabused of their idea that recourse to their common sense will solve everything and this suggests that it will be important to detail how common sense intuitions have led us astray. Abrams does allow that a more gender-specific

the utility of the reasonable person in educating the judge and other decision-makers so that they will be 'reasonable people' in assessing claims of sexual harassment. To effect this transformation and counter the stereotypes that may otherwise prevail, evidence regarding barriers to women's full participation in the workplace and the role of sexualized treatment in maintaining those barriers will be important. Further, it may be necessary to explain how sexual harassment affects women's work as well as how women typically respond to sexual harassment. But understood in this way, the reasonable person standard can provide an important standard of judgement while simultaneously avoiding some of the essentialist dangers of a more particularized standard.

Although many of the positions in the sexual harassment debate are familiar from our earlier discussion, the debate is nonetheless useful for more broadly egalitarian law reform efforts. It reminds us of how critical it is to disentangle the normative ideal of reasonableness from its too-common companion—the notion of what is ordinary or customary. One response suggests abandoning the idea of reasonableness, which has in practice only amounted to the imposition of the male point of view. Another related solution suggests substituting a female point of view (appropriately modified) for the male one. But under both of these solutions the standard of judgement of the *reasonable* person threatens to be subsumed into a description of the *actual* person. And precisely because this effective subjectivization of the standard is broadly unappealing from an egalitarian point of view, it seems more promising to pursue the approaches that consider restructuring the standard to ensure its promise, while simultaneously attempting to sever its dangerous connection to custom. As we shall see, there is a kind of resonance between this approach and egalitarian law reform strategies elsewhere. The underlying commonality resides in the idea that the discretion inherent in a standard of judgement can be shaped and constrained in order to enhance its egalitarian content. Before considering what we can learn from law reform initiatives more generally, let us briefly examine some of the central questions surrounding discretion.

II. The problem of discretion

The problem of discretion has been lurking in the background throughout this entire discussion. Considerable judicial discretion is not only inherent in a standard like the reasonable person or a more general reasonableness standard but is often also positively necessary and even desirable. In fact, H. L. A. Hart noted how a 'reasonableness' standard created space for ordinary moral reasoning.[30] But Hart's

---

standard may be useful in providing judges with the 'jolt' necessary to force them to question their common sense intuitions: ibid 51.

[30] *The Concept of Law* (2nd edn, Oxford: Clarendon Press, 1994) 132–133.

very description reminds us that discretion has a more ominous use: 'ordinary' moral reasoning, as we have seen, may go badly awry—especially where there are widely shared moral mistakes of the kind that characterize discrimination. The troubling confidence of common sense is only the most obvious example of this difficulty. So the inquiry concerns how we can ensure that the space created by 'reasonableness' does not work to undermine the law's egalitarian imperative. Both pragmatically and as a matter of principle, judicial discretion cannot be entirely constrained or obliterated. What is rather called for here is a subtler and more complex enterprise—and a relatively uncharted one as well. The challenge is to determine how we can shape and constrain that discretion. The task is both a positive one—to infuse the judgement space with the overarching values of the larger system—and a negative one—to rule out the uses of that space that would undermine larger systemic values (here equality in particular). For a variety of reasons, this challenge has received limited attention from legal theory. Some general remarks may be helpful before we examine how feminist law reform initiatives might illustrate and even help us to conceptualize some of the difficult questions concerning the exercise of discretion.

Feminists and other egalitarians are notably divided on the question of discretion. This is not surprising. Because strict legal rules and precedents are so often inegalitarian, equality seekers tend to have to ask courts to exercise their discretion creatively by going beyond the strict reading of the precedent or rule. For this reason the 'call to context' has often seemed one of the hallmarks of egalitarian legal reform. However, interest is increasingly also being directed to the question of how discretion has typically been exercised. In the context of sexual assault, for instance, even members of the judiciary began to suggest that 'it was discretion in the trial judges that saturated the law in this area with stereotype'.[31] A similar concern with how discretion is exercised can be seen in many other areas of law as equality seekers increasingly consider how the law may be failing them. This encompasses a broad range of concerns including issues as disparate as the use of discretion in family law,[32] the various areas of criminal law we have discussed

---

[31] *R v Seaboyer* [1991] 2 SCR 577, 707–709, L'Heureux-Dubé J. See also *R v Ewanchuk* [1999] 1 SCR 330, 375 where a similar concern is expressed.

[32] In the family law context, extensive feminist work suggested that judges were exercising their ample discretion in ways that raised worries about gender discrimination. See, for instance, Lenore Weitzman, *The Divorce Revolution: The Unexpected Social and Economic Consequences for Women and Children in America* (New York: Free Press, MacMillan Co, 1985); Lenore Weitzman and Mavis Maclean (eds), *The Economic Consequences of Divorce: The International Perspective* (Oxford: Oxford University Press, 1991); James B McLindon, 'Separate but Unequal: The Economic Disaster of Divorce for Women and Children' (1987) 21 Fam LQ 351. In Canada, the response has been the introduction of child support guidelines to limit the discriminatory gender implications of the exercise of judicial discretion in the family law context: Uniform Federal and Provincial Child Support Guidelines Act 1997, in force in Ontario as O Reg 391/97 under the Family Law Act and the Divorce Act. A similar response was developed in the United States: 42 USCA ss 601 et seq; *Westgate v Westgate* 887 P 2d 737 (Nev 1994) (new child support guidelines intentionally curtail traditional judicial discretion in child support awards). This is but a sample of the very extensive literature on this and related topics across the relevant jurisdictions.

here,[33] and worries about the discriminatory racial impact of sentencing discretion.[34] These difficulties and the responses to them suggest that the most promising way for equality seekers to approach discretion is to reject the traditional dichotomy: discretion should not be repudiated and eliminated, nor should it be wholeheartedly enhanced and celebrated. The task is rather to determine how the discretion inherent in judging can be positively shaped to conform to the overarching norms of the legal system. Attending to the errors of history also illustrates the importance of finally ruling out some uses of discretion that have been particularly problematic.

We can begin to think about the positive shaping of discretion by putting a slightly different spin on Hart's observation about the space for 'ordinary moral reasoning'. There is no doubt that the law does contain such discretionary space. Law's use of terms like 'reasonable' and 'unjust' clearly do invite and even require an inquiry that is not exhausted by the analysis of directly applicable sources of law. Critical legal scholars have called these terms 'weasel words' for just this reason. While frustration with how such terms are commonly infused with meaning (with what Hart more sanguinely referred to as 'ordinary moral reasoning') may tempt us to concur, it also seems possible to think more constructively about shaping this discretionary space. For instance, it is possible to respond to at least some of the difficulties with the implications of 'ordinary moral reasoning' for equality seekers by attending to how the norms of the overarching legal system might help to shape the exercise of discretion in concrete cases. This implicates the deeper connection between the operation of a system of private law and the overarching norms of the constitutional order—including predominantly, equality norms. Although this topic has traditionally received little attention, the question of the influence of constitutional norms is beginning to receive serious attention as constitutionalism itself becomes more expansive.[35] This is because in many of the relevant constitutional orders, even where constitutional norms do not give rise to discrete rights, they nonetheless exert

---

[33] For an illuminating overview in the criminal area, see Victoria Nourse, 'The "Normal" Successes and Failures of Feminism and the Criminal Law' (2000) 75 Chi-Kent L Rev 951 discussing rape, domestic violence, and self-defence.

[34] There is a very significant literature on this question and in particular on the impact of the Federal Sentencing Guidelines in the United States. For two recent contributions, see Shawn Bushway and Anne Piehl, 'Judging Judicial Discretion: Legal Factors and Racial Discrimination in Sentencing' (2001) 35 Law & Society Rev 733 and Rebecca S Henry, 'The Virtue in Discretion: Ethics, Virtue and Why Judges Must Be "Students of the Soul"' (1999) 25 NYU Rev of Law & Social Change 65.

[35] See, for instance, M Moran, 'Authority, Influence and Persuasion: *Baker* and the Puzzle of Method' forthcoming in D Dyzenhaus (ed), *The Unity of Public Law* (Oxford: Hart Publishing, 2003); Lorraine E Weinrib and Ernest J Weinrib, 'Constitutional Values and Private Law in Canada' in Daniel Friedmann and Daphne Barak-Erez (eds) *Human Rights in Private Law* (Oxford: Hart Publishing, 2001) 43; A Barak, *Constitutional Human Rights and Private Law* (1996) 3 Rev Const Stud 218. The German system is typically seen as instructive in this area: B Markesinis, 'Privacy, Freedom of Expression, and the Horizontal Effect of the Human Rights Bill: Lessons from Germany' (1999) 115 LQR 47; Guido Calabresi, *Ideals, Beliefs and Attitudes, and the Law: Private Law Perspectives on a Public Law Problem* (Syracuse, NY: Syracuse University Press, 1985). The leading American case is *New York Times Co v Sullivan* 376 US 254 (1963).

mandatory influence at the level of values. So these constitutional values can accordingly be understood as necessarily shaping and constraining the way that discretion may be exercised within that constitutional order. In Canada, for instance, while the Charter may not apply directly to the operation of the common law, the Supreme Court has consistently affirmed that the common law must nonetheless develop in a manner consistent with Charter values.[36]

This means that in constitutional orders committed to equality, certain kinds of considerations will be ruled out and others positively insisted upon. So, when giving content to terms like 'reasonableness' in a concrete situation, the influence of the overarching norm of equality will help to shape what meanings are possible. At a minimum, the reasonable person must be understood as committed to fundamental constitutional values. So on this understanding, the reasonable person *must* accept the equal moral worth of others. The reasonable person, on this view, could not be a racist or a sexist, for instance. This is because a commitment to the equal moral worth of all is central to the constitutional regimes of all the jurisdictions implicated here, and therefore no beliefs inconsistent with this baseline could be attributed to the reasonable person.

Attentiveness to the values that can be attributed to the reasonable person is important because it makes us aware of an important source of critical leverage within the law. This leverage may help to give the reasonable person a certain degree of priority over her ordinary counterpart. So one implication of this background shaping of values is that some views that are commonly held, and hence ordinary, cannot be attributed to a legal standard[37] (for instance that a woman becomes her partner's property). On this account of discretion, these kinds of views are ruled out. This means that the discretionary space Hart pointed to is not entirely discretionary because it is subject to mandatory values. These values, derived from the larger constitutional order, therefore both positively shape and constrain the 'ordinary moral reasoning' that the judge can invoke in giving meaning to terms that engage broader legal values. And this points to a subtler possibility than what we see in the prevailing debate on discretion. This approach suggests that in and of itself discretion is neither a good nor a bad thing. What matters is how it is exercised and used. It also suggests that we have at least some legal resources to shape and discipline this task and thus to ensure that the exercise of discretion conforms to overall rule of law values.

The fact that overarching norms will sometimes play a role in ruling out certain kinds of considerations and interpretations also directs us to another implication.

[36] So 'the judiciary ought to apply and develop the principles of the common law in a manner consistent with the fundamental values enshrined in the Constitution': *RWDSU v Dolphin Delivery* [1986] 2 SCR 573, 603. See also *Dagenais v CBC* [1994] 3 SCR 835 and *Hill v Church of Scientology* [1995] 2 SCR 1130. The cases and issues are discussed in detail in Moran, 'Authority, Influence and Persuasion' (n 35 above) and Weinrib and Weinrib (ibid).

[37] I would include here the ordinary person as used in provocation because it is a legal standard of judgment and as such cannot be inconsistent with fundamental constitutional values, though it may diverge in other ways from a reasonable person (who would presumably be more capable of self-control, for instance).

It will often not be possible to restructure the exercise of discretion without a fairly clear sense of how it has tended to go awry. Thus, careful examination of the past and its problems will often serve as an important tool for identifying just how discretion may go wrong. An example of judicial recognition of this can be found in *Re Eve*.[38] In that case the Supreme Court of Canada considered whether it should exercise its *parens patriae* jurisdiction to consent to the non-therapeutic sterilization of a young woman with a serious developmental disability. Before making his decision, Mr Justice La Forest examines the history of the treatment of the developmentally disabled and explicitly warns himself of the dangers of decision-making in this area by pointing to the errors of the past. He notes that such a question must be approached 'with the utmost caution' precisely because it 'involves values in an area where our social history clouds our vision and encourages many to perceive the mentally handicapped as somewhat less than human'.[39] *Re Eve* in this way reminds us of the role that the past plays in educating us and illustrates the importance of this for judges as well. In this sense, it also reminds us of the role that litigants and intervenors can play in this important educative task. We may hope that members of the judiciary will follow Mr Justice La Forest's path and explicitly avoid repeating the errors of the past. But the significance of this problem suggests that sometimes more structured methods may be necessary.

Of course the question regarding discretion also implicates the large and difficult issue of the representativeness of the judiciary and other decision-making bodies, in the sense at least of not all being drawn from the same limited segment of society.[40] This is a very significant question in part because it bears very generally on all adjudication (and beyond). And while it is beyond the scope of this work, it is worth reminding ourselves that the question of who judges does bear on the issues here. In addition, to the extent that efforts are being made to ensure diversity on the bench and elsewhere, those efforts feed into this analysis. Closely related to this, judicial education of the kind currently undertaken in most jurisdictions is also an extremely important tool, particularly on issues that may be unlikely to receive a full hearing in any particular case. Nonetheless, the tenacity of troubling uses of discretion in certain areas may sometimes mandate a more directive response. In the family law context, as noted above, frustration with the inability of the courts to make fair awards to women in the wake of divorce ultimately led to rather rigid support guidelines designed precisely to eliminate discretion where it had proved inimical to equality interests. Abrams's attempt to structure the use of discretion in giving content to the reasonable person in the sexual harassment context seems to rest on a similar impulse. As we shall see, feminist law reform in the sexual assault

---

[38] [1986] 2 SCR 388.

[39] ibid 427. Recall also the dissent of Justice Marshall in *Cleburne* on this very point: *City of Cleburne v Cleburne Living Center* 473 US 432 (1985), as discussed in ch 4 above, nn 91–92.

[40] There is a significant literature on this question and on the underlying issue of why such diversity (or, alternatively, representativeness) might matter. For one interesting possibility, see Jennifer Nedelsky, 'Embodied Diversity and the Challenges to Law' (1997) 42 McGill LJ 91.

context also directs our attention to how discretion can be structured in order to enhance equality in those moments where it may be particularly in peril. Let us now turn to consider some more concrete examples of how this kind of restructuring might proceed.

III. RECONSTRUCTING REASONABLENESS

Repeatedly we have seen how the generality, the inaccessibility, and sometimes the politically contentious content of 'reasonableness' makes it susceptible to being interpreted as ordinariness. This turns out to be most problematic in the very cases where it is most likely to occur. Thus, we have noted how when widespread inegalitarian norms are in play, it may well be particularly tempting to read reasonable as ordinary. In part this is because the convergence of beliefs and attitudes that characterizes discrimination provides a relatively plausible and consistent alternative set of norms that may on that ground alone seem an attractive (and more knowable) alternative to some more free-standing conception of reasonableness. Further, such customary norms undoubtedly complicate our ordinary ease with culpability for moral mistakes, and this may make these alternative norms seem fairer and hence more appealing. To the extent that a decision seems fraught with political controversy and complexity, it may also diminish judicial confidence in the very ability to articulate any objective understanding of reasonableness. Ordinary behaviour may thus look attractive as a reading of reasonableness for a whole variety of reasons. However, if we are to ensure that the reasonableness standard lives up to its egalitarian promise, even in a context characterized by discrimination, then it is essential that we find a way to ensure that reasonableness does not get read as ordinariness in these moments when we may be particularly inclined to do so.

The indifference account provides an important piece of a more promising beginning to the inquiry into reasonableness because it enables us to specify just what it is that is unreasonable (indifference to the interests of others) and what is reasonable (appropriate attentiveness to the interests of others). Focusing in this way on the normative core of an objective reasonableness standard will help to ensure that the inquiry is oriented in the right direction. But in a highly charged context like sexual assault where a well-developed set of background norms cuts against the legal rules, our previous analysis suggests that it will not be enough. Instead, it will be necessary to ensure that the meaning of indifference itself is appropriately egalitarian. This can be done by ensuring that the standard is inclusive, rather than specific, as to gender, race, and other relevant characteristics. But it may also be important to be explicit about the egalitarian nature of the normative content of an objective reasonableness test. Where there are powerful customary norms rendering that content especially controversial, it may be necessary to be yet more precise by specifying exactly what an egalitarian who valued sexual autonomy, for instance, might count or not count as consent. Where the egalitarian content of a legal norm is especially controversial, it may also be important to constrain discretion by ruling out particularly common mistakes that might otherwise tempt exercises of that discretion.

A. Specifying the normative content of reasonableness

Let us suppose that indifference to the interests of others is a good general statement of the normative failing that an objective reasonableness standard aims to capture. Clarification of this may well do much of the work needed in many ordinary negligence cases. Recall that when we rephrased the negligence question in *Roberts v Ramsbottom* by asking whether the actions of the defendant betrayed indifference to the interests of the plaintiff, the answer looked very different.[41] Because the risk Mr Ramsbottom imposed was the result of his sudden debilitating stroke, it did not betray indifference to others. Indeed, as discussed above, the indifference analysis helps to explain both why *Roberts* was always controversial, and the ground on which it was subsequently rejected in *Mansfield v Weetabix*.[42] This suggests that focusing the inquiry on indifference will often assist in the application of the objective reasonableness test. And while such explication of the objective component will of course not entirely simplify all judgements about culpability, it will focus the inquiry into objective reasonableness on the right question. An illustration can be found by thinking back for a moment to *McHale v Watson*.[43]

Unlike *Roberts*, *McHale* is a difficult borderline case even when the inquiry is focused on whether Barry's failure to notice the danger his stick-throwing posed to Susan betrayed his indifference to her interests. As discussed in Chapter 2 above, the judgments suggest at least two different ways to read Barry's heedlessness. There are many indications that the heedlessness was due to the cognitive limitations of childhood; thus, the courts intimate that Barry may not have had the foresight, the cognitive power, to understand the danger posed by throwing the stick at the post when Susan was standing immediately behind it. But Barry was an intelligent 12-year-old, and as Menzies J points out in his dissent, the risk of throwing a piece of metal, head high, in the direction of another person would probably been apparent to him had he been paying attention to the implications of his actions for others. Accordingly, it does not seem terribly plausible to read *McHale* as involving a risk that arose because of limited cognitive capacities. In fact, even the majority judges acknowledge the possibility of a prudential mistake when they refer to Barry's lack of 'sense and circumspection',[44] lack of appreciation of the risk, and lack of prudence. All of this language, and much of the discussion of impulsiveness addressed above, suggest that indifference to the interests of others played a significant role in accounting for Barry's heedlessness. Were we to focus on indifference, we may well find Barry responsible. But we cannot stop

---

[41] [1980] 1 All ER 7 (QBD).   [42] [1998] 1 WLR 1263.
[43] (1964) 111 CLR 384; (1966) 115 CLR 199 (Aust HC).   [44] ibid 215–216.

our inquiry here, for *McHale* implicitly raises another possibility that takes us back to our earlier discussion of excusing moral ignorance.

Let us assume that Barry would not have thrown the dart in Susan's direction had he been attentive to her security. The majority decisions hold that Barry cannot be responsible because the standard of appropriate care or prudence is a standard of ordinariness. This is why it is so crucial that Barry's limited capacity for prudence is 'characteristic of humanity at his stage of development'.[45] In fact, the suggestion that ordinary prudential failings count as reasonable under an objective standard echoes the inclination to forgive common moral mistakes that so troubles equality seekers. And *McHale* gives credence to this worry in its suggestion that if boys are routinely oblivious to the needs of others, then an objective reasonableness standard ought not to condemn them. It can be thus be read as supporting the view that common moral ignorance should be excused. We have already addressed this possibility. However, there is a related but narrower way to read this aspect of *McHale* that requires separate consideration.

On this reading (which is arguably more consistent with the law's insistence on the primacy of its own values), the allowance for 'ordinary' moral ignorance is specific to the child. Perhaps we would not ordinarily make allowances for moral ignorance, however widely shared. Nonetheless, it may seem plausible to calibrate the standard of indifference to reflect the ongoing development of the child's capacity for moral judgement. Maybe our understanding of what degree of attentiveness we can reasonably (note, not ordinarily) expect from a child must take into consideration the incomplete cognitive *and moral* development of the child. This may reflect the fact that, in contrast with adults, we cannot condemn the child whose underdeveloped moral capacity is simply the consequence of her stage of development. On this view, 'ordinariness' may simply be an attempt to capture the degree of moral judgement we legitimately expect of a child still in the process of developing her moral sense. In this way, an excuse of understandable moral ignorance may be particularly relevant to children.

But does this account for the courts' exoneration of Barry in *McHale*? This is a complex inquiry, but a few observations may be helpful. To begin with, we would need a more subtle understanding of the moral development of children. But even in the absence of this, the application to Barry does not seem terribly plausible precisely because of his developmental stage. When we ask if we can blame a 12-year-old who throws a sharp object towards another person, the answer seems to be 'yes'. The prohibition against imposing a risk of serious harm on others is relatively easy to grasp. So while we might be inclined to excuse a 6-year-old who said that she did not understand that she should avoid acts that she could foresee threatened harm to another, I think we would attribute blame to an ordinary 12-year-old who forwarded a similar account of her heedlessness. This seems to suggest that while there may be room for some

[45] (1966) 115 CLR 213.

allowance for the ongoing moral development of children, that allowance would probably not explain the exoneration of Barry Watson.

B. The gender of indifference

What does seem to explain Barry's exoneration on this narrower reading of *McHale*'s rationale is a more troubling possibility, and one that helps to make sense of something noted in our earlier discussion of *McHale*. Much of *McHale*'s reasoning suggests that the allowance that the court is making for shortcomings is actually quite specific to boyhood. It may not be coincidental that Kitto J refers repeatedly to the test as requiring Barry only to come up to the standard to be expected of a *boy* of 12.[46] The implication seems to be that we should take into account not simply the moral or prudential limitations of children, but also the more specific (and perhaps more extensive) moral short-comings of boys. In fact, if we phrase the *McHale* test more generally by asking whether a reasonable *child* of 12 would have thrown a metal stick towards another's head, the answer seems to be 'no'. The general test thus seems to weigh in favour of, rather than against, liability. It is only the courts' repeated insistence on boys and boyhood that makes plausible a negative response to the question of responsibility. But it also raises a set of broader concerns.

Are we willing to accept the idea that moral capacity itself is gendered in the way that this seems to imply? Ironically, this 'gendered reasonability thesis' is typically attributed to feminists, especially in the context of sexual crimes.[47] But *McHale* rests on the idea that there is an element of unavoidable moral ignorance that is simply part and parcel of being a boy—perhaps accounting for the fatalism of the majority's view that 'boys will be boys'. However, once we make allowances for moral shortcomings far beyond those strictly attributable to the limited intellectual capacities of the young child, it becomes more difficult to ensure that we are not simply taking account of common failings. Indeed, the most obvious way to read this aspect of *McHale* is that routine common failures to observe care may be given moral and legal weight. This idea, of course, is familiar from our discussion of Fletcher, as are its egalitarian implications.

One response to this would be to insist that if we are indeed to exempt common failings, then they must at a minimum be truly common. In fact, this would be more consistent with the idea that the standard makes allowances for ordinary *human* failings. It is telling that we have difficulty justifying the idea that we should make allowances for ordinary male or ordinary female failings, for instance. In fact the common failings view would rule out taking account of any gender-specific failings: instead, only those failings that are common to both genders could affect the degree of care we think we are entitled to demand

[46] See discussion in ch 2 above, nn 47–61.
[47] Donald C Hubin and Karen Haely, 'Rape and the Reasonable Man' (1999) 18 Law & Phil 113, 119 using the example of Catharine MacKinnon.

of others. Something like this view seems to be behind Hilary Allen's suggestion that in considering provocation, juries should be instructed that they ought to 'consider only such responses as they would regard as equally reasonable in *either* sex, and thus to exclude as unreasonable any response that would not be considered reasonable in both'.[48] Similarly, Donald Hubin and Karen Haely argue that despite possible gender differences in perspective in cases like sexual assault, a gender-inclusive standard like the reasonable person can be seen as an attempt to capture both the empirical possibility and the normative necessity of understanding across those differences.[49] And, as noted above in the context of the sexual assault debate, Abrams insists the reasonable *person* can, if understood inclusively, both express the possibility of moral education and repudiate the essentialist implications of a reasonable woman or man.[50]

A more controversial defence of what is arguably a gender-inclusive standard is found in *A Law of Her Own: The Reasonable Woman as a Measure of Man*.[51] There Carolyn Forell and Donna Matthews argue that in areas involving sex and sexism, we should deliberately use the *reasonable woman* standard (which is in their view a more respectful standard of conduct) to displace the implicit male norm that unavoidably resides in the reasonable person. However, their argument at bottom seems gender-inclusive rather than exclusive because it treats the reasonable woman standard as referring to the higher standard of conduct that the law has typically demanded of women, rather than to a uniquely feminine understanding of reasonableness. The reasonable woman standard is required to elevate the standard of conduct expected of men in sexually charged situations in part because a problematic 'male' norm is so entrenched in the reasonable person that only replacing the person with the woman will yield a more respectful gender inclusive standard of conduct.

An insistence on gender-inclusive normative standards can be understood as expressing in more concrete terms the general assumption, in law and beyond, that except in the case of extreme moral incapacity such as youth and insanity, we are entitled to demand of all the same degree of attentiveness to others. The many gradations of actual moral capacities that undoubtedly exist do not set what we can legitimately expect of others (as opposed to what we actually receive, of course). As suggested in *McHale*, some allowance for the moral development of children may be compatible with this view. But accepting *McHale's* intimation that we should take account of the moral shortcomings inherent in boyhood inevitably undermines our ability to insist on relatively uniform moral and legal standards. Perhaps there are arguments in favour of abandoning the strictness of these moral imperatives. But *McHale* does not take itself to be adopting such a position, nor is it commonly interpreted in that way. In the

---

[48] Hilary Allen, 'One Law for All Reasonable Persons?' (1988) 16 Intl J Sociology of Law 419, 430. Ironically, although he argues against relativizing the provocation standard for race or culture, Ian Leader-Elliott also worries that Allen's proposal would be hard on men, since 'of course' a gender-inclusive standard would result in a higher reasonableness standard: 'Sex, Race and Provocation: In Defence of *Stingel*' (1996) 20 Crim LJ 72, 92 n 118.   [49] Hubin and Haely (n 47 above) 130–134.
[50] n 3 above.   [51] (New York: New York University Press, 2000).

absence of a serious argument that courts are actually committed to the ramifi-cations of this view, we should be reluctant to abandon the law's exacting moral demands, particularly given how significant the equality effects would be.[52]

A number of strains in the debate on objective standards point to the impor-tance of a gender-inclusive normative standard. In the context of the sexual harassment debate, this approach is reminiscent of Abrams's reminder of the conceptual importance of a gender neutral standard. Similarly, in provocation and elsewhere, we can find equality seekers pointing to the possibility that a gender-inclusive standard of judgment may actually enhance equality interests much more than gender exclusivity would. Thus, specifying that any standard be gender-inclusive seems an important element in ensuring an egalitarian stand-ard of judgment. This is because although drawing forward the significance of indifference in the meaning of reasonableness does help to respond to cases like *Roberts*, it will not be enough where a gender or other controversy is in play. If we are to shape the exercise of discretion in order to ensure its consistency with overarching equality norms, then it may sometimes be necessary to do more than specify that indifference is the core normative content of reasonableness. As we have seen, it will often be tempting for decision-makers to invoke gender-specific ideas of appropriate behaviour. This points to the importance of specifying that the meaning of indifference be determined with reference to what counts as appropriate attentiveness to the interests of others in both sexes.[53] Accordingly, anything that would be considered sufficiently attentive by only one gender but not the other, for example, must be counted as indifference.

C. The egalitarian content of indifference

Thus far, we have suggested two different ways in which the exercise of discre-tion might be positively shaped. We began by specifying the meaning of unrea-sonableness: indifference to the interests of others. Because of the complexity of isolating the normative content of an objective reasonableness test, let alone the meaning of the reasonable person, this may be helpful in cases like *Vaughan v Menlove*,[54] *Roberts v Ramsbottom*, and even *McHale v Watson*.

---

[52] Indeed, viewed in this light it seems somewhat ironic that it is feminists who are so often charged with relativizing responsibility to the point of making it disappear. *McHale* illustrates that relatively orthodox legal positions have more in common with such an approach than they may acknowledge, and that there may be good feminist and egalitarian reasons for resisting precisely such a view. Although there are undoubtedly egalitarians who do seek to relativize responsibility in this way, often what is really going on is an attempt to counteract the tendency to 'read down' reason-ableness to ordinariness. Indeed, egalitarian critiques typically aim to correct the way reasonableness tends to get read in the context of discrimination. In this sense then, they do not so much seek to rel-ativize as to *realize* responsibility.

[53] Because criminal law is so often codified, it has more obvious tools to aid the shaping of dis-cretion such as the kind of specific directions to juries and triers of fact than Allen suggests: n 48 above. But a similar method of structuring discretion may well be important even in the private law context where many causes of actions, including negligence, are based on the common law. Some kinds of cases may require more focused guidance though the actual form this takes will necessarily vary with the nature of the concrete area. Undoubtedly, judicial education is also a crucial mechan-ism here.　　　　　[54] (1837) 3 Bing NC 468, 132 ER 490 (CP).

But *McHale* also alerted us to another possibility, a possibility that also shapes the sexual harassment and other debates: the danger that terms like 'indifference' will be interpreted in a gender-specific way. Because such interpretations undermine both the law's own insistence on uniform standards and its broader egalitarian imperatives, it is important to counteract this tendency by insisting on the importance of gender-inclusive standards. But where the egalitarian normative content of what counts as indifference (or its mirror image, appropriate attentiveness to the interests of others) is deeply controversial, more will undoubtedly be required. Recall the controversies about the content of reasonableness in sexual harassment, sexual assault, and elsewhere. In such contexts where the norms are controversial in part because they are in transition, there may well be considerable tension between the egalitarian content of the legal norm and underlying conventional understandings.[55] Thus, it may not be enough to specify that reasonableness refers to appropriate attentiveness to the interests of others and that only what would count as attentiveness in both genders can properly be considered. This is because it may still be tempting for the trier of fact to infuse the idea of appropriate attentiveness with her conception of ordinary or normal attentiveness. In such situations, more definition must be given to the prudential aspect of the standard by making explicit the specifically *egalitarian* normative make-up of the reasonable person. Looking at the most promising features of the sexual harassment debate and at other feminist law efforts provides some further guidance in this endeavour.

Feminist law reform energies are often directed to drawing out the specifically egalitarian normative content of the standard where it is particularly controversial—especially in the context of 'sex crimes' like sexual assault, sexual harassment, spousal homicide, and the like. Thus, in sexual harassment, where the commitments and character of the reasonable person may be in dispute, Abrams suggests it is important to specify that the reasonable person is someone who is enlightened about the barriers to women in the workplace. This may help focus the judge (and ultimately others as well) on the salient feature of the standard in this context. In the process it may also help us to displace some of the unarticulated common sense views of what 'reasonable' (read as ordinary) people might believe about women's role in the workplace. The idea that it may be necessary to specify the egalitarian normative content of the standard where the existence of widespread discriminatory views threatens to undermine that content also plays an important role in feminist law reform efforts in the law of sexual assault. For instance, *A Feminist Review of Criminal Law* suggests that given the difficulties with the idea of reasonableness, the Canadian Criminal Code should stipulate a reasonable person 'who accepts the individual's right to

---

[55] On the relationship between old persistent norms and new legal norms in the law reform context, see Nourse (n 33 above) and Lucinda Vandervort, 'Mistake of Law and Sexual Assault: Consent and *Mens Rea*' (1987–88) 2 CJWL 233. See also Lawrence Friedman, 'Law Reform in Historical Perspective' (1969) 13 St Louis ULJ 351.

sexual autonomy'.[56] Estrich argues that reasonableness can be an important standard if the content of what is reasonable is defined not according to self-interested male conceptions of what is 'reasonable' but rather in accordance with respect for the sexual autonomy of women.[57] Similarly, Forell and Matthews's promotion of a reasonable woman standard is in part a way of insisting on the egalitarian commitments of the idealized agent. For while the egalitarian commitments of the reasonable man or person may not safely be assumed (even if explicitly stated, at least for Forell and Matthews), the normative make-up of the reasonable woman may seem more reliable. Even here, though, the authors suggest that jury instructions can flesh out the idea that a reasonable woman is committed to egalitarian values like autonomy and respect for others.[58]

Feminist law reform efforts place great importance on making explicit the egalitarian content of an objective reasonableness standard when that content may be controversial. This suggests a way to read the amendments to the sexual assault provisions in the Canadian Criminal Code.[59] These provisions were in part the result of extensive feminist law reform efforts and broader consultation. The provisions taken together can be read as making more concrete what an egalitarian understanding about sexual autonomy would and would not count as reasonable in the context of sexual assault. Part of what is striking about the provisions is the amount of detail devoted to precisely these issues. But this should not be surprising. A general statement to the effect that appropriate attentiveness to the interests of others entails respect for their sexual autonomy will often be useful in alerting judges to where they should be critical of 'normal' attitudes. However, where the relationship of the legal norm to the customary one is controversial, it will be necessary to go beyond this to specify just what a reasonable person concerned for the sexual autonomy of others would believe counted—and did not count—as consent. The sexual assault provisions of the Criminal Code can be understood as doing just this.

To begin with, rather than leaving it to the judge to determine what a reasonable person would count as consent, the Criminal Code provisions explicitly define consent as 'the voluntary agreement of the complainant to engage in the sexual activity in question'.[60] Admittedly this simply restates the ordinary meaning of consent in other areas of the law. But recall our discussion in the previous chapter about Al and similar sexual assault problems involving mistaken beliefs in consent. As we saw, in the sexual assault context the use of the term 'consent' by the accused may well obscure the fact that his conception of consent radically diverges from the ordinary legal meaning of the term. Indeed, the significance of this problem shows the importance of insisting that the

---

[56] Christine Boyle, Marie-Andrée Bertrand, Celine Lacerte-Lamontagne, and Rebecca Shamai, *A Feminist Review of Criminal Law* (Ottawa: Ministry of Supply and Services, 1985) 62.

[57] Estrich (n 2 above) 1104.   [58] (n 51 above) xix.

[59] See Canadian Criminal Code RSC 1985, c C-46, and An Act to amend the Criminal Code (sexual assault), SC 1992, c 38 (commonly referred to as Bill C-49).   [60] ibid s 273.1(1).

ordinary definition of consent also prevail in the sexual context.[61] The definition of consent therefore directs the judge to ensure that consent in the sexual context refers to the same kind of voluntary agreement that counts as consent elsewhere. Explicitly defining consent thus helps to displace the 'divergent' meaning of consent that, as we have seen, will too often prevail in its absence.[62] And rather than leaving it to the judge to determine what a reasonable person would count as consent, the definition further specifies the egalitarian normative content of the reasonableness standard by outlining exactly what such a view counts as consent. In so doing, it crucially removes from the judge the opportunity to infuse the definition of consent with her own conception, which may well be influenced by the customary beliefs, myths, and stereotypes discussed in the previous chapter.

Besides defining consent, the Criminal Code provisions can also be read as responding to another feature of the mistaken belief in consent cases discussed in the previous chapter. There we noted that under the ordinary legal definition of consent, and consistent with its role in protecting autonomy interests, the presumption must be non-consent. This in turn requires that consent be affirmatively given and ascertained. But as we noted, in the sexual setting the implicit presumption—sometimes virtually irrebuttable it seems—may be of consent. The Criminal Code provisions also respond to this danger by placing the onus on the accused to take 'reasonable steps, in the circumstances known to the accused at the time, to ascertain that the complainant was consenting'.[63] By emphasizing the responsibility of the accused to ensure affirmative consent, the provision rejects a presumption of consent and thus reaffirms the centrality of the ordinary legal meaning of consent.[64] Although these provisions do not reflect all of the changes urged by feminists, they do seem to provide a concrete example of how one might specify the egalitarian normative content of reasonable behaviour in situations where we know that 'common sense beliefs' are likely to lead to the kinds of mistakes that selectively undermine the rule of law.

---

[61] However, many feminists were critical of the vagueness still inherent in this definition of consent, presumably because of the background effect of custom: Boyle et al (n 56 above). As we have seen, there are powerful customary norms about when sexual intercourse is acceptable that actually undermine the legal requirement of consent. Presumably for this reason, Vandervort also advocates a more explicit definition of consent as 'Mutual exchange of explicit or unequivocal implied consent': Vandervort (n 55 above) 305.

[62] The varying meanings of consent are discussed in Nathan Brett, 'Sexual Offences and Consent' (1998) 11 Can J L Juris 69.   [63] Criminal Code (n 59 above), s 273.2(b).

[64] The provision has been criticized for assuming that 'only the male in a sexual encounter bears responsibility to ensure that the other party is consenting, and only he should be held responsible for any resulting dispute as to consent': A Gold, 'Flawed, Fallacious but Feminist: When One Out of Three is Enough' (1993) 42 UNBLJ 381, 382. But it is perfectly consistent with the ordinary meaning of consent that the requirement of securing it should rest with the person who seeks to engage in an activity that is prohibited unless accompanied by consent. The reasonable steps requirement actually *protects* the accused from bearing legal responsibility for non-consent, so long as he has made a reasonable effort to secure consent.

D. Constraining discretion: Ruling out common mistakes

The sexual assault provisions of the Canadian Criminal Code also illustrate another important point regarding the exercise of discretion. As noted above, the provisions are structured to ensure that discretion is exercised in conformity with egalitarian norms that may be particularly susceptible in a context like sexual assault. In a sense, this is the role of 'positive' specification, for it can be seen as assisting decision-makers by providing at least some of the important overarching norms to guide their exercise of judgement. But the sexual assault provisions also illustrate something equally important: the role of 'negative' specification, or *ruling out* certain exercises of discretion. As discussed in the previous chapter, while judges may generally refuse to give credence to divergent conceptions of legal duties when those conceptions are idiosyncratic, the same cannot be said where the divergent conception is more widely held. So in addition to indicating how discretion *should* be exercised in order to conform to the overall egalitarian imperatives of the legal system, it may equally be necessary to specify how discretion *must not* be used.

As we noted, the mistakes about consent that are so prevalent in the sexual assault context are characterized in part by their systematic nature. We have discussed how such mistakes complicate the application of ordinary legal rules, displace the mistake of law effect, and give rise to rule of law concerns. Identifying the specific ways in which discriminatory customary beliefs may actually override legal norms is therefore an essential task for critical jurisprudence. Only a detailed understanding of this kind will make it possible to develop explicit injunctions to decision-makers to warn against certain kinds of uses of discretion. Fortunately, the one advantage of systematic mistakes is that they are relatively easy to locate and describe. And the importance of specifically identifying such mistakes is nicely illustrated in the process of reforming the sexual assault provisions of the Criminal Code. This is because that process reveals how a close critical analysis of a particularly problematic field, such as we find in feminist analyses of sexual assault, can be vital in ensuring that legislative reforms are attentive to the law's equality interest and to the specific ways in which those interests might be undermined.[65]

---

[65] Although the argument here is that many feminists actually seek—wittingly or not—to secure basic rule of law values, their participation in the legislative reform process has been criticized as the biased domination by an 'interest group': R Martin, 'Bill C-49: A Victory for Interest Group Politics' (1993) 42 UNBLJ 357; Gold (n 64 above). Both articles display considerable outrage at the way legalized standards threaten to displace customary norms about sexual assault. Thus, for instance, Martin argues that criminal law should address 'concrete social reality' (is that custom?) rather than responding to 'changing ideological fashions': ibid 372. Attempts to make the law more egalitarian are often seen as 'biased' precisely because neutrality and reasonableness are so often associated with adherence to the status quo (see, for instance, C Sunstein, *The Partial Constitution* (Cambridge, Mass: Harvard University Press, 1993) discussing 'status quo neutrality'). In the infamous *Plessy v Ferguson* 163 US 537 (1896), the Supreme Court of the United States upheld a Louisiana statute that required railroad companies to provide 'separate but equal accommodations for the white and the coloured races'. Justice Brown, for the Court, held that the 14th Amendment only required the state

The most relevant section in this respect is s 273.1(2), which outlines the situations in which, as a matter of law, no consent is obtained. These provisions preclude a finding of consent where, among other things, the agreement is expressed by someone other than the complainant, where there is an abuse of power or trust, or where the complainant expresses a lack of agreement.[66] Initially, there were two possible interpretations of these provisions. The more limited reading was that while they precluded finding actual consent (which goes to *actus reus)*, they did not similarly restrict the defence of mistaken belief (which goes to *mens rea)*. Thus, an accused could still defend himself by raising a mistaken belief in consent even though his beliefs rested on a situation outlined in s 273.1(2) such as, for instance, that someone else consented on behalf or instead of the complainant. The broader interpretation, urged by feminists, was that the impact of s 273.1(2) was not limited to *actus reus* but also fed into other provisions, and in particular limited the availability of the mistaken belief defence. So, where an accused asserts an honest but mistaken belief based on one of the situations outlined in s 273.1(2), feminist commentators argued that the court should find that this amounted to a mistake of law that could not therefore constitute a defence.[67] Similarly, they insisted that the accused should not be able to argue that he had discharged the 'reasonable steps' requirement by relying on one of the situations outlined in that section. But until the Supreme Court of Canada decision in *Ewanchuk*, the exact relationship between s 273.1(2), on the one hand, and the mistake of 'fact' defence and reasonable steps requirements, on the other, remained unclear.[68]

In *Ewanchuk*, which was the Supreme Court of Canada's first significant consideration of these provisions, the Court unanimously held in favour of the broader interpretation urged by feminists. As a result, the provisions that specify situations where no consent is in fact obtained also limit the beliefs that the accused can invoke in his defence, even for the purposes of the mistaken belief defence. So as Mr Justice Major points out, not all beliefs upon which an accused will rely will serve to exculpate him. Instead, what can count as consent is limited both by the common law and by the sexual assault provisions of the Criminal Code.[69] The consequence is that 'a belief that silence, passivity or

---

to establish that the legislation was reasonable, with reasonableness to be gauged by conformity with 'established usages, customs and traditions'. On this test, the mandatory separation of the two races in public places was reasonable: ibid. The separate but equal doctrine was incrementally challenged by the NAACP until its demise in *Brown v Board of Education* 347 US 483 (1954).

[66] n 59 above.

[67] Christine Boyle and Marilyn MacCrimmon, 'The Constitutionality of Bill C-49: Analyzing Sexual Assault as if Equality Really Mattered' (1998) 41 CLQ 198, 212; Christine Boyle, 'The Judicial Construction of Sexual Assault Offences' in Julian V Roberts and Renate M Mohr (eds), *Confronting Sexual Assault: A Decade of Legal and Social Change* (Toronto: University of Toronto Press, 1994) 136, 152 n 18; Rosemary Cairns-Way, 'Bill C-49 and the Politics of Constitutionalized Fault' (1993) 42 UNBLJ 325, 329.

[68] This suggests that one significant improvement in the drafting of the legislation would have been to clarify that where the accused's 'steps to ascertain consent' involve the situations outlined s 273.1(2), they will not be considered reasonable.   [69] *Ewanchuk* (n 31 above) 355.

ambiguous conduct constitutes consent is a mistake of law, and provides no defence.'[70] The essence of *Pappajohn*, according to Mr Justice Major's majority reasoning, is that the defence of mistake must be available to an accused who acts innocently. On Justice Major's reading, *Pappajohn* remains intact because the morally innocent can still avail themselves of the honest belief defence.

A crucial implication of Major J's decision for our purposes is that we cannot equate honesty and moral innocence in the relatively easy way that *Pappajohn* assumed was possible. An underlying premiss that distinguishes *Ewanchuk* from *Pappajohn* is the view that not all honest beliefs are morally innocent; in fact, the beliefs outlined in s 273.1(2)—and any belief inconsistent with the voluntarist conception of consent—actually inculpates rather than exculpates the person who asserts them. In this sense, it is possible to understand the decision as responding to the difficulty posed by systematic mistakes of law. As discussed earlier, such mistakes, which are often implicated in mistaken beliefs about consent, are much more likely than their idiosyncratic counterparts to escape the application of the mistake of law rule. But *Ewanchuk*'s interpretation of the sexual assault provisions can be read as a significant response to this danger. Not only does the Court insist that the most common 'mistakes' about consent are mistakes of law which do not exonerate, but it also links this to the criminal law's appropriate concern with moral innocence. The underlying assumption is that even an honestly held belief may repudiate the interests of others in such a way that it justifies the attribution of blame. In this way, *Ewanchuk* implicitly recognizes the culpability of moral ignorance. In so doing, it helps to further the project of shaping a more egalitarian conception of responsibility.

Ewanchuk's reading thus ensures that the provisions of s 273.1(2) have broad relevance to the way that judicial discretion is exercised in the sexual assault context. This is crucial given how certain pervasive stereotypes, especially in the context of the defence of mistake, can corrode the egalitarian dimensions of the legal norms. It is in this respect no accident that the specific provisions of that section recite the most common 'rape myths' and stereotypes identified by feminists. As discussed above, these stereotypes are troubling because of how they work to displace the ordinary legal meaning of consent. Here, the ordinary meaning is reasserted in part by specifically ruling out the interpretations that most threaten to undermine it. Accordingly, a brief examination of some of the key provisions of s 273.1(2) will serve as concrete examples of how discretion

---

[70] *Ewanchuk* (n 31 above) 356. In his comment on *Ewanchuk*, Don Stuart criticizes Major J's opinion in this and other respects on the basis that, in Stuart's view, he far exceeded the wording of the legislation. But some of Stuart's reasoning is puzzling. For instance he describes it as startling and unsupported by the legislative provisions to hold that it is a mistake of law to interpret silence as consent: '*Ewanchuk*: Asserting "No Means No"' (1999) 22 CR (5th) 39, 46. However, if the definition of consent is voluntary agreement, which surely involves some sort of positive indication of agreement, then it would indeed be a mistake of law to count silence or passivity as consent. This again echoes the tension between the ordinary and the divergent conceptions of consent discussed above.

can be constrained, in order to avoid the damage that inegalitarian stereotypes may otherwise inflict on legal rights and obligations.

As we have seen, one particularly pervasive mistake about consent invokes the stereotypical belief not only that women are the sexual property of their partner, but that they remain so after the relationship has ended. Because these beliefs are so widespread, claims of mistake based on them will be very unlikely to engage the mistake of law effect for the reasons outlined above. An illustration can be found in *Morgan*. The defence raised in that case actually repudiates the *personal* quality of ordinary legal consent. However, the inclination of the House of Lords, as we have seen, is not to see this as a mistake of law but rather to treat the defence as in principle available as a claim about a mistake of 'fact'. Because such mistakes exonerate only if they are credible, the vociferousness of Mrs Morgan's objection is crucial to conviction. But a credible accused would presumably have been exonerated for an 'innocent' mistake. Section 273.1(2)(a), which precludes consent where 'the agreement is expressed by the words or conduct of a person other than the complainant', seems directed against just this possibility. As *Ewanchuk* implied, an inquiry into honesty does not exhaust the question of culpability. This is because an individual may honestly hold views about others that are at odds with fundamental legal rights. So the defendants in *Morgan* who take the word of a husband for the consent of his wife are, however honest, effectively making an inexcusable mistake of law about the meaning of consent. They believe one adult can consent for another—but it is fundamental to the idea of consent and the idea of personhood that it protects that this is not so. In this way, s 273.1(2)(a) reasserts the 'ordinary' meaning of consent in the sexual assault context by ruling out one particularly common way in which discriminatory stereotypes subvert that meaning. Because this is a legal mistake and hence subject to the invariant standard specified in the legislation, it limits the ability of invidious customary norms about women as sexual property to undermine the legal requirement of consent. Since the provision in this way holds constant the ordinary meaning of consent in a moment where it is particularly susceptible, it can therefore be seen as one means of providing the kind of normative 'fixity' so vital to equality.

Another customary belief that is just as tenacious and of even broader applicability is the myth of 'coy rejection'—that women actually mean 'yes' when they say 'no'. This is exemplified in the idea of violent sexual conquest, which Boyle refers to and which Tur actually invokes when he suggests that a woman's 'protestations of pain or disinclination' may be interpreted by the accused as 'a spur to more sophisticated or ardent love-making'.[71] Section 273.1(2)(d) rules out this stereotype by stating that no consent is obtained where the complainant 'expresses, by words or conduct, a lack of agreement to engage in the activity'. The provision thus effectively accomplishes Estrich's aspiration: 'The law should evaluate the conduct of "reasonable" men, not according to a

---

[71] Richard Tur, 'Rape, Reasonableness and Time' (1981) 1 Oxford J Legal Stud 432, 441.

Playboy-macho philosophy that says that "no means yes," but by according respect to a woman's words. If in 1986 silence does not negate consent, at least crying and saying "no" should.'[72] Similarly, in *Ewanchuk* Madam Justice L'Heureux-Dubé attributes the trial judge's erroneous finding of implied consent to 'mythical assumptions that when a woman says "no" she is really saying "yes", "try again" or "persuade me"'.[73] In her view the reasons of Justice McClung in the Court of Appeal, which place considerable emphasis on the complainant's clothing and personal history, only compound the idea that women exist in a state of presumptive consent. But s 273.1(2)(d), as Madam Justice L'Heureux-Dubé points out, precludes the accused from claiming he had an honest belief in consent where the complainant expressed her non-agreement.[74] The provision is thus a directive to judges to reject certain kinds of beliefs as defences, no matter how honestly held they might be. So this provision too can be seen as part of a specification designed to rule out the uses of discretion that might lead us to miss the very kind of blame egalitarians are most concerned about. And because it limits the influence of discriminatory customary norms by ruling out certain particularly common mistakes that decision-makers might be inclined to make, s 273.1(2)(d) can also be understood as reasserting the ordinary voluntarist conception of consent in the sexual assault context.

The view that women are the sexual property of their former partners is a particularly tenacious stereotype about women and consent. Although some of the substantive provisions discussed above speak to this issue, feminists worried that these may leave intact the 'common sense' inference that once a woman has had sexual relations with a man, she effectively continues to consent—or at least it is credible that he would believe she does—notwithstanding whatever protests she may make. Indeed, this is arguably the best explanation of the impulse to exonerate the accused in *Sansregret*.[75] In response to this danger, s 276 was added to the Criminal Code following *R v Seaboyer*.[76] This provision lists the purposes for which evidence of the complainant's sexual history *cannot* be adduced. It therefore effectively rules out certain uses of the evidence on the ground that they rest on discriminatory myths and stereotypes—most importantly, prior sexual history with the accused.[77] Section 276(3) also explicitly

---

[72] Estrich (n 2 above) 1093.   [73] (n 31 above) 372.   [74] ibid 379.

[75] *Sansregret v R* [1985] 1 SCR 570.

[76] n 31 above. In *Seaboyer*, a majority of the Supreme Court of Canada held unconstitutional the previous 'rape-shield' provisions of the Criminal Code on the ground that they had the potential to violate the accused's Charter right to a full and fair trial.

[77] See the majority decision of Madam Justice McLachlin in *Seaboyer* (ibid). Even the more reflective critics of the new legislation suggest the considerations are different when the prior sexual history concerns the accused: RJ Delisle, 'Potential *Charter* Challenges to the New Rape Shield Law' (1992) 13 CR (4th) 390; D Stuart, 'The Pendulum has been Pushed Too Far' (1993) 42 UNBLJ 349, 350–351. For an opposing view, see M Shaffer, '*Seaboyer v R*: A Case Comment' (1992) 5 CJWL 202, 210 discussing the confluence of *Seaboyer* and *Pappajohn*; TB Dawson, 'Sexual Assault Law and Past Sexual Conduct of the Primary Witness: The Construction of Relevance' (1987–88) 2 CJWL 310; Sakthi Murthy, 'Rejecting Unreasonable Sexual Expectations: Limits on Using a Rape Victim's Sexual History to Show the Defendant's Mistaken Belief in Consent' (1991) 79 California L Rev 541.

directs judges to take into account 'the need to remove from the fact-finding process any discriminatory belief or bias,' as well as 'the risk that the evidence may unduly arouse sentiments of prejudice, sympathy, or hostility in the jury'.[78] These injunctions in a sense furnish judges with warning signs about the danger spots in their exercise of discretion. Thus, these provisions suggest that part of the solution in reformulating reasonableness standards to ensure that they live up to their promise of equality may be found in explicit guidelines that contain and structure judicial discretion. This may be achieved in part by reasserting the ordinary meaning of consent, and in part by making considerations inconsistent with that ordinary meaning 'ultra vires' the judge.

In this way, the debates and the law reform process that engage the problem of sexual assault provide a useful basis on which to conceptualize how we can realize the egalitarian potential of an objective reasonableness standard. Feminists worry that the space for judgement that inevitably resides in standards like those invoking objective reasonableness will be used to draw in discriminatory background understandings of, for example, the appropriate sexual behaviour of men and women. When this happens, whatever egalitarian promise an objective standard may hold is lost—for when reasonableness is read as ordinariness, the law can do no more than enforce social norms. Unfortunately, legal theory in its traditional as well as its critical postures has little to say about this problem. This might seem surprising, since the problem of discretion has been an overarching preoccupation of much recent work in legal theory. But the ensuing debate, which has engaged 'traditionalists' like Dworkin and Coleman, on one hand, and critical legal studies like Duncan Kennedy, on the other, has been so preoccupied with the presence or absence of discretion and what the implications of that may be, that it has barely addressed the problem of how discretion ought to be exercised.[79] The traditionalists who do not view discretion as unbridled do not consider the challenge of reconstruction as a necessary or important question for legal theory. Ironically, however, the critics who see discretion everywhere hold out so little hope for a positive reconstruction that they also provide little guidance. For critical egalitarians this is inevitably unsatisfying. Perhaps for this reason, their concrete efforts to develop responses to particularly problematic exercises of judgment may actually turn out to be more helpful, even in conceptual terms, than most of the apparently more theoretical discussions of discretion.

Examining these law reform initiatives suggests a number of ways to ensure that the individual exercise of discretion conforms to overarching legal principles. Indeed, these efforts can be understood as a nascent project of 'critical reconstruction' that simultaneously recognizes the power of law to pursue egalitarian ambitions and yet thinks critically about how that power might be selectively

---

[78] Criminal Code (n 59 above), s 276(1)(d) and (e).
[79] This point is elaborated in M Moran, 'Right Answers, Wrong Questions: Objectivity, Feminism and the Partiality of Legal Theory' (unpublished manuscript on file with the author).

undermined and hence, perhaps, selectively reshaped as well. Thus, as we saw, where the egalitarian content of the legal norm is controversial, precise guidelines will be essential to shaping and constraining the discretion inherent in judgements about reasonableness.[80] While in some contexts it will be sufficient to clarify the fixed normative content of a reasonableness standard, in others it will be necessary to go beyond this to specify the egalitarian content of the standard. As we have seen, when the exercise of judgment in a particular area has been characterized by systematic mistakes that undermine the objective normative content of the standard, upholding rule of law values may well require ruling out certain exercises of discretion.

IV. Rethinking the Person, Not the Reason

The feminist debates on the reasonable person in these controversial contexts provide important insight into the egalitarian reconstruction of an objective reasonableness standard. Although clarifying normative content and shaping and constraining discretion are undoubtedly helpful, the relevant legal tools also have a crucial bearing on this enterprise. It is to this issue that we now turn. The law's predominant expression of the objective reasonableness standard in its various settings is found in the ubiquitous reasonable person who began this inquiry. At several places along the way we have sidestepped the issues he seems to pose in order to get a sharper sense of the objective reasonableness inquiry itself. But now we must return to the important question of whether the reasonable person is the best way to embody and convey that understanding.

The reasonable person—an idealized person—is the common law's characteristically ingenious solution to the complex problem of articulating a standard of appropriate attentiveness to others across an almost infinite variety of individuals and situations. The genius of the reasonable person is largely found in the way he seamlessly weaves together the normative components of the standard—attentiveness to others—with biographical or empirical qualities— age, intelligence, level of education, mode of transportation, etc. Thus constructed, the reasonable person has the undoubted virtue of making an otherwise abstract normative standard seem familiar and knowable. But these very virtues are inextricably linked to his most serious vices. In fact, the use of an idealized person often seems a poor way to capture the idea of what attentiveness to others requires, precisely because it makes it so difficult to distinguish between those qualities of the idealized person that matter normatively and those that do not. Beyond this, the personification of a normative ideal may

---

[80] This requirement may be particularly difficult, since, as Nourse points out, controversial law reform projects often mask the depth of the underlying controversies through deliberate ambiguity: (n 33 above) 953–961. Read in the light of the text above, this seems to suggest that where precision is most needed it may also be most elusive.

also incline the decision-maker to read ordinariness into the reasonableness component of the standard. These attributes of the reasonable person, though problematic generally, hold special dangers for equality seekers to whom the fixity of the standard is particularly important.

As we have seen, despite the difficulties with the reasonable person, many egalitarians end up insisting on the importance of a gender neutral standard precisely for egalitarian reasons. Recall for instance, Abrams's insistence on the importance of a properly reconstructed reasonable *person* standard in the context of sexual harassment.[81] In the provocation debate, Allen also argues that it is possible to make sense of the notion of a gender neutral legal person.[82] Similarly in 'Rape and the Reasonable Man', Hubin and Haely reject gendered understandings of reasonable agent standards. They point out that if reasonable agent standards are to be used for *mens rea*, and if the gendered reasonability thesis which holds that reasonableness standards are (*pace* MacKinnon) 'gendered to the ground' is correct, then the reasonable man standard must be used for a male accused.[83] This, they suggest, shows that the implications of the gendered reasonability thesis actually counter the very ambitions of the feminists who are its foremost proponents. Ultimately, like Abrams, Allen, and others, Hubin and Haely argue that in principle both men and women can achieve a more egalitarian understanding of the situation.[84]

However much we might laud the tenacity of such efforts it must also be admitted that the reasonable person creates special problems—a kind of double bind—for equality seekers. Insistence on the availability of a gender neutral legal person seems likely to perpetuate the male bias that has so often assumed the guise of the reasonable person. At the same time, however, specification of the particular qualities of the person actually judged carries with it its own set of dangers. The nature of some of these dangers, and the difficulty of resolving them, may lead us to ask whether the reasonable person does not create at least as many problems as he solves for the objective reasonableness standard. We have already noted how puzzling the House of Lords found the reasonable person in the provocation context.[85] But the problems are by no means confined to that admittedly difficult setting. Lord Simon's observation in *Camplin* actually seems to have more general salience: 'A reasonable woman with her sex eliminated is altogether too abstract a notion for my comprehension, or I am confident for that of any jury... [I]t hardly makes sense to say... that a normal woman must be notionally stripped of her femininity before she qualifies as a reasonable woman.'[86] Allen uses Lord Simon's quandary to critique the failure

---

[81] n 3 above.   [82] (n 48 above) 429.

[83] (n 47 above) 118, citing C MacKinnon, *Towards a Feminist Theory of the State* (Cambridge, Mass: Harvard University Press, 1989) 172–183. Hubin and Haely also suggest that it may be possible to dispense altogether with reasonable agent standards.   [84] ibid 131.

[85] *R v Smith* [2001] AC 146, [2000] 2 All ER 289 (HL), as discussed in ch 6 above, n 83.

[86] *DPP v Camplin* [1978] 2 All ER 168, (1978) 67 Cr App R 14, 26. Quoted in Allen (n 48 above) 429.

of the law's moral imagination. And this is indeed important. However, we need not accept all of the implications of Lord Simon's passage in order to admit the difficulty of conceiving of an agent without some implicit gender. Although it may well be possible notionally to strip away or counteract the attributes of the idealized agent that have troubling implications, this does not resolve the question of whether this is the most desirable approach to the objective standard. Many of the egalitarian commentators we have discussed are undoubtedly ingenious in their efforts to get around this worry. Yet Lord Simon's observation about the difficult abstraction inevitably involved in conceiving of a gender neutral legal person does seem to confirm a suspicion that creating an idealized person may not be the best way to capture the law's commitment to an objective reasonableness standard. And the problems he points to are particularly troubling for equality seekers.

Perhaps no stronger evidence can be found for the concern about personification and its egalitarian implications than the difficulties we saw in the sexual harassment debate. There, commentators attempting to counter the potentially inegalitarian effects of the reasonable person often engage in virtually endless specification of the qualities of the actual agent in order to displace the default characteristics of the reasonable person. Thus, they argue in favour of incorporating into the standard many detailed features of the life and biography of the agent—her language, her occupation, her level of education. The resulting approach often seems somewhat tortured, even ridiculous. But this recognition may incline us to overlook the extent to which this is actually necessitated by the very personification of the standard. It is simply that the weaknesses (even the dangers) of personification are most apparent when the reasonable person must be adapted to situations where almost all of its 'default' characteristics seem inapt. It is easy and perhaps tempting to mock the apparently relentless specification of qualities as an example of egalitarianism gone awry, but we should pause before doing so because this attempt to adapt the reasonable person to the demands of a more egalitarian conception of responsibility holds a broader lesson.

As we have seen, the reasonable person is most problematic when used to judge an actual person who is in some significant way very different from her reasonable counterpart. The fact that this divergence has attracted such scrutiny from critical egalitarians hardly seems surprising given that a proper relation between the normative and the non-normative components of the standard is crucial to an egalitarian allocation of responsibility. As we have seen, equality requires a kind of fixity or holding constant of the normative component of the standard. At the same time, we cannot allocate responsibility fairly unless we also ensure that the non-normative elements of the standard reflect the capacities of the agent in roughly the way contemplated by Hart's avoidability inquiry or Honoré's idea of general capacity. When this kind of inquiry takes the form of comparing the actual agent to her idealized counterpart, it inevitably requires some reshaping of the implicit or 'default' characteristics of the idealized person to make her a more apt standard for the actual agent. Only this will establish the kind of relation between the normative and non-normative aspects of the standard that is essential to an egalitarian conception of responsibility.

This importance of the task of reshaping the non-normative attributes of the reasonable person helps to account for the (apparently inordinate) emphasis that equality seekers often seem to place on specifying the various attributes of the person actually judged. Because critical egalitarians generally focus on those who diverge in many ways from the idealized standard, they are more aware of the normative assumptions built into the typical default characteristics of the reasonable person. It seems likely, for instance, that the reasonable person is assumed in the absence of insistence to the contrary to be fluent in the dominant language (probably English), to have a certain level of literacy (to be able to read), a certain level of physical ability, and the like. We cannot properly count these characteristics as normative, however, because we cannot blame an individual who fails to possess these capacities. There is thus no justification for holding any of these factors constant. Of course, often this will not matter, and the difficulties will remain invisible because the person judged will sufficiently resemble the reasonable person. However, as soon as important divergences in these kinds of characteristics appear, there is a risk of misallocating blame under a reasonable person standard that is not properly adjusted to reflect those divergences. To the extent that there are many such divergences, the importance of displacing the non-normative default characteristics increases, although perhaps so too does the difficulty of doing so. On this view, the 'endless specification' engaged in by critical egalitarians actually points to how personification implicitly incorporates (quite literally) into the normative standard all sorts of characteristics that may well be given some kind of normative weight unless specifically displaced.

But is this process of incorporating and displacing non-normative characteristics really the best way to conceptualize a reasonableness standard? The answer surely must be 'no'. We have identified culpable indifference to others as the heart of the objective reasonableness standard and have noted the importance of holding this constant. The reasonable person asks the indifference question by comparing what the actual agent did with what an idealized reasonable (attentive or non-indifferent) person would do in similar circumstances. But this will not properly identify indifference unless the idealized agent is given the non-normative attributes of the actual agent. At the same time, the fixity that equality requires means it is just as vital not to vary the normative attributes of the idealized agent to reflect those of the actual agent. So serious equality problems arise when the relation between the idealized and actual agents is in this way not exact. Viewed as such, it seems unsurprising that the objective standard is persistently troubled by the danger that an attribute that is really descriptive or biographical might be counted as normative. Because personification entails a standard that is part normative and part descriptive and is seamlessly so, it will be extremely difficult to disentangle these different elements. This suggests that the integration that renders personification attractive by making an abstract standard seem more concrete and knowable may be just what leads us astray.

Part of this difficulty with the reasonable person undoubtedly occurs because it offers so little guidance on what actually matters about the idealized person. Personification inevitably entails imputing all sorts of characteristics that are not relevant normatively, and which must therefore be varied in order to engage in a proper inquiry. But if the only attribute of the idealized person that really matters is his level of attentiveness to others, why should we express this in the form of an idealized person with many other attributes that do not bear on the normative question and which must therefore vary depending on the person actually judged? Because the reasonable person is such an oblique way of expressing a normative standard, it leaves open innumerable avenues of error. It is small wonder, then, that in the course of judging someone who differs significantly from the idealized person, decision-makers so often misjudge the relation between the normative element of the standard and its default characteristics—with the consequence that they sometimes fix what they should vary and vary what they should fix. As we have seen, the negligence cases treat intelligence as an aspect of the standard which we must hold firm. This implies that we are entitled to demand intelligence of others, even though closer inspection suggests that this is an untenable claim. Conversely, in provocation and elsewhere even normative qualities like self-control and regard for others were held to vary with the capacities of the accused. The personification of the standard thus turns out to be obfuscatory just when we most need assistance: in the difficult determinations of which aspects of the reasonable person should be held constant and which should be tailored to match the litigant.

There may also be a deeper conceptual problem with a personified standard. The fact that the legal standard is expressed in the form of an idealized person seems at least partially responsible for eliding the crucial difference between *particularizing* a general standard and *subjectivizing* it. Because the standard is expressed as a person, the only way to 'particularize' it is to substitute the attributes of the person actually judged for those of the idealized agent. But since this seems to reshape the standard of judgement itself, by most accounts it looks like subjectivizing. This is exacerbated because the nature of the general norm itself is so poorly expressed in the reasonable person that it is not clear just what one would particularize. Indeed, the way that personification seems to substitute subjectivization for particularization may also help to account for Wilson J's insistence in *Hill*[87] on the fixity of the objective standard that so puzzled us earlier. Perhaps what inclines her to insist on the 'objectivity' or fixity of the objective standard—and what inclines others to view that insistence as important—even though the quality to which she refers really seems to be an ordinary quality of any legal standard, is something more than just the sense that this fixity is especially important to equality. Perhaps it is the fact that where a normative standard is expressed in a personified form (as with the 'ordinary person' test for self-control in provocation which she is discussing) the difference between particularization and subjectivization is

---

[87] *R v Hill* (1986) 25 CCC (3d) 322.

sufficiently compromised that the very objectivity of the standard seems threatened in any attempt to particularize it. In this sense then, it may be that Wilson J's observation speaks as much to the dangers a personified standard poses to the law's commitment to equality as it does to the objective standard itself.

Personification of the standard also poses particular impediments to a more egalitarian conception of responsibility. This arises because of how the default characteristics of the reasonable person tend to mirror those of the privileged in our society—'unmodified', the reasonable person is presumptively white, male, educated, an English speaker, literate, adult, employed, physically able, and the like. This is not to say that he could not be made black, female, illiterate, physically disabled, and so on. The point is rather that the need to displace default characteristics (whenever they do not pertain) places a difficult burden on those who do not share those characteristics. Even identifying what might need to be displaced will be difficult—for such characteristics are rarely even recognized as such until they are challenged. And displacement necessitates insisting on the relevance of some attribute of the person actually judged (not fluent in English, for instance, or not literate). Further, the more the person actually judged differs from the idealized person, the greater the number of qualities that will need to be specified. So because personification builds in default characteristics which are not normative, and because those characteristics are far more likely to reflect the privileged than the disadvantaged, those who are not privileged will have to work harder to ensure that the standard of responsibility is properly applied to them. Even though the aim is to adapt the reasonable person in order to ensure a fair allocation of responsibility (to realize rather than relativize responsibility), this process will often sound like the kind of plea for special treatment or accommodation that undermines those who are forced to engage in it. To the extent that the actual agent resembles the idealized agent and possesses his default characteristics, however, no such burdens are imposed on him.

It will always (and rightly) be difficult to justify employing a conceptual tool that is much more burdensome for some individuals than for others. But it is yet harder to account for why we would place that additional burden on the most disadvantaged. Effectively this is what we do when we insist that it is up to those who do not see themselves in the idealized agent to identify and displace all of its inapt attributes, while by contrast the privileged person who finds herself nicely paralleled by the normative and non-normative attributes of the idealized person faces no such difficulties. This feature of personification means that both the burden of reshaping the standard and the consequent likelihood of the standard going badly awry are far greater in the case of the disadvantaged than the privileged. For this reason, personification effectively poses special difficulties for the disadvantaged. This suggests that it is difficult to sustain an argument for personification of the standard both on specific equality grounds as well as on more general conceptual grounds.

Before we leave the difficulties of a personified standard, we should note one further problem, which though perhaps more speculative is no less important.

Not only does personification obscure which attributes are normative and which are not, but it may also incline judges to misread the normative content by equating reasonableness and ordinariness. As we have discussed, to a significant extent the equation of commonness and correctness (or their inverse, aberrance and wrong) is already closely aligned with our idea of fault even though it may not be conceptually entailed by it. However, personification may increase the temptation to interpret reasonableness by looking to what is ordinarily done. If, as we have noted, it can be difficult to resist treating common behaviour as non-culpable even when the legal standard is clear, this is surely exacerbated by a standard that is vague and ill-expressed. So, decision-makers seeking to determine what an idealized person might do in a concrete situation may well look to infuse common or ordinary behaviour into their assessments of reasonableness. If we are not quite sure what the reasonable person would do, it is far easier to conceive of what the ordinary person would do. In this way, phrasing a normative standard in terms of what an idealized person would do seems to invite the common error of construing the reasonable as ordinary. Indeed, judges accurately describe what they actually do when they refer (as they often do) to the test as involving the person of 'ordinary' prudence, thus effectively equating ordinariness with the core of the reasonable person. The very obviousness and familiarity of the personified form of the standard may in this way facilitate the dangerous extrapolation from the ordinary to the reasonable, a link that we have repeatedly noted.

The fact that the question of objective reasonableness is so often shaped by the question of what we can do with the reasonable person, therefore, seems to impede rather than to further the project of developing a more egalitarian conception of responsibility. The use of a paradigmatic 'person' as a way of encapsulating what kind of behaviour can be counted as reasonable may itself explain at least part of the endemic confusion between the normative and descriptive components of the standard. Critics trying to respond to how the standard gets it wrong often replicate the same difficulty when they use its terms. In part this is because personification makes it so difficult to articulate a standard that is appropriately sensitive to equality without implying some kind of essential moral and epistemological differences among genders, races, and the like. Further, the very familiarity of the reasonable person may tempt us to infer that ordinary behaviour is reasonable. For these and other reasons, it is arguable that further personification of the objective standard is actually a move in the wrong direction. Perhaps equality seekers are better off challenging the personification rather than trying it to make it 'our own'. So although feminists and other egalitarians at times advocate abandoning the 'reason' in favour of more and more finely grained descriptions of the person, this analysis argues instead that we would be well advised, for equality reasons, to consider abolishing not the reason but rather the person created so long ago in *Vaughan*. We may make more progress by instead developing a sharper sense of just what it was about the reasonable person that we so cared about, and by noting where in attempting to realize that promise we have gone consistently and problematically wrong.

A. Some illustrations

Rather than trying to reshape the 'reasonable person' in order to respond to equality worries, this analysis suggests that we should step away from the person and focus instead on the normative content of the standard and how it may be implicated in different kinds of situations. But how would such an inquiry proceed? Part of the appeal of the reasonable person is his broad utility; his usefulness across different inquiries seems to obviate need for a very context-specific analysis of what he is intended to accomplish in any particular situation. So the reasonable person seemed capable of expressing, for instance, an appropriate attentiveness to risk, an appropriate level of self-control, an appropriate degree of resilience, and the like. Despite his common sense appeal, however, our analysis suggests that this utility is largely illusory: although the reasonable person expresses many things, he does so with no great precision. In contrast, because the account here emphasizes the precise normative content of the objective standard, the inquiry that it demands will of necessity be very context-specific. Therefore, it will not be possible to formulate a detailed general answer to the question of how the inquiry into objective reasonableness would proceed after the demise of the reasonable person. Nonetheless, some general guidance and a few illustrations may assist in 'depersonalizing' the inquiry.

Because we cannot assume that the reasonable person actually plays the same role in all of the situations in which he appears, the first step of any such inquiry will require clarifying the exact normative role that the reasonableness standard plays in the particular context. In the context of culpability for negligence, the argument here suggests that the standard is best understood to express a demand for appropriate attentiveness to the interests of others. The real aim of the reasonable person in the law of negligence, on this reading, is to identify culpable indifference. If we are asking the negligence question directly, without the intercession of the reasonable person, we will ask whether the behaviour in question betrays indifference to the interests of others. The implication of our analysis is that where there is such indifference, regardless of how ordinary or common it may be, it must be condemned. This is the fixed normative content of the law of negligence, and it is vital to its egalitarian character.

But although the demands of the law are in this way invariant, they cannot be properly applied to a particular situation without considering the various aspects of that situation that bear on whether those demands have been met. Biography and the other features of the agent that so concern egalitarian critics are important to the inquiry, though not in quite the same way as under a personified standard. Clarifying the nature of the objective normative demand of reasonableness should therefore make it easier to distinguish between the legitimate task of particularizing the standard in the context of a concrete situation, and more troubling one of subjectivizing the standard and thereby undermining the force of the legal demand. In this way, it should be possible to pay attention to context without thereby running the risk of subjectivizing which brings with it many of the implications that are so worrisome on equality grounds. A few brief illustrations may be helpful here.

Recall our earlier analysis of *Roberts v Ramsbottom*.[88] In the last chapter we discussed how focusing on the general normative demand of attentiveness to others (and particularizing that demand) makes it possible to see how the effect of the defendant's stroke in *Roberts* negates the imputation of indifference. In fact, greater attentiveness to how indifference might explain culpability in negligence seems to underlie *Mansfield v Weetabix*,[89] the case that eventually disapproved of Neill J's holding in *Roberts*. In *Mansfield* a defendant who did not know that he was suffering from malignant insulinoma became hypoglycaemic, and this hypoglycaemia severely impaired his ability to drive. As in *Roberts*, he did not lose consciousness and continued to drive, eventually causing a number of accidents. The trial judge and the Court of Appeal accepted that the effect of the defendant's condition was such that he could not be blamed in any way for continuing to drive. After criticizing the distinction between complete and partial loss of consciousness, Leggatt LJ states that the standard must be what could be expected of the reasonably competent driver suffering from the defendant's condition—to do otherwise would be to impose strict liability. But in Leggatt LJ's judgement, recourse to the reasonable person seems to be a way to state the conclusion, not to arrive at it. Instead, the standard of care inquiry focuses on whether the defendant can be blamed for acting as he did.[90] Both Leggatt LJ and Aldous LJ stress that since the defendant was not at fault, he did not fall below the standard of care.[91] So although reference is made to the reasonable person, the conceptual core of the judgement is on the normative failing: the defendant was not indifferent, he cannot be blamed, and therefore he is not liable in negligence.

An indifference-focused analysis also suggests that *Vaughan v Menlove*[92] was correctly decided—despite, rather than because of, the reasons most commonly associated with that decision. The contemporary significance of *Vaughan* is focused on the court's response to Mr Menlove's argument that if he had acted to the best of his judgement, he ought not to be blamed for not possessing 'the highest order of intelligence'. But more attentiveness to the different elements of negligence suggests at least some of the reason for the complexity of *Vaughan*'s legacy. These elements bear on the centrality of indifference. Mr Menlove asks for a reduced standard on the ground that he lacks cognitive capacity. On the analysis suggested above, a claim for an individualized cognitive standard is persuasive: because an individual cannot be blamed for substandard intelligence, he cannot properly be held liable for mistakes that are

---

[88] n 41 above.   [89] n 42 above.
[90] See, for instance, the quote from Lord Wilberforce in *Snelling v Whitehead* to the effect that 'if no blame can be imputed' the action in negligence must fail: The Times, 31 July 1975, HL (E), [1974] CLY 872, quoted in *Mansfield* (n 42 above) 1268.   [91] ibid 1268–1269.
[92] n 54 above.

the result of this failing. But *Vaughan* still seems correct in the result, because whatever intellectual deficiencies Mr Menlove may have had, the accident does not seem attributable to them. He was repeatedly warned of the risk, he actually stated that he would chance it, and as Vaughan J points out 'it was manifest that he adverted to his interest in the insurance office'.[93] All of the judgments indicate that Mr Menlove was in fact to be blamed for the fire that was variously described as the result of his 'gross negligence', procrastination, and the like.

This brings us to the other part of Mr Menlove's claim. Intriguingly, although the basis for his claim is a *cognitive* deficiency, the 'relief' he asks for takes the form of a diminished standard of *judgement*—in other words a diminished normative standard. In effect, he claims that since he is not particularly intelligent he should be held only to his own standard of judgement—in other words his own set of values. But throughout this analysis we have affirmed the centrality of holding firm to legal values: they cannot be tailored to reflect the values of the individual in question without doing violence to the rule of law. So *Vaughan* rightly rejects the defendant's 'best efforts' claim: he cannot insist on setting his own standard of *judgement*, for that is the task of the law.[94] Some of the complexity of *Vaughan*'s legacy turns on this slippage between the nature of the defendant's alleged shortcoming and what attentiveness to that shortcoming is said by him to require. The implication of the indifference analysis is that even if we reject (as we should) the view that diminished intelligence has no bearing on fault in negligence, this in no way entails that individuals set their own standards of prudence or judgement. Thus, we can and should agree with the court in *Vaughan* that individuals cannot insist on being held to their own standards of judgement. The standard of prudence, as Tindal CJ states, is set by the law and so does not vary with the judgement of each individual. Commentators have typically read *Vaughan* as standing for the view that the reasonable person sets both the required level of intelligence and the appropriate standard of judgement, with the result that the individual variations in these capacities are irrelevant to the standard of care. But this analysis suggests that because Mr Menlove's claim elided two very different types of ignorance (moral and non-moral), its rejection led to the overly broad conclusion that ignorance would not be attributed to the reasonable person. The better way to make sense of *Vaughan* is to note that however limited Mr Menlove's intelligence may have been, his actions undoubtedly betrayed extreme self-preference and thus exhibit the indifference that we properly call fault in negligence. It is the focus

[93] ibid 477.
[94] Thus, were Weinrib's equality justification confined to the standard of judgement (as opposed to the level of intelligence) we can demand of individuals, it would seem to provide a compelling account of the private law analogue of the mistake of law rule. In Weinrib's account, as with the mistake of law rule, the egalitarian nature of legal demands necessitates rejection of any claim to be judged according to what are essentially one's own standards: *The Idea of Private Law* (Cambridge, Mass: Harvard University Press, 1995).

on indifference that clarifies what the defendant can and cannot be blamed for. In contrast, attempting to determine what characteristics should and should not be attributed to the reasonable person only seems to complicate the inquiry and at best states the conclusion of the analysis, rather than helping to guide it.

In this sense, it is possible to see how focusing on indifference helps to clarify some of the aspects of the negligence inquiry that seem puzzling under the 'reasonable person' approach. However, this does not respond to all of the worries that egalitarian critics voiced about correcting for implicit bias or lack of knowledge or information. To the extent that the decision-maker may not be well acquainted with the context that is relevant to responsibility, it will be necessary to ensure that this is done. But the focus on indifference provides a better way to understand what may be relevant than does the focus on the attributes of the idealized person. In order to see how this may be so we need a somewhat more complex example. The difficult American criminal negligence case of *State v Williams* serves as an illustration here.[95]

In *Williams*, the Washington Court of Appeals upheld the manslaughter conviction of a mother and father on the ground that they negligently failed to supply their 17-month-old child with necessary medical treatment. The parents were Native American. The father had a grade six and the mother a grade eleven education. Their baby became ill. The lower court describes what happened next:

> The defendants were ignorant. They did not realize how sick the baby was. They thought that the baby had a toothache and no layman regards a toothache as dangerous to life. They loved the baby and gave it aspirin in hopes of improving its condition. They did not take the baby to a doctor because of fear that the Welfare Department would take the baby away from them. They knew that medical help was available because of previous experience. They had no excuse that the law will recognize for not taking the baby to a doctor.[96]

The defendants were convicted at trial and appealed.

Horowitz CJ for the Court of Appeals begins his decision by finding that a conviction for manslaughter does not require wilful conduct. Since simple negligence is enough to support a conviction for statutory manslaughter, all that needs to be proven is a violation of parental duty. The relevant standard asks 'at what time would an ordinarily prudent parent, solicitous for the welfare of his child and anxious to promote its recovery, deem it necessary to call in the services of a physician.'[97] The application of this standard to the facts in *Williams* is complicated because unfortunately in the last week of his life the child became so ill that he would not have survived even if he had been taken to a doctor. So the question was whether the parents should have sought medical care in the week before the baby became critically ill. The medical evidence during this critical period is 'not crystal clear'.[98] During this five-day period, the child was fussy and

---

[95] 484 P 2d 1167 (Wash App 1971).   [96] ibid 1170, quoting the trial court.   [97] ibid 1173.
[98] ibid 1174.

could not keep food down. The swelling in his cheek went up and down and his cheek also turned a bluish colour. The Court states that the defendants did not understand the seriousness of the child's symptoms during this period, nor would an 'ordinary' parent have done so. But the Court, applying the standard of ordinary caution (i.e. the caution exercisable by a man of reasonable prudence under the same or similar condition), finds that the parents were sufficiently put on notice regarding the child's condition to have required them to obtain medical care for the child during the critical period.[99] This failure to observe the standard of ordinary caution sustains their conviction for manslaughter.

Williams is undoubtedly a difficult case, complicated in part by the fact that although the legal standard is satisfied by simple negligence, the consequence is a conviction for manslaughter. But let us focus on whether the parents should have been found negligent and how approaching that question through an indifference analysis may have led to a better, and more egalitarian, analysis than the ordinarily/reasonably prudent parent standard that the Court employs. To begin with, let us set aside the judicial observations about the ignorance of the defendants. There is no suggestion that they lacked intelligence and although they were not particularly well educated that does not seem to bear in any way on the events. In fact, the trial judge observes that no layman would regard a toothache as dangerous to life, suggesting that the Williams were in the same position as most other parents in this respect. The difficulty under the standard seems to arise because the parents' hesitation to take their child to the doctor was one that would not be shared by most 'ordinary' parents. This is because it involved the fear that given their identity as Native American parents, the Welfare Authorities might be particularly inclined to take the view that they were not properly caring for their child. In applying the reasonably prudent parent test, the courts in *Williams* seem to slip, as courts so often do, between what ordinary parents would do and what reasonableness requires.

Both levels of court in *Williams* describe the appropriate test as referring to ordinarily or reasonably prudent parents under the same or similar conditions. But they do not treat the fact of being a Native American parent with a greater fear of the intervention of Child Welfare authorities as part of the 'conditions' in which the idealized parent ought to be placed. However, they do not directly address why this should or should not be a circumstance that feeds into determination of the standard. The trial judge simply states bluntly that the defendants have 'no excuse the law will recognize for not taking the baby to a doctor'.[100] Horowitz CJ is more circumspect, referring to the fear of the authorities and then simply stating that there was no evidence that they were unable to take the child to a doctor. Approaching this case through the lens of the reasonable person

---

[99] 484 P 2d 1167 (Wash App 1971).
[100] ibid 1170, quoting the trial court.

undoubtedly requires consideration of whether the actual parents' fear of the welfare authorities should be attributed to the reasonable parent. The very outcome of the case seems to turn on this question: if we treat the fear as legitimate and attribute it to the idealized parent, then the failure to seek medical care during the period will probably be seen as reasonable given that a layman would not have seen the child's symptoms as life-threatening during the critical period. But how ought we to decide what should be attributed to the idealized parent? Neither the reasonable person test itself nor the reasoning in *Williams* gives us much insight into this inquiry.

The Court in *Williams* seems to assume that because ordinary parents would have sought medical care even long before the symptoms became life-threatening, it was unreasonable for the Williams to fail to do so. Yet the standard of 'ordinary caution' with which the court infuses the reasonable parent standard arguably misleads them in their analysis. This is because unlike 'ordinary' parents the Williams may have had a strong countervailing reason not to seek medical care—and crucially, this reason may actually be consistent with attentiveness to the interests of their child. We would need to know more about the apprehension policies of the Child Welfare authorities in Washington State at that time, and the fate of children taken into care. But it is perfectly plausible that their fear was rational (in the sense of being well founded) and reasonable (in that it was consistent with seeking the welfare of their child). For instance, if children were routinely apprehended at higher rates from aboriginal parents, and often mistreated and neglected in care, the Williams's decision not to take their child to the hospital looks not merely reasonable but correct. Judged from the perspective of their reasonably limited knowledge of the risk posed by a serious toothache during the critical period, the little boy may well have been better off suffering a bit more for a toothache than being taken into care and quite possibly mistreated. If the belief is a reasonable one, ought it to be attributed to the reasonable person even though it is not an ordinary belief? I think our sense would be that it should, but note again that the reasonable person provides no guidance on this difficult question.

Attempting to puzzle through what a more attentive court might do with the reasonable person in a case like *Williams* suggests that we often seem to answer the question of what can and cannot be attributed to the reasonable person by inquiring into whether the relevant belief or characteristic is consistent with attentiveness to the interests of others. In *Williams*, what tempts us to think that their belief should be attributed to the reasonable parent is the fact that it is possible to understand it as consistent with (or even an expression of) attentiveness to the well-being of their child. Think, by contrast, of a parent who notices that her child is extremely ill and yet who decides not to take the child to the hospital because she does not want to miss a big New Year's Eve party. Because it exhibits a form of self-preference, this kind of characteristic would play a very different role under a reasonable person inquiry. The *Williams* case illustrates the difficulty with the use of the reasonable person. But even when we are more attentive, this example suggests that we should attribute characteristics to the reasonable person only where we think those characteristics are consistent with attentiveness to others. If this is so, then it seems the real content of the reasonable person actually draws on the idea of indifference, however obliquely. The inquiry seems much more straightforward if courts instead ask whether the relevant conduct betrayed culpable indifference.

In the *Williams* case, as suggested, this would require a much closer investigation into whether the parents' failure to seek medical care betrayed indifference to the well-being of their child. Asking the question about culpability in this way should also draw attention to the fact that it is unlikely that we can answer the culpability question without knowing more about the context. Was the fear of the parents well-founded? What were the risks to the child if taken into custody? What exactly could we expect the parents to have known about the condition of the child during the critical period? The Court in *Williams* sidesteps all of these questions by focusing on what ordinary parents would have done and then finding these parents negligent because their choices failed to mirror those of ordinary parents. In this way, the reasonable person inquiry makes it all too easy to interpret ordinary behaviour as reasonable. And although the focus on indifference alone will not entirely eliminate this danger, it is more likely to focus the inquiry on the right issues. Rather than struggling over whether the reasonable person should be a Native American and what kind of personal history with child welfare authorities might be attributed to that person, what level of education, and the like, it seems far better to ask whether these parents exhibited indifference to the interests of their child when they hesitated in obtaining medical care because of their fears about the child welfare authorities. Asking the indifference question directly clarifies what we need to inquire into and understand, especially in a context where a belief may be unusual.

Williams remains a difficult case, as do many of the other negligence cases we discussed. The claim here is not that abandoning the personification of the standard will make all such cases easy—it will not. A conceptual tool is not to be judged on whether it makes difficult questions easy, but rather on whether it directs the inquiry to the issues and the evidence that seem most relevant to the outcome. The oddity of the reasonable person, despite his ubiquitousness, is that he does such a poor job at this. At the level of justification, the reasonable person's connection to common sense reasoning makes it all too easy for the reasoning in the negligence inquiry to be conclusory. Focusing on indifference in the negligence context will not eliminate all of the difficulties surrounding the reasonable person. It will not make hard cases easy, and it will not render justification transparent in all cases. But what it arguably will do is focus our attention on the right issues and enable us to ask the right questions about when context and biography matter and when they do not. If fault in negligence without the reasonable person is unfortunately not as picturesque, we may at least hope that it will be more just.

V. CONCLUSION

Focusing on the equality worries about objective reasonableness standards is illuminating. Articulating these worries more sharply helps to conceptualize some of the most perplexing problems with the operation of the standard. Indeed, feminist critiques of the reasonable person confirm the extent to which the standard has typically given judges access to a barely articulated composite of normative and descriptive factors shaped by common sense. It is said that a strength of the standard is that it takes account of ordinary human failings, and yet this very reliance on what is customary or ordinary seems to be at the heart of the problem. Perhaps some 'ordinary' human failings are unproblematic and unsystematic, but as we have seen many are not. An important part of the reconstructive task is to identify where common sense has gone wrong, been unfair or exclusionary, and therefore where and how we should be especially wary of the reasonable person. Indeed, it is arguably because of this that so many critics are prepared to give up on reasonableness standards. Yet the submerged tension between what is reasonable and what is customary can prove fruitful, illustrating as it does that the ideal of reasonableness is not exhausted by notions of what is ordinary or customary. In fact, objective standards of reasonableness hold the potential to express the principle of equal moral worth in those interactions where it may be most subtly and yet most pervasively undermined.

But if this is the strength of the objective standard, that strength is also peculiarly vulnerable. Because the distinctive promise of the standard is found in its ability to challenge and indeed condemn customary beliefs, to the extent that the meaning of reasonableness is derived from conceptions of what is normal or ordinary its promise is lost. As we have seen, too often the meaning of reasonableness is so entangled with conceptions of what is normal or ordinary that we do allow customs to make the law 'their perch, and not their terror'.[101] Again the feminist debate is salutary here: feminist law reform efforts help to illustrate how we can hold objective reasonableness standards to their promise and thus preserve the rule of law. It is crucial to the legitimacy of the standard, as we have seen, to distinguish sharply between its normative and non-normative content. Often, clarifying the normative content of reasonableness in the relevant context will be sufficient to enable the kind of fixity that equality requires. As we have seen, however, in moments where there is deep tension between what is reasonable and what is customarily done, preserving the content and the fixity of reasonableness will necessitate doing more. Specifying the normative content of the standard and correcting for the kinds of systematic errors that critical jurisprudence helps us delineate may go some way to preventing the kind of 'rule of custom' that is so inimical to an egalitarian conception of responsibility.

---

[101] William Shakespeare, 'Measure for Measure' in *The Complete Pelican Shakespeare* (gen ed A Harbage) (New York: Viking, 1979) Angelo: II 1–4, 407.

Ultimately, it will also be crucial to structure and guide the exercise of judicial discretion to avoid the characteristic errors of customary norms.

As we have seen, critics of the reasonable person have often charged that it is the reasonableness component of the test that is problematic for equality seekers. However, while this analysis takes the egalitarian criticisms of the reasonable person as its point of departure, its conclusion points in precisely the opposite direction. Ultimately, it seems more true to egalitarian ambitions to abolish not the reason but instead the person created so long ago in *Vaughan v Menlove*. As a common sense stand-in for a remarkably complex idea, he has perhaps served as a useful kind of shorthand. Undoubtedly the common law would not be as colourful without the slightly frumpy figure that has been the focus of its literary imagination. But the opportunities for efficiencies and for imagination that the reasonable person has long held out may be illusory. Indeed, these very 'strengths' seem intimately linked to his most serious shortcomings. Although he has for well over a century given us a rapid and sometimes picturesque basis and justification for difficult questions of judgement, we may conclude that the reasonable person has lived out the last of his days.

In an increasingly diverse world, the inevitable reshaping of characteristics that such a model person demands comes to seem a futile and ultimately a misguided task. Better instead to ask more directly when our interactions betray the kind of culpable indifference that we properly call fault in negligence. Better to invite openly the necessarily contextual analysis of the quality of the normative choice that particular interactions reveal. And, although critics have sometimes suggested that we abolish the *reason* part of the standard, we may instead see another course before us. Indeed, at the end of the day, we may come to believe that we can fortify the reason by abolishing the person.

Bibliography

Kathryn Abrams, 'The Reasonable Woman: Sense and Sensibility in Sexual Harassment Law' (Winter 1995) Dissent 48

JH Aiken, 'Protecting Plaintiffs' Sexual Pasts: Coping with Preconceptions through Discretion' (2002) 51 Emory LJ 559

Alex Aleinikoff, 'The Constitution in Context: The Continuing Significance of Racism' (1992) 63 Colo L Rev 325

Dolly F Alexander, 'Twenty Years of Morgan: A Criticism of the Subjectivist View of Mens Rea and Rape in Great Britain' (1995) 7 Pace Intl L Rev 207

GJ Alexander and TS Szasz, 'Mental Illness as an Excuse for Civil Wrongs' (1967) 43 Notre Dame L Rev 24

A Alfieri, 'Defending Racial Violence' (1995) 95 Columbia L Rev 1301

Hilary Allen, 'One Law for All Reasonable Persons?' (1988) 16 Intl J Sociology of Law 419

Guido Alpa, 'The European Civil Code: "E Pluribus Unum"'' (1999) 14 Tul Eur & Civ L F 1

JB Ames, 'Law and Morals' (1908) 22 Harv L Rev 97

Michelle J Anderson, 'Reviving Resistance in Rape Law' 1998 U Ill L Rev 953

Appendix A, Muir v Alberta (1996) 132 DLR (4th) 695, Report of the Expert Witness Gerald Robertson, on the Sexual Sterilization Act, SA 1928, c 37

Aquinas, Commentary on the Nicomachean Ethics Vol I (trans CI Litzinger) (Chicago: H Regnery Co, 1964)

D Archard, 'The Mens Rea of Rape: Reasonableness and Culpable Mistakes' in Keith Burgess-Jackson (ed), A 'Most Detestable Crime': New Philosophical Essays on Rape (New York: Oxford University Press, 1999) 213

P Ariès, Centuries of Childhood: A Social History of Family Life (trans R Baldick) (New York: Vintage Books, 1962)

Jody D Armour, Negrophobia and Reasonable Racism: The Hidden Costs of Being Black in America (New York: New York University Press, 1997)

—— 'Race Ipsa Loquitur: Of Reasonable Racists, Intelligent Bayesians, and Involuntary Negrophobes' (1994) 46 Stan L Rev 781

Constance Backhouse, Coloured Coded: A Legal History of Racism in Canada (Osgoode Society, Toronto: Toronto University Press, 1999)

—— 'Married Women's Property Law in Nineteenth-Century Canada' (1988) 6 Law & History Rev 210

—— Petticoats and Prejudice: Women and Law in Nineteenth Century Canada (The Osgoode Society, Toronto: Toronto University Press, 1991)

Gary L Bahr, 'Tort Law and the Games Kids Play' (1978) 23 S Dak L Rev 275

B Baker, 'Provocation as a Defence for Abused Women Who Kill' (1998) 11 Can J L & Juris 193

Susan Bandalli, 'Provocation—A Cautionary Note' (1995) 22 J L & Soc 398

—— 'Women, Spousal Homicide and the Doctrine of Provocation in English Criminal Law' Master of Laws Thesis, Osgoode Hall Law School (1993)

N Kathleen (Sam) Banks, 'The "Homosexual Panic" Defence in Canadian Criminal Law' (1997) 1 CR (5th) 371

A Barak, 'Constitutional Human Rights and Private Law' (1996) 3 Rev Const Stud 218

Charles V Barrett III, 'Negligence and the Elderly: A Proposal for a Relaxed Standard of Care' (1984) 17 John Marsh L Rev 873

PWJ Bartrip and SB Burman, *The Wounded Soldiers of Industry: Industrial Compensation Policy, 1833–1897* (Oxford, New York: Oxford University Press, 1983)

DM Beatty, 'Canadian Constitutional Law in a Nutshell' (1998) 36 Alberta L Rev 605

Derrick Bell, *Faces at the Bottom of the Well: The Permanence of Racism* (New York: Basic Books, 1992)

Mark Bell, 'Mainstreaming Equality Norms into European Union Asylum Law' (2001) 26 E L Rev 20

Leslie Bender, 'A Lawyer's Primer on Feminist Theory and Tort' (1988) 38 J Legal Educ 3

John H Biebel, 'I Thought She Said Yes: Sexual Assault in England and America' (1995) 19 Suffolk Transnat'l L Rev 153

F Bohlen, 'Liability in Tort of Infants and Insane Persons' (1924–25) 23 Mich L Rev 9

Susan Bordo, 'Feminism, Postmodernism, and Gender-Skepticism' in Linda J Nicholson (ed), *Feminism/Postmodernism* (New York: Routledge, 1990) 133

Christine Boyle, 'The Judicial Construction of Sexual Assault Offences' in Julian V Roberts and Renate M Mohr (eds), *Confronting Sexual Assault: A Decade of Legal and Social Change* (Toronto: University of Toronto Press, 1994) 136

—— Marie-Andrée Bertrand, Celine Lacerte-Lamontagne, and Rebecca Shamai, *A Feminist Review of Criminal Law* (Ottawa: Ministry of Supply and Services, 1985)

—— and Marilyn MacCrimmon, 'The Constitutionality of Bill C-49: Analyzing Sexual Assault as if Equality Really Mattered' (1998) 41 CLQ 198

M Brazier and J Murphy (eds), *Street on Torts* (10th edn, London: Butterworths, 1999)

Nathan Brett, 'Sexual Offences and Consent' (1998) 11 Can J L Juris 69

G Brodsky, 'Recent Graduate Student Dissertation and Thesis Abstracts: Transformation of Canadian Equality Rights Law' (2000) 38 Osgoode Hall LJ 669

S Brooks, *Canadian Democracy: An Introduction* (3rd edn, Don Mills, Ontario: Oxford University Press Canada, 2000)

Susan Brownmiller, *Against Our Will: Men, Women and Rape* (New York: Simon and Schuster, 1975)

A Brudner, 'Agency and Welfare in Penal Law' in S Shute, J Gardner, and J Horder (eds), *Action and Value in Criminal Law* (Oxford: Clarendon Press, 1993) 21

Shawn Bushway and Anne Piehl, 'Judging Judicial Discretion: Legal Factors and Racial Discrimination in Sentencing' (2001) 35 Law & Society Rev 733

Paul Butler, 'Racially Based Jury Nullification: Black Power in the Criminal Justice System' (1995) 105 Yale LJ 677

Sir Richard Buxton, 'The Human Rights Act and Private Law' (2000) 116 Law Q Rev 48

Pedro Cabral, 'A Step Closer to Substantive Equality' (1998) 23 E L Rev 481

Naomi R Cahn, 'The Looseness of Legal Language: The Reasonable Woman Standard in Theory and Practice' (1992) 77 Cornell L Rev 1398

Rosemary Cairns-Way, 'Bill C-49 and the Politics of Constitutionalized Fault' (1993) 42 UNBLJ 325

Guido Calabresi, *Ideals, Beliefs and Attitudes, and the Law: Private Law Perspectives on a Public Law Problem* (Syracuse, NY: Syracuse University Press, 1985)

J Cameron, 'Dialogue and Hierarchy in Charter Interpretation: A Comment on *R v Mills*' (2001) 38 Alberta L Rev 1051

Canadian Abridgement, Family Law, XII, 'Status and Capacities of Children', s 2 (Torts) ss a (Child as Tortfeasor) (Toronto: Carswell, 1995, 2001)

G Canguilhem, *The Normal and the Pathological* (trans Carolyn R Fawcett with Robert S Cohen) (New York: Zone Books, 1991)

Jamie Cassels, '(In)equality and the Law of Tort: Gender, Race and the Assessment of Damages' (1995) 17 Advocates' Quarterly 158

Mary C Cerreto, '*Olmstead*: The *Brown v Board of Education* for Disability Rights: Promises, Limits and Issues' (2001) 2 Loyola J Publ Int L 47

Martha Challamas, 'The Architecture of Bias: Deep Structures in Tort Law' (1998) 146 U Penn L Rev 463

—— 'Questioning the Use of Race-Specific and Gender-Specific Economic Data in Tort Litigation: A Constitutional Argument' (1994) 63 Fordham L Rev 73

L Chamzuk, 'Consent: A Relevant Distinction?' (1998) 4 Appeal 22

Arthur Chaskalson, 'Equality & Dignity in South Africa' (2002) 5 Greenbag 2d 189

Jolynn Childers, 'Is There a Place for a Reasonable Woman in the Law? A Discussion of Recent Developments in Hostile Environment Sexual Harassment' (1993) 42 Duke LJ 854

Audrey Chin and Mark Peterson, The Institute for Civil Justice, *Deep Pockets, Empty Pockets: Who Wins in Cook County Jury Trials* (1985) (published for the Rand Corporation Institute for Civil Justice, R-3249-ICJ)

Tim Christian, *The Mentally Ill and Human Rights in Alberta: A Study of the Alberta Sexual Sterilization Act* (Edmonton: Faculty of Law, University of Alberta 1974)

Richard H Chused, 'Married Women's Property Law: 1800–1850' (1983) 71 Geo LJ 1359

KA Clarke and AI Ogus, 'What is a Life Worth' (1978) Brit J L & Soc 1

JF Clerk, *Clerk and Lindsell on Torts* (Gen ed AM Dugale) (18th edn, London: Sweet and Maxwell, 2000)

LD Cohn, 'Sex Differences in the Course of Personality Development: A Meta-Analysis' (1991) Psychological Bulletin 109

A Colby and W Damon, 'Listening to a Different Voice: A Review of Gilligan's *In a Different Voice*' in MR Walsh (ed), *The Psychology of Women: Ongoing Debates* (New Haven: Yale University Press, 1987) 321

Jules L Coleman, 'Mental Abnormality, Personal Responsibility, and Tort Liability' in BA Brody and H Tristram Engelhardt, Jr (eds), *Mental Illness: Law and Public Policy* (Boston: D Reidel Publishing Co, 1980)

—— *Risks and Wrongs* (Cambridge, New York: Cambridge University Press, 1992)

—— 'Tort Law and the Demands of Corrective Justice' (1992) 67 Ind LJ 349

Ronald KL Collins, 'Language, History and Legal Process: A Profile of the "Reasonable Person"' (1977) 8 Rut Cam LJ 311

JR Colombo, *The Canadian Global Almanac, 1998* (Toronto: Macmillan Canada, 1997)

The Compact Oxford English Dictionary (2nd edn, Oxford: Clarendon Press, 1994)

GD Comstock, 'Developments—Sexual Orientation and the Law' (1989) 102 Harv L Rev 1541

—— 'Dismantling the Homosexual Panic Defence' (1992) 2 Law and Sexuality 81

The Concise English Dictionary (London: Cassell/Omega Books, 1982)

G Coss, 'Editorial: Revisiting Lethal Violence by Men' (1998) 22 Criminal LJ 5

—— 'A Reply to Tom Molomby' (1998) 22 Criminal LJ 119

P Crocker, 'The Meaning of Equality for Battered Women Who Kill Men in Self-Defence' (1985) 8 Harv Women's LJ 121 andre douglas pond cummings [*sic*], ' "Lions and Tigers and Bears, Oh My" or "Redskins and Braves and Indians, Oh Why": Ruminations on *McBride v Utah State Tax Commission*, Political Correctness and the Reasonable Person' (1999) 36 California Western L Rev 11

Adrienne D Davis, 'The Private Law of Race and Sex: An Antebellum Perspective' (1999) 51 Stan L Rev 221

TB Dawson, 'Sexual Assault Law and Past Sexual Conduct of the Primary Witness: The Construction of Relevance' (1987–88) 2 CJWL 310

Richard Delgado, 'Rodrigo's Eighth Chronicle: Black Crime, White Fears—On the Social Construction of a Threat' (1994) 80 Va L Rev 503

—— 'Shadowboxing: An Essay on Power' (1992) 77 Cornell L Rev 813

RJ Delisle, 'Adoption, Sub-silentio, of the Paciocco Solution to Rape Shield Laws' 36 CR (5th) 254

—— 'Potential *Charter* Challenges to the New Rape Shield Law' (1992) 13 CR (4th) 390

'Developments in the Law—Race and the Criminal Process' (1988) 101 Harv L Rev 1473

KM DelTufo, 'Resisting "Utmost Resistance": Using Rape Trauma Syndrome to Combat Underlying Rape Myths Influencing Acquaintance Rape Trials' (2002) 22 BC Third World LJ 419

Department of Justice Canada, *Consultations and Outreach, Reforming Criminal Code Defences: Provocation, Self-Defence and Defence of Property*

Department of Justice Canada, 'Reforming Criminal Code Defences' (1998)

DA Donovan and SM Wildman, 'Is the Reasonable Man Obsolete? A Critical Perspective on Self-Defense and Provocation' (1981) 14 Loyola LAL Rev 435

Joshua Dressler, 'When "Heterosexual" Men Kill "Homosexual" Men: Reflections on Provocation Law, Sexual Advances, and the "Reasonable Man" Standard' (1995) 85 J Crim L & Criminology 726

RA Duff, 'Choice, Character, and Criminal Liability' (1993) 12 Law & Philosophy 345

—— *Intention, Agency and Criminal Liability: Philosophy of Action and the Criminal Law* (Oxford: Basil Blackwell, 1990)

—— 'Recklessness and Rape' (1981) 3 Liverpool L Rev 49

Kristie Dunn, ' "Yakking Giants": Equality Discourse in the High Court' (2000) 24 Melb U L Rev 427

Ronald L Dworkin, 'In Defense of Equality' (1983) 1 Social Philosophy and Policy 24

—— *Law's Empire* (Cambridge, Mass: Belknap Press of Harvard University Press, 1986)

—— *Sovereign Virtue: The Theory and Practice of Equality* (Cambridge, Mass: Harvard University Press, 2000)

—— 'What is Equality? Part I: Equality of Welfare' (1981) 10 Phil & Public Affairs 185

—— 'What is Equality? Part II: Equality of Resources' (1981) 10 Phil & Public Affairs 283

M Eberts, 'New Facts for Old: Observations on the Judicial Process' in R F Devlin (ed), *Canadian Perspectives on Legal Theory* (Toronto: Emond Montgomery Publications Limited, 1991) 467

FW Edgerton, 'Negligence, Inadvertence and Indifference: The Relation of Mental States to Negligence' (1926) 39 Harv L Rev 849

Nancy S Ehrenreich, 'Pluralist Myths and Powerless Men: The Ideology of Reasonableness in Sexual Harassment Law' (1990) 99 Yale LJ 1177

S Ehrlich, *Representing Rape: Language and Sexual Consent* (London, New York: Routledge, 2001)

J Ellis, 'Tort Responsibility of Mentally Disabled Persons' [1981] Am B Found Res J 1079

R Epstein, 'A Theory of Strict Liability' (1973) 2 J Leg Studies 151

Susan Estrich, 'Don't Be Surprised If OJ Gets Off Easy', *USA Today*, 23 June 1994, 1A

—— 'Rape' (1986) 95 Yale LJ 1087

KD Ewing, 'A Theory of Democratic Adjudication: Towards a Representative, Accountable and Independent Judiciary' (2000) 38 Alb L Rev 708

Joe R Feagin, Hernan Vera, and Pina Batur, *White Racism: The Basics* (2nd edn, New York: Routledge, 2001)

PW Ferguson, 'Rape and Reasonable Belief—A Limitation on *Morgan?*' (1986) 50 J Crim L 157

—— 'Reasonable Belief in Rape and Assault' (1985) 49 J Crim L 156

K Fierlbeck, 'Redefining Responsibility: The Politics of Citizenship in the United Kingdom' (1991) 24 Can J Political Science 575

LM Finley, 'A Break in the Silence: Including Women's Issues in a Torts Course' (1989) 1 Yale J L & Feminism 41

JG Fleming, *The Law of Torts* (9th edn, Agincourt: The Law Book Company, 1998)

GP Fletcher, *Rethinking Criminal Law* (Boston: Little, Brown, 1978)

—— 'The Theory of Criminal Negligence: A Comparative Analysis' (1971) U Penn L Rev 401

C Forell, 'Reassessing the Negligence Standard of Care for Minors' (Summer 1985) 15 New Mexico L Rev 485

—— and Donna Matthews, *A Law of Her Own: The Reasonable Woman as a Measure of Man* (New York: New York University Press, 2000)

M Foucault, *Discipline and Punish: The Birth of the Prison* (trans Alan Sheridan) (New York: Vintage Books, 1979)

—— *Power/Knowledge: Selected Interviews & Other Writings 1972–1977* (trans Colin Gordon, Leo Marshall, John Mepham, and Kate Soper) (New York: Pantheon, 1980)

P Fournier, 'The Ghettoisation of Difference in Canada: "Rape by Culture" and the Danger of a "Cultural Defence" in Criminal Law Trials' (2002) 29 Man LJ 81

L Francis (ed), *Date Rape: Feminism, Philosophy, and the Law* (University Park: Pennsylvania State University Press, 1996)

GHL Fridman, *Introduction to the Law of Torts* (Toronto: Butterworths, 1978)

—— *The Law of Torts in Canada* Vol I (Toronto: Carswell, 1989)

Betty Friedan, *The Feminine Mystique* (New York: Norton, 1963)

Lawrence Friedman, 'Law Reform in Historical Perspective' (1969) 13 St Louis ULJ 351

WJ Friedman, AB Robinson, and BL Friedman, 'Sex Differences in Moral Judgments' (1987) Psychology of Women Quarterly 11

J Gardner, 'The Mysterious Case of the Reasonable Person' (2001) 51 UTLJ 273

—— and T Macklem, 'Compassion without Respect? Nine Fallacies in *R v Smith*' (2001) Crim LR 623

—— and S Shute, 'The Wrongness of Rape' in J Horder (ed), *Oxford Essays in Jurisprudence* (4th Series, Oxford: Oxford University Press, 2000) 193

C Geertz, *Local Knowledge: Further Essays in Interpretive Anthropology* (New York: Basic Books, Inc, 1983)

Carol Gilligan, *In a Different Voice: Psychological Theory and Women's Development* (Cambridge, Mass: Harvard University Press, 1982)

Alan D Gold, 'Flawed, Fallacious but Feminist: When One Out of Three is Enough' (1993) 42 UNBLJ 381

Wayne Gorman, 'Provocation: The Jealous Husband Defence' (1999) 42 Crim LQ 478

R Graycar, 'The Gender of Judgments: Some Reflections on "Bias"' (1998) 32 UBC L Rev 1

—— 'Women's Work: Who Cares?' (1992) 14 Sydney L Rev 86

E Green, 'The Reasonable Man—Legal Fiction or Psychosocial Reality?' (1968) 2 Law & Soc Rev 241

L Green, *Judge and Jury* (Kansas City: Vernon Law Book Co, 1930)

—— 'The Negligence Issue' (1927–28) 37 Yale LJ 1029

Kent Greenawalt, 'Prescriptive Equality: Two Steps Forward' (1997) 110 Harv L Rev 1265

Jean Grimshaw, 'The "Maleness" of Philosophy' in *Philosophy and Feminist Thinking* (Minneapolis: University of Minnesota Press, 1986) 36

E Groscz, 'Philosophy' in S Gunew (ed), *Feminist Knowledge, Critique and Construct* (London, New York: Routledge, 1990)

WR Habeeb, 'Annotation: Weapons: Application of Adult Standard of Care to Infant Handling Firearms' (1973) 47 ALR 3d 620

Gillian Hadfield, 'Rational Women: A Test for Sex-Based Harassment' (1996) 83 Calif L Rev 1151

Livingston Hall and Selig J Seligman, 'Mistake of Law and *Mens Rea*' (1941) 8 U Chicago L Rev 641

Janet Halley, 'Sexuality Harassment' in Wendy Brown and Janet Halley (eds), *Left Legalism/Left Critique* (Durham, NC: Duke University Press, 2002) 80

Sandra Harding, 'Feminism, Science and the Anti-Enlightenment Critiques' in Linda J Nicholson (ed), *Feminism/Postmodernism* (New York: Routledge, 1990) 83

—— *The Science Question in Feminism* (Ithaca, NY: Cornell University Press, 1986)

—— 'Why Has the Sex/Gender System Become Visible Only Now?' in S Harding and MB Hintikka, *Discovering Reality: Feminist Perspectives on Epistemology, Metaphysics, Methodology, and Philosophy of Science* (Dordrecht, Holland: D Reidel, 1983) 311

FV Harper, F James, Jr, and OS Gray, *The Law of Torts* Vol III (2nd edn, Boston: Little, Brown and Company, 1986)

Angela P Harris, 'Equality Trouble: Sameness and Difference in Twentieth-Century Race Law' (2002) 88 CALR 1923

HLA Hart, *The Concept of Law* (2nd edn, Oxford: Clarendon Press, 1994)

—— 'Legal Responsibility and Excuses' in *Punishment and Responsibility: Essays in the Philosophy of Law* (Oxford: Clarendon Press, 1970) 31

—— 'Negligence, *Mens Rea* and Criminal Responsibility' in *Punishment and Responsibility: Essays in the Philosophy of Law* (Oxford: Clarendon Press, 1970) 146

Jill Elaine Hasday, 'Contest and Consent: A Legal History of Marital Rape' (2000) 88 Cal L Rev 1373

Rebecca S Henry, 'The Virtue in Discretion: Ethics, Virtue and Why Judges Must Be "Students of the Soul"' (1999) 25 NYU Rev of Law & Social Change 65

Bob Hepple, Mary Coussey, and Tufyal Choudhury, *Equality: A New Framework: Report of the Independent Review of the Enforcement of UK Anti-Discrimination Legislation* (Oxford, Portland: Hart Publishing, 2000)

AP Herbert, *Uncommon Law* (London: Metheun, 1935)

RFV Heuston and RA Buckley, *Salmond and Heuston on the Law of Torts* (21st edn, London: Sweet and Maxwell, 1996)

Erick L Hill and Jeffrey E Pfeifer, 'Nullification Instructions and Juror Guilt Ratings: An Examination of Modern Racism' (1992) 16 Contemp Soc Psychol 6

WS Holdsworth, *A History of English Law* Vol III (gen edn, London: Metheun, Sweet and Maxwell, 1966)

OW Holmes, *The Common Law* (ed. MD Howe) (Cambridge, Mass: Harvard University Press, 1963)

T Honoré, 'Responsibility and Luck: The Moral Basis of Strict Liability' in *Responsibility and Fault* (Oxford: Hart Publishing, 1999) 17

J Horder, 'Criminal Culpability: The Possibility of a General Theory' (1992) 12 Law & Philosophy 193

—— 'Gross Negligence and Criminal Culpability' (1997) 47 UTLJ 495

—— *Provocation and Responsibility* (Oxford: Clarendon Press, 1992)

A Howe, '*Green v The Queen*—The Provocation Defence: Finally Provoking Its Own Demise?' (1998) 22 Melbourne U L Rev 466

R Howse, 'Another Rights Revolution? The Charter and the Reform of Social Regulation in Canada' in P Grady, R Howse, and J Maxwell (eds), *Redefining Social Security* (Kingston: School of Policy Studies, Queen's University, 1995) 99

Donald C Hubin and Karen Haely, 'Rape and the Reasonable Man' (1999) 18 Law & Phil 113

Patricia Hughes, 'From a Woman's Point of View' (1993) 42 UNBLJ 341

—— 'Recognizing Substantive Equality as a Foundational Constitutional Principle' (1999) 22 Dalhousie LJ 5

Murray Hunt, 'The "Horizontal Effect" of the Human Rights Act: Moving Beyond the Public/Private Distinction' in J Jowell and J Cooper (eds), *Understanding Human Rights Principles* (Oxford, Portland: Hart, 2001) 161

—— *Using Human Rights Law in English Courts* (Oxford: Hart Publishing, 1997)

EM Hyland, '*R v Thibert*: Are There Any Ordinary People Left?' (1996–97) 28 Ottawa L Rev 145

MA Irvine, 'A New Trend in Equality Jurisprudence?' (1999) 5 Appeal 54

M Jackman, 'Poor Rights: Using the Charter to Support Social Welfare Claims' (1993) 19 Queen's LJ 65

—— 'The Protection of Welfare Rights under the Charter' (1988) 20 Ottawa L Rev 257

F James, Jr, 'The Qualities of the Reasonable Man in Negligence Cases' (1951) 16 Missouri L Rev 1

—— and JJ Dickinson, 'Accident Proneness and Accident Law' (1950) 63 Harv L Rev 769

Sheri Lynn Johnson, 'Black Innocence and White Jury' (1985) 83 Mich L Rev 1611

—— 'Race and the Decision to Detain a Suspect' (1983) 93 Yale LJ 214

C Jung, *Contributions to Analytical Psychology* (trans HG and Cary F Baynes) (London: K Paul, Trench, Trubner & Co Ltd, 1928)

KL Karst, *Belonging to America: Equal Citizenship and the Constitution* (New Haven: Yale University Press, 1989)

—— 'Why Equality Matters' (1983) 17 Ga L Rev 245

Amy H Kastely, 'Out of the Whiteness: On Raced Codes and White Race Consciousness in Some Tort, Criminal and Contract Law' (1994) 63 U Cinn L Rev 269

WP Keeton (gen ed), *Prosser and Keeton on the Law of Torts* (5th edn, St Paul, Minn: West Publishing Co, 1984)

E Keller, *Reflections on Gender and Science* (New Haven: Yale University Press, 1984)

Randall Kennedy, 'The State, Criminal Law, and Racial Discrimination: A Comment' (1994) 107 Harv L Rev 1255

Richard Kidner, 'The Variable Standard of Care, Contributory Negligence and *Volenti*' (1991) 11 Legal Stud 1

Nancy J King, 'Postconviction Review of Jury Discretion: Measuring the Effects of Juror Race on Jury Decisions' (1993) 92 Mich L Rev 63

EB Kinkead, *Commentaries on the Law of Torts* (San Francisco: Bancroft-Whitney Co, 1903)

L Klar, *Tort Law* (2nd edn, Scarborough: Carswell, 1996)

D Klimchuk, 'Circumstances and Objectivity' (1996) 45 CR (4th) 24

—— 'Outrage, Self-Control, and Culpability' (1994) 44 UTLJ 441

Audrey Kobayashi, 'Do Minority Women Judges Make a Difference?' (1998) CJWL 10

Linda Hamilton Kreiger, 'The Content of Our Categories: A Cognitive Bias Approach to Discrimination and Equality Employment Opportunity' (1995) 47 Stan L Rev 1161

W Kymlicka, *Multicultural Citizenship: A Liberal Theory of Minority Rights* (Oxford: Clarendon Press, 1995)

WR LaFave and AW Scott, *Handbook on Criminal Law* (St Paul, Minn: West Publishing Co, 1972)

Lynda Lange, 'Woman Is Not a Rational Animal: On Aristotle's Biology of Reproduction' in S Harding and MB Hintikka (eds), *Discovering Reality: Feminist Perspectives on Epistemology, Metaphysics, Methodology, and Philosophy of Science* (Dordrecht, Holland: D Reidel, 1983) 1

H Laugier, 'L'Homme normal' *Encyclopédie française* 4 (1937)

Law Reform Commission of Canada, *Sterilization: Implications for Mentally Retarded and Mentally Ill Persons*, Working Paper No 24 (Ottawa: Minister of Supply and Services Canada, 1979)

Charles Lawrence, 'The Id, the Ego, and Equal Protection: Reckoning with Unconscious Racism' (1987) 39 Stanford L Rev 317

Law Society of British Columbia, *Gender Equality in the Justice System* (1992)

Ian Leader-Elliott, 'Sex, Race, and Provocation: In Defence of *Stingel*' (1996) Crim LJ 72

Cynthia Kwei Yung Lee, 'Race and Self-Defence: Toward a Normative Conception of Reasonableness' (1996) 81 Minn L Rev 367

Toni Lester, 'The Reasonable Woman Test in Sexual Harassment Law—Will It Really Make a Difference?' (1993) 26 Indiana L Rev 227

PD Lifton, 'Individual Differences in Moral Development: The Relation of Sex, Gender and Personality to Morality' in AJ Stewart and MB Lykes (eds), *Gender and Personality* (Durham, NC: Duke University Press, 1985) 218

AM Linden, *Canadian Tort Law* (6th edn, Toronto: Butterworths, 1997)

—— *Canadian Tort Law* (7th edn, Markham: Butterworths Canada Ltd, 2001)

M Liu, 'A Prophet with Honour: An Examination of the Gender Equality Jurisprudence of Madam Justice Claire L'Heureux-Dubé of the Supreme Court of Canada' (2000) 25 Queen's LJ 417

Claire L'Heureux-Dubé, 'A Conversation about Equality' (2000) 29 Denver J Intl Law and Policy 65

—— 'Lecture: Conversations on Equality' (1999) 26 Man LJ 273

Genevieve Lloyd, *The Man of Reason: 'Male' and 'Female' in Western Philosophy* (London: Methuen, 1984)

Frank M McClellan, 'The Dark Side of Tort Reform: Searching for Racial Justice' (1996) 48 Rutgers L Rev 761

A McColgan, 'In Defence of Battered Women Who Kill' (1993) 13 Oxford J Legal Stud 508

CA MacKinnon, *Feminism Unmodified: Discourses on Life and Law* (Cambridge, Mass: Harvard University Press, 1987)

—— 'Feminism, Marxism, Method, and the State: An Agenda for Theory' (1982) 7 Signs 515

—— 'Feminism, Marxism, Method, and the State: Toward Feminist Jurisprudence' (1983) 8 Signs 635

——*Toward a Feminist Theory of the State* (Cambridge, Mass: Harvard University Press, 1989)

Timothy Macklem and John Gardner, 'Provocation and Pluralism' (2001) 64 Mod L Rev 815

James B McLindon, 'Separate but Unequal: The Economic Disaster of Divorce for Women and Children' (1987) 21 Fam LQ 351

H Maguigan, 'Battered Women and Self Defense: Myths and Misconceptions in Current Reform Proposals' (1991) 140 U Pa L Rev 379

MR Mahoney, 'Legal Images of Battered Women: Redefining the Issue of Separation' (1991) 90 Mich L Rev 1

R Majors and J Mancini Billson, *Cool Pose: The Dilemmas of Black Manhood in America* (New York: Lexington Books, 1992)

B Markesinis, 'Privacy, Freedom of Expression, and the Horizontal Effect of the Human Rights Bill: Lessons from Germany' (1999) 115 LQR 47

TH Marshall, *Citizenship and Social Class* (London, Concord, Mass: Pluto Press, 1992)

D Martin, 'Retribution Revisited: A Reconsideration of Feminist Criminal Law Reform Strategies' (1998) 36 Osgoode Hall LJ 151

Jill Martin, *Hanbury and Martin: Modern Equity* (16th edn, London: Sweet and Maxwell, 2001)

Robert Martin, 'Bill C-49: A Victory for Interest Group Politics' (1993) 42 UNBLJ 357

Robyn Martin, 'A Feminist View of the Reasonable Man: An Alternative Approach to Liability in Negligence for Personal Injury' (1994) 23 Anglo-Amer L Rev 334

Marc Mauer, *The Sentencing Project, Young Black Men and the Criminal Justice System: A Growing National Problem* (Washington, DC: Sentencing Project 1990)

——and Tracy Huling, *The Sentencing Project, Young Black Americans and the Criminal Justice System: Five Years Later* (Washington, DC: Sentencing Project 1995)

MT Mednick, 'On the Politics of Psychological Constructs: Stop the Bandwagon, I Want to Get Off' (1989) 44 American Psychologist 1118

RE Megarry, *Miscellany-at-Law: A Diversion for Lawyers and Others* (London: Stevens & Sons Ltd, 1955)

R Mison, 'Homophobia in Manslaughter: The Homosexual Advance as Insufficient Provocation' (1992) 80 Cal L Rev 133

Susan Moller Okin, 'Justice and Gender' (1987) 16 Phil & Pub Aff 42

——*Justice, Gender and the Family* (New York: Basic Books, 1989)

T Molomby, 'Revisiting Lethal Violence by Men: A Reply' (1998) 22 Criminal LJ 116

Gay Moon (ed), *Race Discrimination: Developing and Using a New Legal Framework: New Routes to Equality?* (Cambridge, Mass: Harvard University Press, 2000)

GE Moore, *Principia Ethica* (ed T Baldwin) (Revised edn, Cambridge: Cambridge University Press, 1903)

M Moran, 'Authority, Influence and Persuasion: *Baker* and the Puzzle of Method' forthcoming in D Dyzenhaus (ed), *The Unity of Public Law* (Oxford: Hart Publishing, 2003)

——'Right Answers, Wrong Questions: Objectivity, Feminism and the Partiality of Legal Theory' (unpublished manuscript on file with the author)

EM Morgan, 'Judicial Notice' (1944) 57 Harv L Rev 269

Jenny Morgan, 'Provocation Law and Facts: Dead Women Tell No Tales, Tales are Told about Them' (1997) 21 Melb U L Rev 237

C Morris, 'Custom and Negligence' (1942) 42 Col L Rev 1147

Sakthi Murthy, 'Rejecting Unreasonable Sexual Expectations: Limits on Using a Rape Victim's Sexual History to Show the Defendant's Mistaken Belief in Consent' (1991) 79 California L Rev 541

T Nagel 'Moral Luck' in Thomas Nagel (ed), *Mortal Questions* (Cambridge, New York: Cambridge University Press, 1979) 24

National Association of Women and the Law, *Stop Excusing Violence Against Women: NAWL's Brief on Provocation* (2000)

Jennifer Nedelsky, 'Embodied Diversity and the Challenges to Law' (1997) 42 McGill LJ 91

New South Wales Attorney-General's Working Party on the Review of the Homosexual Advance Defence, *Review of the Homosexual Advance Defence* (1996)

New South Wales Law Reform Commission Discussion Paper: Provocation, Diminished Responsibility and Infanticide (Sydney: New South Wales Law Reform Commission, 1993)

Margo L Nightingale, 'Judicial Attitudes and Differential Treatment: Native Women in Sexual Assault Cases' (1991) 23 CJWL 71

Note on 'Negligence' (1938) 23 Minn L Rev 628

Note, 'Mental Disability and the Right to Vote' 88 Yale LJ 1644 (1979)

Victoria Nourse, 'The "Normal" Successes and Failures of Feminism and the Criminal Law' (2000) 75 Chi-Kent L Rev 951

—— 'Passion's Progress: Modern Law Reform and the Provocation Defence' (1997) 106 Yale LJ 1331

M Nussbaum, 'Objectification' (1995) 24 Philosophy & Public Affairs 249

D Oliver, 'The Human Rights Act and the Public Law/Private Law Divide' (2000) EHRLR 343

The Oregon Supreme Court Task Force on Racial/Ethnic Issues in the Judicial System, 'Report of the Oregon Supreme Court Task Force on Racial/Ethnic Issues in the Judicial System' (1994) 73 Or L Rev 823

David M Paciocco, 'Subjective and Objective Standards of Fault for Offences and Defences' (1995) 59 Sask L Rev 271

—— 'Techniques for Eviscerating the Concept of Relevance: A Reply and Rejoinder to "Sex with the Accused on Other Occasions: The Evisceration of Rape Shield Protection" ' 33 CR (4th) 365

FT Palgrave's Golden Treasury (Centennial Edn, New York: Mentor Books, 1961)

GE Panichas, 'Rape, Autonomy, and Consent' (2001) 35 Law & Soc'y Rev 231

J Parry, *Mental Disability Law: A Primer* (5th edn, Washington: American Bar Foundation, 1995)

R Parsons, 'Negligence, Contributory Negligence and the Man Who does not Ride the Bus to Clapham' (1957) 1 Melb U L Rev 163

C Pateman, *The Sexual Contract* (Stanford, Calif: Stanford University Press, 1988)

Robert A Pearce and John Stevens, *Pearce and Stevens: Trusts and Equitable Obligations* (London: Butterworths Law, 2002)

Michael L Perlin, *Mental Disability Law: Civil and Criminal* (Charlottesville, Calif: Mitchie Co 1994, Lexis Law Pub Supp 1994)

SR Perry, 'Comment on Coleman: Corrective Justice' (1992) 67 Indiana LJ 381

—— 'The Impossibility of General Strict Liability' (1988) 1 Can J Law & Jur 147

——'The Moral Foundations of Tort Law' (1992) 77 Iowa L Rev 449

——'Protected Interests and Undertakings in the Law of Negligence' (1992) 42 U Toronto LJ 247

P Picher, 'The Tortious Liability of the Insane in Canada . . . with a Comparative Look at the United States and Civil Law Jurisdictions and a Suggestion for an Alternative' (1975) 13 Osgoode Hall LJ 193

T Pickard, 'Culpable Mistakes and Rape: Harsh Words on *Pappajohn*' (1980) 30 UTLJ 415

——'Culpable Mistakes and Rape: Relating Mens Rea to the Crime' (1980) 30 UTLJ 75

SH Pillsbury, 'Crimes against the Heart: Recognizing the Wrongs of Forced Sex' (2002) 35 Loy LA L Rev 845

Wendy Pollack, 'Sexual Harassment: Women's Experiences vs Legal Definitions' (1990) 13 Harv L Rev 35

FW Pollock, *The Law of Torts* (13th edn, London: Stevens and Sons Ltd, 1929)

——*Pollock's Law of Torts* (ed PA Landon) (15th edn, London: Stevens and Sons, 1951)

R Pound, *An Introduction to the Philosophy of Law* (New Haven: Yale University Press, 1954)

A Prenctice et al, *Canadian Women: A History* (2nd edn, Toronto: Harcourt Brace & Company, Canada, 1996)

WL Prosser, *Handbook of the Law of Torts* (2nd edn, St Paul, Minn: West Pub Co, 1955)

F Raday, 'Privatising Human Rights and the Abuse of Power' (2000) 13 Can JL & Juris 103

LD Rainaldi (ed), *Remedies in Tort* Vol II (Toronto: Carswell, 1987)

V Randall, *Women and Politics* (2nd edn, London: MacMillan, 1987)

J Rawls, *Political Liberalism* (New York: Columbia University Press, 1993)

——*A Theory of Justice* (Cambridge, Mass: Harvard University Press, 1971)

Sherene Razack, *Looking White People in the Eye: Gender, Race, and Culture in Courtrooms and Classrooms* (Toronto: University of Toronto Press, 1998)

Judith Resnik, 'Asking about Gender in the Courts' (1996) 21 Signs 952

Restatement (Second) of Torts (St Paul: American Law Institute Publishers, 1965) ss 283C, Comment b (1965)

Arthur Ripstein, *Equality, Responsibility and the Law* (Cambridge: Cambridge University Press, 1999)

GB Robertson, *Mental Disability and the Law in Canada* (2nd edn, Scarborough: Carswell Thomson Professional Publishing, 1994)

WH Rodgers, Jr, 'Negligence Reconsidered: The Role of Rationality in Tort Theory' (1980) 54 S Cal L Rev 1

WVH Rogers, *Winfield and Jolowicz on Tort* (15th edn, London: Sweet and Maxwell, 1998)

J-J Rousseau, *Émile, or on Education (1762)* (trans Barbara Foxley) (London: JM Dent & Sons Ltd, 1955)

C Rover, *Women's Suffrage and Party Politics in Britain 1866–1914* (London: Routledge & Kegan Paul, 1967)

Diana EH Russell, *The Politics of Rape: The Victim's Perspective* (New York: Stein and Day, 1975)

R Savatier, *Traite de la responsabilité civile en droit français civil, administratif, professionel* (2nd edn, Paris: Librairie générale de droit et de jurisprudence, 1951)

S Schiff, 'A *Res Ipsa Loquitur* Nutshell' (1976) 26 UTLJ 451

M Schlanger, 'Injured Women before Common Law Courts, 1860–1930' (1998) 21 Harv Women's LJ 79

EM Schneider, 'Describing and Changing: Women's Self-Defense Work and the Problem of Expert Testimony on Battering' (1986) 9 Women's Rts L Rep 195

—— 'Equal Rights to Trial for Women: Sex Bias in the Law of Self-Defense' (1980) 15 Harv CR–CL L Rev 623

SJ Schulhofer, *Unwanted Sex: The Culture of Intimidation and the Failure of Law* (Cambridge, Mass: Harvard University Press, 1998)

H Schwartz, 'Sex with the Accused on Other Occasions: The Evisceration of Rape Shield Protection' 31 CR (4th) 232

WF Schwartz, 'Objective and Subjective Standards of Negligence: Defining the Reasonable Person to Induce Optimal Care and Optimal Populations of Injurers and Victims' (1989) 78 Georgetown LJ 241

WA Seavey, 'Negligence—Subjective or Objective?' (1927) 41 Harv L Rev 1

DE Seidelson, 'Reasonable Expectations and Subjective Standards in Negligence Law: The Minor, the Mentally Impaired, and the Mentally Incompetent' (1981) 50 Geo Wash L Rev 17

M Shaffer, 'The Battered Woman Syndrome Revisited: Some Complicating Thoughts Five Years After *R v Lavallée*' (1997) 47 UTLJ 1

—— '*R v Lavallée*: A Review Essay' (1990) 22 Ottawa L Rev 607

—— '*Seaboyer v R*: A Case Comment' (1992) 5 CJWL 202

William Shakespeare, 'Measure for Measure' in *The Complete Pelican Shakespeare* (Gen ed A Harbage) (New York: Viking, 1979)

E Sheehy, 'Battered Women and Mandatory Minimum Sentences' (2001) 39 Osgoode Hall LJ 529

C Sheppard, 'Of Forest Fires and Systemic Discrimination: A Review of *British Columbia (Public Service Employee Relations Commission) v BCGSEU*' (2001) 46 McGill LJ 533

J Shklar, 'American Citizenship: The Question for Inclusion' in *The Tanner Lectures on Human Values XI: 1990* (Utah: University of Utah Press, 1989) 388

—— *American Citizenship: The Quest for Inclusion* (Cambridge, Mass: Harvard University Press, 1991)

H Shulman, 'The Standard of Care Required of Children' (1927) 37 Yale LJ 618

H Sidgwick, *The Methods of Ethics* (7th edn, London: MacMillan, 1907)

Reva B Siegel, 'Home as Work: The First Women's Rights Claims Concerning Wives' Household Labor, 1850–1880' (1994) 103 Yale LJ 1073

A Simester, 'Can Negligence be Culpable?' in J Horder (ed), *Oxford Essays in Jurisprudence* (4th Series, Oxford: OUP, 2000) 85

Kenneth W Simons, 'Contributory Negligence: Conceptual and Normative Issues' in David G Owen (ed), *Philosophical Foundations of Tort Law* (Oxford: Clarendon Press, 1995) 85

David A Sklansky, 'Cocaine, Race and Equal Protection' (1995) 47 Stan L Rev 1283

Carol Smart, *Feminism and the Power of Law* (London: Routledge, 1989)

L Snider, 'Feminism, Punishment and the Potential of Empowerment' (1994) 9 Can J L & Soc'y 75

—— 'The Potential of the Criminal Justice System to Promote Feminist Concerns' (1990) 10 Studies in Law, Politics and Society 143

SM Speiser, CF Krause, and AW Gans, *The American Law of Torts* Vol I (Rochester, NY: The Lawyer's Co-operative Publishing Co, 1983)

E Spelman, *Inessential Woman: Problems of Exclusion in Feminist Thought* (Boston: Beacon Press, 1988)

Dale Spender, *Women of Ideas and What Men have Done to Them: From Aphra Behn to Adrienne Rich* (London: Pandora, 1982)

SI Splane, 'Tort Liability of the Mentally Ill in Negligence Actions' (1983) 93 Yale LJ 153

B Spock, *Decent and Indecent: Our Personal and Political Behaviour* (New York: McCall Publishing, 1969)

Tony Storey, 'Right to a Fair Trial by an Impartial Tribunal: Trial by Jury—Ethnic Minority Defendant—Suspected Racial Bias among Jurors' (2000) 5 J Civ Lib 244

Don Stuart, *Canadian Criminal Law, A Treatise* (4th edn, Toronto: Carswell, 2001)

—— '*Ewanchuk*: Asserting "No Means No"' (1999) 22 CR (5th) 39

—— 'The Pendulum has been Pushed Too Far' (1993) 42 UNBLJ 349

KM Sullivan, 'Constitutionalizing Women's Equality' (2002) 90 CALR 735

C Sunstein, *The Partial Constitution* (Cambridge, Mass: Harvard University Press, 1993)

TS Szasz, *The Myth of Mental Illness: Foundations of a Theory of Personal Conduct* (New York: Harper & Row, 1961)

C Tavris, *Mismeasure of Woman* (New York: Simon & Schuster, 1992)

J Temkin, 'Towards a Modern Law of Rape' (1982) 45 Modern L Rev 399

Studs Terkel (ed), *Race: How Blacks and Whites Think and Feel about the American Obsession* (New York: New Press, 1992)

SJ Thoma, 'Estimating Gender Differences in the Comprehension and Preference of Moral Issues' (1986) 6 Developmental Rev 165

Judith Jarvis Thomson, 'Remarks on Causation and Liability' 13 Phil & Publ Aff 101, reprinted in JJ Thomson, *Rights, Restitution, and Risk: Essays in Moral Theory* (Cambridge, Mass: Harvard University Press, 1986) 192

B Thorne, *Gender Play: Girls and Boys in School* (New Brunswick, NJ: Rutgers University Press, 1993)

M Torrey, 'When will We be Believed? Rape Myths and the Idea of a Fair Trial in Rape Prosecution' (1991) 24 UC Davis L Rev 1013

'Torts—Insanity as Defense' 49 ALR (3d) 193

L Tov-Ruach, 'Jealousy, Attention, and Loss' in A Rorty (ed), *Explaining Emotions* (Berkeley: University of California Press, 1980) 465

M Trebilcock, 'Coercion' in *The Limits of Freedom of Contract* (Cambridge, Mass: Harvard University Press, 1993) 78

FA Trindade and P Cane, *The Law of Torts in Australia* (3rd edn, Oxford: Oxford University Press, 1999)

E Tucker, 'The Law of Employers' Liability in Ontario 1861–1900: The Search for a Theory' (1984) 22 Osgoode Hall LJ 213

Richard Tur, 'Rape, Reasonableness and Time' (1981) 1 Oxford J Legal Stud 432

JW Turner, *The Modern Approach to Criminal Law* (London: Macmillan, 1945)

J Tussman and J tenBroek, 'The Equal Protection of the Laws' (1949) 37 Calif L Rev 341

Lucinda Vandervort, 'Mistake of Law and Sexual Assault: Consent and *Mens Rea*' (1987–88) 2 CJWL 233

U Vogel, 'Is Citizenship Gender-Specific?' in U Vogel and M Moran (eds), *The Frontiers of Citizenship* (Houndmils: Macmillan, 1991) 62

George Vuoso, 'Background, Responsibility and Excuse' (1987) 98 Yale LJ 1661

L Walker, 'A Response to Elizabeth M Schneider's "Describing and Changing"' (1986) 9 Women's Rts L Rep 223

Webster's Dictionary of the English Language (Toronto: Wordsworth Editions, 1989)

E Weinrib, 'Causation and Wrongdoing' (1987) 63 Chi-Kent L Rev 407

—— *The Idea of Private Law* (Cambridge, Mass: Harvard University Press, 1995)

—— 'The Special Morality of Tort Law' (1989) 34 McGill LJ 403

—— *Tort Law: Cases and Materials* (Toronto: Emond Montgomery, 1997)

LE Weinrib, 'Canada's Constitutional Revolution: From Legislative to Constitutional State' (1999) 33 Israel L Rev 13

—— and Ernest J Weinrib, 'Constitutional Values and Private Law in Canada' in Daniel Friedmann and Daphne Barak-Erez (eds), *Human Rights in Private Law* (Oxford: Hart Publishing, 2001) 43

Lenore Weitzman, *The Divorce Revolution: The Unexpected Social and Economic Consequences for Women and Children in America* (New York: Free Press, Macmillan Co, 1985)

—— and Mavis Maclean (eds), *The Economic Consequences of Divorce: The International Perspective* (Oxford: Oxford University Press, 1991)

Barbara Welke, 'Unreasonable Women: Gender and the Law of Accidental Injury, 1870–1920' (1994) 19 Law & Social Inquiry 369

C Wells, 'Battered Woman Syndrome and Defences to Homicide: Where Now?' (1994) 14 Legal Studies 266

—— 'Domestic Violence and Self-Defence' (1990) 140 New LJ 127

—— 'Swatting the Subjectivist Bug' (1982) Crim L Rev 209

Robin West, 'Equality Theory, Marital Rape, and the Promise of the Fourteenth Amendment' (1990) 42 Fla L Rev 45

Peter Westen, 'The Empty Idea of Equality' (1982) 95 Harv L Rev 537

LH Wilderman, 'Presumptions Existing in Favour of the Infant in Re: The Question of an Infant's Ability to be Guilty of Contributory Negligence' (1935) 10 Indiana LJ 427

B Williams, *Moral Luck: Philosophical Papers, 1973–1980* (New York: Cambridge University Press, 1990)

G Williams, 'Letter' *The [London] Times* (8 May 1975) 15 col 6

—— *Textbook of Criminal Law* (2nd edn, London: Stevens, 1983)

John M Williams, 'Mistake of Fact: The Legacy of *Pappajohn v The Queen*' (1985) 63 Can Bar Rev 597

P Williams, *The Alchemy of Race and Rights* (Cambridge, Mass: Harvard University Press, 1991)

Susan Wolf, 'Sanity and the Metaphysics of Responsibility' in Ferdinand Schoeman (ed), *Responsibility, Character, and the Emotions* (Cambridge: Cambridge University Press, 1987) 46

C Wong, 'Good Intentions, Troublesome Applications: The Cultural Defence and Other Uses of Cultural Evidence in Canada' (1999) 42 Crim LQ 367

C Woodard, 'Reality and Social Reform: The Transition from Laissez-Faire to the Welfare State' (1962) 72 Yale LJ 286

Stanley Yeo, 'Power of Self-Control in Provocation and Automatism' (1992) 14 Sydney L Rev 3

—— 'Resolving Gender Bias in Criminal Defences' (1993) 19 Mon L Rev 104

—— 'Sex, Ethnicity, Power of Self-Control and Provocation Revisited' (1996) 18 Sydney L Rev 304

Iris Marion Young, *Justice and the Politics of Difference* (Princeton: Princeton University Press, 1990)

—— 'Polity and Group Difference: A Critique of the Ideal of Universal Citizenship' (1989) 99 Ethics 250

—— 'Polity and Group Difference: A Critique of the Ideal of Universal Citizenship' in Cass R Sunstein (ed), *Feminism and Political Theory* (Chicago: University of Chicago Press, 1990) 117

N Yuval-Davis, 'The Citizenship Debate: Women, Ethnic Processes and the State' (1991) 39 Feminist Review 58

Index